MODERN ITALY IN HISTOI PERSPECTIVE

MODERN ITALY IN HISTORICAL PERSPECTIVE

Nick Carter

BLOOMSBURY ACADEMIC

First published in 2010 by:

Bloomsbury Academic

An imprint of Bloomsbury Publishing Plc
36 Soho Square, London W1D 3QY, UK
and
175 Fifth Avenue, New York, NY 10010, USA

CIP records for this book are available from the British Library and the
Library of Congress.

hb ISBN 978-1-84966-333-5
pb ISBN 978-0-34075-901-1
e-ISBN 978-1-84966-029-7

This book is produced using paper that is made from wood grown in
managed, sustainable forests. It is natural, renewable and recyclable. The
logging and manufacturing processes conform to the environmental
regulations of the country of origin.

Printed and bound in Great Britain by the MPG Books Group Ltd,
Bodmin, Cornwall.

www.bloomsburyacademic.com

Contents

Preface

History rarely stands still for long. What we study of the past (i.e. what we consider to be of importance), and the ways in which we study and make sense of it, change as the contemporary world changes. Within every generation, of course, there are also cleavages relating to class, ideology, gender, race, religion and other forms of identity (e.g. national, local), which impact on the way the 'same' past is viewed differently by different groups and individuals. History, I constantly tell students, is, above all else, a *contested* discipline; it is not the trivial pursuit of 'facts' about the past that keeps history alive and makes it interesting, but the ways in which those 'facts' are interpreted and understood.

Historians' changing and competing interpretations of the past of modern Italy (i.e. Italy since unification in 1870) are the focus of this book. Although review articles on aspects of modern Italian historiography (i.e. on what historians have written about Italy's recent past) are quite common in academic journals, and most monographs carry literature surveys as a matter of course, surprisingly few English-language textbooks on modern Italy deal directly or at any great length with the 'history of the history'. There are exceptions. Richard Bosworth's *The Italian Dictatorship* (1998) is a brilliant critical overview of the historiography of Italian Fascism and has rightly been described as 'one of the most informative and entertaining books of the decade'.[1] There are also several very good surveys of modern Italian economic historiography: Vera Zamagni's *The Economic History of Italy* (1993), Giovanni Federico's *The Economic Development of Italy Since 1870* (1994) and Federico and Jon Cohen's *The Growth of the Italian Economy* (2001). But it is slim pickings otherwise. By way of illustration, the best-known general histories of the modern era in English, Denis Mack Smith's *Italy* (first published 1955) and Martin Clark's *Modern Italy* (first published 1982), are excellent but traditional-style interpretative narratives. They do not engage – at least explicitly or at length – with the many historical debates and controversies that surround so much of Italy's past and present. They are not even particularly current: new editions of both works came out in the 1990s, with added chapters to include recent events, but neither saw any revision of the original material; this meant that new and even not-so-new research was ignored.[2] John Foot's *Modern Italy* (2003) is the only general study of the modern period that sets out with the expressed intention to help students 'to understand the ways in which history is continually subject to revision and debate'.[3] An innovative and first-rate study in many respects, the actual coverage of the major historical debates and controversies is, however, disappointingly thin and uneven.

That no book-length overview of the historiography of modern Italy exists in English is not of course reason enough to write one. Such a work is justified, though, on pedagogical and historical grounds. First, the teaching of history at universities (and in secondary schools) over the last twenty years has moved away from a 'this happened then' approach; students are now encouraged to debate and discuss the divergent interpretations of particular phenomena, processes and problems. Textbooks which provide guidance and insights into the different perspectives relating to a particular area of study – in other words, which give the student some idea of the issues and arguments they need to consider – are extremely valuable in this context. Second, the trend in higher education away from year-long courses to semester-length modules has drastically reduced the amount of time students get to spend on a subject. Modularity means students usually complete a course in fifteen weeks or less. Students, if they are going to succeed, really must hit the ground running. *Modern Italy in Historical Perspective* is designed to help them do this. While there may be students who see this type of textbook as a single-source alternative to wider reading – and I caution them against this – many will use it as a launch pad not only for wider reading but also for more critically informed reading; this is the main purpose of the book. Third, the historiography of modern Italy is extraordinarily rich and varied: it merits book-length treatment. Not only have the focus and nature of the historical debates changed over time (and in the chapters that follow I endeavour to give some sense of how and why these shifts have occurred), but the historical arguments and controversies surrounding modern Italy have also been extremely lively, with exchanges between historians often heated and sometimes very personal. There is a particularly strong tradition of polemical writing in Italy, where the type of national historical consensus seen, for example, in Britain (better, England) or the United States, does not exist (a reflection of the comparative weakness of the Italian nation state) and where history has always been highly politicized (indicative of the deep ideological divisions within Italian politics and society). This is not without its problems: politics and history are a dangerous combination and Italian historians have 'often felt the need to line up behind set versions of history, dictated by political considerations'.[4] However, because in Italy 'history was, and is, politics', history really matters there: how historians have interpreted and reinterpreted Italy's past has long helped to shape and sharpen political debate on its future.[5] For their part, Anglophone historians of Italy, although in general less partisan than their Italian counterparts, have rarely shied away from controversy: of the historians already mentioned, both Bosworth and Mack Smith are well known for their ability to provoke – and they are by no means alone, as we shall see.

Structure and content

This work is not comprehensive in its coverage of the historiography of modern Italy. To write such a 'history of the history' of modern Italy would be an enormous, if not impossible, undertaking. Instead, the focus is on those questions that have dominated historical debate for many years and/or are of particular contemporary relevance. Special attention is paid to recent research trends: one of the purposes of this book is to help students to understand and appreciate the current 'state of the art'.

Modern Italy in Historical Perspective is more, though, than simply an extended historiographical essay. One of the objections historians and publishers have to writing historiography (besides the difficulty of the task) is that readers are 'put off' by discussion of historiographical issues; historiography is widely considered to be too hard or – worse – too boring, to inflict on the book-buying public. My counter to this is simple: it depends on one's approach. Certainly, the historiographical gloss that is sometimes applied to general narrative histories helps no one; it only distracts from the narrative and provides very little enlightenment to the reader. It is also true that detailed historiographies can be extremely dry and dull, particularly if there is no critical engagement by the author with the debates they survey. In-depth historiographical treatments often fall down, too, because the author neglects the needs of the general or novice reader who knows little or nothing about the historical period under discussion. In these circumstances, any discussion of debates and interpretations, no matter how insightful or comprehensive, is likely only to leave the reader bewildered, exhausted – and bored. This book is different. I have assumed an intelligent and interested readership with, however, little or no prior knowledge of modern Italian history. Each chapter is thus organized along the following lines:

Introduction. A brief guide to the topic and debates discussed in the chapter.
Framework. A short narrative history of the period/subject.
Debates. A discussion of the relevant historiography.
Assessment. A critical evaluation of the historiography and conclusion.

Narrative and historiography are thus combined, but with the emphasis on the latter. Knowing 'what happened when', the reader can move on with confidence to explore the historical debates over the how and the why. Armed then with both the evidence and the arguments, the reader should be in a position to make sense of *my* arguments and criticisms in the closing assessment section. At no point – and this is the crucial thing – should the reader feel lost.

The periodization of the book is predicated largely on political developments. Part I covers the majority of the 'liberal' period, from 1870 to Italy's entry into World War One in 1915. Part II begins with a discussion of Italy's war and the last years of liberal Italy (1915–22), but its focus is very much on the Fascist era, from Mussolini becoming prime minister in 1922 to his dismissal in the wake of the Allied invasion of Italy in 1943. Part III examines Italy's 'second war', from the (first) fall of Mussolini and Italy's subsequent surrender (also 1943) to the Allies' victory and Mussolini's death in the spring of 1945, before exploring the post-war republican period up to the early–mid-1990s, when corruption scandals engulfed Italy's political class and paved the way for Silvio Berlusconi's remarkable rise to power. Of course, periodization based on political criteria is a somewhat artificial exercise. Politics, as the Russian writer Fyodor Sologub once observed, are the 'momentary froth on the broad surface of life'; and deeper economic, social and cultural trends (what the great French historian Fernand Braudel described as the 'tides of history') do not always fit neatly within timeframes imposed by political developments. Often, too, 'watershed' political moments are not as seismic as they first appear. I am aware of the cross-period relevance of many of the issues covered, and I try to highlight continuities where they exist. Nonetheless, because historians commonly use the 'liberal', 'Fascist' and 'republican' tags, and because the alternatives to such periodization are as, if not more, problematic and contrived, it makes sense to use the former as convenient chronological markers.

Some readers will no doubt bemoan the lack of detailed coverage of certain subjects, and a number of my peers will surely shake their heads at what they see as unforgivable gaps in my reading. Yet, whatever the real or perceived weaknesses of the book, I believe it captures well the vibrancy of historical research on modern Italy. The student who, after reading this, goes on to delve more deeply into the history – and present – of modern Italy will be richly rewarded for their efforts.

By way of acknowledgements, I would like to thank my former colleagues at De Montfort University, Leicester, for their friendship and support over many years (I owe a particular debt of gratitude in this regard to Mark Sandle, David Sadler and David Ryan). For similar reasons, I also must thank Günter Minnerup and Nick Doumanis at the University of New South Wales, Sydney. I am indebted to Christopher Wheeler for giving me the opportunity to write the book in the first place, to Richard Bosworth for his helpful comments on the half-finished manuscript and to my last editor, Tamsin Smith, for her patience and equanimity as I stumbled from one missed deadline to the next.

Modern Italy is dedicated to a number of people: to Peter Van Went and to the memory of Harry Hearder; to my long-suffering partner, Rosemary, and my even longer-suffering parents, Ann and Geoffrey, whose constant love, support – and patience – can never be properly repaid; and finally to my beautiful son, Alexander William, for simply being here.

Nick Carter, Sydney, 2009.

Italy since 1919

After Christopher Duggan, *A Concise History of Italy*. Cambridge: Cambridge University Press, 1994, p. 197.

PART I

LIBERAL ITALY

1 The politics of liberal Italy

> [T]here were moments during these years when past was compared with present, and Italy realized and rejoiced over the extent of her advance.
> BENEDETTO CROCE.

> [T]hey were aiming at the creation of a modern state in Italy, and they in fact produced a bastard.
> ANTONIO GRAMSCI.[1]

Introduction

After centuries of foreign domination and territorial fracture, independence and unity came to the Italian peninsula with remarkable speed in the mid-nineteenth century. Italy's political landscape was completely transformed, 1859–70. The Italy created by the 1815 Vienna settlement – seven separate states under Austrian domination – was destroyed. In 1859, the largest independent state in the peninsula, the north-western Kingdom of Sardinia (commonly referred to as Piedmont), in alliance with France, had driven Austria out of neighbouring Lombardy. In the spring of 1860, the tiny northern duchies of Parma and Modena, the Grand Duchy of Tuscany and the central Italian 'legations' (papal-governed territory around Bologna and Ferrara) were annexed to Piedmont following revolutions in mid-1859 which had deposed the old pro-Austrian

1

rulers. By the end of 1860 the southern Kingdom of Naples, too, had fallen under Piedmont's sway following Garibaldi's famous conquest of Sicily and mainland Naples. Piedmontese forces also occupied the remaining papal territory outside of Rome. In March 1861, King Victor Emmanuel II of Piedmont became King of Italy. Pope Pius IX ruled in Rome and Austria still held Venice, but the rest of the peninsula was now united under the Piedmontese Crown. In 1866, Venice was incorporated into the new Italian kingdom following the Austro-Prussian war (Italy had allied itself with Prussia). In 1870, Italian forces entered Rome after Napoleon III withdrew French forces 'protecting' Pius IX to fight in the Franco-Prussian war. Rome became capital of Italy in September 1870.[2] The Pope's once extensive temporal authority now extended no further than the Vatican gardens.

The political form that the new Italian state took – a liberal-constitutional monarchy (hence the epithet 'liberal Italy') based on a moderate constitution (the Piedmontese *statuto* of 1848), a restricted franchise, and represented by two fluid parliamentary coalitions known as the *destra storica* (Historic Right) and *sinistra storica* (Historic Left) – was challenged from the outset from a variety of sources. First, there were the losers from the unification process: the old deposed rulers, the old regional elites (now smaller fish in a bigger pond) and, most importantly, the Catholic Church. Unification had destroyed the Pope's political power. Pius retaliated by denouncing all forms of 'progress, liberalism and modern civiliza-tion' (the Syllabus of Errors, 1864), by proclaiming papal infallibility (1870) and by rejecting a compromise settlement with the new Italian state (the Law of Guarantees, 1871). The self-styled 'prisoner in the Vatican' refused to recognize the existence of the Italian state and urged Italians not to participate in national political life (1874). Second, there were those who, though nationalists, were unhappy with the form that the new Italy took: the Mazzinian republicans, for example. Third, there were the ideological opponents of the liberal-bourgeois state: the anarchists, the revolutionary socialists and, later, the revolutionary nationalists and revolutionary syndicalists. Finally, there were those who were critical of the way in which the liberal state operated: of the parliamentary horse trading, the political corruption and the state-sponsored political repression that characterized much of the era; of the state's inability to deal adequately with united Italy's many and deep-seated social and economic problems; of its failure to create a sense of national belonging (the much discussed gulf between 'legal' and 'real' Italy, i.e. between state and society).

Many of the contemporary criticisms levelled at the Italian liberal state were repeated subsequently by historians of the liberal period – and were apparently given added weight by the collapse of Italian liberalism after World War One and the rise of Fascism. Wedged between the romanticism of the Risorgimento (unification) and the brutality of the Fascist era, it was easy to look at the liberal period as a failure, one in which Italy deviated from what was assumed to be the 'normal' path of modern state development, represented by the likes of Britain and France, and instead trod its own path towards Fascism. To explain why Italian parliamentary democracy collapsed many historians and observers turned to the 'peculiarities' of liberal Italy's political, economic and social structures.

The critics of the liberal state have not had it entirely their own way, however. Many historians have defended its record. Liberal apologists have traditionally emphasized the scale of the problems facing the new state and have argued that Italy performed as well as could be expected under difficult circumstances. Again, though, the debate has been framed in the light of what came before and, more importantly, after liberalism.

The diametrical verdicts on liberal Italy offered by Benedetto Croce (1866–1952) and Antonio Gramsci (1891–1937), two of modern Italy's intellectual heavyweights, mark the poles of historical opinion on the liberal period, and for many years they defined the nature of the debate about liberal Italy. The past two decades, however, have witnessed a revisionist trend away from these traditional approaches that try to prove or disprove liberal Italy's 'peculiarity', 'deviancy', or answerability for what followed, towards more explicative, and less judgmental, political accounts of the liberal period. The emphasis now is on looking at liberal Italy 'on its own terms'. Just as attempts have been made to detach earlier nineteenth-century Italian history from unification and independence, so historians have attempted to detach the history of liberal Italy from the Risorgimento and from Fascism.[3] In general, these accounts have helped bolster the reputation of Italian liberalism.

Framework

The *destra storica*: government by the 'Right', 1861–76

The *destra storica* was a broad coalition of parliamentary deputies who had supported the Piedmontese moderate liberal-constitutional approach to Italian independence in the 1850s and early 1860s. The *destra* dominated government from the proclamation of the Kingdom of Italy in 1861 until 1876. From 1870, at least, *destra* rule was characterized by austere conservatism in domestic and foreign policy, with the aim of consolidating the new state. At home, great emphasis was placed on balancing the budget (the wars of 1859 and 1866, plus the huge cost of amalgamating so many hitherto separate states, had left united Italy with enormous debts), on maintaining (or imposing) law and order (especially in the south), and on guarding against both 'black' intrigues sponsored by the Vatican and republican agitation encouraged by the heirs of Mazzini. Abroad, Italian governments of the Right after 1870 settled for neutral and pacific diplomacy, in contrast to the extravagant and sometimes reckless foreign ventures and alliances of the previous decade.

The *sinistra storica*: government by the 'Left', 1876–96

The fall of the *destra* in March 1876 and the landslide election victory of the sinistra *storica* under Agostino Depretis later in the year ended the monopoly of political power enjoyed by the Right since 1861. The widely held view that the triumph of the Left – i.e. of the old *Garibaldini* – amounted to a political revolution was not borne out by events. Depretis, who governed for much of the following decade until his death in 1887, did little to alter the basic tenets of government. Domestically, Depretis continued the Right's economic policy of tight fiscal control, and he followed its tough line on law and order, the only difference being that 'red' sedition encouraged by Italian anarchists and socialists gradually replaced clericalism and republicanism as the government's main concern. Nor was Depretis a great reformer. An education bill was passed in 1877 and the franchise extended in 1882 (from 2 per cent to 7 per cent of the total population), but as under the Right no major social legislation was enacted. Foreign policy, however, did become more assertive. Italy abandoned neutrality in 1882 when it entered into a limited defensive alliance with Germany and Austria. The so-called Triple Alliance was renewed (and extended) on a regular basis until 1915. A modest first attempt at Italian empire building in East Africa followed the inauguration of the alliance but ended in military humiliation at the hands of Ethiopian troops at Dogali in 1887.

It was Depretis who instigated the much-criticized practice of *trasformismo*: the 'transformation' of one's political opponents into allies to secure and sustain a parliamentary majority. *Trasformismo*, argued its opponents, stunted the development of genuine political parties, blinded deputies to the national interest, and turned parliament into little more than a clearing-house where a deputy traded his support for patronage.

Trasformismo did not die with Depretis. His successor, Francesco Crispi, who had previously condemned *trasformismo* as 'parliamentary incest', was happy to maintain it once in power. However, Crispi's two periods in office, 1887–91 and 1893–6, did mark a fundamental shift in both the style and substance of government. Crispian politics meant more of everything: greater reforming zeal (Crispi's first ministry saw major reforms of the penal code and of local government, plus the first limited recognition of workers' rights); heavier repression to counter 'red' subversion and social unrest (the brutal crushing of the Sicilian *fasci* in 1893–4 and the subsequent nationwide attack on Italian socialism); higher levels of expenditure; and more frequent accusations of 'parliamentary dictatorship' (a charge previously levelled against Depretis but Crispi strengthened the powers of the prime minister's office and he often ignored parliament). Above all, Crispi instigated the most expansive and ambitious foreign policy of any Italian government since the Risorgimento. Crispi sought to strengthen Italy's alliance with Germany and Austria, he embarked on a programme of massive military expansion, he intensified the long-running rivalry between Italy and France (the Franco-Italian tariff war, 1888–98, just one example), and he relaunched Italian imperialism in East Africa. Crispi's determination 'to make Italy's words heard and respected' abroad ultimately cost him his political career. In 1896, Italian troops were overwhelmed at Adowa by the Ethiopian army. Nearly 5,000 Italian soldiers died, with 1,500 wounded (including 30 soldiers castrated during battle) and 2,000 captured. Crispi, who had staked his political reputation on the venture, resigned.

Government in crisis and transition, 1896–1900

Crispi left behind not only a badly damaged national ego but also a very unstable domestic political situation. His unrelenting persecution of socialism had divided parliamentary opinion. Radical and democratic elements within parliament protested against the level of repression and moved to defend the rights of socialists. Conservative deputies, however, contemplated even more drastic measures of control, most notably Sidney Sonnino's famous call for a 'return to the *statuto*' (1897) entailing a dramatic reduction in the role of parliament with executive power placed in the hands of the Crown. The parliamentary conflict came to a head in the wake of riots in Milan (May 1898). The riots – the culmination of several weeks of protest and unrest across Italy provoked by high food prices and rising unemployment – were met with extreme force by the Italian army (at least 80 civilians were killed). A government crackdown on suspected 'subversives' followed. Shortly afterwards, the Prime Minister, General Luigi Pelloux, proposed legislation aimed at curbing the rights of association and restricting press freedom. The coercion bill brought the parliamentary crisis to a head in 1899–1900. Pelloux, frustrated by radical-democratic filibustering designed to delay the passage of the bill, attempted to force through the measures by the use of royal decree, effectively bypassing parliament. This pushed even moderate deputies to oppose the bill. When the Court of Cassation ruled the use of the royal decree to be unconstitutional, Pelloux chose to appeal to the electorate. Although he won a parliamentary majority, opposition groups registered a massive increase in support. Pelloux resigned in June 1900.

The 'Giolittian age', 1900–14

In contrast to the upheavals and tensions of the 1890s, Italian parliamentary life during the subsequent 'Giolittian age' was, for the most part, relatively stable. Giovanni Giolitti had already held the premiership, albeit briefly, in the early 1890s, but it was as Prime Minister (and Minister of the Interior) in 1903–5, 1906–9 and 1911–14 that he really stamped his authority on parliament.[4] Such was his influence that even when out of office his absence was regarded as merely temporary or even tactical. In many ways, Giolittian politics broke with long-established norms and attitudes. Giolitti revised the traditional state policy of antagonism towards, and repression of, non-liberal forces – socialism, Catholicism, radicalism – choosing instead to open up the liberal system to these forces in an effort to 'absorb' them. Under Giolitti, organized worker and peasant protest was tolerated and press restrictions lifted. Socialist leaders were invited to join the government (they refused), radicals did participate in government, and even the Church ultimately endorsed Catholic participation in national elections on the side of the 'forces of order'. Giolitti was also responsible for a wide range of reforms. A host of social welfare measures were introduced, ranging from general public health reforms (e.g. state provision of quinine to tackle malaria) to the creation of a state monopoly of life insurance (1912). Labour legislation included stricter working conditions for women and children, and the creation of the Supreme Council of Labour (1902). New public holidays were announced and taxation on essential foodstuffs reduced. There was major electoral reform in 1912 (near universal male suffrage more than doubled the electorate to eight-and-a-half million). In addition, there was a huge increase in government spending on public works projects, particularly in the south. Education, agriculture, transport and communications services were also subject to reforms either passed by or initiated under Giolitti.

There were, however, continuities with the not so distant political past. Imperialism was revived in 1911–12 when Italy seized Libya from Turkey and in the process occupied the Turkish-controlled Greek Dodecanese islands. At home, Giolitti, even more so than his predecessors Depretis and Crispi, was accused of manipulating parliament through corrupt electoral practices and *trasformismo*. Liberal parliamentary government was attacked from both the Left and the Right as well as by a small but vociferous body from within Italy's cultural and intellectual élite (see Chapter 3). State repression, too, was not entirely abandoned.

Giolitti resigned as prime minister in March 1914 after Radical party deputies, unhappy with his recent alliance with the Catholic Electoral Union (the so-called Gentiloni Pact), left the government. Giolitti was not expected to remain out of office for long. However, the outbreak of European war in September 1914 and the subsequent 'intervention crisis' in Italy (see Chapter 4) significantly weakened his position. Giolitti did not return to power until 1920, and then only briefly, but with disastrous consequences for the liberal state (see Chapter 4).

Debates

Benedetto Croce and the liberal historical perspective on liberal Italy

Widely regarded as the greatest Italian philosopher of the twentieth century, Benedetto Croce is also a powerful force in modern Italian historiography. English-speaking historians have sometimes come to grief on the rocks of Crocean rhetoric ('I should find it easier to write of Croce's book if I had the least idea what it was all about', confided one reviewer of *History as the Story of Liberty*).[5] However, Croce's key work on the liberal period, *A History of Italy* (1929), is a relatively straightforward – and overwhelmingly positive – narrative account of Italian liberalism.

For Croce, the *destra* was 'a spiritual aristocracy of upright and loyal gentlemen' and 'the exponent of a high ideal'. It successfully balanced the budget – 'a matter of life and death' – and, rightly, imposed political centralization on the country as the only guarantee of unity. The *sinistra* under Depretis, while less dignified, less educated, and less scrupulous than the Right – in short, more *democratic* (Croce considered democracy to be bad for politics) – was nonetheless driven by the same ideas as the *destra*. To Croce then, the development after 1876 of the practice of *trasformismo*, 'a word that seemed ugly and dishonourable' and 'a sign of Italian weakness', was a natural direction for Italian politics to take. Croce noted approvingly the creation of a national army based on the Prussian model, the development of a navy of the 'first rank', and the expansion of the railway system to the benefit of Italian defence, internal security and economic welfare. He accepted economic development was slow but excused this on grounds of the scale of the problems facing Italy. He recognized the failure of the state to remedy the 'southern problem' (the relative backwardness of southern politics, society, economy and culture compared to the north) – indeed, he acknowledged that the *destra* had failed to recognize its existence – but he argued that even in the south significant progress was made in the first two decades after unification. And, with political and economic improvement came social, cultural and moral progress. Italians, Croce declared, became citizens rather than mere subjects.[6]

Croce was less tolerant of the vagaries of Francesco Crispi. Driven by the 'desire to impress himself and others with his own energy', Crispi, according to Croce, pursued unattainable goals, raised 'dangerous passions' at home and abroad and frequently flouted both the spirit and letter of constitutional government. Credulous and impetuous in character, inconsistent and contradictory in policy, Crispi encouraged reactionary tendencies within Italian politics in a lasting way. The brutal suppression of disturbances in Sicily (1893) and Lunigiana (Carrara) in 1894, and the general persecution of socialist organizations that Crispi ordered in their wake, engendered a spirit of reaction in government circles that survived the fall of Crispi himself. The 1898 Milan riots and Pelloux's subsequent attempt to govern without the assistance of parliament were the result. Here, though, Croce was quick to assert the victory of liberalism. True liberals, he argued, had opposed the extent of Crispi's 'war of extermination' waged against socialism, they had opposed the equally heavy-handed tactics of 1898, and had successfully resisted Pelloux. In so doing they had not only saved the liberal state but had also strengthened it by demonstrating to socialists that bourgeois liberalism was not necessarily the enemy of the workers. In this way, 'the first far-reaching step was taken towards a reform which was in effect the fusion between liberalism and socialism'.[7]

There followed, in Croce's words, if not a 'golden age', a period 'in which the idea of a liberal regime was most fully realized'. 'Italian life after 1900 had overcome the chief obstacles in its course', and 'flowed on for the next ten years and more, rich in both achievement and in hope'. Under Giolitti's guidance, political extremism was pushed to the margins of national life. Furthermore, the legislative and administrative reforms introduced by Giolitti were 'really remarkable', and once more, 'as in the early days of unity, Italians abroad were met with congratulations upon the wisdom and the ability of which their country had given proof'. Liberal Italy's maturation was reflected in its foreign policy, too. While the *destra* had been constrained by circumstances to tread a cautious path in international affairs, and Crispian foreign policy had been 'boastful', 'noisy' and ultimately 'barren', Giolittian Italy showed itself to be both 'more enterprising' than the former and 'more practical' than the latter. The Libyan war was, according to Croce, the natural consequence of Italy's growing strength; the success of the campaign confirmed the great strides the country had made since the 'national disaster' of Adowa.[8]

Croce recognized that even in these years 'Liberalism was not a deep and living faith...it had not struck deep roots'. This, though, he attributed to the evils first of positivism and then of irrationalism (i.e. to cultural factors) rather than to any inherent shortcomings within the liberal state (i.e. political factors). Because of these, Italian liberalism lacked the intellectual and critical support 'which would have enabled it to meet any crisis which might arise'. Croce was adamant, however, that there was no crisis of the liberal state prior to World War One; nor (so he later argued) was liberalism in any way responsible for Fascism (see Chapter 4).[9]

Antonio Gramsci and the Marxist historical perspective on liberal Italy

No Marxist writer has had such a profound impact upon the historiography of modern Italy as the Sardinian-born communist Antonio Gramsci. As a socialist propagandist and revolutionary activist in Turin during and immediately after World War One, and more so as a founder and leader of the Italian Communist Party (PCI, est. 1921), Gramsci often touched upon aspects of Italy's history in his writings. The 'Lyons Theses', written with Palmiro Togliatti and presented to the third congress of the PCI in 1926, and 'Some Aspects of the Southern Question', drafted in late 1926, are good examples of Gramsci's interest in Risorgimento history and the structural character of the liberal state. Gramsci's importance to Italian historiography and his wider intellectual reputation rests, however, on the several thousand pages of manuscript written between 1929 and 1935 while he was serving a 20-year prison sentence for his political opposition to Fascism.[10] Published in Italy shortly after World War Two, and in English translation in 1971, Gramsci's *Prison Notebooks* are remarkable for their breadth of subject matter – history, politics, culture, education – and for the depth and originality of their argument and analysis. Yet they are notes, written under prison conditions by a man in extremely bad health. While Gramsci himself periodically revised and reordered them, and later publication entailed their organization along thematic lines, they are inevitably disjointed and convoluted. Consequently, 'few Marxist writers are more difficult to read accurately or systematically than Gramsci'.[11] The task of understanding Gramsci has been made more difficult for the student by the fact that, for reasons which will be explained shortly, 'Gramsci has perhaps suffered more than any Marxist writer since Lenin from partial and partisan interpretation'.[12]

Before we examine Gramsci as historian it is necessary to understand (or at least be aware of) some of his key theoretical concepts: active and passive revolution, hegemony and Jacobinism.

Gramsci identified two types of revolution. The first type was active or 'Jacobin' revolution, sometimes referred to by Gramsci as war of movement/

manoeuvre. By this Gramsci meant a full-frontal assault on the existing political and economic structures of the state and the destruction of the ruling social class whose interests the state represented. For Gramsci, concerned in particular – like any good Marxist – with the rise of the bourgeoisie, the great example of a bourgeois revolution of this type was the 'Jacobin' period of the French Revolution. During this 'active' phase of the revolution, Gramsci argued, the Jacobins – part of the French bourgeoisie – had been the 'hegemonic' social group within France. By hegemony, Gramsci meant the leadership of a social group (or part of a social group) over other social groups (or other parts of the same social group). Hegemony, Gramsci argued, rested primarily on consent – the leading social group exerted an attraction over other social groups.[13] In revolutionary France, the Jacobins had 'imposed' themselves on the rest of the French bourgeoisie (the Girondins). More significantly, the Jacobins, by going beyond the 'narrow' bourgeois concerns of 1789 and appealing to the interests of the urban workers and the peasantry, had established bourgeois 'hegemony' – leadership – over 'all the popular forces' in France. Although this bourgeois-led popular alliance ultimately had broken down, the Jacobins had successfully created a bond between town and country, had destroyed the *ancien régime* and, in doing so, 'created the bourgeois state, made the bourgeoisie into the leading, hegemonic class of the nation, in other words gave the new state a permanent basis and created the compact modern French nation'.[14]

The second type of revolution Gramsci termed variously as 'passive revolution', '"revolution" without a "revolution"', 'revolution/restoration', 'war of position', 'conservation and innovation', 'reformism'. By this Gramsci meant a tactical, gradual 'corrosion' of the *ancien régime* and the modernization of the state to reflect the interests of the rising social class without, however, fundamental change to the social fabric. In the case of 'passive' bourgeois revolution:

> The old feudal classes are demoted from their dominant position to a 'governing' one, but are not eliminated [cf. the French Revolution], nor is there any attempt to liquidate them as an organic whole; instead of a class they become a 'caste' with specific cultural and psychological characteristics, but no longer with predominant economic functions.[15]

Gramsci identified the period 1815–71 in Europe as 'the "passive" aspect of the great [bourgeois] revolution which started in France in 1789'. The vehicle for this 'passive' phase of bourgeois revolution was 'moderate and conservative liberalism'.[16]

Gramsci and the Italian Risorgimento

Gramsci viewed the Risorgimento (here he really meant 1848–61) as a form of 'passive' bourgeois revolution. A parliamentary bourgeois state was created. Capitalism became the dominant economic mode of production. However, there was no 'radical and violent transformation of social and political relations'.

Gramsci, as already noted, did not regard 'passive' revolution as peculiar to Italy. Indeed, for Gramsci, 'The concept of passive revolution seems to me exact not only for Italy, but for other countries which modernized the state by a series of reforms or national wars without undergoing a political revolution of the radical Jacobin variety'.[17] The Italian 'passive' revolution, nonetheless, was implicitly different[18] from other examples, difference that derived from the inherent weakness of Italian capitalism and, by extension, the 'relative weakness of the Italian bourgeoisie' in both a European context and vis-à-vis other social groups (classes) in Italy. Within the emergent Italian ruling class after 1848, it was the Piedmontese liberal-conservative 'Moderate party' of Cavour that had established its hegemony over the democratic 'Party of Action' of Mazzini and Garibaldi. It was the 'moderates' who consequently had determined the approach to the Italian 'national question' and it was in their likeness that the new Italian state was established in 1861. Yet the moderates' intra-class hegemony was not matched by the exercise of bourgeois hegemony over the rest of Italian society, itself a function of the weakness of Italian capitalism. Gramsci argued the moderates were able to exercise only 'limited hegemony' over the feudal classes (the landowners) and the petit bourgeoisie, and 'dictatorship without hegemony' over the popular masses. Contrary to the case of German unification, where 'the bourgeoisie [chose] not to struggle with all its strength against the old regime, but to allow part of the latter's façade to subsist, behind which it can disguise its own real domination', the old feudal classes in Italy remained important after unity because the bourgeoisie lacked the strength to push through its programme alone. 'Their [the moderates'] approach to the national question required a bloc of all the right-wing forces – including the classes of the great landowners – around Piedmont as a state and as an army'. To guarantee capitalist-industrial control of the economy required economic compromises with the great landowners; to reinforce and defend the nation state required further compromises with the landowners and also with the petit bourgeoisie (the latter flooded the ranks of the expanding national bureaucracy). Furthermore, 'at least, if these old classes [the aristocracy] kept so much importance in Germany...they exercised a national function, became the "intellectuals" of the bourgeoisie,' wrote Gramsci. This did not happen in Italy.[19]

The corollary of Italy's 'passive' bourgeois revolution was that the popular classes, the urban workers and the peasants, were essentially spectators of the Risorgimento, their interests and rights ignored or eroded, their protests suppressed with brute force. The Italian bourgeoisie did not attempt to 'lead' the popular classes.

The merit of an educated class, because it is its historical function, is to lead the popular masses and develop their progressive elements...[the Italian educated classes] said that they were aiming at the creation of a modern state in Italy, and they in fact produced a bastard. They aimed at stimulating the formation of an extensive and energetic ruling class, and they did not succeed; at integrating the people into the framework of the new state, and they did not succeed. The paltry political life from 1870 to 1900, the fundamental and endemic rebelliousness of the Italian popular classes, the narrow and stunted existence of a sceptical and cowardly ruling stratum, these are all the consequences of that failure.[20]

In particular, Gramsci emphasized, there was no attempt at agrarian reform in order to gain the support of the peasants. Unlike in the French Revolution there was no union of town and country. In fact, the Risorgimento aggravated the historical division between the two. The industrial north (the 'city') exploited the rural southern peasantry (the 'country') through high taxation and by offsetting the north's large trade deficit against the south's positive trade balance. The southern peasants were reduced to the position of a 'colonial population', while the interests of the southern landowners were protected (through duties levied on imported grain), and the mass of the southern petit bourgeoisie became state employees. Hence, for Gramsci, the 'Southern Question' – the issue of southern backwardness – was itself the product of the Risorgimento:

> [U]nity had not taken place on a basis of equality, but as hegemony of the north over the Mezzogiorno [the south]...the north concretely was an 'octopus' which enriched itself at the expense of the south, and that its economic-industrial increment was in direct proportion to the impoverishment of the economy and the agriculture of the south.[21]

To Gramsci, the practice of *trasformismo* represented the 'parliamentary expression' of Italy's passive revolution, a process begun in 1848 rather than 1876 with the Moderate Party's steady absorption of individual representatives of the Party of Action. It was this 'molecular' form of transformism which characterized the Depretis and Crispi eras, before giving way to a new form of mass transformism after 1900, by which 'entire groups of leftists' effectively passed over to the liberal-conservative ranks. The 'dictatorships' of Depretis, Crispi and Giolitti were the consequences of a form of government which:

> operated as a 'party'...over and above the [political] parties, not so as to harmonize their interests and activities within the permanent framework of the life and interests of the nation and state, but so as to disintegrate them from the broad masses and obtain 'a force of non-party men linked to the government by paternalistic ties of a Bonapartist-Caesarist type'.[22]

In general, Gramsci had little or nothing to say about individual liberal politicians (Depretis, for example, was completely ignored).[23] This is perhaps not surprising, given the emphasis on structures in Gramsci's historical analysis. However, Gramsci did discuss both the Crispian and Giolittian 'dictatorships' within the context of (and to underscore) his general themes. Crispi's 'obsession' with the political and territorial unity of Italy bound him to the southern landowners (whose fear of the peasantry made them enthusiastic unitarians) and made him 'the man of northern industrialization', prepared to sacrifice the south to reinforce the industry which would give Italy its 'real independence'. Crispi's imperialism, too, was rooted in his unitary obsession. To pacify the southern peasantry's demand for land but unready to implement a 'Jacobin' economic solution to the problem, Crispi instead 'conjured up the mirage of colonial lands to be exploited'. While the 'bureaucratic' temperament of Giolitti contrasted with Crispi's 'energetic, resolute and fanatical' character, Giolittian government continued to use the south as 'a semi-colonial market, a source of savings and taxes' in order to reinforce the economy and northern hegemony. The only difference was that Giolitti sought to broaden the 'dictatorship' by the creation of a 'northern urban bloc' of capitalists and workers.[24] Gramsci had explained this shift in an essay written shortly before his imprisonment:

> After the bloody decade 1890–1900, the bourgeoisie was forced to renounce a dictatorship that was too exclusive, too violent, too direct. For there had risen against it simultaneously...the southern peasants and the northern workers.
>
> In the new century, the ruling class inaugurated a new policy of class alliances, class political blocs; i.e. bourgeois democracy. It had to choose: either a rural democracy, i.e. an alliance with the southern peasant...or a capitalist/worker industrial bloc... It chose...the latter solution. Giolitti personified bourgeois rule; the Socialist party became the instrument of Giolitti's policies.[25]

Rather than continue to suppress socialism, Giolitti sought to 'transform' the northern workers (or at least their political representatives) from opponents of the regime into supporters of the system. Giolitti was obliged, however, to modify his 'programme' once the Italian Socialist party (PSI) abandoned reformism in favour of revolutionary 'maximalism' in the wake of the Libyan war, and the introduction of universal suffrage made it impossible to 'control' the southern electorate through 'traditional' forms of individual corruption. In consequence:

> Giolitti changed partners: he replaced the urban bloc by...the 'Gentiloni pact'...a bloc between northern industry and the farmers of the 'organic and normal' countryside (the Catholic electoral forces...spread over the north and the centre); it had additional support in the south as well – at least to an extent immediately sufficient to 'rectify' satisfactorily the consequences of the mass electorate's enlargement.[26]

To summarize Gramsci's thesis:

- The weakness of the Italian bourgeoisie, the absence of fundamental agrarian reform, meant the persistence of strong 'feudal' elements within Italian politics and economy after unification.
- The result (in contrast to the creation of the 'compact modern French nation' following the Jacobin revolution) was the formation of a 'bastard' modern Italian state.
- The incomplete nature of Italy's passive bourgeois revolution produced a flawed process of political and economic modernization based on coercion (of peasants) and compromise (with feudal vestiges and industry).

This was a powerful counter-argument to Croce's liberal paean.

Subsequent historiography

The liberal standard-bearers

After 1945, there was a flurry of activity from historians in defence of liberal politics, in the main working from Croce's original map – the differences were essentially ones of detail and emphasis. These post-war 'liberal' historians were motivated by a variety of factors: their own political attachment to liberal ideals; a desire to defend Croce's reputation, and that of liberal Italy, from the anti-Crocean, anti-liberal, Gramscian school; a determination to defend united Italy's liberal secular traditions from a growing Catholic political culture.

Prominent within the post-war Italian liberal canon was the work of Federico Chabod. In his highly acclaimed *Storia della politica estera italiana dal 1870 al 1896* (1951) – despite its title, a book as much about domestic politics as foreign policy, and with its focus very much on the early 1870s – Chabod set out to explore the many influences (national and international, political, social, cultural and economic) at work upon Italian politics, and to demonstrate how these influences imposed themselves upon the Italian political experience.[27] Chabod threw into sharp relief some of the conundrums facing the Italian political class after unification. How was Rome to be established as the capital of a secular nation state when at the same time it was the historic and symbolic centre of a universal religion? The separation of church and state was one approach (and favoured by the *destra*), but to leave the Church to its own devices risked perpetuating reaction within the Church, while doing nothing to curb papal intrigues against the Italian secular state or lessen the influence of the pontiff over the population. A more vigorous anti-clerical line would put at risk relations with other Catholic countries and stimulate further 'black' conspiracies within Italy. How was Italy to 'modernize' – industrialize, educate, enfranchise – without damaging the integrity of the liberal state itself? Industrialization promised greater prosperity but also meant the creation of a 'working class' and the spread of 'dangerous' ideas: socialism and anarchism. Many viewed secular education as essential if the hold of the Church over a superstitious and ignorant people was to be broken. To others, though, a campaign of mass literacy meant putting the state 'into the hands of its plebeian citizens, the most discontented element, the most presumptuous because of its half-learning, the most deranged and subversive in our society'.[28] On the issue of electoral reform, while a broadened franchise might help to bridge the gap between 'legal' and 'real' Italy, to many the idea of giving the vote to the masses risked turning the countryside 'black' (the peasantry in thrall of the priests) and the cities 'red' (the urban workers controlled by socialist-anarchist agitators). The masses could not be entrusted with the vote. A property or wealth-based franchise, on the other hand, ensured that those entitled to vote represented 'hard work, saving, industriousness, farsightedness'.[29]

Chabod also emphasized how the weight of past Italian greatness hung heavy on the new state. Italian nationalism earlier in the century had drawn strength from the glories of classical Rome and the Renaissance, firstly to emphasize Italy's right to govern itself, secondly in order to contrast past and present Italy and to blame Italy's current lowly status on foreign rule. For many leading nationalists – Gioberti, Mazzini, Garibaldi, for example – Rome had been of particular emotional, spiritual and symbolic importance. The problem for the rulers of Italy after 1870 was how to demonstrate Italy's 'rebirth' as a nation of the first order while at the same time tailoring Italian foreign policy to international and domestic realities. Italy was a new political state and a poor country lacking a powerful and reliable international ally. Consolidation and patience were required.

Step forward the *destra*. The heroes of Chabod's account, the *destra* combined the high ideals of liberty, justice and humanity with a pragmatic approach to domestic and international problems, recognizing the importance of the *juste milieu* – the middle way – and sensibly resisting the dream of imperial Rome reborn. The age of the Right may have seemed prosaic after the poetry of the Risorgimento, but it was vital to the survival and development of the fledgling Italian state.[30]

In stark contrast to the men of the *destra* was the figure of Francesco Crispi. According to Chabod, whereas the nationalism of the *destra* was closely bound up with the pursuit of liberty, Crispi instead embraced the 'mean, jealous and hostile' nationalism of Bismarck's Prussia, one 'closed in on itself...bound up with the reborn spirit of conquest'. Turning his back on the ideals of the Risorgimento, Crispi had played to 'the type of Italian who had not changed for the last two or three centuries, an Italian to whom liberty and unity had come too rapidly and with too much persistence from fortune, an Italian having too little political preparation but a head full of literature and schoolroom memories...an Italian who breathed a false and corrupt atmosphere'. Chabod was scornful, too, of Crispi's efforts to create a new Rome 'powerful and magnificent', his readiness to put authority before liberty, of his lack of perspective and restraint. As Christopher Duggan has noted, Chabod, like Croce before him, was convinced that Crispi had 'wrenched Italy from its true liberal path'.[31]

Alongside Chabod, the Sicilian-born historian Rosario Romeo stands out as the major Italian figure of the post-war liberal historical school. Romeo had close ties to Croce: he was the secretary of the Italian Institute of Historical Studies established by Croce in 1947. Romeo argued it was impossible to 'doubt the leap forward that the new national collectivity achieved in comparison to the somnolent reality of the tiny pre-Unification states, which concealed poverty and impotence behind calm and graceful facades'. This 'leap forward' was founded upon 'the secular and worldly ethics of modern civilization' inherent within the Risorgimento and embodied in Italy's liberal political elite, notably the *destra*. For Romeo, 'writing history was always...the most effective and constructive means of participating in the life and problems of his own time', and, as a convinced liberal and passionate anti-Marxist, Romeo actively sought confrontation with the Gramscian school.[32] According to Romeo, the 'Gramsci thesis' was 'anti-historical'. There had been no possibility of a successful agrarian revolution in 1860 since international opinion simply would not have allowed it, and the vast financial and technical resources required to create a functioning agricultural economy based on small-scale property ownership did not exist. Gramsci, argued

Romeo, was wrong to criticize Italy's ruling élite for its failure to pursue what was an impossible course. Even if an agrarian revolution *had* been possible, its consequences would have been disastrous: it would have retarded Italy's economic development and been detrimental to unity. Unification under the moderates, in contrast, had allowed Italy to transform itself into an industrial, modern state. Romeo acknowledged economic modernization had been at the expense of the agrarian economy and of the southern economy especially. He argued, though, that successful economic modernization always necessitated the exploitation of the rural economy. Moreover, the liberal state had sought to ameliorate the most severe effects of modernization, and the sacrifices made in order to modernize were ultimately balanced by the long-term benefits resulting from that process (see also Chapter 2).[33]

As Chabod and Romeo followed Croce in their praise of the *destra storica*, so other post-war historians of the liberal school shared his admiration for Giolitti. For the Italo-American historian Arcangelo Salomone, for example, Giolittian Italy was 'a democracy in the making'. Working under the precept of 'liberty for all within the limits of the law', Giolitti had overseen a period of great economic progress and social, political and economic reform. In doing so, he had brought Italy once again into 'the vanguard of European civilization. It had been a difficult ascendancy, but a true national resurgence'. The Libyan war, during which, according to Salomone, 'the majority of Italians rallied around their government in an amazing show of solidarity', was a marker of this advance.[34]

Salomone's arguments, put forward in the mid-1940s, were taken up and amplified in the 1970s and 1980s by another Italo-American historian, Frank Coppa. For Coppa, Giolitti was a practical liberal who, unlike most of his peers, understood that if the liberal state was to survive in a new age of mass politics, it 'could only follow a democratic course'.[35] 'In many respects', Coppa declared, 'the Giolittian state was the predecessor of the modern welfare state and Giolitti was in some ways the forerunner of Franklin Delano Roosevelt...both men were essentially democratic figures'.[36] Both Coppa and Salomone played down or excused the less palatable aspects of Giolittian rule: the use of coercion, bribery and fraud in elections, and Giolitti's constant interventions, via the prefecture, in local politics. Giolitti was not the first to employ such methods; such activities had been standard in Italian politics for decades. Moreover, without a strong disciplined party behind him, and confronted by powerful and implacable opponents on both the Left and the Right, Giolitti had little choice but 'to rely upon the solid wall of the state and its administration in order to accomplish many of his [progressive] goals'. Was this not a case, then, of the ends justifying the means?[37]

Post-war critics of the liberal state

From a historiographical perspective, the dominant anti-liberal interpretation within Italy since 1945 has been that of the Marxist school. While the Communist Party consolidated itself as a major political force in post-war Italian politics, Marxist writers expounded and expanded upon Gramsci's ideas. Foremost amongst post-war Marxist interpretations was the work of the economic historian Emilio Sereni.[38] Focusing on the links between the agrarian economy and Italian capitalism, Sereni's *Il capitalismo nelle campagne, 1860–1900* (1947) endorsed Gramsci's politically driven interpretation: Italy had experienced an incomplete bourgeois revolution. The weakness of the bourgeoisie, the absence of a genuine agrarian revolution, the survival of remnants of the feudal order, had all delayed and deformed Italian capitalism:

> The incompleteness of the bourgeois revolution in Italy would not only have important political consequences, leaving the way open to recurrent attacks on the part of the old dominating classes, and maintaining their influence in the political life of the country and in the state machinery itself; but it was to be at the root of all the difficulties and all the internal contradictions of Italian capitalism... For many years to come one would be able to say of Italy what Marx said about the Germany of his time: that 'it suffered both from capitalism and from an insufficient development of the same'.[39]

Subsequent Marxist histories deviated little from this basic model.

Alongside the Marxist school after 1945, a number of liberal Italy's contemporary critics remained to attack its political record. For example, the left-wing democrat and historian Gaetano Salvemini – who had famously described Giolitti as the 'minister of the underworld' in 1910 – condemned Giolitti as 'a corrupter of Italian democracy in the making' in his introduction to Salomone's *Italy in the Giolittian Era*. Giolitti, he argued, had sacrificed the long-term interests of the south in return for the support of the southern conservative elite, and had stunted the nation's political development through his unprecedented interference in local government and the rigging of elections. Emphasizing the gulf between 'legal' and 'real' Italy, Salvemini claimed that while Giolitti was the 'most powerful man in parliament' he was also 'the most unpopular man in the country'. Salvemini's only real regret was that his criticisms of Giolitti (and those of others from the Left) had perhaps helped to lead Italy not towards democracy but to 'militarism, nationalism and reaction', i.e. to Fascism. Given the chance to relive 1900–14, Salvemini wrote, 'I would not omit any of my censures of the Giolittian system, but I would be more indulgent and I would regard with greater suspicion those who found pleasure in my criticism because they wanted to lead Italy in the opposite direction from that which I envisaged for her'. Salvemini's 1952 claim that 'the difference between Mussolini and Giolitti was one of degree and not of kind. Giolitti was for Mussolini what John the Baptist was for Christ: he paved his way', clarified his position.[40]

Many of Salvemini's favourite targets – Giolitti's manipulation of parliament and of elections, southern political corruption and violence (and the 'colonial' status of the south), the insidious role of the prefecture – have all found echoes in later historical accounts, both Italian and Anglo-Saxon, Marxist and non-Marxist. Compare, for example, Salvemini's description of the prefecture as the 'gnawing cancer of Italian democracy' with Ernesto Ragionieri's 1961 assessment of the prefect's job as one of 'systematic control and suffocation of local political life, of assiduous and meticulous interference, which constantly transformed the representative of the state into the representative of the government', and R. C. Fried's 1963 view that the prefecture took 'the leading role in the manufacture of parliamentary majorities'.[41] Compare, too, Salvemini's verdict that Giolitti's management of elections 'surpassed all in clarity of purpose and lack of scruples' with Denis Mack Smith's 1959 claim that methods of 'electoral chicanery' were 'brought to a fine art by Giolitti's election managers'.[42]

Mack Smith, neatly described by Bosworth as an 'Oxbridgean gentleman-radical',[43] is by some distance the best known and most respected (both within Italy and throughout the English-speaking world) 'foreign' historian of modern Italian politics. Similarly, *Italy: A Modern History* has probably been the most influential (and perhaps the most controversial) post-war English-language contribution to the liberal critics' camp.[44]

Mack Smith's account was explicitly a search for the 'flaws...embedded in nineteenth century liberal patriotism and its achievements' which ultimately led Italy to Fascism in the twentieth century.[45] Although certainly not a Marxist, Mack Smith nevertheless attributed liberal Italy's political 'failure' to structural causes. An expansive and expensive foreign policy, driven by considerations of prestige and an obsession with great power status, were the most obvious cause of Italy's ruin. But foreign policy was in itself only a reflection of domestic constitutional deficiencies that precluded healthy political and economic development and which in turn were rooted in social and economic weaknesses. Italians might be 'among the most resilient as well as the most civilized and gifted [people] of any in the world', but Italian liberal politics carried within them the seeds of their own demise. Mack Smith's approach did not prevent him paying handsome tributes to individual politicians (of the *destra's* leaders, Mack Smith wrote 'Seldom in Italian history has the country possessed rulers so talented and incorruptible'; Depretis he considered 'an extraordinary man').[46] However, his thesis emphasized that even 'talented' politicians were obliged to work within – and necessarily contributed to – an inherently defective political system.[47] *Trasformismo*, which destroyed party politics and killed political passions and idealism, was 'rooted in the structure of the Italian parliament'. Efforts to extend political participation (franchise reform in 1882 and 1912) served only to encourage greater centralization and illiberal tendencies. The links between liberalism and Fascism were evident: *trasformismo* characterized both liberal and later Fascist politics; 'parliamentary dictatorship', the consequence of *trasformismo*, 'differed only in degree whether under Cavour, Depretis, Crispi, or Giolitti, or even under Mussolini' in the first years of Fascist rule. Here, of course, was a direct repudiation of the Crocean claim that Fascism was solely a product of World War One, and a rejection of the 'liberal' school's argument that Crispi – the arch-villain of the Croce/Chabod interpretation – represented a hiatus in liberal politics. Mack Smith acknowledged that Crispi, of the leading politicians of the liberal period, was closest to Mussolini in style, temperament and in his approach to foreign and domestic politics. He insisted, however, that Italian liberalism was always susceptible to 'forward and forceful' tendencies in foreign policy at the expense of domestic welfare. Moreover, a constant within liberal politics – and Italian society – was a 'nostalgia for authority', encouraged by the 'ineradicable anarchism' of the Italians themselves. 'Exaggerated individualism, which had been the great glory of Italy, was also her greatest peril. The police state was accepted as an attempt to remedy it, but so rooted was the disease that this remedy only made it worse.'[48]

Not surprisingly, Mack Smith considered Giolitti's decision to go to war with Turkey over Libya in 1911 indicative of the weaknesses of Italian liberalism. The twin issues of prestige (the continuing search for international status) and *trasformismo* (Giolitti's concern to bring anti-liberal nationalist opposition into the liberal parliamentary fold) guided Giolitti's actions. The war achieved neither: international opinion was unimpressed, and Italian nationalists remained openly hostile to 'degenerate' bourgeois liberalism. Moreover, the Libyan war pushed the PSI away from the liberal state: the revolutionary 'maximalist' wing of the PSI defeated the pro-war reformist leadership at the 1912 party congress. Giolitti's efforts to co-opt Italian socialism had failed.

Other critics of the liberal interpretation besides Mack Smith use the Libyan campaign as a measure of the lack of progress and maturity of Italian liberalism. Bosworth, for example, who has written extensively on liberal foreign policy, sees Libya as a consequence of the *failure* of Italian diplomacy to secure Italian 'interests' overseas, a reflection of Italy's position as the 'least of the great powers', rather than as confirmation of Italy's place amongst the European élite. Some historians have brought to discussions about liberal foreign policy the oft-repeated argument we have come across regarding domestic politics: that liberal politicians – and Giolitti in particular – were in hock to the interests of powerful minority interest groups within Italy, in this instance heavy industry and finance. Italian industrialization, so the argument runs, was closely tied to the liberal state's political obsession with great power status: industry developed in response to the state's military requirements. Inherently weak and uncompetitive, heavy industry was from the start reliant upon the state (subsidies, contracts, protection) – but at the same time the state was reliant upon industry if Italy were to become a major international player. The result of this unhealthy mutual reliance was spectacular industrial inefficiency, a 'chronic imbalance' in the Italian economy, and the ability of industry in times of economic difficulty (e.g. during the economic slow-down after 1907–8) to determine state policy. By 1911, 'heavy industry had reached the point of being able to influence political developments'.[49] Seen in this light, the Libyan war represented less the 'maturity' of the liberal state, more the 'flawed' nature of Italian political and economic modernization.

Revisionist trends: Towards a new political history of liberal Italy?

Lucy Riall has commented of contemporary trends in Risorgimento studies: the 'concern of revisionist historiography [has been] to get away from the emphasis on what might have been (and regret why it wasn't) and to concentrate instead on what was'.[50] Revisionist historiography of the liberal period shares this concern.

A consequence of this (in both Risorgimento and liberal revisionism) has been the evolution of a less critical (or dismissive) historiography. Risorgimento revisionism, that stresses unification was not the only possible outcome of the political and social changes in Italy in the first half of the nineteenth century, that dwells on the strength of localism (even amongst that class most associated with unification – the bourgeoisie), and highlights the incomplete and uneven process of modern state formation (centralization, bureaucratization) in pre-unitary Italy, has clear implications for liberal revisionism, too. The complexities and contradictions inherent within Italian unification do not disappear with unity. Awareness of this has encouraged the generally sympathetic – empathetic – approach of revisionist historians of the liberal period.[51]

Much of the revisionist literature has had an institutional or administrative focus. Raffaele Romanelli is perhaps the leading exponent of this approach. Romanelli's work emphasizes the profoundly *liberal* nature of the liberal state. Instead of the liberal state as authoritarian, repressive and suffocatingly centralized – the precursor of Fascism – Romanelli presents it as the embodiment of classical liberal ideals. Liberal institutions were modelled on the progressive Belgian example of 1830 and the Code Napoléon. Liberal policies (e.g. the sale of Church lands, the abolition of collective and communal rights, the end to corporative society, the refusal to run state railways and canals, the justice system built on the individual rights of private property) were designed to encourage private and individual interests. Central, too, to the liberal concept of the state was the idea of local political autonomy. The Provincial and Communal Law (1865), traditionally seen as the basis of the heavily centralized state ('suffocating centralization'), in fact allowed considerable room at the periphery (e.g. important financial autonomy to local government). This was the first time that much of Italy had experienced local self-government (Romanelli calls it an 'explosion of autonomy'). Central powers were assumed by the state, not to control the periphery but, rather, to provide the impulse for liberal mobilization and modernization at the local level. Romanelli emphasizes the weakness of civil society and the aim of Italian liberalism to 'regenerate' this society. From this perspective, the old complaint of excessive bureaucracy is reinterpreted as a complaint against what is perceived as excessive administrative efforts to 'mobilize' Italians. The prefect – so often regarded as the symbol of government authoritarianism and repression – is remade. On the one hand, the prefect is seen as the liberal cheerleader at the local level, prompting and cajoling inexperienced or unwilling local authorities to meet their obligations regarding expenditure on modernizing infrastructures. The apparently 'illiberal' power of the prefect to dissolve municipal councils and to impose a special agent to manage local affairs is seen in this light as one which provided 'the opportunity to make positive provisions for communal services' where local government had been slow to act. Prefectural 'interference' in elections is seen as an effort to 'energize' the electoral process – to get those eligible to register to register, and those registered to vote to vote (turn-out was very low). On the other hand, the prefect is portrayed as the mediator between national and local interests – for example, in the appointment of mayors (who in keeping with continental practice, were both government officials and heads of municipal authorities) – rather than simply the tool of the Ministry of the Interior. The aim of central power was to enforce liberty (to act if necessary as the 'iron hand of liberty' according to senior Interior Ministry officials). Romanelli quotes the leading Piedmontese politician Urbano Rattazzi from 1859 to demonstrate how the liberals saw their mission. Through the prefect, Rattazzi wrote, the government 'sits at the head of the province and commune less to control as to encourage there the development of liberty under the conditions of the law, less to make the hand of central authority felt as to make there appreciated the advantage of having it close, ready and competent'.[52]

The problem for the liberal state was that it could not enforce liberalism. Romanelli describes this as liberalism's 'impossible command': 'I order you to be free.'[53] As a number of historians have noted, political modernization and autonomy were not comfortable bedfellows. Political modernization alienated the old élite, while the newly empowered bourgeois élite at the local level were not necessarily interested in, or aligned with, the national liberal programme.[54] Local/regional autonomy and the 'language of liberty furnished local elites with a fiendishly powerful tool with which to resist the incursions of the centre', to block the liberal revolution from above.[55] Liberal government respect for local autonomy and the weakness of liberal authority at the periphery – the prefect was often an isolated figure – meant the state was unable to enforce its will.

A feature of liberal Italy frequently seized upon by its critics as evidence of its shortcomings is the limited nature of the electoral franchise. Liberal Italy not only lagged behind other 'modern' European states in this regard, but the restricted franchise, so it is argued, meant the gap between 'legal' and 'real' could not be bridged and 'thus just over half a million male voters, dominated by a few thousand influential men, determined the fate of 25 million Italian subjects'.[56] Even these criticisms, however, are turned on their head by Romanelli: the national electorate may have been small, he argues, but even before the 1882 reform act it included all the propertied and professional classes (i.e. the franchise incorporated the same '"civic stratum" of the population' in Italy that had the vote elsewhere in Europe).[57] Romanelli and other revisionists are quick to point out, too, that liberal politicians recognized the need to broaden the suffrage; the question was how to widen participation without damaging the state. Here revisionism treads some old historiographical ground. Although anxious to 'make Italians', and aware that to establish a collective identity required the 'education in liberty' of the masses, the ruling liberal class feared that this would give oxygen to 'anti-system' (i.e. anti-liberal) forces (socialism and Catholicism) which in turn would threaten the liberal institutions which underpinned unification. The perceived threat to the liberal state posed by socialism and Catholicism meant that the politicization of the nation (i.e. the creation of an adversarial political system allowing for the recomposition of social tensions in exclusively political terms) could not be considered. Organized political parties were regarded as potentially threatening to the liberal state. *Trasformismo* was a natural response. By creating a solid parliamentary majority, *trasformismo* was a source of stability: it allowed parliament to meet the immense challenges of unification, to enact necessary reforms, to extend political consensus without undermining the state's structures. Seen in European terms, liberal Italy's response was not unusual. Moreover, if Italian Liberals were guilty of 'failing' to establish a modern mass party (commonly seen by liberal critics as indicative of liberalism's failure to fuse 'legal' and 'real' Italy) then this was part of a broader failure of European liberalism: no such party was created elsewhere either.[58]

Assessment

This chapter has identified three major historical schools of thought on the politics of liberal Italy:

The liberal perspective. Despite some imperfections and weaknesses, the record of the liberal state could be considered generally a success. Liberal Italy was essentially in robust health in 1914.

The Marxist perspective. The inherent structural weaknesses of the liberal state guaranteed its deviation from the 'normal' path of modern state development and ensured its ultimate failure. Some non-Marxist historians, e.g. Denis Mack Smith, also share this view, although for different reasons.

The revisionist perspective. Despite inherent contradictions within the liberal mission, the liberal state developed a series of rational responses – informed by liberalism – to particular political difficulties. Italian political development was merely different from that of other European states rather than deviant. Liberal Italy's ties with, or responsibility for, Fascism are ignored or implicitly rejected.

These different perspectives illustrate nicely Croce's perceptive 1938 comment that 'all history is contemporary history', i.e. the contemporary environment shapes historical interpretation. Regarding Croce's work, we need to bear in mind his own background. Croce had family ties to the *destra storica*: his uncle, Silvio Spaventa, was one of the leading figures on the Right and an old colleague of Cavour. Croce himself was directly involved in liberal politics: he was a senator from 1910; he served twice in Cabinet, including as Education Minister in Giolitti's last government, 1920–1. We should also remember that he wrote his 'splendid apology for liberalism' during the Fascist period.[59] Croce was keen to identify liberal Italy as the true heir of the Risorgimento (the 'masterpiece of European liberalism'; the embodiment of truth and liberty) in order both to challenge Fascism's own claim to the Risorgimento and to isolate Fascism from the 'normal' path of history as the story of liberty (Croce's 'parenthesis' thesis – see Chapter 4). With Gramsci, too, we should not forget that his writing was informed not only by his personal situation (imprisonment) but also by the collapse of the Left in the face of Fascism. Gramsci was concerned primarily with using history to explain the failure of the Left and outline its path to redemption. Chabod's work surveys the history of liberal Italy from the wreckage of World War Two. Romeo and Sereni write as Cold War activists. Mack Smith reflects the Anglo-Saxon Italophile's disappointment with the reality of Italy (Fascism and war) which clashes with their idealized concept of Italians (as civilized and gifted) and which fails to match up to the English example. The generally muted criticism of liberal Italy from post-war American scholars – and their endorsement of Giolitti – is indicative of the conservative cultural milieu of the United States during the Cold War. (There also may be something in Bosworth's argument that the American historians of modern Italy are generally less prone to criticism than their English counterparts because the bulk of American Italianists are, in fact, Italo-American).[60] Finally, it cannot be a complete coincidence that revisionism has taken root against the background of the decline and collapse of post-war political movements and ideologies, themselves the victims of 'post-industrialization' and the end of the Cold War. Revisionism reflects the 'de-ideologizing' trend within contemporary Western society that endorses a pragmatic, technocratic, management-style approach to political problems.

There are problems with each of the historical 'schools' of liberal Italy. The Crocean-liberal approach idealizes both the Risorgimento and the post-unification liberal élite. Liberal historians tend to ignore or excuse the problems of Italian liberalism – the recourse to violence, the evidence of widespread political corruption, the absence of clear political parties representative of wider society, etc. Furthermore, to deny, like Croce, the links between liberal and Fascist Italy is to disregard the very real continuities between the two (just as there were clear continuities between Fascism and the post-1945 republic).[61]

There are fundamental weaknesses in the Gramscian interpretation. At one level, it is easy to see the power of Gramsci's ideas. As with the Marxist interpretation of the French Revolution, Gramsci's concept of the Risorgimento as 'passive revolution' was neat and all-encompassing: it provided an explanation of the weakness of the Italian state, of its reliance upon coercion, of Italy's slow economic development, of the north–south divide, and of the rise of Fascism. The power of Gramsci's thought was enhanced by the fact that after World War Two the PCI – a powerful force in post-war Italy – embraced him as a Communist martyr to the anti-Fascist cause and his writings as the work of a great Communist intellectual (despite Gramsci's isolation from leading Italian Communists from the mid-1920s). Gramsci became 'the Marxist you can take home to mother'.[62] However, and this should not to be taken as academic prejudice, Gramsci was not an historian. His reading of the Italian Risorgimento as a 'revolution without revolution' was, as with all his work, primarily political and concerned with the contemporary world. In many ways, the story of the Party of Action's failure to appeal to the rural masses and its absorption by the moderates is Gramsci's critique of the PSI during the Giolittian age and in the immediate post-war period. His thesis, far less coherent and complete than many secondary accounts suggest, was as much an exhortation to the Italian working class to open itself to the needs of the peasantry – a demand that Gramsci repeatedly made during the 1920s and 1930s – as an historical investigation of the unification process. As Croce commented, one should beware of treating the opinions of political writers as historical judgements. There are, too, key flaws in the basic Marxist historical model that Gramsci adapts to the Italian context. Few historians today would accept unreservedly the Marxian concept of the French Revolution as a 'bourgeois' revolution which destroyed the existing feudal order and gave birth to the 'compact modern French nation'. (Gramsci himself seems unsure on this point, talking of the 'immediate collapse' of the ancien régime in France in the 'great revolution' that began in 1789 but also claiming 'it was only in 1870–1...that all the germs of 1789 were finally exhausted. It was then that the new bourgeois class...defeated...the representatives of the old society').[63] In fact, Gramsci greatly underestimates the power of the 'old orders' in nineteenth-century Europe – it is not accurate to say that 'The old feudal classes are demoted from their dominant position to a "governing" one...they become a "caste"...no longer with predominant economic functions.'[64] Capitalism was not solely the prerogative of the bourgeoisie, nor was the bourgeoisie monolithically capitalist. Gramsci's assertion that 'Rural France accepted the hegemony of Paris', i.e. that French Jacobin hegemony was based on the voluntary consent of the rural masses, is also some way wide of the mark: the 'alliance' between town and country was often forced upon an unwilling peasantry (itself hardly a monolith).[65] The Jacobin model of revolution, against which Gramsci unfavourably judges the performance of the Italian democrats, is thus open to question itself. Beyond this, on the issue of Gramsci's analysis of Italian history, Romeo was right that Gramsci complains of the absence of something (agrarian revolution) that could not happen. For Gramsci to say that the Party of Action 'ought to have allied itself with the rural masses', and 'ought to have been Jacobin', and that 'action directed at the peasantry was certainly always possible', while also admitting that the historical climate after 1815 ruled out Jacobinism in an Italian context and that international circumstances ruled out all but Cavour's approach, demonstrates Gramsci's uncertainty and lack of clarity and consistency on this point.[66] Would the Great Powers have tolerated agrarian reform (land for peasants)? Probably not. It is hard to see 1860 in this light as a missed opportunity.[67] Equally, it is difficult to find evidence to justify the charge of an alliance between the northern industrial bourgeoisie and southern landowners that sold the south into slavery. The idea of a capitalist/worker industrial bloc mediated by Giolitti after 1900 also does not stand up to closer inspection, as Coppa has demonstrated.[68]

Non-Marxist critiques of the liberal period (e.g. Mack Smith's *Italy*) also appear to be wrongly premised. Whereas Gramsci applied the Marxist model of revolutionary France to contrast and highlight the failings of Risorgimento Italy, so Mack Smith appeared to judge liberal Italy against a 'Whiggish' notion of Britain as a model of peaceful, evolutionary and inclusive liberal-democratic parliamentary government. Mack Smith writes that 'It was particularly disturbing that deputies seemed to represent the wrong people', yet British political life, too, was dominated in the late nineteenth century by a powerful and profoundly unrepresentative minority, the landed aristocracy. State force was also used in Britain. Westminster politicians displayed the same schizophrenic tendencies towards socialism as their Roman counterparts, oscillating between repression and concession; and, when faced with their own version of the Italian 'Southern Question' in Ireland, they responded in like fashion. One should be careful not to exaggerate the presence of a functioning democracy in Britain prior to 1914. Put in proper context, the Italian experience looks altogether less 'deviant'.

As we have seen, revisionist historians have questioned liberal Italy's 'deviancy'. The point is an important one. Revisionism, however, does occasionally suffer from a surfeit of goodwill towards the Italian ruling class. In seeking to normalize such 'flaws' as *trasformismo*, and the state's use of the 'iron hand', revisionists are sometimes guilty of failing to exercise critical judgement on the appropriateness (or otherwise) of those actions. As Lucy Riall has pointed out concerning revisionist arguments about the logic of *trasformismo*, 'good intentions' on the part of the Italian parliament 'did not necessarily translate into good government'. Saverio Battente has correctly argued that the Italian state's 'recourse to authority' was certainly not always 'aimed at the growth of civil society' but was 'often an instrument for partisan interests'.[69] In such cases the reluctance of revisionists to criticize suggests identification with those decisions and actions, and amounts to apologism via the back door – the politician's defence of their own decisions/actions becomes the implicit argument of the historian. At such times, revisionism comes close to repeating the failings of Croce and the 'liberal school'.

Where does this leave us? Bearing in mind Mack Smith's dictum 'He is a coward and a dullard who does not risk some interim judgements on the course of history', let us try to reach some conclusions.[70] We cannot deny or ignore the élitist, corrupt and often authoritarian nature of Italian liberalism. Nor can we fail to recognize the distance between 'legal' Italy and 'real' Italy up to 1914: Italy's rulers did indeed fail to exercise 'hegemony' over the greater part of Italy's population. Marxist class-based analysis does not offer an empirically sound explanation for either. Liberal historians offer little in the way of explanation for the former and blame circumstances and parties other than the liberals for the latter. The problems facing the rulers of united Italy were indeed great, and Salomone is right to argue that we must remember that we have a new game after unification, one that the political class have to come to terms with, which the clergy refuse to play, which the peasants do not understand, and the nobility play by their own rules. Salomone quotes Sonnino in 1880 to illustrate his point: 'If our liberals had known the country better perhaps they would not have found the courage to create Italy.'[71] In particular, one should not under-emphasize the immense damage done to the moral authority of the liberal state by the Vatican's opposition to it. As Nicholas Doumanis has written, the Church 'was the one institution that enjoyed real moral authority throughout the country and which was capable of rallying the great mass of the people to the new order. Its refusal to play that role...meant the construction of the Italian nation began with a very serious handicap'.[72] We must bear in mind, however, not only the problems facing the new state after 1870, but also the contradictory task facing the liberal state after unification. Here, revisionism seems to point the way to a more complete understanding of the Janus-like character of Italian liberalism. To borrow from Riall again, the need to establish a modern state (the process of modern state formation) – at the same time an 'inherently authoritarian' exercise and a source of considerable tension and instability – clashed with the need to meet the other great political challenge of the age: the establishment of a political consensus based on representative government. 'Facing the challenges of state formation and liberal consensus simultaneously, Italian liberals had to be pragmatic and conciliatory, and they also had to stand firm against any threat to their position. Arguably, to have any hope of success, they had to come up with exactly the combination of authoritarianism and liberalism with which historians of liberal Italy are so familiar'.[73]

What were the prospects for the liberal state in 1914? Did it still 'have any hope of success'? It would be unhistorical (as well as pointless) to debate whether liberal Italy would have survived the challenges of mass politics, revolutionary socialism, or radical nationalism had there been no war. It is fair to say, however, that the rapid collapse of liberal Italy after 1918 has encouraged historians to exaggerate the weakness of the liberal state on the eve of war. Certainly, the challenges facing Italian liberalism in 1914 were still considerable. Yet Italian liberalism had proved remarkably resilient over the previous half-century. Ultimately, it took a war entirely unlike any other previous conflict – a total war – to bring it to its knees.

2 The economy of liberal Italy

Introduction

There is general agreement that the Italian economy at the time of unification was underdeveloped in comparison with much of northern and western Europe. Nobody would dissent from the view that Italy was a wealthier, more economically advanced, country by 1914 – in other words, that the economy had developed and grown in the five decades since unity. There is, too, universal recognition of the presence of a 'north–south' economic divide in 1870 and the persistence, and aggravation, of this economic 'dualism' over the next half-century and beyond. This, however, is about as far as the consensus extends. The areas of debate can be summarized thus:

- *The nature of change.* Did the changes to the Italian economy represent a fundamental break with previous economic trends (specifically, did rapid economic growth in the Giolittian age mark the 'take-off' of the Italian economy)? Or was growth during the liberal period, including the Giolittian era, more gradual and in line with long-term trends?
- *The extent of Italy's transformation.* Should we emphasize the limited and partial character of Italy's transformation from 'pre-modern' agrarianism to 'modern' capitalism-industrialism? Should we accept the 'magnificent transformation' (Alexander Gerschenkron's description) of the Italian economy while recognizing that Italy still 'could have done better'? Or did Italy do as well as could be expected given domestic and international constraints?

Linked to these are the following issues:

- *The nature of constraints.* Was Italy's development held back by domestic factors? Was the Italian economy the prisoner of a 'backward' agrarian sector? Should we blame the nature and/or role of the state for Italy's economic underperformance? Or was the development of the Italian economy constrained more by international economic factors – Italy's precarious position in the expanding world economy?
- *The reasons for economic growth.* To what extent was growth due to domestic factors? Did agriculture play a positive rather than a negative or merely passive role in Italy's

economic development after 1870? Is the accusation of agricultural backwardness justifiable? Should we source the transformation of the Italian economy (linked primarily to industrialization) to the policies of the state, or to other domestic institutional factors – the role of banks, for example? Or were external factors – the expansion of world trade, emigration – behind economic growth?

Many of the arguments concerning the Italian economy en tout have also played important roles in debates on the 'Southern Question'. The south's inability to match northern Italy's economic development and the increasingly dualistic nature of the Italian economy have often been ascribed to southern economic 'backwardness' and/or to its socio-cultural shortcomings. Equally, the policies of the Italian state have often been highlighted as the cause of the south's 'failure'. Either way, the 'Southern Question' has traditionally cast the south in a negative light with the emphasis on economic stagnation, socio-cultural immobilism and the concept of the south as a passive spectator, or victim, of 'modernization'. More recently, however, revisionist historians have questioned whether it is appropriate even to talk in terms of a 'Southern Question'. To view the south as an economic (or, indeed, social or cultural) monolith is, so the argument runs, to ignore diversity within the region (the revisionist mantra is 'many souths' rather than one 'south'). To focus exclusively on the lack of development is to ignore the very real growth and dynamism of elements within the southern economy and southern society. However, traditional issues – the role of the state and the influence of external and internal factors on southern economic development – remain important features of the debate.[1]

The arguments over liberal Italy's economic performance have deep roots. First, debates have been fuelled by the incomplete and disputed nature of the economic data. On the one hand, limited and fragmented statistics for the first half of the nineteenth century leave room for doubt about the actual state of the economy in Italy prior to unification. It also makes it difficult to judge how well the unified economy performed in comparison, or to what extent subsequent growth represented a continuation of, or break with, existing trends or patterns. On the other hand, the poor quality of the data covering the liberal period means that judgements on economic performance can be, and have been, contested. Contemporary statistics lacked consistency and accuracy, while subsequent estimates have by and large worked off, or modified, data produced by the Istituto Centrale di Statistica (ISTAT) in the mid–late 1950s, data which itself is generally regarded as flawed.[2] Second, ideology has played a major role in economic historiography. Gramsci's political interpretation of the Risorgimento as a 'passive revolution' had clear economic implications, made explicit by Sereni and repeated by subsequent Marxist historians. From the opposite pole, Romeo used economic arguments to attack 'la tesi del Gramsci' and defend the record of Italian liberalism. As with the 'Cold War' debates over the political record of liberal Italy, there was little room for (and little prospect of) consensus. Third, there are issues regarding the utility of measuring and viewing the Italian economy at the national level. National accounts are a crude measure of an economy's performance and tell us little about regional diversity. The trend to regional or 'micro' studies over recent decades has undermined many long-held assumptions about the nature of the Italian economy. At the same time, it has helped to fragment and further confuse the 'macro' picture of Italy's economic development.

Framework

The Italian economy in 1870

What were the defining characteristics of the Italian economy at the time of unification?

Poverty

Italy was a poor country in 1870. Estimates of per capita income, a crude measure of welfare, suggest the average Italian was considerably less well off than his sixteenth-century counterpart. Per capita income in Italy at the time of unification was less than half that of Britain, around 80 per cent that of France and significantly below that of Belgium, Holland and Switzerland. Figures for infant mortality and life expectancy at birth also suggest generally poor quality of life. In 1870, 23 per cent of children born in Italy died within the first year, a higher mortality rate than Romania and Spain. Life expectancy at birth in 1871 was only 32 years – on a par with Austria but well below Britain and Germany (the low-mid 40s).[3]

Agriculture and industry

Italy was an overwhelmingly agrarian economy in 1870. Almost two-thirds of the working population were employed in agriculture. The form of land tenure, the type of agriculture, and the physical and climatic conditions under which farming occurred varied enormously across the peninsula. Small-scale subsistence farming in the mountain regions co-existed alongside large-scale tenant farming on the northern plains, the *mezzadria* (sharecropping) system in the north-east and centre, and the great estates of the south, the infamous *latifondi*. Cereals (wheat and maize) were grown virtually everywhere and dominated Italian agriculture; grapes, olives, citrus fruits and vegetables were the other major crops. Italy did possess particularly fertile and productive agricultural regions – the Po Valley in the north, for example – but much of the peninsula was unsuitable for cultivation. The mountainous regions of Italy, constituting more than one-third of the total agricultural area in Italy, were infertile and prone, especially in the south, to climatic extremes (droughts in summer, torrential rains in winter). Malaria-infested marshland covered great swathes of central and southern Italy. The agrarian economy at the time of unification was unable to support Italy's rural population. There was massive underemployment, a serious problem given the vast and ever-growing numbers of wage-dependent agricultural day labourers. Nor, despite the size of the agrarian economy, was Italy able to feed itself.

Italy's small industrial sector was closely connected to the rural economy and was dominated by foodstuffs, traditional engineering (e.g. smithies), textiles (silk, Italy's largest export, cotton and, to a lesser extent, wool), clothing, leather making and wood working. These were largely cottage-based industries. Heavy or factory-based industry – metallurgy, modern engineering and chemicals – was present only on a very small scale. Women and children made up four-fifths of the industrial workforce.[4]

Limited modern infrastructure

United Italy's social overhead capital (i.e. transport networks and communications, education) was rudimentary. Waterways were generally in poor condition and difficult to navigate, there was no national road network and, despite significant railway construction in the 1860s, including the opening of lines linking Naples via Rome and Florence to Bologna, Italy possessed only a skeleton rail system: 6,429 km of track in 1870. Although Italy compared favourably with the much larger states of Spain, Austria-Hungary and Russia in terms of railway density in relation to total national area, it lagged well behind France, Germany and Britain. Even this limited railway system appears to have been under-utilized: in terms of tonnage transported per kilometre of track, Italy was on a par with Spain but significantly worse than France, Belgium, Austria-Hungary and Britain. One area of transport and communications where Italy did compare well with other European countries was in merchant shipping: the Italian merchant fleet was the third largest in Europe in 1870.[5]

Along with communications, it is appropriate to look at the level of education when assessing the extent of Italy's social overhead capital. Education plays an important role in facilitating economic growth.[6] Yet in Italy in 1870–1, only one in three children between the ages of five and fourteen are estimated to have attended primary or secondary school, a lower rate than Hungary and below half that of France. Illiteracy rates were correspondingly high. Approximately 60 per cent of males and 75 per cent of females over the age of six were illiterate at the time of unification.

Italy's financial infrastructure was also underdeveloped. Unification did not immediately produce a 'national' Italian bank; there were six note-issuing banks in existence in 1870. As Toniolo notes, these were 'the only large banks in the country' and the only 'credit institutions whose dimensions and operative capacity significantly transcended provincial limits'. Beyond the issuing banks, the major bank types in 1870 were the *casse di risparmio* or savings banks (130 nationwide in 1861), and two comparative newcomers: joint-stock banks (36 in 1870) and *banche popolari* (48 in 1870). The dominance of the issuing banks is clear from a comparison of bank assets: the six held two-thirds of all banks' assets. Savings banks accounted for 18.2 per cent of total assets, joint-stock banks for 10.9 per cent and popular banks for a mere 2.3 per cent.[7]

Regional imbalance

National figures hide significant regional variations. Broadly speaking we can identify (from the top down) a north-west, north-east and centre, south and islands economic hierarchy.[8] Regional per capita income at the time of unification was above the national average in the north-west, north-east and centre, and below the national average in the south and islands. In agriculture, while some areas of the south could match the highest levels of northern productivity (measured by yields per hectare), per hectare yield by value was significantly higher in northern and central regions. Underemployment was a key feature of southern agriculture, too, although certainly not a problem restricted to the south. Italian industry was concentrated in the north-west: Piedmont, Liguria and Lombardy were the focus of the Italian textiles industry, and home to Italy's fledgling metallurgical and modern engineering sectors. Italy's best waterways and roads were to be found in the Po Valley and the northern plains. Moreover, the quantity and density of roads in the north and centre far exceeded those of the south where, according to one historian, there was nothing that 'could be really called a road network, from the fall of the Roman Empire onwards'. The railway network, too, was far more extensive in the north. Illiteracy rates in 1871 were lowest in Piedmont (42.3 per cent of men and women aged six and over), Lombardy (45.2 per cent) and Liguria (56.3 per cent) and highest in Basilicata (88 per cent), Calabria (87 per cent), Sardinia (86.1 per cent) and Sicily (85.3 per cent). The enrolment rate in primary schools in 1861 was above 90 per cent in Piedmont, Liguria and Lombardy, below 40 per cent in the rest of Italy and under 20 per cent on the southern mainland. Italy's banks were located almost exclusively in the north and centre of the country.[9]

The Italian economy in 1914

What were the chief characteristics of the Italian economy on the eve of the World War One and how did it compare with that of 1870?

Welfare

Measurements of welfare show that economic conditions had improved significantly since unification. Infant mortality rates were considerably lower (16 per cent in 1911). Life expectancy had risen to 46.6 years (1911). Army conscripts were, on average, several centimetres taller, indicative of improved nutrition. Per capita income was also much higher. Most estimates of Italian national income suggest that Italy experienced, at best, marginal, at worst, no growth in per capita income during the first quarter-century after 1870. Only after 1895 did Italian per capita income increase significantly, and at a rate above that of the major industrial economies. New data, however, indicate that the orthodox picture of little or no increase in per capita income in the first half of the liberal era needs to be revised. According to these figures, there was solid and sustained per capita income growth from the late 1870s to the late 1880s. This runs counter to the conventional view that a collapse in grain prices pushed the agricultural economy and then the national economy into recession during these years, despite concurrent industrial growth. Recent holistic measurements of welfare – for example the Physical Quality of Life Index (PQLI) and the similar Human Development Index (HDI) – also suggest that general welfare improved more substantially and more consistently than old per capita income figures suggest. Nonetheless, Italy in 1914 remained relatively poor in comparison with much of north-west Europe.[10]

Agriculture and industry

The Italian economy experienced significant structural changes between 1870 and 1914. Although still primarily an agriculture-based economy in 1914, the relative importance of agriculture to the economy had declined. Agricultural employment as a percentage of overall employment fell from 61.8 per cent (1881) to 59.1 per cent (1911) while industry's share rose from 20.5 per cent to 23.6 per cent. Similarly, while agricultural product as a proportion of national product dropped from 57 per cent (1870) to 42 per cent (1910), industry's share increased from 18 per cent to 22 per cent. Within the industrial economy, rapid and sustained growth occurred in 'second wave' industrialization sectors from the mid-1890s: metallurgy, chemicals, modern engineering and especially electricity. Nonetheless, Italian industry in 1914 remained dominated by 'first wave' industrialization sectors: around 60 per cent of manufacturing workers were employed in the foodstuff industry, in textiles, or in agriculture-related manufacture (1911 figures). Industrial growth, even during the Giolittian economic boom, was driven as much by the expansion of the cotton and, to a lesser extent, the silk and woollen industries, as by the development of heavy industry. And, while many parts of the textile industry in Italy did undergo significant modernization from the end of the nineteenth century – the cotton and silk industries both witnessed rapid mechanization – textiles remained 'closely tied to the agricultural world that surrounded it'. The Italian economy by 1914 had entered industrial adolescence, not full adulthood.[11]

Infrastructure

Italian governments were enthusiastic railway builders. Italy experienced two major waves of railway expansion between 1870 and 1914. The first, instigated by the *destra* in partnership with private (and often foreign) capital in the 1860s and early 1870s, saw the creation of a national railway system. Over 6,500 km of rail track were laid between 1861 and 1880. The second, paid for by the *sinistra* and intended to create a local rail network, saw another 6,500 kilometres added between 1881 and 1895. The entire system was maintained by the state but used by private companies. Further, more modest, expansion of the network during the Giolittian era meant that by 1913 the Italian railway system boasted 17,500 km of open track (equivalent to 0.064 km of track per square kilometre of territory).[12] By then the Italian state had fully nationalized the railways (1905). Road building took second place to railway construction but even here substantial progress was made. Under the *destra*, 20,000 km of roads were laid between 1861 and 1876; the *sinistra* then extended the road network by more than one-quarter. Further growth during the Giolittian period meant there were 148,000 km of roads covering the country by 1914. Italy on the eve of World War One also possessed over 53,000 km of telegraph lines (cf. 9,860 km in 1861), nearly 10,000 post offices (2,220 in 1861) and almost 90,000 telephone subscribers. This represented a significant development of Italy's communications systems. On the high seas, Italy's merchant fleet remained among the largest in

Europe and was now predominantly steam-based (a relatively late occurrence: most of the fleet still operated under sail in 1900).[13]

Mass education – at least at primary level – had become a reality in much of Italy by 1914, although this is not to say that education provision was adequate. Attendance at primary school was not compulsory until 1877, and even then it was only for two years (extended to three in 1888) and rarely enforced. Nonetheless, by 1911 three-quarters of all six to eleven-year olds were attending primary school; the national illiteracy rate for Italians over six years of age stood at 37.9 per cent.[14]

Italy's financial institutions underwent qualitative and quantitative improvements between 1870 and 1914, although not without periodic crises and setbacks. The most serious crisis, in the late 1880s and early 1890s, involved the six issuing banks themselves and led to the creation of the central Banca d'Italia in 1894.[15] The growth of the banking sector can be seen in the eightfold increase in banks' assets between 1870 and 1914 (although, on its own, this is not necessarily evidence of the increasing efficacy of the banks). The growth in banks' assets was accompanied over the same period by a diffusion of those assets between the various types of banks. By 1914, although the three remaining issuing banks retained the highest percentage of total assets (26 per cent), savings banks and joint-stock banks each accounted for around 20 per cent, while post-office savings banks (set up in 1875) accounted for 16 per cent. We should also note the rapid rise of the so-called 'mixed' or 'German' banks from the 1890s. Established after the demise of the major 'French' banks (the Credito Mobiliare and the Banca Generale, in the banking crisis of the early 1890s), so swift was the development of the four main mixed banks (headed by the Banca Commerciale Italiana (COMIT) and the Credito Italiano) that by 1914 they held approximately 15 per cent of total banking assets.[16]

State intervention

The Italian state became increasingly interventionist in the economy during the liberal period. In 1884 the Italian state funded the establishment of Italy's first steel works at Terni. A year later it made provision for large-scale subsidies to Italian shipping companies and Italian shipbuilders. Free trade was abandoned in favour of protectionism in 1887: the tariff law of that year imposed significant duties on imported iron and steel, textiles and wheat. The state rationalized the banks of issue in the early 1890s. Finally, the Giolittian era witnessed the nationalization of the railways and the introduction of legislation aimed at the regeneration of the southern economy. The level of public spending in Italy, as a proportion of GDP, was one of the highest in Europe, 1870–1913.

Regional imbalance

The economic imbalances between regions evident in 1870 were more pronounced in 1914, especially between the north-west and south. Regional per capita income was one-third above the national average in the north-west, roughly equal to it in the north-east and centre, and only 75 per cent in the south. Per capita income in Liguria was more than five times that of Basilicata or Calabria. Illiteracy rates remained above 50 per cent in every southern region (65.3 per cent in Basilicata, 69.6 per cent in Calabria). In the north-west, illiteracy rates ranged from 11 per cent (Piedmont) to 17 per cent (Liguria). None of the regions of the south came close to the national average for primary school attendance (76 per cent of six to eleven-year olds). In Calabria and Basilicata the rate was below 50 per cent. By contrast, attendance rates in the north-west were nearly 100 per cent; in the north-east and centre they ranged from 70 to 93 per cent. Industrial growth during the Giolittian age was almost exclusively a northern affair. The north-west increased its share of industrial output from an estimated 41 per cent (1889–93) to 54 per cent (1911). Southern industry's share of output fell over the same period from 28 per cent to 17 per cent. In 1911 the north-west contained quarter of the population of Italy, half of Italy's industrial workforce and two-thirds of Italy's 'dynamic' industries (i.e. textiles, metallurgy, engineering, chemicals). The south accounted for only one-fifth of Italy's industrial employment but nearly two-fifths of Italy's population. Estimates of agricultural output also suggest that the growth experienced in the primary sector from the 1890s to World War One was tilted towards the north and centre; southern output grew far more slowly than elsewhere in the peninsula. Underemployment remained endemic in the south, where the average day labourer could expect to work only 120–50 days per annum. It is worth noting, too, that the banking system remained far less developed in the south than in the north.[17]

Debates

Sereni, Romeo and Gerschenkron

There were, of course, debates and controversies prior to 1945 concerning the nature of the liberal economy. Discussion of the 'Southern Question' went back to the 1870s and the investigations of the first *meridionalisti*: Pasquale Villari, Sidney Sonnino and Leopoldo Franchetti, and Giustino Fortunato. Protectionism had been attacked by indignant Free Traders from its instigation. Gramsci took as read the weakness of Italian capitalism, which he linked to the weakness of the Italian bourgeoisie and to Italy's 'bastard' modernization. Liberal cheerleaders, Croce, for example, predictably emphasized the 'natural poverty' of Italy – the absence of raw materials (no coal, very little iron ore) – while at the same time they were keen to stress the extent of economic progress, especially under Giolitti.

Not until the 1950s, however, did economic issues move from the margins to the centre of historical debate regarding liberal Italy. At the same time that the liberal economy became a major topic of discussion for Italian and non-Italian historians of Italy, it also assumed an international prominence that went beyond the confines of Italian history. Crucial to the first development were the works of the Marxist historian Emilio Sereni, and the young liberal historian Rosario Romeo. Central to the second was the Russian-born, Harvard academic Alexander Gerschenkron.

We have already come across Sereni and Romeo. Sereni's thesis, which he developed in the 1930s but only published in 1947, traced the weakness of Italian capitalism after 1870 back to the absence of an agrarian revolution at the time of unification. The failure to create a new peasant land-owning class and to sweep away the 'feudal residues', Sereni argued, reinforced agricultural backwardness, perpetuated rural poverty and, crucially, prevented the development of a domestic consumer market for manufactured goods. Without robust domestic demand a vigorous capitalist economy could not develop. Writing in 1975, Sereni put it thus: 'The concentration of feudal residue in the property relations on the land... takes on, in a large part of central and southern Italy, a sufficient importance so as to seriously inhibit the free development of productive forces'.[18]

Romeo's response to the Marxist interpretation was to attack both the notion of a missed opportunity for an agrarian revolution in 1860 (there was no opportunity) and the idea that such a revolution in landownership would necessarily have advanced Italian capitalism. The creation of a class of small peasant landowners 'would have blocked the development of capitalism in the countryside', involving the 'liquidation of the progressive agricultural sector' and dealing an 'arresting blow' to Italy's economic modernization. Limited domestic demand was not, for Romeo, a significant obstacle to industrialization. Rather, the underdeveloped nature of Italy's economic infrastructure posed much more of a problem. Its expansion and modernization were, according to Romeo, indispensable conditions for industrialization, and it was the unreformed agricultural sector that paved the way for this process.

Romeo argued that there was rapid growth in agricultural production during the 1860s and 1870s, stimulated by the state's policy of trade liberalization and (until the mid-1870s) rising international prices for agricultural goods. Rising output did not translate, however, into higher peasant incomes or increased consumption but into extra profits – surplus capital – for landowners who, taking the opportunity to exploit higher output per capita, raised land rents. Crucially, this surplus capital was forced out of agriculture and channelled into the development of Italy's social overhead capital (railways most importantly) by the tax-and-spend policies of the governments of the *destra*. The qualitative improvements made to the Italian economy by the Italian state in the 1860s and 1870s and funded by agriculture created the 'preconditions for modern economic development', paving the way for limited industrialization in the 1880s and, more importantly, the 'industrial revolution of the Giolittian age'. Romeo admitted that the process 'took place for a long time on a basis of compromise with the semi-feudal elements of the old agrarian world, especially in the south'. He also acknowledged that this meant the development of the urban north at the expense of the agrarian south – the introduction of protectionism, for example, vital for the growth of industry, hit the south especially hard (it pushed up the price of industrial goods and hampered southern agricultural exports). However:

> [T]he challenge facing the participants in the Risorgimento, which they met in the most consistent way, given the constraints inherent in the Italian situation, was to proceed to a forced strengthening of the urban capitalist economy of the north and to the unification of the market, as indispensable premises for the transformation of southern rural areas.

In other words, Romeo turned the Marxist argument on its head: the southern agrarian economy could only be transformed once the urban capitalist economy had been strengthened and a national market created.[19]

Gerschenkron was not interested in the Italian economy specifically. His concern was to understand the nature and pattern of nineteenth-century European industrialization. His basic thesis was straightforward. Gerschenkron argued:

- The more backward a country's economy, the later it would industrialize.
- The later a country industrialized the faster it would industrialize (the greater the chance of a 'sudden great spurt' or a genuine 'industrial revolution' as Gerschenkron put it).
- The later a country industrialized the more the process of industrialization would diverge from previous examples of industrialization. The later industrialization occurred the greater the size of plant, the stress on technology, the emphasis on producer goods, the importance of ideology and the reliance on 'special institutional factors' – banks in the first instance, or the state in the more extreme cases of economic backwardness. Agriculture, which had played a significant role in early industrialization, contributed little in the case of late industrializers.

Gerschenkron argued that, as a general rule of thumb, nineteenth-century Europe displayed increasing degrees of economic backwardness as one moved from the north-west to the south-east across the continent. Gerschenkron identified Britain as the most advanced European economy, Germany as a moderately backward economy relative to Britain and Russia as an example of extreme relative economic backwardness. Along his 'scale of backwardness' Gerschenkron expected Italy to be somewhere between Germany and Russia. Accordingly, Gerschenkron envisaged Italy's industrial 'spurt' would exceed that of Germany but be less vigorous than that of Russia and would take the form of a big initial push (a relatively high rate of sustained industrial growth, immune to cyclical international recession). The focus would be on 'new' heavy industry (and producer goods). Banks or the state would play a determining role in the intensity of the 'push'.

From his analysis – based on his own index of industrial production (1955) – Gerschenkron dated Italy's 'big industrial push' to the period 1896–1908, with average growth of 6.7 per cent per annum. It was, he concluded, concentrated in producer goods. It did, he said, ride out the international recession of 1900. However, the big push was not as big as might have been expected given Italy's late industrialization and relative backwardness: the rate of industrial growth was only just above the German level. The stress on producer goods was nothing compared to the Russian case. In fact, Italian industrialization appeared closer to the German example than the Russian one, even though the indicators of economic backwardness suggested Italy should have been further down the Russian road. Gerschenkron thus set himself the task of explaining not only why industrial 'take-off' occurred, but also why that growth was so anaemic. In answer to the first question he emphasized the role played by the 'mixed' or 'German' banks, especially COMIT and the Credito Italiano. In answer to the second, he blamed the Italian state. The construction of the railways did not foster industrial growth. The 1887 tariff 'slowed down the speed of growth by discriminating against those industries which had the best prospects for growth'.[20] The political élite, dominated by landed interests and the liberal professions, did not possess an industrial ideology. 'Take-off', when it did happen after 1896, did so despite both the *fin-de-siècle* political crisis and Giolitti's later 'conciliatory statesmanship' that favoured the workers at the expense of growth. In sum, 'The Italian government's participation in, and contribution to, the big industrial push in the country certainly fell far short of what we might have expected on the basis of the industrial history of other backward countries such as Russia or Hungary'.[21]

Gerschenkron, not surprisingly, was critical of Romeo, who had praised the role of the state in preparing the ground for an industrial spurt in the 1880s through its development of Italy's economic infrastructure in the 1860s and 1870s. Gerschenkron argued that getting money to fund the development of Italy's infrastructure had never been a problem – foreign investors had always been ready to provide capital for this. The development of Italy's economic infrastructure was not even that important to Italy's industrial take-off: there were, in Gerschenkron's opinion, no 'pre-requisites' for industrialization. The problem, as Gerschenkron saw it, had been how to attract investment into industry. The state had failed in this, and the German banks had eventually assumed the role. Gerschenkron further undermined Romeo's thesis by questioning whether agricultural growth in the 1860s or 1870s had been sufficient to release funds to industry in the first place. He flatly denied, too, that any significant industrialization occurred in the 1880s.[22]

Trends since the 1960s

Evolution vs revolution

Since the 1960s there has been a shift away from the concept of sudden and discontinuous economic growth based on a great industrial 'spurt' in favour of a more evolutionary approach, with the emphasis on cumulative waves of growth and the gradual development of capitalism and industry over the longer period. Luciano Cafagna, for example, has identified processes of economic modernization at work in northern Italy in the early to mid-nineteenth century linked to the cultivation and spinning of silk. Growing foreign demand for raw and spun silk stimulated both commercialization (production for non-local markets) and capitalistic development (modernization of economic infrastructures). From this perspective, the transition to an industrial economy appears 'not so much as a "big spurt" but as a phase characterized by a long period on the verge of transformation'. Italian industrialization progressed by fits and starts rather than leaps and bounds. Although Cafagna has acknowledged the vigour of the *boom giolittiano*, this was, in his opinion, only the latest (and not the last) of several 'peaks' in Italy's industrial development; there was 'no massive turn of the screw concentrated in a small number of years'.[23] It is worth noting, too, that Cafagna links this period of growth as much to external stimuli as internal factors. The expansion of the international economy and the growth of tourism and emigrants' remittances to Italy's balance of payments (these 'invisible' earnings financed the import of necessary raw materials and machinery) were as important to Italian industrialization as protectionism, government intervention, the banks and home-grown entrepreneurial talent.[24]

From a somewhat different perspective, Stefano Fenoaltea has long maintained that Italian industry displayed a clear cycle of growth and decline from unification onwards. In his view, it is meaningless to talk of industrial 'take-off' from the mid-1890s: the *boom giolittiano*, though impressive, was simply part of the industrial cycle (and the 1880s had witnessed similarly buoyant growth). Fenoaltea's own index of aggregate industrial production (2001) based on the most comprehensive set of product-specific and sectoral output estimates yet produced,[25] suggests industrial growth of 2.3 per cent per annum over the period 1861–1913, with peaks in the production cycle in 1865, 1874, 1888 and 1913. Fenoaltea attributes the industrial cycle primarily to patterns of investment in the production of durables (i.e. production connected to industrial sectors such as metallurgy, engineering, mining and construction). The investment cycle itself Fenoaltea links to fluctuations in international capital flows; in particular, the availability or otherwise of British capital exports.[26]

The role of the state

While there are those who see state intervention as crucial to Italian capitalist development and the process of industrialization – Franco Bonelli, for example, has described Italian capitalism as 'state capitalism'[27] – there are many who, like Gerschenkron, question the wisdom of state policies, in particular protectionism and the support given to wheat producers and heavy industry.

Protectionism

When Gerschenkron made his attack on the role of the Italian state his criticism was double-edged. On the one hand, he argued, the state did not intervene enough in the economy; on the other hand, when it did intervene, it merely put more 'obstacles in the road of Italian industrialization' or supported only the 'least deserving branches of industrial activity'. Gerschenkron was particularly critical of the 1887 tariff. The grain tariff was too high, a 'luxury' that Italy 'never should have dared subject the tender plant of its industrial growth to'. The industrial tariff was illogical. Given Italy's lack of coal it would have been sensible to direct protection to new industries with the potential to exploit new technology and low coal demands. Instead, the tariff protected textiles, an old industrial sector with only modest potential to benefit from technological advances, and the coal-guzzling steel industry. To compound the problem, engineering, which in Gerschenkron's opinion was the most suitable recipient of protection, did not get sufficient tariff to offset the cost of duty on iron and steel imports. Chemicals, another area with great growth potential, was ignored altogether.[28]

Subsequent research is divided on the impact of the grain tariff. Coppa has suggested that it was a necessary evil. Although the tariff indirectly translated into higher industrial production costs (higher food prices created pressure for higher wages), to have persisted without protection would have had serious consequences for domestic wheat prices and production and for Italy's balance of trade. Zamagni has argued the increase in cereal prices that resulted from the tariff 'encouraged' the spread of new farming methods and innovations, raising agricultural productivity and output. 'This expansion in the agricultural sector was an important aid to the concurrent industrial boom.' Without the tariff, moreover, 'the flight of peasants away from the countryside would have been even more serious than it was': by bolstering grain prices, the tariff limited agrarian poverty and stemmed emigration.[29] Critics of the tariff, however, suggest it merely served to protect the economic interests of landowners at the expense of the economy (and society) in general. The tariff acted as a disincentive to produce crops more suitable to local conditions (and as an incentive to expand wheat production in areas more suited to other crops). It had a negative impact on welfare, raising the cost of living. Furthermore, by constricting economic growth, it contributed to emigration.[30]

Critics of industrial protectionism have tended to reiterate the views of Gerschenkron: the tariff encouraged dualism within the industrial sector and led to a misallocation of resources. Nonetheless, there is a significant body of opinion that believes the industrial tariff either helped 'to foster industrial expansion' or at least did not adversely affect industrial growth.[31] Zamagni has suggested the steel tariff protected an industry that was vital 'for the completion of the Italian industrial sector and, above all, for the support it provided to the engineering and military sectors'. The 1878 and 1887 tariffs on cotton were a boon to Italian cotton manufacture. Full control of the domestic market meant that, after nearly two decades of slow growth, the cotton industry expanded rapidly: from 900,000 spindles in 1876 to 4.6m spindles in 1913. The number of looms increased from 47,000 to 146,000 between 1896 and 1911. Valerio Castronovo has advanced similar arguments. Multi-sectoral industrial growth, he has suggested, required protectionism. Engineering indirectly benefited from the steel tariff since 'the existence of the [steel] industry helped to reduce the engineering sector's dependence on foreign supplies'. Meanwhile, the tariff-protected cotton industry not only came to dominate the domestic market but was also able to become a major Italian exporter (cotton exports accounted for 9 per cent of all Italian exports by value in 1913). In a different vein, Toniolo has questioned Gerschenkron's claim that tariff protection for steel held the engineering sector back and undermined industrial growth. 'Effective protection for engineering was never negative', and even were the duty on steel to have been replaced by an equivalent subsidy, so lowering input costs in engineering, the increase in engineering output, although significant in itself, would have had minimal impact on industrial output and wider economic growth. According to Toniolo, the failure of engineering to meet the demands of the expanding domestic market in the Giolittian period was not due to the steel tariff but to technological backwardness, small plant size and poor management. More recently Federico and Giannetti have questioned the significance of the industrial protectionism altogether. The industrial tariffs, they point out, were never very high, either in comparison with those of other European countries at the time, with those imposed by the Italian government on wheat, or with those imposed in Italy after the liberal period. Given this, they argue, it is reasonable to conclude that the tariffs had little impact on the development of industry in either a positive or negative sense during the liberal era.[32]

Aside from the specific impact of tariffs on wheat, steel, cotton and engineering, a number of economic historians also see general positives in protectionism. Zamagni admits the immediate effect of the 1887 tariff was negative – the onset of a bitter tariff war with France was a 'major cause' of the deep economic crisis of the early 1890s. However, she argues, the tariff benefited Italy in the long run due to the increasingly 'international' character of its economic relations with other countries after years of heavy reliance on France as an export market and source of investment capital. Castronovo suggests that cotton was able to play an 'avant-garde' role in concentrating the labour force in factories, and in converting a number of provincial banks to industrial finance. Furthermore, 'Protectionism... served to reverse the economic policy of the past and in the long term introduce principles and social roles typical of a more open and dynamic society'. According to Jon Cohen, protectionism encouraged Italian banks to invest in industry: by guaranteeing markets for Italian industrial products the state reduced the risk of industrial investment, i.e. made it a more attractive proposition for financial institutions. Cafagna has described protectionism as the 'only outstanding manifestation of state support for the industrial development' of Italy.[33]

Railways

Gerschenkron argued the failure of the state to take a more active and constructive role in the economy in the 1880s constituted a 'missed opportunity' for early industrial 'take-off'. Had the opportunity been taken, Italy's 'big industrial push' would have displayed 'its full potential force'. One area that Gerschenkron believed the state had failed to exploit, or had actively mismanaged, was the expansion of the railways. The decision to award twenty-year contracts to three private companies to run the railways had, in his opinion, discouraged investment. (What incentive was there for these firms to invest in line and rolling stock if their contracts might not be renewed?) Furthermore, the 1887 tariff penalized the sector most likely to benefit from the growth of the railways: engineering. Consequently, in contrast to other countries, where the railways had an important knock-on effect on industrial growth, the expansion of Italy's railways had no significant impact on industrialization – the great period of railway building was past by the time of

Italy's industrial 'spurt'. State investment in the railways after nationalization in 1905 came too late to influence the pattern of industrial growth.[34]

There has been little dissent from Gerschenkron's general proposition that, despite enormous state investment in railway construction from the 1860s to the 1880s, the impact on economic growth was minimal.[35] Fenoaltea's 1983 study of Italian railways indicated that the building of the railways only acted as a stimulus to the Italian construction industry – materials beyond the 'pick and shovel' variety were imported from abroad – and the railway network itself was too small to have any significant impact on engineering production. High running costs meanwhile discouraged its use and meant the system did 'relatively little to unify the domestic market'. Fenoaltea – a critic of protectionism – even suggested the expansion of the railways had *negative* consequences for Italian industry because it strengthened the hand of those favouring tariff protection for domestic steel.[36]

Economic historians, however, have questioned Gerschenkron's claim that heavy state expenditure on the railways after 1905 had little impact on industrial growth. The need to reconstruct, maintain and improve the mature rail system, it is argued, did create a market for modern industry. Between 1905/6 and 1908/9 the state placed orders for 25,000 freight cars, 3,000 baggage and passenger cars and more than 1,000 locomotives. Domestic manufacturers supplied most of the orders. This 'allowed many engineering firms to invest in new capital equipment and to develop techniques which made them more competitive on world markets after 1910'. It has also been suggested that the stimulus to railway investment provided by nationalization helped to counteract the negative consequences of a major crisis in Italian financial markets in 1907.[37]

Military

Italy's apparently blind pursuit of 'Great Power' status has been highlighted by political historians critical of the liberal state as one of its major failings. Time and money, which could have been more profitably spent on more urgent domestic matters, were wasted instead, so the argument runs, on expensive foreign policy ventures. More alarming still, industries upon which the Italian military relied were able to influence politics adversely. Among economic historians, however, there is a body of opinion that suggests the state's search for military prestige positively influenced Italian industrial growth, at least from the mid-1880s. The construction of the state-owned Terni steel mill in 1884, a project driven by military and strategic concerns, guaranteed Italy a basic steel industry and stimulated the development of associated industrial sectors such as engineering and heavy machinery. The demands of the Italian military provided the Terni works with a steady stream of orders. Defence-related contracts were important, too, to the Italian engineering industry.[38]

Fiscal and monetary policy

The general wisdom is that the fiscal and monetary strategies pursued by Italian governments through the 1870s and 1880s produced mixed results but subsequent policy did facilitate Italy's economic development.[39] In particular, the establishment of the Bank of Italy is seen as an important advance, bringing much needed stability to Italian financial markets and lending invaluable support to industry. The Bank of Italy bailed out the important Società Bancaria Italiana (formerly the Banca Italiana di Sconto) during the 1907 financial crisis, and it co-ordinated the salvage of Italian steel when the sector ran into difficulties in 1911.

Political climate

Fenoaltea once argued that the cycle of industrial growth could be modified by changes in the political environment. Put simply, the presence of a government favourable to industry could help extend and intensify the upward cycle by raising business expectations of a profitable return on industrial investment. Equally, a cyclical downturn could be prolonged and deepened by the presence of a government with little or no interest in industry. Fenoaltea has since abandoned this position in favour of an explanation that instead emphasizes the importance of international capital flows.[40] Nevertheless, political conditions (domestic and international) are held to influence, even if they do not determine, economic activity. Heightened political tensions are seen as a discouragement to investment and economic growth (the Crispian era is highlighted as evidence of this). In contrast, the more stable the political environment the greater the encouragement to investors and economic expansion. For example, the relative political stability of the Giolittian era is seen by some as 'a bonus for the economy itself'. Gerschenkron's complaint that Giolitti's 'conciliatory statesmanship' actually undermined industrial growth because it allowed industrial strife and translated into higher wages is disputed. Although workers' real wages did improve (Cafagna estimates on average by 25 per cent, 1906–13) and consumption rose, the ready availability of labour meant wage increases in industry were contained, and outpaced by productivity gains. The reduction in the unit cost of labour and the subsequent increase in profits and capital accumulation led to new investment in industry and, in consequence, stimulated further industrial growth.[41]

Mixed banks

Gerschenkron, in emphasizing the prime role of the 'mixed' or 'German' banks in Italy's industrial upsurge after 1896, argued they represented a 'great economic innovation'. According to Gerschenkron, the mixed banks:

> took care of an industrial enterprise from its establishment on, supported it over a number of years, collected a number of similar enterprises, waiting patiently for the opportune moment when they could be welded together into a really significant entity; they opened generous lines of short-term credit to their fledglings, knowing full well that short-term funds would be invested long, into fixed capital.

Subsequent research suggests otherwise. The mixed banks were, first and foremost, banks 'more interested in short-term banking and (profits) than in long-term planning of industrial development'. They did not hold particularly large quantities of industrial equities in their portfolios. Their 'importance as suppliers of industrial entrepreneurial talent was negligible' (such talent was not in short supply). Their involvement in industry was neither new nor exceptional (the 'French' banks, had in fact been heavily involved in Italian industry in the 1880s). They did not improve the relative performance of Italian industry. They did not solve the problem of a lack of domestic capital accumulation in industry. Nor were they always well managed: of the four mixed banks, the Banco di Roma frittered investment capital on imperialist speculation in Libya while the Società Bancaria Italiana, as noted, only narrowly avoided bankruptcy in 1907.[42]

This is not to say, however, that today's economic historians discount the role played by the mixed banks in Italy's industrial development. Cohen, for example, has consistently argued the importance of the mixed banks as the 'prime source of external funding for industry'. The mixed banks, he maintains, also gave important technical, financial and managerial advice to industry. Zamagni, too, emphasizes the 'decisive importance' of the mixed banks: they encouraged outside investment in industry, they intervened to help resolve business crises (for example, COMIT and Credito Italiano stepped in to rescue the Italian steel industry in 1911) and they prompted less risk-inclined banks to commit capital funds to industry.[43]

Agriculture

Of Sereni, Romeo and Gerschenkron, only Romeo was prepared to argue that agriculture had played its part in Italy's economic modernization. Even he, however, accepted the continued presence of semi-feudal elements within agriculture. ISTAT estimates for agriculture, meanwhile, undermined his claim that agricultural output had continued to grow beyond the early 1870s. For Sereni, a backward agricultural sector had been a negative influence on Italian economic development, preventing the growth of the domestic market for manufactured goods. Gerschenkron ignored Italian agriculture: a backward agrarian economy, in his opinion, had nothing to contribute to industry.

Backwardness for many years has been regarded as the defining characteristic of Italian agriculture (the one exception being the 'advanced' farming of the northern plains of the Po valley). Backwardness has been viewed as a consequence of:

- The 'feudal' relations between landowners and peasants reflected in the contractual arrangements of sharecropping and the nature of the *latifondi*. These proscribed peasant mobility, discouraged innovation, risk taking and 'rational' economic decision making.
- The 'feudal' preoccupation of landowners with land as a source of status and the derivation of wealth through rents rather than productive exploitation of land.
- The inherent conservatism of the peasantry. This reinforced the institutional tendency towards lack of innovation or risk taking and meant the peasantry viewed commercial agriculture (production for market and profit) with suspicion.

Backwardness, it has been argued, habitually manifested itself in low or no growth in agricultural output (for example, from the beginning of the 1870s to the mid–late 1890s) and in agrarian poverty. Not surprisingly, Italian agriculture has been widely regarded as a 'dead weight on economic expansion'.[44]

Over the past three decades, many aspects of this traditional, negative reading of Italian agriculture have been challenged. Instead, research has emphasized the rationality of economic decision-making in the 'backward' agrarian economies of the centre and south. At the same time, such research plays down the negative image of the *mezzadria* (sharecropping) arrangements and of the *latifondi*. The very 'backwardness' of the peasantry has also been questioned.

Cohen and Galassi have undertaken important research in this regard. Looking at sharecropping in the centre and south, they deny that such practices encouraged the substitution of cheap labour for capital at the expense of productivity. Indeed, they claim that average labour productivity was actually higher in sharecropping areas of central Italy than in the 'advanced' non-sharecropping areas of the north. Cohen and Galassi also insist that the extensive growing of wheat in the centre and the south – a low-yield crop less suited to local conditions, and less profitable, than olives and viniculture – was 'a rational response to non-removable constraints'.[45] Wine and olive yields were extremely volatile, and low yields were not compensated for by rising prices (i.e. there was income volatility). In the absence of crop insurance and credit facilities in the centre and the south, both tenants and landowners sought to spread risk. Hence, in the centre, the mixing of wheat, olives and vines, rather than crop specialization. In the south, where environmental conditions were worse, the possibility of crop failure higher, and credit and crop insurance options virtually non-existent, crop mixing was combined with a system of varied and multiple contracts between tenants and landowners, whereby tenants would hold different contracts with different landowners. The purpose, once again, was to spread the risk for both landlord and tenant. The tenant was able to spread his risk through a variety of contracts, a mix of crops and the geographic spread of areas of cultivation (reducing the risk of localized crop failure). From the landowner's point of view, the reduced risk of tenant failure made the arrangement an attractive one.[46]

Marta Petrusewicz has advanced a similar argument for the southern *latifondi*, for so long regarded by historians as the embodiment of backwardness and the last bastion of feudalism. Based on a detailed study of the Barraco estates of Crotone in Calabria, Petrusewicz argues that the *latifondo* was neither feudal nor capitalist but a combination of the two, an arrangement that was mutually beneficial to both landowner and peasant. Crop diversity and the use of multiple forms of contractual arrangements added up to a rational and flexible approach to estate management in an uncertain economic environment. The production of export-oriented cash crops, which were profitable but also high-risk since yields were by no means guaranteed and the export market was a volatile one, was balanced by extensive wheat growing and land for pasture. This guaranteed the self-sufficiency of the estate (and, importantly, social stability in what was a highly paternalistic system) when yields or export demand fell.[47]

From another perspective, Federico has argued that Italian agriculture at the time of unification was far more market-oriented (the market generally being local) than many traditional accounts assume. A 'fairly dense urban population' and 'the large number of landless labourers' created a market demand for food that was 'satisfied by a supply coming from the sale of small farmers' products, as well as from rents paid in kind by the sharecroppers and from capitalistic farms'. Seventy-five per cent of agricultural output was sold or exchanged. Such a high rate of commercialization places Italy on a par with France and only slightly behind the United States. As Zamagni writes: 'From this point of view, Italian agriculture certainly cannot be considered as backward.' Federico and Cohen argue that commercial activity was not contrary to the natural instincts of the Italian peasantry either. Households often cultivated certain crops specifically for market, and peasants were prepared to take financial risks in order to expand supply in conditions of rising market demand.[48]

Backwardness as an explanation for Italian agriculture's apparent resistance to modern farming methods and mechanization has also been questioned. Federico and Cohen note that in much of Italy 'dry summers made advanced farming impossible while the abundance of labour and the scarcity of capital made mechanization unattractive'. Local conditions also sometimes ruled out the use of new technologies. This did not necessarily make Italian agriculture inefficient. O'Brien and Toniolo have written that '...recognizing the real constraints imposed by soil, climate and terrain on the diffusion of north European and agronomic techniques, there are grounds for believing that the value of Italian agricultural output may not have fallen far short of the optimal obtainable'. In a comparative study of Italian and British agriculture at the turn of the century, they argue that relatively low levels of labour productivity in Italian agriculture disguised relatively high levels of value-added achieved per hectare of cultivated land. This was possible through the efficient use of Italian agriculture's cheapest and most plentiful resource: labour. O'Brien and Toniolo conclude that Italy's agricultural sector could not be said to have underperformed or to have held back the Italian economy. Moreover, the persistence of rural poverty was not a function of agricultural backwardness but of rural overpopulation and the failure of Italian industry to grow rapidly enough to pull labour from the land.[49]

The above should not be taken to mean that innovation and mechanization were total strangers to Italian agriculture. Imports of farm machinery rose in value from under 1m lire (1881) to over 21m lire (1920). The use of fertilizers increased rapidly from the 1880s: the value of imported fertilizers rose from 4m lire (1887) to 60m lire (1908–10), and domestic production of fertilizers increased tenfold. By 1913, the amount of fertilizer used per hectare was higher in Italy than in either France or Britain.[50]

The increasing use of machinery and fertilizers is put forward by way of explanation for the rise in productivity and the strong growth in agricultural output from the mid-1890s to 1914. A number of other causes for agricultural growth in this period have also been advanced (although not necessarily widely agreed upon):

- *Growth in foreign demand.* Further evidence, as Toniolo notes, that 'the Italian agricultural world, far from being static, was able to respond to market signals'.[51]

- *The role of government.* The grain tariff, the establishment of agricultural schools, the provision of agrarian credit, land reclamation schemes – all have been advanced as possible stimuli to agricultural growth.
- *The forced rationalization of Italian agriculture as a consequence of the agrarian crisis of the 1880s.* Agriculture was obliged to adapt.

Did turn-of-the-century agricultural growth have, in contrast to Gerschenkron's view, an impact upon the industrial boom after 1896? The consensus is that it did. For Zamagni, the 'expansion in the agriculture sector was an important aid to the concurrent industrial boom'. Federico and Toniolo believe the thriving agriculture sector helped the industrial surge post-1896 to be more rapid and more resilient than that of the 1880s. Agriculture provided a market for industrial goods and increased agricultural production reduced imports of foodstuffs and contributed to the growth of exports, helping the state to balance its foreign accounts and thus helping financial stability and investment expectations. As has already been noted, the oversupply of rural labour also is seen to have had a positive impact on industrialization: the 'elastic labour supply was...an important condition for the rapid growth in industrial production and investments during the Giolitti years'.[52]

Given the generally positive thrust of recent research on Italian agriculture it is perhaps not surprising that the ISTAT-derived picture of virtual stagnation in agriculture for the thirty-year period from 1870 has been questioned in some quarters, reviving Romeo's (long-discredited) argument for growth in agricultural output up until the 1880s. Indeed, new estimates of agricultural production compiled by Federico indicate that output rose steadily in every decade of the liberal period, including during the so-called 'agricultural crisis' of the 1880s.[53]

Dualism

The reasons for the persistence and intensification of dualism have long been debated. From the beginning, political factors have been a favourite. Salvemini (amongst others) argued that protectionism had squeezed southern exports and strengthened the hand of the conservative landed élite in the south to the detriment of southern economic development. Francesco Nitti declared that unity had been achieved at the expense of the south while the subsequent tax-and-spend policies of the unified state had been inequitable: the southern taxpayer was hardest hit but public expenditure was concentrated in the north. Gramsci claimed that the north's development had been predicated on the 'colonial' exploitation of southern resources, and the existence of an industrial-agrarian 'historic bloc', which protected the southern landowners but meant the impoverishment of the southern economy. Indeed, from Gramsci's point of view, the very form that unification took – the absence of an agrarian revolution – sealed the fate of the south.

Other writers, Giustino Fortunato an early example, have pointed instead to the south's lack of resources, its climate and geography as contributory factors to dualism. More extreme explanations – Alfredo Niceforo's *L'Italia barbara contemporanea* (1898) the most infamous – have emphasized the racial inferiority of the southern population. Socio-cultural explanations, meanwhile, have long been advanced for the existence of the 'Southern Question', from the studies by Villari, Franchetti and Sonnino in the 1870s to the works of Edward Banfield in the 1950s, and Robert Putnam in the 1990s (see Chapter 9). Even some economic historians favour cultural rather than economic explanations for dualism – Brian A'Hearn a forceful example.[54]

As A'Hearn notes, the 'Southern Question' has generated so much discussion that 'the debate itself is almost unmanageable'.[55] Yet much of the debate is based on the same fundamental perception of the south as a single undifferentiated region, characterized by economic (and social) backwardness and immobilism. The south – static, unchanging, agrarian and poor – contrasts with the dynamism of the developing industrial north.

This helps explain why Petrusewicz's analysis of the Baracco *latifondo* generated considerable interest on its first publication in Italian in 1989. Petrusewicz took the most recognizable symbol of southern backwardness – the *latifondo* as a semi-feudal redoubt, based on extensive rather than intensive agriculture, and characterized by landlord absenteeism and the brutal exploitation of the peasant – and not only argued it was a rational socioeconomic set-up given the circumstances but that it functioned effectively for most of the nineteenth century, certainly well into the liberal period.

Petrusewicz's work is a high profile example of the revisionist trend that has characterized many recent studies of the south. At the heart of the revisionist 'movement' is the Istituto Meridionale di Storia e Scienze Sociali (IMES), established in 1986, and its journal *Meridiana*, first published in 1987. The agenda of IMES and *Meridiana* was explicit: to reformulate the way in which the south was studied. The regional problems of development in southern Italy would not be considered only in terms of contrast with the north. The history of the south would not be thought of only in terms of the 'Southern Question'. Rather, the south would be examined on its own terms, recognizing the diversity of the southern historical experience and the potential for and reality of change within that experience. The south was different but it was not necessarily deviant – it moved in the same direction of change as the rest of Europe.

There are certain shared features in revisionist analyses of the southern economy during the liberal era. First, there is the emphasis upon the rationality of southern economic actors and institutions in the context of a difficult, unstable and uncertain economic environment. Second, there is the stress on the changing nature of the southern economy, of the development – at different times and in different regions of the south – of different sectors of the economy, both agricultural and industrial.

Both traits are evident in Piero Bevilacqua's groundbreaking *Breve storia dell'Italia meridionale dall'Ottocento a oggi* (1993). The co-founder of IMES and Director of *Meridiana*, Bevilacqua has been described as 'the spokesperson for the new revisionist history' of the south.[56] In *Breve storia dell'Italia meridionale*, Bevilacqua presents an explanation for dualism that emphasizes external factors: the shortcomings of the liberal state and international trends inimical to southern economic interests.

Bevilacqua's argument runs thus. Southern agriculture, stimulated by the adoption of free trade in the 1860s, saw vigorous sectoral growth over the following two decades (e.g. vines in Puglia, oranges in Sicily) despite only limited qualitative improvements (limited entrepreneurial association, growth based on more intensive use of labour rather than technological innovation). However, the international agrarian depression of the 1880s exposed the limitations of southern agriculture and had a devastating effect on the southern economy in general, not least because of the near total dependency of the economy on agriculture. Despite the presence of relatively dynamic small and medium-size manufacturers, and the growth of some large-scale mechanical engineering and ship-building enterprises, the performance of southern industry since unification – and in contrast to the pre-unitary Bourbon era – had been limited and patchy. The arrest of industrial growth, Bevilacqua suggests, was due in the first instance to national government. Bourbon rule may have been chaotic and contradictory but it did have an industrial strategy and had facilitated the expansion of industry. In contrast, liberal governments from unification until the late 1880s not only did not possess an industrial strategy but they were essentially anti-industrial in outlook. Although the anti-industrialism of Italian liberalism hit all Italian industry, the blow was felt most keenly in the south, where agricultural and social structures were less developed, banks were less common and the internal market more restricted than in the north. The situation was made worse by the fact that European industry was changing in ways that disadvantaged southern industry. Proto-industrialization (i.e. home-based manufacturing) was giving way to major enterprise requiring serious finance and technology, and which was distanced from the agricultural world and its traditions of work. Furthermore, the creation of 'new circuits of inter-regional industrial markets' reinforced the tendency for industry to concentrate in particular areas. Lombardy and Piedmont remained 'attached to the cart' of Europe's industrial area; the south did not. Investment in southern industry dwindled. Weak and inexperienced local government did nothing to arrest the decline. By the time the Italian government finally adopted an industrial strategy with the 1887 tariff, the southern entrepreneurial world was no longer capable of realizing the industrialization of the Mezzogiorno.

The south's economic trajectory was thus set by the time of Italy's industrial surge from the last decade of the nineteenth century. The expansion of industry itself reinforced the 'dualistic' nature of the Italian economy. New industry chose to locate in the north where organized productive forces already existed, in order to take advantage of the resources used by existing industries such as infrastructure, technical and management expertise. The opposite happened in the south where it was precisely the lack of these factors that discouraged the type of large-scale investment required to establish new industrial enterprise. As industrial investment was unattractive in the south the emphasis was placed ever more heavily on agriculture, especially fruit growing. And while northern industry was increasingly capable of self-organization and putting pressure on government, southern industrial entrepreneurs were left with no voice. At the local and the national levels it was agricultural interests that spoke for the southern economy.[57]

Cohen and Federico, who are usually highly suspicious of non-standard economic evidence, have described the arguments advanced by Bevilacqua (and others of the IMES group) as 'very appealing and full of promise'.[58] This is a reflection of the widespread excitement that revisionism has generated within economic and non-economic Italian history circles. There are those, however, who preach caution. Paolo Pezzino, for example, has warned that revisionism runs the risk of becoming a 'simple-minded inversion' of the traditional negative images of the south. John Davis, too, with Bevilacqua's argument in mind, advises against an over-optimistic reading of southern history. Revisionism, he argues, should not exaggerate the capacity for modern economic growth in the south by ignoring or playing down very real internal obstacles (not least the existence of a deeply divided, 'corrupt and self-seeking southern ruling class') to southern development.[59]

Assessment

Economic history has inevitably moved on considerably from the models put forward by Sereni, Romeo and Gerschenkron in the middle decades of the last century. Sereni has rightly been criticized for his assumption that the creation of a smallholding peasant class would have necessarily promoted productivity and ultimately industrialization. As the example of nineteenth-century France shows, a property owning peasantry can act as an impediment to productivity and hinder industrialization. Subsistence farming was the more likely outcome of Sereni's called–for agrarian revolution. Romeo's thesis has long been viewed with suspicion by economic historians, sceptical of his use of the empirical data. Romeo's assertion that agricultural output grew significantly during the 1860s and 1870s did not fit with ISTAT estimates suggesting production flatlined after unification. Although, as noted, new data series suggest agricultural output did grow after 1870, this is not enough to save his argument that agriculture, via the state, supplied the capital needed to modernize Italy's infrastructure as a precondition of Italy's industrial revolution. First, the new data series actually revise down ISTAT estimates of overall agricultural output for the 1860s and 1870s. Second, investment in social overhead capital grew rapidly *after* 1880. This raises doubts as to whether the 'fundamental infrastructure' was actually in place by 1880, as Romeo argued, and suggests that surplus capital cannot have been released for industrial investment as he thought.[60] Third, the idea of economic discontinuity (i.e. of sudden and discontinuous economic growth based on industrial take-off) is no longer sustainable: Italy's industrial development was a gradual process.

Gerschenkron, of course, also can be criticized for his insistence on an Italian 'industrial revolution'. His views on the role of the state, the mixed banks and agriculture in Italy's industrialization process, and his estimates of industrial production, also need to be revised. None of this diminishes the importance of his overall thesis. As O'Brien notes, 'no scholar with Gerschenkron's awesome learning and capacity for generalization has emerged to reconstruct an alternative typology which could serve to draw economic history into a European frame of reference'. However, we do have to recognize the limitations of his model as it applies to Italy.[61]

How should we view the liberal Italian economy? The answer (cautiously advanced) is in an essentially positive light. As Toniolo argues, 'However one judges the backwardness of the country in 1861 and evaluates the characteristics of modern economic growth in Italy, the final results seem considerable.'[62] Not only this, but – if Federico and Fenoaltea are right – growth was steady through most of the liberal period, rather than concentrated in the period from the mid-1890s to 1914. How do we explain growth? The state ultimately played a positive part in Italy's economic development, and certainly one must discount Gerschenkron's argument that the state would have served the economy better had it not intervened at all. At the most basic level, there was clearly a 'direct link between the growth of the state and that of the economy'.[63] The state undoubtedly was a major influence in the development of heavy industry from the 1880s. It promoted the growth of textiles (an important factor in the Giolittian economic boom). It played a key role in the modernization of Italy's economic infrastructure. It (belatedly) facilitated agricultural innovation and growth. This positive assessment of the state's role, however, requires some qualification. Italian heavy industry benefited significantly from state support and protection, but one wonders whether this was the most efficient or productive use of state resources given the evident inefficiency (and the poor quality of product) of Italy's steel, armaments and ship-building industries. The protection given by the state to the textiles industry stimulated the sector's expansion (especially cotton) and contributed to the turn-of-the-century boom but, as Cafagna points out, this limited the potential for sustainable growth: textiles was an 'old' industry with declining long-term market prospects. Many of the economic problems of the interwar period stemmed from this.[64] The state was clearly an important player in the development of Italy's social overhead capital and economic infrastructure: transport, communications and education all saw significant improvements, while the establishment of the Bank of Italy helped bring a measure of stability to Italy's financial sector and helped (certain) industry to ride out crises. Nevertheless, to take the last point first, the founding of the Bank of Italy should not disguise the fact that the opportunity to establish a central bank had been fudged in the 1860s. Moreover, the decision to create one in the 1890s was forced on the government by circumstances largely of the government's making. And while one cannot deny the long-term benefit derived from the rationalization of the banks of issue, it did not immediately remedy Italy's critical monetary and credit situation. As the Editor of the *Gazzetta Piemontese* told Giolitti, all that had happened was that instead of six banks in need of treatment and rehabilitation there were now three 'none the less very sick'.[65] Regarding the development of transport, we can say the railway programme of the 1870s and 1880s had little immediate impact on the wider economy. Rapid expansion was not based on a full and considered assessment of Italy's needs. Silk, which was Italy's main export at the time, hardly provided the heavy freight the railways required. The railways did not serve or create a 'national' economy. The development of the local network in the 1880s often seems to have ignored local needs. Railway stations in the malarial plains and valleys of the south (reasons of economy and ease of construction meant the railways followed contours) sat in glorious isolation miles from the hilltop peasant 'agro-cities'.[66] Nor did the state's favoured method of financing the railways (public–private partnership) encourage consistent investment in the sector. Italian industry did eventually develop to meet the demands of the railways, although even here the knock-on effects could be disastrous,[67] and the renovation of the railways following nationalization in 1905 provided an important boost to industrial growth in the Giolittian period. A national network was required in the long term. However, the manner in which the network developed was extremely inefficient and the main beneficiary appears to have been the north of the country.[68]

Public works projects and state initiatives in general seem to have favoured northern economic development over that of the south.[69] This, however, was not part of a deliberate strategy. We can dismiss claims of 'colonial' exploitation. There is no evidence that the south was taxed more heavily than the north. Per capita spending was no higher in the north than the Mezzogiorno.[70] Nor should we forget the special measures introduced in the Giolittian era aimed exclusively at the south. Of course, it can be argued that per capita spending should have been much higher in the south given that its economic infrastructure was so underdeveloped in comparison with the north's. There is probably some mileage, too, in Bevilacqua's claim that state-sponsored projects in the south worked to northern templates. This meant that southern specialist knowledge and the particular needs of the south were ignored. Southern local administrations were also poorer than many of their northern counterparts, and their capacity to raise revenue more limited. This helps to explain why education provision – the responsibility of local authorities – remained well below northern levels. (Arguably, the biggest encouragement to literacy in the south came not from the state's education policy but from emigration: to enter the United States immigrants had to be able to read and write.)[71] Perhaps the key reason, though, why state intervention had its greatest impact on northern development is a political one. The weakness of the centralized political and administrative system in many of the regions of the south meant that measures taken to develop the local economy were unenforceable. In the north, where local government was less of a novelty and the authority and legitimacy of the new state more widely recognized, state measures were more effective.

What part did agriculture play in Italy's development? As we have seen, the role and character of agriculture have been revised in recent years. Less backward, more rational, more efficient and more prone to expansion than was once thought, agriculture is seen as a contributory factor to economic growth after 1870. Federico summarizes the current consensus well:

> Italy's agriculture seems to have made significant contributions to the broader development process. It succeeded in feeding a growing population with an increasing per capita income and in earning a large, though declining, trade surplus;

it remained for a long time the main outlet for manufactures; and last but not least, it supplied industry with labour and capital, especially during the first phases of its growth.[72]

Two points must be made here, however. First, agriculture's impact upon economic development was not uniform, instead varying from region to region. Second, although peasants and landowners may indeed have acted more rationally than was once thought, we should not disregard the conservatism inherent within, or the institutional limitations imposed upon, parts of the agricultural sector – particularly in the south – that ultimately held back development. Petrusewicz admits the Baracco *latifondo* was unable to respond successfully to changing economic conditions in the latter part of the nineteenth century without undermining the paternalistic social 'guarantee system' (worker security in return for service to the estate) on which it was based. In response to declining income, the Baracco estate adopted a more 'capitalist' approach to production (further specialization in wheat, the introduction of new technology) and in labour relations (the increasing use of unsecured waged labour). Although economic performance improved, the shift away from long-term, fixed salary 'provisionees' to casual, hired labour broke the strong social bonds between *latifondista* and peasant. Social relations worsened, economic stability was compromised and the *latifondo* went into decline: 'when it [the *latifondo*] cast its modernist lot, it dug its own grave'.[73] In his work on the Sicilian citrus trade Salavtore Lupo identifies the same rational pattern of crop diversity and risk spreading as Petrusewicz, and Cohen and Galasso. He also uncovers evidence of significant investment by landowners in an effort to expand production from mid-century. However, as Davis has noted, Lupo also acknowledges that:

> [T]his was not accompanied by structural or organizational change: the Sicilian producers continued to rely on established factors of production, and when their export markets were challenged by rival citrus production in California and Florida they were unable to respond. They had no domestic markets to fall back on, and while they proved well able to organize effective associations for political and commercial lobbying, they were wary of introducing changes in methods of production that might reduce their own control or power, showed little interest in investing in new sectors such as processing industries, and were reluctant to enter into alliance with powerful northern banking and financial concerns for fear that this might jeopardize their autonomy.[74]

Davis is right to suggest that the absence of sustained growth in the economies of the south cannot be blamed entirely on external factors.

Industry, of course, was the key determinant of economic growth in the liberal period. The expansion of industry derived in part from state policies from the 1880s, in part from the performance of the mixed banks, in part from the expansion of agriculture from the 1890s. The inclination is to focus on 'second wave' industrialization. Yet we should not underestimate the dynamism of traditional rural-based industry (primarily textiles) which both before and after unification exploited fully its few comparative advantages – labour (low production costs), size (low investment costs), and location (access to raw materials) – and showed itself open to innovation and new technology.[75]

Clearly, economic growth in the liberal period, and the nature of that growth, had domestic roots. However, both the character and development of the Italian economy were strongly influenced by the international economic environment. We have seen this in obvious ways, e.g. the growth of the international economy at the end of the century which encouraged both industrialization and the expansion of agriculture; the economic 'pull' of the United States which acted as a stimulus to emigration and led to increased remittances from Italian emigrants abroad. To this list we can add others, e.g. the falling price of coal on international markets at the end of the century was of significant benefit to Italian industry, which was largely energy-dependent on foreign coal. The influence of the international economy is seen in more profound ways, too. The northern Italian economy had experienced gradual integration into international markets by the time of unification (and here the comparative advantages noted above which came with the 'ruralization' of industry 'enhanced Italian competitiveness in external markets').[76] The south's reliance on the precarious agriculture-based export trade had an equally significant influence upon the organization of the southern economy and reduced the chances of sustained economic growth in the Mezzogiorno.

This leaves one final observation. The 'peculiarities' of the Italian economy have often been linked to the 'failures' of Italian liberalism and the 'deviant' character of Italy's modernization. The picture presented here, however, challenges both the concepts of economic 'backwardness' and 'flawed' economic modernization. The Italian economy was heading in roughly the right direction between 1870 and 1914, albeit with some delays and setbacks on the way. Serious economic problems remained unresolved in 1914, notably the severe oversupply of labour in the agrarian economy and consequent rural poverty, and the deepening economic imbalances between regions particularly between the north-west and south. Economic growth could not disguise the fact that Italian economic performance still lagged far behind that of its northern and western neighbours. Generally, though, the long-term economic indicators (at the national level at least) were positive. Arguably, it was the combination of international factors (war, world recession) and domestic politics (the rise of Fascism) that delayed further meaningful growth for another forty years.

3 Society and culture in liberal Italy

Introduction

It is necessary when writing about liberal Italian society and culture to stress two points at the outset:

- The enormous diversity of and deep divisions within Italian society. Although Italy was largely free of ethnic or religious differences it was nonetheless a country of marked contrasts: between town and country, between regions, as well as along lines of class, occupation, gender and age.
- The very uneven impact of economic development on Italian society and culture.

It is partly for these reasons that the 'macro' issues which have dominated the political and economic historiography of liberal Italy are largely absent from the socio-cultural arena. Instead, studies reflect the complexity and variety of Italian life and tend to be relatively narrow in their focus and modest in their claims. In addition, historians simply have not studied liberal Italian society and culture in the same numbers, or in as much detail, or for as long, as they have its political and economic characteristics. Compared with political and economic history, social history (history from the 'bottom up') is a relatively new discipline, dating back to the 1960s, and one which Italian historians at least have been generally slow to embrace. Social and cultural historians have also tended to gravitate to (apparently) more exciting periods than the liberal age, the Fascist dictatorship a particular favourite as far as the modern era is concerned (see Chapter 6).

As usual, the following framework section provides a broad narrative overview of the social and cultural history of liberal Italy. In terms of debates, the chapter focuses on three diverse but significant issues. First, it explores changing interpretations of the Italian bourgeoisie, the class most closely identified with the liberal state (and often blamed for its political and economic failures). Second, it looks at the role and status of women in the liberal era, an important but until recently neglected area of study. Third, it examines the debates surrounding the relationship between the so-called 'cultural revolt' of the Giolittian age and Fascism, with particular reference to the connections between Fascism and the leading pre-war avant-garde movement in Italy, Futurism.

Framework

We have already touched on several key aspects of liberal Italian society in the first two chapters. To recap:

- Italians *in general terms* were wealthier, healthier, better fed and better educated in 1914 than they had been in 1870. However, Italy started from a very low base in 1870 and progress was often painfully slow and erratic. There were also great variations across the country along the lines indicated in the 'Introduction' to this chapter.
- Italian society was predominantly rural. Despite the relative decline of agriculture as an employer and producer, industrial Italy retained strong links with the rural economy down to – and beyond – World War One: much of the textiles industry, for example, was located in the countryside. Notwithstanding the growth of 'second wave' industries from the mid-1890s, there were very few modern industrial cities in Italy by 1914; those that did exist were concentrated in the 'industrial triangle' of Turin, Milan and Genoa in the north-west.

Let us now flesh out this picture of Italian society.

Urbanization

Despite the prevalence of the agricultural sector, Italy was a highly urbanized society at the time of unification. Indeed, Italy could boast more towns and cities than nearly any other European country. Most of its major cities had grown considerably between 1800 and 1870. From the 1880s, however, the rate of urban growth accelerated markedly. Milan, for example, with a resident population of 320,292 (1881), had become a city of over 600,000 inhabitants by 1911; Turin's population grew from 249,827 to 416,000 over the same period, Rome's from 275,637 to 522,123, Naples' from 439,911 to 668,633.[1] It was not only Italy's largest cities that experienced rapid growth. The number of towns with populations of between 20,000 and 50,000 more than doubled between 1861 and 1911 (66 to 140). In 1911, there were 27 centres with more than 50,000 residents, 12 more than in 1881.[2] While industrialization explained the rapid growth of towns and cities in Italy's north-west, this was not the case elsewhere. Rome, for example, grew because of its new role as capital, Naples by dint of its already considerable size (it would always be a magnet for southern migrants). In many other instances, towns' populations expanded as their importance as commercial, service and political-administrative centres grew. Most new town-dwellers were local peasant immigrants seeking to escape the grinding poverty and hardships of the nearby countryside. However, the conditions awaiting them in the chronically overcrowded and insanitary new urban slums were often little better than those they had left behind.

Elites

Italy's élite classes, the aristocracy and bourgeoisie, constituted a tiny fraction of liberal Italian society: the former made up less than 1 per cent of the entire population, the latter (defined here as non-titled property owners, professionals, entrepreneurs and civil servants) just 5 per cent.[3]

Aristocracy. The history of the aristocracy in liberal Italy is one of general decline, although historians disagree over the speed, timing and extent of that decline (see the 'Debates' section below). The nobility enjoyed no formal privileges after 1861, unification completing 'a process of devaluation or annulment of noble privileges that had been set in motion in the peninsula in the mid-eighteenth century', and which had intensified under French and then Restoration rule in the first half of the nineteenth.[4] Although the Italian nobility remained a significant force in parliament and government until World War One, its political weight waned over time and was feeble in comparison to that of its British or German equivalents. Similarly, noble representation in the highest ranks of the army declined after 1870, while the numbers of nobles within the officer corps was never more than negligible. Again, this was very different to the situation in Britain or Germany. Only in the diplomatic service did the aristocracy continue to dominate right through the liberal period. Aristocratic wealth, predominantly derived from land, also fell, both in absolute and relative terms, between 1870 and 1914.[5] The Italian nobility after unification was never in any sense 'national': regional nobilities rarely mixed with one another and were deeply divided internally ('old' nobility versus 'new', urban against provincial, rich versus poor, etc.). *Bourgeoisie.* As Franceso Nitti observed in 1905, the Italian bourgeoisie was more 'a bourgeoisie of landed proprietors and professionals than an industrial bourgeoisie'.[6] Land fascinated the bourgeoisie: it confirmed wealth and conferred status; in short, it demonstrated that one had 'made it'. The bourgeoisie's obsession with land meant the Italian middle classes continued to prioritize investment in real estate long after their counterparts in western Europe had made the switch to other more mobile forms of wealth (stocks, shares, bonds).[7] Prestige could also be derived from membership of the 'free' (i.e. independent) professions, law and medicine in particular. Given the size and relative poverty of the Italian population, liberal Italy contained a remarkable number of lawyers and doctors (there were 24,000 lawyers in 1901, quadruple the number in Germany or France; doctors numbered 22,000, equivalent to 6.7 doctors per 10,000 inhabitants, a ratio close to that seen in England and Wales). Such was the status attached by the middle classes to these two 'historic' professions (a lawyer's or doctor's income was often quite meagre) that both were massively oversubscribed. There were, for example, twice as many graduate lawyers as vacancies by the turn of the century. Despite this, and the high levels of graduate unemployment in Italy that resulted, law and medicine remained the most popular subjects at university until 1910, when engineering enrolments exceeded those in medicine for the first time. The primacy of lawyers within the professions – and bourgeois society generally – was reflected in parliament. Although lawyers constituted less than 0.1 per cent of the total population they made up 48 per cent of deputies and senators in 1913; over a quarter of government members, between 1870 and 1913, had legal backgrounds.

Masses

Beneath the élite minority sat the mass of society, the peasantry and the (much smaller) working classes.

Peasantry. Italy, noted the final report of the Jacini Inquiry into the condition of agriculture (1884), displayed 'all the varieties of rural economy from Edinburgh and Stockholm to Smyrna and Cadiz'.[8] The relationship between peasant and land, peasant and landlord, peasant and market, peasant and peasant, varied enormously across the country. Other than poverty, there was very little to link the experiences of the subsistence farmer of the Alpine foothills to those of the *bracciante* (landless day labourer) of the Po Valley, the Tuscan sharecropper to the *latifondo* worker of the rural south. Consequently, and notwithstanding the creation of a national agricultural labourers' union, the Federterra, in 1901, 'The Italian "peasantry" was never a united force, in any sense'.[9]

Rural Italy was marked, nonetheless, by high levels of social unrest. The loss of customary land rights, the privatization of land, the consolidation of landownership in the hands of large landowners and, in some areas at least, the spread of intensive (i.e. capitalist) farming methods – all processes already well underway before 1870 – placed enormous strains on peasant communities throughout the peninsula. Military conscription, high levels of indirect taxation and demographic growth – Italy's population doubled between 1800 and 1910 – placed further pressure on land and resources, and added to the peasants' burden. Widespread, frequent and often violent protest was the result.

In the south, the annexation of the Kingdom of Naples by Piedmont in 1860 had been followed by an explosion of violence in the countryside (the 'Brigands' War'), as expectations of land reform, promised by Garibaldi in 1860, went unrealized and the new state immediately – and unwisely – imposed new taxes and compulsory conscription, both deeply unpopular measures. The brutal way in which the authorities dealt with unrest simply added fuel to the fire. Even with the establishment of (relative) order on the southern mainland by the mid-1860s, the rule of law remained weak in Sicily and the island quickly became associated in the national imagination with violence and criminality (the first official report of the existence of the 'so-called Maffia (sic)' dates to 1865). The full-scale insurrection by Sicilian peasants in 1893–94, triggered by rising rents and land prices against a background of economic collapse, did nothing to dispel the popular stereotype of Sicilians as 'primitive and almost savage', and helped justify the government's authoritarian response (imposition of martial law, dissolution of the *fasci* (labour organizations), internment without trial).[10] Denied voice, hundreds of thousands of impoverished Sicilians chose exit. In the two decades prior to 1914, one in four islanders, the majority young men, left Italy, bound mainly for the United States. They were not alone: over 10m Italians emigrated between 1891 and 1913, the exodus reaching a peak of 872,000 in 1913 (17 per cent from Sicily, 47 per cent from the south).[11]

Rural protest and collective action in the Mezzogiorno did not die with the repression of the Sicilian *fasci* and subsequent emigration. On the Apulian Tavoliere plain, for example, large numbers of highly organized, radicalized, *braccianti* fought a long and bloody class war with the great landowners of the region until suffering a decisive defeat at the hands of Fascist squads in the early 1920s.[12] In general, however, for most of the liberal period, 'The peasant classes [of the south] were more at war amongst themselves than with other sectors of rural society; a war which fed off a terrain of recurring and real contrasts, both economic, psychological and cultural'.[13]

In the north, rural conflict was most intense in the advanced capitalist farming areas of the Po Valley plains, where, as in Apulia, *braccianti* were again at the forefront of protest. *Braccianti* first began to organize collectively during the 1880s, as landowners laid off workers and cut wages in response to falling agricultural prices.[14] Over the next three decades, these peasant leagues and co-operatives became extremely powerful – the region was to become the first stronghold of the Italian Socialist Party – and a bitter and violent class struggle ensued, as landowners and workers battled for control of the local labour market.[15] Unrest even spread to sharecropping areas, despite the fact that the *mezzadria* was habitually described as a model of social harmony. In 1901, sharecroppers joined with *braccianti* in strike action in Emilia-Romagna (a rarity since relations between the two were usually extremely poor). The first ever strike by *mezzadri* in Tuscany followed in 1902.

Working classes. Like the peasantry, the working classes in liberal Italy formed anything but a unified or uniform bloc. As has already been noted, a great deal of manufacture was rural rather than urban-based and was carried out in small workshops or at home, rather than in large-scale factories. Consequently, manufacturing labour, although only a small part of the overall workforce and concentrated in a relatively small geographical area (the north-west), was much dispersed. It was also deeply divided: between town and country, between localities, between skilled and unskilled workers, between male and female labour (the 1881 census counted 4.1m industrial workers; 2.2m were men, 1.9m women). Even when and where large-scale urban factory-based production did develop (in industrial suburbs such as Sesto San Giovanni and Borgo San Paolo on the outskirts of Milan and Turin respectively), the new 'proletariat' was highly segmented according to skills, income, occupation, gender and place of origin. There was also very little contact between the old established urban working classes (artisans and craftsmen) who lived in the heart of the city and the masses of new workers (many of whom were temporary migrants) located on the periphery.

Workers, however, did organize in liberal Italy, and in ever-growing numbers: in mutual aid societies (there were already several thousand of these in Italy by the early 1870s) and co-operatives; in 'resistance leagues' in the 1870s and 1880s; in Chambers of Labour (labour exchanges which also ran co-operative ventures and provided recreational and educational opportunities for workers; the first Chamber was established in Milan in 1890); in political parties (the PSI from the early 1890s, although anarchist and socialist groups had existed since the 1860s); and in trade unions (after the right to unionize was tentatively recognized by the state in 1889). Despite an apparent 'nationalization' of workers' organizations from the 1890s onwards – the PSI was a national party, a national Federation of the Chambers of Labour was set up in 1893, a number of national trade union federations were created in the early years of the twentieth century (FIOM, the metalworkers union, the best known of these), and a national trades union confederation (the General Confederation of Labour, CGL) was established in 1906 – the majority of labour organizations until 1914 were small-scale and local. Worker solidarity was also strongest at the local level. National federations often exercised little or no control over their constituent parts.

Industrial protest, generally over pay and conditions, was also a developing and increasingly insistent feature of liberal Italy, with a shift in the focus of strike activity from 'traditional' sectors, such as textiles, mining and construction, to 'second wave' industries (e.g. metallurgy, modern engineering, electricity etc.), as the latter grew quickly from the 1890s. Metalworkers in particular soon developed a reputation for militancy. Of the 4,543,000 workdays lost to strike action in Italy in 1913, 20 per cent were due to industrial action in this sector.[16] The growth of 'new' industries and the creation of a mass industrial workforce did not automatically result, however, in heightened levels of labour activism. For example, the rapidly expanding industrial suburbs of Sesto saw little strike activity between 1900 and 1910; by contrast, the old working-class districts of Milan 'remained in a state of semi-permanent mobilization'.[17] Skilled workers tended to be far more militant than unskilled labour.

As noted in Chapter 1, for much of the liberal period subversive ideas and popular protest were simply not tolerated by the authorities. Only after 1900 did the government seek more imaginative solutions to social (and political/economic) unrest: a range of social welfare measures was introduced and the suffrage extended; the right to strike was also recognized, prompting a huge upsurge in industrial action. According to official records, there were 17,203 strikes between 1900 and 1914, compared with 2,670 between 1881 and 1899. In 1907, the peak year of strike activity before the war, there were 2,258 strikes involving over half-a-million workers at a cost of 5.5m man-days lost.[18] Government concessions to labour and increasing worker militancy did not sit well with employers. The years down to 1914 saw the emergence of industrial and agrarian lobbies that 'were often explicitly anti-Giolittian, anti-parliamentary, and advocates of direct action against labour protest'.[19]

The role and status of women

In liberal Italy, as across Europe, a woman's place was generally considered to be in the home, as housewife and mother; the public domain was the preserve of men. The concept of separate spheres stemmed from both modern and traditional sources. On the one hand, it was fed by bourgeois notions of respectability, the concerns of working-class men who feared female competition for industrial jobs, and the claims of science (the famous Italian criminologist Cesare Lombroso declared that women were inferior to men in evolutionary terms and were biologically, morally and intellectually suited only for motherhood – which, at the same time, explained their stunted evolutionary development).[20] On the other hand, customary, conservative attitudes regarding women remained deeply entrenched in Italian society and culture, reinforced by the teachings of the Catholic Church: 'the man is the head of the woman, as Christ is the head of the Church,' declared Leo XIII in 1880; a wife 'must be subject and obedient to her husband'.[21] The liberal state, usually only too ready to attack clerical influence, showed little interest in challenging the Church's position in this regard, partly because the 'modern' bourgeois view of women differed little from the traditional Catholic one, partly because the 'private sphere' was seen by laissez-faire minded liberals as an area beyond the remit of government. Liberal efforts to regulate the private sphere effectively began and ended with the 1865 Italian civil code (the Pisanelli law) which for women in some parts of the newly unified country actually represented a step backwards in terms of their rights under the law.[22] The code discriminated against married women in particular. The husband was recognized as 'head of the family' (*capo della famiglia*). A wife had to take her husband's name and his citizenship, and live where he determined. Adultery was designated a crime if committed by the wife but not the husband. The husband had the authority to make all major decisions regarding a couple's children. A married woman could not manage property independently of her husband, even if that property had belonged to her prior to marriage, nor engage in commerce without his prior consent (*autorizzazione maritale*). The code proscribed women's rights in the public sphere, too. Women were excluded from voting or holding public office. They were also barred from many professions, including medicine and law. Although certain aspects of the legislation were relaxed or revoked during the liberal period (notably the abolition of *autorizzazione maritale* in 1919) many of its provisions survived intact until the 1970s (see Chapter 9).

Cultural revolt

In terms of social and political thought, liberal Italy was marked by, in the first instance, the dominance of positivism (the belief in science as the basis of all knowledge) epitomized by the southern studies of the early *meridionalisti*, the élite theories of Vilfredo Pareto and Gaetano Mosca, the criminology of Lombroso and the work of leading reformist socialists such as Filippo Turati. The turn of the century, however, witnessed a full-scale intellectual revolt against positivism, linked in large measure to the 'vast vistas of uncertainty' opened up by science and the rapid social and economic changes produced by recent industrialization and technological innovation.[23] The attack on positivism took two, not always distinct, forms: on the one hand, the philosophical idealism of Benedetto Croce and Giovanni Gentile; on the other hand, the irrationalism of a younger generation of intellectuals who were at the forefront of the emergent nationalist and revolutionary syndicalist political movements, and of a small but influential modernist cultural avant-garde, based in Florence (around the journal *La Voce*), and Milan (the home of Futurism). Bitterly opposed to *giolittismo*, activist, nationalist (albeit in different ways), voluntarist, élitist, anti-parliamentarian, anti-socialist, against 'soft' bourgeois values (love, sentimentalism, feminism, democracy etc.), glorifying youth and war (and embracing the Sorelian myth of regenerative violence), 'obsessed with enthusiasm for the dynamism of modern life', and preaching a message of cultural and spiritual (and thus political) renewal, these were young intellectuals in a hurry, 'excitable men who wrote essays in cultural reviews, with a frenetic message of urgent change. For a few brief years such intellectuals really counted for something in Italy. They gave Italians a new image of themselves: active, passionate and warlike'.[24]

Debates

Rethinking the bourgeoisie

From the liberal period until the 1980s, Italy's bourgeoisie was, in the words of John Davis, 'more widely blamed than studied', held responsible first for the failures of the newly unified state, later for the rise of Fascism (Gramsci's is the best known but certainly not the only interpretation along these lines).[25] The case against the Italian bourgeoisie rested (rests) on the following arguments:

- The Italian bourgeoisie failed to behave like a 'true' bourgeois class, i.e. it was neither a proper capitalist class nor a sufficiently liberal one.[26] As a capitalist class it failed on several counts. First, the bourgeoisie's obsession with land betrayed its pre-modern roots and its unhealthy preoccupation with prestige. The Italian bourgeoisie bought land in order to be like the nobility and, like the nobility, once it possessed land it opted for *dolce far niente*, content to live off rental income.[27] The constant concern with status also explained the upper bourgeoisie's taste for titles (ennoblement), and their passion for the professions. Second, for some time after 1870, the bourgeoisie showed a disdain for/hostility towards industry and industrial development. Only when colonial ambitions came to the fore in the 1880s did it embrace industrialization. Third, the new industrial bourgeoisie that emerged at the end of the nineteenth century showed little appetite for risk taking, preferring instead the protection of the state; like the rest of the middle class, it too exhibited pre-modern attitudes.[28] As a liberal class, the bourgeoisie's shortcomings were reflected in those of a liberal (bourgeois) state plagued by corruption, cronyism, patronage and clientelism[29] and prone to authoritarianism (a fact linked, in Marxist analysis, to the failure of the bourgeoisie to impose itself on the old 'feudal' aristocracy – see Chapter 1).

- The Italian bourgeoisie was not only a small class; it was also divided and weak. Associationism, considered vital to the development of bourgeois cultural identity elsewhere in Europe, was 'concentrated around the 'gentlemanly' figures of the notables without spreading to larger circles'.[30] Associational activity was rarely co-ordinated at a national level, indicative of a weak sense of bourgeois identity in Italy and of the divisions between and within the different bourgeois groups. The inability of the Italian middle classes to organize into political parties was further evidence of this.

Revisionism

Since the 1980s, there has been an upsurge in historical interest in the Italian bourgeoisie (and, indeed, the European middle classes in general). Looked at in cultural as much as economic terms, and in a genuinely comparative European context, a rather different picture of the bourgeoisie emerges from that in traditional accounts.

- Bourgeois landownership and capitalist innovation were by no means exclusive. For example, Alberto Banti has argued that middle-class landowners in the Emilian province of Piacenza, in the Po Plain, responded in typically capitalist fashion to the agricultural crisis of the 1880s, organizing at both the local and regional level[31] to facilitate the introduction and rapid dissemination of new techniques, technologies (e.g. artificial fertilizers) and machinery in order to raise productivity and cut labour costs. Landowners' associations also managed to establish strong ties – and negotiate favourable credit terms – with local banks, thus securing the capital required for innovation. At the same, the associations helped landowners to present a united front in the face of labour unrest.[32] Land for these middle-class landowners 'was seen as an investment that brought not only substantial prestige but also economic profit – especially if it was well managed'. Nor, writes Banti, was this attitude to property limited to the northern bourgeoisie:

> In Naples it was urban real estate that was most attractive to [middle-class] professionals with savings to invest. And although there was perhaps a speculative or parasitical element in their economic behaviour, these professionals paid close attention to the trend in property rents; they were quick to seize the best opportunities for profit, and they were adept analysts of shifts in the economic trend. The assets of the Neapolitan lawyers, as Paolo Macry has observed, displayed 'a strategy which preferred profitability to property as a status symbol'. Of course, in both the north and south of the country, professionals were fully aware of the prestige accruing from property ownership; but their major concern was the yield on their investments, and only secondly its symbolic value.[33]

Looked at in European terms, too, the Italian bourgeoisie's predilection for land does not appear that unusual. As Maria Malatesta has pointed out, 'In France, the bourgeoisie continued to invest in the land throughout the nineteenth century, even if the share of landed property in urban wealth generally diminished, while in late-nineteenth-century England the successful professional often crowned his career by purchasing a rural estate'.[34] The German bourgeoisie behaved in similar fashion.[35]

- Although certain groups within the industrial bourgeoisie lobbied hard for – and secured – state protection (see Chapter 2), others remained committed to free trade, and even set up their own organizations to counter the demands of the protectionist lobbies.[36] In fact, while Italy's industrial class generally came from similar, comparatively humble, social backgrounds and Italian industrial development was concentrated in a relatively small part of the country, 'the entrepreneurial world was, between the end of the nineteenth and beginning of the twentieth century, a variegated world, divided by diverse economic interests, by various associative configurations, sometimes by different political contacts'.[37]

- The authoritarian tendencies of the liberal state are better explained by reference to the challenges of state formation than by notions of 'feudal' residues or a weak commitment to liberalism on the part of Italy's bourgeois political class (see Chapter 1). The fact that sections of the bourgeoisie abandoned or opposed liberalism did not make them any less bourgeois given that liberalism was *not* a defining characteristic of middle-class culture.[38]

However, revisionist studies have confirmed particular aspects of the traditional view of the Italian bourgeoisie. For many years after unification, the Italian middle classes *were* generally hostile towards industry. Industrialization, it was thought, would mean political and social upheaval, as it had in England and France. Besides, the country lacked the necessary resources to develop an industrial base: Italy was an agricultural nation and should remain so.[39] Banti has emphasized how the world of the bourgeoisie was also a deeply fractured one. In the first place, bourgeois horizons were extremely parochial. The middle classes tended to live and work in the towns and cities of their birth. If they bought land, they bought locally. If they organized collectively (as, for example, landowners, entrepreneurs, or professionals) or socialized together in the multitude of recreational, cultural, scientific, educational, sporting and philanthropic societies that sprang up across urban Italy in the late nineteenth century, they did so overwhelmingly at the local level: regional and inter-regional organizations were rare and genuinely national associations virtually unknown before 1900. The strength of localism was also reflected in the political practice of *trasformismo*. Rather than representatives of the 'Nation in general', as the *statuto* had envisaged, deputies acted as the agents of powerful local interests; they traded their support in the *camera* in return for concessions and favours granted to these interests.

The bourgeoisie, though, was divided by more than just localism. The professions, for example, were riven internally by social, territorial, technical-professional and political differences. In medicine, rural-based practitioners earned considerably less than their city counterparts did, while the incomes of city-based doctors varied wildly within individual cities and between regions. The political affiliations of medical professionals, at least in the north and centre, tended to differ with income and status: while the élite within the profession generally backed centrist politics, many of the poorer, lower-status *medici condotti* embraced socialism.[40] Rigid hierarchies within the hospital system and the development of specialist branches within medicine served to splinter further the profession. The many splits within the medical world meant that no broad-based national association representing all doctors was established during the liberal era (instead several professional associations representing particular groups of doctors were created). Similar fractures – with similar consequences – were evident in all the 'free' professions.[41]

Associational life beyond the professions also reflected divisions within the bourgeoisie. The most prestigious recreational clubs were closed to all but the bourgeois élite. Members were co-opted (i.e. to become a member one had to be recommended by an existing member and approved by the remaining membership) and fees were deliberately prohibitive. This élite section of the urban bourgeoisie was highly segmented, too. For example, just over a quarter of the 1,260 members of Milan's three most influential clubs in the 1890s belonged to two of them; only 2.8 per cent belonged to all three. In fact, Banti suggests, élite sociability may have declined in Milan as levels of associationism increased after unification. Whereas 'high society' had once regularly intermingled at receptions held in the salons of Milan's leading ladies, now women were excluded from public life, salon society had gone and the Milanese élite no longer socialized as a single group. As one contemporary observer declared: 'The societies have killed society!'[42] Even among the less exclusive *associazioni di programma* (societies formed on the basis of shared interests or objectives), membership was often by co-option. As with the élite societies, no links existed between similar interest-oriented clubs based in different towns and cities.

The nobility

Revisionist interpretations of the Italian bourgeoisie have impacted on historical debates surrounding the Italian nobility. The traditional view of bourgeois weakness was linked to the idea of continued aristocratic influence/dominance after unification – putting Italy at odds with the (supposedly) standard European model of bourgeois revolution, where the bourgeoisie triumphs over the aristocracy. Revisionism, which stresses the vitality and strength of Italy's bourgeoisie (albeit at the local level) plays down the significance of the nobility: aristocrats after 1870 either experienced precipitous decline or were obliged to amalgamate with the upper echelons of the bourgeoisie, in the process losing their distinct caste identity.[43]

The revisionist notion of an aristocracy *in extremis* has been challenged, however. For example, Anthony Cardoza has argued in a detailed case study of the Piedmontese nobility that a 'pre-modern' Piedmontese nobility was able, through its historical association with the ruling House of Savoy, its continued domination of local politics and civic life (even as it retreated from the national political scene), its strong and binding sense of tradition and service, its ability to make money from rural landownership and its limited exposure to élite bourgeois society, to retain much of its influence, prestige, wealth, as well as its caste integrity, into the first decades of the twentieth century. Only after the World War One, Cardoza suggests, did the Piedmontese nobility, ravaged by the human and financial costs of the war, and confronted by a radically altered and more threatening social environment, lose its distinctiveness and merge with the non-noble notability.[44] Along similar lines, Giovanni Montroni's work on the Neapolitan aristocracy depicts an old urban nobility that survived the collapse of the Bourbon monarchy and retained its influence and distinct identity well into the liberal period.[45] Whether Cardoza and Montroni simply present exceptions that prove the rule, however, is open to question. Cardoza has described Montroni's conclusions as 'highly speculative, since they rest for the most part, upon an excessively narrow base of research'; but Cardoza himself concentrates on a 'core group' of aristocratic families, arguing that it was these 'who set the standards and tone for the [Piedmontese] nobility as a whole up to the Great War'.[46] This 'core group', though, constituted an élite within an élite – the Piedmontese super rich – which was but a tiny percentage (10–15 per cent) of the Piedmontese nobility as a whole. *Their* experience bears out Cardoza's case, but was their experience the same as that of their less affluent fellow aristocrats? The assumption is yes, but the evidence is sketchy.

Women in liberal Italy

It is an obvious fact, but usually overlooked until very recently, that half the Italian population were women. Surprisingly little is known about the position of women in nineteenth century Italy.[47]

More than two decades have passed since Clark noted this particular lacuna in the historical record. In the intervening period, modern Italian women's history has made considerable strides, both in quantitative and qualitative terms. As a result we now know considerably more about the lives of Italian women in both the nineteenth *and* twentieth centuries (see Chapters 6 and 9) than we did in the mid-1980s, although progress has been uneven and much work remains to be done.[48] What of women in liberal Italy?

Whereas women tended to be simply subsumed within discussions of the family and family life, i.e. women were considered of interest only in relation to the private sphere, work over recent decades has thrown much needed light on the 'public' experiences of Italian women in the liberal period. At the same time, it has shown how the private and public spheres constantly impinged on and influenced one another.[49] Here we will focus on three areas of public female activity that have been subject to particular scrutiny: work, education and political activism.

Work

Although women were in theory confined to the private sphere, the reality in late nineteenth and early twentieth-century Italy was that huge numbers of women worked. Over half of all women were classified as economically active in the 1881 census. While the 1901 census indicated a significant decline in the percentage of active women (to 41.2 per cent) this still meant there were several million female workers employed across virtually all sectors of the Italian economy. Historians, moreover, have questioned the extent of the decline in female employment over the liberal period (and beyond), noting how changes to the census classification system rendered women workers increasingly 'invisible'. Many women in liberal Italy worked from home, often on a seasonal and discontinuous basis. This kind of work, recognized in the 1871 census and to a lesser extent that of 1881, was ignored by later statisticians. As a result, hundreds of thousands of women 'even though they continued to contribute to the family and the market economy in a variety of forms', were reclassified as housewives.[50]

In terms of manual work, there were, at least until the beginning of the twentieth century, few restrictions on the type of job a woman could do. Women were a significant presence in the agricultural economy, working on the land whether as part of a family unit (the case in sharecropping areas), or tending small family-owned or rented plots, or as wage labourers (e.g. in the rice fields of the Po Valley, where tens of thousands of casual migrant female workers were employed to sow, weed and harvest the rice crop). Rural women's work often spanned the primary and secondary economies, most obviously in the case of the rural-based textiles industries of north and central Italy. For example, in the silk industry, the most widespread and important of Italy's rural industries in the nineteenth century, the reeling and throwing of the silk had long been women's work. Once employment of a domestic, manual and seasonal nature, in the latter part of the nineteenth century these highly gendered jobs became increasingly factory-based, mechanized and full-time (the same was true of spinning in other textiles sectors). Weaving (of silk or otherwise), largely a male preserve up until mid-century, also became a predominantly female, factory-based (but still rural) occupation after 1870 with the introduction of mechanized looms, although there were still an enormous number of hand-operated home looms in use at the end of century.[51] Large numbers of women were employed in urban-based industries, too, as seamstresses (again, in an increasingly mechanized and factory-based environment), and tobacco workers (12,000 out of a total workforce of just over 13,000 in 1901). Women (and children) could also be found 'even in the heaviest [industrial] jobs and those most hazardous for their health', e.g. in Italy's quarries and mines, on its roads and railways, and 'in highly unhealthy industries like matchmaking, porcelain, and glass'.[52]

Beyond manual work, however, and excluding domestic service (a staple employment for women from the subaltern classes), paid women's work was hard to come by. Legal barriers made it very difficult for married women to set up in business (indicative of this, women owned only 5.3 per cent of manufacturing enterprises in 1911).[53] The small size and slow growth of Italy's tertiary sector, together with the tight restrictions placed on women's employment in the state administration and public services, meant there was little in the way of clerical work.[54] Teaching was the main professional outlet for educated, single women (until the beginning of the twentieth century, female teachers had to resign on marriage). Women, though, were largely restricted to teaching in elementary schools – in fact, elementary teaching was predominantly a female preserve – or at the lowest level of the secondary system, in the *scuole normali*; they were only a peripheral presence in the élite 'classical' schools, the *ginnasi* and *licei*. The same was true in Italy's universities. Beyond teaching – and midwifery (there were c. 14,000 registered midwives in 1900) – there were few other professional career options available to women. A bar on women practising law was only lifted in 1919. Although medicine was opened up to women in the mid-1870s, with the first female medical graduates in 1877, for a long time afterwards women were only allowed to practise gynaecology and obstetrics.[55] Until the end of the nineteenth century, engineering was a strictly male profession (the first female engineering graduate was in 1908).[56] The range of professions available to women is revealing; they were only allowed into areas considered 'female' by nature and tradition, and were largely restricted to dealing with other women. Such roles were entirely compatible with the dominant cultural and social values and hierarchies of the time.[57]

Women were also engaged in the world's oldest profession: prostitution. Although not a crime, prostitution was tightly controlled by the authorities because of the supposed threat it posed to public order, morality and health. The number of registered prostitutes in liberal Italy peaked at over 10,000 in 1881 before falling back to around 6,000 in the Giolittian period. The real numbers, however, were undoubtedly much higher, since many prostitutes were unregistered or 'clandestine'.[58]

Education

Studies of female education in the liberal era reveal a complex and contradictory picture. On the one hand, as Michela De Giorgio has noted, the interest of Italy's ruling élite in the education of women 'was motivated by the wish, repeatedly confirmed, to tear them away from the cultural slavery of the pre-Risorgimento made of ignorance and prejudices, clerical superstition and conservative traditions'.[59] Legislation obliged municipal authorities to provide instruction in equal measure to girls and boys. And, despite the manifest failings of the education system, the impact of schooling on women was undoubtedly positive. Female illiteracy fell significantly, from 81 per cent (1861) to 42 per cent (1911), albeit with significant regional variations e.g. the female illiteracy rate in Turin in 1900 was 21.4 per cent; in Sicily, 77 per cent. Even in Sicily, however, there were signs of the transformative effect of education and literacy on women's lives. In a study of Sutera in Sicily's central-west, Linda Reeder has found evidence of rapidly rising female enrolment rates in both elementary schools and adult education classes during the Giolittian era, coinciding with – and closely connected to – mass male migration to North America. Literacy allowed those women who remained behind to keep in touch with their migrant husbands without the need for expensive and risky third-party intervention (privacy could be an issue). It enabled them, too, to exploit the new economic opportunities provided by the remittances sent back by the male migrants. New, bigger houses were built or bought by the women, and new businesses were established. All of this required forms to be filled out and documents to be read, understood and signed. To be able to read and write also gave these women a new social standing. Literacy, as Reeder points out, was 'a means of claiming membership in the local elites'.[60] More than this:

> The classroom facilitated greater physical and symbolic integration into the nation-state... Classroom lessons, curriculum, and access to newspapers and a national literature relocated rural women within the civic body and national economy. Book learning linked these women to a reservoir of shared historical and cultural symbols, strengthening their sense of national identity. Schoolhouse lessons emphasizing civic obligations introduced rural women to the nation and to their duties as Italian women. The serialized stories and news items published in the daily newspapers offered women direct access to society, politics and culture beyond the village, while advertisements enabled them to purchase the trappings of modern life. These material goods gave women the ability to fashion a new economic role for themselves as consumers in the global economy. Through schooling and literacy they entered into communities defined by written narratives and civic and commercial symbols that transcended the boundaries of kinship and physical proximity that had long shaped rural society.[61]

As Soldani notes, the ubiquitous figure of the female elementary teacher also provided an important external role model for rural women. Although as an outsider the *maestra* might well be viewed with suspicion (if not outright hostility) by the local community, and was often a victim of physical and mental abuse and administrative neglect, she was the messenger of 'new parameters of life', a point of strength 'to sustain and spread knowledge and habits on which to construct new individual and collective strategies, to build bridges between the past and future'.[62]

Nevertheless, 'Discrimination against women began at the level of education'.[63] The elementary curriculum for girls was significantly different to that for boys. Besides literacy, girls took classes in 'feminine' subjects such as personal hygiene, embroidery and home economics. Elementary textbooks hammered home the idea of the obedient daughter and dutiful housewife and mother. This was training for a life of domesticity. Girls were not expected or encouraged to continue school beyond the elementary level. Very few girls (or boys for that matter, though still far more boys than girls) went on to secondary education. If they did, and they remained in the public education system (the vast majority of girls who received post-elementary schooling actually attended private Catholic-run girls' schools, the numbers of which expanded rapidly after unification) then they usually attended the *scuole normali*, where they trained for a teaching career in the elementary schools. The *scuole normali* were almost completely feminized by the turn of the century: of the 21,287 students enrolled in 1899/1900, 19,864 were female. Girls constituted only a tiny minority of students in the *ginnasi* and *licei*, or the technical schools and institutes. A university education was even rarer. University study only formally opened up to women in the mid-1870s, and progress was slow thereafter. There were just 224 female graduates nationwide in 1900, with many Italian universities yet to produce even one. Women made up only 5.8 per cent of university students, 1913/14. The truth was that too much learning was considered a dangerous thing: an educated woman of independent mind was thought unlikely to attract a husband.[64] The fact that, throughout the liberal period, teachers who taught girls were paid less than those who taught boys was a clear demonstration of the inferior cultural value placed on female education.[65]

The women's movement

As Mary Gibson observes, a key element of Italian women's history is its 'emphasis on female consciousness and autonomy'.[66] Thus, as regards women in liberal Italy, although women's historians are quick to note the denial of civil and political rights and the discrimination experienced by women in both the public and private spheres, they are equally keen to dispel the notion of women as necessarily isolated, helpless, passive or docile victims of (male) repression. The most conspicuous example of female 'activism' in the liberal period was undoubtedly the Italian women's movement. This was a broad church ranging from moderate Catholic and lay organizations (e.g. the Women's Union of Catholic Action, established in 1908; the upper-bourgeois and aristocratic National Council of Italian Women, established in 1903) to radical and socialist-feminist groups (e.g. the League for the Promotion of Women's Interests, established in 1881 by the democrat and leading Italian feminist Anna Maria Mozzoni; the National Women's Union, founded by Ersilia Majno in 1899). The women's movement in Italy was small in European terms and a comparative latecomer – the first organizations for female emancipation date to the early 1880s. It was also deeply divided. Catholic and lay bodies, moderate and militant groups, bourgeois and working-class organizations, viewed each other with suspicion and disagreed over methods, aims and priorities (e.g. radicals and socialists quarrelled over protective legislation for working women and children; Catholic women's organizations and, for different reasons, the leading female socialist Anna Kuliscioff, opposed feminists' calls for the legalization of divorce). Generational differences produced further fragmentation.[67] The results obtained were minimal, too. For example, women's organizations pushed hard for the establishment of the national maternity fund to allow working mothers to take paid leave after childbirth. Although such a fund was established under law in 1910, 'its shortcomings were obvious' and many women workers were excluded from the scheme altogether.[68] In other important areas, the women's movement made no progress at all. Liberal Italy remained one of the few European democracies not to allow divorce (a state of affairs that, of course, pleased Catholic sections of the women's movement). Although the suffrage was extended to all adult men during the liberal period, the vote was not granted to women. This remained the case even after World War One, despite expectations in feminist circles that the enormous contribution of Italian women to the war effort would be so rewarded. Nonetheless, the women's movement is considered significant in several respects. Here, after all, were women intervening in the public-political arena as 'conscious historical subjects', capable of effecting change both at the local and national level. The creation of the national maternity fund, for example, followed the establishment of independent maternity funds by women's groups across Italy, the first in Turin in 1898.[69] Nor were such initiatives unusual. The late Annarita Buttafuoco, who wrote extensively on the women's movement in this period, noted 'A number of different experiments...the women workers' mutual aid society; the creation and 'political control' of obstetric first-aid stations; the various departments for assisting needy mothers operated by the organizations of the women's movement', in addition to the local maternity funds.[70] The strong focus on motherhood, a particular feature of Italian feminism in the latter half of the liberal period, stemmed, Buttafuoco argued, from the belief that women's claims to citizenship were best served by embracing rather than denying female difference and in stressing the contribution of women to the life and well-being of the nation as the mothers and educators of future generations of Italians. 'Experiments' such as the maternity funds, then, had to be considered as:

> ...not mere acts of philanthropy. They were a mode of political action: the feminist associations were putting into practice forms of assistance which originated in their thinking about the question of the relationship between motherhood and work, and about the social value of motherhood.[71]

'The objective', Buttafuoco later wrote of what she termed 'practical' or 'social' feminism, 'was not in fact to "integrate" women in the public sphere, leaving the overall framework intact, but rather to redefine the concept and meaning of citizenship'.[72] The 'new woman' promoted by the Italian women's movement, independent and empowered, was a long way from the traditional notion of the *donna di casa*.

Cultural revolt: The case of 'fascinating futurism'

The 'cultural revolt' against positivism has generated a substantial historical literature. Once largely studied as an aspect of high culture and intellectual history, since the 1980s historians have increasingly focused on the connections between the 'cultural revolt', in particular the irrational tendencies evident in the 'age of Giolitti', and post-war Fascism. In this regard, no movement has been given more attention – or been the subject of more debate – than Futurism.

Futurism was effectively created by Filippo Tommaso Marinetti in 1909 with the publication in Paris – on the front page of *Le Figaro* – of Marinetti's *Manifesto of Futurism*. The manifesto was both a cultural and political call to arms, on the one hand glorifying action, struggle, violence, war ('the only cure for the world'), youth and modernity ('the beauty of speed. A racing automobile...'), on the other hand repudiating all aspects of the past ('What is the use of looking behind...?'). Although global in ambition, it was against 'old' Italy that the manifesto was primarily directed: the Italy of museums and libraries ('cemeteries') and 'its gangrene of professors, archaeologists, tourist guides and antiquaries' had to be annihilated; Italian culture and society had to be remade, the nation reborn. In artistic terms, Futurism meant the rejection of all old and conventional (especially bourgeois) forms of expression: standard typography and syntax were abandoned in literature and poetry, harmony and classical instrumentation gave way to dissonance and noise in music, Futurist painting (as well as literature, poetry and music) attempted to capture 'the multitudinous movements, sensations, and scenes that constituted modern life [the concept of *simultaneity*]'.[73] Through art, the Futurists 'affirmed the possibility of living in a different way, the need to renew at the roots people's habits and attitudes, people's perceptions and sensibilities'.[74] In the political sphere, the Futurists' insistent demand for war – they gave enthusiastic backing to the Libyan campaign in 1912 and were among the first to demonstrate against Italian neutrality after war broke out in Europe in 1914 – served similar ends: war would destroy the old corrupt and degenerate Italy; in its stead would emerge a new, modern, great nation.

At one level, the link between Futurism and Fascism is self-evident. The values expressed in the original Futurist manifesto – 'the cult of irrationalism, un-trammelled (male) egoism, the cult of violence and war, an aggressive misogyny' – would all find strong echoes in Fascism.[75] Marinetti was one of a number of Futurists who were present at the founding of the initial *fascio di combattimento* in Milan in 1919, and the political activities of the Futurists and Fascists were closely aligned during the first, difficult months of the new movement; Marinetti even stood as a Fascist candidate in the 1919 national elections. Although Marinetti was to break from Mussolini and Fascism in 1920, he reconciled himself with the regime (1923–24) and went on to become a founder member (and eventually President) of the Royal Italian Academy and served as Secretary of the Fascist Writers' Union. Marinetti volunteered for the Ethiopian War (1935–36) and for the Russian front (1942), and remained loyal to the dictatorship until his death in 1944. For his part, Mussolini, when dictator, publicly acknowledged his debt to Futurism: 'I formally declare that without Futurism there would never have been a fascist revolution'.[76]

As Emilio Gentile has pointed out, however, 'despite the indisputable evidence of Futurist participation in the cultural and political life of the regime, there has been considerable debate...about the nature and significance of this "collaboration"'.[77] Several basic positions can be identified.

First, there are the 'denialists', those who regard Futurism as important but only in artistic terms, as one of the first and most significant modernist avant-garde movements of the twentieth century; political Futurism was, in contrast, an irrelevance – a combination of rhetoric and stunts simply designed to attract an audience.[78]

Second, there are the 'apologists' for Futurism, those who play down the points of contact between Futurism and Fascism, focusing instead on the differences between the two movements and on the evident tensions and disputes between Marinetti and Mussolini. For example, Günter Berghaus argues that Futurism had more in common with the far Left in politics than with the extreme Right, to which Fascism ultimately belonged. According to Berghaus, Marinetti was an 'anarchist who believed in the "destructive gesture of libertarians" and the "healing force of war" as fundamental principles of progress'. Futurism had many admirers on the revolutionary Left, including Gramsci, who in 1921 wrote of the Futurists' 'distinctly revolutionary and absolutely Marxist conception' of the 'need of new forms of art, philosophy, behaviour and language' in 'the age of big industry, of the large workers' city and of intense and tumultuous life'. Futurism aligned itself with early Fascism because of the latter's leftist agenda: Marinetti's (and Futurism's) formal break with Mussolini in 1920 owed to Fascism's increasingly right-wing, anti-worker and reactionary stance. Marinetti later made his peace with Mussolini – a move that dismayed many Futurists – in order to secure Futurism's future in an increasingly hostile, conservative, cultural environment. Futurism was eventually 'tamed' by the regime but this 'did not eliminate Marinetti's critical mind and ability to assess the state of the country with unblinkered eyes'. Furthermore, while Mussolini was keen, in the immediate post-war period at least, to exploit Marinetti's influence and reputation to further his own political ends, privately he dismissed Marinetti as an 'extravagant buffoon'. Throughout the life of the dictatorship, Marinetti's loyalty was always considered suspect by the authorities: an 'antifascist' surveillance file was opened on Marinetti in 1926; all further reports on Marinetti's political activities were sent directly to Mussolini.[79]

Denialist and apologist accounts of Futurism tend to divorce Futurist aesthetics from its politics. By contrast, interpretations of Futurism that emphasize the depth of the Futurist-Fascist relationship are based on the premise that in Futurism (and Fascism) 'culture and politics cannot be readily separated'.[80] Futurism, it is argued, 'sought not merely the *negation* of traditional aesthetic forms of the past', but an aesthetically-inspired 'total' revolution that would transform and transfigure 'the essence and value of life, giving rise to a new art, a new style of life, a new man', in short, a new civilization.[81] Italian hegemony would be thus re-established (Futurism believed in the 'myth of Italianism', that 'Italy was destined to take the role of the great protagonist in the history of the twentieth century').[82] Futurism sought to glorify, conquer and harness the energies (destructive and constructive) of modernity in order to fulfil its totalizing aesthetic-political vision. War was assigned a key role in this process.[83]

Futurism's 'aestheticization of the political', its concept of politics as a total way of life, its commitment to the creation of a 'new man', its determination to master modernity and bend it to the interests of the nation, its masculinism, its cult of youth, its belief in war as a moral imperative: in all these ways, it is argued, Futurism anticipated Fascism; there was 'a fundamental cultural connection'. Futurism and Fascism were not identical and certainly the realities of Fascist power did not correspond exactly with Futurist aspirations, 'But this recognition does not imply that...the culture of Futurism was of a kind that differed fundamentally in its values and its myths from fascist political culture'.[84]

> The Futurists were restless fascists and disagreed with some of the regime's political and cultural decisions. None of them, however, ever questioned the fundamental motifs of the totalitarian state: the primacy of mythical thought, the vitalist realism,

the mystical exaltation of national community, the heroic and warlike pedagogy, the imperial ambitions, or the myth of the Italian nation as the vanguard of a new society. The Futurists were neither deceived nor misled by fascism; they were fascinated by its appeal for the total mobilization of culture to regenerate Italians in a religious cult of the nation and to construct a new society that would leave its mark upon the future in the style of 'Italian modernity'.[85]

Futurism may have anticipated Fascism, and Futurists may have been willing (albeit frustrated) Fascists, but what did Fascism actually take from Futurism? Zeev Sternhell has identified Futurism as an essential element in the birth of Fascist ideology, contributing 'artistic flair, the spirit of youth and boisterousness and the magic of cultural non-conformism'. Others have suggested the Futurists 'developed important *forms* in their performances, notably agit-prop and the spectacle, that formed the basis of later [Fascist] Party methods for crowd provocation and control'. Gentile, meanwhile, has written that 'From Futurism fascism had absorbed a dynamic feeling of modernity that was expressed in the ideal of "continual revolution," an ideal that impelled fascism never to rest content with its accomplishments...[but] to project itself into the future, towards new realities to be constructed.'[86] Against this, though, Walter Adamson has argued that 'Despite the widespread impression that futurism and fascism must have had something to do with one another, Mussolini actually took little from the Milanese avant-garde' other than perhaps 'in matters of propaganda and style, especially in his manner of "seducing" a crowd' – and even here he probably owed more to the post-war exploits of Gabriele D'Annunzio in Fiume (see Chapter 4) than to Futurism. Futurist rhetoric, according to Adamson, 'lack[ed] most of the important commitments – to spiritual discipline, an internal enemy, a new aristocracy, a spiritual Rome – that characterized Mussolini's'. Moreover, Futurism's 'aestheticism and urban sophistication...held little appeal' for the future *Duce* while its 'uncompromising' and 'mindless' *antipassatismo* (hatred of the past) was 'completely alien to him'. Mussolini took to the streets with the Futurists to demand Italian intervention in World War One, and was certainly close to Marinetti, albeit for a short time, in the immediate post-war period. However, in both cases, Mussolini's alliance with the Futurists was tactical: he demonstrated alongside them in 1914 only because they were willing 'to practice an activist *piazza* politics, while more political groups, like the Nationalists, remained hesitant'; his post-war interaction with the Futurists 'aimed at exploiting futurism's considerable appeal among ex-servicemen'. 'At no time was he tempted by an allegiance to futurism'. In contrast, the Futurists 'became ardent fascists': Futurism was influenced by Fascism, not vice versa.[87]

For Adamson, it was from the Florentine avant-garde movement and its mouthpiece, *La Voce*, that Fascism derived its key myths, values and ideas. The myth of two Italies, the first decadent, feminine and degenerate, the second vital, virile, active, but (as yet) without direction or leadership (destined to be provided by a 'new aristocracy'); the quest for a new national-secular religion to fill the spiritual void in modernity; the concept of the internal enemy – 'first' Italy,

Giolittismo, democracy; the idea of war as 'the central vehicle of national and spiritual self-renewal...simultaneously the practical means by which the second Italy will overcome the first and the spiritual means by which the void of modernity will be filled with meaning'; the values of discipline, hardness and duty, and contempt for political parties and doctrine: these were the cultural politics of the Florentine avant-garde and the main 'spawning ground for fascist ideology and rhetoric' – a fact acknowledged by Giuseppe Prezzolini, co-founder and editor of *La Voce* for most of its existence, and by Mussolini himself.[88]

Assessment

The work on Italian women's history and the bourgeoisie since the 1980s is indicative of profound changes within western historiography over the same period. Whereas class was once widely regarded as the key determinant of human relations (thus relegating gender to a secondary role), and classes themselves were dealt with as fairly uniform, stable and coherent identities, today class is viewed as but one of several identities that people carry and which 'press in and react with one another'.[89] On the one hand, this means that historians are now much more aware of the composite and heterogeneous (and often deeply conflicted and fragile) character of class. On the other hand, it means that other identities – including but not limited to gender – have assumed greater significance.

Today's altogether less tidy view of class has undoubtedly helped the historical reputation of the bourgeoisie in liberal Italy. The Italian bourgeoisie aped the lifestyles of the aristocracy, but so did their European counterparts and, as Blackbourn and Eley have argued for the German bourgeoisie, 'It would be misleading to interpret external symbols as a conclusive victory for the archaic values of a traditional caste'.[90] The Italian bourgeoisie harboured anti-modern sentiments, but so did their counterparts in that most industrial, capitalist – and bourgeois – of nations, Britain.[91] The Italian bourgeoisie did not realize its 'historic task' to carry through a full 'bourgeois revolution', but it was not alone: no European bourgeois class did (see Chapter 1). The Italian bourgeoisie was divided, but – again – this was a characteristic common to the European bourgeoisie in general, which has been described as 'diverse and deeply fissured'. Indeed:

> The historian attempting to understand the nineteenth-century [European] bourgeoisie must come to terms with pervasive conflicts among those who defined themselves as 'middle class' as much as with the qualities that made them kin... divisions were so acute that it is tempting to doubt that the bourgeoisie was a definable entity at all.[92]

Little wonder that many historians now prefer the plural 'bourgeoisies' or 'middle classes', to the singular 'bourgeoisie' or 'middle class'.[93]

Of course, it is possible that the fissures within the Italian bourgeoisie(s) were deeper and of more consequence than elsewhere on the Continent. In fact, given the centuries-old political fragmentation of the Italian peninsula prior to unification and the very different histories and economies of the various regions, not to mention the 'closed' nature of many pre-unification states together with the physical barriers to communication (there were few good roads and virtually no rail system; postal services were rudimentary and mail was often censored), it seems probable. The extreme parochialism displayed by the Italian bourgeoisie after 1870 was entirely to be expected: how could it have behaved otherwise? Localism, inevitably, was a defining feature of *all* classes in the newly unified kingdom (see 'Framework' above).

To focus on what divided the Italian bourgeoisie, however, is to run the risk of underestimating or ignoring the 'qualities that made them kin'. The Italian middle classes were defined by a sense of difference: they were not the aristocracy (despite the merging of the *haute bourgeoisie* with the lesser elements of the nobility); and they most definitely were not of the working classes. As the labour movement grew stronger and more militant this 'relational' aspect of bourgeois identity (fear of the masses, fear of socialism) became increasingly important. The term 'bourgeois' began to be used as a term of self-identification ('almost as a battle cry') by agrarian and industrialist groups during the Giolittian era as the threat posed by organized labour grew. It was also around this time that *national* organizations representing bourgeois economic interests first emerged.[94] The bourgeoisie also held, albeit with regional variations, to a common set of cultural values, behaviours and practices. They shared a particular ideal of the family. They believed in the gendered separation of private and public spheres, in certain notions of respectability and in the value of education (and of a particular type of education). They married within their own class.[95] They engaged in the same forms of sociability – theirs was a world of not only clubs and associations (even if these could be a source of division) but also of the café, the theatre, and, increasingly, the department store, of the public park and *passeggiata*, of holidays spent either in the mountains or, from the Giolittian era, on the coast. Finally, and despite their parochialism, the bourgeoisie displayed a strong sense of patriotism.[96] Indeed, as Dickie notes, 'The term "patriotic classes" gets closer to capturing the way Italy's rulers understood themselves than does the term "bourgeoisie"'.[97] The sources of bourgeois patriotism were several: language, literature, the arts, education and, of course, the state (which was both the reflection and source of middle-class power and prestige). That parochialism *and* patriotism should be defining features of the Italian bourgeoisie appears counter-intuitive, yet it is perhaps not so surprising. The concept of 'nation' is, after all, an extremely elastic and malleable one, it possesses many different meanings and can serve many different masters and ends; it can easily accommodate localism. Nor was the bourgeois Italian patriot by any means alone in his failure to match rhetoric with actions.[98]

As regards the role and status of women in liberal Italy, we have seen that historians are still largely engaged in the task of piecing together the history of this, until recently, historically marginalized sex. However, given that Annarita Buttafuoco's declaration 'I hate history as the story of victimization' is a sentiment shared by most other women's historians, it must surely grate when general histories of liberal Italy continue to present women's history in precisely this way (that is, if they do not ignore women altogether).[99] Italian women, of course, *did* experience discrimination, repression, marginalization and hardship, albeit to varying degrees depending on class (in general, women's freedoms increased with social status), geography (women were afforded greater freedoms and opportunities in Italy's towns and cities than in the countryside; the further south one travelled in Italy the more likely women were to be 'trapped' by tradition), family structure, age and marital status.[100] However, as Buttafuoco and others have shown, this is only part of a much bigger picture, one in which women were capable of agency despite the tight political-legal, economic and socio-cultural constraints imposed upon them.[101]

What of our last area of debate, the relationship of Futurism (and indeed of the pre-war cultural avant-garde in general) to Fascism? How one views this is, to a large extent, dependent on how one defines Fascism. If one understands Fascism as essentially reactionary, anti-modern, without ideas or an ideology – and this is (or at least was) a commonly held position (see Chapters 4 and 6), then it is difficult to link it to pre-war modernism (in fact, there is no reason to try and do so). From this perspective, Futurism's role in Fascism can only be seen as either politically (and aesthetically) irrelevant (the denialist position) or as a purely tactical expedient (the apologist view). However, if one agrees (as I do) with the basic thrust of much of recent Fascist historiography, which sees Fascism as an essentially modern movement, holding to a core set of beliefs, myths and ideals, then the search for the roots of Fascist political culture in the cultural (and political) avant-gardist movements of the Giolittian era makes a great deal of sense: Fascism got its ideas from somewhere, and the congruity between key elements of its political culture and rhetoric and that of pre-war avant-gardism is striking. Problems arise, though, if we try to identify precisely the pre-war cultural roots of Fascism. We simply cannot say with any degree of certainty that Futurism *in particular* provided Fascism with x, y and z, or was the preponderant cultural influence on Fascism, for the simple reason that many 'Fascist' Futurist ideas did not originate with, nor were specific to, Futurism:

> The search for an aesthetic-political solution to the problems of liberalism indeed united Marinetti and Mussolini, but this search was not pursued only by them. The advocacy of violence as a purifying force formed a central tenet of Sorel's social theory...the construction of new men characterized the Bolscheviks' [sic] pursuit of socialist society in Russia; an art-inspired form of social order was claimed as a remedy to the crisis of liberalism in the aesthetic culture of *fin-de-siècle* Vienna; the idea of a superhuman *dux* as leader of a mass society had among its illustrious antecedents Friedrich Nietzche.[102]

In the Italian context, we know that like the Futurists, the nationalists, syndicalists and *vociani*, were heavily influenced by Sorel and Nietzche, while the concept of the 'new man' and belief in the transformative power of art were ideas common to both Futurism and the Florentine avant-garde. All of the pre-war avant-garde movements were engaged in the search for a new secular religion of the nation. Given that Mussolini 'drew on nearly every anti-establishment movement or ideology to which he was exposed', any search for the 'real' cultural origins of Fascism is thus bound to be a forlorn one.[103] This means, of course, that one must also treat with considerable scepticism Adamson's claim that the *La Voce* group was the most important of the pre-war avant-garde movements in terms of the ideological orientation it offered Fascism.

It is also a mistake to see Futurism (or the rest of the Italian avant-garde) as a case of 'Fascism in the making'. As Emilio Gentile has written:

> The laboratory of the modernist avant-gardes proposed a series of themes and myths of a new political and artistic culture, motifs that flowed together into fascism after the Great War and contributed to its political culture and its attitude toward modernity. This does not mean, however, that these movements can be defined as proto-fascist, for from the same terrain of Italian modernist culture in the early twentieth century there also developed other syntheses of the same motifs, different cultural and political movements opposed to fascism.[104]

That Gramsci in 1921, as Fascist *squadristi* activity against the Left intensified, should not only write in fulsome praise of 'revolutionary' Futurism but also invite the former *vociano*, Giuseppe Prezzolini, to address a workers' group in Turin, indicates the connection between pre-war avant-gardism and post-war Fascism was not as clear-cut or straightforward as is sometimes assumed.

PART II

FASCIST ITALY

4 Fascist politics

Introduction

From its birth in 1919, debate has raged over the 'true' nature of Italian Fascism. Was it the product of war, of modernization, of capitalism in crisis, of the Left, of the Right, or of both Left and Right? Was it revolutionary or reactionary, the vehicle of a rising or defensive middle class, or of a cross-class constituency? Was Fascism an ideology or an incoherent, contradictory and ad hoc set of ideas determined by circumstances? Was it a form of totalitarianism or a form of politics based on traditional compromise with existing powerful interest groups? Was it, ultimately, little more than a personal monocracy, its fortunes tied to those of Mussolini and destined to die with him? Was the Fascist era characterized more by change or continuity in policy making, political relations, the structure of the state and the nature of state institutions? Was it historically specific – an inter-war phenomenon? The historiography surrounding the meaning of Italian Fascism will be the focus of this chapter. Closely connected to these debates are a second series of questions. Was Italian Fascism *sui generis* or part of a genus? More particularly, were Italian Fascism and German Nazism two sides of the same coin, similar yet different, or entirely separate species? And, connected to this last debate, was Fascist foreign policy driven by ideology or opportunism, was Fascist Italy always destined to become the ally of Nazi Germany or was the alliance the product of very particular circumstances, and was racialism – specifically anti-Semitism – inherent within Italian Fascism or a mere sop to Hitler?

Ideology has played an important part in historical interpretation. The late Renzo De Felice, Italy's best-known historian of Fascism, spent much of his controversial career denouncing the 'fascist mentality' of post-war anti-Fascism and of the Left in particular which, he claimed, prevented discussion and stunted real understanding of the Fascist period. While De Felice's supporters (predominantly on the Right) praised his 'rigorous historical analysis', and applauded the man who had 'restored to Italy part of her history', his critics argued that his self-proclaimed 'scientific' study of Fascism and particularly of Mussolini amounted to apologism, a 'monument for the *Duce*', as Denis Mack Smith famously described it in 1975.[1]

Whatever the relative merits of both arguments – and we shall return to them later – De Felice was justified in his complaint that the historiography of Italian Fascism lagged (and one might add, continues to lag) behind that of German Nazism. Whether De Felice was himself part of the solution or part of the problem remains, however, open to debate.[2]

Framework

War

When European war broke out in 1914, Italy remained neutral. When Italy entered the conflict in May 1915, it was on the side of the Entente – Britain, France and Russia – against its allies of the past thirty years, Germany and Austria-Hungary. In between declaring neutrality and declaring war, the Italian government and parliament had been exposed to the full arsenal of a relatively small but very determined pro-interventionist lobby. In the press and on the streets the interventionists attacked the 'eunuchoid' neutralist position. Among those demanding Italy enter the war and prove itself on the battlefield was the ex-editor of the socialist newspaper *Avanti!* Benito Mussolini, expelled from the neutralist PSI (October 1914) for refusing to toe the party line. When war was declared – after the neutralist parliament had ratified the secretly negotiated Treaty of London that committed Italy to the Entente – the interventionists claimed victory. For Mussolini interventionism was an 'exquisitely and divinely revolutionary' act. The political significance of the intervention crisis and the manner of Italy's entry into World War One has been disputed ever since.[3]

The expectation of a quick victory and easy spoils – the Treaty of London mentioned Trentino, South Tyrol, Trieste, Istria and much of Dalmatia as future Italian territories – was not realized. The hope expressed by interventionists that war would 'make' Italians proved misplaced, too. The PSI refused to support the war. The peasants, with little initial enthusiasm and then increasing reluctance, fought the war. Those on the front line regarded industrial workers, exempt from fighting, with hostility. Everyone hated war profiteers. The war itself was mismanaged from beginning to end by an incompetent military élite assisted by a weak and ineffective central government. Little was done to raise morale or to mobilize the population. Only after the catastrophic defeat of the Italian army at

Caporetto (October 1917), which allowed Austro-Hungarian and German troops to advance deep into Italian territory, did the government take remedial action. A new military leadership was installed, propaganda was used to rally Italians, the economy was brought under strict state control, and relations with the Allies were improved. In the last days of the war, the Italian army won a major victory in the Battle of Vittorio Veneto. However, those who had fought and identified with the war aims – officers drawn from the middle classes, for example – came to view liberal government as an obstacle to national fulfilment.

Peace

(a) *Parliamentary paralysis*
In November 1919, the first post-war national elections took place in Italy, based on a new electoral system of proportional representation. The elections marked the definitive entry of the masses into politics, the birth of mass political parties and the eclipse of the old established liberal groups. The PSI secured 1.8m votes and 156 seats, making it the largest party in parliament. Second to the PSI, the newly formed Catholic Popular Party (the *Popolari* or PPI) won 100 seats.[4] Liberal factions continued to govern but they were unable to do so effectively: there were six different liberal administrations between November 1919 and October 1922.

(b) '*Mutilated victory*'
The Treaty of London had been negotiated with Britain and France, not with the United States, which entered the war in 1917. It was President Woodrow Wilson, however, who set the agenda at the post-war peace conference in Paris, based on the principle of national self-determination. Italy's treaty claims to Dalmatia were ignored. The response of Italy's representatives was to demand, under the same principle, the Italian-speaking port of Fiume on the Dalmatian coast (and not part of the Treaty of London arrangements) in an effort to put pressure on the Americans. Wilson, though, did not give way. Italy's gains from the peace settlement were substantial; the acquisition of Trentino and Trieste (the former of which gave Italy control of the Brenner Pass) greatly strengthened Italy's north-eastern frontier, as did the dismembering of the Austro-Hungarian empire. Nationalists, however, stirred up by the government's posturing at Paris over Fiume, were enraged that Italy had been denied the full fruits of victory. This was the origin of the powerful myth of the 'mutilated victory': that Italy had won the war but lost the peace thanks to its pusillanimous liberal rulers and the duplicity of the 'plutocratic' nations.

(c) *D'Annunzio and Fiume*
The strength of nationalist sentiment was revealed in September 1919 when Gabriele D'Annunzio, Italy's leading aesthete and a national war hero, led a volunteer force into Fiume, beginning a flamboyant 16-month occupation of the city. Liberal politicians felt unable, or unwilling, to interfere. Senior Italian

army officers openly supported the occupation. Only in December 1920 did the Italian government move to expel D'Annunzio – again a step that enraged nationalists.

(d) *Biennio rosso*

Despite D'Annunzio's political cabaret in Fiume, it was the far Left rather than the far Right that seemed to emerge strongest from the war. Membership of the PSI and of the socialist unions exploded in the immediate post-war period, spurred by the economic and social dislocation caused by the war and by the example of the 1917 Russian revolution. There was also an upsurge in worker and peasant militancy. Yet, despite the revolutionary rhetoric of the 'maximalist' PSI leadership and the apparent strength of the socialist movement, Italy during the *biennio rosso* – the 'Two Red Years', 1919–20 – did not experience its own October revolution. The PSI and the socialist unions lacked effective leadership, were bitterly divided over objectives and tactics, and, besides, fought shy of actual revolutionary confrontation with the liberal state. There was also intense hostility between and within the plethora of factions – maximalist, minimalist, reformist, syndicalist, anarchist, anarcho-syndicalist, communist – that made up the Italian Left. The Left, in short, was far weaker than its numbers or activities suggested. The Fascists brutally exposed these weaknesses in the wake of failed factory occupations (September 1920), the last great example of workers' power in Italy in the inter-war period.[5]

(e) *Rise of Fascism*

Launched by Mussolini in March 1919 in Milan, the *Fasci di combattimento* (combat group) appeared stillborn. The 'Fascists of the First Hour', as they were later to be known, were an assorted collection of war veterans, Futurists, and ex-socialists, syndicalists and anarchists, united by the idea of 'revolutionary war' but espousing left-wing republican politics. The movement made little immediate headway. Fascist candidates stood in Milan in the 1919 elections; they won 4,657 votes of the 270,000 ballots cast in the city and no seats. Delighted socialists celebrated the demise of their former colleague by parading a coffin outside the offices of Mussolini's newspaper, *Il Popolo d'Italia*.

Fascism, however, survived. It abandoned its leftist agenda, and by the end of 1920 it boasted around 20,000 members, mainly in the major cities of the north. The *rise* of Fascism, though, dates to late 1920–21 and, in contrast to earlier Fascism, it was essentially an agrarian phenomenon located in the rural heartland of 'red' northern and central Italy. Here, locally led squads of urban-provincial *fasci* (known as *squadristi*) ventured into the countryside to break the power of socialist leagues. Emboldened by the crisis within socialism following the collapse of the factory occupations, sponsored and encouraged by *agrari*, their violence ignored or condoned by the police and local authorities, their numbers swelled by students, and their activities supported by small peasant proprietors anxious to hold on to their land and by landless peasants attracted by the Fascists' promise to widen private land ownership, the *fasci* enjoyed spectacular success through winter and spring.[6] Uncoordinated and certainly not under the control of Mussolini – the provincial leaders (referred to as *ras*) were fiercely independent – Mussolini was ultimately able to use agrarian Fascism to his advantage and to impose some measure of order on the rapidly expanding movement during the course of 1921. First, Mussolini secured Fascism a national profile (and a veneer of political respectability) when he accepted Giolitti's invitation to join the latter's 'National Bloc' list in the May general election. The Fascists duly won 35 seats. Second, in November, Mussolini formally constituted the Fascist movement as a political party, the *Partito nazionale fascista* (PNF), giving the movement greater co-ordination and himself a modicum of control.

As a party, the PNF benefited from the trials, failings and shortcomings of its rivals. The *popolari* lost much of its moral authority when Pius XI, elected in early 1922, turned his back on the PPI. In the summer of 1922, the PPI withdrew support from the coalition government. Meant as a protest at the government's failure to control Fascist violence, the move served only to weaken further the liberal state. Likewise, the failure of a general strike in August 1922, called to demonstrate popular opposition to Fascist terror, only underlined the frailty and divisions of the Left, but did nothing to calm bourgeois fears of a red revolution. Fascist squads responded with a renewed wave of violence and effectively took control of many of the major cities and towns in northern and central Italy. When Mussolini demanded political power in October 1922, the response of the liberal government, and of the King, was to give it to him. The Fascist 'March on Rome' at the end of October 1922 was not a revolutionary seizure of power: Mussolini had already been appointed Prime Minister on the 29th.

Fascism

(a) *Consolidation*

Mussolini was a Fascist prime minister, but he was not Prime Minister of a Fascist Government – his first Cabinet included only three Fascists and this was followed by two years of coalition government. The future of Fascism itself was uncertain. The rapid expansion in PNF membership in the early 1920s and its assimilation of the National Association in 1923 meant that Fascism was a very broad church indeed, ranging from the *ras*, pressing for an end to parliamentary government, to the conservative Right, whose aim was the restoration of law and order and the establishment of strong government. Fascism was, potentially, prone to the same type of internal splits that had so enervated socialism. Mussolini's own position within the party was by no means guaranteed either and he had to work hard to satisfy both his conservative and radical supporters. The *ras*, especially, proved difficult to please, upset that the Fascist 'revolution' was still incomplete. Mussolini moved to placate the *ras* by the creation of a Fascist Grand Council at the close of 1922 (ostensibly a 'shadow' government) and a Fascist militia in early 1923. Not until the late 1920s, however, and some time after the establishment of the dictatorship in 1925–6, was Mussolini able to fully assert his control over both party and *ras*.

(b) *Move to Dictatorship*

The establishment of the dictatorship itself followed hard on the heels of Fascism's first major political crisis, and was less Mussolini's choice than that of party hierarchs. Elections fought under new electoral laws in April 1924 had produced an overwhelming Fascist majority in parliament. Opposition deputies complained of widespread electoral malpractice. The Fascists' response was to murder the reformist socialist leader and outspoken critic of Fascism, Giacomo Matteotti. The 'Matteotti crisis' threatened to overwhelm Mussolini and the government but instead it eased the path to dictatorship. Despite widespread outrage at Matteotti's death, neither the King nor the Opposition were willing or able to engineer Mussolini's removal. Mussolini did take measures against a number of Fascists and temporarily repopulated his Cabinet with a number of non-Fascist appointments. As the crisis receded, however, the *ras* pressed Mussolini (December 1924) to complete the 'revolution' begun with the March on Rome and move decisively against parliament. Faced with the prospect of open revolt from within the PNF, and no doubt attracted to the idea of dictatorship, Mussolini went before parliament (3 January 1925) to claim responsibility for all Fascist violence (including the murder of Matteotti) and to challenge his opponents to remove him. Mussolini did not hide his intentions.[7] The inaction of the King and Opposition made dictatorship inevitable. Over the next two years, full executive powers were given to the head of the government, political opponents were arrested, attacked, or driven into exile, and, ultimately, all other political parties were outlawed. A Special Tribunal was established to deal with political crimes against the state.

(c) *Dictatorship*

A number of key themes were stressed by the regime:

- Corporativism. A concept of syndicalist origin, Fascist corporativism aimed at the resolution of class conflict in the name of national production, i.e. workers and employers combining for the benefit of the state. Society would be organized along productivist lines within industry-specific corporations. The Corporate State would be a 'third way' between capitalism and communism.
- Totalitarianism. Fascism claimed to be a totalitarian regime: 'everything within the state, nothing outside of the state, nothing against the state'. Fascism was to penetrate every aspect of Italian life from cradle to grave, at work and at home. The organization, regimentation, mobilization and fascistization of the masses were the purported aims of the regime. Under Fascism, the individual only existed or had meaning in relation to the state – which itself was indivisible from Fascism. From the mid-1930s, the regime placed increasing emphasis on the totalitarian state and the need to transform Italian society. In this period we see the establishment of a Ministry for Press and Propaganda, the creation of a single Fascist youth movement, the *Gioventù italiana del littorio* (GIL), an increasingly 'Fascist' school curriculum, efforts to change the weak 'bourgeois' habits of Italians (e.g. the introduction of the Fascist salute in place of the handshake), the abolition of the Chamber of Deputies and its replacement by the Chamber of Fasces and Corporations, and steps to

undermine the residual power of the monarchy (e.g. Mussolini claimed the rank of First Marshal of the Empire in 1938, giving him command over the Italian military in wartime).

- **Cult of the *Duce*.** Closely tied to (but not altogether reconcilable with) the object of the totalitarian state was the cult of the *Duce* (leader). Public identification with the figure of Mussolini as Italy's 'man of destiny' was encouraged from the very beginnings of Fascism, not least by Mussolini himself. During the dictatorship, and especially in the 1930s under the guidance of the PNF secretary Achille Starace, disparagingly referred to as Mussolini's 'obedient cretin', Italians were taught to regard Mussolini as omnipotent, omnipresent, immortal (see Chapter 6).[8]

- **Imperialism and war.** Fascism glorified violence, war and the nation-state. It was only natural, then, that the dictatorship should advocate overseas expansion. Foreign policy was Mussolini's personal concern as Foreign Minister, from 1926 to 1929 and from 1932 to 1936. From 1936, foreign affairs became the responsibility of his son-in-law and heir apparent, Galeazzo Ciano. Fascist foreign policy followed an openly aggressive path from the mid-1930s, beginning with the invasion of Ethiopia (1935), and quickly followed by military intervention in Spain alongside Franco's nationalist rebels (1936–9). Albania was invaded in April 1939. A month later, Italy signed the Pact of Steel with Nazi Germany. This committed Italy to militarily support Germany in the event that her ally should 'become involved in warlike complications'. Mussolini hoped there would be no war until 1943. Instead, in September 1939, Germany invaded Poland. Wholly unready for a full-scale European war, Mussolini was forced to declare Italian 'non-belligerency'. Italy finally entered World War Two in June 1940. Ill prepared and badly led, Italian troops were defeated in Greece, North Africa and, alongside German forces, in Soviet Russia.

(d) *Fall of Mussolini*

By the end of 1942 nearly the whole of the Italian merchant fleet had been destroyed, there were acute food and coal shortages, and Allied air raids on northern Italy were increasing. Italy appeared on the verge of defeat. The spring and summer of 1943 saw factory strikes in Turin and Milan (March), the loss of Libya (May) and, finally, the allied invasion of Italy itself (July). Two weeks after Allied forces landed in Sicily, an extraordinary meeting of the Fascist Grand Council (24 July) voted 19:7 in condemnation of Mussolini's conduct of the war and in favour of military powers passing to the King. Mussolini appeared ready to ignore the vote. Instead, on 25 July, he was summoned by Victor Emmanuel, still formally head of state, and dismissed. Mussolini was led away under arrest.

Debates

Meaning and ideology

The ineffective response of liberals, political Catholics, and the Italian Left to the rise of Fascism and the consolidation of Fascist power in the first half of the 1920s was due in no small measure to the incompetence of, and the divisions between and within, the respective political camps. It was also, however, a reflection of their bewilderment at the turn of events and their difficulty in properly understanding the Fascist phenomenon. Certainly, the tendency was to underestimate early (i.e. pre-regime) Fascism. Giolitti believed that Fascism was a useful political ally and could be tamed by exposure to parliament. Others from the Centre and the Right saw Fascism as a short-term palliative necessary to restore law and order in Italy: with the restoration of normality Fascism would no longer be required. Even on the Left – which suffered most at the hands of Fascist violence – the tendency was to see early Fascism as little more than the armed response of agrarian landowners in the face of rural unrest. Again, Fascism was not expected to last.

Part of the problem for contemporary observers – and one that historians have struggled with ever since – was the fact that the Fascists were disinclined to doctrinal elaboration. 'Fascism constructs day by day the edifice of its will and passion', Mussolini stated (March 1921); 'Our programme is simple: we want to govern Italy', he announced (September 1922), declaring at the same time his readiness to abandon republicanism in favour of the monarchy. A formal definition of Fascism (the 'Doctrine of Fascism') was only published in 1932 and was by no means comprehensive; corporativism, for example, was given little space even though it was one of Fascism's 'big ideas'. Nor was the 'Doctrine of Fascism' set in stone: as a form of 'perpetual revolution', Fascism was never to be compromised or restricted by dogma.

Closely related to this point is the question of how seriously we should take Fascism and its claims. Fascism lacked an orthodox ideological basis but did this mean that it had no ideology, or no ideology of its own, or was it a new ideological type? Fascist rhetoric and reality were often two very different things. The much-trumpeted Corporate State failed to materialize. The totalitarian state still accommodated powerful non-Fascist (and potentially anti-Fascist) institutions, the monarchy and the Church being the most obvious examples.[9] The apparently invincible Fascist military machine was humiliated by anti-Fascist volunteer forces in Spain in 1937 and humbled in Greece in 1940–1. However, did the gap between propaganda and practice mean Fascism was merely an elaborate confidence trick; the pursuit and maintenance of power its sole concern? Or did Fascism genuinely strive to remake Italy and Italians in its image, to create the new Fascist man, to make the twentieth century a 'Fascist century'? The search for the 'truth' about Fascism is made all the more difficult by the fact that Fascist policies frequently contradicted one another. Mussolini himself often laid claim to several different and contrary opinions on the same issue at the same time. Whether we should regard these as the actions of a clever politician maintaining his options, or merely those of a mountebank is open to debate.

Marxism and Fascism

That Fascism ever possessed its own identity has been disputed by the Left since the 1920s. Fascism posed particular problems for Marxism – not simply of a practical kind (*squadristi* attacks on the Left, the collapse of socialism, the death, imprisonment or exile of leading Italian socialists and communists) – but of a profoundly ideological character. According to Marx, capitalism, its representative class (the bourgeoisie) and its political superstructure (liberal parliamentary government) would be swept away at the hands of a proletariat brought into existence by capitalism itself. The overthrow of capitalism and the destruction of bourgeois society and politics would usher in communism, an economic system that did not rely upon the economic exploitation of one class by another (the victorious proletariat would be the only class). Where did Fascism fit into this? The logic of Marxism dictated that Fascism could *only* be an aspect of capitalism in crisis, the last throw of a desperate bourgeoisie clinging to power in the face of a rising proletariat. In its cruder forms, as expressed by the Communist International (1933), Fascism was simply the 'open terrorist dictatorship of the most reactionary, most chauvinistic, most imperialist elements of finance capital', the Fascists 'the lackeys, lickspittles of capital'.[10]

Less dogmatic or less Soviet-oriented Marxists – by the 1930s this often meant ex- or marginalized Communist Party members (Trotsky, August Thalheimer, Angelo Tasca examples of the former, Gramsci the latter) – produced more thoughtful (or thought-provoking) assessments of Fascism. However, while they emphasized its roots within the petit bourgeoisie (in contrast to the established Comintern view from the mid-1920s that Fascism was a bourgeois movement which set out to secure a reactionary mass basis) they could not, as Marxists, abandon the basic equation of Fascism with capitalism and, ultimately, as the expression of bourgeois interests. Gramsci will suffice as an example.

Gramsci's early assessments stressed the reactionary, petit bourgeois constituency of Fascism (the 'final incarnation of the petit bourgeoisie') and the bourgeois ends to which it was directed. Fascism, he wrote in 1921, was the 'slave to capitalism and landowners', 'the direct and armed defence of agrarian capitalist interests'.[11] With time, however, Gramsci recognized different strands within Fascism (parliamentary, extra-parliamentary, urban and rural) and the resistance to Fascism of some sections of the 'traditional' and 'industrial' bourgeoisie. The murder of Matteotti, and Fascism's survival of the crisis, though, prompted Gramsci to go further still and declare (November 1924):

> In the last analysis Matteotti's murder is nothing other than the expression and direct consequence of the tendency of Fascism to cease being the simple 'instrument' of the bourgeoisie, but to proceed in a series of abuses, violence and crimes according to its own logic.[12]

Gramsci's subsequent analysis displayed an increasing awareness of Fascism's complexity – it was more than simply capitalism in crisis – and its potential longevity, both views that broke with Comintern orthodoxy. But while Fascism may not have been the 'simple "instrument"' of the bourgeoisie – in *Prison Notebooks* Gramsci defines Fascism as 'modern Caesarism' whereby a mutually 'catastrophic' balance of opposing forces (the bourgeoisie vs the proletariat) is resolved by the intervention of an *outside* third force under the leadership of a 'heroic' personality – it was nonetheless an instrument of capitalism. The 1926 'Lyons

Thesis', written with Palmiro Togliatti, described Fascism as 'an armed reaction' (not a revolution) intent on the immobilization of the working class, favoured by 'the old ruling groups' but peopled by 'the urban petit bourgeoisie, and...a new rural bourgeoisie'. It served, contrary to the interests of the petit bourgeoisie, 'as the instrument of an industrial and agrarian oligarchy, to concentrate control over all the wealth of the country in the hands of capitalism'. Not all sections of the bourgeoisie were reconciled to Fascism ('the organic unity of the bourgeoisie in Fascism was not achieved') but Fascism was 'carrying out the programme of the plutocracy...and of an industrial land-owning minority'. In *Prison Notebooks*, Gramsci toyed with the concept of Fascism as a twentieth-century form of passive revolution, whereby changes were made to the political and economic structure without affecting the social order. 'Is it not precisely the fascist movement which in fact corresponds to the movement of moderate and conservative liberalism in the last century?' he asked. Was not corporativism 'the only solution whereby to develop the productive forces of industry under the direction of the traditional [bourgeois] ruling classes' while at the same time sustaining the illusions of the petit bourgeoisie that Fascism was, in fact, their movement?[13]

For Gramsci, Italian Fascism was the 'revelation' of Italian history, of the Risorgimento. Yet, for all Marxists, fascism (in its generic sense and often denoted by a small 'f') was a 'revelation' of sorts – that is, of bourgeois democracy. As Togliatti was keen to point out, the bourgeoisie might not always have to resort to fascism but still the 'tendency toward the fascist form of government is present everywhere'.[14]

Marxist interpretations of Fascism since 1945 have continued to stress the same essential message of inter-war Marxism (Fascism as the expression of bourgeois-capitalist interests). Although, as in the inter-war period, there has been considerable disagreement over the precise character of Fascism, Italian and generic, the Marxist historiography of Fascism amounts to multiple variations on a common theme.[15]

Non-Marxist accounts of Fascism

Marxists from the beginning had a clear idea of what Fascism represented. To many in the liberal camp, Fascism made far less sense. Some, like Luigi Salvatorelli, shared Marxism's preoccupation with class: Fascism was the 'class struggle' of a petit bourgeoisie, 'wedged as a third force between capitalism and the proletariat'. Fascism was not the 'political projection of capitalist economy', indeed it was hostile towards capitalism, as it was hostile towards the proletariat, since both represented a threat to its interests. However, the fact that the petit bourgeoisie was not a 'real' class – its one common ideological component was nationalism as the negation of class and class struggle – left it vulnerable to conventional bourgeois-capitalist control. For others, Croce among them, class-based explanations of Fascism were mistaken. Fascism was not the movement of one class against another; it found its supporters and backers in all classes. Fascism presented something of a problem for Croce. Like many liberals in the early 1920s, Croce had endorsed Fascism as a short-term solution to post-war 'anarchy'. Only from 1925 did he become an active critic of the regime.[16] But Croce's anti-Fascism also brought into question his historicism. If history really was the story of liberty, and 'of man's positive achievements' as he later put it, where did Fascism fit into this? And if there was nothing wrong with liberal Italy, as he claimed in *History of Italy*, how could one explain the rise of Fascism? By emphasizing the cross-class character of Fascism, Croce was able to absolve the liberal (bourgeois) classes of specific responsibility. By claiming that Fascism was an 'intellectual and moral disease', a 'parenthesis', an 'accident', an 'infection', 'a sickness that arose in the veins of all Europe as a result of the First World War', a 'bewilderment, a civic depression and a state of inebriation caused by the war', Croce was able to separate not only Italian liberalism but also Italy itself (and, on a wider scale, western European culture) from Fascism. Moreover, he was able to reconcile Fascism with history (Fascism was a brief and unexpected detour from the road of liberty represented by secular liberalism), and deprive Fascism of any real substance or positive meaning.[17] Croce also challenged the Fascists' own attempts to portray Fascism as the true heir of the Risorgimento tradition.[18]

Croce's thesis, although perhaps the most famous liberal interpretation of Fascism, was nonetheless criticized from within liberal historical circles. In 1952, Chabod dismissed as unsustainable the idea of Fascism as 'a simple "adventure", inserting itself unexpectedly in the history of Italy almost as if from outside'. Instead, he argued, it was clear that Italian life after unification had carried within it the 'dangerous germs' that 'exploded' in the crisis of 1919–22. However – and here Chabod turned his attack against the 'revelation' thesis – the presence of such germs in liberal Italy did not necessarily lead to Fascism. That they did become decisive elements in the rise of Fascism was the sole fault and responsibility of the men of 1919–22 and not of those of 1860 or 1880. And while it was true that among the guilty were liberal politicians, the 'heirs of the Risorgimento', they were not alone; the socialists and the Catholics – the heirs of the 'anti-Risorgimento', were equally culpable. 'To study the history of Italy between 1860 and 1915', declared Chabod, 'and project onto it...the shadow of 1922 and 1925 and evaluate it only as the function of this shadow, is totally erroneous'.[19]

Chabod's assault on the 'revelation' thesis was directed primarily against the Italian Left. However, the idea of Fascism as the revelation of the structural deficiencies of liberal Italy was not the sole dominion of Marxism. From a distinctly non-Marxist perspective, Mack Smith took a similar line (see Chapter 1), prompting the Italian historian Walter Maturi to complain of the English historian's obsession with the idea that 'everything in Italian history from 1861 on leads to Fascism'.[20] For others, Fascism was less the revelation of liberal Italy's failings but rather of the ancient vices of Italians themselves. Indeed, it was in this sense that Giustino Fortunato first used the term in the early 1920s. In 1930, the leading anti-Fascist and 'liberal socialist' Carlo Rosselli – who was later to be assassinated on the orders of the regime – reached a similar conclusion. Critical of Marxism's view of Fascism as a 'brutal case of class reaction' (a 'facile oversimplification'), Rosselli, borrowing the expression from his old collaborator Piero Gobetti, described it instead as 'the autobiography' of the Italian nation. Italians were 'morally lazy' and passive:

> Out of the deeply sedimented layers of national character and the experience of generations the Fascist phenomenon burst into the light... Look at Fascism as something emerging from the subsoil of Italy and you will see that it expresses the deepest vices, the latent weaknesses, the miseries, alas, of our people, of all our people...[Mussolini] won because he cleverly played the right notes, the ones to which the average psychology of the Italians was extraordinarily susceptible.[21]

But what did Fascism mean in practice? For Marxists it was capitalism in a new guise. For liberals, if anything defined Fascism it was what it stood against – democracy, liberalism, socialism, rationalism, the Risorgimento; it was, in other words, an anti-movement. And little separated the liberal interpretation in this sense from its non-Marxist critics, such as Mack Smith and Salvemini. For Mack Smith, Fascism may indeed have been the revelation of liberal Italy's ills but it did not really stand for anything beyond repression, violence and authoritarianism. It was best defined by what it opposed, it possessed no clear ideas of its own, it was a mass of contradictions, it rarely matched words with deeds (indeed, it rarely bothered to try), it was concerned only with the pursuit of power for its own sake, and it excelled only in propaganda.[22] In this sense, we are not far from Croce's 1925 description of Fascist ideas and policies as:

> ...[A]n incoherent and bizarre jumble of calls to authority and of demagogy, of proclaimed reverence to the law and of violations of the law, of ultramodern concepts and of musty old rubbish, of absolutist attitudes and Bolshevik tendencies, of irreligiousness and approaches to the Catholic church, of an abhorrence of culture and of sterile efforts towards a baseless culture, of mystical mawkishness and cynicism.[23]

Salvemini, one of the few Italian historians in the Fascist period to place principle before employment (he resigned from his chair at Florence University) and perhaps the most high-profile critic-in-exile of Fascism (he left Italy in 1925), did not dissent from this view. (Indeed, he signed Croce's *Manifesto of Anti-Fascist Intellectuals* from which the above quote is taken.) Salvemini excelled at exposing and ridiculing the emptiness of Fascist ideas, rhetoric and claims. Fascism, he argued, was constructed on a number of myths: that it had saved Italy from Bolshevism, that it represented a new social system (corporativism), that it would 'lead the whole world to a higher form of civilization'. In reality, Fascism was an empty shell – 'humbug' – and Mussolini 'an irresponsible improviser, half madman, half criminal, gifted only – but to the highest degree – in the arts of 'propaganda' and "mystification"'. The much-trumpeted (and admired) Corporate State was one of Salvemini's favourite targets. In *Under the Axe of Fascism* (1936) he denounced corporativism as a 'fairy tale'; any attempt to find evidence of the Corporations was like 'looking in a dark room for a black cat which is not there'.[24]

A. J. P. Taylor, admittedly no expert on Fascist Italy, perhaps best encapsulated the non-Marxist, anti-Fascist, consensus on Fascism that lasted from the interwar period until the 1960s. 'Everything about Fascism was a fraud,' Taylor wrote.

'Fascist rule was corrupt, incompetent, empty; Mussolini himself a vain, blundering boaster without ideas or aims'.[25] The gulf that separated Fascist words from deeds, the strutting and posturing of its leader, Italy's disastrous performance in World War Two, all fed into this image of Fascism as 'a comic opera' or 'South American palace revolution'.

There were dissenting voices from the established Marxist and non-Marxist interpretations of Fascism – Dante Germino's 1959 study of Fascist totalitarianism, for example. Totalitarian theory was especially popular in western political science circles in the Cold War environment of the 1950s since it appeared to demonstrate the basic similarity between Soviet Communism and Nazism (the two allegedly shared evil 'totalitarian' characteristics). Fascist Italy, however, was usually given scant attention, or discounted altogether. Germino, though, argued that it deserved to be recognized as a genuine totalitarian system: Fascism 'was a political religion, equipped with the machinery necessary to realize its programme', namely the creation of 'a new ethic, a Mussolinian and Fascist ethic'.[26]

Neither Germino's thesis nor totalitarian theory made much of an impression upon Italian Fascist historiography to begin with. Marxist historians naturally rejected a model that linked Nazism with communism. Even the first generation of archive-based Italian historians of Fascism, such as Alberto Aquarone and Renzo De Felice, disputed the totalitarian reality of Fascism.[27] These young researchers did claim, though, to represent a break with existing Fascist historiography: their primary source-based studies would allow a more profound understanding of Fascism to emerge founded on evidence, rather than ideological predilections or prejudices. It would be possible to study Fascism objectively, allowing the 'facts' to 'speak for themselves'. Was Fascism a simple case of class reaction, a bourgeois phenomenon, a 'fraud', or a totalitarian regime? The documents would tell. As De Felice, who by the end of the 1960s had emerged as *the* authority on Italian Fascism, never tired of saying, 'to define fascism is first and foremost to write its history'.[28]

Renzo De Felice

No other historian of Italian Fascism has written so much, sold so successfully, generated such controversy, or has been so written about as De Felice. Bosworth's observation that 'If a baron ruled over the Fascist segment of the Italian past, it was Renzo De Felice', was hardly meant as a compliment, but the point stands.[29]

De Felice was a poor writer and a difficult read.[30] Yet he carved out an enviable international academic reputation and domestic public profile. His masterpiece – an eight-volume biography of Mussolini written over 30 years (the first volume appeared in 1965, the last and uncompleted volume in 1997, a year after his death) – accounts in large measure for his academic reputation, good and bad, both within and outside of Italy. Crucial, though, to De Felice's rise out of the academic ghetto onto the front pages of the Italian national press and into the world of television was *Intervista sul fascismo* (1975) which sold over 50,000 copies in Italy in less than three months on publication, topping the list of best-selling paperbacks. Twenty years later, his eye for the market was confirmed when *Rosso e Nero* (1995), like *Intervista* a short, interview-based paperback, also became a best-seller. Both books were enormously controversial. *Intervista* was criticized as 'a rehabilitation of Fascism' by the Marxist historian Nicola Tranfaglia, and as '*qualunquismo* historiography', 'objectively philo-fascist' and 'diseducational' by the journal *Italia contemporanea*.[31] So strong was the reaction to *Intervista* that De Felice's friend and colleague Rosario Romeo, likened it to a 'lynching'.[32] *Rosso e Nero* provoked similar outrage (see Chapter 7).

De Felice's death did not silence his critics. Bosworth's *The Italian Dictatorship* (1998) repeated and amplified earlier criticisms of De Felice by the Australian. In 2000, Mack Smith reprised his 1975 assault on De Felice's biography of Mussolini. The best that could be said of De Felice's 'laborious and not very readable' study, he wrote, was that it had 'raised many interesting questions for future generations to debate'. In an interview in 2000 with the Italian daily *La Repubblica*, the Turin-based historian Massimo L. Salvadori repeated Tranfaglia's earlier point that De Felice had opened the way 'to the more or less relative rehabilitation of Fascism'.[33]

De Felice, though, has never been short of supporters. In 1975, the American historian Michael Ledeen, De Felice's interlocutor in *Intervista*, took to the letters pages of the *Times Literary Supplement* in order to rebut Denis Mack Smith's scathing review of *Intervista* and *Gli anni del consenso*, Volume 4 of De Felice's biography of Mussolini.[34] Many other non-Italian historians, including George Mosse and a host of American scholars – Borden Painter junior, A. James Gregor and John Thayer amongst them – have defended De Felice's reputation and method if not every one of his arguments. Within Italy, meanwhile, there are enough supporters of De Felice to constitute, at least in Bosworth's view, an historical 'school'. Chief among the Italian *De Feliciani* has been Emilio Gentile, whose own work we will look at in detail shortly (see also Chapter 6). Gentile's assessment of De Felice as 'a truly exceptional figure'[35] was representative of a significant body of Italian academic and political opinion – in early 1997 the Italian periodical *liberal* named De Felice 'Man of the Year' for 1996.

What had De Felice to say about Mussolini and Fascism that so polarized historical opinion? Little in his first three volumes on Mussolini, covering the period 1883–1929, or in his 1969 work *Le interpretazioni del fascsimo*, could be described as overly controversial or particularly new. *Gli anni del consenso, 1929–1936* (1974) was different. De Felice argued that these were years of mass consensus, when the regime was at its height. The conquest of Ethiopia was Mussolini's 'masterpiece' (*capolavoro*), a personal and popular triumph that amply demonstrated Mussolini's *realpolitiker* skills in international affairs (De Felice was insistent that Fascist foreign policy was predicated on the art of the possible rather than driven by ideology). At the same time, De Felice sought to distance Italian Fascism from German Nazism. The two regimes, he argued, had little or nothing in common.

De Felice's *Duce* of 1929–36 was very different to the one he had portrayed in earlier volumes. Once seen by De Felice as a day-to-day improviser, Mussolini was now presented as a visionary planner. In late 1929, according to De Felice, the Fascist regime entered 'maturity'. Sure of his power following the signing of the Lateran Pacts with the Vatican, but tired of the failings of Italians and aware that the long-term future of Fascism was dependent upon the creation of a new truly 'Fascist' generation, Mussolini, De Felice argued, set out to transform Italian society and create the new Fascist man. Mussolini drew on two sources for moral guidance. First, he adopted the ideas of Giovanni Gentile (the concept of the 'ethical state', the nation as the expression of the state, the historic function of Fascism to 'remake man'). De Felice pointed to the 1932 'Doctrine of Fascism', written by Gentile and Mussolini, as evidence. Second, Mussolini was greatly influenced by the German Oswald Spengler's work on 'Caesarism' (the imminent collapse of western liberal-democratic civilization, the idea of the 'individual Caesar' creating a new civilization). Fascism would be the new civilization, and Italy would lead. But Italians, degraded by centuries of servitude, had to be 'Fascistized' first. Mussolini's task was to induce the Italian people by any means and without delay to be truly Fascist; only then could Italy fulfil its destiny. De Felice pointed to various speeches by Mussolini in the 1930s as proof of Spengler's influence.[36]

Many historians disputed De Felice's interpretation. For now we will concentrate on De Felice's view of Mussolini as the would-be 'constructor of a new civilization',[37] (we will return to the issue of consensus in Chapter 6; foreign policy is dealt with in this chapter). Critics wondered how the man who De Felice had once said had 'no precise idea that morally sustained him and guided him', whose policy had once resembled a kind of 'super-trasformismo', who between 1922 and 1929 had 'confirmed and perfected' the compromise brokered with the traditional ruling class at the time of the March on Rome, had now become the Mussolini-on-a-mission, the leader whose actions were now founded on a 'moral idea'. What had happened to the 'sea of generalities that purported to constitute the ideology of Fascism'? De Felice's evidence was also questioned. Could the 1932 Doctrine really be taken at face value? Many historians considered it mere rhetoric. Was it safe or wise to trust any of Mussolini's public statements? De Felice, his critics suggested, had been duped by, or fallen for, the *Duce*.[38]

De Felice expanded on the themes of *Gli anni del consenso* in *Intervista*. Here, he emphasized the 'enormous' differences between Italian Fascism and German Nazism ('two worlds, two traditions, two histories so different that it is very difficult to unite them in a single discourse'). In doing so he revisited and revised some of his earlier ideas. Fascism was now the revolutionary movement of a 'modern' and 'emerging' rather than a 'castrated' petit bourgeoisie in crisis (the case with German Nazism). Fascism as movement was consequently driven by 'the impulse to renew'. Fascism as ideology was forward-looking, filled with a 'vitalistic optimism' – a belief in progress – in contrast to the 'tragic pessimism' of Nazism. Fascism was the manifestation of a left-wing form of totalitarianism dating back to the French revolutionary 'Terror' of 1793–4, which had used force to change man. Nazism derived from the totalitarian Right, viewing the use of force as necessary to control corrupted man. The Fascist regime was never truly totalitarian, however, unlike Nazism. It was, though, in its way, revolutionary in its drive to mobilize the masses and 'to achieve the transformation of society and the individual in a direction that had never been attempted or realized'.[39]

De Felice's opinion that Fascism and Nazism were different contrasted with Mussolini's own view that 'the goals they [Fascism and Nazism] have sought and reached are the same: the unity and greatness of the people'.[40] Even De Felice, who regarded the concept of generic fascism with suspicion, recognized Fascism and Nazism as the only two true 'fascisms'. His emphasis on the 'vitalistic optimism' of Fascism and its belief in progress had little in common with the widespread notion of Fascism as an 'anti' movement. His view of Fascism as 'the application of the principles laid down in 1789' ran counter to Mussolini's claim that Fascism was the repudiation of the ideals of the French revolution, and surprised those who associated the principles of 1789 with liberty, equality, fraternity.

What really infuriated many of De Felice's critics, however, was his insistence that he was merely presenting the 'evidence' and that it was too early to draw general conclusions, when, in fact, he was all the time interpreting the evidence, choosing the 'facts' and passing judgement. For De Felice to try and hide behind Ranke, to claim to write 'without emotion', with 'serenity...as if one were dealing with events of two, three centuries ago',[41] was viewed as both unacceptable and disingenuous. *Intervista* was published in 1975 at the height of 'black' (right-wing) and 'red' (left-wing) terrorism in Italy. Rumours of a right-wing coup were rife. The communist opposition was gaining in popular support. Elements within the Centre-Right government were considering power sharing with the communists in an attempt to resolve Italy's deepening political crisis. In *Intervista*, De Felice clearly had an anti-communist agenda. Since the late 1950s, De Felice had campaigned against what he regarded as the PCI's rejection of intellectual autonomy, its cultural conformity and its unwillingness to think for itself or to question received wisdom.[42] In his opinion, Marxism sought to impose a strait-jacket on modern Italian historiography, closing the possibility of discussion and ignoring evidence that ran counter to Marxist thought. To find in *Intervista* a reit-eration of these views was not in itself surprising – but De Felice's language was remarkably blunt. Italian culture (De Felice seems to have had in mind academic culture) was 'conditioned and determined by the cultural hegemony of the PCI'. The Marxist anti-Fascist mentality was, in fact, a 'fascist mentality...a mentality of intolerance and of ideological oppression, which seeks to disqualify its opponents in order to destroy them'. The study of Fascism in Italy had been stunted because of this. In a sense, De Felice's arguments could be viewed as simply an apolitical defence of proper historical method rather than as an example of his overt anti-communism. But De Felice could not resist making a direct comparison between 'historical' Fascism (he was convinced that Fascism was a phenomenon limited to Europe between 1918 and 1945) and contemporary Italian communism. Having talked about the failure of the liberal establishment in the early 1920s to 'trans-form' Fascism into a constitutional party, De Felice commented: '[*Trasformismo*] is an operation that, it seems to me, we are seeing again today when a sector of the Italian bourgeoisie talks of the participation of the communists in power, think-ing that this means transforming them into social democrats'. His message was clear. The PCI could not be tamed; it was not interested in parliamentary politics. 'In the course of ten years fascism had achieved a virtual monopoly of power, and the old political ruling class...was almost entirely excluded.' For De Felice, the entry into government of the PCI represented the thin end of the wedge. Just as the Fascists had done in the 1920s so the communists would do in the 1970s, if given the opportunity. This was not the last time De Felice questioned the democratic credentials of the PCI (see Chapter 7).[43]

Revisionist and 'culturalist' readings

De Felice's work was not the only controversial interpretation of Fascism in the mid-1970s. The American political scientist A. James Gregor argued in a number of works that Fascism, led by the profound figure of Mussolini, possessed a clear and coherent ideology of its own (a brand of revolutionary national syndicalism) which it duly implemented once in power. At its heart, Fascism represented a modernizing, mass-mobilizing developmental dictatorship, i.e. a dictatorship committed to the industrialization and modernization of Italy's retarded economic system by whatever means necessary. Production was seen as the key to Italy's greatness, its ability to look after itself and to impose its will on others. Policies might have changed over the years but the aim did not. Fascism may have accommodated the interests of traditional élites but only when those interests coincided with its own. Mass-mobilization – rituals, marches, the cult of the leader – helped to maintain social order, despite the austerity, instability and insecurity engendered by this forced drive to economic maturity, and provided Fascism with a degree of independence from its non-Fascist allies. And, according to Gregor, Fascism succeeded. The Fascist revolution 'carried Italy from the beginning to the conclusion of the drive to economic maturity'.[44] We will look at Gregor's 'developmental dictatorship' thesis in more detail in Chapter 5. Suffice to say that the image of Mussolini as a serious thinker, of the Fascist regime as the revolutionary reality of Fascist ideology, and of Fascism as a success, caused a degree of consternation in more obviously 'anti-Fascist' circles. Gregor, like De Felice before him, was accused of philo-Fascist leanings. There was, according to one critic, a 'strange affinity between Gregor's interpretation and the image of their achievements that the Fascists wished to project. Gregor's Mussolini is not very different from the Mussolini who was always right...the propaganda of yesterday reappears as the scholarly wisdom of today'. The same critic confessed to a feeling of 'moral revulsion' on reading Gregor's thesis.[45] Gregor, for his part, did nothing to deflect such criticisms. His *Italian Fascism and Developmental Dictatorship* (1979) was dedicated 'to the memory of Gioacchino Volpe', Fascism's very own official historian.

Gregor is an extreme example, but his arguments, like De Felice's, are indicative of a broader trend dating from the 1970s to view Fascism (Italian) and fascism (generic) in ways which emphasize its ideological rigour and its novel, creative and utopian aspects.[46] In this regard, amongst the most important influences on Fascist (and fascist) historiography has been the German historian

George Mosse. Since the mid-1960s Mosse has propounded a 'cultural' reading of Nazism – Mosse's specialism – and of fascism. To Mosse, Nazi and fascist ideology drew from a strong cultural and intellectual heritage dating back to the nineteenth century. Fascism also borrowed from the cultural experience of World War One (glorification of war, martyrdom, camaraderie, sacrifice, sense of national community, fulfilment of life through death, class solidarity, etc.). Meanwhile, the 'fascist style' – fascism felt itself to be, and presented itself as, a secular religion and placed great emphasis upon ritual, myth and ceremony – could trace its ancestry back to the democratic ideal of the 'general will' espoused by Rousseau and implemented by the French Jacobins during the 1790s. Fascism, like Jacobinism, was a form of dictatorship in 'which the people worshipped themselves through public festivals and symbols...where religious enthusiasm was transferred to civic rites'. Boasting a revolutionary 'third way' nationalist ideology and culture with a distinct utopian ideal – the creation of the 'new man', the fusion of the spiritual with the political, the fulfilment of the individual within the context of the collective – fascism's 'attitude towards life' struck a popular chord. Social and economic factors were important in the success of fascism, Mosse argued, but cultural factors were pre-eminent.[47]

For Mosse, Italian Fascism was the less ideological, the less serious of the fascist regimes: ritual was not so important, Mussolini was too much a 'man of the world' – too mainstream[48] – and the Italian national character too easy-going for Fascism to match German Nazism. Fascism also derived from fundamentally different national traditions. It was perhaps not surprising then that De Felice should champion Mosse's work in Italy. De Felice, after all, was keen to emphasize the differences between Fascism and Nazism, and, as we have seen, he agreed with a number of Mosse's other conclusions. By the late 1970s and early 1980s, De Felice was demanding a similar cultural analysis of Italian Fascism – that is, of Fascist modernity as an expression of mass society – in order 'for an effective understanding of the Fascist phenomenon'. 'Mosse has begun to do it with very convincing results,' wrote De Felice. 'It is on this path that we must proceed'.[49] How far De Felice himself went along this path is a moot point. His biography of Mussolini was increasingly taken up with foreign policy and war, although he continued to emphasize in *Lo stato totalitario 1936–1940* (1981) the 'cultural revolution' embarked upon by Mussolini to create the 'Fascist man'. The 'culturalist' approach to Fascism nevertheless has made significant inroads in the last two decades and has evolved along two interrelated paths. The first of these is concerned, like Mosse, with the political culture of Fascism (what Mosse describes as 'politics as the expression of a lifestyle, an attitude towards the totality of the human experience').[50] The second is interested more in Fascist cultural policy and production. We will look at the latter in Chapter 6. As regards work on Fascist political culture, the best-known studies are those by Emilio Gentile.

Although well known for advocacy of De Felice,[51] Gentile's method and interpretation owe more to Mosse than to his former colleague at the University of Rome. It is hardly surprising that Mosse, in turn, has been fulsome in his praise for Gentile's work.[52]

Fascism, according to Gentile, was a 'unique synthesis' of the myths of war and the myths of the 'cultural revolt' of the Giolittian era (see Chapter 3). At the heart of Fascist ideology was the utopian ideal of a new civilization and the new Fascist 'soldier-citizen' dedicated to the service of the state. Fascism asserted 'the primacy of politics in every aspect of human life'. By means of totalitarian organization, integration and education – Fascism was a 'totalitarian universe in the making' – the masses would 'absorb the myth of the state as a living reality'. Through the 'sacralization of politics' – Fascism was a 'political religion of the state' – the masses would come to view the state as the 'supreme value'. The state, in turn, would mould the new Fascist man, creating 'a new type of human being, totally dedicated to achieving the political aims of the totalitarian party'. Fascism was the 'first political movement of the century to bring mythical thought to power', believing totally in its ability 'to mould reality and the nature of man in the image of its own myth'. Ideology and style were inseparable: 'the style was the ideology; the forms and the rituals of the organization were both the representation of its myths and their materialization'.[53]

For Gentile, the PNF played the key role within the 'totalitarian logic' of Fascism; it was the prime agent of the new 'state in the making'. The PNF was responsible, as the keeper of the Fascist faith, for the 'socialization' of the Fascist religion through the 'sacralization' of the state, and for propagating the new secular religion, and the cult of the *Duce* within this, through the rituals, liturgy, symbols, festivals, monuments, art and myths of Fascism. It took care of the organization, control and political education of the masses. It was the 'capillary structure' by which the state infiltrated every level of society and penetrated the life of every individual. Omnipresent and irreplaceable, the PNF 'conditioned the existence of millions of men and women'.[54] We will see to what extent Gentile considered Fascism to have 'conditioned' Italian society in Chapter 6.

Gentile's interpretation of Fascism as a political religion has been criticized from within the 'culturalist' camp. From backgrounds in sociology, Simonetta Falasca-Zamponi and Mabel Berezin have offered rival assessments of Fascist political culture. Falasca-Zamponi's work begins from the premise that Fascism was a more complex phenomenon than simply 'politics as religion', and, consequently, 'there are dimensions of fascism that the formula of sacralization does not adequately explain'. To understand Fascism fully, she argues, one must understand the Fascist aesthetic conceptualization of politics. Put simply, for Fascism the world was 'a canvas upon which to create a work of art, a masterpiece completely neglectful of human values'; Mussolini was the 'God-like artist-creator', the (despised) masses his – and Fascism's – raw material. Fascism's aesthetic vision of the world revealed its 'truly totalitarian nature': 'the world is how we want to make it', claimed Mussolini in 1932, 'it is our creation'.[55]

Berezin, too, is critical of Gentile's 'sacralization' thesis which, she argues, presents a 'static view of religion and fascism'. Instead, 'Fascist ritual...was a set of cultural actions that adapted to advance ideological ends' and 'changed in response to shifting political imperatives'. Berezin is also far more interested than Gentile (or, for that matter, Falasca-Zamponi) in exploring the extent to which Fascism's public political identity really penetrated into the private sphere of Italian life. Indeed, Berezin is highly critical of those 'students of political ritual' who blithely assume that 'representations of power equal realities of power'.[56]

Nevertheless, despite her caution, Berezin fits comfortably enough into the culturalist school. The Fascist regime 'attempted to create a fascist political community and identity by merging the public/private self in public political rituals'. Fascism possessed an ideology in the sense that it possessed 'a set of political and cultural practices but not a body of discursive ideas...[Fascists] believed in action and style – ideas that specify means and not ends and that make the ends of fascist action extremely malleable... The Italian fascist commitment to style and action makes ritual action an excellent venue for an analysis of the fascist project'. The words are Berezin's but they could just as easily have been written by Gentile or Mosse, or any one of a host of other 'cultural' historians of Fascism seeking to understand Fascist political culture from within (what Walter Adamson has called the 'internal approach to fascism').[57]

The culturalist school has its detractors. The American historian David D. Roberts, for example, while acknowledging that the focus on spectacle, ritual and rhetoric has 'illuminated important dimensions of [Italian] fascism', is nonetheless critical of the culturalist approach because, in his opinion, it ignores the importance of actual *ideas*. For Roberts, Fascism was the product of a rational critique of the Enlightenment tradition. That said, Fascist ideology was a 'messy mixture' of competing nationalist, syndicalist and Gentilean thought. The fact that these ideas 'did not mesh neatly' meant that Fascism by the end of the 1920s had reached an ideological impasse. This, according to Roberts, explains the increasing centrality of spectacle and ritual – in particular, of the cult of the *Duce* – during the 1930s.[58] Roberts thus still ends up endorsing, albeit in a roundabout way, the view of culturalist historians who argue that Fascism's aesthetic overproduction was ultimately designed 'to compensate for, fill in, and cover up its unstable ideological core'.[59]

A far more resolute and robust anti-culturalist campaign has been waged by Bosworth. For many years an outspoken critic of De Felice, Bosworth has in more recent times railed against the culturalist school. 'In their determination to be apolitical and to treat Fascism on its own terms,' he writes, 'the culturalist historians often credulously report what Fascism said rather than critically exploring what it meant'.[60] For his part Emilio Gentile, whose sacralization-totalitarian thesis has been frequently attacked by Bosworth, has accused the Australian of 'serious errors of fact, inventions, and omissions...[and] an incomplete and distorted representation of the results of research and the historical debate'.[61] We will return to Bosworth and Gentile in Chapter 6.

Foreign policy

Interpretations of Fascism naturally have influenced historical opinion on Fascist foreign policy. Those who have argued that Fascism lacked clear goals and was little more than ad hoc opportunism generally share Salvemini's judgements on foreign affairs: 'He [Mussolini] had no definite plans, but was only trying out different devices day by day according to changing moods. Like the knights-errant of old, he was roaming the world in search of adventure';

> 'Mussolini did not give any importance to the international treaties that he concluded: he signed them, he forgot them and did things his way when he found them inconvenient. He looked for immediate successes, it mattered little if they were real or apparent, short-lived or long-lasting, as long as they served to deceive "the so-called masses", that is, allowed the newspapers recruited by him in Italy and abroad to sing his glories'.[62]

Likewise, in the mid-1970s Mack Smith argued foreign policy was about the preservation and extension of Mussolini's personal power and was 'concerned less with making rational calculations of national interest than with dazzling and fascinating his fellow citizens'.[63] Mack Smith was but the latest in a long line of (mainly British and American) historians to endorse Salvemini's arguments.[64] This 'orthodox' consensus did not rule out interpretative differences of particular events. The Ethiopian campaign, for example, was variously attributed to Fascism's need to restore its faltering reputation at home after a decade of economic failure, to Mussolini's faith in his own propaganda (that Ethiopia would solve Italy's economic problems), his desire for 'war for war's sake', his wish to avenge the Italian defeat at Adowa in 1896, and his jealousy of Hitler and determination 'to match the German dictator'.[65] Nevertheless, the general thrust of the arguments was the same: foreign policy was driven by the egocentricity and opportunism of Fascism and of its leader.

Not everyone, though, who questioned Fascism's ideological rigour was prepared to see its foreign policy as the incoherent and inconsistent product of a prestige-obsessed regime. Writing in the 1960s and 1970s, Alan Cassels argued that although Fascism 'did not possess a clear-cut ideology', its diplomacy and foreign policy were always informed by 'ideological prejudices' – revisionism, nationalism, opposition to democracy and violence. This was as true of the 1920s, when Mussolini was widely regarded as a 'good' European, as of the 1930s, when Fascist Italy adopted an openly aggressive line in foreign affairs. The underlying consistency to Fascist foreign policy was clearly revealed by the occupation of Corfu (1923) which was, according to Cassels, a virtual 'dress rehearsal' for Ethiopia in 1935. The real nature of Fascist foreign policy also meant that the alliance with Nazi Germany in the late 1930s was 'almost predetermined'. Cassels admitted that domestic motives probably influenced individual foreign policy decisions ('It may be that Ethiopia was intended to divert attention from Fascism's failure to cope with the Great Depression at home'), but it did not alter the basic framework within which those decisions were taken. The Ethiopian war and intervention in Spain moreover 'encouraged Mussolini to give full play to rigid, ideological diplomatic thinking'.[66]

Cassels was not alone in detecting an ideological undercurrent and basic coherence to Fascist foreign policy. In the 1970s, for example, Esmonde Robertson argued that 'The ideological aspect of Mussolini's [foreign] policy...was not just window-dressing'.[67] Jens Petersen, like Cassels, noted Mussolini's unswerving commitment to Italian expansion and his predilection for foreign statesmen and political parties who shared his anti-democratic sentiments. Both Petersen and Robertson saw the Ethiopian campaign as a natural consequence of Mussolini's long-term foreign policy ambitions. Indeed, for Petersen the creation of the Italian Empire in Ethiopia in 1936 represented the realization of a plan dating to 1925. The timing of the attack was determined by circumstance. In the mid-1930s, the attention of France and Britain was focused on Germany, while at the same time Germany was not yet strong enough to threaten Italian hegemony in central and southern Europe.[68] For Robertson, too, 'Mussolini was planning a war of aggression long in advance of the invasion of Ethiopia'. Ethiopia became the natural arena for a display of 'Fascist dynamism' of one sort or another once Mussolini understood that there was little prospect of realizing Fascist ambitions in Europe. The German alliance was, for Petersen, 'fast unvermeidlich' ('nearly inevitable'). Robertson also identified a clear 'kinship' between Fascist Italy and Nazi Germany that long predated any formal alliance. (Robertson, however, was at pains to point out the serious political differences that existed over Austria: Hitler's desire for German-Austrian *Anschluss* (union) was seen as a threat to Italian security and to Italian interests in south-east Europe). Robertson believed Italy's involvement in Spain only 'makes sense' if seen in an ideological light: the battle between the revolutionary Right and the revolutionary Left extended to the international plane.[69]

The most determined proponent of the 'foreign policy as the expression of ideology' thesis has been MacGregor Knox. Knox argues that Fascist ideology was not the expression of a particular social group but the creation of Mussolini alone. Far from random opportunism, Mussolini propounded a coherent ideological position, a 'world view' based on 'one underlying assumption' – life as struggle – and 'two political myths' – revolution (the creation of a new civilization) and the nation (national integration and national greatness). Fascist foreign policy sprung directly from the force of these ideas. Foreign policy, in the form of war, was the instrument by which Mussolini sought both to revolutionize state and society (the means by which to destroy the old order and to create the totalitarian state and the 'Fascist man') and to transform Italy into a great power. International and domestic factors constrained Mussolini from following an overtly expansionist foreign policy in the 1920s. The consolidation of the dictatorship at home and the rise of Hitler in Germany, however, allowed Mussolini to instigate more aggressive strategies abroad, in the 1930s, in Ethiopia, Spain and Albania, with the concomitant radicalization of policies domestically (e.g. the racial laws, attacks on bourgeois style and dress) as he sought to impose his 'ferocious totalitarian will'. War in 1940 was the 'Revelation of a long-held vision'. That Mussolini should go to war alongside Hitler was also inevitable. Since Hitler's accession in 1933, Mussolini, 'a fanatic steering by ideology', had been 'set upon a course ever closer to National Socialist Germany'. Mussolini had always seen Germany as Italy's natural ally given his desire to create an Italian empire in the Mediterranean at the expense of Britain and France. The rise to power in Germany of Nazism, so similar to Fascism in structure and dynamics, made such an alliance simply irresistible. From the outset, Mussolini had been prepared to forgo Austria and agree to *Anschluss* in order to draw closer to Berlin. Only 'German pig-headedness', the restraining hand of Victor Emmanuel III, and the need to wait until German rearmament was complete, delayed a military alliance with the Third Reich until 1939. Mussolini's declaration of non-belligerence on the outbreak of war in 1939 could not disguise his determination to enter the conflict at the earliest opportunity.[70]

In an historiographical article on Fascist foreign policy published in the early 1990s, Stephen Azzi identified Knox, Cassels, Robertson, and the Italian historians Giorgio Rumi and Giampiero Carocci, as star pupils of a 'revisionist' school that 'accepted the existence of a coherent Fascist foreign policy' based on treaty revisionism and imperialism.[71] Azzi also placed Renzo De Felice within the same school – a broad school indeed, given that Knox and De Felice disagreed on virtually every other aspect of Fascist foreign policy. In *Intervista*, De Felice suggested that from the mid-1930s Fascist foreign policy was assigned a key role in the creation of the totalitarian state, the means by which Mussolini hoped to accelerate the fascistization of the masses and to eliminate the old establishment.[72] This, in a sense, anticipated Knox's later argument that 'foreign conquest was the decisive prerequisite for a revolution at home'.[73] Similarities between the two approaches end here, however. For Knox, Fascist foreign policy was always tied to ideology, it was inherently aggressive, and the alliance with Nazi Germany demonstrated how close Fascism and Nazism were to one another. For De Felice, foreign policy was independent of ideology, war was not Mussolini's favoured *modus operandi*, and the German alliance was neither inevitable nor something the *Duce* had always wanted. In De Felice's opinion, foreign policy began in traditional and unadventurous mode and remained subordinate to domestic policy until the end of the 1920s. Only when it became clear that domestic policy initiatives to fascistize Italian society had failed did foreign policy become a priority for the regime.[74] However, the desire to use foreign policy to invoke the totalitarian state at home did not mean that Italy abandoned an essentially 'pacific' European strategy. De Felice accepted that war was an integral part of Fascist ideology and imperialism an 'eternal and immutable law of life' (Mussolini's words). The *Duce*, De Felice conceded, also believed that without war, the European Great Powers would never agree to a substantial strengthening of Italy. But, De Felice argued, European war was not on Mussolini's agenda in the 1920s and 1930s: he was a pragmatist – a realist – in foreign affairs who aimed to further Italian imperial interests abroad without upsetting the European balance of power. To this end he conceived of Italy as the *peso determinante* (decisive weight) in European power politics. During the 1930s, Mussolini sought to exploit to Italy's best advantage the tensions between France and Britain on the one side and Nazi Germany on the other by means of a 'pendulum policy', sometimes siding with the former, sometimes with the latter, exacting concessions from both but committed to neither.[75] Up until 1935 – until Ethiopia – the policy 'bore its fruits'.[76]

The Ethiopian campaign was not, in De Felice's opinion, a war at any cost. Mussolini's proposal of a four-power-pact (1933) between Italy, Britain, France and Germany, had been designed to obtain an Anglo-French guarantee of the European peace (a commitment to the containment of Germany) so as to allow Italy to move on Ethiopia. He had followed a deliberate policy of co-operation with Britain and rapprochement with France in 1934–5 in order to clear the ground for an Ethiopian campaign. Even then Mussolini hoped a negotiated conquest of Ethiopia might be possible, so avoiding the need for conflict altogether. When, after the Italian invasion of Ethiopia, the League of Nations imposed sanctions against Italy, Mussolini continued to assure both London and Paris of his continuing friendship – the situation was one of 'crisis yes, rupture no'. Although Mussolini was also quick to emphasize the dangers that the British and French would expose themselves to should they reject his overtures, this was typical of his approach to foreign affairs and designed to bring home to the two powers the importance of Italy's support. Reconciliation was made difficult by the intransigence of the British Foreign Secretary, Anthony Eden[77] – and Italian diplomatic moves towards Germany in 1936 had to be seen in this context – but as it turned out, neither Ethiopia nor Italian involvement in Spain, (a strategic decision) marked a definitive break with Britain or a fundamental shift towards Germany. De Felice pointed to the Anglo-Italian 'Gentlemen's Agreement' of January 1937, and the 'Easter Accords' (April 1938) as evidence. Both constituted a rebalancing of Italy's relations between Germany and Britain, the first after the Italo-German 'Berlin protocols' of October 1936, the second after *Anschluss* in March 1938.[78] The Ethiopian campaign itself was the 'political masterpiece of Mussolini and his greatest success'. Mussolini had demonstrated great self-control in difficult circumstances. He had realistically appraised the risks and benefits of the war. He had shown a 'sense of limit'; a keen understanding of what was possible. He had shown his mastery of the international scene and of the British (Mussolini, not Britain, it turned out, was the real realist). Success in Ethiopia represented still more, however. The war had not been just about prestige or international politics. It had also given Mussolini the opportunity to realize his historical mission: to show to Italy its true vocation and bring together *vox ducis* and *vox populi* in a way that Fascism until then had failed to achieve.[79]

De Felice insisted foreign policy remained predicated on the concept of the *peso determinante* through the second half of the 1930s; Italy's entry into World War Two alongside Germany was not inevitable. Growing anti-Fascism in Britain and especially France, however, undermined Italy's pendulum policy and eventually forced Italy into the German corner. De Felice conceded that ideological links *were* made with Nazism towards the end of the 1930s; he also suggested that increasingly 'Mussolini's "ideology"...had the better of his political sense'.[80] Nonetheless, Mussolini did not commit himself finally and irretrievably to war and Hitler until the spring of 1940. The Munich conference (September 1938) had been used by Mussolini to try to restore Italian equidistance between Britain and France on the one hand, and Germany on the other. The Pact of Steel with Germany in 1939 was an attempt to preserve rather than destroy the European peace – to get Germany to commit to peace, at least in the short run. Even in January 1940, Mussolini hoped to be able to assume once more for Italy the role of European mediator, suggesting

Hitler treat with the British and the French. The impact of the Allied blockade of the Mediterranean, the speed of German conquest in early 1940 and the fall of France, quickly ruled this out, though. Mussolini was now obliged to intervene; not to do so risked German reprisals or at least jeopardized a share of any spoils of war.[81] De Felice maintained that Mussolini nevertheless remained hopeful that news of Italy's intervention would yet bring Britain and France to the negotiating table, where Italy would be an 'arbiter *super partes*, although allied to Germany'. Once at war, Mussolini intended to fight a 'parallel war' rather than a German one, i.e. one directed to serving Italian national interests in the Mediterranean and the Balkans. Mussolini hoped this would allow Italy to emerge from a relatively short and painless conflict in a position to act as a 'point of reference and political association for those European states that did not wish to resign themselves to accept German hegemony more or less passively'.[82]

By the 1980s, then, there was little historical agreement on the essential characteristics of Fascist foreign policy. The old orthodoxy that foreign policy was simply another example of Fascism's magpie-like opportunism might have fallen from favour but it had not been entirely abandoned. Meanwhile 'revisionists' could not agree whether the Fascist foreign policy 'programme' had everything, something, or virtually nothing, to do with Fascist ideology. This was not all. From the distant shores of Western Australia, Richard Bosworth asked 'rather than Mussolini's personality or the ideology of Fascism, was the real key to inter-war Italian [foreign] policy the nation's position among the powers?' Bosworth contended that Italian foreign policy during both the liberal and Fascist eras was conditioned by the same assumption: that Italy was a Great Power and had to behave like one. The constant search for an Empire, for spheres of influence, for control of the Mediterranean, was indicative of this obsession. As representatives of the 'least of the Great Powers', however, all Italian statesmen, Mussolini included, were driven by a volatile mixture of ambition and fear, and obliged to rely on cunning, opportunism, if not outright dishonesty in their pursuit of grandeur. In Bosworth's view, the 1923 Corfu incident was not 'a drastic break with the liberal past'; the Fascist war in Ethiopia '[not] so different from that in Libya in 1911'; Italy's intervention in World War Two 'a classic Italian case of entering a war after it was over, in order to get something at the peace-table, and with the hope in that gathering of confusing and weakening the swagger of the victor'. Churchill's wartime claim that 'One man alone' had been responsible for Italy's subsequent ills was not true. 'Italy's entry into World War Two was not solely Mussolini's responsibility, but was instead the natural result of Italian history'.[83] Continuities between the foreign policies of liberal and Fascist Italy had been identified by other historians, including De Felice, but clearly Bosworth's argument was of an altogether different variety.[84]

An attempt to reconcile the conflicting interpretations of Fascist foreign policy was made in the mid-1990s by H. James Burgwyn. In Burgwyn's view, Mussolini was only a mediocre *Realpolitiker* whose personal ideological predisposition towards authoritarianism and hatred of democracy made, on the one hand, an alliance with Hitler's Germany a possibility but, on the other, ruled out an understanding with Britain and France. Yet ideology was not, in Burgwyn's opinion, the driving force behind foreign policy. Moreover, although Fascism always embraced expansionism and revisionism, and demonstrated an 'enduring hostility toward France' and a 'predilection for Germany', much of Mussolini's approach to foreign affairs carried in it echoes of liberal foreign policy and throughout his dictatorship Mussolini remained essentially an 'old-fashioned' imperialist. Those aspects of Fascist foreign policy that were new to Italy were not unique to Fascism and until the mid-1930s realism, pragmatism, ambition and fear competed against each other to produce a foreign policy characterized by 'inconsistency and improvisation'. It was only after Ethiopia that 'themes that can be described as quintessentially "Fascist" began to affect his diplomacy', and ultimately undermined Mussolini's attempts to maintain equidistance between the great European powers. Mussolini was 'not irresistibly attracted to the Nazi regime', indeed, he had spent much of the first half of the 1930s seeking to rein in Germany and to guarantee Austrian independence. But Ethiopia and then intervention in Spain weakened both Italy's military capability to prevent *Anschluss* and her position as the *peso determinante* in European affairs. Mussolini duly abandoned Austria and drew closer to Nazi Germany, and the more he gravitated towards Hitler 'the less he was able to keep his mind uncluttered of ideological prejudice', and the less capable Italy became of independent action.[85]

Fascism and anti-Semitism

Fascist anti-Semitism has received relatively little attention from historians. It was only in 1961 that Renzo De Felice published the first major study of Italian Jews in the Fascist period and today, while there are several high-quality accounts of Fascism and Italian Jewry in general, and Fascism and the Holocaust in particular, the extent of the literature hardly compares to other areas of Fascist studies, and barely registers in the field of 'Holocaust Studies'. This, despite the fact that during 1938 the Fascist regime formally embraced the concept of biological racism and enacted the most punitive anti-Semitic legislation anywhere in the world outside of Nazi Germany. Historical indifference towards Fascist anti-Semitism mirrors the lack of interest shown at the time in Fascism's racialist turn. The racial laws provoked little outcry within Italy and drew few protests from abroad. The general disinterest – contemporary and historical – in the fate of the Jews under Fascism has, it seems, also fed into a present-day collective forgetfulness within Italy of these events. Italian persecution of the Jews is largely forgotten. The Holocaust only begins in 1943 with the German occupation. *La vita è bella* (*Life is Beautiful*, 1997), Roberto Benigni's Oscar-winning comedy on the Holocaust, epitomizes this selective reading of Italy's past.

The failure to pay much attention to Fascist anti-Semitism stems from the view – aired by contemporaries and historians – that Fascist measures aimed against the Jews were essentially a by-product of foreign policy, specifically of the 'exigencies of the Rome-Berlin Axis'.[86] It is not difficult to see why the racial laws have been interpreted in this light. Prior to 1938 there is little evidence of widespread or deep-seated anti-Semitism within Fascism. Mussolini may have been worried by 'international Jewry' and always suspicious of 'the Jews', but this did not stop him having affairs with Margherita Sarfatti and Angelica Balabanov, both Jewish, nor did it prevent him from appointing Jews to ministerial positions. The Fascist Party had its anti-Semites – some of whom Mussolini tolerated or even indulged (e.g. Giovanni Preziosi and Telesio Interlandi, the latter the editor of the pro-Nazi, anti-Semitic journal *Il Tevere*) – but these were a minority within the PNF and were not usually in positions of authority. The PNF, in fact, attracted Italian Jews to its ranks in the same proportions as it did non-Jewish Italians. A significant number of the 'Fascists of the First Hour' and of the early Fascist 'martyrs' were Jewish, too. 'The Jewish problem does not exist in Italy', declared Dino Grandi (1926). 'Anti-Semitism does not exist in Italy', Mussolini told (the Jewish) Emil Ludwig (1932), at the same time denouncing 'the delirium of race'. 'A specific Jewish problem does not exist in Italy', reiterated the Italian Foreign Office (February 1938).

Nevertheless, in July 1938, the publication of the *Manifesto of Racial Scientists*, written under the direct guidance of Mussolini, announced the arrival of state anti-Semitism in Fascist Italy. 'The concept of race', the Manifesto declared, was 'purely biological'. Italians were Aryans. The 'Italian race' was a 'pure' race. The Jews did 'not belong to the Italian race'. The purity of the Italian race had to be maintained. Anti-Jewish legislation followed in the autumn. The Italian citizenship of all foreign Jews who had settled in Italy since 1919 was revoked; foreign Jews were given six months to leave Italy or its colonies. All Jewish teachers and students were excluded from public schools and universities (those already on university courses were allowed to complete). Mixed marriages, i.e. between Italians and 'non-Aryans', were forbidden. Italian Jews were banned from all public employment. Jewish businesses employing 100 or more persons and Jewish property over 50 hectares were expropriated by the state (amounting to 70 per cent of all Jewish property, valued by the regime at 10 billion lire). Around a quarter of the Italian Jewish population either abandoned Judaism or left Italy over the next five years, devastating the Italian Jewish community.[87]

According to the 'Axis' interpretation, although Mussolini was not an anti-Semite he was always prepared to use and abuse the Italian Jews in his efforts to advance Fascist foreign policy objectives, especially in his attempts first (1933–6) to sustain and then (1937–39) to deepen relations with Nazi Germany. Thus, the anti-Semitic propaganda that surrounded the arrest of several Jewish members of the anti-Fascist *Giustizia e Libertà* (*Justice and Liberty*) movement in March 1934 was deliberately designed to smooth relations with Berlin. The assassination of the Austrian Chancellor, Engelbert Dollfuss, and the attempted Nazi coup in Vienna (July 1934), however, brought the Berlin initiative to an abrupt halt, and rendered redundant the anti-Semitic campaign in Italy. Mussolini moved quickly to re-establish his philo-Semitic credentials: 'I am a friend of the Jews', 'I am a Zionist'.[88]

Ultimately, though, Mussolini felt obliged to choose between Nazi Germany (and the fulfilment of his imperial ambitions) and the Italian Jews. By the late 1930s, it was evident to Mussolini that an alliance with Berlin required Fascism to embrace firmly anti-Semitism in order to eliminate the most glaring contrast in the policies of the two regimes. Rank opportunism allied to breathtaking political amorality lay at the basis of the racial laws. 'On the altar of the alliance with Hitler, Mussolini sacrificed without a moment's thought the Italian Jews, while not believing in their "guilt", so committing a crime morally perhaps even more monstrous than that of the Nazis who – at least – believed in the "guilt" of the Jews', concluded De Felice in his 1961 study. Nearly two decades on, Meir Michaelis offered an equally definite verdict: Mussolini had 'only one reason for persecuting them [the Jews] as a "race" – his ill fated alliance with a Jew-baiter'. For Susan Zuccotti, too, 'Italian anti-Semitism had no ideological base, but was the product of mindless and cynical opportunism'.[89]

The historiography of Fascist anti-Semitism is not quite so clear-cut as this, however. Several historians have suggested that anti-Semitism was inherent within the totalitarian logic of Italian Fascism, its appearance inevitable once the Fascist regime began seriously to pursue its totalitarian agenda from the mid-1930s. Why? First, because Italian Jews were perceived to have divided loyalties, to Italy and to international Judaism; Italian Jews could not then be wholly 'within the state' (and the fact that several leading anti-Fascists were Jewish also suggested to Mussolini that Italian Jews were actually against the state). Second, because Italian Jews were considered the embodiment of the 'bourgeois' mentality – individualist, cynical, materialist – which Fascism, in its drive to transform Italian society, was so keen to eradicate. Third, their persecution could potentially speed up the process of fascistization: a campaign against Italian Jews as the 'enemy within' Fascist Italy would test (and, if successful, harden) ordinary Italians; it would at the very least make Italians 'anxious, nervous...energetic'.[90]

The Ethiopian war has also been suggested as a direct factor in the evolution of Fascist anti-Semitism. Empire brought with it new responsibilities. Italians, Mussolini argued, had to demonstrate their superiority as a 'race' to the Ethiopians, otherwise Italian rule would neither be respected nor tolerated by the native population. 'Empires are conquered with arms but held by prestige,' claimed Mussolini, 'and prestige demands a clear and severe consciousness of race'. Mussolini was also alarmed by news of sexual relations between Italians and Ethiopians and the prospect of a mixed-race colonial population. Anxious to preserve the purity of the Italian *stirpe* (stock), he quickly outlawed miscegenation and, over time, a policy of strict racial segregation was enforced. The jump from a colonial racial policy to the implementation of domestic anti-Semitic legislation was not, it is argued, a considerable one to make.[91]

Assessment

We have identified several key perspectives on Fascism:

The *Marxist* view. Fascism as the product of capitalism in crisis, a screen behind which the bourgeoisie hid the capitalist character of their rule.

The *liberal* (*Crocean*) view. Fascism as a sickness caused by World War One, a parenthesis in Italian history (i.e. nothing to do with the normal course of Italian history).

The *revelation* thesis. Fascism as the revelation of Italian vices, and/or of the flawed process of Italian modernization (a view held, albeit for different reasons, by Marxists and non-Marxists – see Chapter 1).

The *egoist* argument. Fascism as the manifestation of Mussolini's lust for power; an exercise in violence and propaganda (Mussolini as the 'master of make-believe').[92]

The *revisionist/culturalist* view. Fascism as a set of ideas to be taken seriously; a revolutionary, totalitarian, ideology for national rebirth through the radical transformation of society and the creation of the new Fascist man.

We can quickly deal with the second and third perspectives. Croce's interpretation of Fascism as a parenthesis in Italian history simply does not stand up. One cannot divorce Fascism from the long-term Italian historical context, nor is it possible to see Fascism as a contagion caught in the trenches during World War One. Fascism was by no means inevitable and, certainly, World War One was *absolutely* crucial to its development. However, as Chabod and, much more recently, Paul Corner have argued, and as we have seen in Chapter 3, the seeds of Fascism were present in Italy before 1914.[93] The revelation thesis, however, suffers from reading too much into the long-term historical context; reading history backwards it sees all roads leading to Mussolini's Roman Empire.

This leaves us with the Marxist, egoist and revisionist/culturalist schools. Of these, the first two both treat Fascism as so much smoke and mirrors, an elaborate confidence trick: nothing that Mussolini or his cronies said should be taken at face value; for Fascism talk was cheap. The last, the revisionist/culturalist school, by contrast, assumes that Fascism meant what it said. The Marxist and egoist schools find confirmation of their arguments in the gulf between Fascist words and deeds, in the contradiction in policies, in the reluctance (i.e. the inability) of Fascism to define itself, its care to avoid doctrinal elaboration. From this perspective, the purpose of Fascist ritual and spectacle was simply to deflect attention from the fact that Fascism was an ideological empty shell, and to fascinate and divert Italians. In contrast, the revisionists/culturalists are not interested in outcomes, only with how Fascism perceived itself, its view of the world; in particular, ritual and spectacle are seen as crucial to a proper understanding of Fascism. What we have, then, are two very different historical approaches to Fascism: the Marxist and egoist interpretations are essentially external critiques of Fascism; the revisionists/culturalists offer an internal reading of Fascism. It is not surprising that the latter are often accused by proponents of the first approach (particularly by Marxists) of peddling 'flawed histories inextricably linked to the definitions of fascism offered by fascists themselves'.[94] The counter of the revisionists-culturalists is equally predictable: the Marxist and egoist arguments are based on political-ideological prejudice, and politics and ideology get in the way of writing objective history.

What credence should we give to these interpretations? It has already been noted that Marxist interpretations of Fascism have been/are guided as much by Marxist theory as by the historical evidence: Fascism had to be the right hand of capital, the weapon of the bourgeoisie against the working class. Of course, Marxists could point to the fact that in its early years Fascism had served the cause of Italian capital in the fight against socialism and had likewise enjoyed the support of industrial and agrarian interests. Fascism in power also clearly favoured capital over labour, despite the rhetoric of the Corporate State (capital and labour working together for the benefit of the state). That the interests of capital and Fascism often meshed does not mean, however, that Fascism was capitalism in a new guise. At the very least, as Chapter 5 demonstrates, Fascist economics were not always tailored to the interests of big business. As far as our discussion of Fascist politics is concerned, the direction of foreign policy from the mid-1930s hardly corresponded to the wishes of Italian capital. Furthermore, although Fascism enjoyed the (conditional) support of the bourgeoisie, it was never a bourgeois party. In fact, Fascism was instinctively anti-bourgeois: it displayed the same contempt for bourgeois values that had marked the pre-war avant-garde movement.

The egoist argument is attractive because it captures so well, and mocks so effectively, the bluster, bombast and staggering narcissism of Fascism. It is Chaplin's *The Great Dictators* as history. It does not get us very far, however. Let us take Mack Smith's work as an example.[95] Mack Smith presents Fascism as a highly successful authoritarian self-advertising agency, which bullied and bullshitted its way to and through twenty years of power until Mussolini finally began to believe the nonsense he spouted. Mack Smith advises his audience to 'forget about Fascist ideology', since 'Mussolini had no ideology'.[96] It is worth quoting from Mack Smith's conclusion to *Mussolini's Roman Empire* since it encapsulates the egoist argument:

> He [Mussolini] had got used to living in cloud-cuckoo-land, where words and not facts mattered, where the army was judged by its parade-ground performance rather than by anything more substantial, where wars were won not by superior munitions and strategy but by knowing how to manipulate the news so as to give the illusion of strength. It was a world where a skilled publicist could fool most of the people fairly easily... It was an essentially unserious world, where prestige, propaganda, and public statements were what counted... Since the Italian people are not notoriously more gullible than anyone else, one must admit that Mussolini gave a virtuoso performance as an illusionist.[97]

What an incredibly elaborate hoax! As Griffin has commented, from this perspective, 'the countless references in the regime's speeches and books to the values and ideals of Fascism, and all the policies, institutional changes, public works, and social and military campaigns undertaken under Mussolini ostensibly to fulfil them appear...designed to create the illusion of a revolution...to deceive Italians into thinking they were living in a new, exciting era of history'.[98]

Can we seriously believe, though, that a regime could survive and prosper for the best part of two decades on hot air (and castor oil) alone? Mack Smith's intention – and that of the egoist interpretation – is to prick the bubble of Fascist self-importance; instead we end up with a truly remarkable regime, and at its head, a truly remarkable salesman.

Fascism was fraudulent. Fascism was an anti-movement, i.e. it often defined itself in terms of what it opposed. It was also opportunistic, its policies often confused and contradictory. Historians are right to be wary of Fascist claims. All of this does not mean, however, that Fascism was devoid of ideological content, or that we can learn nothing about Fascism from the Fascists themselves. Indeed, to suggest that we can understand Fascism without giving serious consideration to the definitions of Fascism *offered by Fascists* is simply ridiculous. Would any self-respecting historian try to define communism without reference to Marx or Lenin? The overwhelming body of evidence produced by revisionist historians of generic fascism and culturalist historians of Italian Fascism over the past three decades points to one ineluctable conclusion: 'Fascism must be taken as a serious (albeit morally flawed) ideology'.[99] Fascism had an intellectual heritage. It possessed a core body of ideas. It had a (rather vague) concept of the type of society that a Fascist revolution would produce. Fascism did not seek to turn the clock back, it did not look to conserve; rather it sought an alternative modernity to that offered, on the one hand, by capitalist-bourgeois liberal democracy, on the other, by communism. As Eatwell argues, 'the point was to blend economic dynamism and new technology with a less alienating conception of work and social structure'.[100] Fascism was, to use Sternhell's phrase, neither Right nor Left, rather it was an unstable mix of the two, drawing predominantly from revolutionary nationalist and revolutionary revisionist left-wing thought. It was, too – and obviously – a totalitarian concept. When the Fascist philosopher, Giovanni Gentile, said that under Fascism 'the state and individual are identical', he meant it. Ritual, spectacle, myth and rhetoric often served crude propaganda objectives – but they were always essential elements of Fascist totalitarianism. Likewise, the *idea* of corporativism – rather than the reality of the Corporate State (a stick with which to beat the workers) – was, as Roberts points out, 'overtly totalitarian; now even economic roles were to be experienced as political, and public participation would be direct and constant, like it or not'.[101]

It should be no surprise that Fascism often defined itself in terms of what it opposed (anti-liberal, anti-socialist etc.). New political ideologies emerge in response to existing political ideas: liberalism against absolutism, socialism versus liberalism. Fascism was no different; it was an 'anti' ideology certainly, but no more so than its rivals were.

That Fascism was opportunistic hardly makes it unique. The incoherence of Fascist actions and the gap between theory and praxis is mirrored in the histories of many other, supposedly more ideological, regimes, Bolshevik rule in Russia being a prime example. Indeed, Fascism and Bolshevism in power shared a common problem: neither had given much consideration to actual policies before coming to power. The precise means by which the revolution – Fascist or communist – would be made or completed were open to debate. In the Italian case, the precise ends were also a little hazy. Roberts has demonstrated there was considerable discussion, disagreement and divergence between Fascism's leading ideologues before and after the seizure of power. Fascism's problem, as one of its leading thinkers Giuseppe Bottai recognized, was not a lack of ideas but too many.[102] Fascism changed as ideas fell in and out of vogue, and as Mussolini sought to maintain his position by playing off rivals and to maintain party unity by giving encouragement to different political factions within Fascism at different times. Mussolini was the *Duce*, but he understood well his role as party manager, too. He also realized that power had been secured at a price (he could not afford to alienate those influential conservative interests which had supported Fascism's rise) and was forced to acknowledge the structural and institutional constraints on Fascism's freedom of action. Equally, though, he had to keep satisfied the revolutionary wing of the PNF. Mussolini thus tried to balance normality and radicalism – at least until Ethiopia and the example of Hitler persuaded him to abandon the former.

The point I am trying to make is perhaps an obvious one: pragmatism and principle co-existed within Fascism, and within the person of the *Duce* (Mussolini was a 'fully fledged fascist', rather than someone who 'believed in nothing').[103] Until the mid-1930s, Mussolini the politician – that is, the pragmatist – won out over Mussolini the ideologue. But ideology was always there, even if, for many years, certainly during the first decade of Fascism, it often had little to do with the policies pursued by the regime.

Foreign policy

Mussolini's ideological prejudice did eventually get the better of his political caution. The reasons for this are intimately connected to foreign policy and the rise of Nazi Germany.

War was assigned a central role within Fascist ideology. As Knox argues, it was seen by the Fascists as a revolutionary tool, a means by which to transform Italians, to fuse state and society, to make Italy great and to establish Fascism as a 'new type of civilization'. Fascist foreign policy may have echoed that of its liberal predecessors but its roots were very different. During the 1920s and early 1930s, however, foreign policy was based less on ideology than on Mussolini's 'astute political pragmatism'.[104] In international affairs, just as in domestic matters, Mussolini recognized the need for caution: he did not have complete freedom of action. Italy in the 1920s was not strong enough to exert itself militarily (and for many years it lacked the financial resources to develop its military capability). Relations between the European powers – which Italy had always sought to exploit to its advantage – were also not conducive to the furtherance of Italian interests. Britain and France were the dominant powers on the Continent and neither power had anything to gain from helping the Fascist regime to realize its ambitions in the Mediterranean or Middle East, very much British and French spheres of influence. Fascist foreign policy in the 1920s was subversive – Fascist

Italy broke the terms of the 1919 peace treaties by sending arms to Hungary, it took an active interest in Italian irredentist movements in Corsica and Malta, it backed the extremist Heimwehr party in Austria, and it meddled constantly in Yugoslav politics, giving financial support and encouragement to a number of ethnic separatist groups – but, apart from the Corfu incident, it remained pacific.

All this changed with the Nazi assumption of power in Germany in 1933. Here was a regime utterly opposed to the existing national order and committed to the overthrow of the Versailles settlement. The opportunity presented itself to Mussolini to either pursue a policy of equidistance, oscillating between the German and Anglo-French camps to Italy's advantage, or to ally Italy with its powerful northern neighbour and seize control of the Mediterranean and Middle East by military means.

Knox has argued that Fascist Italy always needed Germany if it were ever to become master of the Mediterranean and the Red Sea, and an Italo-German alliance was only a matter of time once Hitler took charge in Germany; after all, the 'similarities in the structures of the regimes and of their foreign policies', made them natural bedfellows. Knox is right, up to a point. If Fascism were to have its war and fulfil its imperial destiny then it could only be in alliance with Germany since it was the British and French who currently commanded those very areas that were marked out for Italian rule. However, the idea that Mussolini was like a dog on heat after Hitler's rise exaggerates the Führer's pulling power. There were several good reasons why Fascist Italy should be cautious in its dealings with Nazi Germany. First, apart from Hitler, there was very little evidence of pro-Fascist/Italian sentiment within Nazism. Second, Mussolini regarded Hitler with a mixture of contempt (Hitler, said Mussolini in 1934, was a 'horrible sexual degenerate, a dangerous fool'), bemusement (the Nazi's fanatical anti-Semitism made little sense to Mussolini nor to the majority of leading Fascists) and alarm (Nazi Germany was a threat to Italian interests in the Balkans; Hitler's desire for *Anschluss* imperilled Italy's chief gain from Versailles: the removal of a powerful neighbour from its north-eastern border). The Austrian question was a very real obstruction to closer Italo-German relations but is glossed over by Knox. Mussolini's proposed four-power-pact in 1933 was, at least in part, designed to guarantee Austrian independence. The *Duce* was also clearly taken with the Austrian Chancellor, Dollfuss ('a man of ingenuity, possessed of real will') and his family (when Dollfuss was assassinated in 1934 his wife and children were on holiday with the Mussolinis). The murder of Dollfuss by Austrian Nazis prompted Mussolini to mobilize Italian troops on the Brenner Pass as a warning to Hitler, and to hold forth on the deficiencies of Nazi doctrine. These were not the actions of a man already determined on a German alliance.

It was because of Mussolini's doubts regarding Germany that Fascist foreign policy between 1933 and 1936 remained 'balanced', sometimes favouring London and Paris, at other times Berlin. However, it runs contrary to all the available evidence to suggest, as De Felice has, that Mussolini continued to pursue a policy of equidistance after Ethiopia. Anglo-French opposition to the war drove a permanent wedge between Italy and the two 'demoplutocracies' (Mussolini's expression).

At the same time, Mussolini took the ineffectiveness of Anglo-French opposition to the invasion – and their equally pusillanimous reaction to the German remilitarization of the Rhineland – as conclusive proof of their decline. By contrast, Mussolini's triumph in Ethiopia (and Hitler's in the Rhineland) demonstrated that the rising powers were Italy and Germany; certainly the momentum and initiative now appeared to lie with Rome and Berlin rather than Paris and London. Ethiopia also showed how useful the Nazi regime could be to Italy. Germany was a vital source of supplies during the period of sanctions; the remilitarization of the Rhineland meanwhile deflected international attention away from Italy and, more importantly for Fascist ambitions in the Mediterranean, left France seriously weakened. The risks associated with a German alliance – the probable loss of an independent Austria, the abandonment of south-eastern Europe to German influence, the danger that Italy would become economically dependent on Germany (official reports in 1937 warned of this) – were outweighed by the potential returns from such a pact: the realization of the Fascist imperial project. As Mussolini told a Hitler aide in early 1936: 'between Germany and Italy there is a common fate. That is becoming stronger and stronger. That cannot be denied. One day we shall meet whether we want to or not. But we want to! Because we must!'[105]

A formal alliance with Nazi Germany was only signed in 1939 but Mussolini was clearly moving in this direction from the time of Ethiopia. The support given by Mussolini to Hitler over the Rhineland in the spring of 1936, the appointment of the (initially) pro-German Ciano as Foreign Minister in June, Mussolini's approval of the Austro-German accords in July, and his end-of-year declaration of a Rome-Berlin 'axis' were but the most obvious early signs of the new trajectory of Fascist foreign policy. Subsequent agreements with Britain and France were not evidence, as De Felice claims, of Mussolini attempting to rebalance Italian foreign policy. Italy's actions in Spain, which included the sinking of British merchant shipping, were not designed to placate the western allies. The so-called 'Gentlemen's Agreement' between Italy and Britain by which Italy agreed to limit intervention in Spain was broken as soon as it was signed (more Italian troops were sent to assist Franco's rebellion). At the same time Italy was busy stirring up Arab anti-British sentiment in the Middle East and military chiefs were left in no doubt that Britain was now Italy's principal enemy and should plan accordingly. By the time of the Easter Accords with Britain in 1938 (Italian troop withdrawals from Spain in return for British recognition of Italy's African empire), Mussolini was irrevocably committed to Germany; his mute acceptance of *Anschluss* in March 1938 is concrete evidence of this. And by committing to Germany he was also – contrary to De Felice's view – committed to war. As Mussolini told Ribbentrop in late 1938, he was determined on an offensive alliance with Berlin 'to change the map of the world'.[106] That Mussolini subsequently tried to delay the conflict with the western powers stemmed not from any desire for peace on his part but from the fact that Italy simply was not yet ready to fight.

Ethiopia and Germany were also both cause and effect of the increasingly ideological character of the Fascist regime from the mid-1930s. The Ethiopian war was, Mussolini told Giuseppe Bottai, a 'revolutionary war', Fascist 'in the commitment to victory by force, and in the deliberate exposure of the nation to the test of war, both a measure and justification of "totalitarian" mobilization and control'.[107] The speed of victory, the enormous groundswell of support for the invasion and the huge boost the war gave to Mussolini's already substantial reputation can only have given the regime, as Morgan notes, 'the confidence and the will to push harder on the pedal of "fascistising" the country, both the premise for and the result of fighting and winning wars'.[108] At the same time, the success of the Nazi revolution in Germany and the deepening understanding between Rome and Berlin from 1936 had an evident impact upon the pace and intensity of Fascism's own totalitarian project. On the one hand, Mussolini was impressed by Nazism's achievements and certainly there was a desire to emulate Hitler and, indeed, to imitate his methods in the second half of the 1930s in order to achieve similar results: the *passo romano*, the Fascist salute, even (to an extent) Fascist anti-Semitism are examples of this. On the other hand, the success of the Nazis in Germany threw into sharp relief the limits of the Fascist revolution in Italy, a fact not lost on younger Fascists or Mussolini. As much as the Ethiopian war gave Mussolini the confidence to press on with his efforts to fascistize Italian society, there was a distinct whiff of desperation about the regime's attempts to create a genuinely totalitarian state in the latter part of the decade.

Fascist racialism must be seen as part and parcel of Fascism's 'totalitarian turn', as part of its drive to make Italians, in Mussolini's words, 'hard, relentless and hateful'. One can also not deny the connection between the acquisition of empire and the development of a Fascist racial conscience: the introduction of anti-miscegenation legislation in 1937 is evidence of this. However, the precise form that official racial policy took in 1938 was first and foremost the consequence of Mussolini's growing fascination with Hitler. The racial laws were not necessary for an Italo-German alliance – the sacrifice of Austria was sufficient measure of Mussolini's good faith and by the summer of 1938 Berlin was as interested in an alliance as Rome was. Nevertheless, the publication of the *Manifesto of Racial Scientists* in July was clearly designed to convince Germany of Fascism's seriousness (Farinacci had been forced to sack his Jewish secretary prior to Hitler's visit in May for this very reason) and of the compatibility of the two regimes. Why else embrace a 'purely biological' concept of race, or describe the Italian race as a 'pure' race of Aryan origin, or expressly identify the Jews as non-Italian/non-European and hence unassimilated and unassimilable? The 'purely biological' racism of the *Manifesto* contrasted with Mussolini's frequently expressed belief, both before and after 1938, that race was 'a sentiment', an essentially spiritual concept. The claim of a 'pure "Italian race"' of Aryan origin clashed with Fascism's oft-repeated view that there was no such thing as a pure race, and its traditional emphasis on the 'Mediterranean' character of Italians. The identification of Jews as irredeemably extra-Italian/European and, by implication, a 'problem', contradicted earlier statements by Mussolini that Italy did not have a Jewish question and his suggestion that Jews could become Italian were they to convert.[109]

To what extent were Fascism and Nazism linked? It is surprising that those who favour the egoist interpretation of Fascism often insist on the ties that bound the two together. Mack Smith, for example, argues that Fascism and Nazism – the latter of which he (rightly) sees as an ideologically driven movement under the control of a fanatic – were in essence the same: 'it goes against common sense' to suggest otherwise.[110] Surely, though, one cannot have it both ways. If we can 'forget about Fascist ideology', how can Fascism be compared to ideological, fanatical Nazism?

Equally contradictory is the De Felicean position that recognizes the ideological character of Fascism (as a movement, at least) but denies any link between it and Nazism. Certainly there were differences between the two – the biological determinism at the heart of Nazism the most profound of these – and there is no doubt that Nazism, which derived from a different national-historical context and was less constrained by institutional and structural factors than Fascism, was more extreme in every way than its Fascist counterpart. Nonetheless, there is an undeniable ideological resemblance which both Mussolini and Hitler recognized.

Why did De Felice seek to distance Fascism from Nazism? Why, for that matter, was he prepared to give Mussolini the benefit of the doubt on so many issues? There are several points to bear in mind when considering this most controversial of Italian historians. First, De Felice's 'soft' view of Mussolini is not peculiar to him, or to the Italian far Right, but enjoys a wider resonance in Italian society. As Luisa Passerini has demonstrated (see Chapter 6), even Italians of an anti-Fascist persuasion who lived through the inter-war period were prepared to buy into the idea of Mussolini as 'a man of the people who was tricked and led astray by Hitler'.[111] Second, De Felice was not an objective historian. His interpretation of the historical evidence was shaped by a deep-seated and increasingly conservative form of patriotism, his growing disillusionment with the post-war Republic and his vehement anti-Marxism. (This latter characteristic was very much linked to the first two: the PCI he considered to be anti-*patria*; the failure of the Italian Republic to instil a strong sense of nationhood and national pride was largely the fault of the communists). As far as De Felice was concerned, at least Mussolini had had the interests of the *patria* at heart: he had wanted to develop a sense of *italianità* in Italians and to make Italy great. Hence De Felice's willingness to excuse or explain away many of the *Duce*'s failings. De Felice's patriotic ardour also accounts for his rejection of any link between Fascist Italy and Nazi Germany, not so much to save the reputation of Fascism as to preserve the good name of Italy: the crimes of Nazism were a strictly German affair.

Although not a philo-Fascist, De Felice is certainly, in the modern parlance, an 'anti-anti-Fascist' and, self-evidently, an apologist for Mussolini (see also Chapter 7). The 'anti-anti-Fascist' accusation has been levelled at many revisionist and culturalist historians of Fascism in recent years. It is an *accusation* – a term of abuse – rather than a mere description of an interpretation/approach that runs counter to the arguments/methodology of traditional 'anti-Fascist' accounts (i.e. of the Marxist, liberal and egoist schools). The implicit (and sometimes explicit) charge is that unwittingly (due to a failure of the historian's critical faculties) or not (because of Fascist sympathies) the 'anti-anti-Fascist' historian has acted as a mouthpiece for Fascism. There are examples of each: Emilio Gentile gets carried away by Fascism's totalitarian rhetoric (see Chapter 6); A. James Gregor wrote for Oswald Mosley's *The European* in the 1950s.[112] However, to label 'anti-anti-Fascist' any attempt to understand Fascism from the inside, which treats the ideas and/or culture of Fascism seriously, is to misunderstand and misrepresent the purpose of such an approach. Martin Blinkhorn has written that 'Ideas... tell us what convinced and thoughtful fascists *wanted* fascism to be; but they do make only a limited contribution towards telling us what fascism actually *was*'.[113] We have long known, though, what Italian Fascism amounted to in practice – 'a coercive yet still shoddy, in some ways superficial regime', as David Roberts puts it.[114] Only a fool (or worse) would dissent from this view. The study of ideas, however, allows us to understand why we ended up with Fascism in the first place and what attracted (often intelligent) people to it. And if we do not properly comprehend Fascism we cannot hope to combat it – or at least its contemporary forms – adequately.

5 Fascism and the economy

Introduction

While much has been written on the liberal economy and on other aspects of Fascism, the Fascist economy has failed to excite historians to the same extent.[1] This is partly to do with the way Fascism has traditionally been viewed. From the orthodox Marxist standpoint, Fascism was the dictatorship of monopoly and finance capitalism. Economic policy therefore did not require much explanation: it was designed simply to serve and mediate between the interests of 'great capital' – financiers, big business and *agrari* – at the expense of the working class, the peasantry and the economy as a whole. However, from the traditional non-Marxist perspective, Fascism meant little more than unprincipled and unbridled opportunism. Economic policy – just like the rest of Fascist politics – was ad hoc, determined by circumstance and devoid of any internal coherence or ideological rationale, despite the insistent claims of Fascist propaganda. Either way, there was little about the Italian economy under Fascism that appeared to warrant in-depth study.

Historical disinterest can also be explained by another factor. Whereas liberal Italy witnessed the 'birth' of the modern Italian economy, the economic significance of the Fascist *ventennio* (the two decades of Fascist rule) was far less obvious. Even if historians were prepared to accept that the economy did actually grow under Fascism – and this was by no means agreed upon – the main structural features of the Italian economy on the eve of World War Two were strikingly similar to those that had characterized it on the eve of World War One. Italy was still a relatively backward, relatively poor and predominantly agrarian economy marked by low levels of private consumption, a small domestic market and geographic and sectoral dualism. Italy's poor performance in World War Two, moreover, appeared to confirm the absence of significant economic progress under Fascism. Italy was poorly equipped and poorly prepared for the conflict, and proved incapable of fighting the sort of campaigns waged by either its allies or opponents.[2]

This does not mean, however, that the Italian economy in the Fascist period is without interesting features, or that debate and controversy have been entirely absent. In keeping with global trends, the inter-war Italian economy experienced unprecedented cyclical volatility, with recession phases lasting longer and hitting harder than at any other time in the first 70 years of the twentieth century. Economic historians have duly investigated how the regime managed the economy in such circumstances. Did Fascist policies prevent, retard or promote modern economic growth in the inter-war period? Did they ameliorate or exacerbate the effects of the Great Depression? What were their effects in the longer term? Did Fascism lay the foundations for the post-war economic miracle? Debate has often been robust. For instance, Pietro Grifone's attack on Salvatore La Francesca's 'absurd' and 'pseudo-historical' study of the Fascist economy – La Francesca had observed some 'productive results' from Fascist economic management – is a masterpiece of Marxist polemic.[3] A. James Gregor's insistence in the mid to late 1970s that Fascist economic policies were largely the function of Fascist 'productivist' ideology and adhered to a long-term developmental strategy provoked a storm of controversy that only abated towards the end of the 1980s.[4] More recently, Rolf Petri's defence of economic policy under Fascism, and his claim for essential continuity between Fascist and post-war Republican economics, have upset some within the Italian economic history community.[5]

Framework

The changing fortunes of the Italian economy in the first half of the 1920s undoubtedly favoured Mussolini and Fascism. A short-lived but severe recession in 1920–1 weakened the labour movement (unemployment rose by over 400,000 in 1921) and pushed 'the productive bourgeoisie and the rural middle classes', hit by falling prices, into the arms of Fascism.[6] By the time of the March on Rome, economic recovery was already well underway but it was Mussolini who reaped the benefits: contemporaries attributed the upturn to the new government, helping at once to establish Mussolini's leadership credentials. Three successive years of vigorous economic growth then facilitated the Fascists' consolidation of power. During the 'boom' years, 1922–5, both industry and agriculture experienced surges in production, fuelled by exports, rising investment, low labour costs and a stock market boom. Physical production rose on average by 5.8 per cent per annum. Growth rates in manufacturing were amongst the highest in Europe and outstripped the United States. Industrial growth was particularly strong in the automobile industry (driven by export-led demand), the 'naturally' protected construction and electricity-generating sectors, and certain textiles (rayon especially). Value-added in the agricultural economy rose on average by at least 3.5 per cent per annum in this period (possibly by as much as 6 per cent).[7]

The surge, however, was not sustainable. Balance of payments problems – the growth of exports never covered the growing cost of capital and raw-material imports sucked in to maintain expansion – put strain on the lira, fuelled inflationary pressures and encouraged short-term speculation at the expense of long-term investment. Attempts in 1925 by Finance Minister Alberto De' Stefani to dampen the economy and to stabilize Italy's finances merely resulted in the collapse of the Italian stock market, a rash of bankruptcies, damage to Italy's banking system (all the big banks were inveterate speculators) and De' Stefani's dismissal. At Pesaro (August 1926), after a summer during which the value of the lira had fallen by 17 per cent to a record low of 153.68 lire to the pound, Mussolini committed the regime to the revaluation and stabilization of the currency. In December 1927, Italy returned to the gold standard, with the lira fixed at 92.46 to the pound, slightly above the target of '*Quota novanta*' ('Quota 90' or 'Q90'), i.e. 90 lire to the pound sterling, set by Mussolini himself. The 'battle of the lira', which involved severe deflationary measures, was accompanied by economic slowdown and then recession, 1926–7, before a brief recovery in industrial production, 1928–9 (although industrial employment in 1929 still remained below that of 1925) and an even shorter-lived upturn in agriculture in 1929.[8]

The worldwide Great Depression of the early 1930s did not spare Italy. As Toniolo notes, the systemic weaknesses within the global economy – fear of productive capacity, non-optimal distribution of resources across areas and sectors, investment funded by banks through increasing indebtedness in international financial markets, the inability to rethink economic problems/ policies – were all present within the Italian economy.[9] Italy was also highly dependent on exports and investment to drive growth, both of which were susceptible to cyclical trends. The loss of overseas labour markets – the United States virtually closed its doors to immigrants in the 1920s – placed further strain on the Italian economy. Emigration had previously gone some way to easing Italy's problems concerning the oversupply (and thus underemployment) of domestic labour, emigrants' remittances had also helped Italy's balance of payments.

During the *grande crisi*, physical production, gross investment and wholesale prices fell dramatically (the first by 10.4 per cent, 1929–33; the latter two each by nearly 30 per cent, 1930–2). Manufacturing industry and construction were particularly hit. Industrial unemployment topped 1m in 1932 and 1933, more than three times the level in 1929, and equivalent to 15 per cent of the industrial workforce. Industrial wages fell by c.15 per cent, as a consequence of government decrees in 1930 and 1934. Looking at falls in manufacturing output and employment, we can see the recession in manufacturing was as severe in Italy as it was in the majority of industrialized countries, the United States and Germany excepted. Although agricultural production remained relatively constant, agricultural prices collapsed. Agricultural salaries fell by 20–40 per cent. The picture is essentially one of stagnation in much of the agrarian economy from the mid-1920s to the mid-1930s.[10]

The Italian economy picked up again from 1935, the upturn generated by massive increases in state expenditure linked to the policies of imperialism, war and autarchy. Industrial growth in this period was tied to heavy industry. Industrial employment returned to 1929 levels at the end of 1936 and continued to grow until the end of 1937 before levelling out until mid-1939.[11] Agriculture also saw recovery, with growth linked primarily to an increase in wheat production.

Key policies

Regarding policy, we can discern three phases in the management of the Italian economy during the Fascist period: the laissez-faire economics of the De' Stefani era, 1922–5; the years of deflation linked to the revaluation of the lira and the return to the gold standard, 1926–34; inflationary-inducing, state-driven, economic expansion tied to the policies of imperialism, war and autarchy from 1935. From the mid-1920s we can also see an increasing trend to state intervention in the economy: control of the labour market, control of trade and exchange, control over price mechanisms, control over the flow of finances to heavy industry.[12]

It is generally accepted that Fascism lacked a clear economic policy, or a policy that differed substantially from that of its predecessors, when Mussolini became Prime Minister in 1922. Certainly, De' Stefani pursued largely orthodox liberal economic strategies. Balancing the budget was the priority. Through cuts in state expenditure, especially military spending, this was achieved by 1925. In many respects, De' Stefani adopted a traditional liberal laissez-faire approach to the economy: deregulation at home, encouragement of international trade (trade agreements with ex-enemies; no return to the grain duty suspended in World War One, a free-floating lira), and tax cuts for businesses. Labour policy was, however, repressive – a feature of the entire Fascist period. Wages were kept low and labour organizations were suppressed, while the tax burden on the rural poor increased.[13]

It is the nature, purpose and outcomes of economic intervention after the establishment of the dictatorship in 1925 that have been at the centre of historical debates regarding the Italian economy under Fascism. In particular, historians have focused on the economic 'battles' waged by the regime – the Battle for wheat (1925), the Battle of the lira (1926) – as well as the *bonifica integrale* (an integrated land reclamation and improvement scheme, announced in 1928), the state's reorganization of Italy's financial and credit systems (1931–3) and the policy of autarchy (economic self-sufficiency, declared in 1936).

Battle for wheat. Launched by Mussolini in order to 'save Italy from the tyranny of foreign wheat', i.e. from dependency on imported grain. Wheat imports costing nearly 4b lire accounted for almost half of Italy's alarming balance of trade deficit between 1924 and 1925. Protective duties on wheat, abolished in 1915, were reintroduced, initially at the rate of 7.5 gold lire per quintal imported, though this was raised considerably in subsequent years. A range of incentives aimed at increasing output and productivity were also introduced. Beyond the duties on foreign wheat, import restrictions were imposed on all agricultural goods from 1926, and export subsidies introduced for certain crops from 1930.

Battle of the lira. The battle to 'rescue' the Italian currency. This entailed, as noted, the revaluation and stabilization of the lira at around '*Quota novanta*' – 90 lire to the pound sterling. Linked, as with the Battle for wheat, to Italy's balance of payments situation, and to the need to re-establish domestic and foreign confidence in Italian financial markets, Q90 was carried through by Mussolini, despite the misgivings of Finance Minister Giuseppe Volpi and Italian industry and business, who feared the negative economic consequences of stabilization at such a high rate of exchange. The 'savage deflation'[14] required to stabilize the currency pushed the Italian economy into recession and certainly adversely affected industrial and agrarian concerns (especially exporters who were already beginning to struggle by 1925–6 and now found themselves priced out of international markets). The cost of deflation, however, was largely borne by Italian labour; 100,000 industrial workers lost their jobs in the year after the Pesaro speech; real wages in industry fell by 10–20 per cent.[15]

Bonifica integrale. Closely tied to Mussolini's 'ruralization' campaign of the late 1920s (his attempt to halt the rural exodus and 'empty' Italy's cities) and, by association, to the Battle for births (the drive to increase Italy's population; urbanization was associated with falling birth rates). Land reclamation schemes were not new to Italy, dating back to the 1880s, although it was only in the Giolittian era that comprehensive reclamation and development packages were put in place. In the Fascist period, the first act concerning land reclamation was introduced in 1923 with more substantial legislation following in 1924. However, it was the 'Mussolini law' (December 1928) that became the centrepiece of the Fascist's 'integral' land reclamation and improvement legislation. Seven billion lire over 14 years was earmarked for the *bonifica integrale*, the financial burden to be shared between the state and the owners of the land on which the projects took place. The *bonifica integrale* was presented as a co-ordinated programme for the modernization of Italian agriculture. The scheme aimed to increase the amount of land under cultivation, replace extensive with intensive forms of agriculture, raise productivity, develop rural communications, construct new 'rural' townships, help reduce agricultural unemployment and reverse the trend to urbanization.[16]

Reorganization of financial and credit systems. Undertaken in the midst of the Great Depression and prompted by the need to rescue Italy's banking system from imminent collapse. Through the creation of the Istituto mobiliare italiano (IMI) in 1931 and the Istituto per la ricostruzione industriale (IRI) in 1933, the state bailed out several of the major commercial banks – and the Bank of Italy itself, which had run into trouble trying to salvage the commercial banks. In the process, the state took a controlling interest in several major industries, relieving the banks of their substantial but worthless industrial share portfolios (the cause of the crisis in the first place). It also became the major supplier of long-term industrial credit, since the banks were either no longer able or no longer allowed to perform this function.[17]

Autarchy. Officially announced in March 1936 at a time when the Italian economy was labouring under the weight of international sanctions imposed by the League of Nations following Italy's invasion of Ethiopia. In fact, many elements of Fascist autarchy – protectionism, import-substitution, state support for or management of

key strategic industries, state-controlled financial intermediation and cartelization –
were already in place by this time.

Debates

We have noted the Comintern's 1933 definition of Fascism as 'the openly terrorist dictatorship...of finance capital...for monopolist capital'. Communism
long 'stressed that fascism was the political expression of a restricted clique of
monopoly capitalists, financiers and landowners – all of whom, in order to preserve their positions, distorted the "normal" pattern of economic development
and impeded the growth of the "progressive" forces of Italian capitalism'.[18] In the
1970s, for example, Pietro Grifone, a lifelong member of the PCI and himself a
victim of Fascism (he was arrested and imprisoned by the Fascists in 1933), was
still able to assert that Fascism 'until the end remained the most direct and consistent expression of "great capitalism", with the Fascist state functioning as the
"political mediator of the class interests of *grande capitalismo monopolistico*". For
Grifone, the idea of economic progress under Fascism was absurd and obscene:
'to mumble...of "development" of the Italian economy in the black *ventennio* [the
twenty years of Fascist rule]...offends the truth'.[19] From the traditional Marxist
perspective, Fascism existed to maintain and defend the existing social order at
the expense of economic progress: 'a fundamental economic stagnation on the
basis of a compromise to conserve a social order at a backward level'.[20] It was, in
essence, anti-economic.

By the early to mid-1970s, however, this orthodoxy was being challenged from
within Marxist circles. Nicos Poulantzas differentiated between Fascism and
state monopoly capitalism, preferring instead to see Fascism as an 'exceptional
state of the capitalist type', in that it possessed 'the distinguishing features of
the capitalist type of state – the relative separation of the economy from politics
and the relative autonomy of the state from the dominant classes and fractions'.[21]
Poulantzas was prepared to accept that there *had* been economic development
along capitalist lines in the Fascist era. Fascism, he wrote, 'really represented
industrial development, technological innovation, and an increase in the productivity of labour'. Similarly, Ernesto Ragionieri claimed that the Fascist period had
witnessed 'rationalization in the capitalistic organization of work'.[22]

Liberal-conservative historians had embraced for some time the idea that the
Fascist era saw the modernization of the Italian economy, especially industry.
Romeo (1961) argued that increasing cartelization and industrial concentration
from the late 1920s and especially during and after the Great Depression had
pushed industry 'towards those forms of oligopoly that are characteristic of the
most mature forms of capitalism'. La Francesca (1972) suggested that, despite
the shortcomings of the regime and the failure and inconsistencies of many of
its policies, the Italian economy under Fascism finally assumed a 'modern and
progressive dimension'. De Felice, perhaps not surprisingly, quoted approvingly

from both Romeo and La Francesca when discussing the economy in his biography of Mussolini.[23]

Such revisionism was not simply an Italian or Continental trend. At the end of the 1970s, for example, the British historian Paul Corner argued in support of both qualitative and quantitative improvements in industry, and stressed the close links between Fascism and capitalist development in Italy. Corner's study was particularly interesting because it challenged the widely held view that Mussolini's ruralization campaign amounted to a rejection of industrialization and modernity.[24] Corner's analysis had three main aspects.

- Fascist agrarian policies always favoured the interests of the great landowners over those of small proprietors. Within this dominant group, however, it was the efficient, productive, flexible, big northern capitalist farmers who benefited the most: capable producers gained more from the high prices and guaranteed market afforded by grain protection. The majority of funds for land reclamation and improvement went to the north and centre, i.e. to the most advanced agricultural sectors. The 'backward' *latifondisti* of the south as a consequence lost ground to their more progressive northern neighbours.[25]

- Despite the rural emphasis of much of Fascist propaganda, agricultural policy was in fact subordinate to industrial policy. The agricultural sector was basically exploited for the benefit of industrial development. For the Fascist regime, the quickest, least problematic means of financing the required restructuring and growth of Italian industry was to facilitate capital accumulation within the advanced sectors of the agrarian economy, which could then be transferred to industry through direct investment (the stock market) or via savings. The major agricultural initiatives – the Battle for wheat, land reclamation – had to be seen in this light, favouring the large northern capitalist landowners within the agricultural economy, but serving the needs of industry above all. The *bonifica integrale*, for example, was as much a policy designed to stimulate the chemical industry (fertilizers) and the makers of agricultural machinery as it was meant to be an impulse to agricultural production. The emphasis on large-scale capitalist agriculture also made sense when related to industrial objectives. Only this sector could be relied upon to embrace technical progress and provide the necessary demand for agrarian-industrial goods. The trend towards monopoly or oligopoly in the industrial sector, backed by protectionist measures, also ensured high product prices and thus big profits for such producers – a good example being the chemical giant Montecatini's control of the fertilizer market.[26]

- While Fascist economic management was far from perfect, the usual criticisms of Fascist agrarian policy and, indeed, of Fascist economic policy *en tout*, started from the wrong premise – comparison with 'normal' forms of capitalist development – and missed the essential point: Fascist economic policy made sense in the context both of Italy's historic capitalist development and the short-term needs of the Italian economy. Italian industrial growth was hampered by three factors: lack of domestic capital, insufficient domestic demand and persistent balance of payments problems (the inability of exports to cover raw-material imports). In the first half of the 1920s these constraints were keenly felt by the Fascist Government. On the one hand, there was the evident need to restructure industry to meet changing global demand (rising demand for modern industrial products such as engineering and chemicals, falling demand for traditional industrial products such as textiles). This required massive investment. On the other hand, the growing balance of payments deficit and accompanying financial instability threatened to scare off both domestic and, more importantly, foreign sources of capital. The reintroduction of the wheat duty in 1925 had been a necessary step to reduce the deficit (to cut raw-material or capital imports would have 'produced an even more profound effect on the economy'). Stabilization via the revaluation of the lira in 1926–7 had been an attempt to attract overseas capital. A short-lived success in that it 'opened the way to American loans', stabilization, however, also killed exports – at a time when the deflationary effects of Q90 and wage controls were reducing internal demand – and ultimately ended in failure when foreign capital dried up after 1929. Domestic capital, always scarce, could not be expected to take up the slack when sales were being squeezed. This was where Fascist agrarian policy fitted in: to stimulate certain key areas of the agrarian economy in order to release funds to industry and to provide a home market replete with guaranteed prices for industrial goods. 'By providing finance for industry through a multitude of channels, by offering a market, and by providing a reservoir of labour, the agricultural sector helped to make possible those qualitative changes of both industrial and financial structures which constitute the main features of the interpretation which rejects theories of economic stagnation and immobility.'[27]

The most radical revisionist thesis of the 1970s, however, was that of A. James Gregor. In several works, culminating with *Italian Fascism and Developmental Dictatorship* (1979), Gregor argued that not only was economic development a feature of the Fascist era but such development was both the outcome of 'autonomous' Fascist policies and the central element of Fascist ideology. Italian Fascism was the first and the 'exemplar' of what he termed 'developmental dictatorship': a 'revolutionary mass-movement regime' whose *raison d'être* was to bring about the 'industrialization of a backward economy' through the fullest exploitation possible of the human and natural resources at its disposal.[28]

According to Gregor, Fascism was the product of heretical Marxism, specifically of Italian revolutionary syndicalism, itself shaped by the particular economic, social and historical condition of Italy. Deriving their analysis from Marx and Engels, Italian revolutionary syndicalists recognized that Italian economic backwardness ruled out imminent socialist revolution – it was impossible to 'jump' to socialism without first passing through capitalism. The immediate need then was to harness the productive elements of Italian society in order to develop Italian capitalism. A revolutionary élite was required to direct this process, in particular to impose 'productivist' discipline on society. A mass-mobilizing myth was required to energize all productive elements, irrespective of class. Syndicalism itself was insufficient for this purpose. The *myth of the nation*, however, had the potential to mobilize all sections of society and to propel Italy towards capitalism. The class struggle was transferred from the national to the international plane: Italy as a 'proletarian' nation competing for resources against the 'plutocratic' nations such as Britain and France. Out of this, Fascism was born.[29]

Gregor argued that Fascism's economic policies – although tailored to circumstance, influenced by tactical considerations and sometimes similar to those pursued by non-developmental or dictatorial governments – all had to be viewed in the light of the regime's ideological commitment to the maximization of national production. While sometimes this meant that Fascist policy also served the interests of Italy's economic élite, 'Fascism was not a "tool" of anyone', and at all times Fascism's primary concern was economic development. The policies of the early 1920s were designed to encourage capital accumulation by deregulation and the control of salaries through the defeat of organized labour, at the same time allowing Fascism to consolidate its hold on power. The Battle of the lira was a 'pretext' used by the dictatorship to move to 'the second phase of Fascism's developmental program' – the withdrawal of Italy from the international marketplace in order to free Italy from economic reliance on its international rivals. (The drive to self-sufficiency [autarchy], wrote Gregor, was, like corporativism and war, a logical consequence of Fascism's emphasis on national development, and its conception of 'proletarian' Italy's 'class struggle' with the plutocracies.) Ruralization was part of Fascism's modernizing ideology. Demographic growth – the fundamental aim of ruralization – was essential if Italy were to compete successfully with the plutocratic nations. To support an expanding rural population required further industrialization and the modernization of the agrarian economy; this was the purpose of the *bonifica integrale*. The Great Depression allowed Fascism the opportunity to extend significantly its direct control over the economy, something that private capital, until then, had been able to resist. The Ethiopian war merely reinforced the trend to industrial concentration, state control, import-substitution and autarchy, which were the dominant characteristics of Fascism from the mid-1930s.[30]

Not only did economic policies match the 'ideological, doctrinal and programmatic commitments' of Fascism, but, claimed Gregor, they were also successful. Early Fascist 'fiscal responsibility' encouraged rapid capital accumulation and investment. Under Fascist influence, industry grew steadily (in terms of both output and productivity) and 'compared favourably with...performances of more resource-favoured industrial states'. Due to the dictatorship's 'serious program of integral modernization', Italy 'had become an industrial nation by 1937', and an 'economically mature society' by 1938. The economic programme of autarchy pursued from 1935 'was not without considerable success', laying the foundation for the post-war 'economic miracle'. Agriculture, too, had seen triumphs. The Battle for wheat ended Italy's dependence on foreign grain. The *bonifica integrale* and 'the technical and scientific modernization of agriculture were...among the most successful efforts of the regime'.[31]

Gregor did acknowledge some of the stresses and strains put on the economy (and society) by Fascism's 'developmental program'. He also recognized that 'By the advent of the Second World War, Fascism had achieved all that could have been achieved of its national economic program'. Only the military defeat of the plutocratic nations, territorial expansion and the final resolution of Italy's raw materials and natural resources problems would allow further growth. Of course, though, Fascist economic policy had all along been designed 'to develop Italy's industrial potential to the level where it could support...aggressive capabilities'.[32]

Gregor's thesis found few adherents. Some academics questioned whether Fascism really had more in common with Bolshevism and Maoism – both identified by Gregor as fellow developmental, and therefore 'fascist', dictatorships – than with Nazism (which could hardly be described as a regime committed to the development of a 'backward economy'). Others queried Gregor's insistence on the ideological coherence of Fascism, the link between ideology and practice, and the importance of national production to Fascism. Gregor's extremely favourable review of the Fascists' economic record was also noted.[33] Certainly, there is no doubt that Gregor overegged his argument and there is indeed much to take issue with in his analysis (see 'Assessment').

In fact, by the time *Italian Fascism and Developmental Dictatorship* was published, a significant and altogether more cautious new strand was emerging within the economic historiography of the Fascist period. Rigorously 'economic' in terms of focus and methodology, these studies brought out the complex and contradictory character of the inter-war Italian economy and set Italian trends firmly within the international economic context. While not constituting a 'school' as such, we can nonetheless identify a number of key figures in the 1970s with this approach: Gianni Toniolo, Piero Ciocca, Jon Cohen, Vera Zamagni and Giuseppe Tattara. All of these contributed to the groundbreaking *L'economia italiana nel periodo fascista* (1976) as well as to a broader collection of essays on modern Italian economic history published in 1973 under the title *Lo sviluppo economico italiano*. Their arguments, first advanced in the 1970s but developed by them – and others[34] – in subsequent decades, can be summarized thus:

- Extreme formulations of stagnation or dynamism are unsustainable. The Italian economy did develop between 1921 and 1938: GDP rose (by an average of 2.2 per cent p.a.), manufacturing grew (by almost 4 per cent p.a.), investment increased (by over 5 per cent p.a.). However, growth was not constant over the period, and the overall picture is one of relative decline, whether compared to long-term Italian economic trends or to the performance of Italy's European neighbours in the 1920s and 1930s.
  - Economic growth between 1921 and 1938 was located almost entirely in the years 1922–5 and 1934–8. Sandwiched between these periods was almost a decade of stagnation.
  - Growth in manufacturing output between 1929 and 1939 did not keep pace with that of GDP, i.e. the Italian economy became relatively 'less industrial' during the 1930s.
  - Growth in investment was concentrated in the period 1922–5. Investment had only a limited impact upon productivity: the increase in output per worker in the industrial sector was in line with that achieved in the 1880s and 1890s and below that of the Giolittian era and after 1945. The most capital-intensive industrial sectors of the 1930s, meanwhile, witnessed only small increases in productivity. On the eve of World War Two, Italy remained a retarded industrial economy relative to its western and northern European neighbours.
  - In terms of GNP per capita, Italy had been 'catching up' with the more advanced economic countries before the Fascist period. This process of 'catch up' – seen again after 1945 – was slowed or even reversed under Fascism.[35]

- The policies of the regime can only be properly understood in the context of the international environment.
    - The stabilization of the lira and Italy's return to the gold standard, together with the timing of the policy, was significantly conditioned by external factors. Many governments had abandoned the gold standard during the war. Post-war inflation and exchange instability saw most of them return their currencies to a gold base in the mid-1920s; indeed, to return to the gold standard was the ultimate in monetary orthodoxy, being seen as the 'cement' of international capitalism. By the end of 1925, all major currencies bar the franc (which followed in 1926) had returned to the gold standard. By 1925, stabilization of the lira was widely regarded within Italian business and financial circles as a necessity – to do otherwise threatened reserves and further inflation. Stabilization of the lira, however, required access to foreign credit – this was needed in order to boost reserves and discourage speculators – which only became available after the resolution of Italy's international war debts in 1925. Stabilization of the lira also first required stabilization elsewhere. Italy, as Toniolo points out, could not 'go it alone' without risking untold damage to the commercial balance. Stabilization of the lira after the stabilization of the other European currencies provided the Italian government with some degree of control over the size of the deficit. The 'Battle for the lira' had its novel features – undoubtedly Q90 was chosen by Mussolini for political and prestige reasons rather than economic considerations – but essentially it was a plan in line with international financial orthodoxy (more than 40 nations returned to the gold standard between 1925 and 1929), and was imposed only when the international context allowed it.[36]
    - Economic policies and trends during the Fascist period which appear novel in the Italian context, such as the Battle for wheat, local development initiatives (e.g. the development of 'special industrial zones' such as Porto Marghera near Venice), autarchy, the rapid acceleration of industrial concentration and cartelization, were often similar in essence to those witnessed elsewhere in Europe at the time. The reimposition of the duty on wheat in Italy was matched by similar measures in Germany (1925) and France (1927). Industrial planning was a feature of the German economy in the 1930s. Autarchic measures were applied in many European countries during and after the Great Depression in order to protect domestic industry from international competition. The trend to monopoly and oligopoly was a feature of inter-war western economies.[37]
- Economic policies and trends during the Fascist period which appear novel in the Italian context were merely variations on policies and trends seen in Italy prior to Fascism. The Battle for wheat was based on traditional grain duties. The integral land reclamation and improvement scheme was an extension of earlier policies. Local development initiatives dated back to the first comprehensive southern development programmes of the early years of the twentieth century. The Giolittian era had seen increasing industrial concentration and cartelization; World War One had accentuated this trend. State intervention in support of 'essential' heavy industry dated back to the 1880s. The differences between pre-Fascist and Fascist economic policies and trends were largely a matter of scale and size: the regime invested and intervened more; existing trends were accelerated.[38] Policies in general also seem to have been reactive rather than proactive, and the part played by Fascists in their realization often rather limited. For example, the IRI, perhaps the most

original feature of state intervention in the 1930s, was originally conceived only as part of a short-term salvage operation, and its management was technocratic rather than Fascist (indeed, IRI President Alberto Beneduce was 'an expert in statistics and a socialist reformer' who had been an adviser to Francesco Nitti prior to World War One).[39]

- The capacity of the regime to follow an 'independent' economic policy, already constrained by international economic factors (see above) was further limited by the nature of the Italian economy itself. The heterogeneity of Italian capitalism, the complexity of Italian society, the backwardness of the Italian economy, the conflicting demands of key economic groups and the ability of these groups to retain a degree of autonomy from Fascism, meant that economic policies were frequently compromise measures designed to reconcile competing interests. 'These often led to sub-optimal solutions whether from the point of view of growth or maximization of profit.' Fascism was not the slave, but neither was it the master, of Italian capitalism.[40]

- While certain aspects of policy did contribute to both short-term and long-term growth, on balance Fascist policies hindered economic expansion. The IRI 'saved' Italy's banking sector, transformed the entire system of financial mediation, and played an important role in the development of Italian industry during the 'economic miracle' of the 1950s. Scientific research undertaken in the 1930s and connected to the policy of import-substitution had important positive repercussions for particular industrial sectors after 1945.[41] However, many of the regime's key economic policies failed to meet their specific objectives, or adversely effected other parts of the economy.

  - Q90. Revaluation and stabilization at 90 lire: £1 may not have been responsible for the recession of the mid-late 1920s – evidence of slowdown can be seen in 1925 – but the deflationary effects of excessive revaluation and wage cuts did, in all likelihood, prolong the crisis.[42]

  - *Maintenance of the gold standard.* The Italian economy's recovery from the Great Depression – far slower than in many countries – was hampered by the regime's reluctance to devalue or to abandon the gold standard, despite the fact that Britain (1931) and then the United States (1933) did both, leaving the lira significantly overvalued. Given this, and the regime's insistence on further wage cuts, recovery could not be driven by exports or by private domestic consumption but instead had to be initiated by public spending. This, however, only occurred from 1934. Although reasons of prestige probably influenced the decision not to abandon the gold standard (this finally happened in 1936), it was probably indicative, too, of a regime that failed to recognize early on the severity of the economic crisis.[43] Fascist policies also had a significant negative impact on technical progress: low wages, the slow rate of recovery in the early 1930s and the decision to cut working hours to combat unemployment all acted as disincentives to productive investment; Italy's increasing isolation from external markets reduced crucial imports of technology. Italy was a bystander in the 'technological revolution' that occurred across much of Europe in the early 1930s as part of industrial restructuring, with important implications for long-term growth. The encouragement given to cartels and the support of inefficient firms also militated against the rationalization of production.[44]

- *The Battle for wheat.* Italy became virtually self-sufficient in wheat by the mid-1930s, producing on average 2m tonnes more of wheat p.a. than in the early 1920s. The amount of imported wheat as a percentage of domestic production fell correspondingly, from an average of 42.3 per cent of domestic yield between 1921 and 1930 to 5.3 per cent p.a. between 1932 and 1941. Yield per hectare also rose markedly. However, productivity increases during the Fascist era were most notable between 1920 and 1924 – prior to the Battle – and between 1930 and 1934 – before the period of official autarchy when wheat self-sufficiency became an 'obsessive priority' for the regime. Wheat production in 1940 was well below the set target. The increase in overall yield was due as much to the increase in the amount of land given over to wheat growing – which accounted for 60 per cent of all arable land by the mid-1930s – as to improvements in productivity. The impact on southern agriculture was particularly startling: a 15 per cent increase in the quantity of land given over to wheat between 1925 and 1939. That the shift to cereal culture was at the expense of traditional – and far more suitable – specialist 'cash crops' (such as fruit and vegetables) helps explain not only the relatively low yield improvements from the mid-1930s (i.e. wheat was increasingly grown on marginal or unsuitable land) but also why fruit production fell, Italy became a net-importer of olive oil and agricultural specialization was set back 'tens of years'. Livestock farming also suffered a precipitous decline as grazing land was turned over to arable use. This, in turn, meant higher livestock – and manure – prices. Any incentive to investment as a consequence of the wheat tariff (the opportunity to profit from the tariff should have encouraged progressive farmers to invest in order to increase yields) seems to have been offset by the high prices of farm machinery and fertilizers, both protected sectors under virtual monopoly control (Fiat and Montecatini respectively). Private investment in agriculture virtually ground to a halt in the 1930s and the process of mechanization did not accelerate. The social consequences of the Battle for wheat were considerable, too. Higher prices for wheat translated into lower levels of per capita consumption. The tariff and the guaranteed prices for wheat may have benefited large northern capitalist farms but they also reinforced the southern *latifondi*. Small farmers meanwhile could not take advantage of the duties since wheat was best grown on a large scale and with the use of labour-saving technology. Condemned to either inefficient wheat production or to the growing of crops for which the market value had collapsed, it was no surprise that many small farmers went bankrupt and had to sell up (as we have seen, Paul Corner considered this a deliberate aspect of the tariff).[45]

- *Bonifica integrale.* The programme never became the public–private partnership envisaged by its creator, Arrigo Serpieri. The threat of expropriation of private land to ensure the co-operation of landowners – included in the 1924 Act – was never a serious option for the regime given that it relied heavily on the support of the agrarian lobby. Repealed in 1925 after protests from landowners, the idea was raised again by Serpieri in the mid-1930s once it had become obvious that landowners were not voluntarily going to commit funds. He was relieved of his duties shortly afterwards. Despite vast amounts of state monies invested in the programme, equivalent to 10 per cent of net investment in public works and 18 per cent of agricultural investment between 1930 and 1934, and the much-publicized success of projects such as the reclamation and settlement of the Agro Pontino near Rome, the *bonifica integrale* realized only modest and uneven returns. For example, the value of agricultural production and yield per hectare rose in the north between 1929 and 1930 and between 1939 and 1941, but provinces which received little funding performed just as well as their better funded counterparts. In contrast, the value of agricultural product and yield per hectare tended to fall in southern provinces, irrespective of the level of expenditure. Increases in population density or in the quantity of land under cultivation – if they occurred – also did not correlate with levels of spending.[46]

- *Local development schemes.* The creation of special industrial zones had little long-term impact other than in the case of Porto Marghera, and here the benefits of industrial development have arguably been outweighed by the colossal damage caused to the local environment.[47]

- *Autarchy.* Despite the positive spillovers associated with some aspects of import-substitution (for example, experimentation in synthetic materials led to the discovery of polypropylene), the pursuit of import-substitutes was often a costly and fruitless exercise, and autarchy in general did not lead to the more efficient use of resources, more effective investment, or higher productivity. Although the development of heavy industry was made a priority, 'autarchic industries emerge on the whole as relatively inefficient'. For example, the growth rate of Italian steel production in the mid-1930s was among the lowest in Europe, and Italy still had to import approximately 6 per cent of its total requirements of iron and steel products in 1938. Output per worker also fell in the iron and steel industry between 1934 and 1938. As Paradisi has written, 'Italian economic autarchy appears particularly costly in comparison to the analogous policies adopted by other industrial nations. The latter temporarily protected an efficient industrial system from international competition. Italy protected, not only in the period 1930–38, an inefficient industrial apparatus that could not be exposed to foreign competition'.[48] Self-sufficiency never extended to raw materials. Italy's new African empire did not yield the natural resources the regime claimed it would. Of industrial raw materials, 79 per cent were still imported in 1939. Italy's retreat from the world economy only made it more reliant on its new ally, Germany, to the extent that 40 per cent of all imports came from Germany by 1940. This was hardly self-sufficiency, nor good preparation for war (Germany was to be far less willing to supply Italy once the Eastern Front opened). Imports, of course, also had to be paid for, yet the loss of export markets meant Italy's ability to do so was reduced. The situation was so serious in 1939 that Italy was forced to sell arms to countries already at war with Germany in order to raise the necessary funds to buy raw materials. Within agriculture, the drive for self-sufficiency in wheat was hindered by the high price of fertilizer. As noted above, the emphasis on wheat production in turn led to a reduction in the amount of pasture and a reduction in the quantity of livestock. This undermined the regime's efforts to raise meat production – as did the duty on imported maize: pig farmers complained that the high price of maize, which was used as feed, ruled out more intensive breeding programmes.[49]

The above represents the current state of play within the economic historiography of the Fascist era: a picture of light and shade certainly, but one that ultimately is critical of Fascism's management of, and impact upon, the economy. The effectiveness of Fascist industrial policies was 'at best dubious'. In agriculture, 'had the regime pursued alternative policies, investment in agriculture would have been greater, agricultural output would have grown more rapidly, and Italian workers would have suffered fewer hardships.' Overall, 'Fascism retarded the economic development of Italy'. Indeed, Fascism was responsible for the relatively modest growth rate of the Italian economy over the course of the twentieth century: 'it was Fascism that went wrong with the growth of the Italian economy in the long run'.[50]

The idea that Fascist policies were favourable to the development and modernization of the Italian economy persists, however, in the work of Rolf Petri. Fascist economic policy, he argues, was consistently directed towards the completion of industrialization. In pursuit of this objective – a national goal at least since the Giolittian era – Fascist economic policies followed what Petri calls a 'neo-mercantilist' agenda: the development of 'advanced' basic industries (steel, chemicals, energy etc.) through state-directed investments and careful management of trade and domestic markets. Echoing the view of Paul Corner, Petri suggests that the introduction of wheat duties in the mid-1920s helped reduce Italy's balance of payments deficit without requiring cuts in energy, capital goods and raw-materials imports, all of which were vital for industrial development. Anti-urbanization and ruralization policies meanwhile were, in his opinion, designed to control – but not stop – the flow of labour from agriculture to industry:

> Only by continuous, but gradual, expulsion of workers from agriculture industrial wages could be kept in a dynamic equilibrium with the improvement of industrial labour productivity. Huge sectoral disparities of income from labour might have distorted capital towards traditional and small-sized consumer goods-producing branches. This might have meant still stronger dependence upon imports and interruption of capital formation in the technologically advanced basic industries... Whatever has to be said on the ideological motivations of Mussolini's anti-urbanism, regulation of labour resources seems to be the ultimate rationale of the demographic, migration and land distribution policies of those years.[51]

As for autarchy, Petri argues this was not so much about preparing the Italian economy for war as it was the long-term development of key industries under 'conditions of a disintegrated world market'. Nor was complete self-sufficiency ever the intention: 'The supreme goal of autarky planning was not obtaining "self-sufficiency at any cost", but minimising the trade balance deficit, stabilising the balance of payments, and achieving technical progress of basic industries'.[52] Judged on these terms, autarchy was a success: Italy actually operated trade balance surpluses in 1941 and 1943, and only a small deficit in 1942; there was significant technical innovation in the steel, chemicals and energy industries.[53] The real benefits to the Italian economy derived from autarchy were only fully felt later, however, with the liberalization of international trade in the 1950s.

Then, thanks to the 'guided' investments and technical improvements in advanced basic industries of the late Fascist period, Republican Italy was able to:

> ...take the role of an equal trade partner and profit from the historically new quality of commercial exchange [trade in similarly manufactured goods]... The investments that probably had contributed to depress the growth figures during the previous periods [because of the distorted allocation of resources to advanced basic industries] *now* turned out to be advantageous for internal industrial production, consumption, and exports. The new panel of Italy's exports permitted the country to release [itself from] the hated role of an inferior supplier of foodstuff and low-quality goods.[54]

Petri sees essential continuity in economic policy between the Fascist and post-war Republican periods. The same group of technocrats who had formulated and directed policy in the state-owned industrial and banking sectors during the 1930s continued to occupy the key decision-making positions in the public sector after 1945 and effectively controlled economic policy until 1960 (for example, Donato Menichella, a senior manager in the IRI under Fascism, was Governor of the Bank of Italy between 1947 and 1960). This group continued to follow the same neo-mercantilist strategy in pursuit of the same national objective after the war as it had done before it. Only the tools employed were different. The new international order and the re-emergence of an integrated world market after 1945 meant the policies of protectionism and autarchy gave way to one of guarded trade liberalization ('as much foreign trade as possible...as much protection [for strategic industries] as necessary').[55]

Petri's claim that innovation in 'advanced' autarchic industries during the 1930s 'enable[d] the performance of the so-called "economic miracle" and the definitive transformation of Italy into an industrialized country', enjoys some support within economic history circles.[56] Critics, however, question the link between Fascist autarchy and post-war growth, and claim Petri's argument for essential continuity in economic policy 'defies logic and flies in the face of the quantitative data'.[57]

Assessment

This chapter has identified three general historiographical perspectives on the Italian economy under Fascism:

The 'stagnationist' position: closely allied to the Marxist school, which argues that Fascism sacrificed economic development in order to preserve the existing social structure.

The 'optimist' position: a broad school including revisionist Marxists, liberals and conservatives, which argues in favour of economic modernization while recognizing the limitations and/or unwelcome consequences of specific policies (even a 'blind optimist' such as Gregor recognized that some policies had negative implications for particular sectors). Sometimes accompanied by an insistence that alternative policies were not an option (e.g. Corner).

The 'sceptic' position: reflecting the current consensus, which recognizes development but only within a picture of relative decline (that is, relative to contemporary international and longer-term Italian economic trends). Acknowledges some positive aspects to Fascist economic management but is hostile to the notion that Fascism helped the Italian economy to develop to its full potential in the inter-war period. The 'sceptics' contend that Fascism held back the Italian economy, retarding the processes of economic modernization and growth.

What should we make of these three interpretations? The simple equation that Fascism = stagnation is untenable. There *is* evidence of economic modernization at least in terms of the development of Italy's economic infrastructure and the growth of 'modern' heavy industry (though not of manufacturing industry as a whole) as a proportion of GNP over the period. The equation that Fascism = backward Italian capitalism resorting to ever more extreme measures to defend its interests is one we have encountered already in Chapter 4. The evidence suggests that, although the interests of landowners and big business were often favoured by Fascism, the alliance was an uneasy one. Each side took what it could, backed down when it had to, and compromised when necessary. Marxists have long argued that 'the historic, dialectic relationship between capital and fascism was not static and therefore from time to time the regime appeared (and was effectively) hostile to this or that group as if one was dealing with an entity superimposed on the class from which it was born and of which it was instead always the direct expression'.[58] The reality appears more complex than this. Fascism was neither capitalist nor anti-capitalist, connected by need but not beholden by nature to Italy's dominant economic class. As to the idea that Fascism was prepared to sacrifice the development of the Italian economy to the needs of social order, this makes little sense when one considers the nature of Fascism, its insistence on the 'nation above all' and its obsession with status and prestige. An Italy feared and respected could only derive from economic strength.

All of this means, of course, that the 'optimists'' insistence on the development of the Italian economy during the Fascist period cannot be gainsaid. What is up for debate – and what the 'sceptics' have questioned – is the extent of the qualitative and quantitative improvements, the degree to which the costs of Fascist policies were outweighed by the benefits of those policies, whether improvements were despite or because of Fascist economic policies, and if the economy would have performed better under different management.

We can certainly take issue with the evidence produced by Gregor in support of his contention that Fascism was a successful 'developmental dictatorship'. It is clear that the (limited) statistical data provided by Gregor is, by and large, misleading. Gregor's figures show an 82 per cent increase in industrial production between 1922 and 1934, but he neglects to say that industrial production

remained below 1929 levels until 1937, or that growth in industrial production as part of GNP was much more in evidence between 1913 and 1925 than
between 1925 and 1938. Gregor notes the growth of iron and steel production
in the 1920s as proof of Fascism's developmental programme, but he does not
acknowledge that production stalled in the 1930s, that there was no integration of the two industries – the steel industry relied upon imported rather
than domestically produced scrap iron – and that production costs in the steel
industry remained extremely high until World War Two, the consequence of
sectoral inefficiency and suggestive of little or no structural rationalization.
Italian industry, it seems, lacked the capacity or the incentives to adapt. Gregor
also suggests that worker productivity increased significantly during the Fascist
period, pointing out that output per worker rose by 47 per cent between 1913
and 1938, but these figures, of course, include growth achieved prior to Fascism
and ignore the fact that the growth rate of gross product per worker was significantly lower between 1921 and 1938 than in either the Giolittian era or during
the 1950s and 1960s.

Nor do Gregor's key arguments stand up. Many of the 'sceptics'' arguments outlined earlier reveal these limitations, but a number of additional
points need to be made. First, the resolution of Italy's war debts and the
stabilization of the lira in the mid-1920s encouraged an influx of foreign,
particularly American, investment in Italy. This was hardly indicative of
a programme designed to liberate Italy from its reliance on international
markets. In fact, the dependency of Italian industry on US credit in the late
1920s left it especially vulnerable following the Wall Street Crash. Second,
protectionism appears to have been tied to events rather than a reflection
of long-term strategy. The Battle for wheat was instigated in response to the
balance of payments crisis. The wave of tariffs introduced in the early 1930s
followed the implementation of similar protectionist measures in Britain
and the United States. Exchange controls were introduced or abandoned
as circumstances dictated. Third, although Italy by 1938 was, as Gregor
suggests, an 'industrial' economy in the sense that industry contributed a
greater percentage to overall GDP than did agriculture (31 per cent: 27 per
cent), in fact, judged on this criterion, Italy was primarily a service economy
(44 per cent of GDP). In terms of employment, however, Italy remained
firmly an agrarian economy: 52 per cent of the labour force in 1936 worked
in agriculture compared to just 25.2 per cent in industry. Whether Italy can
be called an 'economically mature society' on this basis is questionable (as,
indeed, is his claim that Fascism took Italy 'from the beginning' of the drive
to economic maturity – industrialization was well underway by the turn of
the century). Fourth, if Fascist economic policy was indeed meant to advance
Italian industry to the point where it could support 'aggressive capabilities',
then clearly it failed to do so, as World War Two demonstrated. Indeed, Italy
was arguably less prepared for war in June 1940 than in May 1915. Fifth, it
was the demands placed upon the economy by the war itself – a war which, of
course, destroyed Mussolini and Fascism – rather than the policy of autarchy

which provided Italy with the 'new industrial capacity [that] was to furnish the basis for the reconstruction of Italian industry in the post-Second World War period'.[59]

Gregor is a lone voice. Nevertheless, even the more balanced 'optimistic' accounts of the Italian economy under Fascism are problematic. The economic data suggest that the Fascist period saw only very limited qualitative improvements to the economy, and inconsistent and generally unspectacular quantitative growth. This was not entirely Fascism's fault: these were uncertain and often difficult times for the global economy and the Italian economy was hampered by long-standing structural weaknesses. The policies pursued by Fascism, however, did not offer solutions to either the international economic crisis as it affected Italy or to the structural problems of the Italian economy. The decision to develop the Italian economy – in particular, industry – within an increasingly 'autarchic' environment (protectionism, import-substitution, cartelization, oligopoly and monopoly) placed the onus squarely on domestic demand to carry the process of modernization forward. Private domestic demand barely existed, however, a function of low income per capita. The regime, though, from its inception did everything in its power to hold back or even reduce salaries in order to lower production costs (itself not an incentive to industry to modernize or restructure). Public demand – the state – therefore had to carry most of the burden. This in turn was not a stimulus to efficiency, development or structural reform. In sectors favoured by the regime, inefficient firms were able to continue, while efficient businesses engaged in 'non-essential' industrial or agricultural activities were left to survive as best they could. The regime's support of cartels, oligopolies and monopolies discouraged competition and distorted the economy (e.g. price fixing; the exacerbation of dualism because of the increasing relative price differentials between 'essential' and 'non-essential' sectors leading to the transfer and misallocation of resources from the latter to the former; the sacrifice of 'non-essential' sectors; high barriers to entry). The state's role as the major customer of heavy industry put pressure on public finances while balance of payments problems were an inevitable corollary of autarchy undertaken in a country so lacking in natural resources. Italy's withdrawal from the world economy was a one-sided affair; exports fell but Italy still needed to import, and pay for, raw materials. Put simply, this was a regime that by the mid-1930s had led Italy into an economic cul-de-sac.[60] Small wonder that Zamagni felt obliged to conclude that 'fascism represented not only a factor of temporary diversion of resources...but also a gross hindrance to the solution of the structural problems of the Italian economy'.[61]

So we end up at the 'sceptics' position. There is a potential tension between the view (expressed, for example, by Cohen, and Rossi and Toniolo) that economic development would have been more rapid had Fascism pursued different policies, and the argument that Fascism's capacity to 'choose' policy was severely constrained by the international context and the structural characteristics of the Italian economy. If Fascism had little option as regards the policies it followed then it is hard to criticize it for its failure to pursue alternative ones (this is the view of 'optimists' such as Corner). The counter-factual aspect of some 'sceptic' accounts[62] is also problematic: it is very difficult to say with any certainty what *would* have happened *had* the regime behaved differently. Nevertheless, it is clear that 'In strict cost-benefit terms, Italy paid dearly for its fascist experience.' That particular policies may have been to some extent 'forced' upon the Fascist government does not disguise the fact that the regime was responsible for the detailed substance and implementation of those policies. Fascist economic policy making, however, did not show any 'particular breadth of vision, farsightedness and capacity of realization'. As Toniolo notes, Keynes's 1931 observation that 'There is no party in the world at present which appears to me to be pursuing right aims by right methods,' appears particularly pertinent in the Italian case.[63]

6 Society and culture under Fascism

Introduction

The Fascist era fascinates social and cultural historians. Given the regime's totalitarian ambitions, it is not surprising that interest has centred on the *impact* of Fascism upon Italian life. To what extent did the tools of the dictatorship – repression, propaganda, education, the PNF, spectacle, the regimentation and institutionalization of work, leisure and culture – allow Fascism to impose itself upon the Italian national consciousness? Were Italians really prepared to 'Believe, Obey, Fight' as the regime demanded? If not, what was the relationship between ruler and ruled? Did Italians 'consent' to or 'resist' the regime? Did Italians understand Fascism? Was there a recognizably 'Fascist' culture? Do factors other than Fascism better explain social and cultural change in Italy between the wars? In short, how 'Fascist' was Fascist Italy?

Debate has been fierce, with De Felice often a central figure. His claim of a 'mass consensus' behind Fascism between 1929 and 1934 incensed the Italian Left – which contested the implication that the working class had ever been any-thing other than spontaneously anti-Fascist – and challenged the popular view of Italians as the victims of Fascism. Beyond the consensus debate, but not entirely separate from it, a number of other questions have also generated considerable heat. In recent years, culturalist interpretations of Fascism, concerned more with the *nature* of totalitarian culture than its success or failure, have been accused of accepting at face value the totalitarian claims of the regime. Consequently, so its critics claim, 'the culturalist approach...has not provided a sufficiently articulated account of the Fascist experience' and has overshadowed much of the good work produced by social historians.[1] Meanwhile, the growth of racism in Italy since the early 1990s (see Chapter 9) has coincided with historians revisiting well-entrenched notions of the Italians as inherently *brava gente* – good or decent people – a view nourished by the apparently lukewarm response of Italians to the racial laws of 1938 and the high survival rate of Italian Jews and Jews under

Italian occupation during the war. Recent studies have raised questions about the 'innocence' or otherwise of the Italians in the Holocaust, and about the treatment of ethnic groups within Italy (especially of Slovenes in north-eastern Italy) and Italian-occupied lands (particularly the Libyan Arabs, and the Ethiopians).[2] This debate has, in turn, fed back into the issue of whether we can really hope to – or should want to – separate 'ordinary' Italians from Fascism, and is also of relevance to the question of whether Italians have really ever faced up to their past, particularly pertinent given the efforts of the contemporary Right in Italy to 'normalize' Fascism.[3]

Framework

Repression

Fascism worked hard to make its presence felt in all aspects of Italian life. Although the history of Fascism is far less bloody than that of Nazism or Stalinist Russia – death was not the standard penalty for political dissidence – repression was, nonetheless, a fundamental tool of the regime. The police, the *carabinieri*, OVRA (the Fascist secret police) and the MVSN (the Fascist Militia formed out of the *squadristi*) were the main instruments at the Fascists' disposal. By the end of the 1920s the police were visiting thousands of *locali* and businesses and carrying out thousands more checks of individuals and households every week. Some 114,000 new police files were opened on 'subversives' between 1922 and 1943. The Fascist 'Special Tribunal' handed out over 5,000 sentences totalling more than 27,000 years for political crimes between 1928 and 1943. Some 15,000 Italians endured *confino* (internal exile and house arrest) between 1926 and 1943. Leading Fascists were themselves closely observed and some, such as the Fascist *ras* of Bologna, Leandro Arpinati, even ended up in *confino* themselves. Informants were, of course, encouraged. At a more mundane level, toilet graffiti ('Shit on the *Duce!*') was recorded, while books, plays and films were censored. Any sign of political protest was carefully noted. Police even went to the length of collecting and cataloguing hundreds of stamp-size pieces of 'socialist' red paper found scattered over a piazza in one of the slum districts of Turin on May Day 1937. Legislation gave the authorities increasingly wide-ranging powers. The Postal Code of 1936, for example, made it legal to 'look over, copy', and if necessary 'proceed to confiscate', ordinary mail.[4]

Propaganda

The eradication of overt and public dissent was only one aspect of Fascism's attempts to control and colonize Italian society and culture. Control over information was a central concern of the regime, and of Mussolini, who every day read and commented on hundreds of newspaper stories and prefect reports, often intervening in the most banal issues.[5] By 1926, all Opposition newspapers had been closed down or had been obliged to revise their editorial line. Non-party national papers were allowed to exist, but only 'within the orbit of the state'.[6] From the late 1920s, entry into the journalist profession was conditional on membership of the Fascist Order of Journalists. From 1928, newspapers were obliged to rein back on stories damaging to national morale – the reporting of crime, accidents, disasters, the depression, unrest, was suppressed. By 1930, two-thirds of provincial daily papers were under PNF control. During the 1930s, newspapers – whether Fascist or 'independent' – were stripped of any individuality or autonomy. In 1935, the Ministry for Press and Propaganda, later (1937) expanded and renamed the Ministry of Popular Culture (Minculpop), was established to oversee and co-ordinate the management of the mass media (press, radio, cinema).

The press was the only truly national media available to the Fascists in the 1920s, a problem for a regime wedded to propaganda given that one in five of the population was still illiterate in 1931, with the rate rising to almost one in two in some southern provinces. The growth of radio and cinema from the 1920s thus offered Fascism the opportunity to reach a far wider audience than had previously been possible. The regime, however, appears to have at first under-estimated the potential of both new mediums. Although the Fascists operated a licensed monopoly over radio transmissions, the national broadcasting associa-tion was not a public corporation in the same way as the recently created BBC in Britain; revenue from advertising supplemented the income from the licence fee and a levy on radio-set sales. Consequently, there was always a commercial aspect to national radio. The regime moved slowly to exploit the mass potential of radio; only in the 1930s did it encourage the mass production of cheap sets and even then a wireless remained beyond the budget of most Italians. Despite a rapid rise in the number of radio subscribers in the 1930s – from 300,000 in 1932 to 1.2m in 1939 – at the end of the decade Italy still lagged far behind France (4.9m), Britain (8.9m) and Germany (13.7m) in this regard.[7] The politicization of radio was also a relatively late phenomenon: music broadcasts dominated until the end of the 1920s; news and politics constituted a tiny fraction of airtime. This began to change, however, from the early 1930s. Millions listened to Mussolini's proclamation of Empire in May 1936.

Propaganda was an early feature of Italian cinema: from 1926 movie theatres were obliged to carry government newsreels and documentaries produced by the *Istituto Luce* (*L'unione cinematografica educativa*). Main features, however, at least until the mid-1930s, were rarely overtly 'Fascist' in tone, in contrast to the output of the German film industry under Nazism.[8] Italian films instead tended to mimic Hollywood, favouring romantic comedies and farces over serious politi-cal works. In fact, Italian cinema was in crisis throughout the Fascist era, despite huge increases in audiences. Hollywood was to blame, mass-producing films that were both better and cheaper than those made in Italy. The number of Italian films made fell from around 500 per annum. to ten between 1915 and 1930. Almost 90 per cent of films shown in Italy in 1938 were foreign, the majority from America. Partly for 'autarchic' reasons, partly simply to prop up the ailing Italian film industry, the regime made several efforts in the early to mid-1930s to limit the number of foreign films before legislation in 1938, establishing an

Italian monopoly over distribution rights, led US film companies to withdraw from the Italian market. In addition to such protectionist measures, the state also provided financial assistance to the mainly private film industry. The most obvious example of the state's financial largesse was the building of the *Cinecittà* studios on the outskirts of Rome in 1937, paid for with public monies.[9]

Education and youth

The Fascist totalitarian project assigned a central role to the control and indoctrination of youth: the perpetuation of Fascism relied upon the creation of future generations of true believers. However, Fascism's obsession with youth went deeper. Like the pre-war avant-garde, Fascism equated youth with vigour, energy, courage, strength and immortality. It was no coincidence that the Fascist anthem was *Giovinezza* – 'youth'. (This, of course, caused problems for the Fascist hierarchy as it grew older, Mussolini included. The press was not allowed to print Mussolini's age and, when he became a grandfather, it was ordered not to report the news.) In pursuit of the hearts and minds of Italian youth, the Fascist Government followed twin policies: indoctrination via the education system and also through the creation of national Fascist youth organizations. Education was progressively tailored to meet the demands of the regime. From the establishment of the dictatorship, efforts were made to purge the teaching profession of anti-Fascist elements. From 1929, teachers were obliged to swear an oath of loyalty to the regime. University professors had to do likewise in 1931. Membership of the PNF became *sine qua non* for all teachers from 1933. The curriculum became increasingly fascistized, too: 1930 saw the introduction of a single state textbook into every public elementary school; the first two courses in the elementary curriculum introduced in 1934 dealt solely with Italian heroes from Caesar, to Garibaldi, to Mussolini. The Education Minister, Giuseppe Bottai, introduced further measures towards the end of the decade. Every subject at elementary level was linked to Fascism, even maths and grammar. Children were asked after the Ethiopian war: 'The glorious war in Africa lasted seven months. How many days is this?' The slogan 'Believe, Obey, Fight', was used to teach verb conjugations. Indoctrination at secondary level took subtler forms: Fascist culture was taught, D'Annunzio became essential reading, history emphasized the links between past and present Italian greatness, and science was used to reveal the genius of the Italian race. Universities saw the social sciences restructured: law of the Corporate State and Fascist political science were added to the curriculum.

Fascist youth movements, established by the PNF from 1921, were brought together under the control of a new organization, the *Opera nazionale balilla* (ONB) in 1926. Within the ONB, youth was organized into several different groups according to age and sex. Young boys aged 6–8 years enrolled in the 'sons of the she-wolf', moving on to the *balilla* (8–14 years) and the *avanguardisti* (15–18) Girls were served by similar but separate organizations, the *piccole italiane* (8–12 years) and *giovani italiane* (13–18). Rival youth organizations, such as the Catholic scouts, were banned. (Catholic Action was allowed to continue because of its religious aspect; the scouts, however, were considered 'semi-military'.) ONB branches mixed fun with Fascism: trips and rallies, games and military discipline, camaraderie and instruction in the Fascist 'style'. All children entering the ONB were obliged to swear an oath of loyalty to the *Duce*. The ONB oversaw physical education in schools and from 1934 it took direct responsibility for all rural schools with fewer than twenty pupils. After secondary education, the *Gioventù universitaria fascista* (GUF) catered for young Italians in higher education from 18 to 21 years, although female membership of the GUF was discouraged, as indeed were women from further study. The GUF was to groom the next generation of Fascist leaders. For those who did not attend university there was the *fasci giovanili* (established in 1930), 'the fecund nursery for the ranks and cadres of the PNF and the MVSN', according to the then PNF Secretary, Giovanni Giuriati. Following years of bitter rowing between the leaderships of the ONB, GUF and *fasci giovanili*, a new umbrella organization, the *Gioventù italiana del Littorio* (GIL), was established in 1937, directly under the control of the PNF. Membership of the new organization was made compulsory for all children in education. Over 7m children enrolled.

The PNF

Young Italians became members of the PNF proper at 21, an event solemnly marked by the *leva*, a rites of passage ceremony. PNF membership grew rapidly in the first half of the 1920s before efforts to purge the party of both its radical and opportunist elements reduced numbers from 900,000 (1926) to 800,000 (1931). Membership soared again, though, under Starace in the 1930s, peaking at around 2.5m at the end of 1939; it became impossible to work in the public sector or in the professions without a party card.

Spectacle

We briefly touched upon the importance of Fascist spectacle when looking at culturalist readings of Fascism in Chapter 4 – the use of rituals, myths, symbols, monuments, festivals, celebrations, commemorations, rallies, parades, art and architecture to bind Italian society to the Fascist state. Fascism propagated a number of important 'cults' through these means: the cult of the fallen hero and of the martyr, the cult of *Romanità*, and, most importantly, the cult of Mussolini. The cult of the fallen was not new nor unique to Fascism – the memorialization and commemoration of the dead of World War One, for example, was a world-wide phenomenon after 1918. For Fascism, though, the war was a vital element both in its self-representation and in its central messages: Fascism as a movement, party and idea was predicated on the war values of courage, violence, discipline, sacrifice and duty, the subordination of the interests of the individual to those of the state and through this, the self-realization of the individual. The war was to be celebrated for its role in bringing glory to Italy and Fascism to power, its dead to be held up as examples to the living. Thus school-trips took pupils to Italian World War One cemeteries and to the Alpine battle zones, while 'honorary guards' of schoolchildren looked after remembrance parks and monuments dedicated to the fallen. War cemeteries and memorials were built throughout the 1920s and 1930s, their inauguration an opportunity for the Fascists to meld politics with religion, Fascism with the state. Commemoration of the war dead was matched by the remembrance of Fascist 'martyrs' – those who had died for the 'black-shirt revolution' between 1919 and 1922. The roll call of Fascist dead was read on all Fascist anniversaries. An altar in their memory was built on the Capitoline Hill in Rome in 1926. The national headquarters of the PNF and every local branch office contained a shrine to the Fascist fallen. When the *Mostra della rivoluzione fascista* (Exhibition of the Fascist Revolution) to celebrate the tenth anniversary of the March on Rome opened in the capital in October 1932, prominence was given to its own chapel of the martyrs and to the 'altar of sacrifice'.

The cult of *Romanità*, as with the cult of the fallen, was not new or unique to Fascism: Italian nationalists had long argued Italy's right to independence, unification and Great Power status on the basis of Rome's past glories. Again, though, Fascism went further, determined to portray Fascist Italy as the 'new Rome' and Mussolini as the incarnation of Caesar or Augustus. The omnipresent symbol of Fascism, the *fascio littorio* – a bundle of bound rods tied to an axe – was a direct link to ancient Rome, where the *fascio* had been a symbol of authority and unity. The 'Roman salute', the use by the regime of the symbols of the eagle and the wolf, the adoption of Roman military terms (Legionaries, Centurions, Consuls etc.) in the Fascist Militia, the aping of classical architecture, the construction in Rome of the *via dei Fori Imperiali* linking the Colosseum to the Capitoline and to Mussolini's own offices in the Palazzo Venezia – opened on the same day in October 1937 as the *Mostra Augustea della Romanità* to celebrate the two thousandth anniversary of the birth of Augustus – all served to emphasize the links between Italy's past, present (and future) greatness. According to Bottai, Fascism was 'a revolution in the very idea of Rome'.[10]

The most powerful cult, however, was that surrounding the person of Mussolini himself. As Mussolini's political power grew over the Fascist party in the late 1920s and through the 1930s, so too did the cult of the *Duce* (or DUCE, as Starace insisted it be written). Mussolini literally became an 'overwhelming presence'[11] in Italy: posters and stencils of Mussolini could be found on virtually every street; his image featured on millions of postcards, on clothes, it was reproduced in books and on calendars, it found its way even onto bars of soap. Mussolini was photographed as sportsman, musician, intellectual, soldier, peasant, statesman. The lights in his office in the Palazzo Venezia remained on all night, giving rise to the myth that Mussolini never slept. The 1932 *Mostra della rivoluzione fascista* was dominated by Mussolini: the cover of the Exhibition catalogue featured a bust of Mussolini and the repeated call of DU-CE, DU-CE. Through each room of the *Mostra* 'the leader's words drove the historical narrative'.[12] The exhibition was but one example of the increasing tendency to present Mussolini as a 'living God': he was presented to the public as a man *with* but not *of* the people – alone and aloof, often literally raised above the masses on balconies, platforms, on horseback (normally astride a white horse); he was infallible (Italians were constantly reminded that 'Mussolini ha sempre ragione' – Mussolini is always right); even bread provided by Fascist welfare emphasized that Mussolini was no ordinary man – inscribed with the legend 'Pane del *Duce'* (Bread of the *Duce*), the allusion to Christ and the Feeding of the Five Thousand was obvious.[13]

Work and leisure

The Fascist presence was clearly felt in the workplace. In 1925 the Confederation of Fascist Corporations was legally recognized as the sole representative of labour. Non-Fascist unions were dissolved in 1926. In theory, workers and employers were to be united within the framework of the much-trumpeted Corporate State but the Confederation of Fascist Corporations was broken up in 1928 and the interests of employers always took precedence over the demands of the workers. The regime's control over the labour market allowed it to cut industrial and agrarian wages during the late 1920s and early 1930s. Fascism also sought to organize labour outside of the workplace. The *Opera nazionale dopolovaro* (OND), the National After-work Agency, established in 1925, was to prove one of the regime's most popular innovations. Originally conceived as a means by which Fascist ideology and productivist techniques could be disseminated to the masses, by the late 1920s the OND had dispensed with such lofty ambitions in favour of the provision of 'bread and circuses' – welfare assistance and diversionary entertainment – to keep an increasingly impoverished population happy. The OND could boast 4m members by 1939.

The workplace itself was viewed by the regime as very much a male domain. Although early Fascism had toyed with the idea of equal rights for women, Fascist policy towards women throughout the *ventennio* was consistently and profoundly anti-emancipatory in character. From a Fascist perspective, a woman 'was fundamentally defined and confined by her biology'; her role was that of mother and housewife, augmenting the Italian stock and maintaining the family unit.[14] Yet, 'ironically it was Fascism, with its emphasis on virility and the male domination of society, that first sought to engage women on a large scale in the life of the Italian nation'.[15] Women were to be active participants in Fascism, albeit within the context of the home, responsive to the demands of the state. There was a need, then, to mobilize women under Fascism. A number of mass organizations for women were duly established for this purpose. The most important of these were the *Fasci femminili* and the *Massaie rurali*. The *Fasci femminili*, established in the 1920s, was a predominantly urban-based, middle-class movement, involved in charitable work and the promotion of women's moral welfare (i.e. in emphasizing women's biological and family responsibilities). The *Massaie rurali*, established in 1934 and directed by the *Fasci femminili* was, as the name suggests, an organization for rural housewives. The *Massaie rurali* was set up to promote the regime's policies of ruralization, demographic growth and, from 1935, autarchy (it encouraged small-scale farming and craft manufacturing). In pursuit of victory in the 'Battle for births', declared by Mussolini in 1927, the regime – with the support of the Catholic Church – devoted ever more time and money to getting women out of the workplace, up the aisle and into the matrimonial bed. On the one hand, restrictions were placed on women's employment and women's wages were reduced. On the other, a celibacy tax to discourage bachelorhood was imposed on single men in 1927, preference in public employment was increasingly given to married men (especially to those with large families), interest-free marriage loans were introduced in 1937 (the debt written off if a couple produced four children), and marriage and fertility prizes were awarded on the *giornata della madre e del fanciullo* (mother and child day) – an annual event instigated by the regime in 1933 and held two days before Christmas. In a related effort to reduce levels of infant mortality, the regime also pumped funds into the *Opera nazionale di maternità ed infanzia* (ONMI, the National Agency of Maternity and Infancy) established in 1925 to improve prenatal and antenatal care.

Culture

The often brutal character of *squadrismo*, including physical attacks on leading intellectuals such as Piero Gobbetti, early on gave Fascism a reputation as an anti-culture movement. Yet Fascist hierarchs recognized the need to show that Fascism 'besides having faith and muscle also has a brain', and after the establishment of the dictatorship it set out to 'dismantle completely and once and for all the stupid legend of the incompatibility of Fascism and culture'.[16] Initial efforts proved counterproductive. The *Manifesto of Fascist Intellectuals* (April 1925), written largely by Giovanni Gentile and signed by the leading cultural figures within Fascism (though, as Lyttleton notes, not all the 250 signatories could 'claim to represent "culture" or "the intellectuals"') did little to clarify the regime's cultural intentions and served only to provoke an alternative *Manifesto of Anti-Fascist Intellectuals* (May 1925), written by Benedetto Croce and signed by such intellectual heavyweights as Salvemini, Luigi Einaudi and Piero Calamandrei. 'The result of the two manifestos was undoubtedly a moral defeat for Fascism.'[17] Despite this early setback, the regime continued to emphasize that 'Fascism is not anti-intellectual or anti-culture', though it sought 'to infuse culture with the severe and profound spirit of discipline which is found in the barracks'.[18] Consequently, the second half of the 1920s saw the creation of the National Fascist Institute of Culture (established in 1925) under Gentile, the Royal Italian Academy (announced in 1926, inaugurated in 1929), and the Corporation of Intellectuals, later reconstituted and renamed the Confederation of Professionals and Artists, membership of which was an essential precondition of Fascist patronage. Existing cultural institutions such as the highbrow *Società Dante Alighieri* were also fascistized. Further Fascist cultural organizations were established in the 1930s. Only in the mid-1930s, however, specifically with the creation of the Ministry of Popular Culture, did Fascism begin to insist on cultural uniformity.

The Fascist state also made its presence felt in the cultural sphere as an enthusiastic and generous patron of the arts. It promoted theatre and opera: state-funded *carri di tespi* (thespian cars) and *carri lirici* (lyric cars) toured the country bringing drama and opera to the masses; the OND encouraged amateur dramatics; traditionally bourgeois theatre houses were opened up to the working class with cut-price 'theatrical Saturdays'. The visual arts were well served by state patronage, too. Major exhibitions of the visual arts were staged in Venice, Rome and Milan (the Venice *Biennale*, of which the Venice Film Festival – first held in 1932 – was a part, had an international reputation). Artists could also take advantage of major state commissions. The state was a consumer of art: throughout the 1930s a '2 per cent' rule applied to all state building projects, i.e. 2 per cent of the overall construction's costs were to be spent on art. Such projects were, of course, also good business for favoured architects. Finally, there were the one-off celebrations of Fascism, the *Mostra* of 1932 the best example, on which no expense was spared and which engaged the services of a number of prominent Italian artists, architects and designers.

Debates

De Felice and consensus

We have looked at *Gli anni del consenso*, the fourth volume of De Felice's biography of Mussolini, in Chapter 4. We have seen how De Felice's presentation of Mussolini as would-be architect of a new Fascist civilization and his insistence on Mussolini's realist conception of international affairs generated considerable controversy at the time and subsequently. There was a third element to De Felice's study that provoked as much debate: his claim that in the years 1929–34 there existed a 'mass consensus' (*consenso di massa*) behind Fascism. In the wake of the Lateran accords, and despite the onset of the Great Depression:

> The great majority of Italians did not substantially question the authority of the state; the 'moral model' of fascism was largely accepted...the politics of the regime on the whole did not appear dangerous, irrational...the man in the street, the 'good citizen', finally, had as yet relatively little direct contact with the party, and so his private life was not touched by it – for the moment – or very rarely and then not in a heavy manner...the benefits, real or presumed, which the regime procured for him were on the whole greater than the disadvantages... All things considered, it is correct to affirm that the five year period '29–34 was for the regime and, in substance, also for Mussolini, the moment of greatest consensus and of greatest solidity.[19]

Although the regime would later bask in the popular acclaim which accompanied the conquest of Ethiopia in 1936, by then the consensus behind Fascism was, according to De Felice, less 'complete' than that of the earlier period. Italians were more worried about the future, desirous 'to draw breath' after the war, and uncomfortable with the apparent direction of domestic policy (the regime's totalitarian aspiration to transform Italian society; the intrusion of the state into the private sphere). Even then, however, the regime was never in any serious difficulty, he argued; there was no reason to believe that it might fall in the near future.

The working class

By 'consensus', De Felice did not mean that the mass of Italians had become 'true fascists', active participants in the political life of the country and 'propulsive elements' within the structure of the regime.[20] Instead, he argued, the regime had achieved only the 'passive fascistization' of Italian society. Consensus equalled compliance, conformity, the (conditional) support of the masses for the regime.[21] Nevertheless, it did mean that the regime had been successful in bringing those social groups previously hostile or indifferent to Fascism – here De Felice really meant the working class – within its orbit. The acquiescence of the working class, De Felice wrote, could be shown by an examination of demonstrations that took place between 1929 and 1933. This, he argued, indicated that collective protest, whether work-related or to do with issues beyond the factory, was always 'exquisitely economic' in character. The unemployed demanded work or assistance, the employed protested against the tax burden, but there were never political protests directed against the regime or Mussolini. De Felice pointed out that even in Turin, Italy's most industrial city and a former socialist stronghold, women on a protest march of the unemployed were reported to have shouted 'Viva il *Duce*! But we want to eat!'[22]

According to De Felice, those workers who remained employed during the Depression years actually had little cause for complaint. While industrial salaries fell in nominal terms (i.e. pay packets were reduced), in real terms (i.e. in terms of their purchasing power) they either increased or, at least, remained unaltered. This was because the fall in the cost of living (the fall in prices) either matched or exceeded the fall in nominal wages between 1929 and 1935. On this basis, argued De Felice, 'It is difficult to sustain that living conditions of employed industrial workers worsened in the years of the Great Depression'.[23]

The working class, De Felice acknowledged, did not adhere to Fascism, but it had little option other than to accept Fascism. The underground PCI within Italy was brought to its knees in the early 1930s because of a concerted police crackdown against militant organizations. Other anti-Fascist groups were too small to be of significance or, like the PCI, were broken by the police. Besides, claimed De Felice, the workers were aware not only that the Great Depression was a global crisis, and were thus to an extent resigned to the situation in which they found themselves, but they also recognized that the regime and the PNF *were* taking measures to mitigate its effects. Public works projects employed hundreds of thousands of men. The *dopolavoro* provided cheap recreational activities and entertainment and social assistance. Even the Fascist syndicates seemed able to defend workers' interests. Workers thus came to see some *advantage* in Fascist organizations. And what was true for the working class, De Felice wrote, was equally true for the rest of Italian society. The results of plebiscitary elections in 1934, in which Italians were asked to endorse the list of new parliamentary deputies selected by the Fascist Grand Council, were 'truly unanimous' and 'corresponded to the Italian reality of that moment': over 96 per cent of the electorate voted, more than 10m in support of the regime, just 15,000 against.[24]

De Felice was not the first to identify a popular consensus behind Fascism – foreign journalists, for example, had written in a similar vein at the time. De Felice's claim in the mid-1970s, however, certainly hit a nerve. Many Italians clung to Churchill's notion of 'one man alone' when remembering Fascism (if they chose to remember it at all) – the idea that Italians were not responsible for Fascism and, indeed, could be regarded as its victims (an example of what Ruth Ben-Ghiat terms collective 'memory (re-) construction').[25] At a general level, then, De Felice's interpretation was unlikely to be particularly welcome. In emphasizing the acquiescence of the working class in particular, however, De Felice deliberately challenged the Marxist/PCI historical orthodoxy that emphasized 'the dogged and stubborn resistance of the industrial working class to the blandishments of the regime'.[26] In the post-war Republic, the 'spontaneous' anti-Fascism of its members and constituents gave the PCI both political legitimacy (the 'right' to govern) and a first line of defence against attacks from conservative opponents, notably the Christian Democrats, who questioned its democratic and patriotic credentials. (Had not the PCI 'saved' Italy from Fascist and Nazi dictatorship; had not the sacrifices of the PCI made possible the new Italy?) Not for the first time, De Felice's reading of Italy's recent history had contemporary political resonance. The Marxist response to *Gli anni del consenso* (and the subsequent *Intervista sul fascismo*) was, as we have seen, predictably hostile.

Marxists, it should be noted, did/do not necessarily believe that the Italian working class were able to resist successfully *all* Fascist incursions. In his 1935 series of lectures on Fascism, Palmiro Togliatti, the leader-in-exile of the PCI, admitted the success of the *dopolavoro* in attracting working-class participation. 'What do local *dopolavori* do?' he asked. 'They carry on a whole series of activities. The benefits the workers have are manifest... We cannot inveigh against the worker who agrees to enter...for the mere fact that the Fascist symbol is on the door'. Togliatti urged communist cells in Italy to infiltrate *dopolavoro* clubs precisely because they were frequented by the working class. In 1946, Emilio Sereni wrote that Fascism had 'disorganized' the working class, commenting that 'disorganized masses necessarily are and become less conscious masses'. In the 1990s, De Felice's contemporary and arch-critic, Nicola Tranfaglia, acknowledged that the working class under Fascism had been 'constrained to oscillate between acceptance of the rites and norms of the dictatorship and protest often subterranean and indirect'. Tranfaglia was even prepared to accept that 'the new generations – those born and educated during the regime – accept[ed] the passwords and the astonishing promises of the *Duce* and for them...one can speak of enthusiasm and of faith', although this quickly dissipated in the face of war and the German alliance. None of this, however, amounted to a real and true consent since there were no alternatives from which to choose.[27]

Not all Marxist historians have conceded as much. For example, Tobias Abse (1996) has insisted that the notion of a 'high degree of working-class acceptance of, or complicity with, Fascism' is mistaken, despite the popularity of the *dopolavoro* with a 'very significant minority' of the workforce. According to Abse, a 'subversive tradition' (*tradizione sovversiva*) existed within the Italian working class that effectively immunized it from Fascism. This was a working class which had long since demonstrated its alienation from the state and the nation (it had opposed the war in 1915) and its anti-Fascist credentials (in 1921–2 it had ignored the 'absurd pacifism' of the PSI leadership and the sectarianism of the PCI bosses and instead had united in 'mass violent resistance' against the Fascist squads). Neither Fascism's unions nor its youth and mass leisure organizations were able to legitimate it in the eyes of the working class. Because of the backwardness of Italian industry, 'Taylorist' and 'Fordist' mass production techniques, which encouraged interworker competition, made little headway in Italy and thus 'older working-class traditions based on collective identity and shared antagonism to the employer, associated with *sovversivismo*' survived. That the *tradizione sovversiva* of the working classes remained intact through the Fascist period was demonstrated, Abse argued, in the 'remarkable' mass strikes directed against the regime in Turin and Milan (March–April 1943) following Allied bombing raids. Abse suggested that only the existence of a *tradizione sovversiva* could explain why the Italian working class did not unite behind the war effort after the bombings in the same way that the British and German working classes did in similar circumstances. Here, then, was a modern Marxist counter to the 'avowedly apologetic' interpretation of Fascism offered by De Felice.[28]

Abse, in his portrayal of a heroic Italian working class standing united and alone against Fascism, was clearly fighting the historiographical tide by the mid-1990s, his work following in the wake of influential studies by Luisa Passerini and Victoria de Grazia that questioned the solidarity of the Italian working class in the inter-war period and its ability to resist Fascism.[29]

Passerini's groundbreaking research (conducted between the late 1970s and early 1980s) on popular memory and Fascism, and based on the oral testimonies of 67 Turin workers, sought to reconstruct the everyday experience of working-class life under Fascism. For Passerini, the (Marxist) stereotype of a working class 'totally opposed to the existing order', was without foundation. The reality was of a working class internally divided 'along the lines of age, skill, family social position', of which a 'large part' was 'only marginally or occasionally concerned with politics'. Furthermore, in the accounts given by her interviewees there were 'important signs of acceptance' of Fascism, and a marked ambivalence towards the figure of Mussolini himself. Even acts of hostility towards Fascism, such as anti-Fascist jokes, graffiti, parodies and songs, could not be seen simply 'as acts of resistance to Fascism', but also 'as compensations for the fact that people had pragmatically accepted the regime'. Equally, though, to talk of working-class 'consent' was misleading since individuals were engaged in a process of constant negotiation with the dictatorship. 'In their day-to-day choices,' wrote Passerini, people 'took account of the demands made on them by the regime, and the resources it offered, assessing in turn what it was opportune to accept and what not'; 'Every day everyone negotiates spaces of advantage or resistance with Fascist power...according to the moment, to family traditions, to the relations of force'. Sometimes this might entail a public but not a private commitment to Fascism (e.g. the boy who stopped misbehaving on *Balilla* parades to spare his father from being reproached by the authorities for his son's ill discipline). At other times, it might involve a private acceptance of, but not a public involvement in, Fascism (e.g. the man who, thanks to the good offices of a family acquaintance in one of the Fascist unions, did not himself have to join the union). Either way, it was representative of the 'deep conflict within individuals and hence also within the collectivity in the face of the dictatorial regime', a fact that previous studies of the working class had failed properly to understand or recognize.[30]

From a more traditional 'top-down' historical perspective, Victoria de Grazia's 1982 investigation into the origins, evolution and role of the *dopolavoro* and the creation of a 'culture of consent' within Fascist Italy also concluded that the working class had not remained insensible to the regime's efforts to 'reach out to the people' in the 1930s. For the working class, the effects of the nationalization of popular culture were extremely damaging.[31] Fascism proved adept at appropriating previously autonomous popular pastimes which had taken place at the local level and had 'lent cohesiveness to the working class community', repackaging them in a national, non-class-specific context within the ambit of state authority. Thus, for example, the game of *bocce* (bowls), 'closely identified with working-class sociability', and (because of the many local variations in rules) parochialism, was transformed into a 'national' sport by the OND, with a nationwide network of provincial and regional bodies abiding by a single code. This was not all. Besides 'the assimilation of previously autonomous working-class associations into the mainstream of national life', the *dopolavoro* entailed the 'homogenization of popular culture through contact with the mass media; the separation of recreational clubs from job-related organizations and union halls; the depoliticization of leisure pursuits'. (De Grazia argued that efforts by the PCI to infiltrate *dopolavoro* clubs in order to politicize the working class came to nothing not least because it was difficult to give political meaning to a demand for more sports.) De Grazia also identified a generational crisis within the working class. Young workers in the 1930s, with no direct experience of the 'red years', familiar only with Fascist organizations and 'consumers' of leisure (provided by the state) in a way that older workers were not, were necessarily distanced from the post-war 'red' generation.[32] While not actively Fascist, neither were they anti-Fascist.[33] In De Grazia's opinion, the *dopolavoro* achieved its aims: it fostered 'passivity, ignorance, individualism, traditionalism, evasion', which was enough for a regime that for much of the time 'was perfectly satisfied with silence, no matter whether this masked indifference or disapproval'. Of course, given that the OND did not possess a political bone in its elephantine body, it was unable actually to mobilize the masses – a problem for the regime at it pursued increasingly radical (and unpopular) domestic and foreign policy objectives in the mid-late 1930s.[34]

Other studies of the Italian working class, produced in the late 1980s and 1990s, reinforced the picture of class fragmentation in the face of Fascism. According to Maurizio Gribaudi and Giuseppe Berta, generational divisions fatally undermined working-class solidarities in Turin.[35] From a more general perspective, Paul Corner emphasized how existing tensions between skilled and unskilled workers, 'old' established workers and 'new' immigrant workers, urban-based workers and worker-peasant 'commuters' (those who continued to work on the land as well as in the factories) were exacerbated under Fascism. New work practices, he argued, helped to fracture old loyalties. High unemployment from the late 1920s bred competition for jobs – competition that tended to favour young workers over older labour.[36] The desperation of many workers meanwhile presented the regime with the opportunity to 'assert itself among the working class in a way which had not previously been possible' through its welfare, assistance, recreational and public works programmes. In this sense, the Depression 'served to reinforce the hand of dictatorship'. Did the working class support Fascism? Corner thought not (he was particularly keen to dismiss De Felice's claim that workers' standards of living had risen during the 'years of consensus' and thus had cause to back the regime). Fragmented, defeated and isolated, the 'relative quiescence of the Italian working class' – its 'resignation, passivity, even impotence' – during the years of the Great Depression had, however, to be acknowledged. The 'politicization of the working class in an anti-fascist direction' – in fact, the establishment of the working class as a serious, sustainable political force – had to wait until the catastrophe of World War Two and occupation.[37]

The attitude of the working class towards Fascism was but the most contentious aspect of De Felice's 'mass consensus' thesis. Leaving aside whether or not De Felice was right to talk of the 'passive fascistization' of the working class, what was the impact of Fascism upon other significant sections of Italian society? The middle classes and the petit bourgeoisie were the Fascists' natural constituencies. The industrial and agrarian élites sided with the regime. Youth, most historians agreed with De Felice, was Fascist by default (it knew nothing else) but in the main young people were not dedicated followers of Fascism. Was it possible to argue, though, that the peasantry accepted Fascism? De Felice had next to nothing to say on the subject. And what of Italian women – the silent majority in De Felice's account (there were more women than men in Fascist Italy but *Gli anni del consenso* was very much a *his*tory) – how did they experience and respond to Fascism?

The peasantry

> The gentry were all Party members, even the few...who were dissenters. The Party stood for Power...and they felt entitled to a share of it. For exactly the opposite reason none of the peasants were members; indeed, it was unlikely that they should belong to any political party whatever, should, by chance, another exist. They were not Fascists...or anything else. Such matters had nothing to do with them; they belonged to another world and they saw no sense in them.
>
> To the peasants the state is more distant than heaven and far more of a scourge, because it is always against them... Their only defence against the state and the propaganda of the state is resignation, the same gloomy resignation, alleviated by no hope of paradise, that bows their shoulders under the scourges of nature.
>
> For this reason, quite naturally, they have no conception of a political struggle.[38]

In 1935, the anti-Fascist intellectual Carlo Levi was sentenced to internal exile in the Basilicata region of southern Italy. Levi's memoir of his *confino*, in a part of Italy forsaken – so its inhabitants said – even by Christ, was published immediately after World War Two to universal and lasting acclaim. Levi's depiction of a world 'hedged in by custom and sorrow, cut off from History and the state, eternally patient...without comfort or solace, where the peasant lives out his motionless civilization on barren ground in remote poverty, and in the presence of death', remains a remarkable literary and moral *tour de force*. Its impact in political, social and historiographical terms has been considerable. The reawakening of the 'Southern Question' – or what Levi described as the 'death-like existence' of the peasantry – after twenty years of Fascist neglect was due, at least in part, to Levi's work. Nonetheless, Levi reinforced the traditional view of the southern peasant as backward, superstitious, irrational and premodern. Only in recent decades has this perspective been challenged by historians (see Chapters 2 and 9). Levi's account offered a powerful critique, too, of the limits of Fascist power. The southern peasant class was indifferent to the conquest of Ethiopia and considered Rome 'the centre of a foreign and hostile world'. The local élite was 'Fascist' in name only. The one monument to Fascism in the village was the unused public toilet.[39] Historical research has yet to gainsay Levi in this respect.[40] A couple of examples will suffice: Jonathan Steinberg's 1986 study of Calabria in the early Fascist era and De Grazia's work on the OND which looked at length at Fascism's attempts to use the mass leisure organization to (in Mussolini's words) 'penetrate the vast masses of silent and industrious peasants'. Steinberg found little evidence of Fascism within Calabria prior to the March on Rome, a fact he attributed to the poverty and backwardness of the region.[41] He did discern, though, a tenacious, flexible and unscrupulous local ruling class quick to adapt itself to Fascism (as it had done to liberalism and was to do, after 1945, to Christian Democracy) in order to retain power. Calabrian politics thus remained, to all intents and purposes, unaltered.[42] For the poor, illiterate, dialect-speaking peasant majority nothing changed, at least not for the better. The peasantry remained 'beyond the reach of Fascism' for the lifetime of the regime. De Grazia, meanwhile, had found that lack of funds allied to the absolute poverty of the peasants, the rigid caste and patronage system of southern society, the lack of pre-existing peasant organizations on which the OND could build, and the resistance of traditional southern élite and bourgeois associations to the encroachment of the OND, meant the *dopolavoro* made little headway in the rural south. There were, for example, only 39 peasant members of the OND in Basilicata in 1927; there were just 76,664 peasant members of the OND in the whole of the south and islands (out of an active agricultural population of 3.3m) in 1932. *Dopolavoro* clubhouses, if they existed, 'were rarely supplied with radios or reading materials, or sponsored the organized pastimes common in the north'; instead they 'served simply as a gathering place, its members frequently without even a card as token sign of allegiance to the regime'.[43]

De Grazia also questioned the depth of the relationship between Fascism and the peasantry of northern and central Italy. In the north, the creation of a mass peasant middle class of smallholders around the time of World War One and concentrated in Lombardy, Emilia and in the Veneto had provided Fascism with many of its first supporters; these new landowners did not intend to let the social-ists deprive them of their property. Yet, as De Grazia noted, Fascist deflationary policies from the mid-1920s forced many small farmers who had purchased land on credit to sell up – despite the fact that land values had, in some cases, halved. Actual enthusiasm for Fascism – never widespread – was thus short-lived.[44] The OND, however, was always more successful in attracting peasant members in the northern countryside than in the south, helped by those factors that were largely absent in the Mezzogiorno: a tradition of peasant organization, 'modern' socio-economic conditions, a landowning class and a local bourgeoisie generally well disposed towards the OND, and 'the combination of novel urban recreational pastimes and aids to agricultural improvement' offered by many northern (but few southern) *dopolavoro* clubs. Even in the north, though, rural membership grew slowly and the presence of the *dopolavoro* varied considerably from one area to the next.[45]

The regime idealized the rural community, but all accounts concur on the pro-gressive impoverishment of rural society under Fascism as the prices of many agricultural products collapsed and rural wages fell, the latter by as much as 40 per cent in the early 1930s. Even De Felice recognized that in the first half of the 1930s, 'in respect to other sectors, agriculture finished up the most disad-vantaged... As to the living and working conditions in the various agricultural categories, it is easy to understand how, in a general situation of this type, no substantial changes were seen and, in fact, often worsened on the economic level'.[46] Fascism, it would seem, hardly satisfied even the basic needs of the peas-ants – and yet, De Felice had argued, popular consensus rested in part on the Fascists' ability to benefit rather than disadvantage Italian society.

Women

The consensus issue, such a prevalent feature of studies of the working class under Fascism, rarely features in the historiography of women in the Fascist era.[47] Instead, studies tend to echo Passerini: women's experiences of Fascism were necessarily varied (within and between classes and according to age, geogra-phy, family, education, marriage status, the number of children, the relationship to the world of work); their responses to Fascism were complex and contradictory, the product of day-to-day, issue-by-issue, negotiation with the regime. Historians have also been quick to point out that the experiences of women under Fascism should not be conflated with women's experience of Fascism. As Perry Willson has written, 'Politics in Fascist Italy failed to have the great impact on daily life that "Big Brother" theorists of totalitarianism might have us believe'. Indeed, in Willson's detailed account of women's working life at the Magneti Marelli factory in Sesto San Giovanni near Milan, Fascism is very much in the background.[48]

What is the picture that emerges from the historical studies of women under Fascism? Fascist policies consistently and deliberately discriminated against women. Only as wives and, more importantly, mothers, did Italian women enjoy the support of the regime. Nonetheless:

- *Women were often confronted by contradictory and confusing Fascist messages.* Women were to be both modern and traditional – they were encouraged to participate in Fascist mass organizations, to compete and participate in sports, but at the same time they were told to accept the 'passive domesticity' of motherhood. Women were important to Fascism, and by extension, the state, as 'prolific mothers' but were not recognized as citizens. Working women were castigated for abandoning their proper duties but the often 'arduous quest' for state welfare also took women away from the home and undermined the integrity of the family unit.[49]
- *While women were prepared to engage with Fascism they were also ready to ignore Fascist policies and laws.* Women's organizations did recruit in large numbers. The *Massaie rurali* boasted a membership of 2.5m in 1942. There were over 1.3m girls and women enrolled in the various groups of the *Fasci femminili* by 1934. Women were active in these organizations, too: a quarter of members took part in the 6,000 training programmes provided by the *Massaie rurali* in 1937. And women did listen to Mussolini. In March 1936, for example, thousands of women responded to the *Duce*'s call to help finance the war effort in Ethiopia by giving up their wedding rings – and any other items of gold – to the dictatorship. Over 2,000 kg of gold were collected. However, most women simply refused to go along with the Fascists' demographic campaign, the 'Battle for births', launched in 1927. The long-term decline in birth rates continued throughout the Fascist period: from 39 births per thousand people in the 1880s to 29.9 (1921–5), 27.1 (1926–30), 24 (1931–5), 23.4 (1936–40) and 19.9 (1941–5). So lacklustre was the response to the campaign that in 1933 the *Duce*, whose original declared aim had been to increase the population to 60m by 1950, was forced to set a revised target of 50m. Economic realism and sociocultural factors explain women's resistance. Economic hardship obliged many women to work and encouraged couples to practise birth control. The financial incentives to have large families were, for most women, insufficient compensation for the cost of raising several more children. Falling birth rates accompanied growing literacy and urbanization, both long-term trends that Fascism was unable to reverse. Passerini has also argued that for the working-class women of Turin the idea of large families was negatively associated with 'southerness' and thus frowned upon. The most drastic form of birth control – abortion – was commonly practised during the Fascist period (Passerini has suggested abortion rates actually increased in Turin) despite being declared a crime against the Italian 'stock' and punishable by imprisonment. The lack of information available to women about birth control – the dissemination of such information was itself a criminal offence – may also have contributed to a rise in the number of abortions. Women's refusal to follow Fascist strictures on procreation was not, according to Passerini, evidence of political dissent, even though in her study many female interviewees attached an anti-Fascist meaning to their actions. Passerini attributed this to 'The constant stress on the importance of anti-fascism in Italian history in the last decades, and, more recently on the question of the liberation of women'.[50] Many women, primarily for economic reasons, also carried on working throughout the Fascist period, despite the regime's active discouragement through legislation and propaganda. Female employment as a proportion of the working population did fall

under Fascism – part of a long-term trend – but in the 1930s women still constituted over a quarter of the workforce.[51]

- *Modern mass consumer culture and traditional Catholicism presented women with alternative messages to Fascism.* The values, behaviour and appearance of the modern urban American woman portrayed in Hollywood movies and the new pulp magazines competed with – and won out over – the submissive, passive, rural and maternal image of women put forward by Fascism. Associated with this, De Grazia has talked of the 'fundamental tension between the collectivist imagery of massed forces and the pursuit of exclusiveness and individuality typical of the workings of the modern fashion industry', which emerged (albeit slowly) during the inter-war period. The state also found it difficult to regulate female leisure time, if and where it existed. Traditional gender segregation (especially strong in the south) meant women generally did not use the male-dominated OND; only 10 per cent of OND members in 1930 were women. Instead, women's leisure was bound up either with the home – sewing and embroidery were popular – or, particularly in the case of urban women, with 'the free floating sociability of commercial cultural pastimes'. This new, 'unabashedly secular, [and] cosmopolitan' mass culture was 'the real pacesetter in forming the new girl peer culture'. Cinema, in particular, afforded 'a kind of imaginary space...[offering] possibilities of individual development practically impervious to the clumsy discipline of traditional state, community, or familial authorities'. As regards the Church, at least half a million girls and women were enrolled in Catholic organizations at the end of the 1930s and the Church remained an important social centre in rural areas. Church views on women more often than not chimed with Fascist policies but Catholic culture and the Vatican's anti-modernizing agenda were still distinct from, and sometimes contrary to, the message of Fascism. For example, the Fascist determination to, as De Grazia puts it, 'put female youth on public display' in rallies, gymnastic exhibitions and sports competitions was condemned as immoral by the Church.[52]

- *It is possible to identify positive aspects to the female experience in the inter-war years.* Not just commercialization but also industrialization and urbanization were important modernizing influences on many Italian women during the inter-war period. Some women who worked found self-value and dignity as workers. Others saw their status within the family improve because of their employment in industry. Paul Corner, looking at the role of women within share-cropping families of northern Lombardy, has argued that the importance of the industrial economy in the early twentieth century meant that factory work, once regarded as 'women's work' and subordinate to agriculture ('men's work'), began to attract growing numbers of male workers and thus took on a new significance for men. This, and the increasingly capitalist and entrepreneurial outlook of share-cropping families in the early twentieth century – which ultimately was to give rise to the economic success story of the 'Third Italy' after 1945 – meant that work by women and their ability *to earn* received greater recognition from male family members. The result, Corner suggests, was a less subordinate role for women within the family and a corresponding decline in the authority of the male head of the household.[53]

  Although clearly misogynist, Fascism did provide women with new opportunities. For many girls the mass Fascist youth organizations and associated recreational activities provided a social space away from the family for the first time. The encouragement given to women by the Massaie rurali to produce goods for market consumption ultimately allowed peasant women an independent source of income and hence a greater degree of autonomy; many women did benefit from the modernization and professionalization of antenatal and postnatal healthcare through ONMI. None of this is to deny or diminish the generally repressive political, social, economic, cultural and political context within which Italian women lived – any benefits accruing to women as women (as opposed to mothers or wives) from Fascist organizations or policies were purely unintentional from the regime's point of view. Rather, it demonstrates that women were not simply passive victims of Fascism, or of dominant social mores. Nor is it meant to imply that women's experiences can be generalized. Some but by no means all women found work to be a positive experience. ONMI's presence and influence varied wildly across the country and affected women in radically different ways. Mass consumerism affected urban women more than their rural counterparts (De Grazia says that working-class girls were particularly avid consumers of magazines and movies). Middle-class girls were more exposed to Fascism than were working-class or peasant girls because they stayed in school longer. The influence of Catholicism remained strongest in rural Italy.[54]

Fascism and culture

The study of Italian culture under Fascism is marked by basic agreement on the actuality of Fascist cultural policy but significant disagreement over how this should be interpreted as, over the last two decades, culturalist readings of Italian Fascism have increasingly challenged traditional views of Fascism as acultural or even anti-cultural.

All historians agree that in the field of high culture – the 'arts' (i.e. painting, sculpture, architecture, drama, music, serious literature) – Fascism was not especially repressive. For most of the *ventennio* there existed 'a relatively open cultural climate'. Censorship and regulation certainly existed, but the state preferred the carrot (commissions, prizes, subsidies) to the stick, or simply left cultural producers alone 'to live undisturbed at the margins of society'.[55] Fascism did not prescribe or proscribe particular aesthetic styles. Indeed, what marks out high cultural production under Fascism from that under Nazism or Soviet communism is its sheer diversity. There was no 'state art', for example; instead, modernists (Futurists, Rationalists, Neo-Impressionists, Expressionists, Abstract artists), competed with the 'Magic Realists' of the *Novecento* movement ('Magic Realism' combined elements of modernism with traditional themes), the more conservative naturalist-realist *Strapaese* movement (eulogizing *ruralità*) and the decidedly retro Neo-Classicists (who spent their time aping the ancients). The 1932 *Mostra* featured major contributions from the Rationalists, the *novecentisti*, the *strapaesani* and the Futurists.

Similarly, in the realms of 'low' or 'popular' culture – light entertainment (cinema, radio and popular theatre) – there is little evidence of a clear Fascist presence (it is difficult to comment on popular literature because so little has been written on the subject). The 1932 Venice *Biennale* staged its first Film Festival in the presence of glamorous Hollywood stars Greta Garbo and Lionel Barrymore. In 1935, Walt Disney's *The Band Concert,* featuring Mickey Mouse, left Venice with the golden medal for best animation. Even after foreign cartoons were banned in Italy in 1938, Disney strips continued to be published and Mickey – known as *Topolino* in Italy – continued to feature in his own comic until early 1942. Mussolini himself apparently found time to watch the Disney film of *Pinocchio* in 1940.[56] Radio advertising was banned in 1937 but the broadcasting association (EIAR) got round this with the introduction of programme sponsorship, ensuring that a commercial presence was maintained. The thespian and lyric cars may have covered tens of thousands of miles and performed in front of millions of spectators, but they brought mainly traditional theatre and opera to the masses.

What should we make of Fascism's attitude towards, and role and influence in, cultural production? How should we interpret its policy of 'aesthetic pluralism'?[57] This largely depends on how one perceives Fascist ideology. For Marxists it represented yet another example of Fascism's elaborate use of smoke and mirrors to confuse and defeat the masses. From the liberal/non-Marxist 'egoist' perspective that Fascism lacked any ideological consistency or coherency, the absence of a clear statement of Fascist culture, and the 'proliferation of conflicting styles' in, for example, visual arts, finds its explanation in that very lack of ideological rigour. If Fascism was unable to define itself then how could it have a definable culture? Taking this one stage further, if Fascism did not steer by ideological compass, but was driven instead by opportunism and pragmatism, then should not its cultural politics be seen in this light, too? Fascism, so the argument runs, was anxious not to alienate Italian intellectuals, especially since the public relations disaster of the *Manifesto of Anti-Fascist Intellectuals.* By its generous patronage of the arts, by welcoming any artist or intellectual who was prepared to pay lip service to Fascism, the regime acquired a degree of cultural legitimacy both in Italy and abroad, and the acquiescence of the intellectual and artistic community at home. Culture, then, was simply another instrument of propaganda and control, modernism a convenient cloak so long as it suited the regime's interests to appear modern. If anything, Fascism was instinctively anti-culture, and anti-modern: its brutality, its obsession with *ruralità* and *Romanità,* its growing preference in the 1930s for neo-classical design (ending up with the 'hyper-Romanism' of the never completed EUR project[58]) and its alliance with anti-cultural, anti-modern Nazism all seem to point in this direction. The conclusion? 'There was no such thing as a "Fascist culture"'; Fascism was 'the negation of culture', 'Fascist culture can for the most part be held to be either just culture or just Fascism'; 'Where there was culture there wasn't Fascism, where there was Fascism there wasn't culture'.[59]

From the newer culturalist perspective of Fascism as a modernizing, active ideology centred around the utopian ideals of national renewal and rebirth, and the realization of the 'new man' within the totalitarian state, the view is somewhat different. Fascist aesthetics were much more than propaganda. It was only through 'aesthetic over-production', an 'over-abundance of theatricality', that Fascism, which possessed an 'ideological core' (aims) but refused to or could not elaborate a philosophical system (means), was able to construct, define and realize itself.[60] Fascism was not 'anti-culture' it *was* culture. The most obvious forms of this – the rituals, symbols, myths, cults and ceremonies of Fascism – we have already looked at. According to the culturalist historians, Fascism was to be a 'way of life', a 'faith', a 'political religion'. These were not empty slogans designed to give the Italian people a sense of identity and the illusion of participation whilst simultaneously exploiting them, or to disguise the vacuum at the heart of Fascism as many claimed.[61] The 'aestheticization of politics', the '"theatricality" of public display', were to engage and transform ordinary Italians, fusing politics and society within the organic 'ethical state', and giving rise to a new national community, a 'renewed flowering of the Italian creative genius'. 'In fascism', wrote George Mosse, 'power *had to* [my emphasis] express itself visually'.[62]

From a culturalist perspective, the aesthetic pluralism that characterized cultural production under Fascism could be explained in a number of ways. Jeffery Schnapp, for instance, suggested that Fascism's aesthetic overproduction helped 'to explain why the Italian regime...tended towards an "eclecticism in spirit" in its cultural policies, encouraging a proliferation of competing formulations of fascist modernity, among which Mussolini felt free to choose as a function of expediency or circumstance'. The important role that expediency and circumstance played in determining Fascist cultural policy is noted in a number of other accounts. For Marla Stone, Fascist culture was 'shaped by shifting economic, social and rhetorical priorities'. It was 'the product of a constant negotiation between the dictatorship's goals and cultural tastes of artists and spectators', designed to project 'a malleable, undefined image of itself which could be read as simultaneously revolutionary and authoritarian, changing and stable, urban and popular', in order to attract the widest possible cultural constituency. The success of the Exhibition of the Fascist Revolution – 3m visitors between 1932 and 1934 – demonstrated the advantages to the regime of such a policy. The lack of a state art allowed the event's organizers to call upon the services of the best modern Italian artists and architects, and engage them in an official cultural enterprise, thus lending a cultural legitimacy to the exhibition and to the regime. By not favouring any single aesthetic style the regime bred competition within Italy's artistic community, each movement seeking to extend its influence, rather than disaffection with the regime. The various contributions by different modernist groups gave the exhibition a modern, vibrant image, and made it the cultural event of the year. The range of styles, meanwhile, catered to a broad spectrum of tastes. This and careful marketing of the event by the regime, including cheap train-exhibition packages, ensured large crowds. Emily Braun has noted that Fascism, by granting high culture a significant degree of autonomy, not only guaranteed the support or acquiescence of Italian artists and intellectuals but, through the aesthetic quality of the work produced by those artists ('free to create but obliged to serve'), was able to talk of a new era of Fascist Italian cultural primacy and genius. As Giuseppe Bottai commented, 'the unlimited vastness of content and plurality of forms gives the Italian artistic tradition a universal value and an influence a thousand times larger than its national territory'.[63]

Culturalist historians seeking to explain the lack of 'Fascist' theatre have likewise noted how the regime often tailored its cloth according to circumstances.[64] Traditional theatre going, they point out, was essentially a middle-class ritual and the middle class was Fascism's core constituency. Fascism did not wish to alienate its supporters, therefore Fascism, as a rule, left theatre alone.[65] Popular theatre was, potentially, a different matter but stage plays with Fascist themes were not usually very good and audiences were largely unimpressed. The idea of a 'theatre of masses for masses' suggested by Mussolini in 1933 – Mussolini had in mind 'a theatre with a capacity of 15,000–20,000 seats', and drama capable of stirring 'great collective passions' – was attempted, with disastrous results in 1934. *18BL*, a play in which a Fiat truck (the eponymous 18BL) was the chosen vehicle to get over a series of rather crude political messages, involved 2,000–3,000 amateur actors, an air squadron, an infantry brigade, a cavalry brigade, 50 trucks, 8 tractors, 4 field and machine-gun batteries, 10 field radio stations, and 6 photo electric units. It played to an audience of 20,000 spectators on the banks of the River Arno in Florence. The aim of *18BL* was to be ritual (to allow youth to re-enact the war and the March on Rome) and inaugural (to preview a 'Fascist' society). It 'failed abysmally'. Critics hated it, the audience did not understand it, people could not see or hear properly, many simply were bored by the whole experience.[66] 'Theatre of masses for masses' was abandoned after one night.

Fascism, nonetheless, 'produced its culture', much of it with a modernist tinge, which gave form to Fascist spiritual values. For example, Braun's study of the one-time *novecentisto* Mario Sironi concludes that his style 'evoked the instinctive and irrational aspects of human experience, most specifically the mystical, collective life of the nation', values that were central to Fascism. Stone meanwhile argues that Fascist exhibitions sought to nationalize culture. The aim was to make high culture available to the masses and to open up élite culture to new mass artforms, such as cinema, while at the same time mobilizing Italians – the cultural producers and the popular masses – behind the Fascist project of cultural and national renewal. Mark Antliff, the co-editor of *Fascist Visions: Art and Ideology in France and Italy* (1997), a work which includes contributions from (amongst others) Braun, Gentile, Stone and Adamson, suggests that Fascist aesthetics served modern and revolutionary ends even when they appeared conservative or reactionary; the past was utilized for its 'mythic appeal as a catalyst for the radical transformation of present society'. Little wonder then that one of the leading historians of generic fascism, Roger Griffin, has been quick to see recent studies on Fascist cultural production as confirmation of his argument that Fascism was a coherent ideology based upon the core myth of national palingenesis (rebirth). Fascist culture may have taken many different forms – Griffin recognizes that the 'boundless nebulousness' of the core myth admitted 'any number of nuanced permutations at the level of surface rationalization' and he notes that Mussolini did not much care about the precise means by which rebirth was achieved – nonetheless, he insists, Fascists regarded cultural regeneration as an essential constituent of national rebirth. Furthermore, 'it can be empirically proved that the underlying assumption of all artists and intellectuals who devoted their creativity to the regime was that they were contributing to the "rebirth of Italy" and the "regeneration of western civilization"'.[67]

Fascism: A cultural revolution?

While culturalists argue that a cultural revolution – the creation of a 'total' culture, of a totalitarian state (an organic 'ethical' state) – was central to the Fascist project, they, like social historians, are generally sceptical of the results achieved. Griffin, for example, argues that the Fascist totalitarian experiment was always doomed to failure. The ambiguity inherent in the core myth of national palingenesis allowed several competing fascisms to exist simultaneously, while Mussolini – who might have been able to impose a single orthodoxy – chose instead to mediate between the different groups, acting in the great Italian political tradition as a 'super-*trasformista*'. Even had Mussolini acted differently, however, the realization of the totalitarian state would have remained beyond his grasp: the creation of a total culture in an age of growing secularization, internationalization and individualism was, according to Griffin, an 'irremediably utopian' idea.[68]

Falasca-Zamponi, too, recognizes 'fascism's inability to control the Italians totally', pointing to the challenge posed to Fascism by consumerism, and noting how the fragmented nature of Italian society meant that the impact of Fascism was far from uniform across the country. Like Griffin, Falasca-Zamponi also recognizes how the 'multiple narratives' within Fascism allowed for 'diversity, difference and contradiction'. Mabel Berezin, meanwhile, cautions against assuming 'that regimes have total power...that publics passively receive regime messages'. Berezin makes the point that many Italian men – even sincere Fascists – saw themselves first as Catholics and sons; Fascism, in other words, did not colonize the private sphere and this 'limited what was ideologically possible on the part of the regime'.[69]

Berezin is also highly critical of the assumption – implicit in the work of Schnapp, Braun and Stone, and clearly articulated by Griffin – that those who produced 'Fascist culture' were necessarily Fascists themselves, or were genuinely inspired by Fascist ideals. For Berezin, 'When the State is the principal source of artistic patronage, the savvy young artist...seizes the main chance. This opportunism was not unique to artists; it characterized the behaviour of many from scientists to the local bricklayer. It is not surprising that in the quest for scarce resources artists fought, disagreed, came up with ludicrous innovations'.[70] The implications of this are important. If those engaged in the production of Fascist culture were not really Fascists, then it is hardly surprising that Fascism was unable to 'bridge high art with popular culture in order to awaken the spiritually inert of the new Italy and so help generate the 'new Fascist man'.[71]

If the consensus among culturalists is that the Fascist totalitarian project remained unrealized and unrealizable and that the majority of Italians, even if they consented to Fascism, were not in any meaningful way 'transformed' by Fascism, there is at least one eminent historian within the culturalist camp who argues to the contrary. In keeping with other culturalist accounts, Emilio Gentile wrote in *The Sacralization of Politics* that 'Fascist rituals and celebrations wished to educate in order to convert...to conquer and mould the moral consciousness, the mentality and the mores of the people, right down to its most intimate feelings about life and death'.[72] In contrast with most other culturalist readings, however, Gentile claimed (or appeared to claim) that Fascism achieved its objective. For two decades under Fascism, Gentile stated:

> The piazzas of Italy...were transformed into a huge stage on which millions celebrated – as one, *to a single beat* [my emphasis] – the national holidays, the régime's anniversaries, the triumphs of the 'revolution', the cult of the fallen, the glorification of heroes, the consecration of symbols, the appearances of the *Duce*... People and nation were bound up in a thick web of symbols.

By the end of the 1930s, 'totalitarian politics had successfully worked its ideology among the masses'.[73]

It is this particular culturalist reading of Fascism that Bosworth has attacked so insistently. Gentile, according to Bosworth, 'totally fails to grapple with the difference between words and deeds'. Drawing on his own research, Bosworth has argued instead for '"webs of insignificance", of normality, tradition and commerce', rather than the 'triumphant intrusion of totalitarian politics'. Italians, he has argued, 'seem to have been as moved by the structures of the histories of the Italies as by the influence of the political event of Fascism'.[74]

Bosworth has not limited his criticisms to Gentile, however. The 'anti-anti-Fascist' culturalist school was, in Bosworth's opinion, collectively guilty of the same offences as its leader, that is, of charting 'webs of significance which, it has been alleged, bound the Fascist state to Italian society and so brought cultural revolution'. Indeed, according to Bosworth, 'The culturalist school of recent historiography has more and more confidently asserted the reality of a cultural revolution in Fascist Italy'. Bosworth was also prepared to name and shame. Falasca-Zamponi, Berezin, Stone and Schnapp, and the entire cast of writers who had published in the thirtieth anniversary edition of the *Journal of Contemporary History* in 1996, were all part of the conspiracy to pervert the course of (anti-Fascist) history.[75] As should be apparent already, Bosworth's charge against the wider culturalist school is entirely without foundation.[76] What of the case against Gentile? Here Bosworth is on firmer ground. The bold assertions contained in *The Sacralization of Politics* are just that – assertions. Gentile produces no evidence beyond a handful of quotes, mainly (but not exclusively) from official records to support his claims. Even these are far from conclusive. Gentile quotes a communist militant in 1932 to the effect that 'Fascism has managed to influence a fair part of the masses with its ideology'. But what does 'influence' mean? And how many is a 'fair part of the masses'? (Interestingly, in a later article by Gentile this phrase is translated as 'the greater part of the masses'.) Gentile also quotes another communist source: 'whoever has to live in Italy has to adopt the Fascist *label*' (my emphasis), but again the meaning is ambiguous. In a situation where to do anything other than 'adopt the Fascist label' could mean unemployment, exile, imprisonment or even (though rarely) death, paying lip service to Fascism was perfectly understandable. In fact, even Gentile frequently appears to be unsure as to the reality of Fascist totalitarianism. Gentile has written both before and since *The Sacralization of Politics* that there are 'no examples of totalitarian experiments that were not subject to limitations, obstacles and resistance'. He has described as 'absurd' the Fascist attempts to mould Italians and has declared that the 'Fascist religion...failed to achieve its aim'. He has at various times admitted that Fascism made little headway with the secularized, the religious, the ill-treated (those who suffered at the hands of Fascism), those who clung to non-Fascist political traditions, or those who came from the backward areas of Italy – specifically the south. He has admitted that it is 'difficult to say' what effect the PNF, which, he says, extended its tentacles into every area of Italian life, had upon the collective Italian conscience.[77] In *The Sacralization of Politics*, Gentile also admits that the cult of Mussolini dwarfed the Fascist cult and that while ordinary people identified with Mussolini they never understood Fascism, but he does not pause to consider the significance of such a state of affairs. The logical conclusion to be drawn from this is that the cult of the *Duce* got in the way of the totalitarian objective of Fascism – if people did not understand Fascism how could they be fascistized?[78] The incoherence and inconsistency evident in Gentile's arguments stem from the fact that his aim is to understand rationally the irrationality of Fascism – a task he excels in – not to judge its effects, a task for which his particular expertise/interests and his methodological approach ill prepare him.

Italians: *brava gente*?

Historians argue over popular attitudes towards Fascism and Fascism's impact upon society and culture, but all agree that by the second half of the 1930s dissent and dissatisfaction in Italy were becoming more prevalent. The usual explanations for this are the increasingly intrusive nature of Fascist legislation, the racial laws of 1938 and the drift towards Nazi Germany and war. The fact that many Italians who until then had embraced, accepted or tolerated Fascism began to question (if not yet turn against) the regime suggests there was a point beyond which they were not willing to follow the dictatorship. The conclusion that many historians have drawn from this is that Italians, despite their many faults, were essentially *brava gente* (good people).

Italy's 'good' Holocaust particularly seems to lend itself to this kind of interpretation. Although Lynn Gunzberg has argued that there was no real opposition to the racial laws,[79] nonetheless there was clearly little support for the legislation either, even from within Fascist ranks: 1,000 PNF members were expelled from the party for displaying 'overt' Jewish sympathies, while newly created Centres for the Study of the Jewish Problem attracted only 864 PNF recruits. The fact that the great majority of Italians rejected racial doctrine is confirmed by the experience of foreign Jews in Italian-occupied territories between 1941 and 1943, and of Italian Jews in Nazi-occupied northern and central Italy between 1943 and

1945. According to Jonathan Steinberg, no Jew under Italian jurisdiction was given up to the Germans, despite German pressure, between the start of the war and the Italian surrender. Some 85 per cent of Italian Jews survived the German occupation – along with Denmark the highest survival rate in occupied Europe. There are many examples of individual Italians helping Jews, both in Italy and abroad, at considerable risk to their own safety.[80]

A number of reasons have been advanced to explain why Italians did not embrace Fascist anti-Semitism. There were not many Italian Jews (only 45,000, less than 1 per cent of the population). They were highly integrated into Italian society – they looked like other Italians, they dressed like other Italians, they often married non-Jewish Italian families, they did not live in separate Jewish communities. There were no large concentrations of Jews. They were not particularly linked with or envied for their involvement in Italian finance and banking, or the medical and legal professions. They fanned out across the political spectrum. Their patriotism was unquestioned (given that legal restraints on Italian Jews were removed at the time of unification they were usually deeply patriotic and fervent supporters of the monarchy). In short, non-Jewish Italians did not regard Italian Jews as being in any way different to the wider population, or a threat to the nation. During the war, other factors also came into play. There was, in Steinberg's opinion, a 'considerable dose of calculation' in Italian officials' reluctance to hand over Jews to the Germans: as the war wore on and defeat seemed increasingly likely, it made sense to consider the reaction of the victorious Allies. Steinberg also suggests that the senior ranks in the Italian army were ill disposed to act against Jews because for many years prior to the racial laws, Italian Jews had held senior positions within the armed forces and had been accepted by their peers. Indeed, Steinberg talks of a 'conspiracy to save Jews' within the Italian services.[81] As to the high survival rate of Italian Jews under German occupation, this has been explained with reference to the relatively short period of occupation (at most 18 months), the fact that those who aided Italian Jews could see their help would only be needed over the short term (after all, the Allies were on their way), because the small number of Italian Jews made it easier for sympathetic non-Jewish Italians to help with shelter, food and documents, and because Italian Jews had money with which to buy help; unlike their Eastern European counterparts, 'they were not impoverished by years of ghettoization'.[82]

Frequently, though, accounts of Italy's Holocaust return to the notion of Italians as good people by way of explanation. Hannah Arendt, writing in 1963, encapsulates this view: 'What in Denmark was the result of an authentically political sense, an inbred comprehension of the requirements and responsibilities of citizenship and independence...was in Italy the outcome of the almost automatic general humanity of an old and civilized people'.[83]

Subsequent historians have followed Arendt in suggesting that 'The whole story of Italian Fascism and the Jews reveals the central humanity and resistance of the Italian people'. Even Mussolini was 'too much of an Italian' to approve of the Final Solution, his refusal indicative of 'the reassertion of a deep Italian virtue: the triumph of old humanitarian values over new Fascist principles'.[84]

The ideas of Italians as inherently 'good people' and of humanity as an Italian national characteristic are well-established concepts, too, in popular fiction and film – *Captain Correlli's Mandolin* an obvious example. Here, the Italian occupation of the Greek island of Cephalonia is marked by the Italians' love of life (especially music, food and women). The humanity and compassion of the Italians stands in stark contrast to the calculated brutality of the Germans. While the novel is essentially a fictional tale based upon historical events, Nick Doumanis's excellent oral history of the Italian occupation of the Dodecanese islands reveals a popular memory of the Italians which is strikingly similar: 'the Italians were good'.[85]

Nevertheless, there are those who question the *italiani = brava gente* equation.[86] Here the focus is on evidence that reveals the complicity of 'ordinary' Italians in Fascism's crimes. For example, the concept of 'almost automatic general humanity' sits uncomfortably with the deportment in the early 1930s of over 100,000 Libyans to concentration camps. The majority of internees died in what has been described by one historian as an act of 'authentic genocide'.[87] Nor does it sit well with the war crimes committed in Ethiopia, including the use of poison gas, acts not of Fascist squads but rather of the 'un-fascistized' Royal Italian Army. Questions have been asked, too, about the innocence of Italians in the Holocaust. Historians have estimated that up to 5,000 people (many of them Slovenes) were killed at the Risiera di San Sabba concentration camp near Trieste, between October 1943 and May 1945. A further 20,000 were deported to camps outside of Italy. While Risiera was established and run by the Nazis, evidence suggests 'widespread collaboration and the Nazis' reliance on Triestine citizens and institutions' for the functioning of the camp. Popular anti-Slavism, rather than Fascism, was behind this.[88]

As to the idea that 'if everyone under a Hitler dominated Europe were to have comported themselves like the Italians, the genocide would have been impossible',[89] it has been pointed out that without the Fascist racial laws, and the complicity of many Italians, the Germans would have been unable to track down Italian Jews. Instead, the addresses and names of Italian Jews were already catalogued and many Jews were already interned or under house arrest by 1943.[90] Michele Sarfatti has challenged the claim that Italian occupying forces did not surrender any Jews under their authority to German forces: 51 Central European Jews were handed over in Pristina, the capital of Kosovo, in March 1942; in July 1943 the decision was taken to hand over all German Jews in Italian-occupied south-east France – only the fall of Mussolini a few days later meant the hand-over did not occur.[91] Some historians have also called for the notion of the 'assimilated Jew', of the 'hidden Jew...literally invisible within Italian culture', to be reconsidered. Anti-Semitism was inherent within Catholicism (there was a Jewish ghetto in Vatican-controlled Rome until 1870). From the early nineteenth century through to the mid-1930s, the Jew was popularly portrayed in Italian literature as a corrosive, invisible, dishonest, money-fixated presence. Although many Italian Jews did indeed see themselves as assimilated, others grew up in an environment that was 'at times friendly, more often hostile, always alien'. The racial laws 'took root in a fertile terrain: the hearts and minds of the mass of Italians'.[92]

Assessment

As Alexander De Grand has argued, the 'myth of the good Italians' should be laid to rest.[93] The inherently good Italian is a stereotype, not an historical explanation. Italian humanity was selective. Yes, there were Italians who helped Jews at considerable personal risk. But the reason why Fascist anti-Semitism made little impact on the majority of Italians was that Jews simply were not perceived as a threat: there was no 'Jewish problem', no matter how hard the regime tried to convince the population otherwise. In contrast, popular resentment of the Slovenes easily translated into brutal repression.

Another persistent myth, that 'one man alone' – Mussolini – was responsible for all Italy's ills also must be rejected. 'The Italians collectively can be seen as morally responsible for the creation and long-term survival of the regime in one way or another'.[94] There is little evidence of unambiguous, consistent, or spontaneous popular anti-Fascism – including from within what was a defeated, leaderless and divided working class. At the same time, though, we should treat with scepticism De Felice's claim of a 'mass consensus' behind the regime. As the works of Passerini, De Grazia, Corner, Willson and others have clearly demonstrated in relation to popular attitudes towards Fascism, relations between ruler and ruled were extremely complex. At both the individual and group level, a single action could simultaneously demonstrate resistance to, and compromise with, Fascism, while 'Rejection of and discontent with some areas of the regime's activity [e.g. the Battle for births] could co-exist with acceptance and enjoyment of others [e.g. the OND, Fascist organizations], an ambivalent mix of attitudes'.[95] Mass consensus implies the existence of widespread and general support for Fascism. The evidence produced by Passerini and company indicates this is a gross simplification.[96]

What this all points to is the failure of the Fascist cultural revolution. Fascism did not create a totalitarian state. Italian society did not 'become Fascist'. We have already seen considerable evidence that testifies to the limits of the Fascist project. There is much more. Take the example of Italian youth. As soon as children were able to leave school (at fourteen), many left Fascism. In 1936, three-quarters of schoolchildren aged 8–14 years old were enrolled in Fascist youth organizations but only one in two males aged 18–21 remained members. The number of children involved in Catholic youth groups grew by more than 50 per cent in the 1930s despite the restrictions placed upon them by the Fascist government. If we look at the newspaper reading habits of Italians we can see a preference for traditional rather than Fascist papers: the *Corriere della Sera*, despite its emasculation under the Fascists, still outsold the official mouthpiece of Fascism, *Il Popolo d'Italia*, by a ratio of 6:1 in 1933. The circulation of the Vatican-based (and thus independent) *Osservatore Romano* actually grew in the

Fascist period. Meanwhile, in the area of Fascist demographic policy, despite the barrage of legislation aimed at stemming rural-urban migration and propaganda designed to reconcile the peasants to life on the land, the flight from the countryside continued apace. As Carl Ipsen notes, the failure of Fascist demographics demonstrates the regime's 'inability to extend its influence to the more intimate areas of social behaviour'.[97]

The clearest indication of the limits of Fascism, however, is the response of Italians to events leading up to and following the outbreak of war. Italian crowds cheered Mussolini the peacemaker on his return from the Munich conference in September 1938. Chief of Police Arturo Bocchini noted in 1939 that '*all Italy loathes war* and the people do not want to fight for the Germans'. When Mussolini declared Italy's non-belligerence (he refused to use the word 'neutrality') thousands of Italians celebrated. Letters from conscripted soldiers suggest that when Italy did eventually go to war in 1940 there was little enthusiasm among those called up to fight. Humiliating military defeat abroad, acute food shortages at home (rationing was only belatedly introduced) and the damage inflicted on northern Italian cities by allied bombing translated into growing public disquiet, culminating in the mass strikes in Turin and Milan in the spring of 1943, the first major industrial action in Italy for two decades.[98] Evidently, the majority of Italians had not absorbed the Fascist mantra, 'Believe, Obey, Fight'.

Why the Fascist ideal remained unrealized (and unrealizable) is relatively easy to explain. First, Fascism was never able to impose itself upon the socio-economic élites that had helped bring it to power. Nor was the Fascist state strong enough to confront effectively the power of the monarchy or the Catholic Church. Throne and altar remained important non-Fascist (though not necessarily anti-Fascist) forces within Italy throughout the *ventennio*. The King, not the *Duce*, was head of state (and, of course, it was Victor Emmanuel who eventually sacked Mussolini). It was wishful thinking on the part of Bottai when he described the monarch as 'king of a Totalitarian state, embodiment of an organized people'.[99] As regards relations with the Vatican, although the Lateran pacts helped legitimize Fascism in the eyes of many Italians, they also recognized the independent interests of the Church.

Second, the Italian state was historically weak at the periphery (see Chapter 1). The Fascist state, like its liberal predecessor, was obliged to govern through local élites that were often indifferent, if not actually hostile, to the interests and objectives of the state.

Third, the Fascist Government had to rely upon an inherited state apparatus, that is, on the existing bureaucracy, judiciary and military. It was not feasible to conduct a root and branch purge of suspect political elements within these bodies (although Jews were removed from public office in the wake of the racial laws). Conservative/nationalist in outlook and thus sympathetic to many of the aims of Fascism they may have been, but they were not Fascist. Let us take the examples of the bureaucracy and the army. At a superficial level, the state bureaucracy was politicized: membership of the PNF became a condition of employment in the state administration in the late 1930s. However, the vast influx of civil servants into the PNF seems to have had the effect of depoliticizing the party rather than fascistizing the civil service. Evidence suggests that state officials ignored many Fascist directives, e.g. the instruction that all public employees use the Roman salute instead of the handshake.[100] Clientelism and patronage continued to influence placements and promotions. In short, as one Italian historian of the Italian state administration has written, the bureaucratic culture remained 'that of the liberal era'.[101] As for the Royal Italian Army, even though army officers were required to join the PNF from 1936, and Mussolini in 1938 took for himself the position of Commander-in-Chief of the Italian military in wartime, it remained closely linked to the monarchy. The senior ranks also demonstrated a distinct coolness towards Fascism. Army commanders were wary of the Fascist militia and often unhappy with the poor supply and quality of military equipment provided under Fascist auspices. Many officers remained freemasons despite a ban on freemasonry. A survey conducted in the late 1930s of the main government ministries listed 375 senior army personnel, including 25 generals, as suspected anti-Fascists within the Ministry of War (only one other ministry reported more than one hundred anti-Fascist suspects). As a German military observer noted, the army served Fascism 'as long as crown and Fascism went hand in hand...[but] in a conflict between the king and the *Duce* the officer corps would decide for the monarch'.[102] This happened in 1943.

Fourth, the nature of Italian Fascism itself was an obstacle to the creation of a totalitarian state and to the realization of the Fascist revolution. Fascism contained too many competing 'fascisms' ever to be able to impose a total culture. Mussolini's reluctance to establish a single orthodoxy had its practical advantages (as we have seen, for example, in the sphere of cultural production) but the confusion of ideas within Fascism and the nebulousness of its core myth left it open to interpretation. If Fascists were unable to agree on the form and style of Fascism it was not surprising that ordinary Italians struggled to understand the message.

In contrast, Italians *were* able to identify with the figure of Mussolini. There is considerable evidence attesting to the power of the cult of the *Duce*.[103] However, faith in the *Duce* did not necessarily translate into belief in, or an understanding of, Fascism. Arguably, *mussolinismo* was at the *expense* of Fascism; as Bottai complained, 'You cannot create Fascism because of Mussolini'. The major casualty of *mussolinismo* was, of course, the PNF. By the 1930s, the party – as a display at the 1932 *Mostra* declared – was 'everywhere', but it was far from a cohesive revolutionary vanguard. Instead, it was a mass party, which had been stripped of its radical elements in purges conducted during the late 1920s. The one organization potentially up to the task of fascistizing society and creating the totalitarian state had been neutered long before the 'totalitarian turn' of the late 1930s.[104]

The 'totalitarian turn', as has already been suggested (Chapter 4), was indicative of a growing sense of dissatisfaction within Fascism at the meagre gains from over a decade in power. Until then the regime had practised what De Grazia calls 'selective totalitarianism': 'The Italian Fascists were generally not inclined to expend excessive energy regulating groups that posed no obvious threat to their rule. Nor did they seek to extend state or party control into areas of civic life where a responsive audience would have served no immediate political or economic end'.[105] Inevitably, this meant that Fascism's impact across society was extremely uneven. For many Italians, Fascism was not a way of life, nor necessarily a constant, or dominant, presence and influence in everyday life.

Fifth, the economic, social and cultural diversity of Italy worked against the logic of totalitarianism. As we have seen, exposure to Fascism varied according to all manner of factors, including class, wealth, geography, employment, age and gender. In addition, pre-existing cultural identities, practices and loyalties proved extremely difficult to eradicate (if the regime tried to do so): popular (working-class) culture may have been impoverished but it survived; long-standing client–patron relations persisted; familial and parochial interests continued to be prioritized over those of party or nation, even within the Fascist hierarchy.[106]

Finally, Fascism did not enjoy a cultural monopoly in Italy, rather it had to compete with traditional Catholicism on the one hand and battle against the rising tide of modern mass consumer culture on the other. Moreover, the regime had little control over the means of cultural production. High cultural production remained in private ownership, its output largely untouched by Fascism. Nor was it 'nationalized' to any great extent; the OND, for example, had nothing to do with high culture. True, some high cultural events, such as the Venice *Biennale*, which had once catered only for élite audiences, were opened up to the masses (or at least to the middle classes). But the *Biennale's* transformation stemmed less from any desire to give the event a 'Fascist and national character', as Marla Stone has suggested,[107] and more from the commercial and personal political motives of its organizer, the Venetian businessman Giuseppe Volpi. A former ally of Giolitti, Volpi had benefited greatly from his contacts within the liberal establishment and had amassed a huge personal fortune (and accumulated enormous local political power) by the time of Mussolini's accession. By transferring his loyalties to Fascism – he joined the PNF in mid-1923 – Volpi ensured that his wealth and influence continued to grow. Volpi's stewardship of the *Biennale* must be seen in this context. For their part, the Fascists, like the Giolittian liberals before them, made use of Volpi because he represented real power at the local level and was a leading figure within the Italian business community.

If high culture was not Fascist, low cultural production, too, maintained a significant degree of autonomy (cinema, as we have seen, remained in private ownership and was dominated by American film) and did not, for the most part, embrace explicit or uniquely Fascist themes.

Contrary to what Griffin has claimed, it cannot be 'empirically proved' that 'all the artists and intellectuals who devoted their creativity to the regime', believed in its 'core myth' of national rebirth. Artists and intellectuals needed to earn a living; for many it was surely a matter of common sense rather than ideological fervour to cosy up to a regime that liked to identify itself with, and was prepared to spend large sums of public money on, the arts. Granted, there were those who genuinely believed they were contributing to the regeneration of Italian and western civilization, but a belief in art's ability to transform is not peculiar to Fascism. Nor can the idea that cultural regeneration is an essential element of national rebirth be viewed as especially Fascist; one need only look at the pre-war Italian avant-garde to see this. Not surprisingly then, works supposedly inspired by Fascist ideals were often more run-of-the-mill nationalist than Fascist in character.[108] To talk of a Fascist culture – of a culture that was recognizably and distinctly Fascist – is to claim more than the evidence allows.

III
ITALY SINCE 1943

7 Italian politics from the fall of Mussolini to the rise of Berlusconi

Introduction

When Milanese entrepreneur Silvio Berlusconi became Italian Prime Minister in April 1994, he completed perhaps the most rapid ascent to national political power of an individual ever seen in a democratic country. Only in January had Berlusconi announced his interest in standing for election, launching his very own party, Forza Italia (Go Italy), in the process. His victory, at the head of an unusual right-wing coalition (the 'Freedom Pole') containing the pro-autonomy Lega Nord (Northern League) and the neo-Fascist Movimento sociale italiano-Alleanza nazionale (Italian Social Movement-National Alliance [MSI-AN]), marked the end of a remarkable five years in Italian political history. In early 1989 the Italian political landscape looked much like that in 1948, when the first post-war elections to be held in Italy under the new republican constitution had returned a coalition government controlled by the Christian Democrats (DC) and a communist (PCI)-led Opposition. Although governments came and went with bewildering speed – there was, on average, more than one administration per year between 1948 and 1987 – their political make-up barely altered over the decades. The DC was always in government, in coalition with all or some of the other, smaller, centre parties (the Social Democrats [PSDI], the Liberals [PLI] and the Republicans [PRI]). Occasionally, the governing coalition also included the Socialist Party (PSI). Every prime minister until 1981 was a Christian Democrat. The PCI, always the second largest party in parliament, was never able to muster enough support to break the DC stranglehold.

Between 1989 and 1994, however, the stability that had characterized post-war politics broke down in spectacular fashion. By the 1994 general election, the DC and PCI no longer existed. Although the minor parties struggled on, they did so in much reduced circumstances; the PSI, for example, had suffered two major splits and polled only 2.2 per cent of the vote in 1994. Against this, the brand-new 'media-mediated personality-party'[1] Forza Italia took 21.1 per cent of the vote, the previously taboo MSI-AN 13.5 per cent and the anti-system Lega 8.4 per cent. Adding to the picture of political rupture, the new parliament consisted of a largely virgin political class. A third of deputies claimed to have no previous experience in party or electoral politics. Most senators were first-timers. The social-economic composition of the new parliament was also significantly different, with many more deputies drawn from the private sector.[2] Little wonder, then, that commentators referred to the 1994 election as the beginning of a 'Second Republic'.

The crisis that engulfed the Italian political system between the late 1980s and early 1990s has been explained with reference to long-term factors and short-term triggers that will be explored in this chapter. But the crisis also provoked intense historical (and, this being Italy, political) debate over the very origins of the Republic itself, in particular over the nature and significance of the Italian Resistance between 1943 and 1945. The Resistance had been the founding myth of the 'first' Republic. The example of the popular, cross-class, cross-party, patriotic 'War of Liberation' against Nazi-Fascism had provided the moral basis for Italy's political renewal after the war. Anti-Fascism had been the fundamental principle underpinning the post-war constitution. It had also lent legitimacy to those post-war political parties which could demonstrate their anti-Fascist (i.e. their Resistance) credentials, and denied it to those which could not (e.g. the neo-Fascist MSI, formed in 1946). The collapse of the post-war order in the early 1990s, however, and in particular the demise of the PCI, the party most closely associated with the Resistance tradition, prompted historians to revisit the events of fifty years earlier. New assessments of the Resistance now played down the idea of a popular patriotic war of liberation; instead, it was a catastrophic 'civil war' fought by a minority of Italians, with 'unpatriotic' partisans on the one side, and Italian (Fascist) loyalists on the other. In the long-term, so revisionists claimed, the Resistance myth and anti-Fascism had exercised a debilitating influence on Italian politics and, more generally, the nation's moral fibre. The now defunct PCI was held responsible, accused of manipulating the historical record for its own base political motives. Once again, De Felice was a pivotal figure in the resulting debate and controversy. His attack in *Rosso e Nero* (1995) on the 'Resistance vulgate', provoked outrage on the Left and firebombs were thrown at his house (fliers left at the scene claimed that *Rosso e Nero* was 'a shot aimed at our historical memory').[3] The new and not-so-new Right in Italian politics, however, welcomed the revisionist 'anti-anti-Fascist' Resistance line, not only as a stick with which to beat the Left (the PCI had re-emerged as a social democratic party, the Democratic Party of the Left [PDS], in 1991), but also as a means to establish their own legitimacy.

Framework

The end of the Fascist dictatorship

Mussolini's dismissal and the fall of the Fascist regime were not the result of a popular rising but rather the work of the monarchy, senior military personnel and recently dismissed Fascist hierarchs (Bottai, Ciano, Grandi). Mussolini's arrest, the immediate dissolution of the PNF and the Chamber of Corporations, and the appointment of Marshall Pietro Badoglio as Prime Minister, did not mean, however, an immediate end to dictatorship or repression. Badoglio made clear that new political parties would not be allowed for the duration of war; strikes were also forbidden and the military ordered to shoot those who disobeyed. Nor did Mussolini's fall mean the immediate end of the war – 'la guerra continua', announced Badoglio, although secret talks were taking place with the Allies at the same time as the Italian government was assuring Germany of its continuing support. After 45 days of indecision, Italy eventually signed an armistice with the Allies (8 September), by which time Hitler had poured troops into northern and central Italy. German forces occupied Rome (10 September). Mussolini was liberated from his mountain-top prison by German airforce units two days later. Taken first to Germany for discussions with Hitler, he was then flown back to Italy to take charge of the occupied territory, officially christened the Italian Social Republic (RSI) but better known as the Republic of Salò, after the small town on Lake Garda where the Administration was based.

The Resistance

The armistice marked the start of the Italian Resistance. On 9 September, six anti-Fascist parties established the Comitato di liberazione nazionale (Committee of National Liberation, CLN) in Rome, in an effort to mobilize popular resistance in the city against the advancing German army. From the beginning of 1944, the northern Resistance was placed under the general control of the Comitato di liberazione nazionale per l'Alta Italia (Committee of National Liberation for Upper Italy, CLNAI, based in Milan). Partisan brigades were formed along political-ideological lines and organized within a vertical military command structure. Relations between the CLN/CLNAI, the royal government in the south (the King, his ministers and senior military personnel had fled Rome prior to the German assault on the city) and Allied command were frequently strained. The CLN parties at first refused to work with the monarchy, demanding Victor Emmanuel's immediate abdication. Only after the communist leader Palmiro

Togliatti unilaterally declared the PCI's readiness to participate in Badoglio's Administration (the so-called *svolta di Salerno*, March 1944) did the other CLN parties compromise: they would join the government but Victor Emmanuel would 'retire' once Rome was liberated; a decision would be taken on the future of the monarchy after the war. Rome fell in June 1944. Victor Emmanuel's son, Umberto, became Lieutenant General. The CLN parties now flexed their political muscle: Badoglio was forced to resign and a CLN Government formed under the old reformist socialist Ivanoe Bonomi. The British government was outraged. It had little interest in the partisan movement (other than concerns regarding its communist elements) and no faith in the 'extremely untrustworthy band of non-elected political comebacks' – Churchill's description – that made up the new Administration. In British eyes, the Italians were defeated enemies, even though now 'co-belligerents' (the royal government had finally declared war on Germany in October 1943), and were to be treated – and behave – as such. The 'Bonomi affair' was one of the few times the CLN was able to ignore the Allies, helped in this instance by divisions between the British and Americans. Ultimately, though, both the CLN Government in the south and the CLNAI in the state were dependent upon the British and American forces. By the Protocols of Rome (December 1944) the CLNAI, in return for desperately needed Allied funds, gave up direct command of the Resistance and agreed to surrender its authority in the state to Supreme Allied Command upon liberation.

The Italian Social Republic

Although the RSI had the institutional trappings of an autonomous state – ministries were quickly established, the Fascist party was reconstituted (with almost 500,000 members), the republic had its own security forces – and many of the old Fascist hierarchs were present, the real power lay with the German occupiers. Mussolini understood this only too well. 'He was,' as Clark writes, 'an old man, defeated in life, wasted by sickness...bullied by the Germans, without friends and without hope'.[4] The RSI collapsed with the final defeat of the German army in Italy in the spring of 1945. Mussolini was caught trying to escape by communist partisans and shot (28 April 1945). His body was taken to recently liberated Milan and hung on public display in piazzale Loreto, where 15 partisans had been executed the previous summer.

The creation of the post-war Republic

After the Allied victory and prior to the establishment of the Republican constitution at the end of 1947, Italy was governed by multi-party coalitions of increasingly conservative character. A progressive but weak centre-left government under Ferruccio Parri lasted from June to November 1945, to be followed by a DC-led coalition under Alcide de Gasperi. Although the left-wing parties (the PCI and PSI) remained within the government, there was little tolerance of social protest. The decision was also taken – by Togliatti, as Minister of Justice – to grant a general amnesty for those who had been closely involved with Fascism. This allowed many Fascist war criminals to escape punishment, and the bureaucracy, judiciary and security services to remain virtually unchanged. With the onset of the Cold War, De Gasperi excluded the PCI and socialists from government (May 1947), thus breaking the anti-Fascist unity that had lasted from the days of the Resistance.

Major constitutional and institutional changes still did occur, however. June 1946 saw the end of one of the oldest royal dynasties in Europe when a referendum on the monarchy went against Umberto by 12.7m to 10.7m votes. Italy was now a republic. Over the next 18 months, a Constituent Assembly, elected by universal suffrage (including votes for women), drafted a new constitution. This came into force on 1 January 1948. Under its provisions, a chamber of deputies would be elected every five years, a senate every seven. Elections would be based on proportional representation. A president would be elected every seven years but the post would be largely ceremonial. The first part of the constitution was, as Piero Calamandrei commented, 'the spirit of the Resistance translated into juridical formulae'.[5] For example, workers' rights (including the 'right to work') and the principle of regional autonomy were recognized, and provision was made for popular referenda. Many of the radical elements of the constitution were immediately frustrated, though, by the ruling (February 1948) of Italy's highest court, the Court of Cassation, that they were 'programmatic provisions', to be actuated only at a later, undetermined, date. This was a triumph for the forces of conservatism within the Italian state. Consequently, a Constitutional Court was established only in 1956 and the independence of the judiciary only formally guaranteed with the creation of the Supreme Council of the Magistracy (CSM) in 1958; regional autonomy and popular referenda became realities in the 1970s.

By 1948, Italian politics was a microcosm of the wider Cold War: on the one hand, the centre-right DC, backed to the hilt by the Vatican and the United States; on the other, the left-wing 'Popular Front' consisting of the PCI, which looked towards Moscow, and the PSI. Communism/anti-communism was the central issue in the bitterly contested general election of April 1948, won by the DC. It remained a critical element in elections for the next four decades.

The politics of the Republic, 1948–89

The basic rationale of all DC coalitions after 1948 was simple: to defend Italian democracy from the supposedly anti-democratic PCI. The PCI's only chance for power in Italy was to make alliances with other parties in order to construct a parliamentary majority against the DC. The centre-party bloc, especially when joined by the PSI – the PCI's most likely political partner – made this impossible. Post-war Italy was a 'special democracy', a 'blocked' political system where, to many, the main Opposition party was not seen as a legitimate alternative to the existing government and hence where there could be no alternation in government.

This is not to say the Communist Party had no influence within Italian national politics. As a highly organized mass party in control of local government over large swathes of central Italy, the PCI could not be ignored completely. In the mid-1970s, as the national communist vote surged against a background of economic crisis and intense social-political unrest (see Chapters 8 and 9), the DC was even obliged to negotiate with the PCI in order to maintain its hold on government. In return for communist non-opposition to the DC Government, the DC made a number of policy concessions and extended the practice of *lottizzazione* – the sharing-out between the governing parties of key positions within Italy's enormous public/semi-public sector – to include the PCI.

During the 1970s, the DC's 'stuttering reformism',[6] its involvement in a number of major corruption scandals (although nothing like on the scale of the 1990s) and the public warring between DC factions led to 'the draining of that massive reservoir of public esteem that the DC had acquired during the 1950s and 1960s as the guarantor of Italian democracy and the godfather of the Italian economic miracle'.[7] The increasingly popular view of DC was of 'a divided, dishonest, not very modern party'.[8] Secularization and the 'crisis of catholic subculture' linked to the economic miracle and social transformation of Italy from the 1950s (see Chapter 9) further eroded the DC's traditional support base. Consequently, the DC's election fortunes became ever more dependent on the anti-communist vote, i.e. what it opposed rather than what it stood for. This was not a problem – as long as there remained a communist threat. By the 1980s, however, the PCI appeared benign: it had long since abandoned the revolutionary road to socialism, its slow electoral advance (1948–76) had been abruptly reversed in 1979, it had few allies in parliament and, with the death of its leader Enrico Berlinguer in 1984, it lost its greatest political asset. Communist Party membership remained strong, but the PCI offered neither a real alternative to parliamentary democracy nor a realizable 'democratic alternative' to the DC.

The DC's own relatively poor electoral showing in the 1980s was partly due to the declining value of the anti-communist card. A small percentage of DC voters felt 'released' to vote for other 'cleaner' centre parties (the case in 1983) or for regionalist, single-issue or protest parties (in 1987). The DC also found it impossible to embrace fashionable 'modern' right-wing free-market ideology, and thus could not appeal to a new constituency. 'Modernising' talk alarmed its traditional electorate. More to the point, the DC was symbiotically tied to the state-run economy and bureaucracy. For the DC to have 'rolled back the frontiers of the state' would have been equivalent 'to the self-amputation of both legs'.[9]

In contrast to the two major parties, the PSI, which in the 1970s had appeared to be in decline, experienced an electoral revival in the 1980s. Its electoral growth coincided with the dumping of socialist baggage and the embracing of modernizing rhetoric under the leadership of the highly ambitious Bettino Craxi. Elected as Party Secretary in 1976, Craxi sought not only to make the PSI a permanent party of government but also to challenge DC control. In 1983, after parliamentary elections that saw the DC's vote fall by over 5 per cent (the result of the DC's first and last experiment with neo-conservative ideas), he became the first socialist and only the second non-DC prime minister in the Republic's history – even though the PSI had won just 11.4 per cent of the vote. Craxi's arrival as a political force intensified competition between the parties for control of the public and semi-public sectors and political corruption grew exponentially during the 1980s. The DC-PSI alliance remained intact for the rest of the decade, but it was, as Ginsborg notes:

> ...not a political alliance based on mutual trust, parity, or programmatic accord. It is, rather, riven by suspicion, by personal rivalry, by an eternal jockeying for position. It makes any strategic planning next to impossible, wastes an extraordinary amount of time and energy and leads inexorably to weak rather than strong government.[10]

The inability of the two main governing parties to govern effectively – or honestly – would soon be ruthlessly exposed.

Debates

The fact remains, though, that despite all its problems and growing public disaffection, the post-war political system appeared secure at the beginning of 1989; nobody anticipated its imminent demise. How and why did it occur? There are several explanations.

The collapse of the communist bloc and the end of the Cold War

Many commentators have noted the 'devastating' consequences of the end of the Cold War for the old political order. For the PCI the impact was immediate. After years of internal wrangling as to the meaning of 'true socialism', suddenly, with the collapse of communist governments across eastern Europe in 1989, 'the communist alternative [to democracy] had been made bankrupt'.[11] Just days after the fall of the Berlin Wall, (9 November 1989), the PCI leader Achille Ochetto declared his intention to dissolve the party. The collapse of Italian communism was at first welcomed by the governing parties who took it to mean that their political hegemony was secured. This, some observers have suggested, explains the extraordinary complacency of the DC and PSI leaderships through 1990–2 as the storm clouds gathered.[12] In fact, the dissolution of the PCI 'unblocked' the party system. With the communist 'threat' gone, so too had the underlying reason for many moderate Italian voters to 'hold their noses' – as they had been famously instructed to do by the journalist Indro Montanelli in the 1970s – and continue to vote for the DC and its coalition partners. Instead, they now had the opportunity to register their discontent with the traditional governing parties via the ballot box, not by voting for the new PDS – unthinkable – but for the centre or right-wing opponents of the old parties who were in favour of fundamental political and/or economic change.[13] This phenomenon was seen most clearly in northern Italy with the spectacular gains made by the Lega Nord at the expense of the DC and PSI, first in regional and local elections in 1990 and 1991 respectively, then in the April 1992 general election when the Lega won 8.7 per cent of the national vote, 17.3 per cent of the vote in the north. With this latter success, the Lega 'destroyed in one fell swoop the monopoly of power achieved by the

Christian Democrats and the Socialist Party in Lombardy, Venetia and some areas of Piedmont'.[14] This seriously undermined the position of both the main governing parties (a quarter of Lega voters in 1992 had voted for the DC in 1987, one in ten for the PSI). The DC vote suffered similarly in Sicily at the hands of another 'anti-party' movement, the Rete.

The April 1992 election, while damaging to the major parties, still returned a DC-PSI coalition government. The DC won 29.7 per cent of the vote, the PSI 13.6 per cent, marginally down on its 1987 showing but still higher than at any other time since 1963. Twelve months later, however, and even the Prime Minister, the socialist Giuliano Amato, was talking of the 'death of a regime'.

Academics agree that it was the convergence of several separate but nonetheless mutually reinforcing issues between 1992 and 1993 that ultimately brought down the old order.

Fiscal crisis and the impact of Maastricht

By the beginning of the 1990s, the Italian state was running out of money. The level of public debt, 71.99 per cent of GDP in 1983, had risen to 100.50 per cent in 1990 – in part a reflection of the remarkable growth in levels of political corruption during the 1980s – by which time Italy's national debt constituted a third of the debt of the whole European Community. Until 1992, Italian governments had dealt with the problem by ignoring it. However, the convergence criteria laid down for membership of a Single European Currency by the Maastricht Treaty on European Union (February 1992) – and Italy's failure to meet any of the requirements – at last concentrated minds. 'The result was a sort of national panic.' In response, the new government pushed through a series of deeply unpopular austerity measures in the second half of 1992, cutting spending, raising taxes and clamping down on tax evasion. Recession, rising unemployment, and Italy's forced withdrawal from the European Exchange Rate Mechanism (ERM, September 1992) – membership of which was itself a condition of Economic and Monetary Union (EMU) – increased public alarm and discontent.[15]

'Clean hands' and Tangentopoli

The 'clean hands' (*mani pulite*) investigations by Milan magistrates into political corruption, which began in early 1992 and gathered pace over the next two years, were instrumental in the collapse of the old political order, revealing as they did quite breathtaking levels of bribery at all levels of the political process. Hundreds of national parliamentarians and local and regional politicians soon found themselves under investigation. The leaders of all the governing parties had to resign; Craxi eventually fled the country to avoid arrest. Magistrates in the spring of 1993 estimated that the cases then under investigation involved *tangenti* (bribes or kickbacks) totalling £70b, two-thirds of Italy's public debt. In a separate development to the *Tangentopoli* scandals – *Tangentopoli* literally means 'kickback city', a reference to Milan where the first anti-corruption cases were prosecuted – anti-Mafia magistrates in Sicily also uncovered evidence of substantial collusion between DC politicians and organized crime. In the most high-profile case, magistrates in April 1993 notified the six-times DC prime minister of Italy Giulio Andreotti that he was under investigation for links to the Mafia.

Why the Milan magistrates were allowed to carry out their investigations in the first place – or to put it another way, why the political class did not prevent them, as it had many times before – is open to debate. Some observers have stressed the significance of the political rise of the Lega at the same time as the 'clean hands' investigations were beginning in Milan. The success of the Lega broke the PSI stranglehold on Milan and gave the magistrates space to work in.[16] The PSI in Milan – which was the focus of the initial *mani pulite* investigations – was faced with allegations of corruption at the same time as its local political power was ebbing away. Indeed, one can speculate that the decline in the political fortunes of the PSI in Lombardy (and the north generally) in the local elections of 1990 actually encouraged business to question the value of continuing to pay *tangenti* (or *tangenti* on the scale they were being asked to pay) to a party whose hold over local power seemed to be increasingly insecure.

It has also been argued that for the *mani pulite* investigations to have taken off as they did required the coincidence of the PSI (as the initial focus of the investigations) and Milan (as the centre of those investigations). The PSI's startling rise under Craxi to the heart of national government in the 1980s allowed the party to indulge in corruption on a massive scale. Milan, as Craxi's personal power base, was particularly exploited. But the PSI – and Milan – represented the soft underbelly of the party political establishment. The PSI's rise to political prominence was a relatively recent one. Its corrupt relationship with (predominantly northern) private business was, therefore, less well established and less stable than, for example, that between the DC and (predominantly southern) state-reliant business in which the ties of loyalty in the corrupt exchange were older and stronger (enforced if necessary by criminal organizations). The PSI's approach to corruption was more businesslike than that of the DC, where the nature of corruption was more personal. Craxi, for example, employed a set of 'auditors' – and sometimes even intervened himself – to check the accuracy of PSI representatives' declarations on levels of bribes received, and to acquire information on firms not yet 'donating' to the party. Power within the PSI ultimately resided with Craxi, unlike in the DC where the power structure was less linear and hence the location of power more diffuse. Would a southern businessman have been so ready to break his corrupt pact with a DC official? Would an investigation into allegations of local corruption involving the DC have moved so quickly (if at all) to the national level? Probably not. In the first *mani pulite* case in Milan, however, it was a PSI official who was 'betrayed' by a businessman. In turn, he implicated other PSI officials in Milan – including Craxi's son, the Secretary of the Milan PSI. The link then between the local and national political leadership of the PSI was a relatively easy one to make. Once the web of corruption involving the PSI began to unravel, it quickly drew in the DC and the other governing parties because these shared control of the major sources of corruption: the public and semi-public sectors.[17]

A third explanation that crops up regularly in accounts of *Tangentopoli* is the independence of the Italian judiciary. The judiciary elects two-thirds of the Supreme Council of the Magistracy and it is the CSM's responsibility to promote and discipline judges. Prosecuting magistrates are not answerable to the Justice Minister and prosecution is supposed to be mandatory for all reported offences; a decentralized system of judicial authority also makes it difficult to predict the pattern of prosecution. Nevertheless, although theoretically independent, the judiciary up to the 1990s was at the mercy of the political establishment. Investigations of corruption were often suppressed. The majority of the judges on the CSM were also sympathetic to governing parties, so important posts – Rome especially – went to the 'right' people (the Rome magistrature was known as the *porto delle nebbie* [foggy port] where any cases potentially damaging to the governing parties were quietly shelved). If necessary, parliament used the privilege of immunity to block investigations: the Chamber of Deputies approved only 34 of 224 judicial requests for authority to proceed with enquiries against deputies between 1987 and 1992; the senate approved 9 of 113 requests. The successful 1987 PSI-sponsored referendum on the civil responsibility of the judges, which made judges financially responsible for their mistakes, underlined the dominance of the politicians over the judiciary.[18]

Clearly, the judiciary could hardly have even begun their investigations in 1992 without the crisis of the political élite already touched upon (and which the actions of the magistrates then intensified).[19] Guido Neppi Modona, however, has pointed out how procedural changes relating to the judiciary introduced in 1989 also worked to the advantage of the *mani pulite* pool. These gave prosecuting magistrates 'increased and more active investigative powers' and 'the ability to develop free, informal and secret investigations (i.e. without being obliged to inform the suspected person and without having to invite them to nominate a defence lawyer) until that point that suspicions could be transformed into precise elements of accusation'. Neppi Modona further suggests that 'Changes in the judicial structure contemporary to the entry into force of the new code also legitimized the establishment of groups of magistrates coordinated among themselves in order to follow full-time particularly delicate and complex lines of investigation'. The *mani pulite* pool of magistrates was 'a precise expression of these very useful forms of co-ordination'.[20] Equally, the magistrates' willingness to exploit their power of preventive custody (a suspect could be jailed for up to three months without charge) against subjects used to impunity contributed to their success in breaking the bond between corrupter and corrupted.[21]

Public opinion is also often highlighted as an important factor in the magistrates' favour. Public opinion was a significant factor in forcing the Amato Government in March 1993 (and the first Berlusconi Government in July 1994) to drop legislation aimed at curbing the powers of the judiciary. The 'star' status conferred upon leading magistrates (Antonio Di Pietro being the most obvious example) gave investigators some immunity from political smear campaigns designed to undermine their authority. The magistrates' frequent and highly successful use of preventive detention even during preliminary investigations, i.e. before charges had been laid – which was an infringement of civil liberties and not the purpose for which preventive detention was intended – would not have been possible without the public's consent.[22]

Public support for the magistrates is attributed to several factors:

- The austerity drive launched by the Amato Government in the wake of Maastricht massively increased the level of indirect taxation. Public anger with the Government over tax hikes was heightened when the scale of political corruption was revealed by the *mani pulite* investigations.
- The brutal Mafia killings of leading anti-Mafia investigating magistrates Giovanni Falcone (May 1992) and Paolo Borsellino (July 1992) in Sicily provoked a wave of solidarity with the magistrates' offensive against graft (in the state) and organized crime (in the south). It also helped to legitimize the sweeping powers of the magistrates in the eyes of the public.
- Magistrates deliberately avoided tackling widespread illegality connected to clientelism – i.e. illegality involving 'ordinary' Italians.

Electoral reform

After more than a year of *Tangentopoli* revelations, Italians were given the opportunity to pass judgement on the old governing parties via the ballot box in eight popular referendums held in April 1993. The fact that there were eight such votes itself demonstrated the public mood: for a referendum to be held in the first place required a petition of half-a-million signatures. Italians had already used a referendum to express their disillusionment with the existing political system in June 1991, when they had ignored the advice of both the DC and PSI leaderships and voted overwhelming in support of electoral reform of the chamber of deputies. A new voting system was used for the lower house in the 1992 general election but, despite widespread calls for a fundamental overhaul of Italy's electoral laws, further measures were not immediately forthcoming. Mark Gilbert has suggested that had the governing parties after April 1992 embraced even only the *rhetoric* of reform, they might have survived.[23] As it was, the April 1993 referendums delivered them a devastating blow. The level of turnout and the size of the 'yes' majorities in each of the referendums was remarkable. For example, 77 per cent of the electorate voted on the main question of electoral reform of the senate, of which 82.7 per cent voted for reform – equivalent to 60.4 per cent of eligible voters. A vote against the existing electoral system was a vote against the existing political order. Faced with such a massive vote of no-confidence, the Amato-led DC-PSI-PSDI-PLI coalition government collapsed. The Bank of Italy's Governor Carlo Azeglio Ciampi became the first non-partisan prime minister in the history of the Republic, heading up a caretaker government of 'technocrats'. Ciampi pushed through new electoral laws for both houses of parliament in August 1993. By then, municipal council elections in June 1993 had confirmed the public mood of April; the DC secured less than 19 per cent of all votes cast, the PSI a mere 3.7 per cent.[24] The DC formally dissolved itself in January 1994.

Longer-term explanations

Explanations of the collapse of the post-war political order by reference to visible, tangible and largely short-term causes by no means monopolized academic, political and public debate on the Italian crisis. Accounts that connected Italy's most recent 'failure' with its *historical* failure to become a 'proper' nation, that is, to develop a sense of national identity and (flowing from this) a sense of civic responsibility, also were – and remain – extremely popular. In this search for 'what went wrong', the usual suspects were identified: parochialism, familism, anticlericalism, Catholicism, foreign influence and occupation, geopolitics, traditions of oligarchic government, the north-south divide and so on. Their origins were located in Italy's distant past: the Risorgimento, the Counter-reformation, Machiavelli, Frederick II, Ancient Roman, even pre-Roman times.[25]

These sorts of arguments were, of course, hardly original (and, one could argue, rather pointless). From a similar position, but of greater contemporary significance, were those writers who connected the collapse of the First Republic to the lack of national identity by reference to a much more recent historical event: the Resistance, 1943–5.

Back to the future: The Resistance

The Resistance, as we have noted, was central to the genesis of the First Republic, the source from which it drew its legitimacy and from which those post-war parties active in the anti-Fascist struggle derived their right to govern. It was perhaps not altogether surprising, then, that the demise of these parties and the collapse of the post-war political system should spark renewed and critical interest in the events of 1943–5.

Among those writing on the Resistance in the early 1990s – from historians with a long-standing interest in the subject, e.g. Guido Quazza and Claudio Pavone, to those who were relatively new to the field, e.g. Ernesto Galli della Loggia and Renzo De Felice – there was, at one level, general agreement. The Resistance, the Republic's foundation myth, had failed to establish itself as an inclusive national experience; it had been unable to provide Italians with a sense of common history. The Resistance, as taught in schools, as usually portrayed on television and film, and officially remembered on 25 April (Liberation Day), was a popular patriotic fight for freedom from the Nazi German occupiers and their Fascist sidekicks (those Italians who fought for the RSI were 'fanatics, drifters, criminal gangs... beyond all reason and outside history').[26] The victory of the Resistance in this interpretation marked the triumph of good (the majority of Italians) over evil. Yet Liberation Day, as the respected historian Pietro Scoppola lamented in the mid-1990s, was for many Italians simply a holiday rather than a remembrance or celebration of a decisive 'point of departure for the reconstruction of Italian democracy'.[27]

There was little consensus, however, over the reasons for the failure of the Resistance tradition, and bitter disagreement as to the significance, and meaning, of the Resistance itself.

The role of the PCI

There is no doubt that, of all the post-war parties, the PCI most closely identi-fied itself with the Resistance, and not without reason. The PCI could trace its anti-Fascism back to the early 1920s (although for many years the party was a source of division within the anti-Fascist movement). Communist partisans had been the majority within the Resistance movement after 1943. It had been the PCI leader Palmiro Togliatti who, in recognizing the monarchy in the spring of 1944, had broken the potentially damaging stand-off between the CLN and the royal government in the south, paving the way for a broad united front against Nazi-Fascism. The communists had been loyal members of the all-party governments after liberation. From the late 1940s, with the onset of the Cold War, the Resistance took on an increasing significance for the PCI. First, it enabled the party to defend itself against DC accusations that it was control-led from Moscow and opposed to the democratic system. Second, it provided the basis for the communists' own claim to the right to govern, a right which was being denied to it; after all, had it not led a popular (but, the PCI claimed, essentially working-class) and progressive movement in a patriotic war of national liberation? Third, it allowed the PCI to accuse the conservative and in many ways authoritarian DC of betraying the ideals of the Resistance and of the constitution.

Raking over the ashes of the First Republic – and of Italian communism – in the early 1990s, many historians saw the PCI's post-war 'appropriation' of the Resistance as the root cause of the failure of the Resistance to serve as a founding myth, as a new symbol of national identity. By its 'decades-long effort to hegem-onize the Resistance heritage', the PCI sacrificed a national myth to party ends.[28] Other political parties were written out of Resistance history, which in turn meant they played down the importance of the Resistance (not until the 1960s was the Resistance taught in schools). By peddling its own Resistance history, the PCI also encouraged rival versions of the Resistance to circulate. The neo-Fascists responded by declaring the Resistance to have been a 'civil war' between compet-ing groups (Fascist vs communist) for control of the state, rather than a patriotic war of national liberation. By this, the neo-Fascists claimed moral parity with the partisans. More seriously, in the 1960s and 1970s, a new generation of Marxists bought into the idea of the 'Resistance betrayed', pointing the finger of blame this time at the PCI leadership itself; this group turned to violence and 'red' terrorism, citing the Resistance as inspiration (see Chapter 9). An official state-sponsored 'popular' anti-Fascist interpretation of the Resistance did emerge in the 1960s and 1970s as the DC turned first to the socialists and then to the PCI for sup-port, but the Resistance was by now contested terrain. The PCI, albeit with some assistance, had, to use an American historian's analogy, 'chopped down' the Italian 'cherry tree'.

Criticism of the Italian Communist Party extended to its version of events, too. Such criticism was not new – and had come not only from political groups of the far Right and Left but also from respected historians.[29] In the early 1990s, however, with the PCI no longer in a position to defend itself, it became open season: the non/anti-communist press, television, political parties and historians revelled in exposing the hypocrisies of the party whose very ideology, so the argument ran, had been shown with the collapse of Soviet communism to be a fraud. Considerable attention was given to 'red' violence during and after the war. The 'triangle of death' around Modena, where, in the months following liberation, communists had killed several hundred (perhaps even several thousand) Italians – by no means all Fascists – was a particular favourite with the media. Much was also made of the support given by the PCI to Tito's pro-Yugoslav communist forces operating in the far northeast of Italy during 1945. Both instances were taken as evidence of the PCI's prioritization of ideology over patriotism, of 'class war' over 'war of national liberation'. Togliatti's patriotism was closely scrutinized, too: his refusal to help Italian prisoners of war held in Russia indicated that his loyalties were to Stalin rather than the Italian people; the *svolta di Salerno* was at Stalin's behest, part of Soviet strategy rather than for the good of Italy. The PCI's anti-Fascism, then, was neither democratic nor patriotic. It had served, however, to give the party what De Felice had some years earlier described as 'a patina of democracy' and a (false) claim to legitimacy.[30] Even its anti-Fascist credentials could be questioned. While the PCI paraded its anti-Fascism in the post-war period – and consistently blocked moves to a 'national reconciliation' – at the same time it took in thousands of new recruits from Fascist ranks, even Fascists of the 'last hour', from the RSI . Little wonder that what De Felice termed the 'aggressively hegemonic' *vulgata resistenziale* of the PCI had left many Italians unmoved during the life of the First Republic.

Despite the sins of the PCI and the failure of the founding myth of the Resistance, there were historians who continued to argue that the values and purpose of the Resistance still carried moral weight. Claudio Pavone, for example, whose work on the Resistance had first allowed 'respectable' society to talk of it as a 'civil war' (previously regarded as a no-go, neo-Fascist position), argued that the 'unity of the Resistance' retained its moral value.[31] Others argued that, if purged of its mythic and celebrative elements, a more honest 'warts and all' Resistance history could still stimulate within Italians a 'feeling of democratic citizenship and a national identity'.[32] James Miller's comments are characteristic of this position:

> Fortunately, the Resistance myth, though seriously battered by political manipulation and scholarly revision, still offers something to Italians...the Resistance remains one of the brightest moments in united Italy's 150-year political history. It offers Italians a set of values and of experiences that are worthy of emulation in any democratic society. By coming to terms with the breadth of positive and negative experiences included in the Resistance – individual courage, idealism, civil war, massacres, betrayal and cowardice – Italians are in a position to face their future with a more secure hold on their past. The myth may yet prove a useful political tool for democratic, post-communist and post-Fascist Italy.[33]

Revisionism and the Resistance

The idea that the Resistance could or should serve as the lodestar of a Second Republic and the basis for the spiritual renewal of the nation was not universally accepted, however. It is in this context that Renzo De Felice made his last and perhaps most controversial contribution to national historical debate.

By the early 1990s, De Felice was reaching the end of his biography of Mussolini, preparing the final volume that would cover the last two years of the war. An established media personality by this time, De Felice did not wait to complete his biography (in the event published posthumously and unfinished in 1997) before delivering his verdict on the German and Allied occupations, the RSI and the Resistance. First in a series of newspaper and magazine articles and then, in 1995, in *Rosso e Nero*, De Felice argued not only that the Resistance had failed to supply post-war Italy with a sense of collective identity but it could never have done so given its real historical character. The 8 September represented not so much the beginning of Italy's finest hour (the Resistance) but rather a 'national catastrophe'. Instead of conducting themselves heroically in defeat, Italians went on 'moral strike': the King and his government fled Rome; the Italian army in occupied zones was left to its fate; the army in Italy simply disintegrated. These events, symptomatic of the ethical-political weakness of national sentiment, of the failure of a self-serving bourgeoisie to fulfil its historic task of nation build-ing, and of the technical, moral and intellectual deficiencies of the military and political hierarchy of Fascism, had, De Felice insisted, marked and undermined for ever the national collective memory. 'A large part of Italy welcomed...defeat', De Felice said, quoting the writer Corrado Alvaro. 'Solidarity and patriotism and the sense of individual responsibility was dispersed and killed.'[34]

The subsequent Resistance could not put the Humpty Dumpty of the Italian nation back together again. The Resistance was not a popular movement. There were a few thousand activists in the first months after 8 September, rising to 110,000 partisans by October 1944 (De Felice placed his trust in official Fascist estimates of the 'bandits'' strength rather than those of the Resistance itself). The number of partisans fell away over the winter of 1944–5 before, in the final weeks leading up to liberation, many Italians suddenly discovered they too were partisans and donned the red neckerchief. At this point, the Resistance could claim 200,000 members. In comparison, the number of Italians fighting for the Salò republic totalled over half a million. Either way, most Italians were not involved. According to De Felice, survival was their primary concern. The major-ity of Italians in the north occupied what he called a 'grey zone' between the partisans and the Salò Fascists, favouring neither side in the 'civil war'. Italians in the south, meanwhile, were entirely divorced from the proceedings. As such, De Felice argued, any attempt to create a national unity based on anti-Fascism after the war could only be divisive, the source of a collective identity crisis, since it excluded the largest part of the population.[35]

Worse still, not only was the Resistance vulgate of a popular war of national liberation historically inaccurate (De Felice also played down the military importance of the Resistance) and mainly to the benefit of the unpatriotic and anti-democratic PCI whose presence in the Republic sullied post-war democracy, but it prevented any attempt to address the 'lacerating trauma' that 8 September represented for most Italians.[36] The Italian nation had lived in denial for half a century, hence the lasting failure to reconstitute Italy's moral fibre.[37]

There were a number of 'if only' moments in *Rosso e Nero*. If only there had been an Italian De Gaulle, a patriot and soldier able 'to summon Italians to the defence of the *patria*' in September 1943, then at least the nation would have lost with honour. If only Salò had not existed, then the Resistance would have assumed a national hue, it would have been a natural patriotic revolt. If only the two main political parties at the war's end and subsequently had been more patriotic and less concerned with *realpolitik*, then Italy's post-war ethical-political degeneration – ending up in *Tangentopoli* – might have been averted. For De Felice, so it appeared, the whole period September 1943–April 1945 had to be judged by patriotic criteria: to what extent had the actions of individuals, classes, parties been governed by their love of Italy? The King, the Fascist élite, the Italian military leaders, Togliatti, the PCI, the DC, the bourgeoisie, all failed the patriot test. Those who passed included Alfredo Pizzoni, the first President of the CLNAI, who, De Felice argued, had been kicked out by the communists in 1945 because he was too patriotic and too liberal. The pass list also featured – rather more controversially – Mussolini, the old Fascist *filosofo* Giovanni Gentile, and Prince Junio Valerio Borghese, head of the feared *Decima Mas* (X-Mas) group that had fought a particularly bloody campaign for the RSI. Mussolini, claimed De Felice, had returned to power not because he sought revenge against the Italians, or was moved by political ambition, or was interested in reviving Fascism, but because he wanted to 'put himself at the service of the *patria*'. Mussolini wished to save northern Italy from the same fate as Poland, to maintain the territorial integrity of the north (threatened by piecemeal German annexation) and to redeem Italy's national honour by continuing to fight alongside its ally. Gentile meanwhile had worked to preserve the moral fabric of the nation, to contain the civil war, and had been prepared to die for his country. As for Borghese, though he had tortured partisans, and was an undoubted reactionary (years later he organized an attempted military *coup d'état* against the Republic), he was not, in De Felice's opinion, a Fascist but 'a nationalist that thought to fight a non-political, almost personal, war, for the honour of the *patria*'. De Felice did not spell it out, but the clear implication of his argument was that some aspects of Salò had as much to offer Italians in terms of moral or ethical-political values as did the anti-Fascist Resistance.[38]

De Felice's was not a lone voice. Ernesto Galli della Loggia, for example, described 8 September as 'la morte della patria' – 'a tragedy for the Italian nation state and therefore of the entire Italian people'. There were no moral or ethical-political lessons to be learned from the Resistance. The presence of the 'anti-national' PCI within its ranks meant it was impossible to view the Resistance as a movement founded on national identity, as the basis of a common civic sense. The Resistance had obscured the reality of Italy's defeat. Instead, the myth that 'Italy too won the war' gained currency when, in fact, Italy had only been liberated courtesy of the Allies, had been made to pay for losing, and had suffered a 'radical demotion in terms of international status'. Furthermore, the anti-Fascist basis of the Republic had excluded as many Italians as it included, undermining any sense of national identity. Lacking a De Gaulle-type figure capable of unifying the nation, the political parties post-war had presided over a 'gigantic work of denationalization'. The monopolistic claims of the post-war anti-Fascist parties to represent the 'idea of nation' excluded those who had previously supported Fascism or, in 1946, had voted for the continuation of the monarchy. The stress on anti-Fascism post-1945 had allowed the Left, specifically the PCI, to exert a pernicious influence over intellectual and cultural debate.[39] Ploughing a similar furrow, Romolo Gobbi argued that specific character defects of the Republic could be traced directly to the Resistance. The practice of *lottizzazione*, for example, owed its origins to the CLN's sharing out of the principal public offices between its constituent parties after liberation. A precedent was thus set 'between the antifascist parties that characterized all the political history of the Republic born of the Resistance'.[40]

Assessment

In an interview given by Silvio Berlusconi in September 2003 to Nicholas Farrell of the *Spectator* magazine, the Italian premier stated that 'Mussolini never killed anyone,' and had 'sent people on holiday to confine them' during his 'benign dictatorship'. In the ensuing controversy, Luca Volonté, the leader of the Christian Democratic Union Party, and part of the Forza Italia-led governing coalition, claimed: 'Anti-fascism is a value that unites. It unites the majority [in parliament]. It unites the government with the opposition. It unites the country. To split over that which unites is senseless'.[41] Clearly, though, anti-Fascism did not unite in parliament; for much of the new political Right, anti-Fascism had little meaning in a post-Cold War, post-ideological, post-Fascist world. Nor did it unite – and, if De Felice and Galli della Loggia were to be believed, nor had it ever united – the country.

It is in this context that one can properly see the dangers of 'anti-anti-Fascism' and understand the concerns of historians such as Bosworth. It is extraordinary that in the mid-1990s, Gian Enrico Rusconi felt the need to ask (albeit rhetorically): 'To be a democrat in Italy today is it still necessary to be an anti-Fascist?'[42] De Felice's droll observation that an 'anti-Fascist habit does not make a democratic monk'[43] is certainly justified, but anti-Fascism was/is an essential element of the democratic constituent just as surely as anti-democracy was/is part of the Fascist one.

In place of the anti-Fascist Resistance myth, a neopatriotic *vulgata* appears to be under construction, where the Resistance is the original sin rather than the original virtue of the Republic and the PCI its black heart, behind virtually all of Italy's post-war ills.

De Felice and other neo-patriots have accused the 'aggressively hegemonic' Left of putting ideology before historical truth. Certainly, one cannot deny that many communist historians were guilty of using history for political ends, producing far from balanced or accurate accounts of the Resistance and the PCI's role in events. But so wrapped up in the *bandiera tricolore* are some 'neopatriotic' accounts that basic moral considerations are cast aside and the historical record reworked, sometimes – as in the case of De Felice – in the most extraordinary fashion. Let us look again at De Felice's four patriots: Pizzoni, Mussolini, Gentile and Borghese. Of the four, only Pizzoni is from the Resistance camp and he is included to demonstrate the ideological and unpatriotic character of the PCI. As regards Mussolini, the fact remains that the establishment of Salò under the *Duce* was excellent propaganda for the Nazi regime, and its consequences – civil war and the prolongation of the international conflict on the peninsula – deleterious to Italy. The idea that Mussolini had no thoughts of revenge is also highly questionable. As Mack Smith writes:

> Mussolini's vindictive cruelty and attenuated patriotism were further exposed in 1944 by his attempt to make the Germans destroy Rome by defending it street by street. He had a particular grudge against the Romans because of their jubilation over his arrest in July 1943. Much to his disgust the German generals left Rome and Florence more or less intact, for reasons which he called sentimental and irrelevant...he encouraged the Germans to destroy the main ports of Venice, Genoa and Trieste... This was a strange kind of patriotism.[44]

In the cases of Gentile and Borghese, in *Rosso e Nero* De Felice had argued that both were, in different ways, champions of the idea of 'national pacification' in order to preserve unity of mind and to avoid the excesses of civil war. Yet Gentile made repeated calls for death to traitors, and Borghese was more than happy not just to kill but also torture his partisan victims. De Felice's portrayal of Borghese and the X-Mas group as an apolitical, patriotic band fighting to restore Italy's honour fails to do justice to Borghese's record. From September 12 1943, X-Mas was part of the German Wehrmacht. Borghese was happy to take contributions for his new journal *L'Orizzonte* from the rabid anti-Semite – and (in Mussolini's opinion) 'repulsive human being' – Giovanni Preziosi. Borghese may not have been a member of the Fascist Party, but he did join the neo-Fascist MSI after the war. His wartime crimes earned him a life sentence in 1949.

Neopatriotic history of this stripe is surely a dead end. De Felice certainly was not opposed to democracy; indeed, he talked of De Gasperi's 'great historical merit of having carried over the idea of democracy that was asserting itself in twentieth-century Italy – roughly speaking before and after the Great War – an idea that Fascism had with its revolution first defeated, then trodden underfoot'.[45] Nevertheless, one is left wondering whether De Felice, like that fanatical nineteenth-century Italian patriot Francesco Crispi, might have been prepared, in certain circumstances, to exchange democracy for authoritarianism in defence of the *patria*.

How should we view the Resistance and the PCI's involvement within the partisan movement and the post-war Republic? It should be noted at the outset that there *is* a negative side to the Resistance myth. As with the myth of the 'good' Holocaust (see Chapter 6), it has encouraged Italians to forget about the two decades of dictatorship in Italy prior to the Nazi occupation and to avoid moral responsibility for Fascism. It is no coincidence that 'When Italians talk about the war, it is always about the last year of the war, about the Resistance, the German occupation. You don't hear about the invasion of Ethiopia, Albania, and Greece, or about the Racial Laws'.[46] Such collective amnesia is unhealthy.

This, however, should not detract from the historical and symbolic importance of the Resistance. While it is undeniable that the partisan movement was small in absolute terms, at its height boasting around 200,000 activists, relative to other Resistance movements it was one of the largest in occupied Europe. Nor could the partisans have survived without the tacit support of a significant portion of the unarmed civilian population. Looked at in these terms – and bearing in mind the many kinds of 'civil resistance' offered by unarmed Italians, e.g. the help given to thousands of escaped Allied prisoners after September 1943 – the Resistance was a popular movement.[47] It should also be remembered that the Resistance entailed enormous sacrifice: an estimated 50,000 partisans were killed between September 1943 and April 1945. And while the Resistance certainly did not liberate Italy – as the Protocols of Rome demonstrate, the Resistance needed the Allies – it was still a very significant thorn in the side of the German and Fascist authorities. In the summer of 1944, the Resistance held all the Alpine valleys, the hill zones of Piedmont and Lombardy and a great part of the Apennine valleys; it also tied down almost a quarter (26 divisions) of German and Fascist forces in the north. Between June and August 1944, partisans killed some 5,000 Germans.[48] Was the Resistance a civil war? Of course it was. As is the case in all such conflicts where the normal rules of warfare do not apply, it was also a particularly bloody and violent struggle, with atrocities committed by both sides. It is no surprise, either, that in those regions of northern Italy where twenty years earlier 'Fascist squads had been particularly vicious...the civil war was more violent and the after-effects of the Liberation lasted longer'.[49] But the Resistance was far more than a civil war. Rather, as Pavone argues, it was three wars in one:

> If the German enemy was considered the prime element, it took on the character of a patriotic conflict. If, alternatively, attention was drawn to the Fascist enemy it looked more like a civil war. If from fascism as a political enemy the line was traced back to the bosses and masters (the capitalists and the landowners) as the social enemy that had created and nurtured Fascism...it took on the distinct characteristics of a class conflict.

Although 'The three characteristics of the struggle were closely connected and easily confused', indeed, few partisans fought just 'one war'. 'The main objective remained that of delivering Italy from Fascism, ally and accomplice of Nazism.'[50] The Resistance, then, was primarily seen *by the partisans themselves* as a 'war of national liberation'. It was also viewed, as both Quazza and Pavone point out, as part of a wider European civil war: a war of and for civilization. As a PDS deputy commented in 1994, in a television discussion of the Italian 'civil war', 'the ideals for which they [*Salòists* and partisans] died were profoundly different and only one set of values is worthy of our respect'.[51] The Resistance does indeed still have much to offer contemporary Italy.

The Resistance, in the shape of the CLN, also deserves credit for driving Italian politics into the modern age. The 1946 constituent assembly was elected on the basis of universal suffrage, including women. The subsequent Republican constitution, although in hindsight not without its problems (e.g. proportional representation led to unstable coalition government) was, in many ways, a progressive document, even if it took several decades for some aspects to be realized in practice. That a constitution was even agreed upon, despite considerable political differences between the parties and the onset of the Cold War, suggests that the experience of working together during the war paid immediate dividends in the post-war period. Unlike Greece, post-war Italy did not descend into a partisan civil war.

The PCI's role in the Resistance and the Republic has been, as we have seen, subject to much criticism. In fact, so long is the list of the PCI's alleged failings – it was an unpatriotic and anti-democratic party; it was responsible for deflowering the Resistance myth, preventing national reconciliation and stifling Italian culture; it could be blamed for clientelism, *lottizzazione* and *partitocrazia* (rule-by-parties) – that one might be forgiven for thinking:

> ...that Italy had been governed by five Togliatti and several Berlinguer ministries... that the elections of 1948 had been won by the Popular Front, and that Alcide De Gasperi...had been off doing missionary work in Africa. In fact, postwar Italy was dominated by Christian Democracy and American-inspired popular culture, not the 'Marxist Vulgate'... All of this should be painfully obvious...'[52]

It is true that after 1948 the PCI sought to manipulate the Resistance myth for its own ends – to the detriment of the Resistance as a national tradition. But it is also understandable given the post-war political context and the PCI's bitter struggle with the DC. In an increasingly conservative environment, the Resistance was the PCI's most obvious defence against DC attacks, and its most obvious grounds for demanding that the rights of workers be recognized. Nor can one seriously dispute that the PCI did have a significant and generally positive role in the Resistance and in the creation of the Republic. Although the PCI under Togliatti certainly looked to Moscow for leadership, advice and guidance, Stalin was happy to let the PCI fend for itself and Togliatti was realist enough to understand that social revolution was not on the cards, either under the cover of the Resistance or after liberation: at the very least, the Allies would not permit it. In fact, Togliatti – and whether the direction came from Stalin or not is really neither here nor there – placed winning the war and maintaining unity between all sides involved in the 'war of liberation' above all other considerations. As Ginsborg points out, there were many benefits to this approach. Unity between the CLN was essential for the effectiveness of the Resistance in the north. By bringing the CLN into the Badoglio Government, Togliatti greatly strengthened its position vis-à-vis both the Kingdom of the South and the Allies. Furthermore, his course of action helped to secure the legality of the PCI, and guarantee it a central role in the political process between 1945 and 1947. However, by risking nothing on the major social and political questions – while their opponents 'continued to pursue their objectives with all the means at their disposal' – the communists allowed themselves to be 'completely outflanked by the Allies and by the conservative forces in Italian society'. From this perspective, if the PCI was guilty of anything, it was of playing too straight and too narrow.[53]

Was the PCI an anti-democratic party? Despite its formal adherence to revolutionary Marxism there is no evidence that the PCI leadership ever seriously considered pursuing anything other than a reformist road to socialism – hence the hard Left's criticisms of the PCI in the 1960s and 1970s and its recourse to violence and direct action, and the PCI's willingness to deal with the DC in the mid-1970s. In fact, the only real challenges to the democratic Republic after 1945 came from right-wing elements (the armed forces and security services) within the state itself. Arguably, by maintaining the patina of revolution, the PCI managed only to frighten the moderate majority in Italy and ensure that it remained unelectable; in so doing it failed in its role as Opposition to oblige the DC to govern properly.

To what extent was the Resistance or the PCI responsible for the character defects of the Republic? The claims that *partitocrazia* and the practice of *lottizzazione* derive from the CLN's example at the end of the war are easily dismissed. As Pavone and Neri Serneri point out, such arguments, besides ruling out the possibility that events over the next (or, indeed, previous) decades might have had a bearing on the development of these phenomena, also fail entirely to understand the historical context in which the decision to share out offices was taken. 'On coming out of a Fascist, totalitarian, one-party system, the plurality of parties, rather than their abandonment, was a much greater sign of change.'[54] The politicization of the state did not begin with the Republic; it was a feature of both the liberal and Fascist periods. Nor was clientelism the invention of the post-war political parties. It is perhaps not surprising, then, that these traditions were also a feature of the post-war Republic, especially when we bear in mind the extraordinary continuity in the apparatus of the state between liberal, Fascist and Republican Italy. The Resistance removed the monarchy and the Republican constitution was a genuinely democratic innovation, but the bureaucracy, the judiciary and the security services remained largely untouched after 1945. Togliatti has been blamed for this as well: as Justice Minister, it was he who had announced the wide-ranging political amnesty in 1946, effectively bringing to an end any hopes of a clean sweep of the state administration. Togliatti, however, had little choice. At the end of the war the bureaucracy and the judiciary had been tasked with purging themselves; their own complicity in Fascism, though, meant little was done. Furthermore, a root and branch purge was simply not practicable, it would have paralysed the state administration. It did mean, however, that Fascist and, indeed, pre-Fascist mentalities persisted, and institutional renewal in a modern, democratic sense was stymied.[55] It also meant that post-war trials against those accused of war crimes inevitably favoured the Fascist over the partisan. Borghese, for example, managed to have his trial moved from Milan to

Rome where his family carried considerable influence; although found guilty and sentenced to life imprisonment, he was allowed to go free immediately. RSI units were later given 'belligerent' status – a right denied to partisans, who were treated as common criminals. In the case of seven Fascist 'Black Brigade' members who were charged with raping and killing a female partisan messenger before impaling her corpse in a vineyard, the judge ruled that rape was not torture, knifing was not a heinous act and impalement was just insult to a corpse.[56] So much for left-wing hegemony.

One further point should be made regarding the growth of clientelism, *lottizzazione* and *partitocrazia* in Republican Italy. If blame for the spread of these tendencies *is* to be apportioned amongst the post-war political parties then it must surely fall mainly on the shoulders of the governing parties and the DC in particular. These were, after all, in control of the spoils system.

This assessment has not yet paid much attention to the debates surrounding the immediate causes of the collapse of the old orders in the early 1990s. I will limit myself to three main observations in this context. First, although it is true that the two main parties were undoubtedly in decline in the 1980s, to claim, as some have done, that 'all the conditions for [political] change existed' by the late 1980s, is to ignore the fact that nobody in the late 1980s could – or did – anticipate fundamental change in the foreseeable future. Ginsborg in his much-praised *A History of Contemporary Italy* (1990) described the 1980s as 'a period of great political continuities'. Leonardi and Wertman in 1989 forecast that the DC's 'unparalleled record among parties in Western democracies of remaining in power for the entire post-war period is very likely to be extended well beyond the late 1980s'.[57] Second, and related to the first point, the collapse of the First Republic was dependent on a remarkable confluence of mutually reinforcing factors: the end of the Cold War, the rise of the Lega, the financial crisis exposed by Maastricht, *Tangentopoli* and the referendum on electoral reform. Third, public support, as we have seen, was important to the success of the *Tangentopoli* investigations; but *Tangentopoli* and, indeed, the whole political crisis, did not involve any serious public debate about the responsibility of ordinary Italians for the mess that Italy found itself in. As Ginsborg notes, 'There was a crucial failure, or refusal, to connect the themes raised by the magistrates with the power structure and culture of Italian society... Ordinary Italians were never forced to ask themselves how much the culture of *Tangentopoli* – clientelism, corruption, nepotism, tax evasion – was *their* culture'. Italians saw themselves (and Italian business also portrayed itself) simply as the victims of a corrupt political class. Moreover, many Italians did not really identify with 'the austerity, ethical rectitude and idea of service to the state' which characterized the *mani pulite* pool of magistrates. Contemporary northern Italian society had instead embraced 'the full hedonism and romanticism of late twentieth century consumption'. Notions of civic trust and responsibility had shallow roots in the south (see Chapter 9).[58]

Opinion polls conducted at the height of the *Tangentopoli* scandals (from mid to late 1993) suggested that Italians were more worried about job insecurity, political uncertainty and new taxes than they were that there might be a 'wipe of the sponge' for those implicated in *Tangentopoli* – despite government attempts to do precisely this earlier in the year. In polls taken in 1994, only 23 per cent of respondents considered corruption to be 'the most important problem facing Italy'. These figures would seem to bear out Ginsborg's assessment that the public's support for *mani pulite* did not mean a deep-rooted commitment to its ideals (a return to legality). Indeed, traditionally, respect of the law has never been high in Italy. An opinion poll of August 1994 revealed that some 30 per cent of Italians still considered fiscal evasion acceptable.[59] Tax evasion in the 1990s cost the Italian government an estimated 100,000b lire per annum.

Perhaps the clearest sign of the limits to Italy's 'revolution', however, has been the remarkable political career of Berlusconi. Italians voted him into office in 1994, 2001 and again in 2008. This, despite Berlusconi's close ties to the old regime (in particular to Craxi), his alleged involvement in *Tangentopoli*, masonry and with the Mafia, his blatant use of political office to curb the powers of the magistrates and to change the law in order to block investigations into his business affairs, his portrayal of the magistrates as 'red togas' seeking to impose a left-wing government on Italy, and his efforts to overturn the electoral reforms of the early 1990s – brought in because of *Tangentopoli*. Berlusconi's success suggests that many Italians have been more than willing to draw a veil over the recent past.[60]

8 The post-war Italian economy

Introduction

The post-war period is relatively unexplored territory for economic historians of Italy; surprisingly so, given the extraordinary expansion of the Italian economy after 1945. The bare facts demonstrate post-war Italy's 'spectacular catch-up'.[1] Between 1950 and 1989, the Italian economy grew on average by 4 per cent p.a. Consequently, by the end of the 1980s, Italy had nearly caught up the major European economies in terms of GDP; indeed, much fuss was made of the fact that Italian GDP actually surpassed that of the UK for the first time in the late 1980s. As the twentieth century drew to a close Italy was the world's sixth largest economy, accounting for nearly a fifth of the new euro-zone economy; globally, 4 per cent. Italian income per capita had quintupled within half a century. Less than a third that of the United States in 1950, by 1995 it had risen to more than two-thirds of the US level, and was on a par with the UK.[2] Between 1960 and 1990, only Spain and Ireland of the twenty-four member states of the Organization for Economic Cooperation and Development (OECD) experienced higher rates of growth in income per capita – and both started from much lower levels of economic development than Italy.[3] By the mid-1990s, life expectancy was higher in Italy that in Britain, Germany and the United States.

'Catch-up' also entailed fundamental changes to the structure of the Italian economy. Agriculture employed 44 per cent of the workforce in the 1940s; in 1997, less than 8 per cent. Agricultural product represented 23 per cent of GDP in 1945; by the early 1990s, 5 per cent. Centuries-old patterns of rural life were swept away within 20 years of the end of World War Two: the *latifondi* were broken up during the 1950s; sharecropping contracts were made illegal from 1964; millions of peasants, including vast numbers of former day-labourers, left the countryside for Italy's towns and cities, or emigrated.[4] Many internal migrants ended up in industry. By 1961, the so-called secondary economy employed 38 per cent of the working population, more than in agriculture (30 per cent) and services (32 per cent). Italy, however, was an 'industrial economy', in the sense of an economy based on large-scale heavy industry, 'Fordist' mass-production techniques and an unskilled mass workforce, for a remarkably short time. From the 1970s, not only did the number of workers in industry fall as a percentage of the overall labour force (39.5 per cent in 1970; 32.2 per cent in 1995) but also the trend within industry (especially manufacturing) was towards smaller firms. In 1971, 24 per cent of workers in manufacturing were employed in firms with over 500 employees; in 1991, 13 per cent. Over the same period, the percentage of manufacturing workers employed in firms with less than 500 staff rose from 76 per cent to 87 per cent. By the 1990s, 71.4 per cent of the industrial labour force (manufacturing and non-manufacturing) worked in firms with less than 250 employees, and almost a quarter in firms with less than ten employees. Of the world's advanced economies, only Japan shared the Italian preference for small rather than large-scale industry.[5]

Linked to this was another peculiar feature of the late twentieth-century Italian economy: the growing importance of low-tech/labour-intensive 'traditional' and artisan-based manufacturing, such as textiles and clothing. This bucked the trend seen in other advanced economies towards high-tech/capital-intensive industry. Mainly small to medium-size enterprises (SMEs), these firms were typically family-owned and concentrated in north-east and central Italy where they tended to form regional pockets of specialization (so-called 'industrial districts') producing just one product or several related products, with a strong export orientation. Their phenomenal success from the 1970s meant that, by the 1990s, the 'Third Italy' (i.e. neither the 'First Italy' of the north-western industrial triangle, nor the 'Second Italy' of the relatively backward south) had become the engine room of the national economy and the country's wealthiest region.

How and why Italy became a major player in the post-war global economy are two of the key questions that economic historians/historians have sought to address. Questions have also been asked, however, about the underlying health of the economy since 1945. Here attention has focused on the persistence of two major imbalances in the Italian economy. First, regional dualism, namely the north–south divide. Second, sectoral dualism, i.e. the significant differences in productivity between sectors, in particular between privately owned, export-oriented manufacturing – the SMEs of Third Italy but also some of the older, larger Italian firms, primarily located in northern and central Italy – and the inefficient, protected and predominantly southern-based services sector, in which the state was a major presence. In these respects, we are dealing with some very familiar economic historiographical issues: the 'Southern Question', the role of the state in the Italian economy and the influence of external factors in Italian economic growth.

Framework

Post-war reconstruction

Although Italy's transport and communications networks and housing stock were badly damaged during World War Two, Italian industry emerged from the conflict relatively unscathed and, in fact, had benefited during the war from substantial investment. It was perhaps not too surprising then, that Italy should experience rapid economic growth immediately after the war as reconstruction efforts got underway; the economy grew by 25 per cent in 1946, 14.5 per cent in 1947. American dollar aid in the form of the European Recovery Programme (ERP, commonly known as the Marshall Plan, 1948–52) helped to sustain economic growth through the late 1940s. By 1950, GDP had recovered to its 1939 level, with growth over the entire reconstruction period (1945–50) averaging 11.2 per cent p.a.[6]

Trade liberalization and European integration

Italy's participation in the Marshall Plan was indicative of a clear line in post-war Italian economic policy: to tie Italy into a US-led capitalist-industrial economic bloc based upon the liberalization of trade. Italy quickly signed up to Bretton Woods (whereby western nations agreed to a system of fixed exchange rates pegged to the value of the dollar), the International Monetary Fund (IMF) and the World Bank. Italy was also a founder member of the Organization for European Economic Cooperation (OEEC) in 1948. More significantly, in the 1950s, Italy was a signatory to the Treaty of Paris (1951) establishing the European Coal and Steel Community (ECSC), western Europe's first foray into economic integration, and was one of the original six members of the European Economic Community (EEC) created in 1957, the forerunner of the European Union (EU).

The 'economic miracle', 1950–63

Italy was not undeveloped in 1950; it already had a well-established industrial base. Nevertheless, the rapidity and extent of economic change between 1950 and 1963 was remarkable. As Cohen and Federico note, 'Rates of growth of GDP, GDP per capita, total factor productivity and output per worker were higher and more sustained than at any time in the country's history'. If we just take GDP and labour productivity (output per worker):

- GDP grew on average by 5.9 per cent p.a. between 1950 and 1963 (6.3 per cent p.a. between 1958 and 1963), peaking in 1961 when the economy grew by 7.6 per cent. In western Europe, only the West German economy experienced more rapid growth.
- Industrial productivity grew on average by 7.2 per cent p.a. between 1949 and 1959, the fastest such growth in Western Europe. Agricultural productivity rose by 4.7 per cent p.a. over the same period.

Industrial production increased by 270 per cent between 1948 and 1962, growing on average by over 8 per cent p.a. between 1950 and 1963. Steel production tripled, car production increased tenfold (to over 1m vehicles p.a.), electricity output doubled. Industrial output as a percentage of GNP rose from 4 to 12 per cent between 1951 and 1964.[7]

Perhaps, as Zamagni has argued, the real 'miracle' of these years was that Italian industrial goods at last were able to penetrate markets in which the Italian state was not the primary customer – new overseas markets and the domestic consumer market. Accounting for 60 per cent of all Italian exports in 1938, by 1960 industry's share had risen to 90 per cent. This after a decade of extremely rapid export growth (Italian exports grew on average by 11.4 per cent p.a. between 1949 and 1963, peaking at over 20 per cent in 1957 and 1960) during which Italy's share of world exports increased (i.e. Italian exports grew at faster rate than global exports). Metal-engineering goods dominated industrial exports. The incredible growth of domestic private consumption during the 1950s (it grew almost as much between 1948 and 1963, as between 1861 and 1948) and of private consumption per capita (having grown by only a third between 1861 and 1948, it doubled over the next 15 years) meant that for the first time there was also a real home-grown demand for Italian industrial products. The burgeoning market for consumer goods (especially consumer durables, e.g. televisions, cars) is evident from the statistics. In 1954, there were 88,000 television licence holders; in 1958, 1.2m; in 1964, 5.22m. In 1950, there were 347,000 private cars and 700,000 motorcycles on Italian roads; in 1964, 4.67m and 4.3m respectively. Accompanying the growth of industrial output, productivity and demand, industrial investment grew on average by 6 per cent p.a. between 1951 and 1958, and by 14 per cent p.a. between 1958 and 1963.[8]

Although agricultural output grew in absolute terms during the 1950s, as a percentage of national income it fell significantly, from 27.5 per cent of GDP (1949) to 13 per cent (1960). Productivity gains in the primary economy were largely due to the huge reduction in the agricultural labour force linked to mass migration. Over 3m permanent or part time agricultural workers left the land between 1951 and 1963. By the early 1960s, more people were employed in the secondary and tertiary sectors (industry and services) than in agriculture. Italy had 'finally joined the league of industrial nations'.[9]

It was not all change in the Italian economy during the miracle years. Salaries remained low (real wages rose by less than 2 per cent p.a.) and unemployment remained high (in an era of virtual full employment elsewhere in western Europe, Italian unemployment never fell below 2.6 per cent p.a.).[10] The wealth gap between north and south widened. The state also remained a significant player in the Italian economy, particularly industry. The IRI (see Chapter 5) invested heavily in the modernization of utilities during the 1950s (the electricity industry was actually nationalized[11] in 1962). Its steel subholding company, Finsider, oversaw the creation of a major new integrated steelworks at Cornigliano (Genoa) in the early 1950s. Its engineering subholding company, Finmeccanica, controlled and directed investment in twenty major companies, including Alfa Romeo. The state-owned Azienda generale italiana petroli (AGIP) established in 1926, greatly expanded its operations after 1945 before being subsumed into the state-holding company Ente nazionale idrocarburi (ENI) in 1953; this in turn became a major player in the oil, gas and chemicals sectors. So extensive were the state's industrial concerns by the mid-1950s that a ministry for state holdings was established. It is estimated that by the mid to late 1950s public enterprise accounted for more than a quarter of gross fixed investment in industry in Italy. If we take into account all the different forms of state intervention, the state was responsible for more than half of total gross fixed investment.[12] While industry was the main beneficiary of the state's generosity, agriculture also received state help. Under a series of agrarian reforms passed in 1950, hundreds of thousands of hectares of unused land, much of it in the south, was bought up by the state and resold – on favourable terms – to peasant landowners and *braccianti*. In the same year, the Cassa per il Mezzogiorno (Casmez) was created with the immediate aim of developing southern infrastructure and modernizing agriculture. Later in the 1950s, Casmez shifted its attention to the industrialization of the Mezzogiorno, or at least of designated 'development zones' within the south. Between 1957 and 1975, Casmez spent an estimated 8.433b lire (at 1975 prices) to this end.[13] State enterprises were obliged to direct 40 per cent of total investment and 60 per cent of new investment towards the south (these thresholds were raised from 1971 to 60 and 80 per cent respectively). Financial incentives (tax concessions, soft loans) were also offered to private industry to establish or expand factories there. Virtually all funds were channelled into large-scale heavy industrial projects. Over the next two decades, a number of major industrial plants were established in the south.

Trouble and strife, 1963–83

Although GDP grew on average by 4.8 per cent a. between 1963 and 1973, the Italian economy during the mid to late 1960s and early 1970s was clearly beginning to falter. In 1963, balance of payments difficulties and rising inflation – the consequence of a tightening labour market and increasing worker militancy which pushed up wages, costs and prices – led the Bank of Italy to implement a monetary squeeze; further deflationary measures followed in 1964. Deflation brought to an abrupt end the years of extraordinary growth. The economy did recover – exports, in particular, were buoyant for the rest of the decade – but the annual rate of GDP growth, after picking up in 1966 and 1967 to levels akin to the 'miracle' years, declined steadily thereafter and in 1971 fell sharply to less than 2 per cent. The slow-down of the economy was also evident in the rates of growth of output, productivity, investment and employment: all were lower between 1963 and 1973 than in the previous ten-year period. Wages, however, rose rapidly. King estimates that industrial wages increased by 77 per cent between 1964 and 1971, and labour costs (including social security payments) by as much as 90 per cent.[14] Industrial (and social) unrest also grew, culminating in the 'hot autumn' of 1969, when nearly 1.5m workers went on strike, demanding improved working conditions and greater union influence in the running of the factories.[15]

The decade 1973–83 was one of recurrent crises in the Italian economy, marked by rampant inflation, rising unemployment, a weak and volatile currency, an acute balance of payments deficit and growing public debt. GDP grew on average by 3.2 per cent p.a. between 1973 and 1980 (in fact, taking the 1970s as a whole, the Italian economy performed relatively well compared with the rest of western Europe) but economic growth was of the 'stop-go' kind. The Italian economy tipped into full-blown recession in the early 1980s, growing by only 0.6 per cent p.a. between 1980 and 1983. By 1983, unemployment stood at 8.8 per cent (1970: 4.9 per cent), the rate of inflation at 14.8 per cent (1970: 5.3 per cent), the public debt at 69 per cent of GDP (1971: 38 per cent).

Italy's problems in these years stemmed from a number of sources. On the domestic front, rising wages hit profits, pushed up prices and fanned inflation (the situation was exacerbated by the agreement between unions and employers in 1975 to automatically adjust wages to price increases every three months); government attempts in the 1970s to spend its way out of recession added to inflationary pressures. The public debt rose as extensive and costly social welfare measures were introduced, without a corresponding rise in taxation; government efforts to prop up or rescue Italy's ailing big industrial enterprises increased the debt burden. The Italian economy was also rocked by two external shocks: the end of fixed exchange rates pegged to the dollar (in the early 1970s, the United States first devalued and then floated the dollar) and the quadrupling of oil prices in the winter of 1973–4 (a second round of price hikes followed in 1979–80). After an unsuccessful attempt in the early 1970s to fix the lira against other European currencies, its value had plummeted. The falling lira pushed the cost of raw material and energy imports up even before the oil crisis. The *combined* effect of a weak lira and high oil prices provoked a serious deterioration in Italy's balance of payments. At the same time, rising import costs and ever-higher wages drove the annual rate of inflation into the high teens. In an attempt to tackle the balance of payments crisis, the Bank of Italy instigated (April 1974) a severe credit squeeze in order to contain domestic demand and reduce imports. The shock to the economy was considerable: GDP actually shrank in 1975 by 2.5 per cent, the first time since the war that Italy had experienced negative economic growth. Italy's balance of payments situation subsequently eased but inflation remained a serious problem into the 1980s, peaking at over 20 per cent in 1980 in the wake of the second oil crisis. Only after Italian membership of the European Monetary System (EMS, 1979) was the value of the lira stabilized and the government forced to take inflation seriously (membership of the EMS ruled out the use of inflationary policies to increase demand, the favoured tactic of Italian governments in the 1970s).

Growth, crisis, reform, 1983–90

The mid to late 1980s saw a sustained recovery in the Italian economy. GDP grew on average by 3 per cent p.a. between 1984 and 1990, above the rate of most other advanced industrial countries. Both private domestic and foreign demand increased significantly (the growth rate of private consumption exceeded that of GDP, exports rose by 5 per cent p.a. – though not enough to prevent Italy from carrying a significant balance of payments deficit throughout the period). Share prices soared on the Italian stock market, the *borsa*. At the same time, inflation moderated, eventually settling at around 6 per cent p.a. (still, though, significantly above the western European average).

It was the definitive rise of the Third Italy, however, that gave Italy's economic revival in the 1980s its own particular character. The late 1970s and the recession of the early 1980s witnessed major changes to Italy's industrial landscape. Large-scale industry, which had been hit particularly hard during the 1970s by the rising price of raw material imports and the mounting cost of labour, restructured and rationalized operations. Capital-intensive investment saw the introduction of labour-saving technology, production was decentralized and large cuts were made in the size of the workforce (in this regard the victory of management over workers in the FIAT strike of 1980 was of immense significance). The number of workers employed in large industry fell by a fifth between 1980 and 1984; by 1987, nearly 1m jobs had been lost since the start of the decade.[16] As big industry downsized, small and medium-sized firms became more important. While some SMEs were actual or virtual subsidiaries of larger industrial enterprises (i.e. connected to the process of decentralization mentioned above), many others were independent, specialist companies of the type outlined in the 'Introduction.' SMEs were not new: small, specialized industry was present in the north-east and centre in the 1920s and 1930s, and even in the era of 'Americanization' after World War Two the vast majority of manufacturing firms were small or medium-size rather than large-scale concerns. Proto-industrial districts meanwhile had begun to emerge during the 1950s and 1960s.[17] It was only in the 1970s, however, that the existence and economic value of the Third Italy was properly acknowledged; the Italian economy's ability to grow during those difficult years had been largely predicated on the performance of the SMEs and industrial districts of the Third Italy. In the 1980s (and 1990s), despite strong competition from the Far East, these firms continued to carve out new markets overseas, driving forward Italian exports. The Third Italy was the great Italian economic success story of the late twentieth century.

Yet, even during the 1980s boom, the Italian economy was not free of problems. The 'Southern Question' re-emerged. The income per capita gap between the north-centre and south, which had closed or remained stable since the 1960s, began to widen once more: GDP per capita in the south fell from 60 per cent to 57 per cent of that in the north and centre between 1983 and 1987. For the first time since 1945, unemployment in the south constituted more than half the national total.[18] In 1980, the unemployment rate in the south had been just four percentage points above that of the north and centre; by 1987, the gap had widened to more than 10 per cent. By then it had been clear for some years that state efforts to industrialize the south had failed. Since the 1960s, levels of investment in the south had outstripped those in the north, and several public enterprises and major private companies, including FIAT, had built new factories in the

Mezzogiorno. However, there was little spontaneous local industrial development around these 'poles' – or 'cathedrals in the desert', as their critics disparagingly referred to them. The focus on the development of heavy industry in the south also meant that high oil prices and the collapse of world steel markets in the 1970s had a devastating impact on the industrial economy of the Mezzogiorno. As in the north, southern Italy saw major de-industrialization during the late 1970s and early 1980s – but there was nothing like the same expansion of SMEs. Even Casmez was shut down in the mid-1980s after incurring massive losses. This was not the end of what was called 'extraordinary intervention' by the state in the south – the policy was only formally abandoned in the early 1990s – but subsequent state spending in the Mezzogiorno was channelled into welfare support rather than industrial investment.

The other major issue of the 1980s was the alarming growth of the public debt: 58 per cent of GDP in 1981, by 1991 it had risen to 102 per cent, i.e. it actually *exceeded* GDP. Interest charges on the public debt by this point accounted for 23.1 per cent of public expenditure. Having shown virtually no interest during the 1980s in the problem or its sources, the governing parties finally took action in 1992, their hand forced by the demands of the Maastricht Treaty and the subsequent refusal of the international money markets to continue to tolerate such financial indiscipline. Maastricht had set down the details, convergence criteria and timetable for Economic and Monetary Union (EMU). Italy wanted to be part of the proposed single currency from its inception (due to be launched in 1999) but in 1992 it failed to meet any of the entry requirements, including that public debt should not exceed 60 per cent of GDP. Faced with the prospect of being left outside the single currency zone – an unpalatable prospect for such a major European trader and founder member of the EEC – the Italian government in the summer of 1992 announced a range of emergency austerity measures designed to cut costs and raise income. Further cuts followed in the wake of Italy's unceremonious exit from the Exchange Rate Mechanism (September 1992), when the Italian lira was targeted by international currency speculators precisely because of the high public debt-to-GDP ratio. Special intervention in the south – a policy dating back to the formation of Casmez in 1950 – was ended. So deep were the cuts overall that the budget deficit was reduced by 60b dollars in a single year. Austerity measures were pursued right through until 1999. Privatization – only rarely seen during the 1980s – raised 56.4b dollars between 1993 and 1999, as successive governments sold off shares in dozens of former state-owned enterprises.[19] Remarkably, Italy was able to join the single currency on its launch in 1999 (although it still failed the debt-to-GDP test).

Membership of the single currency came at a price, though. The Italian economy shrank in 1993 and subsequent GDP growth lagged behind that of all its European competitors for the remainder of the decade. The unemployment rate – already high at the beginning of the 1990s (over 10 per cent) – rose to 12 per cent in 1995 and remained in double figures thereafter. Most unemployment was also long-term, i.e. the majority of the unemployed remained out of work for over a year. Female, youth and southern unemployment rates were particularly alarming: 15 per cent of women, a third of young adults and a fifth of the popula-tion in the south were unemployed at the end of the 1990s.[20] At the same time, the employment rate (the percentage of working-age Italians – 14–64 years – actually employed) was staggeringly low. In 1995, just over half of the potential working population was in work – or at least in 'regular' employment (i.e. in declared and contracted work). The employment rate was lower still amongst women (36 per cent), young adults (26.1 per cent) and adults aged 55–64 years (27 per cent). Even allowing for the extremely large underground economy (the source of 'irregular' employment for thousands of Italians) this represented a huge waste of resources and compared very unfavourably with other major economies.[21]

Debates

Explaining growth

Post-war reconstruction

The Marshall Plan did not kick-start reconstruction; as we have seen, the Italian economy grew quickly immediately after the war. However, by making dollars available to the Italian government, Marshall Aid did allow the recovery to continue at a time when balance of payments difficulties threatened to choke expansion (like most western European countries after 1945, Italy found itself importing huge quantities of US capital goods for reconstruction purposes without being able to pay for those goods). Marshall Aid was also an important, though not crucial, additional element in GNP between 1948 and 1952.[22] Did the Italian government make effective use of ERP funds? Opinion is divided. Critics argue the Italian government failed to formulate a clear and coherent long-term develop-ment strategy beyond pumping money into heavy industry, while its decision to pursue a deflationary policy after 1947 stymied growth and investment – in other words, wasted the opportunity for expansion afforded by ERP – and unnecessar-ily perpetuated high levels of unemployment. According to De Cecco, the Italian economy was only rescued 'from the doldrums in which its leaders had placed it' by the growth of the international economy in the early 1950s, stimulated by the Korean War (1950–53).[23] Apologists, though, suggest the Italian government's pro-posals for Marshall Aid, submitted to the OEEC in 1948, were 'not totally lacking in inspiration'. The basic idea – to raise productivity and boost exports through tar-geted investment in industries producing capital goods – was sound, while results were generally good: industrial output increased by 49 per cent between 1948 and 1952 – above target – and there was significant expansion in the productive capac-ity of the metallurgical, chemical and energy sectors. In particular, the ERP-funded Sinigaglia plan for the development and modernization of the Italian steel indus-try, of which the construction of the Cornigliano plant was a key element, was a 'resounding success'. Steel output rose rapidly during the 1950s to meet growing domestic and overseas demand. Italian steel, so long a byword for inefficiency, became internationally competitive; Italy even became a net exporter of steel.[24]

As to the deflationary monetary policy implemented by the Budget Minister Luigi Einaudi in 1947 and broadly followed by Italian governments throughout the 1950s, its supporters argue that economic growth slowed only briefly in 1948, while the benefits of the policy were both substantial and long-lasting. The taming of inflation – which had threatened to spiral out of control after the war – and the devaluation and stabilization of the lira at a competitive rate had a positive knock-on effect on savings, investment, exports and balance of payments. Moreover, the settled macro-economic climate created by the so-called *linea Einaudi* favoured long-term economic expansion, free from the growth-curtailing effects of rising wages and prices. It is also suggested that while government policies in the late 1940s did little to ease Italy's chronic unemployment problem, it was with good cause: industry had to be modernized if the economy were to continue to grow once Marshall Aid ended; in the short term, at least, development rather than expansion had to be the government's primary objective. Besides, the Italian government had a strategy (of sorts) to deal with unemployment: emigration. The 1948 plan presented by Italy to the OEEC envisaged a net population outflow of 800,000 over the following four years. Not only would this reduce unemployment but it would also help the balance of payments (it was envisaged that emigrants' remittances would cover around 10 per cent of import costs). Federico Romero has argued that one of the main reasons why successive Italian governments in the 1950s were such enthusiastic supporters of European integration was because they believed – mistakenly as it turned out – that it would lead to the liberalization of Continental labour markets, thus making it easier for Italy to export its surplus workforce.[25]

The economic miracle

In fact, most economists and economic historians have long regarded Italy's labour surplus as a permissive factor in the 'economic miracle', helping to sustain the 'supergrowth' of the 1950s. The argument is relatively straightforward. The abundance of labour meant Italian industry was able to attract new workers while keeping wage increases to a minimum. The additional revenue derived from the output of each new worker exceeded the cost of employing that worker, thus increasing profits and encouraging investment. Investment brought productivity gains and an increase in output. Wages remained stable as the workforce grew because: (a) there was readily available labour; and (b) productivity gains derived from new investment in machinery and equipment meant that worker numbers increased relatively slowly. All this translated into higher profits and a new wave of investment in what was a 'virtuous circle' of growth. The ability of firms to self-fund investment was important given the weakness of Italy's stock market, the absence of merchant banks and the fragmented nature of the banking sector.[26] Furthermore, the reservoir of labour upon which industry drew came from the relatively backward agrarian economy; the reallocation of labour from low-productivity agriculture to high-productivity industry in itself meant that overall productivity in the economy grew rapidly. The impact on GDP was immense. According to one estimate, the reallocation of labour from agriculture to industry accounted for over 20 per cent of Italian growth between 1950 and 1962.[27]

The elastic supply of labour kept wages down and helped to generate profits and investment, but it is not regarded as the *cause* of the economic miracle: there had always been an excess of labour in Italy but never before had the economy experienced such prolonged or rapid growth. On its own, an abundant labour supply was insufficient to stimulate economic expansion; it did not explain how the Italian economy entered the 'virtuous circle' in the first place.

Many economic historians have argued that Italian industry was able to realize huge productivity gains by exploiting the technology gap with the United States and, to a lesser extent, western Europe, which had been created by the Great Depression, Fascist autarchy and war.[28] Rapid modernization encouraged the process of resource reallocation (i.e. the transfer of labour from low-productivity agriculture to high-productivity industry) and fed into the 'virtuous circle' of growth outlined above. It is often pointed out, though, that previous opportunities to play technological catch-up had not always been taken.[29] What was different about the 1950s?

Here economic historians have been keen to emphasize the favourable domestic economic context created by the *linea Einaudi* and the benign international economic environment created after the war under the leadership of the United States.[30] The liberalization of trade in the capitalist world and increased economic cooperation and integration in western Europe – both processes pushed relentlessly by Washington and embraced by Italian governments after 1945 – greatly facilitated the exchange of ideas, the spread of innovation and the transfer of technology. The expansion of world trade, which accompanied liberalization, enabled Italian firms to specialize and to realize significant economies of scale, increasing their international competitiveness and boosting exports; at the very least, it obliged Italian industry exposed to foreign competition to modernize in order to survive. Important, too, was the fact that the United States successfully sold the message 'you too can be like us' to western Europe, Italy included. There was a general acceptance of the American model of consumption based on a mass market for consumer durables such as cars, televisions, washing machines etc., and the cautious adoption of US 'productivity ideology' based on the use of technology and 'Fordist' production methods. In such a climate of expansion – and stability (international currency markets were unusually settled during the 1950s) – business confidence could only be high. The rate of investment, closely linked to market forecasts, rose. The Italian entrepreneurial 'animal spirit' was released.[31]

The growth of exports was once seen as the key demand-side element in the economic miracle (in fact, as the motor of the miracle). In this version of the 'virtuous circle' of economic growth, exports, investment, productivity and output were all locked in a mutually reinforcing upward spiral. Low wages and an undervalued lira allowed exports to grow. Domestic productivity improved as producers responded to the growth in foreign demand by investing in new capital stock to increase production, resulting in economies of scale. Rising productivity generated higher profits and made producers even more internationally competitive (to the extent that they could cut prices and still increase profits), prompting further investment, scale economies, productivity gains, etc. Rising exports also helped to keep the balance of payments in equilibrium, allowing Italy to import the raw materials it required without creating inflationary pressures within the economy. This in itself may have helped raise the level of investment since it created expectations of smooth and long-term growth. However, as Cohen and Federico note, 'The case for export-led growth has fared poorly'. Although exports as a percentage of GDP increased during the period, their overall share of GDP remained relatively small – too small to have driven growth. Furthermore, there appears to have been little linkage between export performance and levels of output and investment. The oil-refining industry, for example, witnessed rapid output growth but negative investment growth; exports increased in absolute terms but barely rose as a proportion of production, indicating the importance of rising domestic demand in the expansion of the sector. Textiles, however, saw exports as a percentage of output increase significantly even though output and investment performed poorly. It is also noted that invisible earnings from tourism and emigrant remittances exceeded merchandise exports for much of the period.

Today, most analysts regard *internal* demand factors – the growth of investment connected to the enormous post-war demand for housing, rising demand for consumer durables and massive state intervention in the economy – as integral to economic growth in the first years of the miracle (1951–7). Exports, it is widely believed, were important only in the period 1958–63, after the creation of the EEC, by which time Italian manufacturing had become internationally competitive because of rapid domestic investment linked to internal demand (see below).[32]

Investment as a percentage of GNP rose rapidly in Italy during the 1950s and early 1960s, from around a fifth in 1950 to more than a quarter by 1962.[33] The highest rate of growth was in housing investment as years of pent-up demand combined with post-war mass migration from the countryside to the towns to create a construction boom. By itself, housing investment did little to increase productive capacity, but rapid household formation did generate a considerable domestic consumer market for durables, 'the production of which enjoyed particularly large returns to scale at the prevailing technology', increasing investment in, and output of, manufacturing, notably engineering. The existence of a strong domestic market for durables also meant there was no need for employers to sacrifice profit to higher wages in an attempt to stimulate demand; this in itself acted as an incentive to invest.[34] How did rapidly rising consumer demand for durables – at a rate not only well above that of private consumption generally but also of GDP – square with only modest wage increases and persistent unemployment during the 1950s? In the first place, it is argued, new household formation obliged workers to buy furniture, domestic appliances, etc. Second, durables became less expensive relative to essential goods (e.g. foodstuffs) as productivity gains in the sector drove down costs and prices (a trend not so evident in subsidized agriculture). Consequently, consumer demand shifted from basic to non-basic goods. Third, as noted earlier, there was the American consumption model that Italians were encouraged to aspire to; and here the growth of consumer credit in the 1950s was a considerable boon.[35]

State investment is often seen as the primary propulsive domestic demand-side factor behind economic growth up to 1957. We have already noted the enormous contribution of the state to investment in Italy during the 1950s, particularly in industry. Posner and Woolf's conclusion is not unusual: 'It follows that the role and significance of the public sector was very great, both on its effect on the rate of economic growth, and on the direction which that growth was to take: since it is from industrial investment that the main fruit of economic progress grows'.[36] One estimate suggests that total government spending between 1955 and 1965, accounted for 18 per cent of the actual growth rate of GNP in these years.[37] Nevertheless, as Cohen and Federico note:

> One caveat is necessary. A number of economists have observed that investment decisions by public-sector firms were often based on notions of public interest or loss minimization, neither of which would ensure an efficient use of scarce capital...it may be correct to argue that, while public-sector firms did contribute to high rates of capital formation, a reallocation of investable funds from public- to private-sector firms would have increased the rate of economic growth.[38]

Looking at the period 1958–63, the coincidence of very strong GDP growth, very high rates of industrial investment and very strong export performance (exports increased on average by 14.5 per cent p.a. with the rate of growth of merchandise exports exceeding that of invisibles for the first time) is sufficient for many historians to argue for the existence of the type of export-led 'virtuous circle' of growth described earlier. The creation of the EEC in 1957 is seen as fundamental to this. The presence of a large western European market encouraged Italian manufacturers in what was now a modern but still low-wage economy to increase production, realize scale economies, enjoy productivity gains and higher profits and make further additions to the capital stock. Certainly, the proportion of Italian exports going to other EEC member countries shot up (23 per cent of exports in 1955; 40.2 per cent in 1965).[39]

Explaining slow-down and imbalances, 1963–93

As we have seen, the Italian economy continued to expand from the mid-1960s to the early 1990s at a rate that, if poor in comparison with the miracle years, was nevertheless impressive relative to Italy's long-term economic performance and still amongst the highest in contemporary Europe. The fact remains, however, that the rate of economic growth, the investment ratio (investment as a percentage of GDP) and the rate of productivity growth all declined decade on decade. Historians have generally shown little interest in explaining post-miracle growth (the success of the SMEs of the Third Italy the one real exception), preferring instead to focus on what caused growth to slow and the roots of Italy's economic problems (inflation and unemployment, the huge public debt, growing geographic and sectoral dualism). The emphasis here is on 'what went wrong' with the Italian economy rather than on what continued to go right.

Mitigating factors

Economic historians recognize that some slackening in the pace of growth was inevitable. Economic gains from playing 'catch-up' could only lessen over time as the technology gap closed between Italy and the more advanced western economies. The productivity increases stemming from the reallocation of labour from agriculture to industry were certain to diminish as the agricultural and industrial workforces approached optimum size. High-demand growth linked to massive internal migration and the rapid process of household formation was bound to tail off once the economy reached equilibrium. The wage moderation of the 1950s was destined to end, too, as the economy grew and surplus labour was absorbed; an increasingly inelastic labour supply usually meant higher wages.[40]

The favourable international economic conditions that facilitated miracle growth could not be expected to last indefinitely either. Stresses in the global economy began to manifest themselves during the 1960s. The final collapse of the Bretton Woods system of fixed exchange rates (1971–3) and the first oil crisis (1973–4) marked the definitive end of a 'golden age' of capitalism. The monetary instability, inflationary pressures and general climate of economic uncertainty occasioned by the slow death of Bretton Woods could only have a negative impact on business confidence and economic growth both in Italy and abroad. The oil crisis meanwhile ended the very favourable terms of trade that most western countries – Italy included – had enjoyed since the early 1950s. During the 1950s and 1960s, the costs of raw materials, including oil, had fallen relative to the price of industrial products. For Italy, a country with few natural energy or raw material resources of its own, this trend had been particularly beneficial and had clearly helped growth. Conversely, the abrupt hike in oil prices meant a rapid deterioration in Italy's terms of trade and balance of payments. Inflation rocketed as costs rose and profits evaporated. Energy-intensive heavy industries were hardest hit – and it was the rapid development of precisely these industries which had underpinned the extraordinary post-war growth.[41]

Domestic political and societal factors

Italy's economic slow-down, then, was, in part, the consequence of economic events and trends largely beyond its control. However, economic historians also attribute slow-down and the growing problems of the Italian economy from the mid-1960s to non-economic variables originating within Italy itself, in particular to: (a) the failings of the Italian political system; and (b) the shortcomings of Italian society.

The state and the economy

Missed opportunities. Economic historians have identified several missed opportunities (*occasioni mancate*) since 1945 – the immediate post-war period, the 1960s and the mid-late 1980s – when the political parties failed to take advantage of favourable economic and political circumstances to press ahead with much needed structural reforms. The failure to reform, it is argued, precipitated and perpetuated imbalances in the economy and ultimately stymied growth.

The post-war 'extraordinary compromise'. The argument that an opportunity was missed immediately after 1945 to carry out fundamental – even revolutionary – structural and institutional change in Italy is not a new one; it has a particularly long heritage within the Italian Left, disappointed with the meagre returns from the PCI's policy of national solidarity in the mid-1940s.[42] More recently, however, the traditional thesis of a post-war *occasione mancata* has been reworked by Fabrizio Barca. A senior government economist, as well as an economic historian of considerable repute, Barca's concern is not Italy's failure to turn to the Left after 1945, but rather the failure to transform Italian capitalism in a liberal and social democratic direction, bringing it closer to the type of economic regime seen elsewhere in western Europe.[43]

According to Barca, the fact that there was no radical break after the war contributed to both rapid reconstruction and the economic miracle. First, the decision to entrust to the autonomous public bodies (*enti pubblici*) of the Fascist period, such as the IRI, the task of driving post-war industrial development, paid immediate dividends.[44] Experienced managers from the Fascist era, possessed with a 'sense of mission', and given virtually 'sovereign power', took the reins of the 'strategic aces' of the industrial sector – iron and steel, petrochemicals, telecommunications – with considerable success in the 1950s. Second, the continuation of an industrial relations system based on relations of force (cf. the types of 'social contract' seen elsewhere in western Europe between capital and labour), when combined with the oversupply of labour and the weakness/ meekness of the PCI, helped to contain wages and restrict workers' rights during the miracle – to the benefit of profits, investments and growth.[45]

This was a far from satisfactory state of affairs, however. The 'extraordinary compromise' – Barca's description of the agreement between the very diverse social, political and economic forces involved in the post-war settlement in Italy to keep things much as they found them (the decision to liberalize trade the major exception) – meant vital reforms necessary for the healthy long-term development of the economy were ignored. The ordinary public administration was left untouched, ill-attuned to the needs of a developing and modernizing economy. The fiscal system remained unchanged, incapable of collecting and spending public monies effectively, equitably, or efficiently. There was no attempt to overhaul Italy's lacklustre financial markets. Crucially, there was also no move to establish clear 'rules of the game' – norms of behaviour that would enable the development of modern, open, fair, predictable and competitive domestic markets (no anti-trust legislation was enacted, no modern commercial code was introduced, there was no reform of labour markets).[46]

Was this a missed opportunity? No and yes, Barca suggests. On the one hand, the immediate post-war period was perhaps not the time to introduce sweeping economic changes. Indeed, all sides involved in the 'extraordinary compromise', from the United States government to the PCI, understood that root and branch reform threatened reconstruction; and neither the Right (including the US), fearing a communist surge if recovery efforts stalled, nor the Left, believing that the Italian capitalist economy needed further development before conditions would be ripe for socialist revolution, were prepared to risk this. In a sense, then, there was no immediate opportunity for change. On the other hand, the opportunity *did* exist to make sure that the choices made at the end of the war were only temporary; that once reconstruction was complete, 'ordinary' instruments of regulation and control – based on effective public administration, established market rules etc. – would come into force. In Barca's opinion, *this* was the opportunity missed. Why was it not taken? Because none of those involved in the 'extraordinary compromise' had enough faith in reform. Some groups were actually opposed in principle to the idea of a regulatory state (e.g. radical liberals, conservative industrial groups). Some doubted the capacity of Italy's political and entrepreneurial classes to push through the necessary measures or to make them work (e.g. 'Nittian' technocrats). Some simply did not see the need to look beyond the *enti pubblici* (e.g. the influential 'Christian-social' wing of the DC). Others, already suspicious of the public bureaucracy, fretted that reform of state structures and functions would mean further bureaucratization (e.g. the PCI).[47]

None of this mattered too much in the short-run. Low wages during the 1950s helped profits and allowed the great family-owned private corporations to self-finance investment. At the same time, the task of the managers of the state-owned enterprises and newly created public agencies such as Casmez was relatively straightforward: to facilitate reconstruction, to develop infrastructure, to promote growth. All this changed from the 1960s, however. Rising costs and falling revenues meant that large family-run firms could no longer rely on profits to fund investment. This, combined with the weakness of the Italian stock market and the lack of corporate regulation, meant the long-standing practices of pyramiding[48] and cross-share ownership[49] intensified as families sought to generate investment funds by other means. According to critics such as Barca, family capitalism and the prevalence of pyramiding and cross-share ownership have been detrimental to the efficiency of the private corporate system and to the Italian economy at large over recent decades. Pyramiding and cross-shareholding have meant there is little external monitoring of firms' performance: ordinary investors are powerless to force a firm to disclose information, and they do not have the option of supporting take-over bids (thus registering their disapproval of existing management) since take-overs are impossible. The threat of take-over, it is argued, obliges management to deliver profits and dividends to ordinary shareholders, i.e. it forces management to perform. Instead, in the Italian case, management has often reflected the interests of the dominant shareholders rather than those of the corporation as a whole.

The state-owned corporate sector also ran into difficulties from the 1960s. SOEs had performed well during the economic miracle, but they had not operated according to any predetermined plan, nor had their activities been subject to close investor scrutiny (i.e. scrutiny by the state on the behalf of taxpayers) for the simple reason that the necessary monitoring mechanisms did not exist. From the late 1950s and early 1960s, the DC moved to resolve both weaknesses, not through reform and regulation but by subjecting the managers of public enterprises to direct political control and turning state companies into the instruments of economic planning: the DC wanted to see balanced economic development; the *enti pubblici* would be directed to this end. There were also, of course, significant political benefits for the DC. In an economy without any established 'rules of the game', the discretionary power wielded by the party would be immense.[50]

The colonization of public enterprise by the DC (and its allies) during the 1960s undermined the efficiency and integrity of the state sector. New managerial appointments often came from within the parties. State companies were required to pursue multiple and changeable targets, making it both more difficult for managers to manage effectively and harder to judge results. SOEs were also exploited as a source of party funds.[51] The state-owned corporate sector was in a degenerative condition long before the external shocks of the 1970s pushed energy-intensive heavy industry – and thus the majority of SOEs – into full-blown crisis.[52]

The 1960s. The failure of state-owned industry in the 1960s is seen as indicative of a more general failure by successive centre-left governments between 1964 and 1969 to take advantage of 'the breathing-space provided by a moderation in demand pressures and by healthy balance of payments to consolidate the achievement of the previous decade and a half'. Despite interminable discussions over the need for and content of economic and institutional reform, there was actually very little in the way of meaningful new legislation. Blame is widely apportioned. Salvati suggests the anti-capitalist rhetoric of the PSI (now part of the coalition government) – which it adopted in an attempt to match that of its left-wing rival, the PCI – frightened business. Italian capitalists consequently opposed reform. They also stopped investing. Private investment in plant and equipment dried up in the 1960s in what he describes as a 'strike of capital'. Investors speculated abroad, or they bought government bonds, but they did not invest in productive capacity: the investment ratio, which had exceeded 26 per cent between 1962 and 1963, fell back to 24 per cent in 1969. Ginsborg is highly critical of the DC leadership's failure to look beyond narrow party political concerns and give its consistent support to proposed reforms. He and others also note how the reform programme never recovered from the shock of an attempted coup in 1964 by the head of the *Carabinieri*, General Giovanni De Lorenzo, an act that clearly demonstrated the extreme conservatism of much of the state apparatus and its hostility to change. Socialist leaders rushed to the side of the DC, forsaking reform in order to preserve democracy – and to maintain their places in government. According to Rey, the Centre-Left's failure to enact reforms meant that any attempt by government to use demand management to stimulate economic growth foundered on the twin rocks of bureaucratic inertia and fiscal system failings. Weak and ineffective macro-economic policy acted, in turn, as a further disincentive to investment.[53]

The 1980s. The failure to reform in the mid to late 1980s in Italy is widely regarded as a 'remarkable missed opportunity' to redress the 'fundamental anomalies in the economic fabric' of the country.[54] This was a period of sustained economic growth against a background of expanding world trade (stoked by burgeoning US demand), falling oil prices and the revival of integration in western

Europe (the Single European Act [1986] for the long-delayed completion of the single market). Domestically, it was also a time of relative political calm and social stability. Terrorism (see Chapter 9) had petered out. Bettino Craxi became Prime Minister in 1983 and remained in office for nearly four years, an eternity in Italian politics. Industrial relations were much improved (largely because of the weakening of the unions following the collapse of the 1980 FIAT strike and subsequent mass redundancies). Given such a favourable economic, political and social context, it should have been possible to reform and modernize the economy. For the first time since the economic crisis of the early 1970s, government did not have to spend enormous sums of money on welfare, subsidies and bailouts in an effort to contain social disorder and to minimize economic hardship.[55] Now it had the resources and the freedom to tackle Italy's long-standing economic problems, to raise productivity levels and to lay the basis of a genuinely competitive and flexible economy.[56] Instead, the imbalances in and difficulties facing the Italian economy became more acute and intractable.

Public expenditure grew as a percentage of GDP (37 per cent in 1980, 51 per cent in 1990) but very little of this was designed to boost productivity and foster long-term growth. Annual expenditure on social policy consistently accounted for over a fifth, in some years more than a quarter, of total spending between 1983 and 1991. Most of this went on financing Italy's extraordinarily generous pensions system (which became even more generous and subject to widespread abuse during the 1980s).[57] The payment of interest on the mushrooming public debt was the other major outlay and the fastest growing: 7.9 per cent of public expenditure in 1979, 28.1 per cent in 1993. Against this, spending on research and development, despite increasing rapidly in the first half of the 1980s, remained relatively low in international terms (by 1990 it constituted 3–5 per cent of GDP compared with 10–11 per cent in France and 18 per cent in Germany) and yielded little.[58] Social capital formation remained below its optimum level for the entire period. State spending in the south increasingly took the form of transfer payments (i.e. income support measures) rather than investment in productive capacity. The Italian public education system remained in desperate need of reform and funds.[59]

Public enterprise witnessed some restructuring and successes in the 1980s – the IRI and ENI moved into the black for the first time in years – but measured in terms of share of value added, fixed capital investment and employment, it still comprised 19 per cent of the total economy in 1990, well above that of its western European neighbours and barely down on a decade earlier.[60] Meanwhile, public administration grew relentlessly (13.4 per cent of the active workforce in 1981, 18.1 per cent in 1990) but without any improvement in the quality of public services, which remained a disgrace.[61] The private service sector (naturally protected from foreign competition, tightly regulated by the state and, as a consequence, almost as inefficient as its public counterpart) also expanded rapidly. In the early 1980s, it employed a little over a third of the active workforce; in 1990, 42.6 per cent. Together, the public and private service sectors accounted for 65.3 per cent of GDP. So inefficient were these sectors – productivity rates barely improved in either sector during the 1970s and 1980s – and yet so important were they to the Italian economy, it was inevitable that overall productivity growth in the economy also remained depressed. This had a significant knock-on effect on GDP. According to Rossi and Toniolo, 'given a service sector as efficient as the British one and the UK's level of corruption, Italy's [economic] growth in the 1970s and 1980s would have been on average one yearly percentage point higher than it actually was'.[62] The lack of competition in the services sector also helped to keep inflation high. Sassoon estimates that inflation in the sheltered sector of the Italian economy – essentially public and private services and construction – was 139.1 per cent between 1982 and 1990, compared with 79.1 per cent in those sectors exposed to foreign competition.[63]

Although taxes rose, taxation failed to keep pace with expenditure (fiscal revenue amounted to 25 per cent of national income in 1989; total state spending in 1990 stood at 52 per cent of GNP). Fiscal reforms introduced in the 1980s in an effort to improve the efficiency of the tax system had a negligible impact. So lax was tax enforcement that tax avoidance became endemic. It is estimated that tax evasion in 1991 amounted to 15 per cent of GDP. The impact of this on the public debt was considerable. One contemporary study found that 'if tax evasion in Italy since the 1970s had been at United States levels, the debt-to-GDP ratio in the 1990s would be about 80 per cent; if tax evasion had been at UK levels, the debt ratio would be 60 per cent'; instead, it was 102 per cent.[64]

It is the failure of successive governments to get to grips with the public debt that is seen by most commentators as the most glaring and unforgivable 'missed opportunity' of the 1980s since 'from an economic point of view there was plenty of room in the expansionary years to redress public finances'.[65] Why was the opportunity not taken? Why, indeed, was so little done to modernize or rebalance the economy during these 'years of "thoughtless prosperity"'?[66]

Many accounts note how at a fundamental level the 'endemic and degenerative interpenetration of the state, political parties and public enterprise in Italy' ruled out any prospect of real change.[67] All the major parties – including the PCI – materially benefited from the system of *lottizzazione* (see Chapter 7); reform was not in their interests. It is also pointed out that, with the political decline of the PCI during the 1980s, the *pentapartito* – the five governing parties – began to behave with a growing sense of impunity, increasingly confident that they could not be turned out of government or otherwise held to public account. A decadent political class shamelessly plundered the resources of the state (and, indeed, of the economy as a whole) for its own benefit and those of its supporters.[68] Clientelism spread to every corner of Italy's public institutions further compromising their effectiveness.[69] 'The loss of control over public spending took place in a context of 'waste, administrative inefficiency and, as became clear in the first half of the 1990s, diffuse corruption'.[70]

The failure of 'extraordinary intervention' in the south. Economic policy in the south has changed dramatically since the early 1990s. Today there is no ministry for the Mezzogiorno, no southern development agency (at least not of the Casmez type), no special state funding. Major public enterprises in the south have been privatized. Public spending in the south has been cut dramatically.[71] The state has not abandoned the south (not quite) but traditional top-down policy making for the Mezzogiorno is now a thing of the past. There are many reasons for this shift in approach. Italian governments have had to rein in expenditure in order to get a grip on public finances. New European competition rules have forced an end to subsidies. The rise of the anti-southern Lega Nord has made other parties wary of adopting or endorsing policies that could be considered pro-south. Essentially, though, 'extraordinary intervention' ended because it was a discredited policy, universally regarded as a costly failure – and not just in economic terms. True, as leading contemporary southern revisionists such as Piero Bevilacqua have been keen to emphasize, by the 1990s, the south had seen enormous economic change since the 1950s, much of which could be traced back to state initiatives. Irrigation and land reclamation projects had helped to transform large sections of southern agriculture. Public works schemes had modernized communications and led to dramatic improvements in hygiene. Education had been significantly improved. In fact, the population of the south by the end of the 1980s was considerably wealthier, healthier, taller, better educated and more literate than in 1950.[72] Nonetheless, after four decades of public investment in the Mezzogiorno, the southern economy had not only failed to catch up with that of the north and centre but, since the 1970s, the gap between the two had actually widened. Statistics from the mid-1990s make dismal reading:

> Around 36 per cent of the Italian population live in the eight regions of the Mezzogiorno, and they produce 24 per cent of GDP. Per capita income is 55 per cent of that in the north-centre.
>
> [...] The unemployment rate in the south is more than 15 percentage points higher than in the north-centre...the activity rate is lower...the employment rate is among the lowest in Europe. Southern families are on average 30 per cent poorer than families in the north, although the average size of the family is bigger; according to a 1991 study, only 4 per cent of families possess financial assets other than bank deposits and state bonds (16 per cent in the north). Poverty is more widespread, and inequality within the region...is greater in the south than in the north-centre. The incidence of the agricultural sector on employment is more than double that of the north-centre (12 per cent against 5 per cent in 1998 [sic]) and that of industry less than half (14 against 29 per cent); in the service sector, the weight of public services, already considerable at the national level, is greater still in the south. Exports account for 8 per cent of GDP, compared to the 25 per cent in the north-centre, primarily because of the limited weight of industry. According to available reconstructions, the Mezzogiorno presents a permanent deficit on the commercial balance.
>
> Only the rate of investment has been, for long periods, higher in the south than in the north-centre... Nevertheless, the productivity of both capital and labour in southern enterprises are, according to various studies, significantly below the national average.[73]

This was only half the picture. Public services were worst in the south. Health care was dire. In Campania, for example, there were only 3.5 hospital beds per thousand inhabitants in 1988; in Liguria in the north-east there were 8.2 beds per thousand of population. Inadequate health provision was reflected in relatively high infant mortality rates: 30 per cent higher in the south than in the rest of Italy (infant mortality in the south accounted for half of Italy's total). Local government in the south was far less efficient. A 1991 study reached the alarming conclusion that 'local administrative structures in the south are generally characterized by a degree of inefficiency which is even greater than that generally associated with the central administrative apparatus'. Clientelistic and/or criminal ties determined virtually all appointments and contracts. Crime itself appeared to be a southern disease. Two-thirds of all crimes took place in the south. Serious crime was far more prevalent here than elsewhere: of the 3,726 reported cases of murder, attempted murder, manslaughter, infanticide and kidnap in Italy in 1990, 2,470 occurred in the south. Over 80 per cent of these were in Sicily, Calabria, Puglia and Campania, those regions most associated with organized crime. In addition to their negative social effects, the low level of institutional performance and the strong presence of criminal groups within southern institutions, economy and society together represented serious obstacles to self-propelling growth. 'The fact remains', wrote a despairing Michele Salvati in 1999, 'that fifty years of policies for the Mezzogiorno, and in a context of economic development on the whole very favourable, still consign, to the new century and to Europe, a "Southern Question"'.[74]

The south's experience since 1945 is often referred to as one of 'modernization without development': major economic and social change was not accompanied by a widening of the south's economic base nor did it fundamentally alter or improve the way in which southern society was organized or operated. We will look at the sociocultural and institutional aspects of this phenomenon in Chapter 9. For now, we will concentrate on the economy. The state figures prominently in many explanations.

- The post-war decisions to liberalize trade and to promote industrial development were almost exclusively to the benefit of the industrialized north. Northern industry, often generously assisted by the state, was in a position to produce the type of goods that richer nations required, and to exploit the opportunity afforded by access to international markets to achieve scale economies, resulting in higher productivity, increased output and bigger profits. Northern industry's close proximity to the major West German and French markets gave it a particular advantage. In contrast, southern industry, tied to local markets, geographically on the periphery of Continental Europe, and after 1945 in desperate need of reconstruction, was left by the state to plough its own ever-diminishing furrow for over a decade. State funds for the industrialization of the south only became available for the first time in 1957, by which time 'the industrial world, Italian and European, had marched on to more vast and unheralded frontiers'.[75]

- The expansion of northern industry after 1945 was in large measure dependent on the exploitation of the south's one real resource: labour. At the height of the 'economic miracle' between 1958 and 1963, more than 900,000 southerners left their homes for the northern cities. This brought funds into the south as migrants sent money home, and helped relieve chronic unemployment and underemployment in the region. However, it also denuded the south of its most dynamic and productive workers (mainly young males).[76]

- Even when the state appeared to be assisting the south it was giving with one hand while taking away with the other and, more often than not, was really helping the north. First, 'extraordinary intervention' was not that extraordinary. Sassoon estimates that Casmez expenditure between 1951 and 1981 equated to just 0.85 per cent of national income in that period. Bevilacqua meanwhile notes that extraordinary spending on the south was instead of, not in addition to, ordinary regional funding. In 1988, for example, the south received only 25.6 per cent of state funds.[77] Second, southern agriculture, although markedly improved because of state intervention in the 1950s, was at the same time held back by the lack of an agricultural policy for Italy. Several commentators remark how the obsession with (northern) industry and European integration prevented successive governments from formulating a rational strategy for the primary sector. Most damagingly, it meant that little was done to protect Italian farming interests within the EEC. The complicated European system of quotas, subsidies and prices for farm produce meekly agreed to by the Italian authorities in the 1950s and early 1960s clearly favoured northern European agricultural products (meat, dairy goods etc.) over southern ones (fruit and vegetables). EEC subsidies to Italian producers were only a fraction of those paid to the richer farmers of Holland, Germany and France.[78] Third, state investment in southern infrastructure helped to modernize the south but also contributed substantially to economic growth in the north. Public works contracts in the south went to northern firms, while the process of modernization created new markets for northern manufactured goods (e.g. road construction in the south increased demand for cars built in the north – there was a twentyfold increase in the number of private cars in the south between 1961 and 1971). Fourth, as regards state industrial policy in the south after 1957, the generous system of subsidies and loans designed to attract northern industrial investment in the south simply encouraged northern firms to build capital-intensive plants in the Mezzogiorno. These plants generated relatively few jobs in the area and the type of employment they offered did not require or produce a skilled workforce. Furthermore, although located in the south, plants were geared entirely to the business needs of the mother company in the north. The industrialization of the south in the 1950s and 1960s was fundamentally an exogenous process, an 'imported' industrial revolution. Funds were allocated in Rome. Industry came from outside of the region. The raw materials used by the new plants came from abroad. The goods these plants produced went north or for export. Backward or forward linkages with the local economy simply did not develop.[79]

The state's subsidies policy is also considered to have stifled competition and development in the south in another way. Signorini explains:

> Discretionary subsidies...distort the incentives for the most enterprising peo-ple in a way that is detrimental to long-term development...in a less developed area, [since] many people may come to think that the surest way to make money is not to start a business that would be successful in the market, but to start one that would be amply subsidized. So their efforts will be devoted to maximizing monetary initiatives rather than market profits. Furthermore, if entrusted to dishonest individuals, discretionary initiatives will also encourage corruption, which is a brake on long-term development.[80]

Finally, it is pointed out that after the economic crisis of the 1970s, the state abandoned the idea of developing the south. While state funds were directed towards the restructuring of heavy industry in the north, monies for the south were now used to prop up demand for northern industrial goods and to maintain consensus in the Mezzogiorno via increased welfare payments, public works programmes, and the creation of thousands of new jobs in the public sector (all accessed through personal, political or criminal ties). State investment in the south's productive economy dried up. This not only stunted economic development in the south but it also had serious implications for southern civic life (see Chapter 9).[81]

There are those, however, who see the modern 'Southern Question' as a problem of the south itself: economic change was not accompanied by more solid processes of economic (or social-institutional) development in the south after 1945 because southern society was not up to the task. The premodern (vertical rather than horizontal) structure of social relations in the south had stopped it from following in the economic footsteps of the north. Southerners were incapable of seeing beyond the short-term, narrow interests of their immediate family and of working together for the greater good (what Edward Banfield in the 1950s famously described as the 'ethos' of 'amoral familism'). The inability to cooperate was rooted in centuries-old patterns of behaviour; the south was locked in a 'no-trust equilibrium'. This not only made it impossible 'to create the system of interaction and networks which now make industrial districts in Tuscany and the rest of central and northern Italy vital actors in the regional and international economy', but it also created an environment in which the Mafia could flourish. (According to one interpretation, the Mafia existed as a producer and seller of protection as a substitute for trust; of course, at the same time, the presence of the Mafia prevented the development of 'normal' market rules).[82] Seen from this perspective, the state's policy of industrializing the south (and the expectation that industrialization would in turn transform southern social and institutional structures) was wrong-headed. Only once southern Italian society and institutions had changed could the south hope to experience 'real' economic growth. Throwing money at the south was not only a waste of time and resources but it also exacerbated old patterns of behaviour (clientelism, corruption, crime) and encouraged dependency within the Mezzogiorno.

Society and economy

It is not only the 'Southern Question' that is attributed to sociocultural factors. Rossi and Toniolo have claimed that *most* of Italy's economic problems from the mid-1960s onwards 'can ultimately be traced back to a less than satisfactory adjustment of Italian society to the economic reality created by largely unanticipated rapid growth', in the 1950s. This created a situation where both employers and workers (and not just institutions and administration) were ill-attuned to the needs of what was now a developed economy. To start with, employers in the 1960s refused to modify their traditionally combative approach to industrial relations, provoking worker unrest. Then, after the workers' victory in the 'Hot Autumn' of 1969, the unions imposed a series of settlements on employers (and the Italian government) that were extremely damaging to the long-term health economy. The argument that the Italian labour movement must take much of the blame for the problems of the Italian economy in the 1970s (and beyond) is one that is often made. Zamagni, for example, complains that the unions 'flirted for too long with the idea of being able to impose successfully whatever bargain they could reach, without any thought of compatibility with the existing state of the Italian economy'. What were the consequences of the unions' actions? First, the labour market grew ever more inflexible: it became almost impossible for employers to sack workers, to hire workers at will, or to change working practices. Productivity suffered. Unemployment, especially youth unemployment, rose (employers became wary of taking on young workers because it was such an open-ended commitment). The underground economy, in which workers had no rights and from which the government received no tax revenue, grew. Second, wages soared because of indexation, generating enormous inflationary pressures and undermining the ability of Italian firms to compete in international markets. Third, welfare measures conceded by governments during the 1970s (but without corresponding tax rises) in an attempt to buy off social discontent 'set a time bomb into the state budget' which was finally triggered in the 1990s. The new and extremely generous pension provision also further depressed an already low employment rate, effectively reducing the economy's productive capacity.[83]

Italians, it is argued, were also complicit in the financial crisis of the state in the early 1990s and the resulting economic downturn. Despite the manifest failings of the state, there had been no popular clamour in the 1980s for fundamental structural reform, nor had Italians been overly concerned with the burgeoning public debt. Indeed, it is pointed out, many Italians actually benefited from the maintenance of the status quo. Small business and the self-employed were able easily to circumvent labour and tax laws. Big business could call on the state for support and favours. Middle-class investors made handsome profits from the purchase of government guaranteed, tax-exempt and high-yield treasury bonds (Buoni Ordinari del Tesoro [BOTs]) even though these only served to increase the size of the public debt since the state had to borrow more to pay the high rates of interest they offered. The state was also a major – and very generous – employer. Civil servants made up 17 per cent of the workforce in 1990 (cf. 13 per cent in 1974). Once employed by the state it was almost impossible to be sacked. Not only did state employment mean a job – and therefore a salary – for life, it also brought with it extraordinary pension entitlements: it was possible, for example, for women working in the public sector to retire on a full pension before the age of forty (so-called 'baby pensioners'). Secure in their work, many *statali* also moonlighted in undeclared second jobs in the private sector or the black economy. This, of course, suited the private sector since these were workers 'outside market rules and outside trade unions' control'. The state was a particularly important source of employment in the south. According to Cassese, 70 per cent of civil servants in the early 1990s were southerners (although the south accounted for only 34 per cent of the total population). At the same time, many out-of-work southern Italians, because of state welfare transfers, were able to participate in the consumer boom of the 1980s despite being unemployed (or, at least, not officially employed). The 'system' then, despite its many obvious faults, was widely accepted. Besides, opposition was both pointless and potentially self-harming. In the end, it took the external 'shocks' of Maastricht and the collapse of the lira in 1992 to force the government to face up to its financial responsibilities.[84]

The SMEs and industrial districts of the Third Italy

Economists' perceptions of Italy's SMEs have changed markedly since the 1950s and 1960s. Viewed then as indicative of Italy's continuing economic backwardness – the inefficient by-product of over-regulation, government subsidies and limited credit opportunities – by the 1980s and 1990s small had become beautiful; 'molecular capitalism' was heralded as the salvation of the Italian economy. Not that SMEs were necessarily more efficient, competitive or dynamic than larger firms; in fact, when measured by productivity, investment per worker and export capacity, bigger usually meant better.[85] Where SMEs excelled, though, was in the context of industrial districts.

According to ISTAT figures, there were 199 industrial districts in 1991. Although the precise number is disputed, all estimates indicate a rapid growth in their numbers since the 1970s.[86] Industrial districts in the late twentieth century have been recognized as a major source of:

- *Manufacturing employment.* It is thought that between 1.7m and 2.2m people worked in industrial districts at the beginning of the 1990s. One estimate suggests that the workforce in industrial districts increased fivefold between 1951 and 1991, compared with only a 50 per cent increase in manufacturing employment over the same period.[87]
- *Exports.* Industrial districts accounted for an estimated 22 per cent of Italian exports in 1995. Producers within industrial districts were in many cases world export leaders in their particular niche markets. For example, the province of Treviso in the Veneto region of north-east Italy dominated the world ski and motorbike boot trade; other districts led the way in textiles, clothing, furniture, shoes, ceramics and – demonstrating the fact that the industrial districts were more than modern-day craft centres – spectacles, medical equipment and precision engineering.[88]
- *Wealth creation.* Of the 199 industrial districts identified by ISTAT in 1991, 68 were located in the Veneto and Marche regions (34 in each). In 1951, the per capita income of the Veneto was 88 per cent of the national average; in 1997, nearly a quarter above the mean. John Foot notes that at the end of the twentieth century there were 10,000 'lire billionaires' in Treviso province alone. Further down Italy's eastern seaboard, Marche once numbered amongst the country's poorest regions. Per capita income in 1951 was only 75 per cent of the national average, below that even of Sardinia. In 1997, it was above the mean, while Sardinia's relative position over the same period had worsened. Italy's wealthiest region measured by per capita income in the late 1990s was Emilia-Romagna, renowned for its industrial districts specializing in knitwear (at Carpi) and ceramics (at Sassuolo). Only Lombardy of

the regions of the old 'industrial triangle' remained in the top five, its continuing prosperity closely linked to the 42 industrial districts located there, specializing in textiles and clothing and engineering.[89]

SMEs located within industrial districts were also found to be more profitable, more productive and more likely to export than Italian firms of a similar size producing similar goods and using similar technology but based outside of such districts. Wages were thought to be higher in district-based SMEs and unemployment levels lower in those regions where industrial districts were prevalent.

Why were Italy's industrial districts so successful? Commentators habitually refer to their flexibility, the degree of interfirm cooperation within districts and the externalities they generated. First, specialization at different stages of the same production process meant firms could respond quickly to changes in demand and tastes. Second, there was a strong sense of community and mutual trust between firms located in industrial districts, which resulted in considerable cooperation between firms. This helped flexibility, it allowed for the rapid dissemination of technical and market information and it meant that even when businesses were in direct competition with one another there was a tendency to work together (or at least not work against one another), for example, in the setting of prices. Third, SMEs located in industrial districts were able to do without the internal economies of scale enjoyed by larger firms because of the significant external economies that derived from membership of a district. The presence of a local labour force specialized in particular aspects of the production process increased productivity. Firms benefited from the expertise of local financial intermediaries (*commercialisti*) and banks, both of whom possessed a detailed knowledge of individual firms and of the district itself. Firms were able to wield considerable influence over suppliers because of the market power of the district as a whole. Through the industrial districts, in which advertising and marketing were often co-ordinated, firms were able to present themselves to buyers virtually as a single shop for a particular product, but where that product was available in a myriad of different styles and brands.[90]

Given the record of Italy's industrial districts in the 1980s and 1990s it is little wonder that they were often put forward by economists and politicians alike as models of post-Fordist best practice, 'glorified', in the words of John Foot, 'as perfect examples of hyper-efficient capitalism'.[91] The Third Italy was even held up as an international exemplar at the 1997 G7 summit in Denver.[92] It should be noted, however, that even in the 1990s there were those who worried that past performance was no guarantee of future success. What of the threat posed by competition from the low-wage economies of south-east Asia, where the quality of product had dramatically improved but production costs remained extremely low? Would not industrial districts break up as Italian firms relocated or outsourced to eastern Europe where, once again, labour costs were a fraction of those in Italy? What was to stop the larger firms in industrial districts – the Benettons of this world – simply swallowing up the smaller businesses? Would not the districts suffer from the inevitable rationalization of the European banking system in the wake of the creation of the eurozone? The fear here was that local banks would disappear, devoured by the large multinational banks and depriving the districts of their traditional source of finance; as for the big banks, they would have neither the expertise nor the inclination to bother with small businesses, preferring instead to deal with large firms. Was it not the case that recent advances in technology favoured large companies over SMEs, allowing them greater flexibility in production and removing one of the main advantages of the industrial districts? Were not large companies better able to respond to the challenges of globalization? At a more fundamental level, would not the Italian economy in the end pay for its failure to follow the high technology route of the other advanced industrial nations? In response, admirers of the Third Italy model pointed out that 'the unusual structure of the Italian manufacturing industry has not hampered its growth so far', noting, too, the industrial districts' remarkable resilience and capacity to adapt in the face of rapid changes in technology and market conditions.[93]

Assessment

How and why did Italy become a major player in the post-war global economy? The conventional wisdom runs thus: strong economic growth during the 1950s and 1960s was due to the same 'simultaneous – and improbable – occurrence of a number of favourable factors' that underpinned rapid economic growth across much of western Europe.[94] In no particular order these were: high demand (domestic and international), high rates of investment (private and public), stable macro-economic conditions (both at home and abroad), the capacity to boost productivity through the employment of new technology and the reallocation of labour from agriculture to industry, favourable terms of trade, and trade liberalization and economic integration. Growth rates in this period were higher in the relatively backward Italian economy because it was playing catch-up with its more advanced neighbours.

Growth slowed in subsequent decades. The rapid advances associated with catching up diminished as the Italian economy matured. The advantageous economic circumstances of the miracle years evaporated. The far more difficult conditions of the 1970s and 1980s revealed and exacerbated structural weaknesses in the Italian economy that had gone unnoticed or had been ignored during the years of unprecedented and untamed growth. Italy's political and public institutions were found wanting. Italian society struggled both to come to terms with the changes wrought by the miracle and to face up to the new economic challenges of the post-miracle era. Yet, despite its problems, the Italian economy continued to expand; in fact, up until the 1990s, Italian economic growth rates were among the highest in the western world. This was possible largely because of the remarkable dynamism of the industrial districts and SMEs of the Third Italy.

There is nothing fundamentally wrong with this account. However, it does suggest that, other than the entrepreneurial skills demonstrated by the small and medium-sized Italian firms of the north-east and centre, Italians could claim little credit for what was, after all, a remarkable economic achievement. In fact, economic growth often seems to have been despite rather than because of the efforts of ordinary Italians and their leaders. As the *Economist* put it in 1993: 'Except for being rotten, it [the Italian economy] is a success'.

As we have seen, the Italian state is most often held up to ridicule. Virtually all accounts highlight the incompetent, inefficient, immobile, profligate and increasingly corrupt nature of the political system and the public sector. There are, indeed, many, many reasons to be highly critical of the state's performance. Yet, the economic record of the Italian state during the life of the 'First Republic' was not all bad. Trade liberalization and Italy's commitment to European integration were bold gambits in the immediate post-war years: the Italian economy was relatively underdeveloped and thus susceptible to foreign competition, and Italy 'had a much lower degree of trade dependence with the rest of the original EC than any other members'.[95] They both, however, yielded significant long-term economic dividends in terms of modernization and economic growth. Moreover, while Italy consistently failed to punch its weight at the European Community level, sometimes to the detriment of national economic interests (the case in agriculture), on several occasions participation in the integration process forced/helped governments to take difficult – but necessary – economic decisions. Membership of the EMS meant governments had to rein in inflation in the 1980s. More importantly, EMU obliged Italy's politicians in the 1990s to try and get to grips with public spending and the public debt while at the same time it eased the passage of a programme of (for Italy) radical economic reform which would otherwise, in all probability, have been blocked. Because virtually all Italians agreed that Italy had to be part of EMU, the government was able to use the 'blunt instrument' of the convergence criteria 'to remove partisan, ideological and political considerations from the discussion of drastic measures'; to oppose reform was seen to be against the national interest.[96]

State intervention was also not the complete failure it is often considered to have been. Examples of successful intervention do exist, e.g. the Sinigaglia plan, the performance of SOEs such as ENI in the 1950s and the modernization of southern infrastructures during the early years of Casmez. True, intervention from the 1960s was generally hopeless. Still, though, there is a case for arguing that state protection and subsidies played a significant part in the remarkable growth in the number of SMEs and the success of industrial districts in later decades.[97]

It is also worth considering the alternatives available to Italian policymakers for much of the post-war period. Private industry was not strong enough to carry the Italian economy after World War Two; the state should certainly have done more to encourage its development, but in the absence of a strong private corporate sector, the state was forced to take the lead. It would have been strange, too, in a era when state intervention, whether in the form of public ownership or Keynesian demand management, was the norm across western Europe, for the Italian state not to have taken an active role. Moreover, in a European context many aspects of Italian state intervention do not appear that unusual. The economic record of Italian SOEs since the war looks neither particularly good nor especially bad when compared with that of public enterprise elsewhere in Europe: France did better, Britain worse. State-owned enterprise made up a significant part of the Italian economy but for most of the post-war period its share was not remarkable when judged in European terms (it was below that of public enterprise in France, a little higher than in Britain or West Germany).[98] In terms of macro-economic policy, Aldcroft has noted that 'Italy's experience in demand management in the 1950s and 1960s was not dissimilar to that of other countries'.[99] Later policy mistakes in the 1970s, notably the decision to use bailouts to prop up the economy in order to preserve jobs rather than lay the foundations for future growth by investing in new infrastructure and technology, were not failings peculiar to the Italian state. As Eric Hobsbawm has observed, 'The policies of most governments and the politics of most states, assumed that the troubles of the 1970s were only temporary... Essentially the story of that decade was one of governments buying time'.[100] Italian policymakers had a tendency to stick their heads in the sand, but they were not alone.

If it is possible to make a case (of sorts) in defence of the state, one can also (just about) portray the south – routinely seen as the most serious and intractable of all Italy's economic problems – in other than funereal terms. It is pointless to deny that the south when looked at as a whole presents a grim economic picture. The south is no longer poor in the way it was fifty or sixty years ago, but poverty is still a problem (see Chapter 9) and nearly every economic indicator continues to show the south lagging far behind the rest of the country. (In 2006, for example, the employment rate in the south was 46.6 per cent; the unemployment rate, 12.2 per cent. In Italy as a whole, the employment rate was 58.4 per cent, the unemployment rate, 6.8 per cent.)[101] Before we write off the south entirely, however, we must remember the southern revisionists' mantra: not one south, many 'souths'. There have been southern economic success stories. In Abruzzo, small and medium-sized firms specializing primarily in traditional goods proliferated in the last decades of the twentieth century. Per capita income rose significantly: just 73 per cent of the national average at the start of the 1970s, by 1997 it had reached 89 per cent. Unemployment in the region at the end of the 1990s was below the national rate.[102] Signorini and Visco have pointed to similar small-firm-based development in Molise as well as in parts of Campania and Puglia. Certainly, it would be foolish to read too much into this, after all, the 'changes affect only a few areas and are often quite small'.[103] There were – are – still more things wrong than right with the economy of the south (or as the *Economist* described the situation in the south in 1997: 'Not as bad as it was, but plenty left to do').[104] Nonetheless, these changes are important, suggestive of a southern vitality that is often overlooked and perhaps justifying the opinion of those who see a '"bias towards hope" for the south today'.[105]

The flipside of economic and non-economic historians' focus on the failings and problems of the post-miracle Italian economy has been their tendency to draw an exaggerated picture of the Third Italy as its saviour. The SMEs and industrial districts of the Third Italy have been extremely important to economic growth.

However, to hold them up as 'perfect examples of hyper-efficient capitalism' is to ignore the fact they 'epitomize both the strengths *and the weaknesses* [my emphasis] of the country's industry...its dynamism, receptivity, and design genius, on the one hand, and its resistance to growth, excessive reliance on family links, and opaque financial and governance structures, on the other'.[106] These weaknesses are closely linked. The emphasis on family ownership means there is a tension between growth (which usually entails external investment) and control. The fact that small businesses have for years used creative accounting 'to show the taxman as little as possible', and have circumvented costly employment legislation by employing irregular labour, is a hindrance to expansion since it rules out the stock market as a source of growth funds. Going public, as De Cecco and Ferri point out, 'is everywhere an operation based on disclosure', which is precisely what SMEs try to avoid.[107]

The prevalence of SMEs within the economy also helps to explain Italy's poor record of investment in research and development, which most observers agree has contributed to lower rates of productivity growth in Italy and declining economic competitiveness. Because of their size, and the nature of their product, Italian SMEs have not the money, time, or motivation to undertake large R&D projects.

Finally, it appears that many of the fears expressed in the 1990s regarding the future of industrial districts are now being realized. Hadjimichalis notes how intense global competition has led many small businesses either to shift all or part of their production overseas, to eastern Europe and Asia, or replace Italian workers with skilled but much cheaper (and often illegal) immigrant labour, in order to cut costs. Mergers and acquisitions have also become more prevalent, greatly reducing the number of firms and resulting in an increased concentration of capital and control. Just how effective this has all been is debatable. Italian economic growth between 1990 and 2005 was the slowest in the European Union. Italy's share of international trade fell by 25 per cent between 1990 and 2003. In 2005, Italy ranked only 47th in the World Economic Forum's annual competitiveness league table (it had ranked 26th in 2001).[108] This, of course, is not all or primarily the fault of the Third Italy, but it does suggest that the heyday of Italian 'molecular capitalism' has passed. Just as we need to take care not to exaggerate Italy's economic weaknesses since 1945, so we must beware of overplaying its strengths.

9 Post-war society and culture

Introduction

Unprecedented social and cultural change accompanied the remarkable growth and transformation of the Italian economy from the 1950s. In the immediate post-war period Italy was still, despite the growth of industry over the preceding fifty years, predominantly a poor, low-consumption, rural, religious, peasant society. Day-to-day life for many Italians had altered little since the beginning of the twentieth century or, for that matter, since unification. By contrast, the Italy of the *Sessantotto* – the students' revolt of 1968 that marked the beginning of a decade of intense, and often violent, social and political ferment – was fundamentally an industrial-urban, mass consumer society, far more affluent and considerably less devout than that of the mid-1940s. Fast-forward to the mid-1990s, and the picture was very different again. Many of the traits of late-1960s Italian society – secularism, enrichment, consumerism, urbanism – were still evident, indeed, they had been accentuated, but the age of the 'industrial society', of class politics, of collective action and organized labour, was over. Italy had joined the ranks of 'post-industrial' nations. The following framework section details the changes within Italian society and culture.

There were, however, obvious continuities between 'old' and 'new' Italian society. The family, for centuries 'the first source of power' in Italy, remained, despite significant changes in its size and structure, 'a central focus of social and self-identification and allegiance'.[1] Although scholars acknowledge the value of strong kinship relationships in Italy – family networks provide a vital safety net in a country where the state cannot be relied upon to provide welfare support; the family unit is the foundation stone of the Third Italy – they have been far more interested in counting the costs of such ties. The *southern* family has been subject to particularly close academic scrutiny ever since Edward Banfield used the phrase 'amoral familism' in the late 1950s to describe what he saw as the narrow pursuit of short-term family interests over long-term community needs in the south. Amoral familism, he argued, was the key to understanding southern backwardness. The idea that there is 'something deeply wrong with the southern Italian family'[2] has persisted because enormous economic and social change in the south since the 1950s has not led to a significant widening of its economic base nor – and this is what concerns us here – has it fundamentally altered the way in which much of southern society operates. The south at the end of the twentieth century still had, in the words of Percy Allum, the 'civic conditions of an underdeveloped country'.[3] Politics continued to serve individual or family rather than community interests. Old patterns of 'vertical' (patron–client) social relations endured. Public services were generally awful. Local and regional government were often terrible. Organized crime was a huge problem in certain regions (Sicily, Calabria, Campania, Puglia). Civil society – i.e. the arena of uncoerced associationism and collective action independent of the family, state or market and widely considered to play a vital role in the maintenance and enhancement of democracy – was extremely restricted. There were far fewer voluntary organizations in the south than in the north and much lower rates of participation.[4]

The southern family is not the only suspect in the search for the roots of the south's 'uncivicness'. Robert Putnam, for example, has suggested that the south was essentially a prisoner of its past; distant historical events had shackled the Mezzogiorno to a political culture based on patronage and clientelism from which the region had never broken free. For Putnam, as for Banfield, the causes of southern backwardness were located in the south itself. In contrast, there are those – and here the southern revisionists are well represented – who emphasize the importance of exogenous factors: to understand why post-war southern society has experienced 'modernization without development' one must look outside of the south.

Of course, southern backwardness is a relative concept: the south appears backward in comparison to the north and centre. Yet civil society in northern and central Italy at the beginning of the 1990s, while more robust than in the south, looked weak when compared to that in other developed nations. Moreover, as *Tangentopoli* – predominantly a northern phenomenon – demonstrated, northerners could hardly be described as model citizens. 'Uncivicness' was, at the end of the twentieth century, a general Italian problem rather than a specifically southern one. Nor was it a new issue: three decades before *Tangentopoli*, Gabriel Almond and Sidney Verba had described Italian political culture as 'one of relative unrelieved political alienation and of social isolation and distrust'.[5]

Italian commentators writing in the 1990s took great delight in enumerating and excoriating the many shortcomings of their compatriots, while simultaneously trying to explain them. The respected author and literary critic Pietro Citati captured the prevailing mood in a short essay published in *la Repubblica* in early 2000:

> In the newspapers at least, Italians have never before inflicted upon themselves such bloody wounds. They have no civic sense, they have no inner life, they don't love their country, they don't love God, they have no faith, they don't pay taxes,

they don't read books: they are frivolous, arrogant, corrupt, empty, pompous, megalomaniacs, mythomaniacs, spendthrifts, immoral, stupid. They have dreadful politicians, industrialists without imagination, sailors without patience, uninformed journalists, writers without talent, directors without a public, and above all abominable literary critics who every day pollute the entire nation. And then they haven't had the Protestant reformation which would have saved them from the tyranny of the Church. And they haven't had the French revolution which would have allowed them to know freedom, leaving aside the glittering guillotine. And they haven't had the Russian revolution, which would have allowed them to know equality, forgetting the blood spilt. In sum, the Italians have had nothing and have nothing. They are there, with their old cities, their old towns, ravens, greedy, perched on the ruins [*rapaci appolaiati sulle rovine*]. This, or something similar to this, columnists and writers say nearly every morning. As the eminent novelist Giuseppe Culicchia summarizes, ours, pardon me, 'is a country of shit'.[6]

Inside and outside of Italy (certainly in the United Kingdom), the political success of the 'new' Right, Silvio Berlusconi's Forza Italia party and its allies, Alleanza nazionale and the Lega Nord, in the early to mid-1990s, also set alarm bells ringing, at least on the Left. Berlusconi's 1994 election triumph was seen as evidence of the power of television in Italy and of the vulnerability of Italians to media manipulation, and confirmation of the long-standing claim by 'apocalyptic' intellectuals that mass culture produced conformity, uniformity and conservatism.[7] The strong performance of the 'post-Fascist' Alleanza nazionale in the south was said to demonstrate the weakness of democratic values in the Mezzogiorno and the susceptibility of southern Italians to authoritarian politics.[8] The rise of the Lega Nord – racist, sexist, homophobic and bitterly critical of the south – suggested that prejudice was deeply ingrained in the 'Third Italy' of the north-east, the Lega's heartland. Indeed, some believed the anti-southern sentiment whipped up by the Lega in the north in the early to mid-1990s to be so virulent that a repeat in Italy of the terrible events then unfolding in Yugoslavia could not be ruled out. As one troubled observer wrote: 'Although the conflict between north and south in Italy has not ended in bloodshed, it is developing in a similar manner to that in Eastern Europe...there is currently a marked return to the divisive arguments of the nineteenth century, but with even greater malice'.[9] Other commentators, even if they did not subscribe to the notion of a Balkan-style bloodbath in Italy, nevertheless still considered the break-up of the nation a real possibility.[10]

Not all assessments of *fin-de-siècle* Italian society were so bleak. The leading British historian Paul Ginsborg, for example, while deeply concerned by the intensification of familistic and other 'uncivil' tendencies since the 1970s, nonetheless took heart from what he saw as small but growing 'virtuous minorities' within Italy, involved in a range of organizations dedicated to the defence and renewal of Italian democracy at both the local and national levels.

The southern social question (why modernization without development?), the weakness of civil society and civic life in Italy in general, and the state of Italian society at the end of the twentieth century, are the issues that are covered in the debates and assessment sections of this chapter.

Framework

Society and culture during the economic miracle: The 1950s and early 1960s

The economic miracle transformed Italian society and culture. Millions of Italians abandoned the land for towns and cities in search of work and a better life. Millions migrated from southern to northern Italy (and overseas) for similar reasons. And for many Italians, migrants and non-migrants alike, the 'golden age' of the Italian economy *did* bring enormous material improvements. The 1950s and 1960s saw rising living standards and heralded the birth of a mass consumer society. Consumption of consumer durables grew enormously. Italians ate more (the consumption of chicken, beef and veal doubled during the 1950s; that of coffee and sugar increased threefold) and lived longer (average life expectancy rose between 1951 and 1971 by five years for men and eight years for women). They also spent more time and money than ever before as cultural consumers. Per capita spending on forms of cultural entertainment (e.g. theatre, cinema, concerts, spectator sports) almost doubled in the 1950s.[11] There was a huge and rising demand for paper-based entertainment, too. In the 1960s, 34 magazine titles and 120 children's comics generated combined sales of 10b lire. It was the advent of television, though, that had the most profound impact on cultural consumption. Regular broadcasts on the one state-run channel only began in 1954; by 1964, one in two Italian families owned a television set. The growth of television did much to aid the spread of 'standard' Italian across the country. It also played a key role in what Forgacs calls the 'revolution of rising expectations': although television output reflected the socially conservative attitudes of its Christian Democrat masters, programmes and advertisements still pushed the values of modern consumerism.[12]

Rapid change inevitably brought with it considerable social and cultural dislocation. Isolated and already impoverished agricultural communities suffered from the rural exodus as it was predominantly the young and able who left. New urban immigrants had to endure very difficult conditions: many felt alienated and disoriented in their new surroundings, working conditions were poor, and there was considerable prejudice shown towards southern immigrants in the north. One reason why southerners were unwelcome in the northern cities – and a major problem for all new arrivals – was the shortage of urban housing and the enormous strain placed on already stretched educational, social and health services by mass migration. Housing shortages had developed during the Fascist period and become acute during the war. Modest building programmes in the late 1940s did little to ameliorate the situation. The subsequent massive influx of people into Italy's towns and cities – not just in the north (where, for example, the population of Turin grew by 61 per cent between 1951 and 1971) but also in Rome (a 60 per cent increase between 1951 and 1971) and further south (in Sicily, Palermo's population grew by 20 per cent between 1951 and 1961) – created a crisis of national proportions.[13] A housing boom in the late 1950s and early

1960s did much to close the gap between supply and demand, but there was little attempt by either local or national government to manage this new wave of urban development. Uncontrolled and often illegal building speculation saw historic centres destroyed or irreparably damaged, public and green spaces within towns built over and the surrounding countryside consumed. It was on the new urban periphery that many migrants were eventually housed. Their accommodation, usually apartments in vast high-rise estates, represented a huge improvement on what most had left behind – after all, new flats had electricity, central heating, running water and an internal toilet. Many of the estates, though, were, as Ginsborg notes, 'no more than concrete deserts', built without even the most basic community amenities and services.[14] It was hardly surprising that 'a significant part of the new working class in the new metropoli became embittered by the personal costs of the transition to an industrial way of life, believed itself to be exploited, and was simply hostile to the assembly line and the businessmen who ran it'.[15]

Mass protest and unrest in the late 1960s and 1970s

Conflict was never far from the surface in post-war Italy. The mid to late 1940s saw urban workers protesting against high unemployment and inflation, and widespread and prolonged unrest in the southern and central Italian countryside. These actions achieved little, though, and in the 1950s the use of strong-arm tactics by employers and the state, combined with a weakened union presence, served to mute protest.[16] From the beginning of the 1960s, however, there were signs that the balance was shifting away from the authorities. In the summer of 1960, after police shot dead antigovernment demonstrators in Sicily and Reggio Emilia, outraged public opinion forced the resignation of the DC Prime Minister, Fernando Tambroni. The early part of the decade saw union membership rise rapidly and labour militancy increase. The Italian political establishment now seemed to recognize the need for change. The 'opening to the Left' by the DC in 1963, which brought the socialists into government, suggested that major reform was a real possibility. The political reform process, however, did not satisfy expectations. The socialists backed away from instigating structural changes after an attempted right-wing coup in 1964.

For many young Italians who had grown up during the 'great transformation' of the economic miracle, the failure of reform confirmed their view of the Italian establishment as obsolete and irrelevant. Dismissive of the traditional parties and impatient for change, Italian youth were soon to take matters into their own hands. The Italian industrial working class meanwhile grew tired of the ineffective reformism of its political and union leaders. The workers were to be the other main protagonists in the tumultuous events of the late 1960s.

The *Sessantotto*

The general failure of education reform and new government proposals to restrict access to university sparked the student rebellion of 1968. Students across Italy mobilized, occupying the universities. Lectures were disrupted or boycotted, 'counter-courses' set up and student assemblies established. Student protest also spread to the upper secondary school sector.

The student movement, though, was about more than just education. Inspired by the wartime Resistance movement and radicalized by contemporary international events – in Cuba, Vietnam, China and South America – it promulgated an alternative anti-authoritarian, libertarian and collectivist vision of society based on Marxist-Leninist and/or Maoist principles. The students' revolt came to a head in March 1968 when students from the University of Rome and local high schools beat back riot police to regain control of the Faculty of Architecture in what was dubbed the 'Battle of Valle Giulia'. For some historians, the Rome students' violent victory over the police marks the real beginning of the 'cycle of protest' that was to last for over a decade, and which finally closed in October 1980 with antistrike demonstrations at FIAT.[17]

During 1968 and 1969, many student activists, convinced of the revolutionary potential of the situation, abandoned their studies and turned their attention to mobilizing the industrial working class. Revolutionary groups (the 'new Left') mushroomed, Lotta continua (Continuous Struggle) the most influential. For a short time, at least, the new Left was successful in spreading the message of imminent revolution to the factory floor. Its influence over organized labour diminished, however, once the unions moved to reassert their control in late 1969. Union leaders did not abandon reformism. Rather, by taking a tough and uncompromising line in disputes – most notably during the metalworkers' strike of the 'hot autumn' of 1969 – they were able to extract major concessions from employers and re-establish the reputation of unionism within the factories. The metalworkers' victory was to have a profound effect on industrial relations over the next few years, tipping the balance of power in favour of the unions and away from the employers and the state.

New social movements

The ideals and values expressed by the activists of 1968–9 were to spread far beyond the confines of Italy's universities and factories to involve all sections of society over the next few years. Ginsborg, for example, writes of how small-scale collectives, "red" markets, kindergartens, restaurants, surgeries, social clubs, etc., opened (and often shut) one after another'.[18] Mass rent strikes and housing occupations were also staged across the country in protest at high rents and squalid conditions. Even the unemployed of Naples organized to demand an end to the corruption and clientelism that permeated the city's labour market – a rare example of collective action in the south in this period.

The most significant of the new social movements, however, was the women's movement. Women's rights and gender issues were rarely discussed in post-war Italy prior to the *Sessantotto*. Women had been granted the vote immediately after the war and the 1948 constitution spoke of equality before the law regardless of sex, of equal rights in the workplace and in marriage and of the right of women to stand for public and elective office. At the same time, though, the constitution confirmed the 'essentially family-based function' of women, discriminatory legislation against women dating back to the liberal and Fascist eras remained on the statute books, and neither the DC nor the PCI seriously questioned the traditional role and status of women as homemakers.[19]

Women's lives were changing, though. After the war, the spread of the culture of consumption and of modern cultural forms meant that even in areas of rural Italy where women's roles continued to be shaped by tradition, there were still 'changes in sexual attitudes and norms, a greater freedom in dress codes and language (with more sexual licence and greater intimacy)'.[20] The growth of female education in the 1950s and 1960s also carried within it the seeds of women's emancipation. Urbanization, too, had an enormous effect on women's lives. As Ginsborg notes, 'The transfer to the cities undoubtedly gave women greater freedom from traditional family hierarchies and a greater autonomy in a whole number of ways'.[21] The spread of electrification and mains supply water, plus the growing market for modern household appliances, eased the domestic burden for women. The decline in the size of the average Italian family during the 1950s and 1960s (4 in 1951, 3.3 in 1971) presumably also helped in this regard. At the same time, however, there were downsides to modernity. Female employment fell during the economic miracle. For women who lived on the new housing estates and did not go out to work, autonomy often meant isolation. The lack of communal amenities discouraged socialization. The absence of public transport made it difficult to travel to see friends. The arrival of the refrigerator meant the end of the daily shop, traditionally a social exercise where women met other women. Television, too, although it 'increased sociability *within* the family...led to greater *social* isolation within the neighbourhood and the city'; the family sat down together to watch TV but went out less often.[22]

Viewed against this background of institutional inertia and sociocultural change, the *Sessantotto* represents a watershed in post-war Italian women's history. In its challenge to authority, stress on personal autonomy and freedom, and promotion of alternative, egalitarian forms of organization, 1968 suggested the *possibility* of radical change in gender relations. Women activists, however, turned away from the student and new Left organizations, once it became clear that these were 'revolutionary in the confrontation with capitalism, [but] reformist towards the patriarchal system'.[23] Instead, they adopted a separatist agenda, seeking liberation from, rather than integration into, a society and culture dominated by men. 'Women must not be defined in relation to men', declared the manifesto of Rivolta femminile, one of the first and most important Italian feminist groups, formed in Rome in 1970. 'Equality is an ideological attempt to enslave women further... We communicate only with women.' Small, informal, 'consciousness-raising' separatist groups emerged across Italy in the early 1970s in which women were encouraged to see themselves 'as women, laying claim to a gendered identity and seeking to understand and live out that identity'.[24] The concern was 'to change society beginning with the individual's personal life'.[25] With self-awareness came control, or the demand for control, over their bodies and lives; 'the personal is political', a very popular slogan of the time, 'did not mean the privatization of the feminist debate, but rather the politicization of an area of life previously [regarded as] separate'.[26] Nowhere was this better demonstrated than in the campaign to legalize abortion in the mid-1970s. In 1975 the Italian Women's Liberation Movement (MLD), one of the few feminist groups with direct links to a political party (the Radicals), secured the half-a-million signatures required to force a referendum on the existing anti-abortion law. Although no referendum was held – instead, parliament legalized abortion in 1978 – the issue brought hundreds of thousands of Italian women out onto the streets during 1975–6 in support of the 'right to choose'.

All forms of collective action, however, lost momentum and entered into decline in the late-1970s. This was indicative of a general crisis within the Left (both new and old), intimately connected to the growth of Italian terrorism in these years.[27]

Terrorism

Italian terrorism emerged at the end of the 1960s, initially as a weapon of the extreme Right. Neo-Fascists, with ties to the Italian security services, perpetrated the first terrorist outrage in post-war Italy: the bombing of the Banca Nazionale dell'Agricoltura in Piazza Fontana, Milan (December 1969). According to Della Porta, 'black' terrorist attacks left fifty dead and 351 wounded between 1969 and 1974.[28] Black terrorism was one part of the so-called 'strategy of tension' pursued from the late 1960s to the mid-1970s by forces on the extreme Right (active within and outside of the state) with the objective of bringing Italy 'back on track' after 1968. 'Black' terrorist massacres were often blamed on the far Left – Piazza Fontana a case in point – with the purpose of generating a public outcry that would render impossible any agreement between the DC and PCI, force an authoritarian turn-about by the state and, perhaps, even justify a military coup.

In fact, genuine acts of left-wing ('red') terrorism were relatively few and far between in the first half of the 1970s. Red terrorism, like its black counterpart was a by-product of 1968: those involved were convinced that revolution was imminent; all that was required was 'one supreme "voluntarist" act' to bring it about.[29] The main (but still very small) red terrorist group engaged in the 'armed struggle' against the state during this period was the Brigate rosse (Red Brigades [BR]), established in 1970. Until 1974, the BR limited its actions to kidnapping and robbery; nobody was killed. Between 1974 and 1976, although it was behind several high-profile kidnappings – and killings – BR activity was sporadic. By 1976, the organization was in deep crisis; police infiltration of the group over the previous two years had resulted in the arrest of most of its leadership.

The year 1976, however, proved a turning point in the fortunes of the BR. First, the revolutionary groups of the new Left were humiliated in the June general election and folded soon after. Second, the decision of the PCI leadership to cooperate with the DC 'government of national solidarity', rather than use its new electoral strength to push for major corrective reforms (the PCI had just won its largest ever share of the popular vote, 34.4 per cent), was seen on the extreme Left as a final, unforgivable, act of ideological betrayal. For some former new Left activists, and younger militants who had grown up surrounded by social and political conflict and economic crisis, terrorism was now seen as the only way 'to continue the struggle'. This brought the BR much-needed new members. Reinvigorated, the BR launched a savage assault on the Italian state: in 1978, it carried out over a hundred actions, killing 16 (more than in all previous years put together) and wounding 18. The most notable victim of the BR's new 'strategy of annihilation' was the leading DC politician and former Prime Minister Aldo Moro, who was kidnapped (March 1978) and then murdered (May) by BR activists in Rome. Terrorist murders – red and black – continued into the early 1980s, when the problem was finally brought under control by state authorities.[30]

The post-industrial era from the 1980s onwards

In contrast to the left-wing, anti-capitalist, collective ethos of the *Sessantotto* and the 1970s, Italian society and culture in the 1980s was characterized by rampant individualism and an insatiable desire to consume.

Private consumption in Italy grew rapidly during the mid to late 1980s. In part, this was due to economic factors: strong GDP growth, rising wages in the expanding public sector, profits from investments in safe government treasury bonds or from shares traded on the booming Italian stock market. It was also, though, the consequence of societal trends – notably the relative and absolute decline of the working class and the rapid expansion of the urban middle classes. According to Sylos Labini, the urban middle classes grew as a percentage of the active population from 38.4 per cent in 1971 to 46.4 per cent in 1983, to 52 per cent in the early 1990s.[31] Ginsborg has noted how since the early years of the economic miracle many of those within the *ceti medi* had been 'attracted by the bright lights of consumerism and the possibility of individual advancement'. Their ascendancy in the 1980s signalled a general sea change in social attitudes.[32]

Commercial television, too, had an important role to play in shaping consumer habits. Television was essentially a state-run monopoly until the 1980s, with control of the three public channels divided between the DC, PSI and PCI according to the principle of *lottizzazione*. In the 1980s, however, private commercial stations took root and flourished. Coinciding with the arrival of colour television, commercial broadcasters gave Italians what dour, political, monochrome, state-run TV did not: (extremely) cheap and cheerful TV (soaps, quizzes and cabaret shows etc., the latter types usually featuring dozens of scantily clad, very young women). The growth of commercial TV was extraordinary. By 1990, the three major commercial channels, *Canale 5*, *Rete 4* and *Italia 1* – all owned by Silvio Berlusconi – held a 45 per cent share of the national audience. Not only were the shows broadcast on commercial TV overtly aspirational and acquisitive in content but the thousands of advertisements shown during and between programmes – 1,500 per day in the mid-1980s, more than the rest of Europe put together – inevitably influenced patterns and levels of consumption.[33]

The growing affluence of Italians in the 1980s and their determination to spend can be seen in their obsession with the motor car. In 1980, there was one car on the road for every three Italians; in 1990, one for every two. Within

Europe, only Germany had more cars per head of population. Consumption was conspicuous in other ways, too: by 1990, Italians were eating on average twice as much meat per annum as they had in the late 1960s.

The amount of time and money Italians could and did devote to cultural consumption continued to rise. The numbers of Italians participating in sport grew rapidly, from 6 per cent of the population in the 1970s to 22 per cent by the end of the 1980s. Revenue linked to sporting activities (ticket sales, clothing, fitness club membership etc.) increased by 60 per cent between 1979 and 1989. By the end of the decade, per capita spending on sport in Italy was the highest in Europe.[34] Daily newspaper circulation figures, static since the 1950s, also ballooned during the 1980s, from 5m to 6.5m. Magazines and weeklies, long popular in Italy, continued to sell in enormous quantities, sales bolstered by new titles dealing with what Ginsborg calls the 'four principal, interconnected realms of modern Italian consumption': pleasure, knowledge, the body and the home.[35] *Fumetti* – comic books – also remained tremendously popular with both Italian children and adults alike.[36] It was television, though, that dominated cultural consumption in the 1980s. The extraordinary awfulness of Italian TV (both state-run and commercial) did not seem to dampen Italians' enthusiasm for the small screen – by 1990, the average Italian spent 25 hours per week watching TV.[37] The home entertainment market, stimulated by the introduction of colour TV (the percentage of Italian families with a colour set more than doubled between 1980 and 1985) received a further boost during the 1980s with the advent of video. Video sales and rentals were to prove vital new sources of revenue for Italian film companies that since the mid-1950s had been fighting a losing battle with TV for audiences.

Numbers were also a major concern for the Catholic Church. Since the mid-1950s, when roughly two in three Italians attended mass at least once a week, the proportion of the population attending mass regularly had fallen sharply, to approximately 40 per cent by the late 1960s, 30 cent by the early 1990s. By then, one in ten Italians did not even consider themselves Catholics. The rate of decline was even more astonishing given Italy's ageing population: people usually become more religious as they grow older; the elderly are most likely to go to church. Consumerism, urbanization and migration are commonly held accountable for the Church's diminishing flock. The Vatican oscillated between modernization and tradition in its efforts to reverse the secular trend, not just in Italy but also across the developed world. The brief pontificate of Pope John XXIII (1958–63) witnessed the reorientation of Vatican policy away from direct political intervention in Cold War Italian politics and towards a more inclusive, spiritual and accessible brand of Catholicism. In contrast, John Paul II (1978–2005) steadfastly refused to compromise on 'traditional' Catholic values and was eager to embrace the type of popular devotional cults that the Second Vatican Council inaugurated by John XXIII in 1962 had sought to undermine.[38] Both approaches, in their own way, helped to strengthen the Church internally. However, Catholicism's hold over Italian cultural life – although still remarkable when viewed in a European context – continued to weaken.[39]

One cannot conclude a survey of the changes in post-war Italian society and culture without noting Italy's late-century transformation from a country of mass emigration to one of mass immigration. From unification until 1973, more Italians left Italy annually than returned. Until the early 1980s, more Italians went to live and work abroad every year than immigrants settled in Italy. Indeed, Italy barely had an immigrant population before the 1980s: only 147,000 foreigners had a 'permit to stay' (*permesso di soggiorno*) in Italy in 1970, the figure rising to 200,300 in 1979. The 1980s and especially the early 1990s, however, saw a dramatic increase in these numbers: 450,200 (1986), 781,200 (1989), 923,625 (1992), 1,095,622 (1996). Including illegal immigrants, the total immigrant population was believed to be close to 1.5m by the end of the century, equivalent to 2.5 per cent of the Italian population.[40] The vast majority of these new immigrants were what were disparagingly referred to as *extracomunitari*, i.e. from outside of the European Union (mainly from Africa and Asia in the late 1980s; from Eastern Europe during the 1990s). The rapid increase in immigration created considerable resentment and fear within Italian society. This manifested itself, on the one hand, in discrimination and violent attacks against immigrants; on the other, in calls for tighter immigration controls and for stronger measures to curb immigrant crime – immigrants were popularly associated with criminality. Of the main political parties, the Lega Nord was particularly insistent in its opposition to further immigration.

Debates

The south

'Modernization without development': A question of culture and history?

The Putnam controversy. The Lega, despite its clear xenophobia, was, fundamentally, an anti-*southern* party. The south, it claimed, had sponged off the north for years, benefiting from state handouts – bribes – paid for by hardworking northern taxpayers. It was because resources had been squandered on the south that northerners were now being asked to pay even higher taxes. Southerners were either thieves or *mafiosi*: there was no point trying to help people who could not even help themselves.

In its crusade against the south, the Lega found an unlikely – and unwitting – academic ally: Harvard University professor Robert Putnam. In *Making Democracy Work: Civic Traditions in Modern Italy* (1993), Putnam compared the performance of regional governments across Italy since their creation in 1970. Putnam found that those in the north had performed well (i.e. were alert to the needs and demands of the local population and effective and efficient in their response), those in the south, badly. The same seed on different soils, Putnam observed, had produced different results. Why? According to Putnam, good government required good citizens. Wherever one found an 'active, public-spirited citizenry', one would find responsive, effective public institutions. The civic spirit of a community could be easily measured – by the number of voluntary associations per head of population, by the proportion of the population that read a newspaper and by the percentage turnout in referendums (the higher the figures the stronger the spirit). Judged by these criteria, the most civic regions were in northern (and central) Italy; the least civic were all in the south.[41]

Why should civicness be a characteristic of communities in the north but not in the south? Putnam's explanation was simple: history and culture. The Norman conquest of the south in the twelfth century set a pattern for social and political behaviour in the Mezzogiorno lasting up to the present day. Absolutist, feudal Norman rule imposed a hierarchical structure on southern society based on vertical relations of authority; ordinary people were subjects rather than citizens. The Church, itself based on the principles of hierarchy and obedience, was a major institutional presence. By contrast, at the same time in the north and centre there was a shift away from feudalism towards self-government and the evolution of communal republicanism. Here the people were citizens rather than subjects and the Church only one institution among many (the guilds). Horizontal bonds of mutual trust and cooperation took root and grew stronger over time (what Putnam referred to as the accumulation of 'social capital'). By the fourteenth century a 'civic tradition' had been firmly established, one that not even a series of unfortunate events over the next few centuries – the Black Death, war, the collapse of the republics, foreign rule and the reintroduction of feudalism – could completely destroy. Consequently, the north and centre were 'receptive to the first breezes of renewed progress…that whispered along the peninsula in the second half of the eighteenth century'. The south, however, without a civic history, slipped into a state of 'desolate anarchy' – and never recovered. The pursuit of individual needs and goals always took precedence over those of the community, while the weak always sought the protection of the powerful rather than of their peers, whom they competed with and mistrusted. Horizontal forms of cooperation were impossible in such conditions. Democratic values could not take root. The Mafia flourished.[42]

In Putnam's interpretation, north and south were thus set on very different paths long before the modern era. In contemporary Italy, good regional government was dependent on the civic virtue of its citizens. The civicness of those citizens was determined by the strength of the region's civic heritage, its stock of social capital. 'Social patterns plainly traceable from early medieval Italy to today turn out to be decisive in explaining why, on the verge of the 21st century, some communities are better able than others to manage collective life and sustain effective institutions'.[43]

Not only was a region blessed with a civic past likely to blessed with a civic present and by good government but it was likely, in Putnam's opinion, to be economically advanced precisely because of its tradition of civicness.[44] This was, of course, all good news for the north and centre. With history against it, though, the south's political, economic and social prospects looked distinctly bleak. As one progressive president of an 'uncivic' region pointed out, 'This is a counsel of despair! You're telling me that nothing I can do will improve our prospects for success. The fate of the reform was sealed centuries ago.'[45]

Making Democracy Work drew considerable criticism. Critics attacked Putnam's methodology, in particular his tendency to lump regional data together, hiding in the process significant inter-regional variations in performance within the north-centre and south. Such differences, it was argued, were important. Putnam had claimed that good government depended on good citizens; he had also divided Italy into two diametrically opposed, internally homogenous, cultural entities – the virtuous north-centre and the uncivic south. Given this, one would expect there to be little variation in institutional performance between regional governments *within* each area. The fact that there *were* such disparities suggested: (a) that the presence or absence of civic traditions was not the key determinant of good government in a democracy; and/or (b) that the sociocultural landscapes of the north-centre and south were more complex and varied than Putnam thought. Critics also took issue with Putnam's determinism and essentialism. Putnam had argued that sociocultural values once established were very unlikely to change over time; hence, even though the north had experienced several centuries of virtually identical rule to the south, northern society had remained fundamentally different to that in the Mezzogiorno. Recent history, though, suggested otherwise. The rise of Fascism in the agrarian north and centre in the early 1920s ran 'counter to the assumption of continuity in civic tradition' (furthermore, the phenomenon of agrarian Fascism pointed to the presence of deep town–country and class divisions within Putnam's idealized 'community').[46] The 'clean hands' investigations of the early 1990s, which had revealed widespread political corruption and extensive 'premodern' patron–client relations in the north, also cast doubt on Putnam's thesis. As for Putnam's verdict on the south, even Robert Leonardi, who had worked with Putnam over many years, found it 'too pessimistic'. Writing in the mid-1990s, Leonardi pointed out that communal elections held in the south in 1993 had swept away much of the corrupt ruling class and brought into office a new cohort of political leaders. According to Leonardi, the new political order had 'demonstrated a significant ability to change the nature of local public policy'. Moreover, 'Where local institutions have shown their ability to produce collective [public] goods, it has a positive impact on the patterns of social values, and over time it helps to build up social capital'. This ran directly counter to Putnam's own argument that (in Leonardi's words), 'attempts to change the internal logic of the system [of values in the south] will be long and difficult', if not impossible.[47]

Nonetheless, Putnam's arguments did find a receptive audience. *Making Democracy Work* proved enormously popular with the Italian media and the serious Anglophone press. Much of this (in Italy, at least) owed to the zeitgeist. Publication coincided with the end of extraordinary intervention in the south, the Mafia murders of judges Falcone and Borsellino, the *Tangentopoli* scandals (which, though they revealed endemic corruption in the north, were interpreted by some 'as a sign of how deeply the north had been "infected" by southern ills') and the rise of the Lega. Putnam reflected the popular mood.[48]

Putnam's success, however, was due to more than just the spirit of the times; he was tapping into well-established *historical* representations of the south. His portrait of the south as static, unchanging, perhaps unchangeable; his judging of the south against northern criteria (and finding it wanting); his view of the south as a *problem*: all were hallmarks of traditional *meridionalismo*. Moreover, since the 'discovery' of the southern problem in the late nineteenth century many *meridionalisti* had identified 'an almost genetic "backwardness" in southern society', habits which had become so deeply ingrained over time as to be an integral part of the southern character or 'way of being'.[49] Individualism, distrust, honour, cleverness (*furberia*) were essential elements of the southern psyche. In many ways, then, Putnam was simply dressing up old arguments in new clothes.

The Banfield legacy: 'Amoral familism'. Putnam's analysis of the south also bore similarities to the controversial but highly influential work of another American scholar: Edward Banfield's *The Moral Basis of a Backward Society* (1958).

Banfield's findings were based on fieldwork conducted during the period 1954–5 in 'Montegrano' (real name Chiaromonte), a village in Basilicata. The purpose of the study was simple, if ambitious: to explain the causes of extreme poverty and backwardness in the south (although Montegrano was only a small village, Banfield considered it to be 'fairly the "typical" south').[50] From his time in Montegrano, Banfield reached the following conclusions:

- The Montegranesi were 'prisoners' of a 'family-centred ethos', 'amoral familism'. The product of poverty, humiliation and extreme anxiety, amoral familism led each individual to 'maximize the material, short-run advantage of the nuclear family' – according to Banfield, the dominant family structure in the village and the south generally – '[and] assume that all others will do likewise'. In the 'tireless and cunning pursuit' of familial advantage, the interests of the wider community were ignored. Favours, if granted, were never freely given; there was always some obligation on the part of the receiver. 'The satisfaction of being thought well of would not, for most people, outweigh any advantage that could be had without danger by trickery or other unfair means.' Even offspring, once married, were regarded with suspicion by their parents, as potential competitors. This was all very different, he suggested, to the situation in the north. There one found large, extended, families who had rented and worked the land together for generations and understood the value of organization, cooperation and discipline. Amoral familism was, Banfield declared, 'a fundamental impediment to...economic and other progress', in Montegrano and, by extension, the south. In contrast, the model of the extended northern patriarchal family had much to recommend it.[51]
- Amoral familism in Montegrano and the south was self-perpetuating and difficult to break (certainly, it could only be broken through external agency). If poverty could be overcome, communications between north and south improved, the geographical and occupational mobility of labour increased and manual labour destigmatized, then 'a new spirit would soon be evident'. But, wrote Banfield, 'Obviously...these changes are not likely to occur'. Instead, he argued, the south's only possible hope lay in the devolution of government from Rome, first to the provincial prefects whose job it would be to establish community initiatives at

the local level, and then, once the lesson of cooperation had been absorbed by community leaders, to local institutions. Even if such measures were tried – and Banfield considered it most unlikely that they would be – there still 'would be no dramatic improvement' in the condition of a village like Montegrano; it was simply too isolated and lacking in resources to pull itself out of poverty, 'even if the villagers cooperated like bees'. Moreover, the ethos of amoral familism was so well entrenched in Montegrano (and across the south) that even 'Under the most favorable conditions it might take two or three or four generations' to dissipate. This was, as Banfield conceded, a 'cheerless note' on which to conclude – but it was 'necessary' to do so.[52]

Subsequent research has discredited many of Banfield's arguments. Studies have shown that although the nuclear family prevailed across much of the south, it was far from the only form of family organization – in fact, virtually all types of family structure, including the extended peasant family, could be identified. Moreover, the shape and character of the family unit was not fixed; instead, it could change over time as circumstances altered and new opportunities or challenges emerged. Analyses of larger, less isolated southern settlements than Montegrano also revealed evidence of solidarities and collective identities beyond kin ties even where the family structure was predominantly nuclear. Montegrano's problems were, in fact, those of any isolated, poor village; similar social structures and relations were just as likely to exist in remote mountain regions of the north as elsewhere in the south.[53]

'Modernization without development': A question of politics?

Gabriella Gribaudi: Against familism. One of the most trenchant critics of familism in recent decades has been Gabriella Gribaudi. For Gribaudi, writing in the early 1990s, familism was a 'completely useless' concept. Banfield, she argued, had not properly understood the society he was studying; his findings were unreliable. Certainly, the model of amoral familism could not be sensibly applied to the south generally (for the sort of reasons noted above). This, though, was exactly what had happened, giving rise to the enduring stereotype of the familistic southern family. In the stereotype, however, the southern family was quite different to that described by Banfield. Whereas Banfield had identified familism with the nuclear family, in the stereotype the extended patriarchal family was considered familist. How had this happened? Gribaudi attributed it to the common association of modernization with growing individualism and the nuclearization of the family. By contrast, the extended patriarchal family was widely considered to have been the dominant 'traditional' Mediterranean family form – and a constraint on individual (and commercial) initiative; in other words, it was seen as an obstacle to modernization. Because familism was associated with backwardness, and backwardness with the traditional extended patriarchal family, it was easy for the former to become confused with the latter. 'Hence Banfield's argument was unwittingly turned on its head'.

In Gribaudi's opinion, the stereotype stood even less scrutiny than Banfield's original thesis. Not only was the extended family not all-pervasive but 'Anyone who has observed and studied southern society impartially knows very well that the patriarchal family practically does not exist there'. Gribaudi further insisted that while kinship ties were indeed strong in the south they were no stronger there than elsewhere in Italy. The peculiarity of the southern case lay in the fact that, in certain specific areas of the south, informal kin networks had 'invaded the channels that link communities with the political centre', weakening civic society and undermining collective identities in the process. 'Only in this sense,' wrote Gribaudi, 'can we speak of the pervasiveness of the family' in the south; for this, the central organs of the state, which accepted and legitimized such networks at the local level, had to bear responsibility.[54]

Piero Bevilacqua: The contemporary state and southern civic weakness. Numerous studies highlight the state's role in the stunting – weakening – of civic life in the south since 1945. It is, of course, an interpretation clearly at odds with the cultural-historical explanations offered by Banfield and Putnam. The contrast with Putnam is particularly stark. Putnam argued that institutions, at least in the short to medium term, had little influence on social values; the civicness or uncivicness of a community depended on its history, not on the contemporary political environment.[55] State-centric accounts, by contrast, insist that 'the political system... has an enormous power in conditioning the social life of the Mezzogiorno'; in fact, the contemporary south is what 'the Italian political system has wanted it to be, or at least has ended up making it'.[56] Piero Bevilacqua, for example, has argued that the degradation of southern civic culture, a process traceable to the 1970s, went hand in hand with the progressive degeneration of the Italian political system (see Chapter 7). The south was particularly affected because the state was the major economic actor and prime source and distributor of funds in the Mezzogiorno. Since the agrarian reforms of the early 1950s, the DC, which by dint of its monopolization of national political power controlled those funds, had been able to dominate southern political life, dispensing grace and favours in return for votes and political fealty. Until the mid-1970s, the economic benefits of state intervention had (just about) outweighed the political and social-institutional costs: at least funds had been directed towards the development of the south. This was not the case subsequently, however. Instead, state funds, distributed through the new regional governments, were used to prop up the southern economy and maintain political consensus (see Chapter 8). Welfare payments increased and jobs were created in the public administration – for those with the right political connections. The rise of the PSI under Craxi exacerbated the situation: here was a political rival to DC hegemony in the south, determined to play the DC at its own game and embed itself in the Mezzogiorno through the control and disbursement of resources. 'Through this, public institutions were bent more fully and profoundly than in the past to the private interests of groups, factions, notables.' Increasingly this involved organized crime. Nourished and protected by their political patrons, criminal groups also had little to fear from Italian justice which, constrained by lack of funds and weak legislation, was unable to impose law and order in the south. Civic society could not remain immune to these developments. Bevilacqua admitted that the 'southern public spirit' had never been strong. Now, though, it was dramatically enfeebled. While the great majority of southerners aspired to a higher quality of civil life, the relative weakness of the southern economy obliged many to privilege personal and private ties over collective identities and loyalties. High youth unemployment was a major factor in this regard. Entry into the job market was dependent upon contacts and favours. Rather than a 'rite of passage', the moment when an individual stepped out of the confines of the family and into the wider world, getting a job 'branded' young southerners with the mark of a favour received which one day would have to be repaid. The new young worker had obligations to a powerful patron, not to society in general or to the state. In fact, the more the state via the political parties invaded southern life the more it lost legitimacy in the eyes of southerners and helped to undermine popular respect for the law. Rapid urbanization which overwhelmed small-town administrations and destroyed old community identities, the death of the Left (and of collective values linked to socialist/communist ideology) and the growth of the 'me' culture during the 1980s had also accelerated, in Bevilacqua's opinion, the disintegration of southern civic sense and sensibilities.[57] This was a rather dispiriting conclusion to a book that had consistently stressed how far the south had come over the past 200 years.

Quo vadis Italy?

As we noted in the Introduction to this chapter, many writers in the 1990s despaired of the state of Italian civic culture in general terms, not just in the south. Putnam's upbeat assessment of civic conditions in contemporary northern and central Italian society could not easily be reconciled with the facts of *Tangentopoli*. 'Uncivicness' was a nationwide problem rather than simply a southern question. In seeking to explain this sorry state of affairs, Italian commentators in particular often fell back on well-worn negative stereotypes concerning Italian 'national character'. Italians were 'anarchic sheep, allergic to any rule of civic co-existence', 'individualistic', 'afraid only of the stick and of the shepherd's dog'. These, of course, were the same stock stereotypes habitually and specifically applied to southern Italian society (in times of crisis Italy assumes 'southern' characteristics). As with the 'Southern Question', there was also a strong tendency to assign centuries-old roots to such character flaws: the Italian 'way of being' originated in Roman times, or in the Middle Ages, or in the Counter-Reformation; recent history was largely irrelevant in this sense. And, just as the south was often compared with an ideal-type north (and found wanting), so Italy was compared unfavourably (as it had been so many times before) to the ideal-type of an apparently 'civilized' country – for example, the United States or Britain.[58] Even when modern history was taken into account it was usually to bemoan, in the style of Gramsci, either what had *not* occurred in Italy (her missing revolutions) or *had* happened but in only bastardized form.[59] Such analyses not only made the current crisis seem inevitable but effectively ruled out the possibility of future improvement.

Not all scholars, though, were prepared to endorse such a 'desperate vision'[60] of Italian history. In this regard, the works of Paul Ginsborg, probably the best – and certainly the best known – Anglophone historian of contemporary Italy, deserve particular consideration.

Paul Ginsborg: Italian history, familism and civic culture reconsidered

As Charles Maier has noted, Ginsborg's history of contemporary Italy (and, indeed, his interpretation of the modern period generally) offers an 'intriguing' mix of the 'Left' narrative of Italian development, rooted in the works of Salvemini and Gramsci and full of (more or less inevitable) failures, injustices and missed opportunities, and the 'liberal' paradigm, inspired by Croce, with its emphasis on progress and achievement (see Chapter 1).[61] Ginsborg's thesis is also very interesting, in historiographical terms, for another reason: his reworking of the hackneyed but (in his view) still 'useful'[62] concept of familism.

Ginsborg and the 'Left' narrative

For Ginsborg, the outcome of the Risorgimento represented the defeat of the 'revolutionary' progressive and enlightened elements of the bourgeoisie (the republicans and democrats) by conservative bourgeois forces (led by the moderates). As a result, the 'new' Italian state created by unification was, in many ways, not that new at all. Old patron–client and kinship relations dominated. Italy's ruling political class was deeply suspicious of, if not actually hostile to, the idea of civil society. The state was staggeringly inefficient, ineffective, negligent, self-referential, resistant to reform, seemingly deaf to the needs of Italian families – and entirely lacking popular legitimacy. Despite subsequent regime change (liberal–Fascist–republican) and the extraordinary transformation of the Italian economy in the 1950s and 1960s, the basic characteristics of the Italian state and its relationship with 'real' Italy remained essentially unaltered through the twentieth century.

In circumstances where the state was widely distrusted and civil society weak, it was not surprising, Ginsborg suggested, that ordinary Italians should concentrate their attention on the family, which was both 'strongly cohesive', and 'the single structure...over which they could exercise some control'. However, 'the accentuation of exclusive family values and action', where 'the interests of the family are counterposed to those of the other principal moments of human association' – familism in other words – served only to further undermine the development of Italian civil society and deform the relationship between citizen and state.[63] This bond was not one based on reciprocal obligations; instead, the state was regarded both with hostility, suspicion and contempt, and as a resource to be exploited for private ends. Familism thus overlapped with and reinforced the twin evils of patronage and clientelism.

Despite Ginsborg's insistence on the centrality of familism to any meaningful discussion of the relationship between family, civil society and the state, his understanding of familism differed significantly from Banfield's in several key respects. First, while Banfield regarded familism as a southern phenomenon, Ginsborg saw it in *national* terms: 'familist' tendencies were evident in northern and central Italy, not just the south. Second, whereas Banfield specifically linked familism with the nuclear family, for Ginsborg the type of family was largely unimportant. As we have seen, Ginsborg held the state historically responsible for the 'inward-looking phenomenon' of familism. The Church, too, he argued, shared some of the blame. For a long time after unification, it had encouraged Italians to distrust the state and its institutions. Moreover, in its teachings it had always 'stressed the pre-eminence of the family over society' (or, as Pope Pius XII put it in September 1951, 'the family is not there to serve society; it is society which is there to serve the family').[64] Third, in contrast to Banfield, who saw familism as a constant, Ginsborg suggested that familistic tendencies fluctuated over time. The Resistance and the collective movements of the late 1940s and 1970s demonstrated that private familial concerns had not always been placed ahead of, or necessarily clashed with, the interests of the wider community. Fourth, and most important, while Banfield – and subsequent scholars who had used the term[65] – associated familism with backwardness, Ginsborg considered it 'a phenomenon intrinsically connected to modern society'.[66] Since the economic miracle of the 1950s, familism had been 'accentuated in considerable measure' by aspects of urbanization, the privatization of family leisure time (the rise of home entertainment), the growth of private transport (the rise of the car) and of family-based enterprise, and the trend towards smaller families – in short, by 'modern economic and social conditions'. The acquisitive 1980s in particular had witnessed the 'rejection of any attempt to place the family in a collective context'.[67]

Ginsborg and the 'liberal' narrative

For Ginsborg, though, the history of modern and contemporary Italy was more than simply a résumé of its vices. Certainly, there was nothing inevitable or immutable about the course that events had taken. Italian history was 'perhaps best presented in terms of deep and unresolved *conflicts*, which allow for a variety of cultural and institutional outcomes'.[68] Thus, while he endorsed the 'Left' view of Italian unification as a victory for conservative bourgeois forces, Ginsborg also acknowledged that progressive elements within Italian society and politics had remained active (and not altogether without influence) down to the present day. The ideals of the Resistance movement, for example, had, inspired the post-war Republican constitution, which had offered a powerful 'vision of what the Republic should have been, even if it was not'. The Communist Party in the contemporary era had (for the most part) 'taught a vision of politics based on self-sacrifice, honesty, social equity and efficiency'. The *Sessantottini* had attempted 'to change the predominant values of a rapidly changing society'. From the 1970s onwards, 'virtuous minorities' within the state (e.g. reformist magistrates, Bank of Italy officials) had worked hard to bring about reform of the public administration. Finally, the rapid growth during the 1980s and 1990s of new forms of associationism in Italy, including the south, which were free from political or religious influence had 'given new vigour and independence to horizontal linkages in civil society', and as such had made 'an important contribution to the growth of Italian democracy'.[69]

Vital to the development of this autonomous and pluralistic civil society in the last decades of the twentieth century had been the input of 'critical and "reflexive"' elements within the Italian *ceti medi* (middle classes). Broadly left-wing, they were 'concentrated for the most part amongst teachers, public sector technicians and management, educated women who have recently entered the labour market, the lower ranks of the professions, students and some of those who work in the media and in information technology'.[70] According to Ginsborg:

> Instead of being swept away by the intense rhythms, the enrichment and the material consumption of the modern world, this middle class has shown a growing awareness of global dangers, of the damage wrought by unthinking consumption on the quality of everyday life, of the connections between private choices and public consequences.[71]

Civil society did not extend much beyond the middle-class *riflessivi*, however. The new associations of the 1980s and 1990s failed to attract working-class or lower-middle-class support. Even within the ranks of the middle classes the *riflessivi* were greatly outnumbered by a 'rampant and even irresponsible *ceto medio*', narrow-minded, avaricious, self-absorbed, familist and – more often than not – self-employed.[72] There were many other reasons, too, to fear for the 'delicate plant' of Italian civil society on the eve of the new millennium.[73] For instance, the *riflessivi* lacked a strong political voice. By contrast, 'Berlusconi's piloted and privatized version of Italian democracy' coincided exactly with the interests and values of the *rampanti* (Berlusconi was the archetypal *rampanto*).[74] More worryingly, the concentration of media ownership in the hands of Berlusconi posed a grave threat to freedom of information and the diffusion of knowledge, both of which were vital to the health of civil society and, of course, to the proper functioning of democracy. Furthermore, the 'deeply conformist, repetitive and uncritically consumer-oriented' message of Italian television, the main – and for many Italians, the only – form of cultural consumption, discouraged exactly the kind of debate and autonomy of judgement that civil society attempted to stimulate. It also went a long way, in Ginsborg's opinion, to explaining Berlusconi's political success.[75] Nonetheless, the existence of the *riflessivi*, the growth of a 'plural and critical civil society' from the 1980s, 'the material wealth of a majority of the population, the striking change in the condition of many Italian women in the last three decades, spreading educational opportunity, increased access to information of every kind, [and] the introduction of the theme of democratic participation in the recent teachings of the Catholic church', all suggested there was 'much in modern Italian society which favours the growth of a democratic culture within Italian families'.[76] This was a very different conclusion to those accounts that stressed only the negative tendencies within recent Italian history and society.

We will consider Ginsborg's general argument, as well as his views on family, Church, state and modernity, in the assessment part of this chapter. We should note here, however, that his portrayal of two contrasting Italian middle classes – one 'good', educated, broadly left-wing and working in the public sector, the other 'bad', right-wing and (literally and metaphorically) working for itself – has been much (and deservedly) criticized. Some critics noted how the middle classes *en masse* bought into state treasury bonds in the 1980s, despite the obvious damage the BOT system was causing to state finances, structures and services (see Chapter 8).[77] Others questioned the 'reflexivity' of Ginsborg's much-lauded public-sector professionals:

> In the absence of any concrete evidence...the reader has to presume that these social groups are judged to be more civic-minded simply by virtue of their being relatively underprivileged or constituting a 'caring' profession. One has only to think of all those school teachers in Italy who earn a considerable income, often undeclared for tax purposes, by giving private lessons to the wealthiest pupils, leaving the poor to fend for themselves, to start nurturing serious doubts on the validity of this type of generalization.

Similarly, Ginsborg's dislike of Italy's small entrepreneurs merely because they were most interested in making money appeared a simple case of prejudice; after all, was not 'capital accumulation...the very essence of a western capitalist society'?[78]

Ginsborg's suggestion that left-wing voters (middle-class or not) made better citizens than their right-wing counterparts also seems highly tendentious. In a survey conducted in 1994 of two Lombard towns, one traditionally communist or 'red' (Sesto San Giovanni), the other Catholic or 'white' (Erba), Anna Cento Bull found a majority of both left-wing *and* centre-right Catholic party voters in Sesto supported the idea of paying higher taxes in exchange for better services. This was not the case amongst either PDS or DC/PPI voters in Erba. Moreover, while PDS voters in both towns were generally more tolerant of outsiders than non-PDS voters, still a 'substantial minority' of PDS supporters in 'red' Sesto expressed 'exclusionary, even racist, views' (25 per cent supported a policy of repatriation of extra-EU immigrants).[79] Other studies have shown that left-wing local authorities, too, have been guilty of racism in their dealings with immigrants.[80]

Assessment

This chapter has explored the debates surrounding the following issues:

The persistence of deeply uncivic conditions in the south despite rapid economic and social change after 1945: The south's history, the southern family, the Church, the state: each has been used to explain the post-war southern phenomenon of 'modernization without development'.

The weakness of civil society and civic life in Italy in general at the end of the twentieth century: Again, accounts have stressed the deleterious effects of one or more of the following: history, family, the Church, the state. Particular aspects of modern mass culture, together with certain socioeconomic trends evident since the era of the economic miracle, are also considered to have exacerbated the problems of uncivicness and social disconnection.

The state of Italian society at the end of the twentieth century (and beyond): Assessments have ranged from the alarmist/apocalyptic (the end of Italy/the Balkanization of the peninsula), to the merely pessimistic/fatalistic (Italy as a 'country of shit'), to the guardedly optimistic (the Ginsborg position).
Let us re-examine the arguments.

Southern uncivicness/the weakness of Italian civil society and civic life

History

History and the 'uncivic' south. The weight of history sits heavily on the south.
For many writers – Putnam is by no means alone[81] – the south is what it is because of what it once was. Although the south at the end of the twentieth century possessed the trappings of a developed consumer-based society, in reality southern society remained, for distant historical reasons, wedded to a set of values and behaviours dating back to a much earlier time. This is a dubious argument. While it is certainly true that social practices can become habitual (customary) over time, and as a result can persist long after the conditions which created them have disappeared, the idea of a 'cultural lag' lasting several *centuries* seems (to put it mildly) unlikely. Moreover, as Jane and Peter Schneider have pointed out, by projecting an image of the south frozen 'in a mould of the past', such accounts serve only to essentialize the southern character. There is, we are meant to believe, an immutable, fundamentally antimodern and 'backward', southern type; the particular circumstances of time and place are ignored. From here, it is easy to fall into cliché and generalization, caricature and prejudice.[82]

Time and place – historical *context* – are vital to a proper understanding of why 'traditional' 'southern' cultural values and behavioural patterns have endured. The work of the Schneiders is instructive in this regard. In *Culture and Political Economy in Western Sicily* (1976), a study based on extensive fieldwork conducted in the small rural town of 'Villamaura' (real name Sambuca di Sicilia), the Schneiders suggested that the prevalence of the old cultural codes of family honour (*onore*), 'instrumental' friendship (*amicizia*)[83] and cleverness (*furberia*) did not prove the existence of a Sicilian psychosis. Instead, their persistence over time was a reflection of the fact that for centuries Sicily had been dominated by, and dependent on, outside political forces and had occupied a precarious position in the world economy. Sicilian cultural codes, they argued, had developed in the first place as means to an end: survival. These codes had remained important up to the present day because the basic conditions of subjugation, dependency and uncertainty under which Sicily laboured had not fundamentally changed, the post-war transformation of Sicilian society and the economy notwithstanding: 'If traditional codes persist it is because, nurtured by dominance in the past, they still respond to dominance today'.[84]

The Schneiders, at least in their later works, were nevertheless at pains to point out that honour, friendship and cleverness were not the *only* cultural values found in Sicily and that change *was* possible. Sicilians were not 'forever locked in an archaic ambience of (Mafia-friendly) *clientelismo*, fatalism, vendetta, patriarchy, honour and shame'.[85] For example, in *Reversible Destiny* (2003) which charted the judicial and popular anti-Mafia campaigns in Palermo during the 1980s and 1990s, the Schneiders demonstrated how civil society could grow even in a city dominated by a corrupt political class in collusion with organized crime. The crackdown by magistrates on the Mafia in these decades, and the emergence of a citizens' anti-Mafia movement, they argued, could be linked in a general sense to the modernization of Sicily since World War Two and the concomitant expansion of the urban, educated, professional, middle classes. The late-century success of the anti-Mafia crusade in Palermo, though, was intimately connected to the end of the Cold War, 'whose global arrangements had fostered close ties between Mafiosi and national, as well as regional political protectors', and to the subsequent collapse of Italy's two main parties, the DC (which had dominated Sicily since the 1940s) and the PCI.[86] The demise of the DC cost the Mafia its main political ally; the passing of the PCI meant it could no longer even justify itself as a bulwark against communism. At the same time, both the European Union and United Nations were becoming increasingly involved in the fight against organized crime. In these radically changed circumstances, the Italian judiciary was able to move decisively against the Mafia. In January 1992, the Italian Supreme Court confirmed the guilty verdicts that had been handed down to dozens of Mafiosi in the so-called 'maxi-trials' of the mid-1980s. In the wake of the Supreme Court's ruling, Salvo Lima, the long-time Mayor of Palermo, DC Deputy and Mafia ally was murdered because of his failure to protect Cosa Nostra from prosecution (in the past, Mafiosi appeals against convictions had nearly always been successful). The subsequent Mafia assassinations of judges Falcone and Borsellino (May and July 1992) signalled not so much the strength of the Mafia but rather the desperation of its leadership. In early 1993, Totò 'Shorty' Riina, the 'boss of bosses' and a fugitive from justice since the late 1960s, was arrested. The success of the magistrates' war on the Mafia during the 1990s was mirrored in the growth of the anti-Mafia social movement, and the latter's ambitious plans to regenerate the historic centre of Palermo and implement anti-Mafia educational programmes in schools.

Although the movement has lost a great deal of momentum in recent years – its decline coinciding with the growing political influence of Forza Italia in Sicily – the Schneiders, in an article published in early 2006, refused to be downcast:

> ...we do not delude ourselves with the belief that the antimafia process is linear and continuous. As engines of change, social movements wax and wane, take fire during periods of crisis and recede as activists and followers yield to the pressures of their everyday lives. True to form, 'normalization' has become the watchword in Sicily. Yet we remain convinced the events of the 1980s and 1990s gave ample support for the possibility that political corruption and Mafia predation can be scaled down. Things are not what they used to be during the heyday of the sack of Palermo

and the triumph of the Corleonesi [Mafia family], and they will never be that way again: the antimafia process has decisively altered the resources and framework for prosecuting organized crime. To date, at least, there is really no evidence of the reconstitution of a virulent Mafia – and much evidence that, for the first time in history, the police and judiciary have at last created a formidable obstacle to this happening. Perhaps most important, the antimafia process has changed the conversation, criminalizing a phenomenon that once enjoyed wide public tolerance, if not respect and support.[87]

The subsequent arrest and imprisonment of Riina's successor, Bernardo 'The Tractor' Provenzano (April 2006) and then of *his* replacement, Salvatore Lo Piccolo (November 2007), both of whom had been wanted by the Sicilian police for decades (Provenzano since the early 1960s), would seem to bear out the Schneiders' arguments.

The size and energy of the anti-Mafia social movement of the 1990s clearly showed that when circumstances presented Sicilians with the opportunity to cast aside what can be termed 'practical' morality, many (although by no means all, or even a majority) spontaneously and independently chose to organize themselves in pursuit of the common good. It is also worth pointing out that anti-Mafia activism was just one example of a new spirit of associationism and cooperation across the south in the last decade or so of the twentieth century. We have already touched on the emergence of southern 'industrial districts' in Chapter 8. At the same time, the number of voluntary organizations in the south grew rapidly, and more quickly than in the north: of the 6,000 associations in the south in the mid-1990s (estimated total membership of 700,000) two-thirds had been established since 1980.[88] We can safely assume that the underlying reasons for this are essentially the same ones that explain the Palermo phenomenon.

History and the weakness of contemporary Italian civil society. Although Italian society at the end of the twentieth century in certain ways resembled that of much earlier times – for example, the particularism of Italians is evident in writings dating back to the fifteenth century – this does not mean the dye was cast hundreds of years ago. Accounts which trace the causes of Italian civic weakness to events (or lack thereof) in the dim and distant past need to be treated with caution. History, of course, is very important, but context is everything: and it is the modern and contemporary historical context that matters here.

Family

It is tempting to agree with Norberto Bobbio's observation that Italians have squandered too much time and energy on the family, leaving little of either for society or the state.[89] The empirical evidence indicates a continuing and remarkably strong attachment amongst Italians to the family and traditional family values. Moreover, surveys conducted in the 1990s revealed very low levels of institutional trust in Italy generally and, in the south, where family ties were considered strongest and traditional values were most widely held, very low levels of interpersonal trust. It is hardly surprising, then, that many writers have assumed 'a strong correlation between a family-centred cultural characteristic and social mistrust',[90] and that the all-consuming focus on the family 'explains the lack of public spirit in Italy, and even of the concept of the public good'.[91]

In reality, however, things are more complicated than this. First, as Ginsborg has pointed out, there are numerous instances where family values have been linked to collective or community-based action.[92] Second, despite the continuing importance of family ties and the persistence of traditional family values, changes within the Italian family over the post-war period have arguably made it a more democratic and open institution. Certainly, there appears to be some merit in Arnaldo Bagnasco's argument that, as the 'long' family (i.e. with children remaining at home well into adulthood) has established itself, '[t]he way in which hierarchies are perceived within the family has changed, with consequences upon processes of socialization: the values of obedience and hierarchy make way for those of discussion and agreement, *both in the family and in society* [my emphasis]'.[93] Ginsborg, too, has acknowledged that:

> Any lingering image of the closed nature of the Italian family – all work, rest and socializing with relations – has given way to a reality where individual members of the family relate more and more to their peer groups and the outside world. The family remains united at the level of income and overall strategy, but its individual members often go their own way at the level of consumption and free time.[94]

Of course, this does not mean that family members automatically go out and join associations or actively participate in civic life, but the opportunity is there and the growth of associationism in Italy in the latter part of the twentieth century (and the lead role played by young Italians in this growth) suggests they often do. Third, historians and social scientists have long recognized the importance of strong family ties in the Third Italy. Yet social networks of friends, neighbours and work colleagues are also extremely important here, levels of interpersonal trust are high, and there is a strong predisposition to associate. In other words, the evidence indicates *no* strong correlation between a family-centred culture and social mistrust. Little wonder, then, that Cento Bull has suggested 'it is time to stop blaming the strong Italian family for uncivicness, clientelism and patronage'.[95]

What of the role of the family in southern Italy? Is there excessive identification with the family to the detriment and exclusion of the wider community? First, let us clarify what the 'southern family' exactly means: it was – is – predominantly nuclear in structure (in some regions, such as Puglia, overwhelmingly so); the vast majority of people lived, and continue to live, in simple households made up of parents and their children.[96] In this sense, at least, Banfield's Montegrano was, indeed, 'fairly the "typical" south'. Beyond this, however, it is very difficult to generalize about the southern family, still less draw firm conclusions about its behaviour. Certainly, '[w]e do not have sufficient empirical evidence to claim that generally the structure of the southern family prevents people from extending trust and solidarity beyond the family network'.[97] For example, in a study of inner-city Naples, Gribaudi found simple-structure artisanal families fully engaged in the life of the local community residing alongside members of the criminal – and in structural terms, very complex – Mariano clan, part of the Neapolitan Camorra.[98] Similarly, in *Fertility of the Poor* (1996), the Schneiders described a remarkably open, dynamic, egalitarian and progressive artisanal community in twentieth-century Sambuca, based around the local Workers' Club (*circolo degli operai*).[99] Again, the typical family was nuclear. We cannot even say with any certainty that the south is more family-centred than the north and centre: in the 1990s, the Third Italy recorded the highest proportion of young adults still living at home; people here also met with kin more frequently than in the south.[100]

This does not mean the family is not important in the south – it is – but it is equally, if not more important, elsewhere in the peninsula. Nor should we conclude that familism does not exist there: it does. It also feeds modern clientelism.[101] However, it is neither the 'southern condition', nor an exclusively southern problem. As Antonio Mutti writes, '[a] differentiated analysis of the southern family is needed, which explains where familism is an obstacle to modernization, where it is only a marginal phenomenon and where a family-based particularism more open to people outside the family can help economic development, like in "Third Italy"'.[102]

Church

In *Making Democracy Work*, Putnam not only criticized the Catholic Church as an institution (it had played a key role in sustaining feudal rule in the south and, by extension, in perpetuating southern uncivicness; it was characterized by vertical bonds of authority and hierarchy and stressed obedience and 'the acceptance of one's station in life') but he also claimed that – in Italy, at least – 'religious sentiments and civic engagement seem to be incompatible'. The more religious the individual the less civic-minded they were likely to be ('Churchgoers seem more concerned about the city of God than the city of man').[103] Ginsborg, too, with his gaze fixed firmly on the contemporary period, found the Church and its teachings had offered little succour to civil society: not only did it encourage familist behaviour, '[b]ut the culture it preached *vis-à-vis* authority was fundamentally that of submission and docility'. The Catholic ritual of asking particular saints to intervene on one's behalf also looked suspiciously like a religious version of clientelism.[104] Although Ginsborg recognized that social activism (welfare, education, cooperatives etc.) had been a feature of Catholicism in Italy since the late nineteenth century, he argued that for Church leaders, the primary objective of Catholic associationism for most of the twentieth century had not been the growth of civil society but rather the defence of the family 'against the Communist menace and the threats of modern society'.[105] Even under Pope John Paul II, who was keen to encourage a strong, active and critical citizenry in Italy capable of holding government to account (as in his native Poland), the Church remained a heavily centralized, hierarchical and undemocratic organization wedded to a concept of society (and family) that was profoundly inegalitarian.[106]

Many of these criticisms of the Church cannot be gainsaid: the Catholic hierarchy has often set a poor example to its flock.[107] More problematic is Putnam's claim that religion (specifically Catholicism) and civicness did not mix in Italy.

Putnam found that 'manifestations of religiosity' were higher in the south than elsewhere in Italy and linked this to its lower levels of civicness. Yet, while it is generally accepted that 'Italy's southern regions present higher levels of religious practices and identification with the church than elsewhere in the country', the connection between religiosity and uncivicness in the south is not as straightforward as Putnam assumes.[108] The south has a long history of uncivicness, but there is plenty of evidence to show that southern Italians have not always been devout Catholics. For example, the south of the 1930s was deeply uncivic (see Chapter 6) but at the same time it was barely Catholic. Carlo Levi's memoir of his political exile in Basilicata during the mid-1930s records the local priest complaining: 'No one comes to church... I say my mass to empty benches'. The Istituto nazionale di economia agraria noted a similar lack of enthusiasm among Sicilian peasants in a study conducted a couple of years earlier. What existed in the south was, as Ginsborg writes, 'a widely diffused pagan religiosity...separate from the structure and social doctrines of the Catholic church'.[109]

The negative correlation between Catholicism and civicness identified by Putnam does not stand up in historical terms. For the contemporary period, too, his argument looks weak. In her study of Erba and San Sesto Giovanni, Cento Bull found practising Catholics in 'white' Erba were not only far more likely to participate in apolitical associations than lay townspeople (non-practising Catholics or non-believers), but 'the more religious the respondent, the more likely they were to be active participants, and vice versa'.[110] Furthermore, if we accept Putnam's argument, it is hard to know what to make of the estimated 5m practising Catholics in Italy – 12 per cent of the adult population – currently involved in some form of association-based activity: does not this constitute a crucial dimension of civic engagement? Putnam argued that Catholic associationism effectively ceased in the late 1960s with the catastrophic collapse of Catholic Action, the "civic" face of Italian Catholicism'; 'In today's Italy,' he wrote, 'the civic community is a secular community'.[111] Yet, even if we ignore the 3m or so 'hard-core' Catholics (i.e. those who belong to organizations of a strictly religious/spiritual nature), this still leaves approximately 2m Catholics active in Catholic voluntary welfare groups 'whose common and distinctive trait', according to Franco Garelli, perhaps Italy's foremost authority on contemporary Italian Catholicism, 'is represented by a commitment to social goals and ties of solidarity (expressed both on a local level and in international cooperation)'. Furthermore:

> Most of the members of these associations are driven toward engagement and solidarity by a specific religious sensibility, but the factor of faith is for the most part not taken into consideration – in these milieux – as a discriminating or determining factor for this type of affiliation and involvement. In this context, a part of these groups feels slightly ill-at-ease in the current phase of the Italian church, believing as they do that the accentuation of identity issues now under way in Catholic milieux may prove to be more of a source of division than a resource for mobilization. Moreover, they fear that the heavy emphasis now being placed on religious values (admittedly within the context of a society that is quite open to this type of appeal, given the great disquiet and fear now felt in that society) may

eventually shift the impulse toward charity that is a basic element of the Christian message to a secondary role. In other words, for these groups the danger is that a model of Catholicism may be established that places more emphasis on religious identity (although that does satisfy the need for meaning and affiliation) considered as an end in itself than on taking into consideration the needs and conditions of the weaker members of society; more directed toward finding a legitimacy in society and to establish itself in relation to formal culture than to dirtying its hands in combating the miseries of the world.[112]

While the Catholic Church as an *institution* has hampered, and in some ways continues to obstruct, the growth of civil society, it appears that, at least at a *grassroots* level, many Italian Catholics have been working towards precisely this goal, inspired by solidarist values derived by universalist Catholic principles.[113] The influence of Catholicism on the development of Italian civic and civil society in the contemporary era must be seen as both complex and contradictory.

State

Institutions affect the ways in which individuals and groups become activated within and outside established institutions, the level of trust among citizens and leaders, the common aspirations of political community, the shared language, understanding, and norms of the community, and the meaning of concepts like democracy, justice, liberty, and equality.[114]

There can be little question that state institutions have been a major obstacle to the development of civic life and civil society in Italy, especially in the south, since 1945. Simply put, a well-functioning modern democratic state makes certain demands upon its citizens (e.g. to respect the law, to pay taxes, to defend the nation should the need arise etc.) In return, it assumes a range of responsibilities: to protect its citizens from external threats, to maintain law and order and to be responsive to (and effective in addressing) societal needs and concerns (social, economic and political). In contrast, the post-war Italian state has demanded much of its citizens (for instance, Italians are subject to tens of thousands of laws; they are very heavily taxed; military service was compulsory for men until 2005) but it has manifestly failed to meet many of its obligations. Consider law enforcement. As we have seen in Chapter 7, for many years the state military and security services contained elements actively opposed to the democratic process and prepared to subvert the rule of law if necessary. For its part, the judiciary, at least in the first few decades of the Republic, while nominally independent, was an extremely conservative (and male) body, closely aligned to the governing parties and deeply antipathetic towards the Left. Although the judiciary became, in social terms, a much more diverse institution after 1968, it remained highly politicized; in fact, if anything, it became *more* political, as judges and prosecutors began to divide and organize along partisan lines. The political ties of, and political rivalries between, factions within the judiciary often compromised the fairness and effectiveness of criminal investigations (which are led by magistrates) and the impartiality of judges.

The legal system failed Italians in many other ways, too. The enormous number of state and regional laws, all written in impenetrable legalistic jargon and full of clauses, subclauses and references to other laws, created what John Foot describes as a 'legal labyrinth' which 'was incomprehensible to the vast majority of citizens'.[115] On top of this, the legal process was extraordinarily slow. Foot notes that by 1994 the average civil case lasted nearly three years, with only a third ever reaching a conclusion; the average length of penal cases was only marginally better: 27 months. Even then, Italy's lengthy appeals process meant many more years could pass before a final judgement was handed down. (In fact, a well-represented and wealthy defendant – Berlusconi being a case in point – could reasonably expect to be able to spin out the appeals procedures until the statute of limitations expired on the charges, resulting in automatic acquittal).[116]

The politicized nature of the judiciary and the rank inefficiency and unfairness of the legal system were features characteristic of the entire state administration. We have seen in Chapters 7 and 8 how the governing parties, the DC in particular, colonized the entire administrative apparatus and gradually acquired complete control of para-state agencies. Jobs were awarded not on merit but according to political or kinship ties. Public funds, contracts, permits and services were used to construct extensive patron–client networks.

The use of public money and services in this way helps, of course, to explain why the quality of public administration in post-war Italy was so awful: the 'public interest' was rarely considered. Moreover, an administrative system based on *raccomandazione* (recommendation) rather than merit was inevitably going to be slow and inefficient. Employees might not be up to the job, or, because they were 'well protected', simply indolent. Certainly, because of the patronage system, there was very little incentive for an official to do their job properly, let alone consider professional development, since it had no bearing on their career prospects. Inefficiency and inertia were also the products of a highly centralized system (meaning a lack of autonomy at the local level) and over-regulation: the Italian bureaucracy was awash with rules and red tape. On the one hand, this discouraged initiative (public officials were loathe to make decisions). On the other hand, it meant that, for a private citizen, even the most simple of tasks could require trips to several different state offices, generating copious amounts of forms and involving a great deal of waiting around:

> One recent study suggested that two weeks of every working year are lost by Italians in queues and bureaucratic procedures. The calculation went that since Italians need, on average, 25 visits to various offices each year, the equivalent of almost 7000 minutes are spent queuing. That would be a normal year; if you want to apply for a job, it's best to put aside a week or ten days, in order to gather the correct documents, pay for them to be stamped and so on... As much as 2,000 billion lire is spent annually by Italians just to certify their status (car owner, divorced, resident at a particular address etc). It's not just slow: it's exceptionally slow. It's been nicknamed the *lentocrazia*, the 'slowocracy'.[117]

What has all this to do with civic values and civil society? Because it asked much of its citizens but delivered very little, the post-war Italian state was never able to command the loyalty or respect of its citizens (a tough ask anyway, given that it had come near to complete collapse in 1943 and had rarely enjoyed mass support since unification). As Italians did not trust the state – and because state institutions were, as a rule, so inefficient – many citizens showed little sense of civic duty. Why pay taxes when the state misused public funds? Why adhere to the law when the state failed to uphold it? Furthermore, because the public administration functioned on the basis of personal ties and informal contacts rather than as an impartial 'rational authority' based on impersonal rules, and because of the ineptitude of public services, it was almost inevitable that 'patron–client relations, the exchange of favours, the use of kin and friends, became an accepted way for families to negotiate and traverse the bureaucracy'.[118] This created a vicious circle. Because of its systemic failings, the state invariably failed to meet the needs and concerns of the wider community. However, because the system held out 'the possibility of individual gain to all those who can succeed in forging a personal tie, however tenuous, to the holder of power',[119] it was one that many Italians were prepared to tolerate, or even exploit, for personal (or familial) advantage. In this way, civil society was undermined. Ginsborg's thesis, at least as regards the role of the state, is fundamentally correct.

It was in the south that the shortcomings of the post-war Italian state were felt most keenly and were most damaging to civic life and civil society. Nowhere, for example, was justice more beholden to and constrained by politics than in regard to the Sicilian Mafia. For decades after the war, both the judiciary and law enforcement agencies failed to confront the Mafia. Magistrates regularly failed to investigate Mafia crimes properly, and judges were very reluctant to convict Mafiosi should a case make it to court. When magistrates (or the police and Carabinieri) *did* show a willingness to combat Mafia activity, they rarely enjoyed official support or protection – in fact, quite the opposite – and were often left fatally exposed to Mafia retribution. The result was that, until the maxi-trials of the mid-1980s, the Mafia was able to operate with impunity in Sicily and grow largely unchecked, with devastating consequences for wider Sicilian society.

The failure of the state to combat organized crime in Sicily was due to two key factors. First, and most importantly, it was a consequence of the post-war 'alliance' between the Mafia and the Christian Democrats, and the dominance by the latter of island politics and public institutions. Local party chiefs received votes and backhanders (plus, in the early days especially, help in bringing communist activists to heel and maintaining the social and political order), in return for which they sheltered the Mafia from the law and provided privileged access to the public resources and services under their control. The extent of the ties between Sicilian politicians and Mafiosi was revealed in the early 1990s when magistrates laid charges of corruption or collusion with the Mafia against more than half of the deputies in the Sicilian regional parliament. A further 17 national parliamentarians were similarly indicted.[120] Second, as John Dickie points out, it was because of the solipsism of Italy's public institutions. For many politicians and their allies in the magistracy, the ability to wield power over rivals within the state was simply more important than the pursuit of justice.[121]

The DC replicated its domination of Sicily across the mainland south. DC politicians and officials thus controlled the enormous sums of money that flowed into the south from central government coffers from the 1950s on, and which were so vital to the modernization of the southern economy, as well as entry into the public administration, which was such an important source of employment in the south, given the relative weakness of the private sector. The south, then, as Bevilacqua argued, was more at risk of contamination from the degenerate Italian state than was the rest of Italy, so heavily dependent was its economy on the DC-run state and para-state agencies for investment, jobs, and, from the 1970s, welfare handouts.

Together with the fact that the state allowed and encouraged organized crime to flourish in parts of the south, it was little wonder that southerners, in general, displayed so few signs of 'civicness', or that civil society was weak. Bevilacqua was not the first to note how young Italians in the south had little choice but to embrace clientelism. In the early 1970s, Percy Allum commented how 'Neapolitan youths know that the achievement of their aspirations and ambitions depends upon membership of the government parties, or, more specifically, the dominant governing party, the DC'.[122] In the 1980s, Amalia Signorelli found that students in the province of Salerno articulated civic values, but were nonetheless resigned to the fact that, if they wanted to get on in life, they would have to play by the rules of patronage. Who they knew would be far more important than what they knew.[123] In such circumstances, where vertical relations are privileged over horizontal social ties, civic values are suffocated and civil society undermined. Similarly, because southern public administration, even by Italian standards, was so awful but southerners were so reliant upon its resources, it was scarcely surprising that clientelistic contacts were so widely utilized.[124]

Let us look at one final example of the debilitating influence of the Italian state on southern civic life. The south in the early 1990s had the lowest levels of tax payment (of any kind) to the state in the country. Tax evasion was rife. In part, this was due to the inefficiency of the tax system; in part, because the ruling parties were prepared to ignore the problem in order to maintain consensus in the south. It was also due, though, to the fact that many legal businesses, at least in regions where organized crime was strong, were subject to a parallel system of taxation: the payment of protection money. Because the state could not guarantee the rule of law and because public institutions in the south (and, by extension, the economy) did not operate according to 'normal' rules, businesses were obliged (and in some cases were willing) to pay for private protection (not only protection from the criminal organizations themselves, but also from competitors, thieves and so on).[125] Such an environment was clearly not conducive to the spread of civic values or the development of civil society.[126]

Modernity

Earlier in the chapter it was noted how Ginsborg linked the persistence (indeed, the revival) of familism – and the weakness of civil society – in the contemporary era to modernizing trends in Italian society and the economy. 'Much in the modern world...forcefully invites families to be more passive and detached, more concerned above all with themselves.' The huge new housing estates that mushroomed from the late 1950s had, in Ginsborg's opinion, served to isolate families. The rise of the motor car had signalled the privatization of travel; even when Italian families did leave the house and ventured into the wider world, they did so in a way that kept them largely insulated from it. Television had first glued Italian families to the sofa and then sold them an idea of the family that was itself 'distinctly *familist* in the sense of putting its own acquisitive interests first, and very rarely being portrayed as willing to sacrifice some part of these for the good of civil society, let alone the state'. (Ginsborg joked that by the 1990s it was easier to watch *Neighbours* than be neighbours.) As for the growing number of small, family-based firms, 'if you've got family and work overlaid on each other, you've got a pretty good recipe for people caring fundamentally about family'.[127]

Is Ginsborg right? There is little to take issue with regarding his comments on the isolating effects of post-war urban development (although, as John Foot observes, isolation could have its benefits, too: it was arguably preferable to the 'enforced intimacy' of the old working-class housing areas).[128] His views on the privatization of travel appear commonsensical. On the matter of family and work, however, it is necessary to repeat that associationism is particularly strong in precisely those areas of Italy where family and work *are* overlaid. As to the impact of television, there are several points to make. Yes, Italians do watch an awful lot of (awful) television: nearly 27 hours a week on average in 2000. This surely can only have a negative impact on levels of civic engagement. (Putnam has found this to be so in his investigation of civic decline in the United States.)[129] Yes, much of what is aired on Italian television does nothing to encourage the viewer to think beyond his or her own family's material needs and interests (or, for that matter, to think at all). In more general terms, one can only agree with Ginsborg (and many other commentators) that the concentration of media ownership in Italy since the 1980s has been an extremely unhealthy development, both in cultural and political terms. In the first case, it has denied space to 'alternative' culture(s): compared to the 1960s and 1970s, the Italian mass media now operates within a very narrow cultural framework. In the second case, there is no question that Berlusconi has used his extraordinary control of the media, and television in particular, to discourage journalistic freedom of expression and to further his political career. In 2002, for example, two leading RAI presenters who had been critical of Berlusconi prior to his 2001 election victory subsequently had their shows taken off air by a new RAI board all but handpicked by the new Prime Minister.[130] During the 2006 Italian general election campaign, Italy's independent Communications Authority ordered two of Berlusconi's TV channels, Italia 1 and Rete 4, to pay fines totalling €500,000 for repeated bias in their news coverage. (In truth, news programmes on Berlusconi's television stations have *never* provided balanced political coverage.) For Berlusconi, the importance of TV could not be exaggerated: 'if something is not on television it doesn't exist! Not a product, a politician or an idea.'[131]

While it would be wrong to argue that television does not influence the behaviour and attitudes of viewers, we need to recognize that there are limits to the power of *la tivù*. The far from flawless electoral record of *La Sua Emittenza* himself is evidence of this: Berlusconi has contested five general elections, he has won three (1994, 2001, 2008) and lost two (1996, 2006); his second Government, 2001–6, suffered very heavy defeats in European and regional elections.[132] True, in 2001, Berlusconi enjoyed the lion's share of television coverage leading up to polling day, and Forza Italia duly claimed 29.5 per cent of the vote (up from 20.6 per cent in 1996) making it by far the largest party in the *camera*. There is also evidence to suggest that the more time Italians spent in front of the television the more likely they were to vote for Berlusconi. One study found that among ex-DC women voters, 'an astonishing 75 per cent of those who watched four or more hours of television a day voted for Mr Berlusconi in 2001, while only 40 per cent of those who watched two hours or less did so'.[133] However, most of Forza Italia's gains came at the expense of its coalition partners, the Alleanza nazionale and the Lega Nord, not the Centre-Left Opposition; voters showed themselves to be extremely reluctant to switch their allegiances from one coalition to the other.[134] Television certainly helped Berlusconi, but only up to a point. As Forgacs has written, Berlusconi's rise 'does not prove that Italy is now ruled by and through television'.[135]

There are a number of reasons why television does not rule in Italy. First, not all Italians watch television all of the time, nor do they all watch Berlusconi's Mediaset networks. Second, for many Italians, TV is but one of several media sources they access for news or entertainment. We have already noted the increase in newspaper readership in the 1980s; in the late 1990s, there were signs that rising Internet use was beginning to take viewers away from television; moreover, recent studies suggest young Italians are increasingly favouring the radio over TV.[136] The Internet, of course, is far less of a 'controlled' medium than television (or, for that matter, the press). Italian radio has nothing like the concentration of ownership that one sees in the television industry. Third, as Agnew points out:

> ...opinions are also still formed in everyday interaction with other people, notwithstanding their joint reliance on increasingly homogenized national sources. People in different social groups and operating in different milieux interpret what they encounter in viewing television in radically different ways. However persuasive television often appears, the best attempts at persuasion often backfire when people bring their own 'common sense' and identities to bear in interpreting what they see.[137]

Fortunately, we are not usually (quite) as dumb as the programmes we watch.

Italian society at the end of the twentieth century (and beyond)

Despite many predictions to the contrary, the Italian nation state has survived the collapse of the First Republic and the rise of the Lega Nord, not to mention the challenges posed to its authority and power by globalization and European integration. There has been neither a Czechoslovakian-style 'velvet divorce' of north and south, nor – the worst-case scenario – have we seen the Balkanization of the peninsula. In fact, there was very little chance that Italy would fragment in the mid-1990s. The Lega worked hard to promote the idea of the north as fundamentally different from the rest of Italy (and thus justify its demand for northern self-determination). In reality, though, Italy was, in terms of ethnicity, religion, ideology, language and culture, a relatively homogenous country (certainly, as regards the latter three, far more so than at any point since unification, thanks to television, mass education and internal migration). The usual causes of (or excuses for) territorial fragmentation or disintegration did not exist. Furthermore, although one in five northern Italians voted for the Lega in the 1996 general election – at a time when the party had abandoned federalism and was demanding northern independence – there was very little enthusiasm for secession. One contemporary survey revealed that only one in ten Lega voters actually supported the idea of an Italian confederation of independent republics.[138] When Lega leader Umberto Bossi subsequently announced (September 1996) the establishment of an independent northern state of Padania, only 300,000 people participated in the mass demonstrations staged to coincide with the declaration. As Nick Doumanis notes, this hardly amounted to a popular endorsement.[139]

Indeed, the Lega's obsession with Padania in the second half of the 1990s undoubtedly contributed to the catastrophic decline in its electoral fortunes from mid-decade. (In 2001, the Lega picked up just 3.9 per cent of the vote, compared with 10.8 per cent in 1996. This represented a loss of 2.5m votes.)[140] In the early 1990s, the Lega's anti-Rome, pro-autonomy rhetoric had chimed with, and given political expression to, the 'feelings of grievance and even rage' harboured by many small business owners in the industrial countryside of the north-east towards a central state seen as parasitic, inefficient, indifferent and a hindrance to the growth and competitiveness of small industry at a time of expanding global markets.[141] In other words, there had been a 'striking symmetry between the political and economic programme of the Lega Nord and the needs and demands of industrial districts as repeatedly expressed by economic experts close to the districts'.[142] The new emphasis on Padania, however, 'involving a shift from an attack on the institutions of the Italian *state* to an attack on the idea of Italy as a *nation* – failed to find an echo among northern industrial districts where autonomy was supported [only] because "it is useful, not to create nations or peoples in opposition to the nation state"'.[143] Although the Lega abandoned its secessionist agenda for devolution shortly before the 2001 election, the damage had been done. Berlusconi's Forza Italia was the main beneficiary of the Lega's failure to maintain its position as the mouthpiece of the small-town, small-scale producers of the north-east.[144]

While apocalyptic assessments of *fin-de-siècle* Italy have proved wide of the mark, the pessimists' position also looks weak. Certainly, there was (and remains) a great deal 'wrong' with Italian society. As will be clear by now, civic virtue was/is in short supply. Moreover, efforts by groups of 'ordinary' Italians to make society both more 'civic' and 'civil' have frequently been deliberately impeded, if not completely undermined, by the state, and/or by fellow citizens who have felt threatened by change. For example, the anti-Mafia movement in Sicily in the 1990s soon found itself at odds with a large section of the Palermo working class, which was concerned that efforts to eliminate the considerable Mafia influence in the construction industry would threaten jobs. (Building firms with suspected Mafia ties were to be barred from tendering for public contracts.) Business interests and significant sections of the Palermo middle class, '"conditioned" by relationships of contiguity with the Mafia that had permeated Palermo society throughout the postwar period', also proved unwilling to denounce Mafia activity.[145] The electoral success of Forza Italia in Sicily in the 1990s and subsequently must be understood in this context. Forza Italia made clear from the start its hostility towards the anti-Mafia pool of magistrates, part of its wider campaign against the 'red togas' investigating Berlusconi (see Chapter 7). As Judith Chubb has observed, 'it is clear that for many people the campaigns for legality and the moralization of public life had gone too far and that Berlusconi's attacks on the magistrates fell on increasingly receptive ears'.[146] In fact, the success of Forza Italia nationally can be seen as evidence of a similar depressing trend across the entire country (see Chapter 7).

Italian society at the end of the twentieth century remained marked by profound gender inequality and inequity. Italian feminism in the 1970s did alter gender relations in Italy, a fact reflected not only in the new abortion law and in legislation covering the family (1975) and women at work (1977), but also in the growing number of women staying on at school, attending university and pursuing careers. Oral and written testimonies from women also 'confirm that great changes in relations between women followed in the train of 1970s feminism...in the great majority of cases a central theme is the making and celebration of relationships between women...or else the forging of symbolic links with cultural forms in which women had found, and were finding, self-expression'.[147] Nevertheless, Italy has remained 'a country in which gender relations are still often formed in the mould of an underlying masculinism'.[148] This is most obvious in the media's representation of women as either sexual objects (the ubiquitous dancing girls on television, the semi-naked models who grace the covers of even 'highbrow' magazines), or simply as wives and mothers, but it can be seen in a number of other ways, too. For example, although the percentage of women in the workforce grew quickly during the 1980s, the female employment rate in the early 1990s was still low in a western European context and female unemployment high. Furthermore, many of the new entrants were poorly paid and much of the work was in the unregulated 'submerged' economy.[149] Married women, working or not, continued to perform the majority of household chores (cooking, cleaning, shopping, looking after the children, caring for sick relatives and so on). Women also continued to be severely under-represented within the political sphere – after the 1992 elections, for example, there were only 82 women in the *camera* and senate combined. Women were noticeable only by their absence in the constitutional debates of the early 1990s.[150] Little has changed in the intervening years. In 2006, female unemployment in Italy stood at 8.8 per cent, against a general rate of 6.6 per cent, while the female employment rate of 46.3 per cent lagged far behind the overall employment rate of 58.4 per cent, itself the fourth lowest in the EU. In a survey of 48 countries by the International Labour Organization, Italy came above only Cyprus, Egypt and South Korea for female share of legislators, senior officials and managers.[151] Little wonder that Italy has been described as 'the land that feminism forgot'.[152]

The picture of Italian society at century's end is equally troubling if we look beyond gender-related issues to questions of social exclusion and poverty. Let us take just one example of social exclusion: that of disabled people. In 1999, the employment rate of disabled persons in Italy was 20.8 per cent (EU average: 44 per cent). Among EU countries, Italy ranked third from the bottom in accessibility for the disabled, ahead of only Greece and Portugal. Although 15 per cent of Italian households included a disabled person, only 2 per cent of Italians reported actually going to school with one.[153] As regards poverty, despite the general affluence of Italian society, 2.6m Italian families in 1999, equivalent to 11.9 per cent of all households, were classified as 'poor' (i.e. living below the official poverty line). One million families, 4.8 per cent of all households, were considered to be living in conditions of 'absolute poverty'. As usual, the problem was particularly acute in the south: nearly a quarter of all southern families were living below the poverty line; two-thirds of all poor households and three-quarters of all households living in conditions of absolute poverty were located in the south. Lack of work was, of course, a major contributory factor: the unemployment rate in the south in 1998 stood at 23 per cent, well above the national average of around 12 per cent (in the north, by contrast, the unemployment rate was 6 per cent).[154]

One could go on, but the point should be clear by now: it is not difficult to present Italian society as deeply, perhaps irredeemably flawed. To focus exclusively on the failings of Italian society, however, is to see only part of a bigger picture. Tremendous change *for the better* has occurred since World War Two. Moreover, as Doumanis writes, large numbers of ordinary Italians have consistently 'demonstrated an interest in making the nation work *despite* the state, and most substantial political, legal and social reforms...have been the result of pressure "from below"'.[155] Seen from this perspective, Ginsborg's guarded optimism appears justified.

Postscript

Modern Italian History at the End of the 'noughties'

There is no doubt that modern Italian history outside of Italy is an understudied and undervalued subject, certainly in comparison with the histories of the other 'great' European powers of the nineteenth and twentieth centuries (Germany, Russia, Britain and France). Modern Italy barely registers a presence on bookshop shelves (or in many publishers' catalogues). The wider media meanwhile seem unaware that modern Italy actually has a history. The problem is one of perception. Outside of Italian Studies, modern Italian history and contemporary Italian affairs are rarely treated as serious subjects. The assumption is that modern Italy represents the triumph of style over substance. Take the example of Mussolini. Despite decades of revisionism, the popular view of the *Duce* is still that of an 'Ice Cream dictator', frivolous, frothy, ultimately ridiculous, and mostly harmless. (In this regard I was struck by a recent discussion [November 2009] on the BBC Radio 4 *Today* programme of Mussolini's World War One links to British Intelligence, in which the veteran broadcaster John Humphries – with the willing assistance of his interviewee, the historian Peter Martland – reduced Mussolini to a sex-obsessed political opportunist, a clownish figure.) For the most part, the mass media treats the current Italian premier, Silvio Berlusconi, in similarly light-hearted fashion, despite the deeply worrying political implications of the Berlusconi 'project' noted by Ginsborg and others.

Ridicule and contempt breed ignorance. For example, in Britain in the late 1990s – long before sex scandals brought him to the public's attention – awareness of Berlusconi was so limited that even Jeremy Paxman, the anchor of the BBC's flagship *Newsnight* programme, appeared not to know that Berlusconi had entered politics, let alone had been Prime Minister. (Paxman mocked a student contestant on *University Challenge* for suggesting this.) *Italia moderna?* The popular perception was and remains of pizza, pasta and piazza politics, of football, fashion and Mafia. The élite view of Italy – little changed since the beginnings of the Grand Tour – is of opera, art and ancient ruins. From this perspective, Italy has a history – but it is not modern.

Nevertheless, there are some reasons to be cheerful. Modern Italian history has enjoyed something of a 'surge' in recent years. In the early 1990s, there were no specialist modern Italian history journals in English, nor had there been since the demise of the short-lived *Journal of Italian History* over a decade earlier. Now there are two journals dedicated to the study of modern Italy, each with a strong historical element: the American-dominated *Journal of Modern Italian Studies* and the British-based *Modern Italy*. Both journals celebrated their tenth anniversaries in 2005. *Modern Italy*, the journal of the Association for the Study of Modern Italy, has expanded twice since then, from two to four issues per year, indicative of an increase both in the number of submissions to the journal and an expanding readership. Furthermore, and as we have seen here, a new generation of historians (and other specialists) of modern Italy has injected fresh life into the subject, revisiting, rethinking, and revising old debates and orthodoxies, and opening up new and fascinating lines of historical enquiry in the process. Let us hope that the seriousness and intelligence that they, like their predecessors, have brought to the historical study of modern Italy finally feeds through into the wider public domain.

Glossary

Agrario (plural: agrari) · Landowner.

Alleanza nazionale · Lit. National Alliance. Right-wing political party established in 1994 out of the old neo-Fascist Movimento sociale italiano (MSI). Merged in 2008 with Forza Italia (see below) to create Il popolo della libertà, under the leadership of Silvio Berlusconi.

Anschluss · De facto annexation of Austria by Nazi Germany, March 1938.

Autorizzazione maritale · Lit. 'marital authorization'. Part of the Italian Civil Code of 1865. Under the law, a married woman could not manage property or enter into a business transaction independently of her husband. Repealed in 1919.

Avanti! · Lit. 'Forward!' Official newspaper of the Italian Socialist party (est. 1896, closed in 1993).

Banche popolari · Lit. 'People's banks'. Small local cooperative banks.

Biennio rosso · Lit. 'Two Red Years'. Peak years of socialist agitation after World War One, 1919–20.

Bonifica integrale · Land reclamation and improvement scheme. Launched in 1928.

Bracciante (plural: braccianti) · Landless rural day labourer.

Brigate rosse · Lit. 'Red Brigades'. Revolutionary left-wing terrorist group (est. 1970).

Buoni ordinari del tesoro (BOT) · Government treasury bonds.

Camera dei deputati · Chamber of Deputies. Lower house in the Italian parliament.

Carabinieri · Military corps with policing duties.

Cassa per il Mezzogiorno (Casmez) · State-run body (est. 1950) with responsibility for stimulating economic growth in the Italian south. Abolished in 1986.

Cassa di risparmio (plural: casse di risparmio) · Savings and loans bank.

Clientelismo · Clientelism. The exchange of resources between a patron and their clients. The patron distributes favours (e.g. protection, employment, contracts etc.) to clients in return for political fealty (votes).

Confino · Fascist-era punishment of internal exile and internment for those found guilty of 'political crimes'.

Comitato di liberazione nazionale (CLN) · The Committee of National Liberation. Cross-party wartime anti-Fascist resistance organization established in Rome, September 1943.

Comitato di liberazione nazionale per l'alta Italia (CNLAI) · The Committee of National Liberation for Upper Italy. Cross-party wartime anti-Fascist resistance organization established in Milan, November 1943. Responsible for the coordination of the northern Italian resistance movement from January 1944.

Cosa Nostra · Lit. 'Our thing'. Term for the Sicilian Mafia.

Democrazia Cristiana (DC) · Italian Christian Democratic party (est. 1943).

Destra storica · Lit. Historic Right. Broad coalition of parliamentary deputies who had supported the Piedmontese moderate liberal-constitutional approach to Italian independence in the 1850s and early 1860s. Dominated government from the proclamation of the Kingdom of Italy in 1861 until 1876.

Duce · Leader (from the Latin 'dux'). Used by Mussolini.

Extracomunitari · Term for non-EU immigrants in Italy.

Fascio (plural: fasci) · Lit. 'bundle'. Term used to designate a group.

Fasci di combattimento · Lit. Combat groups. Name given to early Fascist groups. The first *Fascio di combattimento* was established in Milan by Mussolini in March 1919.

Fasci femminili · Lit. 'Women's groups'. Fascist organization for Italian women (est. 1920).

Fasci giovanili · Lit. 'youth groups'. Fascist organization for young Italian men, aged from 18 to 21 (est. 1930).

Fascio littorio · Tightly bound bundle of rods tied to an axe head. Ubiquitous symbol of Fascism (signifying unity, force and justice).

Federterra · National agricultural labourers' union.

Forza Italia · Lit. 'Go Italy'. Political party created by Silvio Berlusconi in 1994.

Ginnasio (plural: ginnassi) · Elite type of Italian secondary school.

Giustizia e libertà · Lit. 'Justice and Liberty'. Main anti-Fascist movement in Italy during the Fascist period.

Giolittismo · Similar to *trasformismo* (see below). Term used to describe the management and manipulation of parliamentary majorities under Giovanni Giolitti.

Gioventù italiana del Littorio (GIL) · Lit. Italian youth of the Lictor. Organization established in 1937 to oversee and control Fascist youth movements.

Gioventù universitaria fascista (GUF) · Fascist university students' association (est. 1922).

Istituto Luce (L'Unione cinematografia educativa) · Fascist-controlled documentary film and newsreel production/distribution company (est. 1924).

Istituto mobiliare italiano (IMI) · Italian Securities Institute. Established in 1931 to provide medium and long-term financing to industry in the wake of a major banking and credit crisis.

Istituto per la ricostruzione industriale (IRI) · Institute for Industrial Reconstruction (est.1933). Created in response to the financial and economic crisis of the early 1930s, the IRI bought up virtually worthless bank-owned shares in struggling industrial companies and took a controlling stake in the banks themselves.

Istituto nazionale di statistica (ISTAT) · Italian National Institute of Statistics (est. 1926).

Latifondista (plural: latifondisti) · Large estate owner in southern Italy (see *latifondo* below).

Latifondo (plural: latifondi) · Type of large landed estate found in southern Italy.

Lega Nord · Contemporary northern regionalist party (est. 1991).

Liceo (plural: licei) · Elite type of senior secondary school.

Linea Einaudi · Name given to the monetary restrictions introduced in 1947 by Luigi Einaudi, Governor of the Bank of Italy, in an effort to curb inflation.

Lottizzazione · The sharing-out between the major post-war political parties of key positions within the Italian public/semi-public sector.

Mani pulite · Lit. 'clean hands'. Investigations by Milanese magistrates into political corruption in the city (began in 1992). Gave rise to the 'Tangentopoli' scandals (see below) that heralded the collapse of the post-war political system in the early 1990s.

Massaie rurali · Fascist organization for rural housewives (est. 1934).

Medico condotto (plural: medici condotti) · General practitioner employed on a non-permanent basis by a municipal authority.

Meridionalismo · The study of the 'Southern Question'.

Meridionalisto (plural: meridionalisti) · Student of the 'Southern Question'.

Mezzadria · Sharecropping system.

Mezzadro (plural: mezzadri) · Sharecropper.

Mezzogiorno · The Italian south.

Mostra della rivoluzione fascista · Rome-based exhibition to celebrate the tenth anniversary of Fascist rule (1932).

Mussolinismo · Lit. 'Mussolinism'. The personality cult that developed round Mussolini.

Milizia voluntaria per la sicurezza nazionale (MVSN) · Lit. 'Voluntary Militia for National Security'. Armed wing of the Italian Fascist party (est. 1923).

Opera nazionale balilla (ONB) · Umbrella organization for Fascist youth movements (est. 1926). Replaced by the Gioventù italiana del Littorio (GIL) in 1937.

Opera nazionale dopolavoro (OND) · Lit. 'National After-work Agency'. Fascist organization providing adult leisure and recreational facilities (est. 1925).

Organizzazione per la Vigilanza e la Repressione dell'Antifascismo (OVRA) · Fascist secret police.

Padania · Term used by the regionalist Lega Nord to describe its 'nation' of northern and central Italy.

Partitio comunista italiano (PCI) · Italian Communist party (est. 1921).

Partito nazionale fascista (PNF) · National Fascist party (est. 1921).

Partito popolare italiano (PPI) · Catholic Popular party (est. 1919).

Partito socialista italiano (PSI) · Italian Socialist party (est. 1892).

Partitocrazia · 'Party rule'. Term used to describe the control of state institutions and the public administration by the governing parties of the post-war Italian republic.

Passo romano · Lit. 'Roman step'. Fascist name for the German military 'goose step', introduced in Italy in 1938.

Il Popolo d'Italia · Official Fascist party newspaper.

Qualunquismo · Term meaning distrust of, and apathy towards, politics. Derived from the short-lived post-World War Two political party, the *Fronte dell'uomo qualunque* (Common Man's Front).

Quota novanta (Q90) · Lit. 'quota ninety'. Policy announced by Mussolini in August 1926 to revalue the Italian lira at the exchange rate of 90 lire to the pound sterling.

Ras · Name given to provincial Fascist leaders (term of Ethiopian origin).

Risorgimento · Lit. 'resurgence'. Name given to the process of Italian unification in the mid-nineteenth century.

Salò · Town on Lake Garda and headquarters of the puppet Fascist government in German-occupied Italy, from September 1943 to April 1945.

Scuola normale (plural: scuole normali) · Lit. 'normal school'. Upper secondary level teacher training school. *Scuole normali* were renamed *istituti magistrali* in 1923.

Sessantotto · Students' revolt of 1968.

Sessantottini · Participants in the students' revolt of 1968.

Sinistra storica · Lit. 'Historic Left'. Heterogeneous political grouping including former followers of Garibaldi, opposed to the ruling moderate-conservative *destra storica* (Historic Right see above) which governed Italy from 1861 to 1876. Succeeded the Right in government in 1876.

Squadrista (plural: squadristi) · Fascist squad member.

Squadrismo · Acts of political violence perpetrated by Fascist squads.

Statuto · Piedmontese constitution of 1848, adopted as the constitution of Italy after 1861. Replaced in 1948 by Republican constitution.

Svolta di Salerno · Lit. 'turn of Salerno'. Term given to the decision of Communist Party leader Palmiro Togliatti (March 1944) to reverse his party's policy of non-collaboration with the royal Italian government in Allied-occupied southern Italy.

Tangentopoli · Lit. 'Kick-back city' or 'Bribesville'. Name given to the Italian political corruption scandals of the early 1990s, which began in Milan in 1992. (See also 'mani pulite' above.)

Tangente (plural: tangenti) · Lit. 'bribe or kick-back'. (See also Tangentopoli.)

Trasformismo · Lit. 'transformism'. The process whereby one's political enemy is 'transformed' into a political ally through the judicious use of favours. A practice particularly identified with Liberal Italy under the governments of the *sinistra storica* (Historic Left see above).

Ventennio · Lit. 'twenty years'. The two decades of Fascist rule in Italy, 1922–1943.

Notes

Preface

1 John Whittam, 'Fascism and anti-Fascism in Italy: History, Memory and Culture', *Journal of Contemporary History* 36(1) (2001), p. 165.
2 Denis Mack Smith, *Modern Italy: A Political History* (Ann Arbor: University of Michigan Press, 1997); Martin Clark, *Modern Italy* (London: Longman, 2nd edn, 1995). A third edition of Clark's work was published in 2008. According to the publisher's online catalogue, it includes updated sections on liberal and Fascist Italy, 'in the light of recent scholarship and changes in historiographical approach', and increased coverage of the 1980s and 1990s.
3 John Foot, *Modern Italy* (Basingstoke and New York: Palgrave Macmillan, 2003), p. 2.
4 Foot, *Modern Italy*, p. 5.
5 Philip Morgan, *The Fall of Mussolini: Italy, the Italians, and the Second World War* (Oxford: Oxford University Press, 2007), p. 233; John A. Davis, 'Modern Italy – Changing Historical Perspectives since 1945', in Michael Bentley (ed.), *Companion to Historiography* (London and New York: Routledge, 1997), p. 591.

Chapter 1 The politics of liberal Italy

1 Benedetto Croce, *A History of Italy, 1871–1915* (Oxford: Clarendon Press, 1929), p. 230; Antonio Gramsci, in Quentin Hoare and Geoffrey Nowell Smith (eds), *Selections from the Prison Notebooks of Antonio Gramsci* (London: Lawrence and Wishart, 1971), p. 90.
2 Prior to Rome the Italian capital had moved from Turin (1861) to Florence (1865).
3 As an excellent introduction to the revisionist trends in Risorgimento historiography see Lucy Riall, *Risorgimento: The History of Italy from Napoleon to Nation State* (Basingstoke: Palgrave Macmillan, 2009).
4 Giolitti also held the influential post of Minister of the Interior during the Zanardelli ministry of 1901–03.
5 Derek Beales, *The Risorgimento and the Unification of Italy* (London: Longman, 2nd edn, 1981), p. 15.
6 Croce, *A History of Italy*, pp. 5, 19–20, 45, 51, 60, 70.
7 Croce, *A History of Italy*, pp. 178–9, 192.
8 Croce, *A History of Italy*, pp. 214, 225, 230–1, 261–2.
9 Croce, *A History of Italy*, pp. 252–3.
10 Arrested in 1926 and tried in 1928, Gramsci was granted unconditional release from prison on health grounds in April 1937. He died a few days later. During his trial the prosecution is alleged to have demanded: 'We must stop this brain from working for twenty years.'
11 John A. Davis (ed.), *Gramsci and Italy's Passive Revolution* (London: Croom Helm, 1979), p. 13.
12 Hoare and Nowell Smith, *Selections from the Prison Notebooks*, p. xciv.

13 Although Gramsci did admit that hegemony could be based on a 'combination of force and consent...without force exceeding consent too much', it could not exist on force ('domination') alone.

14 Hoare and Nowell Smith, *Selections from the Prison Notebooks*, p. 79.

15 Hoare and Nowell Smith, *Selections from the Prison Notebooks*, p. 115.

16 Antonio Gramsci, in David Forgacs (ed.), *A Gramsci Reader: Selected Writings 1916–1935* (London: Lawrence and Wishart, 1988), p. 266.

17 Quoted in Paul Ginsborg, 'Gramsci and the Era of Bourgeois Revolution in Italy', in Davis (ed.), *Gramsci and Italy's Passive Revolution*, p. 46.

18 Implicitly different since Gramsci does not name particular examples of passive revolution elsewhere in Europe, though from his comments he certainly must have had Germany in mind.

19 Hoare and Nowell Smith, *Selections from the Prison Notebooks*, pp. 83, 101; Forgacs, *A Gramsci Reader*, pp. 257–8.

20 Hoare and Nowell Smith, *Selections from the Prison Notebooks*, p. 90.

21 Hoare and Nowell Smith, *Selections from the Prison Notebooks*, p. 71.

22 Forgacs, *A Gramsci Reader*, p. 268.

23 Depretis remains a relatively unstudied political figure – perhaps due to the prosaic nature of politics relative to the excitement of unification and immediate consolidation of the state, and the extravagance of the subsequent Crispian era.

24 Hoare and Nowell Smith, *Selections from the Prison Notebooks*, pp. 67–8, 93–4.

25 Forgacs, *A Gramsci Reader*, pp. 175–6.

26 Hoare and Nowell Smith, *Selections from the Prison Notebooks*, pp. 95–6.

27 Republished in English translation in 1996 by Princeton University Press under the title *Italian Foreign Policy: The Statecraft of the Founders*. Chabod had originally intended this volume to act as an introduction to four volumes of 'standard' diplomatic history. These, though, were never written.

28 Sidney Sonnino (1881), quoted in Chabod, *Italian Foreign Policy*, p. 227.

29 Marco Minghetti (1881), quoted in Chabod, *Italian Foreign Policy*, p. 318.

30 Chabod, *Italian Foreign Policy*, pp. 377, 414, 420, 464.

31 Chabod, *Italian Foreign Policy*, pp. 114, 243, 255; Christopher Duggan, 'Francesco Crispi, "Political Education" and the Problem of Italian National Consciousness, 1860–1896', *Journal of Modern Italian Studies* 2(2) (1997), pp. 142, 144.

32 Rosario Romeo, quoted in Giuseppe Galasso, 'Rosario Romeo (1924–1987)', *Journal of Modern Italian Studies* 4(2) (1999), pp. 258, 267.

33 Romeo's key works in this regard are *Risorgimento e capitalismo* (Bari: Laterza, 1959), and *Dal Piemonte sabaudo all'Italia liberale* (Turin: Einaudi, 1963). Romeo dedicated the last twenty years of his life (he died in 1987) to writing a three-volume biography of Cavour (*Cavour e il suo tempo* (Bari: Laterza, 1969–84)) – a eulogy to the principles and practices of moderate liberalism. For a positive appraisal of Romeo's career see Galasso's article cited above.

34 A. W. Salomone, *Italy in the Giolittian Era: Italian Democracy in the Making, 1900–1914* (Philadelphia: University of Pennsylvania Press, 2nd edn, 1960), pp. 97, 101, 106.

35 Frank J. Coppa, 'Giovanni Giolitti: Precursor of Mussolini?', *Italian Quarterly* 27(104) (1986), p. 47.

36 Frank J. Coppa, *Planning, Protectionism and Politics in Liberal Italy: Economics and Politics in the Giolittian Age* (Washington: Catholic University of America Press, 1971), p. 107. Coppa's contention that Giolitti was essentially a 'democratic figure' is challenged by Alexander De Grand, *The Hunchback's Tailor: Giovanni Giolitti and Liberal Italy from the Challenge of Mass Politics to the Rise of Fascism, 1882–1922* (Westport: Praeger, 2001a). See also Alexander De Grand, 'Giovanni Giolitti: A Pessimist as Modernizer', *Journal of Modern Italian Studies* 6(1) (2001b), pp. 57–67.

37 Salomone, *Italy in the Giolittian Era*, p. 109; Coppa, *Planning, Protectionism and Politics in Liberal Italy*, pp. 107, 251 (quote from p. 107).

38 Gianni Toniolo has described Sereni as the 'greatest interpreter of the Gramscian tradition'. Gianni Toniolo, *An Economic History of Liberal Italy 1850–1918* (London: Routledge, 1990), p. 135.

39 Sereni (1947), quoted in Toniolo, *An Economic History of Liberal Italy*, p. 138.

40 Gaetano Salvemini, 'Introductory Essay', in Salomone, *Italy in the Giolittian Era*, pp. xv, xx–xxi. Salvemini's 1952 comments are quoted by Salomone, pp. 131–2.

41 Salvemini, 'Introductory Essay', p. xviii. Ragionieri and Fried are quoted in Nico Randeraad, *Authority in Search of Liberty: The Prefects in Liberal Italy* (Amsterdam: Thesis Publishers, 1993), p. 163.

42 Salvemini, 'Introductory Essay', p. xix; Denis Mack Smith, *Italy: A Modern History* (Ann Arbor: University of Michigan Press, 1959), pp. 220–1.

43 R. J. B. Bosworth, 'Historiography', in Gino Moliterno (ed.), *Encyclopaedia of Contemporary Italian Culture* (London: Routledge, 2000), p. 269. Less polite than Bosworth in his description of Mack Smith was the Italian historian Walter Maturi, who referred to the Oxford academic as a 'rigid English puritan'. Walter Maturi, *Interpretazioni del risorgimento: lezioni di storia della storiografia* (Turin: Einaudi, 1962), p. 684.

44 *Italy: A Modern History* provoked considerable controversy within Italy due to its less than flattering assessment of the Italian ruling class. Mack Smith had already attracted attention in Italy for his ground-breaking 1954 study of relations between Cavour and Garibaldi in 1860, which had attacked a number of Italian nationalist myths. See Denis Mack Smith, *Cavour and Garibaldi: A Study in Political Conflict* (Cambridge: Cambridge University Press, 2nd edn, 1985).

45 Mack Smith, *Italy*, p. v.

46 Mack Smith, *Italy*, p. vii, 103, 137.

47 For example, Mack Smith commented of Giolitti's legacy: 'if he left politics in a not altogether healthy state, it was existing traditions and institutions rather than himself which were primarily responsible'. Mack Smith, *Italy*, p. 285.

48 Mack Smith, *Italy*, pp. 119, 135, 200, 286–7.

49 R. J. B. Bosworth, *Italy and the Approach of the First World War* (Basingstoke: Macmillan, 1983), pp. 74–5; R. A. Webster, *Industrial Imperialism in Italy 1908–1915* (Berkeley: University of California Press, 1975), p. 204.

50 Lucy Riall, review of *Storia d'Italia I*, by G. Sabbatucci and V. Vidotto (eds), *Journal of Modern Italian Studies* 1(3) (1996), p. 458.

51 Even the reputation of Crispi, for so long reviled by both liberal and Marxist historians (and most in between) and once claimed by the Fascists as one of their own, has been rescued by the revisionists. See Christopher Duggan, *Francesco Crispi, 1818–1901: From Nation to Nationalism* (Oxford: Oxford University Press, 2002). In contrast to the traditional picture of Crispi as a megalomaniac, Duggan presents Crispi as honest, sober and self-controlled, principled and pragmatic, very much a man of his time, and prepared to sacrifice personal and material gain (Crispi lived most of his life in financial penury and died in poverty) in his efforts to educate Italians in liberty and nationhood.

52 Raffaele Romanelli, *Il comando impossibile: stato e società nell'Italia liberale* (Bologna: il Mulino, 1988), pp. 7–30. A useful work in English on the role of the prefecture is Nico Randeraad's 1993 study, *Authority in Search of Liberty*. For a more general treatment by Romanelli on the role of the Italian state see 'Centralismo e autonomie', in Raffaele Romanelli (ed.), *Storia dello stato italiano* (Rome: Donzelli editore, 1995), pp. 125–86.

53 Romanelli, *Il comando impossibile*, p. 8.

54 Marco Meriggi has pointed out that although bourgeois power derived from the nation, the Italian bourgeoisie was 'for the most part immersed in a local universe'. 'Even on the occasions of maximum rhetorical sublimation of the nation,' Meriggi writes, 'the loyalty of the notability to the local town, to the city from which the bourgeoisie starts, never gets lost'. Many of the apparent symbols of bourgeois nationalism – e.g. the bureaucracy, the university system – were, in fact, instruments of bourgeois localism. Marco Meriggi, 'Introduzione', in Marco Meriggi and Pierangelo Schiera (eds), *Dalla città alla nazione: borghesie ottocentesche in Italia e in Germania* (Bologna: il Mulino, 1993a), pp. 18–19.

55 Christopher Duggan, review of *Sicily and the Unification of Italy*, by Lucy Riall, *English Historical Review* 114(459) (1999), p. 1346.

56 Roger Absalom, *Italy Since 1800: A Nation in the Balance?* (London and New York: Longman, 1995), p. 57.

57 Raffaelle Romanelli, 'Political Debate, Social History, and the Italian *Borghesia*: Changing Perspectives in Historical Research', *Journal of Modern History* 63(3) (1991), pp. 723–4. As Eric Hobsbawm has noted, the extent of the franchise was not necessarily a reliable indication of the degree of democratization in a particular country. Germany, for example, boasted a parliamentary assembly (Reichstag) elected by universal suffrage, but its powers were minimal in comparison with the unelected upper house (Bundestag) and those of the Chancellor. Eric Hobsbawm, *The Age of Empire 1875–1914* (London: Weidenfeld & Nicolson, 1987), pp. 85–7.

58 Fulvio Cammarano, 'Nazionalizzazione della politica e politicizzazione della nazione. I dilemmi della classe dirigente nell'Italia liberale', in Meriggi and Schiera (eds), *Dalla città alla nazione*, pp. 139–163; Lucy Riall, 'Progress and Compromise in Liberal Italy', *Historical Journal* 38(1) (1995), pp. 205–13; Christopher Duggan, 'Politics in the Era of Depretis and Crispi, 1870–96', in John A. Davis (ed.), *Italy in the Nineteenth Century* (Oxford: Oxford University Press, 2000), pp. 154–180.

59 The phrase is Mack Smith's. See Denis Mack Smith, 'Benedetto Croce: History and Politics', *Journal of Contemporary History* 8(1) (1973), p. 56.

60 Bosworth, 'Historiography', p. 270.

61 Liberal critics of liberal Italy *do* exist. See, for example, Guido de Ruggiero, *The History of European Liberalism* (London: Oxford University Press, 1927). According to de Ruggiero, the Right (i.e. the *destra storica*):

> 'confined liberty to the narrow political caste which took actual part in public life and even...came to identify liberty with the state itself. Now it is certainly true that the state is the highest and most complete creation of human freedom; but only if the state is the term or culminating point of an ideal process connecting it with the individual, nourishing it and nourished by it in a constant interchange of influences... This was not the state brought into existence by the Right. No one who remembers how far the men of the Right and their successors were prepared to go in justifying reactionary excesses by appeals to the principle of the state can fail to recognize what degradation the original ideal had in practice undergone' (p. 327).

62 Jackson Lear, quoted in Bosworth, 'Historiography', p. 269.

63 Hoare and Nowell Smith, *Selections from the Prison Notebooks*, pp. 119, 179.

64 Hoare and Nowell Smith, *Selections from the Prison Notebooks*, p. 115.

65 Hoare and Nowell Smith, *Selections from the Prison Notebooks*, p. 79.

66 Hoare and Nowell Smith, *Selections from the Prison Notebooks*, p. 74.

67 Cf. Ginsborg, 'Gramsci and the Era of Bourgeois Revolution', pp. 60–1.

68 Coppa, *Planning, Protectionism and Politics in Liberal Europe*. Gramsci received little help from subsequent Marxist scholars. The lack of a substantial Marxist critique of Gramsci's historical writing – the result, according to Paul Ginsborg, of an 'excess of deference' – meant the ossification rather than the development of his ideas. This, as Ginsborg rightly says, 'is nothing but a disservice to Gramsci himself' (Ginsborg, 'Gramsci and the Era of Bourgeois Revolution', p. 46). Gramsci would have disapproved of such deference – as he complained of dogmatic Marxism in 1918: 'Marx did not write a nice little doctrine, he is not a Messiah...[he] is for us a master of spiritual and moral life, not a shepherd wielding a crook.' Forgacs, *A Gramsci Reader*, pp. 36, 39.

69 Riall, 'Progress and Compromise in Liberal Italy', p. 210; Saverio Battente, 'Nation and State Building: Recent Historiographical Interpretations (1989–1997): Unification to Fascism', *Journal of Modern Italian Studies* 5(3) (2000), p. 314.

70 Mack Smith, *Italy*, p. vii.

71 Sonnino, quoted in Salomone, *Italy in the Giolittian Era*, p. 10.

72 Nicholas Doumanis, *Italy* (London: Arnold, 2001), p. 110.

73 Riall, 'Progress and Compromise in Liberal Italy', pp. 211–12.

Chapter 2 The economy of liberal Italy

1 For an excellent introduction to revisionist literature on the 'Southern Question' see Jonathan Morris, 'Challenging *Meridionalismo*: Constructing a New History for Southern Italy', in Robert Lumley and Jonathan Morris (eds), *The New History of the Italian South: The Mezzogiorno Revisited* (Exeter: University of Exeter Press, 1997), pp. 1–19.

2 For problems with the ISTAT estimates see Jon Cohen and Giovanni Federico, *The Growth of the Italian Economy 1820–1960* (Cambridge: Cambridge University Press, 2001), pp. 8–11; Toniolo, *An Economic History of Liberal Italy*, pp. 3–8.

3 Vera Zamagni, *The Economic History of Italy, 1860–1990* (Oxford: Clarendon Press, 1993), pp. 29–30, 39–41; Toniolo, *An Economic History of Liberal Italy*, p. 50; B. R. Mitchell, *International Historical Statistics: Europe 1750–1993* (London: Macmillan, 4th edn, 1998), pp. 121–2, 750–6.

4 Mack Smith, *Modern Italy*, p. 44.

5 Clive Trebilcock, *The Industrialization of the Continental Powers, 1780–1914* (London: Longman, 1981), p. 440; Toniolo, *An Economic History of Liberal Italy*, n. 9, p. 157; Mitchell, *International Historical Statistics*, pp. 710–14.

6 Zamagni, *The Economic History of Italy*, p. 192.

7 Toniolo, *An Economic History of Liberal Italy*, pp. 58, 76; Zamagni, *The Economic History of Italy*, pp. 133–41.

8 North-west includes Piedmont, Liguria, Lombardy; north-east and centre includes Veneto, Emilia, Tuscany, Marches, Umbria and Latium; south and islands includes Abruzzi, Campania, Apulia, Basilicata, Calabria, Sicily and Sardinia. Alfredo Giuseppe Esposto, 'Estimating Regional Per Capita Income: Italy, 1861–1914', *Journal of European Economic History* 26(3) (1997), p. 587.

9 Toniolo, *An Economic History of Liberal Italy*, pp. 58, 76; Zamagni, *The Economic History of Italy*, pp. 14–15, 23; Simon P. Ville, *Transport and the Development of the European Economy, 1750–1918* (London: Macmillan, 1990), p. 17; Richard Eckaus, 'The North–South Differential in Italian Economic Development', *Journal of Economic History* 21(3) (1961), p. 291; Clark, *Modern Italy*, p. 36.

10 Cohen and Federico, *The Growth of the Italian Economy*, pp. 9–12; Stefano Fenoaltea, 'The Growth of the Italian Economy, 1861–1913: Preliminary Second-Generation Estimates', *European Review of Economic History* 9(3) (2005), pp. 273–312.

11 Cohen and Federico, *The Growth of the Italian Economy*, p. 13; Trebilcock, *The Industrialization of the Continental Powers*, p. 433; Luciano Cafagna, 'Italy 1830–1914', in Carlo M. Cipolla (ed.), *The Fontana Economic History of Europe, Volume 4: The Emergence of Industrial Societies. Part One* (London: Collins-Fontana, 1973), p. 306; Zamagni, *The Economic History of Italy*, p. 83.

12 Trebilcock, *The Industrialization of the Continental Powers*, p. 440. The United Kingdom had reached a similar density in the 1860s, Germany in the 1880s and France in the 1890s. The Italian rail system was, however, far more developed than, for example, those in Austria-Hungary, Spain or Russia.

13 Mitchell, *International Historical Statistics*, pp. 717, 735–42; Zamagni, *The Economic History of Italy*, p. 162. Road figures exclude local roads.

14 Clark, *Modern Italy*, p. 36; Zamagni, *The Economic History of Italy*, p. 195.

15 The creation of the Bank of Italy did not mean the establishment of a central bank as such – two other note-issuing banks remained in existence until the 1920s – but the new bank's resources and responsibilities did mean it quickly became the linchpin of the Italian financial system.

16 Zamagni, *The Economic History of Italy*, pp. 140, 147. The term 'mixed' bank was applied to those banks 'that provided short-, medium- and long-term credit at the same time; they were 'universal' rather than specialized in nature, providing all the services a client could possibly require' (Zamagni, *The Economic History of Italy*, p. 147). This type of bank originated in Germany, hence the term 'German' bank; this was particularly apposite in the Italian case since COMIT was the creation of German bankers and was set up under German management.

17 Zamagni, *The Economic History of Italy*, pp. 39, 195; Toniolo, *An Economic History of Liberal Italy*, p. 122; Alfredo Giuseppe Esposto, 'Italian Industrialization and the Gerschenkronian "Great Spurt": A Regional Analysis', *Journal of Economic History* 52(2) (1992), pp. 357–8; Brian A'Hearn, 'Institutions, Externalities and Economic Growth in Southern Italy: Evidence from the Cotton Textiles Industry, 1861–1914', *Economic History Review* 51(4) (1998), p. 734; Esposto, 'Estimating Regional Per Capita Income', p. 593; Francesco L. Galassi and Jon S. Cohen, 'The Economics of Tenancy in Early Twentieth Century Southern Italy', *Economic History Review* 47(3) (1994), p. 593.

18 Sereni (1975), quoted in Jon S. Cohen and Francesco L. Galassi, 'Sharecropping and Productivity: "Feudal Residues" in Italian Agriculture, 1911', *Economic History Review* 43(4) (1990), p. 646.

19 Rosario Romeo, *Risorgimento e capitalismo* (Bari: Laterza, 2nd edn, 1963), pp. 29, 32, 120–1; Rosario Romeo, 'Lo sviluppo dell'economia italiana dopo l'unificazione', first published 1965 and reprinted in Rosario Romeo, *L'Italia unita e la prima guerra mondiale* (Rome-Bari: Laterza, 1978), pp. 72, 74; Alexander Gerschenkron and Rosario Romeo, 'Debate with Romeo, November 1961, Naples', in Alexander Gerschenkron, *Continuity in History and Other Essays* (Cambridge, MA: Harvard University Press, 1968), p. 115; Toniolo, *An Economic History of Liberal Italy*, p. 137.

20 Alexander Gerschenkron, *Europe in the Russian Mirror: Four Lectures in Economic History* (Cambridge: Cambridge University Press, 1970), p. 125.

21 Alexander Gerschenkron, *Economic Backwardness in Historical Perspective: A Book of Essays* (Cambridge, MA: Harvard University Press, 1962), p. 83.

22 Gerschenkron, *Economic Backwardness in Historical Perspective*, chs 1, 4, 5 and pp. 353–64; Gerschenkron, *Continuity in History and Other Essays*, ch. 5.

23 Cafagna (1965), quoted in Valerio Castronovo, 'The Italian Take-off: a Critical Re-examination of the Problem', *Journal of Italian History* 1(3) (1978), p. 499; Luciano Cafagna, 'La questione delle origini del dualismo economico italiano' (1989), available in translation in Giovanni Federico (ed.), *The Economic Development of Italy since 1870* (Aldershot: Edward Elgar, 1994), pp. 649–50.

24 Cafagna, 'Italy 1830–1914', pp. 306, 318, 322; Federico (ed.), *The Economic Development of Italy*, p. 647.

25 For example, Fenoaltea's estimate for total manufacturing output is obtained from information derived from nearly 200 newly constructed product-specific series; Gerschenkron based his estimate for total manufacturing production on just eleven.

26 For a detailed introduction to Fenoaltea's arguments (present and past) see his excellent 'Notes on the Rate of Industrial Growth in Italy, 1861–1913', *Journal of Economic History* 63(3) (2003), pp. 695–735.

27 Bonelli argues for a long economic upswing prior to unification, with its roots in the agrarian economy (Italy's role as an exporter of primary products to more developed economies). Agricultural accumulation, however, did not act as a spur to agricultural modernization or to the wider transformation of the Italian economy. Rather, the agricultural surplus was used to buy land and securities, or was converted into liquid assets (holdings of gold and silver). Unification broke this long-established pattern. The state, through taxation, land sales and bond-issues, drew surplus capital out of the agrarian sector, using it to develop the country's infrastructure and industrial basis (shades of Romeo). Agricultural depression in the 1880s, however, entailing the loss of foreign markets and an end to agricultural accumulation, meant the state lost its one internal source of finance and increased its reliance on foreign capital. At the same time, the state adopted a more hands-on approach to industrial growth, becoming the main investor in, and client of, the Italian steel and ship building industries and using tariff protection to sustain textiles. Bonelli, echoing the view of Cafagna, insists that state-driven industrialization during the Giolittian era was ultimately only sustainable because of the remittances from emigrants and tourism, which helped to balance the cost of industry-related imports. Franco Bonelli, 'Il capitalismo italiano. Linee generali di interpretazione' (1978), available in translation in Federico (ed.), *The Economic Development of Italy*, pp. 99–142.

28 Gerschenkron, *Economic Backwardness in Historical Perspective*, pp. 80–2.

29 Frank J. Coppa, 'The Italian Tariff and the Conflict between Agriculture and Industry: The Commercial Policy of Liberal Italy, 1860–1922', *Journal of Economic History* 30(4) (1970), p. 750; Zamagni, *The Economic History of Italy*, pp. 62, 116.

30 Fenoaltea, 'Notes on the Rate of Industrial Growth in Italy', pp. 715–16. For an overview of the debates see Cohen and Federico, *The Growth of the Italian Economy*, p. 41.

31 Jon S. Cohen, 'Italy 1861–1914', in Rondo Cameron (ed.), *Banking and Economic Development: Some Lessons of History* (Oxford: Oxford University Press, 1972), p. 70.

32 Zamagni, *The Economic History of Italy*, pp. 89, 115; Castronovo, 'The Italian Take-off', pp. 496, 501; Toniolo, *An Economic History of Liberal Italy*, pp. 108, 145; Giovanni Federico and Gianni Toniolo, 'Italy', in Richard Sylla and Gianni Toniolo (eds), *Patterns of European Industrialization* (London: Routledge, 1991), p. 207; Giovanni Federico and Renato Giannetti, 'Italy: Stalling and Surpassing', in James Foreman-Peck and Giovanni Federico (eds), *European Industrial Policy: The Twentieth-Century Experience* (Oxford: Oxford University Press, 1999), pp. 127–8. See also Giovanni Federico, 'Protection and Italian Economic Development: Much ado about Nothing?', in Jean-Pierre Dormois and Pedro Lains (eds), *Classical Trade Protectionism, 1865–1914* (London: Routledge, 2006), pp. 193–218. This article was originally accessed online at <http://www.iue.it/HEC/People/faculty/Profiles/federico-publications.shml>.

33 Zamagni, *The Economic History of Italy*, p. 123; Castronovo, 'The Italian Take-off', pp. 496, 510; Cohen, 'Italy 1861–1914', pp. 71–2; Cafagna, 'Italy 1830–1914', p. 321.

34 Gerschenkron, *Economic Backwardness in Historical Perspective*, pp. 79, 84, 362–4.

35 See, for example, Cafagna, 'Italy 1830–1914', pp. 290, 325; Zamagni, *The Economic History of Italy*, p. 165; Albert Schram, *Railways and the Formation of the Italian State in the Nineteenth Century* (Cambridge: Cambridge University Press, 1997), p. 5.

36 Stefano Fenoaltea, 'Italy', in Patrick O'Brien (ed.), *Railways and the Economic Development of Western Europe, 1830–1914* (London: Macmillan, 1983), pp. 50, 76.

37 Cohen, 'Italy 1861–1914', p. 71; Fenoaltea, 'Italy', p. 50; Federico and Toniolo, 'Italy', p. 208.

38 Zamagni, *The Economic History of Italy*, pp. 94–5, 166; Federico and Toniolo, 'Italy', p. 208.

39 The success of the *destra* in balancing the budget in 1876 is widely regarded as important, although the need to raise revenue was responsible for the hasty and badly handled sale of Church lands in the late 1860s/early 1870s, and the reintroduction of the hated grist tax. The decision in 1866 to abandon the Gold Standard is thought to have made a 'permanent contribution to economic growth' by the subsequent increase in the use of paper money and bank deposits. Public debt, however, was never brought under control (in 1876 the public debt amounted to 92% of GDP) and represented a major drain on public expenditure. The situation was made worse by the government's decision to return to the Gold Standard in 1883 – in order to give gold backing to Italian banknotes the government was forced to take out a huge international loan in gold. Public debt was only brought under control in the early twentieth century through what Luigi Luzzatti (Minister of the Treasury for much of the 1890s and early 1900s) modestly called the 'heroic management of the country's finances and monetary circulation'. Toniolo speculates the return to the Gold Standard may have sown the seeds of the banking crisis in the early 1890s by increasing the 'already serious liquidity problems' of two of the banks of issue. See Toniolo, *An Economic History of Liberal Italy*, pp. 64, 81; Rondo Cameron, 'Introduction', in Cameron (ed.), *Banking and Economic Development*, p. 19; Zamagni, *The Economic History of Italy*, pp. 176, 179.

40 For a full and frank explanation of his change of heart see Fenoaltea, 'Notes on the Rate of Industrial Growth in Italy', pp, 702, 706–7.

41 Toniolo, *An Economic History of Liberal Italy*, pp. 86, 111, 140–2; Castronovo, 'The Italian Take-off', pp. 507–8; Gerschenkron, *Economic Backwardness in Historical Perspective*, pp. 85–6; Federico and Toniolo, 'Italy', p. 207; Cafagna, 'Italy 1830–1914', p. 303.

42 Gerschenkron, *Economic Backwardness in Historical Perspective*, p. 88; Gerschenkron, *Continuity and Other Essays*, p. 108; Federico and Toniolo, 'Italy', pp. 205, 211; Toniolo, *An*

Economic History of Liberal Italy, p. 113; Fenoaltea, 'Italy', p. 59; Zamagni, *The Economic History of Italy*, pp. 148–50; Castronovo, 'The Italian Take-off', pp. 495, 502; Pierluigi Ciocca and Gianni Toniolo, 'Industry and Finance in Italy, 1918–1940', *Journal of European Economic History* (special issue) 13(2) 1984, pp. 117–18.

43 Cohen, 'Italy 1861–1914', p. 81; Cohen and Federico, *The Growth of the Italian Economy*, p. 59; Zamagni, *The Economic History of Italy*, pp. 148–50.

44 R. Zangheri (1969), quoted in Patrick K. O'Brien and Gianni Toniolo, 'The Poverty of Italy and the Backwardness of its Agriculture before 1914', in Bruce M. S. Campbell and Mark Overton (eds), *Land, Labour and Livestock: Historical Studies in European Agricultural Productivity* (Manchester: Manchester University Press, 1991), p. 387.

45 Galassi and Cohen, 'The Economics of Tenancy in Early Twentieth Century Southern Italy', p. 595.

46 Cohen and Galassi, 'Sharecropping and Productivity', pp. 646–56; Galassi and Cohen, 'The Economics of Tenancy in Early Twentieth Century Southern Italy', pp. 585–600. See also: Adrian Lyttleton, 'Landlords, Peasants and the Limits of Liberalism', in Davis (ed.), *Gramsci and Italy's Passive Revolution*, pp. 110–12.

47 Marta Petrusewicz, *Latifundium. Moral Economy and Material Life in a European Periphery* (Ann Arbor: University of Michigan Press, 1996); Marta Petrusewicz, 'The Demise of Latifondismo', in Lumley and Morris (eds), *The New History of the Italian South*, pp. 20–41.

48 Giovanni Federico, 'Introduction', in Federico (ed.), *The Economic Development of Italy since 1870*, p. xvi; Giovanni Federico, 'Mercantilizzazione e sviluppo economico italiano (1860–1940)' (1986), available in translation in Federico (ed.), *The Economic Development of Italy*, pp. 305–19; Zamagni, *The Economic History of Italy*, p. 57; Cohen and Federico, *The Growth of the Italian Economy*, p. 36.

49 Cohen and Federico, *The Growth of the Italian Economy*, p. 34; John A. Davis, 'Remapping Italy's Path to the Twentieth Century', *Journal of Modern History* 66(2) (1994), p. 296; O'Brien and Toniolo, 'The Poverty of Italy and the Backwardness of its Agriculture before 1914', pp. 408–9.

50 Cohen, 'Italy, 1861–1914', p. 88; Cohen and Federico, *The Growth of the Italian Economy*, p. 34.

51 Toniolo, *An Economic History of Liberal Italy*, p. 104.

52 Zamagni, *The Economic History of Italy*, p. 62; Federico and Toniolo, 'Italy', p. 212; Toniolo, *An Economic History of Liberal Italy*, p. 111.

53 Giovanni Federico, 'Heights, Calories and Welfare: A New Perspective on Italian Industrialization, 1854–1913', *Economics and Human Biology* 1(3) (2003a), pp. 289–308; Giovanni Federico, 'Le nuove stime della produzione agricola italiana, 1860–1910: primi risultati ed implicazioni', *Rivista di Storia economica* 3(19) (2003b), pp. 359–81. Both articles were originally accessed online at <http://www.iue.it/HEC/People/Faculty/Profiles/federico-publications.shtml>. The widely held and long established view of the 1880s as a particularly dismal decade for Italian agriculture is challenged by both Federico's findings and those of Fenoaltea relating to industry. The collapse of international grain prices combined with apparently falling per capita calorific intake in Italy, rising emigration rates, and the gloomy contemporary accounts of landowners led historians to see the 1880s as a period of immense economic hardship for the rural population. Federico, however, has shown that the evidence for falling per capita calorific intake is fundamentally flawed. Fenoaltea, meanwhile, has demonstrated that consumption of non-durables such as clothing actually rose in the 1880s, an unlikely scenario if the population was actually starving. Fenoaltea links rising levels of consumption to the falling price of imported grain. Italy, he argues, was not adversely affected by the collapse of the international grain market since it was not a grain exporter. In fact, the falling price of imported grain drove down the cost of living, translating into higher real wages for the majority of Italians – hence the growth in consumption, at least until the introduction of the pernicious 1887 tariff. Fenoaltea, 'Notes on the Rate of Industrial Growth in Italy', pp. 717–19. See also Cohen and Federico, *The Growth of the Italian Economy*, pp. 32–3.

54 A'Hearn, 'Institutions, Externalities and Economic Growth in Southern Italy', pp. 734–62; Brian A'Hearn, 'Could Southern Italians Cooperate? *Banche popolari* in the *Mezzogiorno*', *Journal of Economic History* 60(1) (2000), pp. 67–93. A'Hearn's conclusions are 'broadly consistent with a qualified version of Putnam's thesis', i.e. that the failure to establish 'networks of civic engagement' left the south in a 'no trust equilibrium' in which extensive impersonal forms of economic co-operation – such as capital investment in industry, banking – were impossible.

55 A' Hearn, 'Institutions, Externalities and Economic Growth in Southern Italy', p. 735.

56 John A. Davis, review of *La modernità squilibrata del Mezzogiorno d'Italia*, by Francesco Barbagallo, *Breve storia dell'Italia meridionale dall'Ottocento a oggi*, by Piero Bevilacqua, and *Nord e sud. Non fare a pezzi l'unità d'Italia*, by Luciano Cafagna, *Journal of Modern Italian Studies* 1(1) (1995), p. 152.

57 Piero Bevilacqua, *Breve storia dell'Italia meridionale dall'Ottocento a oggi* (Rome: Donzelli editore, 1993), chs. 2 and 3.

58 Cohen and Federico, *The Growth of the Italian Economy*, p. 29.

59 Paolo Pezzino, 'Local Power in Southern Italy', in Lumley and Morris (eds), *The New History of the Italian South*, p. 47; Davis (review of Barbagallo, Bevilacqua and Cafagna), pp. 155; Davis, 'Remapping Italy's Path to the Twentieth century', pp. 296–300; John A. Davis, 'Casting off the "Southern Problem": Or the Peculiarities of the South Reconsidered', in Jane Schneider (ed.), *Italy's 'Southern Question': Orientalism in One Country* (Oxford and New York: Berg, 1998), pp. 205–24.

60 Fenoaltea, 'Notes on the Rate of Industrial Growth in Italy', n. 26, p. 704.

61 Patrick K. O'Brien, 'Do We Have a Typology for the Study of European Industrialization in the XIXth Century?', *Journal of European Economic History* 15(2) (1986), p. 325.

62 Gianni Toniolo, *An Economic History of Liberal Italy*, p. 149.

63 Marcello de Cecco, 'The Economy from Liberalism to Fascism', in Adrian Lyttleton (ed.), *Liberal and Fascist Italy* (Oxford:, Oxford University Press, 2002), p. 72.

64 Cafagna, 'Italy 1830–1914', p. 306.

65 L. De Rosa, 'Unity or Plurality? Italian Issuing Banks, 1861–1893', *Journal of European Economic History* 23(3) (1994), p. 473.

66 In fact, malaria was a major problem in railway-building programmes in the South. See Frank M. Snowden, 'Fields of Death: Malaria in Italy, 1861–1962', *Modern Italy* 4(1) (1999), p. 27.

67 Martin Clark writes that one of 'the most important effects on the Italian economy [was] probably the demand for sleepers, causing deforestation over vast areas'. Clark, *Modern Italy*, p. 28.

68 Fenoaltea, 'Italy', p. 96.

69 The Baccarini law of 1882, for example, which made provision for local and central government financial support for land reclamation schemes, was only successful in the lower Po valley (leading to very profitable cultivation in wheat). It had far less of an impact in the malarial belts of central Italy or in the south. Bevilacqua estimates that between 1870 and 1921 over 1m hectares of land were reclaimed for agriculture in the north at a cost of 102m lire. In the south, however, the amount of land reclaimed amounted to only 633,000 hectares, despite expenditure of 261m lire. Much of the work carried out in the south was undertaken by northern industry, too. Whatever the reasons (Bevilacqua, not surprisingly blames the state; Zamagni points out that while most of the cost of the work in the sorth was met locally, the state was the sole financier of southern projects), the net benefit to the north is clear. Bevilacqua, *Breve storia dell'Italia meridionale*, pp. 56–8; Zamagni, *The Economic History of Italy*, pp. 50–1.

70 Cafagna, 'La questione delle origini del dualismo economico italiano', p. 645.

71 Bevilacqua, *Breve storia dell'Italia meridionale*, p. 61; Mack Smith, *Modern Italy*, p. 216.

72 Federico, *The Economic Development of Italy*, p. xvi.

73 Petrusewicz, 'The Demise of *Latifondismo*', p. 39.

74 Davis, 'Casting off the "Southern Problem"', p. 214. Salvatore Lupo, *Il giardino degli aranci: il mondo degli agrumi nella storia del Mezzogiorno* (Venice: Marsilio editori, 1990); Salvatore Lupo, 'Tra società locale e commercio a lunga distanza: la vicenda degli agrumi Siciliana', *Meridiana* 1(1) (1987), pp. 81–112.

75 Davis, 'Remapping Italy's Path to the Twentieth Century', p. 295.

76 Davis, 'Remapping Italy's Path to the Twentieth Century', p. 295.

Chapter 3 Society and culture in liberal Italy

1 Figures are from the statistical appendices to Giovanni Sabbatucci and Vittorio Vidotto (eds), Storia d'Italia. Vol. 2. Il nuovo stato e la società civile, 1861–1887 (Rome-Bari: Laterza, 1995), p. 572, and Storia d'Italia. Vol. 3. *Liberalismo e democrazia, 1887–1914* (Rome-Bari: Laterza, 1995), p. 578.

2 Francesca Socrate, 'Borghesie e stili di vita', in Sabbatucci and Vidotto (eds), *Storia d'Italia*. Vol. 3., p. 399.

3 Alberto Mario Banti, *Storia della borghesia italiana: l'età liberale (1861–1922)* (Rome: Donzelli editore, 1996), p. 49; Socrate, 'Borghese e stili di vita', p. 365.

4 Banti, *Storia della borghesia italiana*, p. 52.

5 Banti, *Storia della borghesia italiana*, pp. 52–5.

6 Banti, *Storia della borghesia italiana*, p. 65.

7 Maria Malatesta, 'The Landed Aristocracy during the Nineteenth and Early Twentieth Centuries', in Harmut Kaelble (ed.), *The European Way: European Societies during the Nineteenth and Twentieth Centuries* (New York and Oxford: Berghahn, 2004), p. 51.

8 Banti, *Storia della borghesia italiana*, p. 69.

9 Foot, *Modern Italy*, p. 113.

10 The description of Sicilians as 'primitive and almost savage' appears in Alfredo Niceforo's *L'Italia barbara contemporanea* (1898). Quoted in John Dickie, *Darkest Italy. The Nation and Stereotypes of the Mezzogiorno, 1860–1900* (New York: St Martin's Press, 1999), p. 3.

11 Emigration, albeit on a less dramatic scale than in the period 1891–1913, had been strong through the 1870s and 1880s, with an estimated 4m Italians leaving the country. The pattern of emigration during this period, however, was significantly different to that after 1890: most emigrants were from the north-east, with the majority making for other European countries. Many left for good. In contrast, the majority of emigrants after 1890 returned home at some point.

12 Frank Snowden, *Violence and the Great Estates in the South of Italy: Apulia, 1900–1922* (Cambridge: Cambridge University Press, 1986).

13 Piero Bevilacqua (1984), quoted in Paul Ginsborg, *A History of Contemporary Italy: Society and Politics 1943–1988* (London: Penguin, 1989), p. 34.

14 The *braccianti* have been described – with good reason – as the poorest and most vulnerable of all rural classes. Because of a chronic oversupply of labour, a *bracciante* worked on average just 180–200 days a year, sometimes much less. Zamagni calculates that in the Bologna area, the number of working days could fall as low as 100–20. To achieve an income sufficient to live above subsistence levels (solely in terms of food consumption) a day labourer needed to work a minimum of 280 days. Zamagni, *The Economic History of Italy*, pp. 198–9 and n. 69.

15 In an effort to counter the influence of the 'red' leagues and co-operatives over the peasantry, the Catholic Church established its own rival organizations in Lombardy and Venetia. This was the origin of the 'red' and 'white' subcultures that characterized much of north and central Italy after 1945.

16 Lorenzo Bordogna, Gian Primo Cella, Giancarlo Provasi, 'Labour Conflicts in Italy Before the Rise of Fascism, 1881–1923: A Quantitative Analysis', in Leopold H. Haimson and Charles Tilly (eds), *Strikes, Wars, and Revolutions in an International Perspective: Strike Waves in the Late Nineteenth and Early Twentieth Centuries* (Cambridge: Cambridge University Press, 2002), p. 231.

17 Carl Levy, 'The Centre and the Suburbs: Social Protest and Modernization in Milan and Turin, 1898–1917', *Modern Italy*, 7(2) (2002), p. 181.

18 These figures underplay the extent and degree of labour militancy since they only include 'economic' strikes; politically motivated strike action, such as the 1904 general strike, is not recorded. Bordogna et al., 'Labour Conflicts in Italy', pp. 217, 220, 224.

19 Paul Corner, 'State and Society, 1901–1922', in Adrian Lyttleton (ed.), *Liberal and Fascist Italy* (Oxford: Oxford University Press, 2002), p. 25.

20 Perry Willson, 'Introduction: Gender and the Private Sphere in Liberal and Fascist Italy', in Perry Willson (ed.), *Gender, Family and Sexuality: The Private Sphere in Italy, 1860–1945* (Basingstoke: Palgrave Macmillan, 2004), p.3; Mary Gibson, 'Labelling Women Deviant: Heterosexual Women, Prostitutes and Lesbians in early Criminological Discourse' in Willson (ed.), *Gender, Family and Sexuality*, pp. 92–3.

21 Michela De Giorgio, 'The Catholic Model', in Geneviève Fraisse and Michelle Perot (eds), *A History of Women in the West*, vol. IV (Cambridge, MA, and London: Harvard University Press, 1993a), p. 172.

22 Victoria de Grazia, 'How Mussolini Ruled Women', in Françoise Thébaud (ed.), *A History of Women in the West*, vol. V (Cambridge, MA, and London: Harvard University Press, 1994), pp. 125–6.

23 Michael Biddiss, 'Intellectual and Cultural Revolution, 1890–1914', in Paul Hayes (ed.), *Themes in Modern European History 1890–1945* (London and New York: Routledge, 1992), p. 88.

24 Quotes from Emilio Gentile, 'The Conquest of Modernity: from Modernist Nationalism to Fascism', *Modernism/Modernity*, 1(3) (1994), p. 63; Clark, *Modern Italy*, p. 173.

25 Davis, 'Remapping Italy's Path to the Twentieth Century', p. 301.

26 See, for example, Clark, *Modern Italy*, p. 29.

27 Banti, *Storia della borghesia italiana*, p. 228.

28 Marco Meriggi, 'The Italian "borghesia"', in Jürgen Kocka and Allan Mitchell (eds), *Bourgeois Society in Nineteenth-Century Europe* (Oxford: Berg, 1993b), p. 433.

29 Patronage and clientelism are closely linked phenomena. Patronage involves the control and discretionary distribution of resources by a relatively rich and powerful patron to dependent individuals or groups (clients), in order to maintain and strengthen the position and power of the patron. Clientelism is the process by which dependent individuals or groups use their ties to a patron in order to access those resources.

30 Romanelli, 'Political Debate, Social History, and the Italian *Borghesia*', p. 727.

31 The Federconsorzi, the Italian Federation of Agricultural Associations, consisting of societies from Reggio-Emilia, Lombardy and Tuscany, was established in Piacenza in 1892.

32 Alberto Mario Banti, *Terra e denaro: una borghesia padana dell'Ottocento* (Venice: Marsilio editori, 1989). See also: Banti, *Storia della borghesia italiana*, p. 274.

33 Alberto Mario Banti, 'Italian Professionals: Markets, Incomes, Estates and Identities', in Maria Malatesta (ed.), *Society and the Professions in Italy, 1860–1914* (Cambridge: Cambridge University Press, 1995), p. 241.

34 Maria Malatesta, 'The Italian Professions from a Comparative Perspective', in Malatesta (ed.), *Society and the Professions in Italy*, p. 22.

35 David Blackbourn and Geoff Eley, *The Peculiarities of German History* (Oxford: Oxford University Press, 1984) p. 231.

36 Banti, *Storia della borghesia italiana*, p. 170.

37 Banti, *Storia della borghesia italiana*, p. 178.

38 Jürgen Kocka, 'The Middle Classes in Europe', in Kaelble (ed.), *The European Way*, p. 32.

39 Banti, *Storia della borghesia italiana*, pp. 143–4.

40 Banti, *Storia della borghesia italiana*, p. 302.

41 'Hence, from the point of view of both occupational trajectories and economic situation it is difficult to portray the world of the nineteenth-century Italian professions as a homogenous and cohesive milieu'. Banti, 'Italian Professionals', p. 247. See also Maria Malatesta, 'Gli ordini professionali e la nazionalizzazione in Italia', in Meriggi and Schiera (eds), *Dalla*

città alla nazione, pp. 173–8; Adrian Lyttleton, 'The Middle Classes in Liberal Italy', in Davis and Ginsborg (eds), *Society and Politics in the Age of the Risorgimento. Essays in Honour of Denis Mack Smith* (Cambridge: Cambridge University Press, 1991), p. 224.

42 Banti, *Storia della borghesia italiana*, pp. 187–8.

43 For example: '[T]he importance of the nobility in post-unification Italy was, on the whole, rather modest'. Alberto Mario Banti, 'Note sulle nobiltà nell'Italia dell'Ottocento', *Meridiana*, 19 (1994), p. 17. See also: Meriggi, 'The Italian "Borghesia"', p. 435.

44 Anthony L. Cardoza, *Aristocrats in Bourgeois Italy: The Piedmontese Nobility, 1861–1930* (Cambridge: Cambridge University Press, 1997a).

45 Giovanni Montroni, *Gli uomini del Re: la nobiltà napoletana nell'Ottocento* (Rome: Meridiana Libri, 1996).

46 Cardoza, *Aristocrats in Bourgeois Italy*, p. 8. For Cardoza's critique of Montroni, see *Journal of Modern Italian Studies*, 2(1) (1997b), pp. 95–7 (quote p. 96).

47 Clark, *Modern Italy*, p. 33.

48 The practitioners of women's history in Italy, for example, have found acceptance and recognition from the mainstream historical community much harder to come by than have their colleagues in the United Kingdom and the United States. Furthermore, 'early modern Italian historians of women and gender have been much more successful in making an impact than those studying more recent times'; and a surprising number of general surveys of modern Italy – both Italian and English (John Foot's *Modern Italy* a case in point) – still fail to address gender issues. For snapshots of the state of women's history in Italy see Michela De Giorgio, 'Women's history in Italy (nineteenth and twentieth centuries)', *Journal of Modern Italian Studies*, 1(3) (1996), pp. 413–31; Mary Gibson, 'Introduction to Special Issue: Annarita Buttafuoco (1951–99) and Women's History in Italy', *Journal of Modern Italian Studies*, 7(1) (2002), pp. 1–16; Perry Willson, 'From Margin to Centre: Recent Trends in Modern Italian Women's and Gender History', *Modern Italy*, 11(3) (2006), pp. 327–37 (the quote above is from Willson, p. 329).

49 Gibson, 'Women's History in Italy', pp. 6–7.

50 Silvana Patriarca, 'Gender Trouble: Women and the Making of Italy's "Active Population", 1861–1936', *Journal of Modern Italian Studies*, 3(2) (1998), p. 153.

51 Simonetta Ortaggi Cammarosano, 'Labouring Women in Northern and Central Italy in the Nineteenth Century', in Davis and Ginsborg (eds), *Society and Politics in the Age of the Risorgimento*, p. 164. For more on women workers and the Italian silk industry see Anna Cento Bull, 'Lombard Silk-spinners in the Nineteenth Century: An Industrial Workforce in a Rural Setting', in Zygmunt G. Baranski and Shirley W. Vinall (eds), *Women and Italy: Essays on Gender, Culture and History* (Basingstoke, Macmillan, 1991), pp. 11–42; Patrizia Sione, 'From Home to Factory: Women in the Nineteenth-century Italian Silk Industry', in Daryl M. Hafter (ed.), *European Women and Preindustrial Craft* (Bloomington and Indianapolis: Indiana University Press, 1995), pp. 137–52.

52 Ortaggi Cammarosano, 'Labouring Women', pp. 157, 181.

53 Maura Palazzi, 'Economic Autonomy and Male Authority: Female Merchants in Modern Italy', *Journal of Modern Italian Studies*, 7(1) (2002), p. 29. Women proprietors were more common in the retail sector but, as Jonathan Morris points out for Milan, 'The trades in which women were most heavily represented...were the most precarious in terms of financial stability, often carried out from a barrow or a stall.' Jonathan Morris, *The Political Economy of Shopkeeping in Milan, 1886–1922* (Cambridge: Cambridge University Press, 1993), p. 42.

54 Estimates suggest there were only 40,000 female white-collar workers in Italy in 1911, a 'derisory' figure in comparison to the major industrialized powers. Michela De Giorgio, *Le italiane dall'unità a oggi: modelli cuturali e comportamenti sociali* (Rome-Bari: Laterza, 2nd edn, 1993b), p. 460. On the conditions of employment for women in the state railway, telegraph and postal services see Simonetta Soldani, 'Lo stato e il lavoro delle donne nell'Italia liberale', *Passato e Presente*, 9(24) (1990), pp. 33–4.

55 Malatesta, 'The Italian Professions', pp. 14–15.

56 Michela Minesso, 'The Engineering Profession, 1802–1923', in Malatesta (ed.), *Society and the Professions in Italy*, pp. 190, 204.

57 Soldani, 'Lo stato e il lavoro delle donne', p. 42.

58 For more on prostitution in liberal Italy see Mary Gibson, *Prostitution and the State in Italy, 1860–1915* (New Brunswick and London: Rutgers University Press, 1999).

59 Michela De Giorgio, *Le italiane dall'unità a oggi*, p. 411.

60 Linda Reeder, 'Women in the Classroom: Mass Migration, Literacy and the Nationalization of Sicilian Women at the Turn of the Century', *Journal of Social History*, 32(1) (1998), p. 110.

61 Reeder, 'Women in the Classroom', p. 112.

62 Soldani, 'Lo stato e il lavoro delle donne', p. 40. Soldani says the midwife (*levatrice*) performed the same function as the *maestra* in this regard. See also Simonetta Soldani (ed.), *L'educazione delle donne: scuole e modelli femminili nell'Italia dell'Ottocento* (Milan: Franco Angelli, 1989).

63 Ortaggi Cammarosano, 'Labouring Women', p. 180.

64 De Giorgio, *Le italiane dall'unità a oggi*, pp. 417–18, 420, 437, 461–2, 464.

65 Soldani, 'Lo stato e il lavoro delle donne', p. 43.

66 Gibson, 'Women's History in Italy', p. 5.

67 On the arguments over protective legislation see Soldani, 'Lo stato e il lavoro delle donne', p. 54. On divorce see Mark Seymour, 'Keystone of the Patriarchal Family? Indissoluble Marriage, Masculinity and Divorce in Liberal Italy', *Journal of Modern Italian Studies*, 10(3) (2005), pp. 302–9.

68 Annarita Buttafuoco, 'Motherhood as a Political Strategy: the Role of the Italian Women's Movement in the Creation of the *Cassa Nazionale di Maternità*', in Gisela Bock and Pat Thane (eds), *Gender Politics: Women and the Rise of the European Welfare States, 1880s–1950s* (London: Routledge, 1991), p. 189.

69 Gibson, 'Women's History in Italy', p. 5; Buttafuoco, 'Motherhood as a Political Strategy', pp. 183–7.

70 Buttafuoco, 'Motherhood as a Political Strategy', pp. 180–1.

71 Buttafuoco, 'Motherhood as a Political Strategy', p. 181.

72 Buttafuoco (1997), quoted in Patrizia Gabrielli, 'Protagonists and Politics in the Italian Women's Movement: A Reflection on the Work of Annarita Buttafuoco', *Journal of Modern Italian Studies*, 7(1) (2002), p. 84.

73 Anne Bowler, 'Politics as Art: Italian Futurism and Fascism', *Theory and Society*, 20(6) (1991), p. 779.

74 Simonetta Falasca-Zamponi, 'The Artist to Power? Futurism, Fascism and the Avant-garde', *Theory, Culture and Society*, 13(2) (1996), p. 47.

75 John Pollard, *The Fascist Experience in Italy* (London: Routledge, 1998), p. 15.

76 Gentile, 'The Conquest of Modernity', p. 55.

77 Emilio Gentile, 'Political Futurism and the Myth of the Italian Revolution', in Günter Berghaus (ed.), *International Futurism in Arts and Literature* (Berlin and New York: Walter de Gruyter, 2000), p. 2.

78 Gentile, 'Political Futurism', p. 3; Walter L. Adamson, 'Contexts and Debates. Fascinating Futurism: The Historiographical Politics of an Historical Avant-garde', *Modern Italy*, 13(1) (2008), p. 70.

79 Günter Berghaus, *Futurism and Politics: Between Anarchist Rebellion and Fascist Reaction, 1909–1944* (Providence and Oxford: Berghahn Books, 1996), pp. 61, 118, 183, 282. See also Adamson, 'Fascinating Futurism', p. 73.

80 George L. Mosse, 'The Political Culture of Italian Futurism: a General Perspective', *Journal of Contemporary History*, 25(2–3) (1990) p. 253.

81 Bowler, 'Italian Futurism and Fascism', p. 765; Gentile, 'The Conquest of Modernity', p. 77.

82 Gentile, 'Political Futurism', p. 4.

83 Mosse, 'The Political Culture of Italian Futurism', p. 256; Gentile, 'The Conquest of Modernity', p. 72.

84 Gentile, 'The Conquest of Modernity', pp. 56, 58.

85 Gentile, 'The Conquest of Modernity', p. 79.

86 Bowler, 'Italian Futurism and Fascism', p. 785; Zeev Sternhell, *The Birth of Fascist Ideology: From Cultural Rebellion to Political Revolution* (Princeton: Princeton University Press, 1994), p. 30; Gentile, 'The Conquest of Modernity', pp. 74–5.

87 Walter L. Adamson, 'Modernism and Fascism: The Politics of Culture in Italy, 1903–1922', *American Historical Review*, 95(2) (1990), pp. 387–8; Walter L. Adamson, 'The Language of Opposition in Early Twentieth-century Italy: Rhetorical Continuities between Prewar Florentine Avant-gardism and Mussolini's Fascism', *Journal of Modern History*, 64(1) (1992), pp. 50–2.

88 Adamson, 'The Language of Opposition', p. 31; Walter L. Adamson, *Avant-Garde Florence: From Modernism to Fascism* (Cambridge, MA and London: Harvard University Press, 1993), pp. 4, 141, 257; Adamson, 'Modernism and Fascism', p. 390.

89 Patrick Joyce (1995) in John Tosh (ed.), *Historians on History* (Harlow: Pearson Education, 2000), p. 275.

90 Blackbourn and Eley, *The Peculiarities of German History*, p. 231.

91 Lucy Riall, *Sicily and the Unification of Italy: Liberal Politics and Local Power* (Oxford: Clarendon Press, 1998), p. 22.

92 Peter Gay, *Schnitzler's Century* (London: Allen Lane, 2001), pp. 4–5.

93 Kocka, 'The Middle Classes in Europe', p. 18.

94 Banti, *Storia della borghesia italiana*, pp. 304–5, 321.

95 Although sometimes they only married within their own particular social group. Francesca Socrate notes how the Milanese entrepreneurial class rarely entered into marriages with members of the professional or bureaucratic middle classes. Socrate, 'Borghesie e stili di vita', pp. 391–2.

96 See Banti, *Storia della borghesia italiana*, pp. 213–26; also Bruno Tobia, 'Associazionismo e patriottismo: il caso del pellegrinaggio nazionale a Roma del 1884', in Meriggi and Schiera (eds), *Dalla città alla nazione*, pp. 227–47.

97 Dickie, *Darkest Italy*, p. 18.

98 As John Davis has written about the Italian working classes of the period: 'the acceptance of socialist politics [did not] necessarily change individual patterns of behaviour. The language of equality and emancipation does not seem to have changed gender relations amongst the Turin workers, whose families continued to reflect old patriarchal divisions of labour...while women and children from socialist families often continued to attend Mass although externally rejecting the influence of the Church'. John A. Davis, 'Socialism and the Italian Working Classes in Italy before 1914', in Dick Geary (ed.), *Labour and Socialist Movements in Europe before 1914* (Oxford, New York and Munich: Berg, 1989), p. 225.

99 A good recent example of this tendency is John A. Davis, 'Economy, Society, and the State', in Davis (ed.), *Italy in the Nineteenth Century*, pp. 259–60. Buttafuoco's remark is quoted by Gibson, 'Women's History in Italy', p. 5.

100 Davis (see previous footnote) recognizes that 'the towns were the principal theatres of social and cultural change' (p. 256), but he does not consider the new opportunities for women that could stem from such change. For example, there are clear signs that the world outside the home actually became more accessible for middle-class women during the liberal period, mainly due to the physical transformation of the city at this time. The construction of new *viale, piazze, gallerie*, the introduction of street lighting, the establishment of department stores etc., all opened up and lit up the city, creating new spaces suitable for respectable women. Urban bourgeois notions of what constituted 'respectable' female behaviour also became notably more relaxed, as Emilia Nevers, author of *Il galateo della borghesia* (*The Book of Etiquette of the Bourgeoisie*), noted in the 1916 edition:

> 'Once upon a time – I note that I am writing principally for ladies in this paragraph – there were many reasons why women rarely went out: the practice of sending girls to school was not so established; there were no public lectures, no skating, no bicycle-clubs, no meetings for charitable, educational or literary reasons, or at least these occurred less frequently or were differently arranged'. (Quoted in Ann Hallamore Caesar, 'About Town: The City and the Female Reader, 1860–1900', Modern Italy, 7(2) (2002), p. 136).

Visitors to the Mezzogiorno frequently commented on the 'invisibility' of women in the south. Even after World War One, when the founder of the women's branch of Youth of Catholic Action suggested opening branches of the association in Palermo, the city's hierarchy objected on the grounds that 'young women do not go out alone, even after marriage'. See De Giorgio, *Le italiane dall'unità a oggi*, pp. 19, 92, 95.

Anna Cento Bull has shown how important family structures could be in shaping gender relations and women's experiences of work in the textile areas of northern Italy. See Bull, 'Lombard Silk-spinners'.

101 See, in addition to the works already referenced, Annarita Buttafuoco, *Le Mariuccine: Storia di un'istituzione laica, l'Asilo Mariuccia* (Milan: Franco Angelli, 2nd edn, 1988); Elda Gentili Zappi, *If Eight Hours Seem Too Few: Mobilization of Women Workers in the Italian Rice Fields* (Albany, NY: State University of New York Press, 1991). Buttafuoco's groundbreaking study explores the history of the *Asilo Mariuccia*, a women's shelter established in by Ersilia Majno in 1902 with the purpose of re-educating young Milanese women engaged in prostitution. Zappi shows how the women rice field weeders of the Po Valley, although only casual workers, successfully organized themselves in the last two decades of the nineteenth century to demand better hours, conditions and wages.

102 Falasca-Zamponi, 'The Artist to Power?', p. 41.
103 Quote from Adamson, 'Modernism and Fascism', pp. 361–2.
104 Gentile, 'The Conquest of Modernity', p. 59.

Chapter 4 Fascist politics

1 Renzo de Felice, *Intervista sul fascismo* (Rome-Bari: Laterza, 1975), pp. 7, 109–11; *Rosso e Nero* (Milan: Baldini and Castoldi, 2nd edn, 1995), pp. 45–6. *Intervista sul fascismo* appeared in English translation in 1976 as *Fascism: An Informal Introduction to its Theory and Practice* (New Jersey: Transaction Books). The cited praise of De Felice is from Michael Ledeen's Introduction to *Fascism* (Ledeen interviewed De Felice for *Intervista*) and A. James Gregor's *Phoenix* (New Brunswick: Transaction Publishers, 1999). Both are, coincidentally, American historians. For Mack Smith's critique of De Felice see 'A Monument for the Duce', *Times Literary Supplement*, 31 October 1975.

2 For a critical perspective, see R. J. B. Bosworth, *The Italian Dictatorship: Problems and Perspectives in the Interpretation of Mussolini and Fascism* (London: Arnold, 1998), pp. 131–2. For the view from the other side of the fence see Emilio Gentile, 'Renzo De Felice: a Tribute', *Journal of Contemporary History* 32(2) (1997), pp. 143, 148, 150.

3 For a sample of the different perspectives on Italian neutrality and intervention see Mack Smith, *Modern Italy*, pp. 255–67; Clark, *Modern Italy*, pp. 181–5; W. A. Renzi, 'Italy's Neutrality and Intervention into the Great War: a Re-examination', *American Historical Review* 73(5) (1968), pp. 1414–32.

4 The Giolittian liberals claimed 168 seats but hardly constituted a 'party'.

5 It is perhaps not surprising that some of the most critical accounts of the 'failed revolution' and the collapse of the Left in the face of Fascism come from within the Marxist camp. For an early example see Gramsci's assessment in Hoare and Nowell Smith (eds), *Selections from the Prison Notebooks of Antonio Gramsci*. For the official Italian Communist Party view of the occupation of the factories see Paolo Spriano, *The Occupation of the Factories: Italy, 1920* (London: Pluto Press, 1975) translated by the late, great, stuttering Welsh Marxist historian Gwyn A. Williams. For a more recent Marxist interpretation of the Left's failure to combat Fascism see Tobias Abse's analysis of Livorno in 'The Rise of Fascism in an Industrial City: The Case of Livorno, 1918–1922', in David Forgacs (ed.), *Rethinking Italian Fascism: Capitalism, Populism and Culture* (London: Lawrence and Wishart, 1986). Abse argues for a heroic working class let down by national leaders unable to agree on a united anti-Fascist front. A useful, non-Marxist, account is supplied in English by Martin Clark, *Antonio Gramsci and the Revolution that Failed* (London and New Haven: Yale University Press, 1977).

6 Paul Corner's study of Fascism in Ferrara estimates that membership of the socialist leagues in the region fell from 70,000 members to virtually none between autumn 1920 and spring 1921. In contrast, Fascist support grew rapidly: a crowd of 20,000 turned up to see Mussolini when he visited Ferrara in April 1921. Paul Corner, *Fascism in Ferrara, 1915–1925* (Oxford: Oxford University Press, 1974), p. 138. See also: Corner, 'State and Society, 1901–1922' (2002a), pp. 40–1.

7 Adrian Lyttleton, *The Seizure of Power: Fascism in Italy 1919–1929* (London: Weidenfeld & Nicolson, 2nd edn, 1987), pp. 265–6.

8 See, as useful but very different introductions to the myth of Mussolini: Denis Mack Smith, 'Mussolini, Artist in Propaganda', *History Today* 9(4) (1959), pp. 223–32; Simonetta Falasca-Zamponi, *Fascist Spectacle: The Aesthetics of Power in Mussolini's Italy* (Berkeley: University of California Press, 1997), pp. 42–88. Fascist totalitarianism and the cult of the *Duce* are examined in more detail in Chapter 6.

9 Victor Emmanuel III remained head of state throughout the Fascist period. The Catholic Church, although attracted by some aspects of Fascism (its anti-socialist, anti-feminist, pro-family policies, for example) and prepared to treat with the regime (under the Lateran accords of 1929, the Church finally formally recognized the existence of the Italian state), nevertheless vigorously defended Catholic subculture (e.g. Catholic Action) and criticized Fascist racial legislation.

10 Quoted in Roger Griffin (ed.), *International Fascism: A Reader* (London: Arnold, 1998a), pp. 59, 65.

11 Quoted in Renzo De Felice, *Interpretations of Fascism* (Cambridge, MA: Harvard University Press, 1977), pp. 121–2.

12 Quoted in Richard Bellamy and Darrow Schecter, *Gramsci and the Italian State* (Manchester: Manchester University Press, 1993), p. 73.

13 For Gramsci's Lyons thesis and prison notes on Fascism as a form of passive revolution and of Caesarism see Forgacs, *A Gramsci Reader*, pp. 142–149, 266–7, 269–72. For Thalheimer see De Felice, *Interpretations of Fascism*, pp. 34–5. For Trotsky see Griffin, *International Fascism*, pp. 67–74, 298. For a discussion of Tasca's ideas see Bosworth, *The Italian Dictatorship*, pp. 51–2.

14 Togliatti, *Lectures on Fascism*, p. 5.

15 See, for example, Abse, 'The Rise of Fascism in an Industrial city', p. 54. For a range of post-1945 Marxist accounts of generic fascism see Griffin, *International Fascism*.

16 On Croce's early support for Fascism, see Mack Smith, 'Benedetto Croce', pp. 47–9.

17 Benedetto Croce, 'Chi e "fascista"?', in Renzo De Felice (ed.), *Il Fascismo. Le interpretazioni dei contemporanei e degli storici* (Rome-Bari: Laterza, 2nd edn, 1998), pp. 397–401; De Felice, *Interpretations of Fascism*, pp. 14, 26; David Ward, *Antifascisms: Cultural Politics in Italy, 1943–46* (Cranbury, NJ: Associated University Presses, 1996), pp. 70–4.

18 This particular fight Croce had waged since the publication of Giovanni Gentile's 'Manifesto of Fascist Intellectuals' in April 1925, which had claimed Fascism to be 'a recent and ancient movement of the Italian spirit', and had compared Fascism to Mazzini's 'Young Italy' movement of the 1830s. In his 'counter manifesto', published the following month, and signed by leading anti-Fascist intellectuals, Croce retorted: 'We turn our eyes to the images of the men of the Risorgimento…and it seems as if we see their offended and disturbed faces as they hear the words uttered and the acts carried out by our Italian adversaries'. Quoted in Ward, *Antifascisms*, pp. 54–5.

19 Chabod (1952) quoted in Romeo, *L'Italia unita e la prima guerra mondiale*, pp. 176–7; De Felice, *Interpretations of Fascism*, pp. 165–6.

20 Maturi, *Interpretazioni del risorgimento*, p. 688.

21 Carlo Rosselli, *Liberal Socialism* (Princeton: Princeton University Press, 1994), pp. 104, 108.

22 Denis Mack Smith, 'Mussolini, Artist in Propaganda'.

23 Quoted in De Felice, *Il fascismo*, p. 400.

24 Gaetano Salvemini, *Under the Axe of Fascism* (London: Victor Gollancz, 1936), pp. 114, 117, 119. See also: Stephen Corrado Azzi, 'The Historiography of Fascist Foreign Policy', *The Historical Journal* 36(1) (1993), p. 189. For another superb 'egoist' interpretation of Fascism by an Italian contemporary of Mussolini see Luigi Barzini, *The Italians* (London: Penguin, 1968), pp. 171–9.

25 Taylor (1964), Quoted in Azzi, 'The Historiography of Fascist Foreign Policy', p. 193.

26 Quoted in Bosworth, *The Italian Dictatorship*, p. 56.

27 Alberto Aquarone, *L'organizzazione dello stato totalitario* (Turin: Einaudi, 1965).

28 De Felice borrowed the phrase from Angelo Tasca's *The Rise of Italian Fascism* (1938).

29 Bosworth, *The Italian Dictatorship*, p. 17.

30 Philip V. Cannistraro – a close friend of De Felice – admitted De Felice's prose 'was often so turgid and dense as to make it inaccessible to all but the most serious specialists'. Philip V. Cannistraro, 'Jacobinism, Marxism, and Fascism: The Historiographical Trajectory of Renzo De Felice', *Italian Quarterly* 36(141–2) (1999), p. 25. One historian recently described De Felice's biography of Mussolini as 'appallingly written history'. Philip Morgan, *Italian Fascism 1915–1945* (Basingstoke: Palgrave, 2nd edn, 2004), p. 6.

31 'Qualunquismo' is a reference to the short-lived post-war political party, the Fronte dell'uomo qualunque (Common Man's Front), which attracted many ex-Fascists.

32 De Felice, *Fascism: An Informal Introduction*, p. 17; Renzo De Felice, *Breve storia del fascismo* (Milan: Mondadori, 2001), p. xiii.

33 Denis Mack Smith, 'Mussolini: Reservations about Renzo De Felice's Biography', *Modern Italy* 5(2) (2000), p. 210; De Felice, *Breve storia*, p. xv.

34 *Times Literary Supplement*, 9 January 1976. Mack Smith ('A Monument for the *Duce*') had 'scrutinized' De Felice's judgements 'in the light of common sense' and had concluded that they were 'nonsense'. Ledeen – a very controversial figure in his own right – has remained a passionate supporter of De Felice. See, for example, Michael Ledeen, 'Renzo de Felice and the Question of Italian Fascism', *Society* 38(4) (2001), pp. 75–7, in which Ledeen takes issue with MacGregor Knox's unflattering verdict on the final volume of De Felice's biography of Mussolini ('In the Duce's Defence', *Times Literary Supplement*, 26 February 1999). Knox had variously described De Felice's arguments as 'profoundly eccentric' and 'peculiar'; his magnum opus, 'disorderly' – and a 'gigantic wreck'.

35 Gentile, 'Renzo De Felice: A Tribute', p. 139.

36 Renzo De Felice, *Mussolini il duce (I): Gli anni del consenso 1929–1936* (Turin: Einaudi, 1974), pp. 25–6, 35–53, 54.

37 De Felice, *Gli anni del consenso*, p. 53.

38 For a penetrating critique of De Felice along these lines see MacGregor Knox, 'The Fascist Regime, its Foreign Policy and its Wars: An Anti-anti-Fascist Orthodoxy?', *Contemporary European History* 4(3) (1995), pp. 347–65.

39 De Felice, *Intervista sul fascismo*, pp. 24, 41, 74, 103.

40 The point is made in Charles Delzell's Introduction to De Felice, *Interpretations of Fascism*, p. ix.

41 De Felice, *Intervista sul fascismo*, p. 112.

42 De Felice had himself been a member of the PCI in his youth – he had even been arrested in 1952 for his political activities – but he had grown disillusioned with academic Marxism by the mid-1950s and had left the party after its refusal to condemn the Soviet invasion of Hungary in 1956.

43 De Felice, *Intervista sul fascismo*, pp. 7, 45, 110.

44 A. James Gregor, *Interpretations of Fascism* (New Jersey: General Learning Press, 1974a), p. 202.

45 Roland Sarti, review of *Italian Fascism and Developmental Dictatorship* and *Young Mussolini and the Intellectual Origins of Fascism*, by A. J. Gregor, *American Historical Review* 86(1) (1981), p. 169.

46 Readers are directed to the works of Stanley Payne, Zeev Sternhell, Roger Eatwell and Roger Griffin as examples *par excellence* of this trend in generic fascist studies. Payne has defined fascism as 'a form of revolutionary ultra-nationalism for national rebirth that is based on a primarily vitalist philosophy'. For Sternhell, fascism was a revolutionary

synthesis of organic nationalism and anti-Marxist socialism, a 'system of ethics and aesthetics...a complete ideological system' which sought 'a moral revolution, a profound transformation of the human spirit' and the creation of 'a communal, anti-individualist civilization'. Eatwell has described fascism as 'an ideology that strives to achieve social rebirth based on a holistic-national radical Third Way'. In the Sisyphean pursuit of a single-sentence definition of fascism, Griffin has settled on fascism as 'a political ideology whose mythic core in its various permutations is a palingenetic form of popular ultra-nationalism'. See Stanley Payne, *A History of Fascism* (Madison: University of Wisconsin Press, 1995), p. 14; Zeev Sternhell, *Neither Right nor Left: Fascist Ideology in France* (Princeton: Princeton University Press, 1986), pp. 27, 29, 270, 272–3; Roger Eatwell, 'What is Fascism?', *History Review* 26 (1996), pp. 29–35; Roger Griffin, 'The Palingenetic Core of Generic Fascist Ideology', January 2000. This article was accessed online at <http:// ah.brookes.ac.uk/resources/griffin/coreoffascism.pdf>. It can also be found in Alessandro Campi (ed.), *Che cos'è il fascismo? Interpretazioni e prospettive di ricerche* (Rome: Ideazione editrice, 2003), pp. 97–122. For a scathing Marxist attack on the 'new consensus' see Dave Renton, *Fascism: Theory and Practice* (London: Pluto Press, 1999).

47 George L. Mosse (ed.), *International Fascism: New Thoughts and Approaches* (London: Sage, 1979), pp. 4, 25–6. See also: George L. Mosse, 'Fascism and the French Revolution', *Journal of Contemporary History* 24(1) (1989), pp. 5–26.

48 According to Mosse (1980), Mussolini was, like Hitler, a consummate politician, but unlike his German counterpart, 'he was not oppressed by the weight of a heavy ideological baggage and by an apocalyptic vision. Hitler judged every important problem in eschatalogical terms and its solution had to be, in his opinion, absolute and definitive. For Mussolini, the future was something undetermined which in virtue of a vague concept of a new Fascist man would surely have had a positive solution'. Quoted in Renzo De Felice, *Storia degli ebrei italiani sotto il fascismo* (Turin: Einaudi, 4th edn, 1993), p. vii.

49 Quoted in Emilio Gentile, 'Paths to an Interpretation: Renzo De Felice and the Definition of Fascism', *Italian Quarterly* 36(141–42) (1999), pp. 65, 68.

50 Mosse, 'The Political Culture of Italian Futurism', p. 253.

51 See Gentile, 'Renzo De Felice'; Emilio Gentile, *Renzo De Felice. Lo storico e il personaggio* (Rome-Bari: Laterza, 2003).

52 In Italy and abroad, the new historiography points to the need to proceed with new criteria for the historicization of fascism. Historians who share this leaning can adopt Mosse's position: "The chief problem facing any historian is to capture the irrational by an exercise of the rational mind. This becomes easier when the irrational is made concrete through rational acts within the terms of its own ideological framework." The myths, organizations, institutions and mass politics of fascism form the "ideological framework" which will allow the historian to understand rationally the fascist irrationality. This cultural attitude does not overlook social situations. The task of the historian is to understand how, in given social situations, the people's choice is directed towards some myths rather than others, even when this conflicts with their own objective interests.

Emilio Gentile, 'Fascism in Italian Historiography: In Search of an Individual Historical Identity', *Journal of Contemporary History* 21(2) (1986), pp. 203–4. For his critique of De Felice's views on the totalitarian nature of Fascism see Gentile, 'Paths to an Interpretation'. Mosse described Gentile's *The Sacralization of Politics in Fascist Italy* (Cambridge, MA: Harvard University Press, 1996) as 'Among recent works on fascism...one of the most original and essential contributions'.

53 Emilio Gentile, 'From the Cultural Revolt of the Giolittian Era to the Ideology of Fascism', in Frank J. Coppa (ed.), *Studies in Modern Italian History: From the Risorgimento to the Republic* (New York: Peter Lang, 1986), pp. 113, 115–16; Emilio Gentile, 'Fascism in Power: The Totalitarian Experiment', in Lyttleton (ed.), *Liberal and Fascist Italy*, pp. 143, 157; Emilio Gentile, 'The Problem of the Party in Italian Fascism', *Journal of Contemporary History* 19(2) (1984), p. 256.

54 Gentile, 'The Problem of the Party in Italian Fascism', pp. 268–9.

55 Simonetta Falasca-Zamponi, *Fascist Spectacle*, pp. 7–8, 13–14, 16, 187.

56 Mabel Berezin, *Making the Fascist Self: The Political Culture of Interwar Italy* (Ithaca: Cornell University Press, 1997), pp. 50, 195, 251. Claudio Fogu provides a very brief but useful discussion of the differences and similarities between the works of Gentile, Falasca-Zamponi and Berezin. See Claudio Fogu, '"To Make History": Garibaldianism and the Formation of a Fascist Historic Imaginary', in Albert Russell Ascoli and Krystyna von Henneberg (eds), *Making and Remaking Italy: The Cultivation of National Identity Around the Risorgimento* (Oxford and New York: Berg, 2001), p. 204.

57 Berezin, *Making the Fascist Self*, pp. 7, 30; Walter L. Adamson, 'Fascism and Culture: Avant-gardes and Secular Religion in the Italian Case', *Journal of Contemporary History* 24 (1989), p. 429.

58 David D. Roberts, 'How Not to Think about Fascism and Ideology, Intellectual Antecedents and Historical Meaning', *Journal of Contemporary History* 35(2) (2000), pp. 185–211.

59 Jeffrey T. Schnapp, *Staging Fascism: 18BL and the Theater of the Masses for Masses* (Stanford: Stanford University Press, 1996), p. 6

60 Bosworth, *The Italian Dictatorship*, p. 27.

61 Gentile, 'The Totalitarian Experiment', p. 263.

62 Quoted in Alan Cassels, *Mussolini's Early Diplomacy* (Princeton: Princeton University Press, 1970), p. 391, n. 4; and in De Felice, *Gli anni del consenso*, p. 336, n.1.

63 Denis Mack Smith, *Mussolini's Roman Empire* (London: Longman, 1976), p. 82.

64 See Azzi, 'The Historiography of Fascist Italy', pp. 189, 193. Nor was Mack Smith the last. See, for example, Clark, *Modern Italy*, p. 280, for a more recent but very similar perspective.

65 Salvemini, *Under the Axe of Fascism*, p. 427; Mack Smith, *Mussolini's Roman Empire*, p. 68; Azzi, 'The Historiography of Fascist Italy', p. 195. It should be noted that Salvemini also suggested that Mussolini saw the Ethiopian war as a way to give the restive 'Left' Fascists the 'real' Fascist revolution they wanted – a point picked up in later interpretations.

66 Cassels, *Mussolini's Early Diplomacy*, pp. 125, 396; Alan Cassels, *Fascist Italy* (London: Routledge and Kegan Paul, 1969), pp. 71, 84, 89–90.

67 Esmonde Robertson, *Mussolini as Empire Builder: Europe and Africa, 1932–36* (London: Macmillan, 1977), p. 2.

68 For a discussion of Petersen's work see H. James Burgwyn, 'Recent Books on Italian Foreign Policy in the 1930's: A Critical Essay', *Journal of Italian History* 1(3) (1978), pp. 535–53.

69 Robertson, *Mussolini as Empire Builder*, pp. 2, 5, 49, 93; Petersen, quoted in Burgwyn, 'Recent Books on Italian Foreign Policy', p. 551.

70 MacGregor Knox, 'Conquest, Foreign and Domestic, in Fascist Italy and Nazi Germany', *Journal of Modern History* 56(1) (1984), pp. 5, 8, 40; Knox, 'The Fascist Regime, its Foreign Policy and its Wars', pp. 359, 362, 364.

71 Azzi, 'The Historiography of Fascist Italy', pp. 188, 190.

72 De Felice, *Intervista sul fascismo*, p. 69. There is far less explicit linkage between the two in *Gli anni del consenso*.

73 Knox, 'Conquest, Foreign and Domestic, in Fascist Italy and Nazi Germany', p. 57.

74 De Felice, *Intervista sul fascismo*, p. 69.

75 This was not an entirely new idea – both Salvemini and Ivone Kirkpatrick (*Mussolini: Study of a Demagogue*, London: Odhams, 1964) for example, had previously argued along similar lines.

76 De Felice, *Breve storia*, p. 70.

77 Eden was 'politically...a colourless figure, objectively inferior to the responsibility placed upon him and to the fame that he at length won'. De Felice, *Gli anni del consenso*, p. 668.

78 De Felice, *Gli anni del consenso*, p. 689; De Felice, *Intervista sul fascismo*, p. 70; *Breve Storia*, pp. 74–5.

79 De Felice, *Gli anni del consenso*, pp. 642–3.

80 De Felice, quoted in Knox, 'The Fascist Regime, its Foreign Policy and its Wars', p. 354. See also: De Felice, *Breve storia*, pp. 76, 85–6.

81 De Felice, *Intervista sul fascismo*, pp. 72–73, 88; De Felice, *Breve storia*, pp. 75–6, 88, 91, 94.

82 De Felice, quoted in Knox, 'The Fascist Regime, its Foreign Policy and its Wars', p. 356. De Felice was not alone in blaming the British for Italy's aggression and ill-fated alliance with Hitler's Germany. See, for example, Rosaria Quartararo, *Roma tra Londra e Berlino, La politica estera fascista dal 1930 al 1940* (Rome: Bonacci, 1980); Rosaria Quartararo, *L'Anschluss come problema internazionale. Le responsabilità anglo-francesi* (Rome: Jouvence, 2005); James J. Sadkovich, 'Understanding Defeat: Reappraising Italy's Role in World War Two', *Journal of Contemporary History* 24(1) (1989), pp. 27–61.

83 Bosworth, *Italy and the Wider World*, pp. 37, 42, 50, 52; Bosworth, *The Italian Dictatorship*, p. 100; Bosworth (1983), quoted in Azzi, 'The Historiography of Fascist Italy', p. 196.

84 De Felice saw links between early Fascist foreign policy and that of the liberal period. He also argued that the *peso determinante* was not that far removed from traditional policy in the pre-Fascist era, especially the 'Italian vocation for the policy of the "waltz"' (i.e. the idea that Italy should dance with everyone). De Felice, *Gli anni del consenso*, p. 340.

85 H. James Burgwyn, *Italian Foreign Policy in the Interwar Period, 1918–1940* (Westport: Praeger, 1997), pp. xii, xiv, xvii, 24, 35, 54, 142, 155, 168, 224, 228.

86 Meir Michaelis, *Mussolini and the Jews. German-Italian Relations and the Jewish Question in Italy, 1922–45* (Oxford: Clarendon Press, 1978), p. viii.

87 Joshua D. Zimmerman, 'Introduction', in Joshua D. Zimmerman (ed.), *Jews in Italy under Fascist and Nazi Rule, 1922–1945* (Cambridge: Cambridge University Press, 2005), p. 5.

88 Michaelis, *Mussolini and the Jews*, pp. 68–9. See also Joel Blatt, 'The Battle of Turin, 1933–1935: Carlo Rosselli, Giustizia e Libertà, OVRA and the Origins of Mussolini's Anti-Semitic campaign', *Journal of Modern Italian Studies* 1(1) (1995), pp. 33, 45.

89 Renzo De Felice, *Storia degli ebrei sotto il fascismo*, p. 462. De Felice identifies several other minor or lesser influences on Fascist anti-Semitism but states on more than one occasion that the racial legislation was determined essentially by Mussolini's desire to 'eliminate the most strident contrast in the policies of the two regimes' (pp. 247, 252). Michaelis, *Mussolini and the Jews*, p. 125; Susan Zuccotti, *The Italians and the Holocaust* (London: Peter Halban, 1987), p. 40.

90 The quote is from Germino, *The Italian Fascist Party in Power*, quoted in Michaelis, *Mussolini and the Jews*, p. 124. Similar arguments have been advanced by Michael Ledeen (for further details see Michaelis, *Mussolini and the Jews*, pp. 124–5). More recently, Emilio Gentile has written that the Fascist concept of the totalitarian community meant it was 'totally coherent...to radicalize the principle of discrimination [against "bad" citizens] to the point of adopting anti-Semitic legislation' (Gentile, *The Sacralization of Politics*, p. 101). See also Enzo Collotti, who argues that 'the question of anti-Semitic racism forms one of the components of that process of totalitarian acceleration...after 1936'. Enzo Collotti, 'La politica razzista del regime fascista' (1998). <http://www.novecento.org/interCollotti.html>.

91 See, for example, Morgan, *Italian Fascism*, pp. 200–1. Interestingly, De Felice, a staunch defender of the 'Axis' interpretation, seems at the very end of his life to have embraced this explanation of Fascist anti-Semitism. In *Rosso e Nero*, De Felice stated: 'Whoever has the patience to examine the first edition of *Storia degli ebrei*...will find, in the chapter in which I speak of the beginnings of Fascist racism, many arguments except one: the very tight relationship between racial legislation and the conquest of empire. I had not immediately understood the most important thing. I discovered it during research for my biography of Mussolini' (*Rosso e Nero*, p. 155) Later editions of *Storia degli ebrei sotto il fascismo* had noted the influence of Ethiopian racial policy on the development of Fascist anti-Semitism, but had considered it to be a 'minor' factor (see, for example, the 1993 edition, p. 239). De Felice in *Rosso e Nero* also argued that another 'one of the strongest motives' for the racial laws was Mussolini's conviction that they would give a new dynamism to Fascism, bringing on board the younger generation of Fascists who were anti-Semitic and who attributed the failure of the Fascist revolution to the absence of a clear racial policy (pp. 156–7). He did not mention the role of the German alliance.

92 Barzini, *The Italians*, p. 174.

93 Paul Corner, 'The Road to Fascism: An Italian *Sonderweg?*', *Contemporary European History* 11(2) (2002b), pp. 273–95.

94 Renton, *Fascism*, p. 29.

95 Mack Smith, of course, argues the Fascism-as-revelation thesis as well as the egoist case.

96 John A. Davis and Denis Mack Smith, *Mussolini and Italian Fascism* (Coventry: Warwick History Videos, 1991).

97 Mack Smith, *Mussolini's Roman Empire*, p. 252.

98 Roger Griffin, 'How Fascist was Mussolini?' This article was originally accessed online at <http://ah.brookes.ac.uk/resources/griffin/mussolinifascist.pdf>. It can also be found in *New Perspective*, 6(1), 2000, pp. 31–5.

99 Eatwell, 'What is Fascism?', p. 29.

100 Eatwell, 'What is Fascism?', p. 33. See also Zeev Sternhell, *The Birth of Fascist Ideology*, pp. 6–7.

101 Roberts, 'How Not to Think about Fascism', p. 196.

102 John Whittam, *Fascist Italy* (Manchester: Manchester University Press, 1995), p. 81.

103 Griffin, 'How Fascist was Mussolini?'; Jonathan Steinberg, *All or Nothing: The Axis and the Holocaust, 1941–1943* (Routledge: London and New York, 1990), p. 241.

104 Robert Mallett, *Mussolini and the Origins of the Second World War, 1933–1940* (Basingstoke: Palgrave Macmillan, 2003), p. 16.

105 Mallett, *Mussolini and the Origins of the Second World War*, p. 66.

106 MacGregor Knox, 'Fascism: Ideology, Foreign Policy and War', in Lyttleton (ed.), *Liberal and Fascist Italy*, p. 130.

107 Bosworth, *Mussolini*, p. 309; Morgan, *Italian Fascism*, p. 175.

108 Morgan, *Italian Fascism*, p. 175.

109 On the evolution of the *Manifesto* see Aaron Gillette, 'The Origins of the "Manifesto of Racial Scientists"', *Journal of Modern Italian Studies* 6(3) (2001), pp. 305–23.

110 Davis and Mack Smith, *Mussolini and Italian Fascism*.

111 Luisa Passerini, 'Oral Memory of Fascism', in Forgacs (ed.), *Rethinking Italian Fascism*, p. 192.

112 Renton, *Fascism*, p. 27.

113 Martin Blinkhorn, 'The Author's Response', *Reviews in History*, 2001. This article, a reply to a review by Tobias Abse of Blinkhorn's *Fascism and the Right in Europe* (London: Longman, 2000), was accessed online at <http://www.history.ac.uk/reviews/paper/blinkhornMartin.html>.

114 Roberts, 'How Not to Think about Fascism', p. 189.

Chapter 5 Fascism and the economy

1 The 1970s represent the high-water mark of historical studies of the Italian economy under Fascism, and most of the few major economic studies of the inter-war period date from this time. Little interest had been shown in the subject since the end of the war, a point noted by Pierluigi Ciocca and Gianni Toniolo (eds) in their Introduction to *L'economia italiana nel periodo fascista* (Bologna: il Mulino, 1976), one of the first comprehensive studies of the economic history of Fascism. Since the 1970s, interest and debate have again waned. This is reflected in the limited treatment given to the Fascist period in recent general surveys of the modern Italian economic history, e.g. Federico (ed.), *The Economic Development of Italy* and Cohen and Federico, *The Growth of the Italian Economy*. Of recent works, the best and most comprehensive coverage of the inter-war economy available in English is provided by Zamagni, *The Economic History of Italy*. However, Gianni Toniolo's 1980 study, *L'economia dell'Italia fascista* (Rome–Bari: Laterza), remains probably the most useful book-length work on the subject.

2 On the poor performance of the Italian wartime economy see Fortunato Minniti, 'L'industria degli armamenti dal 1940 al 1943: i mercati, le produzioni', and Andrea

Curami, 'Tecnologia e modelli di armamento', in Vera Zamagni (ed.), *Come perdere la guerra e vincere la pace: l'economia italiana tra Guerra e dopoguerra, 1938–1947* (Bologna: il Mulino, 1997), pp. 55–148 and 149–84 respectively.

3 Pietro Grifone's article, first published in the journal *Politica ed economica*, 4 August 1972, appears as an appendix in his *Capitalismo di stato e imperialismo fascista* (Milan: Mazzotta, 1975).

4 See, for example, Roland Sarti's review of Gregor's *Italian Fascism and Developmental Dictatorship* and *Young Mussolini and the Intellectual Origins of Fascism*, in the *American Historical Review*, 86(1) (1981), pp. 169–70. Jon Cohen later dedicated an entire article to a repudiation of Gregor's 'developmental dictatorship' thesis. Jon S. Cohen, 'Was Italian Fascism a Developmental Dictatorship? Some Evidence to the Contrary', *Economic History Review* 41(1) (1988), pp. 95–113.

5 See, for example, Douglas J. Forsyth's review of Petri's *Storia economica d'Italia. Dalla Grande Guerra al miracolo economico (1918–1963)* (Bologna: il Mulino, 2002), in the *Journal of Modern Italian Studies*, 8(1) (2003), pp. 113–15.

6 Zamagni, *The Economic History of Italy*, pp. 239–40.

7 Figures are from Toniolo, *L'economia dell'Italia fascista*, pp. 31, 59–60, 70. Toniolo gives extensive coverage to the boom years, 1922–5, pp. 31–74.

8 Toniolo, *L'economia dell'Italia fascista*, pp. 127–30.

9 Toniolo, *L'economia dell'Italia fascista*, pp. 136–7.

10 Toniolo, *L'economia dell'Italia fascista*, pp. 141, 145, 147; Ciocca and Toniolo, 'Industry and Finance in Italy', p. 128; Ciocca and Toniolo, 'Introduzione', p. 17. For data on salaries see De Felice, *Gli anni del consenso*, pp. 67–72.

11 Toniolo, *L'economia dell'Italia fascista*, p. 28.

12 Ciocca and Toniolo, 'Introduzione', p. 17.

13 Nicola Rossi and Gianni Toniolo, 'Catching Up or Falling Behind? Italy's Economic Growth, 1895–1947', *Economic History Review* 45(3) (1992), p. 545; Paul Corner, 'Fascist Agrarian Policy and the Italian Economy in the Inter-war years', in Davis (ed.), *Gramsci and Italy's Passive Revolution*, p. 241.

14 Toniolo, *L'economia dell'Italia fascista*, p. 116.

15 Roland Sarti, 'Mussolini and the Italian Industrial Leadership in the Battle of the Lira 1925–1927', *Past and Present* 47(2) (1970), p. 111.

16 For details of the *bonifica integrale* see Jon Cohen, 'Un esame statistico delle opere di bonifica intrapese durante il regime fascista', in Gianni Toniolo (ed.), *Lo sviluppo economico italiano* (Rome-Bari: Laterza, 1973), pp. 351–5.

17 For details of the banking crisis and the creation of the IMI and IRI see Ciocca and Toniolo, 'Industry and Finance in Italy', pp. 131–4.

18 Corner, 'Fascist Agrarian Policy', p. 240.

19 Grifone, *Capitalismo di stato e imperialismo fascista*, pp. 152, 155.

20 V. Foa, quoted in Corner, 'Fascist Agrarian Policy', p. 240.

21 Nicos Poulantzas (1974), quoted in Griffin (ed.), *International Fascism*, p. 88.

22 Quoted in Toniolo, *L'economia dell'Italia fascista*, p. 5.

23 Both quotes given here can be found in De Felice, *Gli anni del consenso*, pp. 97, 179.

24 For example, Lyttleton (*The Seizure of Power*, p. 354) believed 'The policies of "rurality" and the demographic battle marked a significant turn away from the objectives of modernization'. Renzo De Felice (*Gli anni del consenso*, p. 149), who argued that the ruralization campaign was a central element in Mussolini's efforts to 'transform' Italian society, denounced the attempt as 'absurd, anachronistic and anti-historical, a confused jumble'. Emilio Sereni talked of 'the transformation of Italian society in an agrarian direction' under Fascism (quoted in Corner, 'Fascist Agrarian Policy', p. 242).

25 Corner, 'Fascist Agrarian Policy', pp. 246–54.

26 Corner, 'Fascist Agrarian Policy', pp. 257–60, 262–3.

27 Corner, 'Fascist Agrarian Policy', pp. 256, 265–6, 268.

28 See A. James Gregor, 'Fascism and Modernization: Some Addenda', *World Politics* 26 (1974b), pp. 370–84 (extracts can be found in Griffin [ed.], *International Fascism*, pp. 127–37); A. James Gregor, *Interpretations*; A. James Gregor, *Fascism and Developmental Dictatorship*, (Princeton: Princeton University Press, 1979).

29 'Italian Fascism was the natural child of revolutionary Marxism, and revolutionary syndicalism was its midwife'. Gregor, *Developmental Dictatorship*, p. 97.

30 Gregor, *Developmental Dictatorship*, pp. 115–16, 148–9, 155–6, 265–81; *Interpretations*, pp. 198–9.

31 Gregor, *Developmental Dictatorship*, pp. 117, 143, 145, 158, 161, 264; *Interpretations*, p. 197, 'Fascism and Modernization' in Griffin (ed.), *International Fascism*, pp. 133–4.

32 Gregor, *Developmental Dictatorship*, pp. 158, 161–2; *Interpretations*, p. 198.

33 In addition to the criticisms levelled at Gregor by Sarti and Cohen (n. 4), see also: Lyttleton, *Seizure of Power*, pp. 437–8; Knox, 'Conquest, Foreign and Domestic, in Fascist Italy and Nazi Germany', p. 4.

34 See, for example, Federico and Giannetti, 'Italy: Stalling and Surpassing', pp. 132–5.

35 Giuseppe Tattara and Gianni Toniolo, 'L'industria manifatturiera: cicli, politiche e mutamenti di struttura (1921–37)', in Ciocca and Toniolo (eds), *L'economia italiana nel periodo fascista*, p. 155; Toniolo, *L'economia dell'Italia fascista*, pp. 10–11; Rossi and Toniolo, 'Catching Up or Falling Behind?', pp. 551–2.

36 Toniolo, *L'economia dell'Italia fascista*, pp. xi–xii, 99–102, 126; Sarti, 'Mussolini and the Italian Industrial Leadership', pp. 97–100. Q90 is usually seen as an example of Mussolini demonstrating his authority over Italian big business which favoured stabilization at a rate closer to 120 lire to the pound, and as a prestige measure – a strong currency equated in Mussolini's eyes to a strong country.

37 Jon Cohen, 'Fascism and Agriculture in Italy: Policies and Consequences', *Economic History Review* 32(1), p. 71; Federico and Giannetti, 'Italy: Stalling and Surpassing', p. 134; Mariangela Paradisi, 'Il commercio estero e la struttura industriale', in Ciocca and Toniolo (eds), *L'economia italiana nel periodo fascista*, p. 323.

38 Federico and Giannetti, 'Italy: Stalling and Surpassing', p. 132.

39 Zamagni, *The Economic History of Italy*, pp. 236, 300–1; Toniolo, *L'economia dell'Italia fascista*, p. 247; Cohen, 'Was Fascism a Developmental Dictatorship?', pp. 106–7.

40 Toniolo, *L'economia dell'Italia fascista*, p. xiv–xv; Ciocca, 'L'economia italiana nel contesto internazionale', in Ciocca and Toniolo (eds), *L'economia italiana nel periodo fascista*, pp. 49–50; Cohen, 'Was Fascism a Developmental Dictatorship?', p. 97; Roland Sarti writes of a process of 'continual give and take between the Fascist and the industrial leaders', *Fascism and the Industrial Leadership in Italy, 1919–40*, (Berkeley: University of California Press, 1971), p. 5.

41 Toniolo, *L'economia dell'Italia fascista*, pp. xv–xvi, 244–68; Ciocca and Toniolo, 'Industry and Finance in Italy', pp. 133–6; Federico and Giannetti, 'Italy: Stalling and Surpassing', p. 135.

42 Tattara and Toniolo, 'L'industria manifatturiera', p. 156.

43 Zamagni, *The Economic History of Italy*, pp. 252–3. This contrasts with De Felice's claim that Mussolini immediately understood the significance of the crisis and acted accordingly.

44 Rossi and Toniolo, 'Catching Up or Falling Behind?', pp. 551–2; Toniolo, *L'economia dell'Italia fascista*, pp. xii, 11; Ciocca, 'L'economia italiana nel contesto internazionale', pp. 39–40; Sarti, 'Mussolini and the Italian Industrial Leadership', p. 107.

45 Clark, *Modern Italy*, p. 269; Toniolo, *L'economia fascista*, pp. 128, 306, 309, 311, 314; Vera Zamagni, *The Economic History of Italy*, p. 260; Ciocca, 'L'economia italiana nel contesto internazionale', p. 42; Cohen, 'Fascism and Agriculture in Italy', pp. 72, 78–9.

46 Cohen, 'Un esame statistico delle opere di bonifica intraprese durante il regime fascista', pp. 351–72; Ciocca, 'L'economia italiana nel contesto internazionale', p. 42; Toniolo, *L'economia dell'Italia fascista*, pp. 156–7.

47 Federico and Giannetti, 'Italy: Stalling and Surpassing', p. 134. For a summary of the environmental consequences of Porto Marghera see Simonetta Tunesi, 'Italian Environmental Policies in the Post-war Period', in Patrick McCarthy (ed.), *Italy since 1945* (Oxford: Oxford University Press, 2000), pp. 127–9.

48 Paradisi, 'Il commercio estero e la struttura industriale', p. 323.
49 Federico and Giannetti, 'Italy: Stalling and Surpassing', p. 135; Ciocca and Toniolo, 'Introduzione', p. 18; Toniolo, *L'economia dell'Italia fascista*, pp. xiii, 301, 314, 323–4; Zamagni, *The Economic History of Italy*, p. 271.
50 Federico and Giannetti, 'Italy: Stalling and Surpassing', p. 135; Cohen, 'Fascism and Agriculture in Italy', pp. 70, 71; Rossi and Toniolo, 'Catching Up or Falling Behind?', p. 552.
51 Rolf Petri, 'A Technocratic Strategy of Industrial Development in Italy, 1935–60'. <http://www.ub.es/histeco/Activitats/Petri.pdf>. This paper, given to the Departament d'Història i Institucions Econòmiques, Universitat de Barcelona, 7 April 2005, summarizes the arguments and evidence put forward in Petri, *Storia economica d'Italia* (see n. 5).
52 Petri, 'A Technocratic Strategy', pp. 25–6.
53 Petri, 'A Technocratic Strategy', pp. 14–15, 29, 31–5.
54 Petri, 'A Technocratic Strategy', pp. 11–12.
55 Petri, 'A Technocratic Strategy', pp. 5, 17–21, 26–8, 37–8.
56 See, for example, Zamagni, *The Economic History of Italy*, pp. 292–3, 321; Vera Zamagni, 'Introduzione', in Zamagni (ed.), *Come perdere la guerra e vincere la pace*, p. 10. See also Ruggero Ranieri's review of *Storia economica d'Italia*, in *Business History* 45(2) (2003), p. 115.
57 Forsyth, *Journal of Modern Italian Studies* 8(1) (2003), p. 115; Cohen and Federico, *The Growth of the Italian Economy*, pp. 25, 69.
58 Grifone, *Capitalismo di stato e imperialismo fascista*, p. 152.
59 Zamagni, *The Economic History of Italy*, p. 291.
60 Similar arguments are made by Ciocca, 'L'economia italiana nel contesto internazionale', pp. 44–7, and Lyttleton, *The Seizure of Power*, p. 441.
61 Vera Zamagni, 'La dinamica dei salari nel settore industriale', in Ciocca and Toniolo (eds), *L'economia italiana nel periodo fascista*, p. 351.
62 See, for example, Cohen, 'Fascism and Agriculture in Italy'.
63 Toniolo, *L'economia dell'Italia fascista*, pp. xiii, xviii.

Chapter 6 Society and culture under Fascism

1 Bosworth, *The Italian Dictatorship*, p. 29.
2 See, for example, Angelo Del Boca, *Italiani, brava gente? Un mito duro a morire* (Vicenza: Neri Pozza, 2005); Davide Rodogno, 'Italian brava gente? Fascist Italy's Policy towards the Jews in the Balkans, April 1941–July 1943', *European History Quarterly* 35(2) (2005), pp. 213–40; H. James Burgwyn, 'General Roatta's War against the Partisans in Yugoslavia: 1942', *Journal of Modern Italian Studies* 9(3) (2004), pp. 314–29; Lidia Santarelli, 'Muted Violence: Italian War Crimes in Occupied Greece', *Journal of Modern Italian Studies* 9(3) (2004), pp. 280–99. See, too, the contributions to R. J. B. Bosworth and Patrizia Dogliani (eds), *Italian Fascism: History, Memory and Representation* (Basingstoke: Macmillan, 1999).
3 On the question of the failure of Italians to face up to atrocities committed by Italians during the Fascist period see Claudio Pavone, 'Introduction', *Journal of Modern Italian Studies* 9(3) (2004), pp. 271–9; Filippo Focardi and Lutz Klinkhammer, 'The Question of Fascist Italy's War Crimes: The Construction of a Self-acquitting Myth (1943–1948)', *Journal of Modern Italian Studies* 9(3) (2004), pp. 330–48. For a somewhat different perspective, see Robert Ventresca, 'Debating the Meaning of Fascism in Contemporary Italy', *Modern Italy*, 11(2) (2006), pp. 189–209.
4 De Felice, *Gli anni del consenso*, p. 83, n.1; Gentile, 'Fascism in Power', p. 157; R. J. B. Bosworth, '*Per necessità famigliare*: hypocrisy and corruption in Fascist Italy', *European History Quarterly* 30(3) (2000), pp. 363, 370; Luisa Passerini, *Fascism in Popular Memory: The Cultural Experience of the Turin Working Class* (Cambridge: Cambridge University Press, 1987), pp. 70–1, 95, 102.
5 De Felice, *Gli anni del consenso*, pp. 21–2.

6 Quoted in Lyttleton, *The Seizure of Power*, p. 397.

7 Victoria de Grazia, *The Culture of Consent: Mass Organization of Leisure in Fascist Italy* (Cambridge: Cambridge University Press, 1981), pp. 155, 276, n. 7.

8 LUCE newsreels from the Fascist period can be viewed at <http://www.archivioluce.com>.

9 David Forgacs, *Italian Culture in the Industrial Era 1880–1980. Cultural Politics, Politics, and the Public* (Manchester: Manchester University Press, 1990), pp. 68–72.

10 Gentile, *The Sacralization of Politics*, p. 77.

11 Falasca-Zamponi, *Fascist Spectacle*, p. 82.

12 Marla Stone, *The Patron State: Culture and Politics in Fascist Italy* (Princeton: Princeton University Press, 1998), p. 162.

13 See Emilio Gentile, 'The Theatre of Politics in Fascist Italy', in Günter Berghaus (ed.), *Fascism and Theatre: Comparative Studies on the Aesthetics and Politics of Performance in Europe, 1925–1945* (Oxford: Berghahn, 1996b), pp. 84–5. For a brief description and pictorial evidence of Fascism's urban propaganda see Diane Yvonne Ghirardo, 'Città fascista: surveillance and spectacle', *Journal of Contemporary History* 31 (1996), pp. 347–72.

14 Perry R. Willson, 'Women in Fascist Italy', in Richard Bessel (ed.), *Fascist Italy and Nazi Germany: Comparisons and Contrasts* (Cambridge: Cambridge University Press, 1996b), p. 80.

15 Carl Ipsen, *Dictating Demography: The Problem of Population in Fascist Italy* (Cambridge: Cambridge University Press, 1996), p. 145.

16 The quotes are by Farinacci and Mussolini respectively, both from 1925. Quoted in Berghaus, *Futurism and Politics*, pp. 224–5.

17 Lyttleton, *The Seizure of Power*, p. 383.

18 Forges Davanzati (1926), quoted in Philip V. Cannistraro, 'Mussolini's Cultural Revolution: Fascist or Nationalist?', *Journal of Contemporary History* 7 (1972), p. 122.

19 De Felice, *Gli anni del consenso*, p. 55.

20 Indeed, argued De Felice, the 'active fascistization' of the population was impossible since Starace, on the orders of Mussolini, was engaged in the 'political liquidation' of the one organization that could have been used to bring about 'the complete and definitive fascistization of the country' – the PNF. According to De Felice, the PNF lost its political character through Starace's decision to open up membership to all-comers (membership of the PNF had been controlled for much of the 1920s) and his efforts to turn the party into a bureaucratic organ of the state populated by, at best, patriots, at worst, opportunists. The depoliticization of the PNF was deliberate: the intention was to cement Mussolini's personal political authority. Fascism effectively became *mussolinismo*, the regime increasingly identified with the person of the *Duce*. The long-term impact on Fascism was negative. Fascist youth – from whose ranks were supposed to come the next generation of Fascist leaders – either saw the PNF merely as a means of employment and personal advancement or, if genuinely politicized, grew frustrated with the apparent ossification of Fascism. For this latter group, the inability to change Fascism from within – Mussolini did not tolerate debate – led to apathy and resignation or (increasingly from the mid-1930s) rebellion. For Mussolini, too, the political liquidation of the PNF weakened his own position: he was forced to rely on the most traditional – i.e. non-Fascist – elements of the regime, in the first instance, the bureaucracy, which was neither interested in the active fascistization of society, nor unconditionally supportive of the *Duce*. Moreover, by reducing Fascism to the cult of Mussolini, the basis of the regime itself became more precarious, tied to the fortunes and successes of one man. De Felice, *Gli anni del consenso*, pp. 180–1, 199, 218–46.

21 De Felice, *Gli anni del consenso*, p. 199.

22 De Felice, *Gli anni del consenso*, p. 81.

23 De Felice, *Gli anni del consenso*, p. 75.

24 De Felice, *Gli anni del consenso*, pp. 88, 95, 198, 313.

25 Ruth Ben-Ghiat, 'Liberation: Italian Cinema and the Fascist Past', in Bosworth and Dogliani (eds), *Italian Fascism*, p. 83.

26 The characterization is that of Tobias Abse, 'Italian Workers and Italian Fascism', in Bessel (ed.), *Fascist Italy and Nazi Germany*, p. 45.

27 Togliatti, quoted in Morgan, *Fascist Italy*, p. 159; Sereni, quoted in De Grazia, *The Culture of Consent*, p. 229; Nicola Tranfaglia, *Storia d'Italia. Vol. 22. La prima guerra mondiale e il fascismo* (Turin: UTET, 1995), pp. 547, 671.

28 Abse, 'Italian Workers and Italian Fascism', pp. 42, 46, 49–52, 58–9. See also Abse, 'The Rise of Fascism in an Industrial City', for a discussion of the 'mass violent resistance' of the working class to Fascism in 1921–2.

29 Abse's basic thesis, that the 'subversive traditions' of the Italian working class both united and protected it from Fascism (indeed, from any sources of authority), has been taken up by Antonio Sonnessa in his work on working-class resistance to Fascism in the early 1920s. See Antonio Sonnessa, 'Working Class Defence Organization, Anti-Fascist Resistance and the *Arditi del Popolo* in Turin, 1919–22', *European History Quarterly* 33(2), 2003, pp. 183–218; Antonio Sonnessa, 'The 1922 Turin Massacre (*Strage di Torino*): Working Class Resistance and Conflicts within Fascism', *Modern Italy*, 10(2), 2005, pp. 187–205. Sonnessa is a former student of Abse's.

30 Passerini, *Fascism in Popular Memory*, pp. 5, 71, 111–12, 126, 129, 136, 139, 141; Passerini, 'Oral Memory of Fascism', pp. 192–3, 195.

31 In a later work, De Grazia referred to the 'dictatorship's torment of working people'. *How Fascism Ruled Women. Italy, 1922–1945* (Berkeley: University of California Press, 1992), p. xii.

32 De Grazia, *The Culture of Consent*, pp. 168–9, 186, 235, 238, 243.

33 This brings to mind Piero Calamandrei's observation on the eve of World War Two that Italian youth 'are not fascist, but they are not really antifascist. Instead, they are anti-antifascist. They consider the antifascists to be pains in the neck'. Quoted in Alexander De Grand, 'Cracks in the Façade: The Failure of Fascist totalitarianism in Italy 1935–9', *European History Quarterly* 21(4) (1991), p. 517.

34 De Grazia, *The Culture of Consent*, pp. 20, 224, 226–7.

35 Maurizio Gribaudi, *Mondo operaio e mito operaio. Spazi e percorsi sociali a Torino nel primo novecento* (Turin: Einaudi, 1987); Giuseppe Berta, *Conflitto industriale e struttura d'impresa alla FIAT, 1919–1979* (Bologna: il Mulino, 1998). See also Giuseppe Berta, 'The Interregnum: Turin, FIAT and Industrial Conflict Between War and Fascism', in Chris Wrigley (ed.), *Challenges of Labour: Central and Western Europe, 1917–1920* (London: Routledge, 1993), p. 120.

36 'The political significance of this kind of generational change', Corner wrote, 'is all too obvious'. Paul Corner, 'Italy', in Stephen Salter and John Stevenson (eds), *The Working Class and Politics in Europe and America, 1929–1945* (London: Longman, 1990), p. 160.

37 Corner, 'Italy', pp. 154, 160, 162, 168.

38 Carlo Levi, *Christ Stopped at Eboli* (London: Penguin, 1982), pp. 77–8.

39 Levi, *Christ Stopped at Eboli*, pp. 11, 50, 77, 121.

40 See Bosworth, *The Italian Dictatorship*, pp. 133–9.

41 Steinberg argued that there was a 'minimum level of economic and social development above which masses can be mobilized and below which they cannot'; the Calabrian peasantry fell below that minimum. Jonathan Steinberg, 'Fascism in the South: The Case of Calabria', in Forgacs (ed.), *Rethinking Italian Fascism*, pp. 83, 85.

42 A more recent study of Calabria, although dealing primarily with the period 1943–48, reaches the same conclusion as Steinberg. See Jonathan Dunnage, 'Policing and Politics in the Southern Italian Community, 1943–48', in Jonathan Dunnage (ed.), *After the War: Violence, Justice, Continuity and Renewal in Italian Society* (Market Harborough: Troubador, 1999), pp. 36–8.

43 De Grazia, *The Culture of Consent*, pp. 95, 100–1, 121, 125–6.

44 De Grazia, *The Culture of Consent*, p. 97.

45 De Grazia, *The Culture of Consent*, pp. 104–24.

46 De Felice, *Gli anni del consenso*, p. 153.

47 Willson, 'Women in Fascist Italy', pp. 81–2; De Grazia, *How Fascism Ruled Women*, pp. 11–12.

48 Perry Willson, *The Clockwork Factory: Women and Work in Fascist Italy* (Oxford: Clarendon Press, 1993), p. 12.

49 Perry Willson, 'Women in Fascist Italy', p. 81; De Grazia, *How Fascism Ruled Women*, pp. 94, 147.

50 Perry Willson, 'Cooking the Patriotic Omelette: Women and the Italian Fascist Ruralization Campaign', *European History Quarterly* 27(4) (1997), p. 536; De Grazia, *How Fascism Ruled Women*, pp. 46, 59, 77–8; Perry Willson, 'Flowers for the Doctor. Pro-natalism and Abortion in Fascist Milan', *Modern Italy* 1(2) (1996a), p. 47; Passerini, *Fascism in Popular Memory*, p. 181.

51 Willson, 'Women in Fascist Italy', p. 86; De Grazia, *How Fascism Ruled Women*, p. 166. For more on women's attitudes to Fascism see Elda Guerra, 'Memory and Representations of Fascism: Female Autobiographical Narratives', in Bosworth and Dogliani (eds), *Italian Fascism*, pp. 195–215. There were, of course, women who were convinced and loyal Fascists through to 1945. See, in this context, Maria Fraddosio, 'The Fallen Hero: The Myth of Mussolini and Fascist Women in the Italian Social Republic (1943–5)', *Journal of Contemporary History* 31(1) (1996), pp. 99–124.

52 De Grazia, *How Fascism Ruled Women*, pp. 130, 132, 213; Victoria de Grazia, 'Nationalizing Women: The Competition between Fascist and Commercial Cultural Models in Mussolini's Italy', in Victoria de Grazia (ed.), *The Sex of Things: Gender and Consumption in Historical Perspective* (Berkeley: University of California Press, 1996), pp. 342–3, 352; Victoria de Grazia, 'Mass Culture and Sovereignty: The American Challenge to European Cinema', *Journal of Modern History* 61 (1989), p. 86.

53 Willson, *The Clockwork Factory*, p. 245; Paul Corner, 'Women in Fascist Italy. Changing Family Roles in the Transition from an Agricultural to an Industrial Society', *European History Quarterly* 23(1) (1993), pp. 51–68.

54 De Grazia, *How Fascism Ruled Women*, p. 109; Willson, 'Cooking the Patriotic Omelette', p. 541; Perry Willson, *Peasant Women and Politics in Fascist Italy: The Massaie Rurali* (London and New York: Routledge, 2002), p. 172; Willson, 'Flowers for the Doctor', p. 47; Willson, 'Women in Fascist Italy', p. 87; Lesley Caldwell, 'Reproducers of the Nation: Women and the Family in Fascist Policy', in Forgacs (ed.), *Rethinking Italian Fascism*, pp. 128–33.

55 Ruth Ben-Ghiat, 'Italian Fascism and the Aesthetics of the Third Way', *Journal of Contemporary History* 31(2) (1996), p. 310; Lino Pertile, 'Fascism and Literature', in Forgacs (ed.), *Rethinking Italian Fascism*, pp. 170–1.

56 Marla Stone, 'Challenging Cultural Categories: The Transformation of the Venice Biennale under Fascism', *Journal of Modern Italian Studies* 4(2) (1999), pp. 184, 192; Forgacs, *Italian Culture in the Industrial Era*, pp. 55, 62–3.

57 Stone, *The Patron State*, p. 5.

58 The EUR (*Esposizione universale di Roma*) – scheduled to open in 1942 – was intended to be a 'vast, marble exhibition metropolis', built to celebrate the twentieth anniversary of the March on Rome. See Stone, *The Patron State*, p. 254–5.

59 Pollard, *The Fascist Experience in Italy*, p. 67; Lyttleton, *The Seizure of Power*, p. 378; E. Papa (1958), quoted in Lyttleton, *The Seizure of Power*, p. 511, n. 67; Norberto Bobbio (1982), quoted in Bosworth, *The Italian Dictatorship*, p. 155.

60 Schnapp, *Staging Fascism*, p. 6; Stone, *The Patron State*, p. 4; Roger Griffin, 'Staging the Nation's Rebirth: The Politics and Aesthetics of Performance in the Context of Fascist Studies', in Berghaus (ed.), *Fascism and Theatre*, p. 26.

61 See, for example, Doug Thompson, 'The Organization, Fascistization and Management of Theatre in Italy, 1925–1943', in Berghaus (ed.), *Fascism and Theatre*, p. 99; Lyttleton, *The Seizure of Power* 31(2) (1996), p. 379.

62 Berghaus, 'Introduction', in Berghaus (ed.), *Fascism and Theatre*, p. 4; Griffin, 'Staging the Nation's Rebirth', pp. 24–5; Roger Griffin, 'The Sacred Synthesis: The Ideological Cohesion of Fascist Cultural Policy', *Modern Italy* 3(1) (1998b), p. 15; George L. Mosse, 'Fascist

Aesthetics and Society: Some Considerations', *Journal of Contemporary History* 31(2) (1996), p. 245.

63 Schnapp, *Staging Fascism*, pp. 6–7; Stone, 'Challenging Cultural Categories', pp. 185, 203; Marla Stone, 'Staging Fascism: The Exhibition of the Fascist Revolution', *Journal of Contemporary History* 28(2) (1993), pp. 227, 238; Emily Braun, 'The Visual Arts: Modernism and Fascism', in Lyttleton (ed.), *Liberal and Fascist Italy*, pp. 198–9, 214–15.

64 Professional theatre remained in private hands and committed to what Mussolini disparagingly referred to as 'theatre of adultery' – the love triangle dramas favoured by bourgeois audiences – rather than 'Fascist' theatre (one estimate suggests that 90% of plays produced during the Fascist period had no discernible Fascist element).

65 Berghaus, 'Introduction', pp. 5–6; Griffin, 'Staging the Nation's Rebirth', p. 23.

66 Pietro Cavallo, 'Theatre Politics of the Mussolini Regime and their Influence on Fascist Drama', in Berghaus (ed.), *Fascism and Theatre*, p. 115; Schnapp, *Staging Fascism*, pp. 7–8, 21, 78–83; Mario Verdone, 'Mussolini's "Theatre of the Masses"', in Berghaus (ed.), *Fascism and Theatre*, p. 138.

67 Emily Braun, 'Expressionism as Fascist Aesthetic', *Journal of Contemporary History* 31(2) (1996), p. 287; Stone, 'Challenging Cultural Categories', pp. 186–8; Mark Antliff, in David D. Roberts, Alexander De Grand, Mark Antliff and Thomas Linehan, 'Comments on Roger Griffin, "The Primacy of Culture: The Current Growth (or Manufacture) of Consensus within Fascist Studies"', *Journal of Contemporary History* 37(2) (2002), p. 268; Griffin, 'The Sacred Synthesis', p. 15; Griffin, 'How Fascist was Mussolini?'. For more by Griffin on this issue see 'Notes towards the Definition of a Fascist Culture: The Prospects for Synergy between Marxist and Liberal Heuristics', *Renaissance and Modern Studies* 42 (2001) (originally accessed on-line at <http://ah.brookes.ac.uk/resources/griffin/fasaesthetics.pdf>); 'The Primacy of Italian Culture: The Current Growth (or Manufacture) of Consensus within Fascist Studies', *Journal of Contemporary History* 37(1) (2002), pp. 21–43.

68 Griffin, 'The Sacred Synthesis', p. 19.

69 Falasca-Zamponi, *Fascist Spectacle*, pp. 141, 190–1; Berezin, *Making the Fascist Self*, pp. 246, 248.

70 Mabel Berezin, review of *Staging Fascism*, by Jeffrey T. Schnapp, *Journal of Modern Italian Studies*, 3(3) (1998), p. 337. Berezin is not alone in questioning the motives of Italian cultural producers under Fascism – see Walter Adamson's suspicions regarding Margherita Sarfatti, Mussolini's lover and the force behind the *novecento* movement. Walter L. Adamson, 'Avante-garde modernism and Italian Fascism: cultural politics in the era of Mussolini', *Journal of Modern Italian Studies*, 6(2) (2001), pp. 238–41, 245.

71 Griffin, 'The Sacred Synthesis', p. 18.

72 Gentile, *The Sacralization of Politics*, p. 160.

73 Gentile, *The Sacralization of Politics*, pp. ix, 98.

74 Bosworth, *The Italian Dictatorship*, p. 21, n. 50; R. J. B. Bosworth, 'Venice Between Fascism and International Tourism, 1911–45', *Modern Italy* 4(1) (1999), p. 18; Bosworth, 'Hypocrisy and Corruption in Fascist Italy', p. 377. See also Bosworth's excellent social history of the Fascist era, *Mussolini's Italy: Life under the Dictatorship, 1915–1945* (London: Allen Lane, 2005).

75 Bosworth, 'Hypocrisy and Corruption in Fascist Italy', pp. 357, 376; Bosworth, *The Italian Dictatorship*, pp. 25–6.

76 Interestingly, although Bosworth casts a wide net in his search for guilty culturalists he overlooks Günter Berghaus, who actually seems to fit the profile described by the Australian. In *Fascism and Theatre*, Berghaus writes: 'Many reports on Fascist mass meetings testify that the rituals did produce awe of, and willingness to submit to, the greater power of the Fascist system and its leader'; 'Fascist rituals could indeed be like magical rites that led to trance and possession states' – 'ecstasy and fervour', that 'canalized' into Fascist organizations and institutions'. Günter Berghaus, 'The Ritual Core of Fascist Theatre: An Anthropological Perspective', in Berghaus (ed.), *Fascism and Theatre*, pp. 51, 55–6.

77 Gentile, *The Sacralization of Politics*, pp. 98, 149; Gentile, 'Fascism in Power', pp. 143, 164–5; Gentile, 'Fascism in Italian Historiography', p. 201; Emilio Gentile, 'Fascism as Political Religion', *Journal of Contemporary History* 25(2–3) (1990), p. 248; Gentile, 'The Problem of the Party in Italian Fascism', p. 269.

78 Gentile, *The Sacralization of Politics*, p. 150.

79 Lynn M. Gunzberg, *Strangers at Home: Jews in the Italian Literary Imagination* (Berkeley: University of California Press, 1992), pp. 6, 9.

80 Steinberg, *All or Nothing*, p. 4; Zuccotti, *The Italians and the Holocaust*, p. 5; Nicola Caracciolo (ed.), *Gli ebrei e l'Italia durante la guerra 1940–45* (Rome: Bonacci editore, 1986).

81 Steinberg, *All or Nothing*, pp. 169, 213, 222–4.

82 Zuccotti, *The Italians and the Holocaust*, pp. 274, 277–8.

83 Quoted in Steinberg, *All or Nothing*, p. 6.

84 Roderick Kedward, 'Afterword: What Kind of Revisionism?', in Forgacs (ed.), *Rethinking Italian Fascism*, p. 203 (Kedward is paraphrasing the view of Leon Poliakov); Michaelis, *Mussolini and the Jews*, p. 414; Gene Bernadini, 'Anti-Semitism', in Philip Cannistraro (ed.), *Historical Dictionary of Fascist Italy* (Westport: Greenwood Press, 1982), p. 30. See also H. Stuart Hughes, *Prisoners of Hope: The Silver Age of the Italian Jews 1924–74* (Cambridge, MA: Harvard University Press, 1983), p. 14; Zimmerman, 'Introduction', p. 2.

85 Louis de Bernières, *Captain Corelli's Mandolin* (London: Minerva, 1996); Nicholas Doumanis, 'Dodecanese Nostalgia for Mussolini's Rule', *History Today* 48(2) (1998), p. 17. For the full account of the Dodecanese experience of Fascism see Nicholas Doumanis, *Myth and Memory in the Mediterranean: Remembering Fascism's Empire* (London: Macmillan, 1997). Very similar to *Captain Corelli's Mandolin* in its portrayal of 'good Italians' is Gabrielle Salvatores' 1991 Oscar-winning film *Mediterraneo*.

86 In addition to those texts referenced in the following endnotes which deal with the 'myth of the good Italian', readers are directed towards the works of Enzo Collotti, e.g. Enzo Collotti and Lutz Klinkhammer, *Il fascismo e l'Italia in guerra: una conversazione fra storia e storiografia* (Rome: Edizione Ediesse, 1996,) Alexander De Grand, e.g. *Fascist Italy and Nazi Germany*, and David Bidussa, *Il mito del bravo italiano* (Milan: Saggiatore, 1994). See also n. 2.

87 Angelo Del Boca, quoted in Bosworth, *The Italian Dictatorship*, p. 4.

88 Glenda A. Sluga, 'The Risiera di San Sabba: Fascism, Anti-Fascism and Italian Nationalism', *Journal of Modern Italian Studies* 1(3) (1996), pp. 406–10 (quote p. 406). See also Glenda Sluga, 'Italian National Identity and Fascism: Aliens, Allogenes and Assimilation on Italy's North-eastern Border', in Gino Bedani and Bruce Haddock (eds), *The Politics of Italian National Identity* (Cardiff: University of Wales Press, 2000), pp. 163–90. On anti-Slavism as an element of continuity in Italian nationalist discourse through the twentieth century see Glenda Sluga, 'Italian National Memory, National Identity and Fascism', in Bosworth and Dogliani (eds), *Italian Fascism*, pp. 178–94.

89 Caracciolo, *Gli ebrei e l'Italia durante la guerra*, p. 21.

90 See Alexander Stille, *Benevolence and Betrayal: Five Italian Jewish Families under Fascism* (London: Jonathan Cape, 1992), p. 349.

91 Michele Sarfatti, 'Fascist Italy and German Jews in South-eastern France in July 1943', *Journal of Modern Italian Studies* 3(3) (1998), pp. 318–28.

92 Gunzberg, *Strangers at Home*, pp. 282, 284

93 De Grand, *Fascist Italy and Nazi Germany*, p. 83.

94 Jonathan Dunnage, 'Facing the Past and Building for the Future', in Dunnage (ed.), *After the War*, p. 90.

95 Philip Morgan, '"The Years of Consent?" Popular Attitudes and Forms of Resistance to Fascism in Italy, 1925–1940', in Tim Kirk and Anthony McElligott (eds), *Opposing Fascism. Community, Authority and Resistance in Europe* (Cambridge: Cambridge University Press, 1999), p. 179.

96 In fact, De Felice provided no real evidence to support his own case. His argument that the 'exquisitely economic' nature of dissent in the early 1930s demonstrated working-class acceptance of Fascism is based on dubious logic given the impossibility of open political

protest. His claim that the overwhelming vote in favour of the regime in the 1934 plebiscite revealed the extent of the consensus behind Fascism is utter nonsense. What other result could seriously be expected in a one-party authoritarian state? The plebiscite tells us absolutely nothing about popular attitudes towards Fascism. Police reports are also hardly reliable indicators of levels of dissent. There were good reasons why those writing the reports should seek to play down unrest (not least to demonstrate to their superiors that they had matters under control). Equally, 'By criminalising so many activities or at least making then a matter for police surveillance and intervention, the regime created "dissenters" and inflated "dissent". Police measures hit people who, in acting as they did, probably had no intention of seeking to "subvert" the Fascist state'. Morgan, 'Popular Attitudes and Resistance to Fascism', pp. 167, 171.

97　Clark, *Modern Italy*, pp. 243, 255; Morgan, *Fascist Italy*, p. 89; Ipsen, *Dictating Demography*, pp. 118–19, 184.

98　Bosworth, *Mussolini*, p. 356; Dunnage, *Twentieth Century Italy*, pp. 117–18. A detailed account of the Italian Home Front, 1940–3, is provided by Morgan, *The Fall of Mussolini*, pp. 34–84. For a useful discussion of the Turin strikes see Tim Mason, 'The Turin Strikes of March 1943', in Jane Caplan (ed.), *Nazism, Fascism and the Working Class* (Cambridge: Cambridge University Press, 1995), pp. 274–94.

99　Bosworth, *Mussolini*, p. 348.

100　Dunnage, *Twentieth Century Italy*, p. 106; Farrell, *Mussolini*, p. 239.

101　G. Melis (1993), quoted in Foot, *Modern Italy*, p. 101.

102　Steinberg, *All or Nothing*, pp. 209–10.

103　The success of the cult of Mussolini is vividly demonstrated by Barzini:

> 'I remember him [Mussolini] one day, during military manoeuvres in the Langhe [in southern Piedmont], in 1932, walking through a vast bare plain of yellow stubble surrounded by distant green hills, trees and the steeples of village churches. Peasants came running from all sides, red-faced, panting, to see him, touch him, shout to him. One of his secretaries followed him with a leather envelope, the exact size of thousand-lire bills, to hand out banknotes to the more miserable with the gesture of a gambler dealing out cards. Soon enough Mussolini was leading a parade of thousands of frenzied and gesticulating followers. He showed no expression on his face except the usual wooden determination'.

Barzini, *The Italians*, pp. 169–70.

104　See n. 20.

105　De Grazia, *The Culture of Consent*, p. 20.

106　Bosworth, 'Hypocrisy and Corruption in Fascist Italy', pp. 371–5. See also Bosworth, *Mussolini's Italy*. According to a popular joke of the time, the initials PNF stood for 'per necessità famigliare' ('for family reasons').

107　Stone, 'Challenging Cultural Categories', p. 189.

108　See, for example, David Forgacs, 'Nostra patria: Revisions of the Risorgimento in the Cinema, 1925–52', in Ascoli and Henneberg (eds), *Making and Remaking Italy*, pp. 257–76; Cannistraro, 'Mussolini's Cultural Revolution'.

Chapter 7 Italian politics from the fall of Mussolini to the rise of Berlusconi

1　Jörg Seisselberg, 'Conditions of Success and Political Problems of a "Media-mediated Personality-party": The Case of *Forza Italia*', *West European Politics* 19(4) (1996), pp. 715–43.

2　Leonardo Morlino, 'Crisis of Parties and Change of Party System in Italy', *Party Politics* 2(1) (1996), pp. 17–18; Richard Katz and Piero Ignazi, 'Introduction', in Richard Katz and Piero Ignazi (eds), *Italian Politics: The Year of the Tycoon* (Boulder: Westview Press, 1996), p. 22.

3　Quoted in Charles F. Delzell, 'Renzo De Felice: An Overview', *Italian Quarterly* 36(141–42) (1999), p. 20.

4 Clark, *Modern Italy*, p. 310.

5 Quoted in Oreste Massari, 'La Resistenza', in Gianfranco Pasquino (ed.), *La politica italiana: dizionario critico 1945–95* (Rome-Bari: Laterza, 1995), p. 515.

6 Ginsborg, *A History of Contemporary Italy*, p. 377.

7 Putnam, Leonardi and Nanetti (1981), quoted in Roberto Leonardi and Douglas Wertman, *Italian Christian Democracy* (London: Macmillan, 1989), p. 185.

8 Leonardi and Wertman, *Italian Christian Democracy*, p. 186.

9 Donald Sassoon, 'The 1987 Elections and the PCI', in Roberto Leonardi and Piergiorgio Corbetta (eds), *Italian Politics: A Review* (London: Pinter, 1989), p. 143.

10 Ginsborg, *A History of Contemporary Italy*, p. 419.

11 Morlino, 'Crisis of Parties', p. 7.

12 For example, Mark Gilbert, 'Italy's Third Fall', *Journal of Modern Italian Studies* 2(2) (1997), p. 224. Gilbert suggests that 'the political elite's misunderstanding of the mood of the country was the immediate cause of Italy's systemic crisis: with less inebriated hands on the tiller, the ship might never have run onto the rocks'.

13 Martin J. Bull, 'The Great Failure? The Democratic Party of the Left in Italy's Transition', in Stephen Gundle and Simon Parker (eds), *The New Italian Republic: From the Fall of the Berlin Wall to Berlusconi* (London: Routledge, 1996), p. 159; Gianfranco Pasquino, 'Political Development', in McCarthy (ed.), *Italy Since 1945*, p. 82; Paul Ginsborg, 'Explaining Italy's Crisis', in Gundle and Parker (eds), *The New Italian Republic*, p. 35. One of the most forthright and earliest formulations of this argument was advanced by Angelo Codevilla in 1992: 'as soon as they [the Italians] were able to junk the system safely, they set about the task with gusto'. Quoted in Gilbert, 'Italy's Third Fall', p. 222.

14 Donald Sassoon, '*Tangentopoli* or the Democratization of Corruption: Considerations on the End of Italy's First Republic', *Journal of Modern Italian Studies* 1(1) (1995), p. 130.

15 Ginsborg, 'Explaining Italy's Crisis', p. 22; Sassoon, '*Tangentopoli* or the Democratization of Corruption', pp. 136–7.

16 Ginsborg, 'Explaining Italy's Crisis', p. 30.

17 Nick Carter, 'Italy: The Demise of the Post-war Partyocracy', in John Kenneth White and Philip John Davies (eds), *Political Parties and the Collapse of the Old Orders* (Albany: State University of New York Press, 1998), pp. 79–80.

18 David Nelken, 'A Legal Revolution? The Judges and *Tangentopoli*', in Gundle and Parker (eds), *The New Italian Republic*, pp. 194–7; Mark Gilbert, *The Italian Revolution: The End of Politics, Italian Style?* (Boulder: Westview Press, 1995), p. 128.

19 Ginsborg, 'Explaining Italy's Crisis', p. 27.

20 Guido Neppi Modona, 'Tangentopoli e mani pulite: dopo le indagni, i processi', in Paul Ginsborg (ed.), *Stato dell'Italia* (Milan: il Saggiatore/Mondadori, 1994), p. 527.

21 Vito Marini Caferra, 'La corruzione', in Pasquino (ed.), *La politica italiana*, p. 411.

22 Neppi Modona, 'Tangentopoli e mani pulite', p. 528.

23 Gilbert, 'Italy's Third Fall', p. 224.

24 Gilbert, *The Italian Revolution*, p. 159.

25 For a discussion of these ideas see Silvana Patriarca, 'Italian Neopatriotism: Debating National Identity in the 1990s', *Modern Italy*, 6(1) (2001), pp. 24, 28–30.

26 The quote is from the television documentary *I giorni della nostra storia*, (Rai, 1974), quoted in Simona Monticelli, 'National Identity and the Representation of Italy at War: The Case of *Combat Film*', *Modern Italy* 5(2) (2000), p. 139.

27 Pietro Scoppola, *25 aprile. Liberazione*, (Turin: Einaudi, 1995). An extended extract from the introduction to Scoppola's work, from which this quote is taken, is included in Philip Cooke, *The Resistance: An Anthology* (Manchester: Manchester University Press, 1999), pp. 175–80 (quote from p. 177).

28 J. E. Miller, 'Who Chopped Down that Cherry Tree? The Italian Resistance in History and Politics, 1945–1998', *Journal of Modern Italian Studies* 4(1) (1999), p. 39.

29 For example, Guido Quazza, a former partisan and a leading left-wing historian of the Resistance, had for many years queried a number of the PCI's claims. Quazza argued the

majority of partisans, including those from the working class, were 'existential' rather than political anti-Fascists, i.e. were not committed to any political party or programme and had not always opposed Fascism. In these cases anti-Fascism was not spontaneous but a process, a gradual realization there were alternatives to Fascism. Guido Quazza, 'La guerra partigiana: proposte di ricerca', in Francesca Ferratini Tosi, Gaetano Grasini, Massimo Legnani (eds), *L'Italia nella seconda mondiale e nella Resistenza* (Milan: Franco Angeli, 1988). An extended extract from this work is included in Cooke, *The Resistance*, pp. 44–51.

30 Quoted in Roland Sarti, 'De Felice's Mussolini and the Historiography of Fascism', *Italian Quarterly* 36(141–2) (1999), p. 51.

31 Claudio Pavone, 'Le tre guerre: patriottica, civile e di classe', in Massimo Legnani and F. Vendramini (eds), *Guerra, Guerra di Liberazione, Guerra Civile*, (Milan: Franco Angeli, 1990), pp. 35–6.

32 Scoppola, quoted in Cooke (ed.), *The Resistance*, 179.

33 Miller, 'Who Chopped Down that Cherry Tree?', p. 49.

34 De Felice, *Rosso e Nero*, pp. 31–3, 35, 44, 45–6.

35 De Felice, *Rosso e Nero*, pp. 48–53, 57, 59–60.

36 De Felice, *Breve storia*, p. 124.

37 De Felice, *Rosso e Nero*, p. 61.

38 De Felice, *Rosso e Nero*, pp. 40, 107–8, 109, 114–16, 122–5, 133.

39 Ernesto Galli della Loggia, *La morte della patria. La crisi dell'idea di nazione tra Resistenza, antifascismo e Repubblica* (Rome-Bari: Laterza, 1996), pp. 22, 40–4, 62–3, 72–3; Ruth Ben-Ghiat, Luciano Cafagna, Ernesto Galli della Loggia, Carl Ipsen and David I. Kertzer, 'History as it Really Wasn't: The Myths of Italian Historiography', *Journal of Modern Italian Studies* 6(3) (2001), pp. 402–19; Patriarca, 'Italian Neopatriotism', p. 24.

40 Romolo Gobbi, *Il mito della Resistenza* (Milan: Rizzoli, 1992). An extended extract from this work, from which this quote is taken, is in Cooke (ed.), *The Resistance*, pp. 172–5 (quote from p. 173).

41 John Hooper, 'Mussolini Wasn't that Bad, Says Berlusconi', *Guardian*, 12 September 2003.

42 Gian Enrico Rusconi, *Resistenza e postfascismo* (Bologna: il Mulino, 1995), p. 7. Andrea Mammone has recently gone further: 'Nowadays, it is no longer compulsory to be anti-Fascist in order to be genuinely democratic'. Andrea Mammone, 'A Daily Revision of the Past: Fascism, Anti-Fascism, and Memory in Contemporary Italy', *Modern Italy* 11(2) (2006), p. 216.

43 De Felice originally made the comment in an interview for the *Corriere della Sera*, 27 December 1987. Quoted in Borden W. Painter junior, 'Renzo De Felice and the Historiography of Italian Fascism', *American Historical Review* 95(2) (1990), p. 403, n. 54.

44 Mack Smith, 'Mussolini: Reservations about Renzo De Felice's Biography', p. 209.

45 De Felice, *Rosso e Nero*, p. 76.

46 Ugo Caffaz, quoted in Alexander Stille, 'A Disturbing Echo: Anti-Semitism, Fifty Years after Mussolini's Infamous Racial Laws Took Effect, is an Issue Again', *The Atlantic* 263(2) (1989), p. 20.

47 On the help given to Allied fugitives, see Roger Absalom, 'Allied Escapers and the *Contadini* in Occupied Italy (1943–5), *Journal of Modern Italian Studies* 10(4) (2005), pp. 413–25. On 'civil resistance' in German-occupied Italy see Anna Bravo, 'Armed and Unarmed: Struggles without Weapons in Europe and in Italy', *Journal of Modern Italian Studies* 10(4) (2005), pp. 468–84.

48 Massari, 'La Resistenza', p. 509; Absalom, *Italy since 1800*, pp. 173–4; Clark, *Modern Italy*, p. 315; Guido Quazza, 'The Politics of the Italian Resistance', in Stuart J. Woolf (ed.), *The Rebirth of Italy 1943–50* (Harlow: Longman, 1972), p. 28.

49 Claudio Pavone, 'The General Problem of the Continuity of the State and the Legacy of Fascism', in Dunnage (ed.), *After the War*, p. 11.

50 Pavone, 'The General Problem of the Continuity of the State', p. 11; Claudio Pavone, *Conoscere la Resistenza* (Milan: Unicopoli, 1994). An extended extract from this work, from which the latter quote is taken, is in Cooke, *The Resistance*, pp. 64–9 (quote p. 67).

51 Piero Fassino, quoted in Miller, 'Who Chopped Down that Cherry Tree?', p. 39.
52 Alexander De Grand, review of *Italian Fascism: History, Memory and Representation*, by
   R. J. B. Bosworth and P. Dogliani (eds), *Journal of Modern Italian Studies* 4(3) (1999),
   pp. 456–7.
53 Ginsborg, *A History of Contemporary Italy*, p. 47.
54 Pavone, 'The General Problem of the Continuity of the State', p. 15; Simone Neri Serneri,
   'A Past to be Thrown Away? Politics and History in the Italian Resistance', *Contemporary
   European History* 4(3) 1995, p. 380.
55 Franco Ferraresi, *Threats to Democracy: The Radical Right in Italy after the War* (Princeton:
   Princeton University Press, 1996), pp. 17–18; Pavone, 'The General Problem of the
   Continuity of the State', pp. 17–18.
56 Ferraresi, *Threats to Democracy*, pp. 18–20, 209, n. 16.
57 Ginsborg, *A History of Contemporary Italy*, p. 418; Leornardi and Wertman, *Italian Christian
   Democracy*, p. 245.
58 Ginsborg, 'Explaining Italy's Crisis', pp. 27–32.
59 *Panorama*, 28 August 1993, 5 August 1994, 16 September 1994.
60 For more on Berlusconi's Italy see: Tobias Jones, *The Dark Heart of Italy: Travels Through
   Time and Space Across Italy* (London: Faber and Faber, 2003); Paul Ginsborg, *Silvio
   Berlusconi: Television, Power and Patrimony* (New York: Verso, 2004). The (absurd) claim
   made by Berlusconi and others on the Right that the *mani pulite* investigations were
   no less than an attempted left-wing coup is repeated in Stanton H. Burnett and Luca
   Mantovani, *The Italian Guillotine: Operation Clean Hands and the Overthrow of Italy's First
   Republic* (Lanham: Rowman and Littlefield Publishers, 1998). When Berlusconi became
   Prime Minister for the third time in April 2008 it was at the head of a new political
   party, Il popolo della libertà (People of Freedom Party, PDL), incorporating both Forza
   Italia and Alleanza nazionale, as well as a number of small centre-right parties.

Chapter 8 The post-war Italian economy

1 Vera Zamagni, 'Evolution of the Economy', in McCarthy (ed.), *Italy since 1945*, p. 42.
2 Zamagni, 'Evolution of the Economy', p. 43; Nicola Rossi and Gianni Toniolo, 'Italy',
  in Nicholas Crafts and Gianni Toniolo (eds), *Economic Growth in Europe since 1945*
  (Cambridge: Cambridge University Press, 1996), p. 427; Luigi Federico Signorini, 'Italy's
  Economy: An Introduction', *Daedalus* 130(2) (2001), p. 68.
3 Carlo D'Adda and Bruno Salituro, 'Le politiche economiche', in Pasquino (ed.), *La politica
  italiana*, p. 480.
4 For a useful survey of these changes to Italian agriculture see Foot, *Modern Italy*, pp. 113–30.
5 Ginsborg, *A History of Contemporary Italy*, p. 216; Paolo Carnazza, Alessandro Innocenti
  and Alessandro Vercelli, 'Small Firms and Manufacturing Employment', in Andrea Boltho,
  Alessandro Vercelli and Hiroshi Yoshikawa (eds), *Comparing Economic Systems: Italy and
  Japan* (Basingstoke: Palgrave, 2001), p. 160; Zamagni, 'Evolution of the Economy', p. 56.
6 Zamagni, *The Economic History of Italy*, p. 321; Rossi and Toniolo, 'Italy', p. 439; Nicholas
  Crafts and Gianni Toniolo, 'Postwar Growth: An Overview', in Crafts and Toniolo (eds),
  Economic Growth in Europe Since 1945, p. 4.
7 Cohen and Federico, *The Growth of the Italian Economy*, p. 87. Figures are from Rossi
  and Toniolo, 'Italy', pp. 441–2; Alan Milward, *The European Rescue of the Nation-State*
  (London: Routledge, 2nd edn, 2000), p. 230; M. V. Posner and S. J. Woolf, *Italian
  Public Enterprise* (London: Gerald Duckworth, 1967), p. 113; Zamagni, 'Evolution of the
  Economy', p. 49; Dunnage, *Twentieth Century Italy*, p. 149. Ginsborg provides a telling
  example of the great leap forward in industrial productivity during the 'economic
  miracle': in 1947, the washing machine manufacturer Candy produced one machine per
  day; in 1967, one machine every fifteen seconds. Ginsborg, *A History of Contemporary
  Italy*, p. 215.

8 Vera Zamagni, 'The Italian "Economic Miracle" Revisited: New Markets and American Technology', in E. di Nolfo (ed.), *Power in Europe II. Britain, France, Germany and Italy and the Origins of the EEC, 1952–57* (Berlin and New York: Walter de Gruyter, 1992), pp. 198–9, 205; Forgacs, *Italian Culture in the Industrial Era*, p. 125; Ginsborg, *A History of Contemporary Italy*, pp. 214, 239.

9 Milward, *The European Rescue of the Nation-State*, pp. 230, 236; Zamagni, 'The Italian "Economic Miracle" Revisited', p. 201; Cohen and Federico, *The Growth of the Italian Economy*, p. 87.

10 Rossi and Toniolo, 'Italy', p. 442.

11 Nationalized industry was quite rare in Italy after 1945. In most cases of public ownership, the state owned a controlling share in companies rather than the company outright.

12 Posner and Woolf, *Italian Public Enterprise*, p. 14; Cohen and Federico, *The Growth of the Italian Economy*, p. 94.

13 Clark, *Modern Italy*, p. 358.

14 Russell King, *Italy* (London: Harper and Row, 1987), p. 47.

15 In 1962, 1,848 working days per 1,000 workers were lost because of strike action, seven times the EEC average; in 1969, 3,013 working days per 1,000 workers were lost through strikes, 13 times the EEC average. Sergio Ricossa, 'Italy 1920–1970', in Carlo M. Cipolla (ed.), *The Fontana Economic History of Europe. Contemporary Economies, Part One* (Glasgow: Collins/Fontana, 1976), p. 313.

16 Zamagni, *The Economic History of Italy*, p. 339; D'Adda and Salituro, 'Le politiche economiche', p. 489.

17 Zamagni, 'Evolution of the Economy', p. 44; Fabrizio Barca, Katsuhito Iwai, Ugo Pagano, Sandro Trento, 'Divergences in Corporate Governance Models: The Role of Institutional Shocks', in Boltho et al., *Comparing Economic Systems*, pp. 35–6. The historical roots of the industrial districts are neatly summarized in Franco Bianchini, 'The Third Italy: Model or Myth?', *Ekistics*, v. 350–1, 1991, pp. 337–8.

18 Bevilacqua, *Breve storia dell'Italia meridionale*, p. 120.

19 Amongst the major privatizations of the 1990s were the banks Credito Italiano (1993) and Banca Commerciale Italiano (1994), sold off by the IRI, the investment lender, the IMI (1994–6), Telecom Italia (1997), the oil and gas company, ENI (1995–8), and the electricity company ENEL (1999). In 2000, even the IRI was closed down.

20 The problems of long-term, female and youth unemployment were, of course, particularly acute in the south.

21 Yuji Genda, Maria Grazia Pazienza and Marcello Signorelli, 'Labour Market Performance and Job Creation' in Boltho et al., *Comparing Economic Systems*, pp. 138–9; Luigi Federico Signorini and Ignazio Visco, *L'economia italiana* (Bologna: il Mulino, 1997), pp. 26–30.

22 Milward estimates that Marshall Aid added an extra 5.3% to GNP in 1948–9. Over the period covered by the Marshall Plan (1948–52), ERP funds accounted for approximately 2% of Italian GNP. Alan Milward, *The Reconstruction of Western Europe, 1945–51* (London: Routledge, 1984), pp. 102, 480; Ginsborg, *A History of Contemporary Italy*, p. 159.

23 Ginsborg, *A History of Contemporary Italy*, p. 159; Marcello de Cecco, 'Economic Policy in the Reconstruction Period 1945–51', in Woolf (ed.), *The Rebirth of Italy*, pp. 178–80; Donald Sassoon, *Contemporary Italy: Politics, Economy and Society since 1945* (London: Longman, 2nd edn, 1997), pp. 24–5.

24 Vera Zamagni, 'Betting on the Future: The Reconstruction of Italian Industry, 1946–1952', in J. Becker and F. Knipping (eds), *Power in Europe? Great Britain, France, Italy and Germany in a Postwar World, 1945–50* (Berlin and New York: Walter de Gruyter, 1986), pp. 291–3; Zamagni, *The Economic History of Italy*, pp. 327, 330; Zamagni, 'Evolution of the Economy', p. 45; Federico and Giannetti, 'Italy: Stalling and Surpassing', pp. 136–7.

25 Zamagni, 'Betting on the Future', pp. 289, 294; Ricossa, 'Italy', pp. 293–4; George Hildebrand, *Growth and Structure in the Economy of Modern Italy* (Cambridge, MA: Harvard University Press, 1965), p. 43; Andrea Boltho, 'Convergence, Competitiveness and the

Exchange Rate' in Crafts and Toniolo (eds), *Economic Growth in Europe since 1945*, p. 118; Federico Romero, 'Migration as an Issue in European Interdependence and Integration: The Case of Italy', in Alan Milward et al., *The Frontier of National Sovereignty: History and Theory 1945–1992* (London: Routledge, 1993), pp. 33–58.

26 The state, of course, did provide funds to industry, but predominantly to large firms.

27 E. F. Denison (1967) in Derek H. Aldcroft, *The European Economy 1914–2000* (London and New York: Routledge, 4th edn, 2001), p. 139.

28 Rossi and Toniolo, 'Italy', p. 441; Barry Eichengreen, 'Economy', in Mary Fulbrook (ed.), *Europe since 1945* (Oxford: Oxford University Press, 2001), pp. 113–14.

29 Massimo di Matteo and Hiroshi Yoshikawa, 'Economic Growth: The Role of Demand', in Boltho et al., *Comparing Economic Systems*, p. 46.

30 In addition to the stable macro-economic conditions created in the wake of the *linea Einaudi*, reference is often made to the fact that the trades union movement was divided and weak, DC political control was firmly established and the PCI did not object to the economic development of the country, expecting the inherent contradictions of capitalism to make themselves quickly apparent. See, for example, Di Matteo and Yoshikawa, 'Economic Growth', p. 54.

31 As Paul Hoffman, the American in charge of the European Cooperation Administration (ECA) established to administer Marshall funds, commented in his memoirs: 'They [the West Europeans] learned that this [the United States] is the land of full shelves and bulging shops, made possible by high productivity and good wages, and that its prosperity may be emulated elsewhere by those who will work towards it'. David W. Ellwood, *Rebuilding Europe: Western Europe, America and Postwar Reconstruction* (London and New York: Longman, 1992), p. 227. See also Rossi and Toniolo, 'Italy', pp. 441–2; Zamagni, 'The Italian "Economic Miracle" Revisited', pp. 204–5, 209–15; Cohen and Federico, *The Growth of the Italian Economy*, pp. 91–2; Ginsborg, *A History of Contemporary Italy*, p. 213; Federico and Giannetti, 'Italy: Stalling and Surpassing', p. 138.

32 K. J. Allen and A. A. Stevenson, *An Introduction to the Italian Economy* (London: Martin Robertson, 1974), pp. 59, 62; Cohen and Federico, *The Growth of the Italian Economy*, p. 93; Di Matteo and Yoshikawa, 'Economic Growth', p. 55; Zamagni, 'The Italian "Economic Miracle" Revisited', pp. 208, 216, 224–5.

33 Posner and Woolf, *Italian Public Enterprise*, p. 13.

34 Rossi and Toniolo, 'Italy', p. 441; Zamagni, 'The Italian "Economic Miracle" Revisited', pp. 201, 205.

35 Zamagni, 'The Italian "Economic Miracle" Revisited', pp. 202–5.

36 Posner and Woolf, *Italian Public Enterprise*, p. 14.

37 B. Hansen (1969) in Milward, *The European Rescue of the Nation-State*, p. 34. Milward considers 'The calculation is necessarily a rather narrowly based one. It cannot take into account for example the effect of high and predictable levels of government expenditure on mood and the climate of investment... When government consumption and expenditure took up so much larger a share of national income, the psychological influence of the government's general stance towards the economy could be of great consequence (p. 34).'

38 Cohen and Federico, *The Growth of the Italian Economy*, p. 100.

39 Guido Rey, 'Italy', in A. Boltho (ed.), *The European Economy: Growth and Crisis* (Oxford: Oxford University Press, 1982), p. 511; Cohen and Federico, *The Growth of the Italian Economy*, p. 93; Allen and Stevenson, *An Introduction to the Italian Economy*, p. 63; King, *Italy*, p. 44; Ginsborg, *A History of Contemporary Italy*, p. 214; Zamagni, 'The Italian "Economic Miracle" Revisited', pp. 208, 216.

40 Di Matteo and Yoshikawa, 'Economic Growth', pp. 43, 60; Rossi and Toniolo, 'Italy', p. 443.

41 See Aldcroft, *The European Economy*, pp. 194–8, for a general discussion of the impact of the end of Bretton Woods and the oil crisis on the west European economy.

42 Fabrizio Barca, *Il capitalismo italiano: storia di un compromesso senza riforme* (Rome: Donzelli editore, 1999), p. 63.

43 Barca, *Il capitalismo italiano*, p. 64.

44 Barca, *Il capitalismo italiano*, p. 34.

45 Barca, *Il capitalismo italiano*, p. 61.
46 Barca, *Il capitalismo italiano*, pp. 5–65; Barca et al., 'Divergences in Corporate Governance Models', p. 32.
47 Barca, *Il capitalismo italiano*, pp. 14–22, 57–8, 64–5.
48 Pyramiding is a system of corporate ownership which allows the controlling shareholder in one firm to exercise control over other firms without having to own more than a bare majority of shares in those firms (in its most basic form, investor A owns a controlling stake (>50% of shares) in Firm B, Firm B owns a controlling stake in Firm C which in turn owns a similar percentage of shares in Firm D, and so on). As Dermot McCann explains in 'The "Anglo-American" Model, Privatization and the Transformation of Private Capitalism in Italy', *Modern Italy*, 5(1) (2000), p. 51:

> By spreading the voting rights of minority shareholdings over a large number of firms and concentrating those of the entrepreneurs in the company at the top of the pyramid, this model allows the entrepreneurs to obtain control over the greatest possible amount of other people's capital with the smallest possible amount of their own. Through the manipulation of this mechanism, families have been able to raise funds on the stock market by issuing shares in a swathe of firms without losing control of them. It has been estimated that in the case of the Agnellis [the owners of FIAT], the family controls approximately 16 units of other investors' capital for every one unit it has itself invested.

49 Cross-ownership of shares protects the interests of the dominant shareholder in a pyramidal group. 'If, for instance, 12 corporations get together and hold 5 per cent of each others' shares (but their own), simple arithmetic [(12−1) × 0.05 = 55 per cent] tells us that a majority block of each corporations' shares can be effectively insulated. These 12 corporations would indeed become their own owners, at least as a group, and be immune from any take-over attempts.' Barca et al., 'Divergences in Corporate Governance Models', p. 18. In Italy since the 1960s, the major family-owned firms, with the financial assistance of the big Italian banks and through the good offices of Italy's one great merchant bank, Mediobanca, have bought each other's shares for precisely this purpose.
50 Barca, *Il capitalismo italiano*, pp. 87–91, 94.
51 Barca, *Il capitalismo italiano*, p. 106; Barca et al., 'Divergences in Corporate Governance Models', p. 33.
52 Fabrizio Barca and Sandro Trento, 'La parabola delle partecipazioni statali: una missione tradita', in Fabrizio Barca (ed.), *Storia del capitalismo italiano dal dopoguerra a oggi* (Rome: Donzelli editore, 1997), p. 217. A similar critique of state intervention can be found in Posner and Woolf, *Italian Public Enterprise*, Chapter 7. Posner and Woolf argue that though money was spent on long-term development projects, most notably in the south, actual policy varied from year to year, depending on the whims of ministers and the short-term needs of the government. 'The Italian public sector', they conclude (p. 128), was 'a machine without a driver. It is a machine of considerable potential, which has achieved some notable successes, but which remains above all a machine with little conscious direction'. See also Ginsborg, *A History of Contemporary Italy*, pp. 284–5.
53 Rey, 'Italy', pp. 516–18; Michele Salvati, 'Dal miracolo economico alla moneta unica europea', in G. Sabbatucci and V. Vidotto (eds), *Storia d'Italia. Vol. 6. L'Italia contemporanea dal 1963 a oggi* (Rome-Bari: Laterza, 1999), pp. 324–5, 336–7; Ginsborg, *A History of Contemporary Italy*, pp. 281–3; Rossi and Toniolo, 'Italy', p. 443.
54 Sassoon, *Contemporary Italy*, p. 81; Silvio Lanaro (1992) quoted in Rossi and Toniolo, 'Italy', p. 448; Salvati, 'Dal miracolo economico', p. 386.
55 Giulio Sapelli, *L'Italia di fine secolo. Economia e classi dirigente: un capitalismo senza mercato* (Venice: Marsilio editore, 1998), pp. 14–15. For a scathing attack on state subsidies and bail-outs in the 1970s see Federico and Giannetti, 'Italy: Stalling and Surpassing', pp. 141–2.
56 Sapelli, *L'Italia di fine secolo*, p. 15; Rossi and Toniolo, 'Italy', p. 449.
57 Vincent della Sala, 'Hollowing Out and Hardening the State: European Integration and the Italian Economy', *West European Politics* 20(1) (1997), p. 28.

58 Sassoon, *Contemporary Italy*, p. 81; Federico and Giannetti, 'Italy: Stalling and Surpassing', p. 143. Writing in 1984, Franco Bonelli was highly critical of the state's failure to invest in information technology:

> From this standpoint, it is natural to make a comparison with what was achieved at other times, specifically thanks to state intervention, in the fields of iron and steel and electricity. We cannot avoid the question of what destiny would have overtaken Italy if, at the end of the nineteenth century and the beginning of the present one, the attention of the ruling classes had remained concentrated on the traditional sectors which had led the way in the first English Industrial Revolution, instead of paying attention to the emerging ones, more or less "heavy" and more or less capital-intensive, even when it seemed that the costs of providing them were enormously high.

Franco Bonelli, 'Stato ed economia nell'industrializzazione Italiana dale originial "Welfare state"' (1984), available in translation in Federico, *The Economic Development of Italy since* 1870, pp. 626–33 (extract p. 633).

59 Rossi and Toniolo, 'Italy', p. 449; Bevilacqua, *Breve storia dell'Italia meridionale*, p. 120; Sassoon, *Contemporary Italy*, p. 81.

60 McCann, 'The "Anglo-American" Model', p. 47. The turn-around in the fortunes of the IRI under the direction of former economics professor, later Italian Prime Minister and EU Commission President Romano Prodi, was remarkable. In 1980, it sustained losses of 2,200b lire, equivalent to 6% of national income. David Edge and Valerio Lintner, *Contemporary European Economics, Politics and Society* (Harlow: Prentice Hall, 1996), p. 179.

61 'Whenever one stepped into the field of public services, one sank immediately into a bog.' Paul Ginsborg, *Italy and its Discontents: Family, Civil Society, State, 1980–2001* (New York and London: Penguin, 2003), p. 10. Mail took weeks rather than days to reach its destination., Telecom Italia took on average more than five months to connect new subscribers, Italian railways employed a staggering 100 workers per kilometre of rail track (twice that of France). Pierella Paci, 'Italy', in David A. Dyker (ed.) *The National Economies of Europe* (London and New York: Longman, 1992), pp. 91–3.

62 Rossi and Toniolo, 'Italy', p. 450 (see also pp. 429, 446).

63 Rossi and Toniolo, 'Italy', p. 449; Sassoon, *Contemporary* Italy, p. 77.

64 Sabino Cassese, 'Hypotheses on the Italian Administrative System', *West European Politics* 16(3) (1993), p. 326; Ginsborg, *A History of Contemporary Italy*, p. 423; Della Sala, 'Hollowing Out and Hardening the State', p. 27.

65 Zamagni, 'Evolution of the Economy', p. 53.

66 Clark, *Modern Italy*, p. 394.

67 McCann, 'The Anglo-American Model', p. 49.

68 Pasquino, 'Political Development', pp. 80–1.

69 Cassese estimates that of the 600,000 new recruits to the civil service between 1973 and 1990, 350,000 were employed without having taken the requisite entrance exams – in other words, they were found positions through family ties and political affiliations. The majority of these came from the south where diminishing opportunities for graduate employment in either industry or the professions left open only a career in public administration. According to Cassese, the 'southernization' of the civil service further undermined the efficiency of the public sector. First, it created imbalances (too many staff in southern offices, too few in the north). Second, it led to an exponential growth in the number of posts, since in the south 'the level of importance of an official is not indicated by responsibilities, but by the number of subordinates which he or she commands'. Third, it produced a new generation of dissatisfied and demotivated public employees 'happy to have found a "place"...unhappy because...[they] are part of a machine that does not work; and since there are no other openings there will be no chance of going anywhere else'. Fourth and perhaps most significantly, it produced a civil service 'characterized by the values typical of the less developed and less industrial south, which favours...the diffusion of a "possessive" attitude towards the office'. Cassese, 'Hypotheses on the Italian Administrative System', pp. 319–20, 323–5.

70 Signorini and Visco, *L'economia italiana*, p. 81.

71 Lidia Greco, 'Institutional and Industrial Changes in the Italian South: The Case of Brindisi', *Modern Italy* 8(2) (2003), pp. 192–3; Fabrizio Barca, 'New Trends and the Policy Shift in the Italian Mezzogiorno', *Daedalus* 130(2) (2001), pp. 97–8.

72 Bevilacqua notes that in just 25 years (1950–75), family incomes virtually tripled, consumption per capita more than doubled, life expectancy increased by more than a third (49 to 68 years), infant mortality rates fell by three-quarters (82–20.6 per thousand), the average height of southern male conscripts rose by 4.7 cm, the proportion of southerners holding a degree increased from 1% to 2.6% (and those with a school-leaving certificate or a secondary school certificate rose from 3.32% and 6.21% to 10% and 21% respectively) and illiteracy rates dropped from 24% to 11%. These trends continued over the next decade or so. Bevilacqua, *Breve storia dell'Italia meridionale*, pp. 108, 116–18, 121. See also Piero Bevilacqua, 'New and Old in the Southern Question', *Modern Italy* 1(2) (1996), p. 89.

73 Signorini and Visco, *L'economia italiana*, pp. 96–7.

74 Bevilacqua, *Breve storia dell'Italia meridionale*, p. 122; Ginsborg, *Italy and its Discontents*, p. 22; Bodo and Sestito (1991) quoted in Zamagni, *The Economic History of Italy*, p. 372, n. 89 (see also p. 374); Robert Leonardi, 'Regional Development in Italy: Social Capital and the Mezzogiorno', *Oxford Review of Economic Policy* 11(2) (1995), pp. 167, 170–2; Salvati, 'Dal miracolo economico', pp. 420–1.

75 Bevilacqua, *Breve storia dell'Italia meridionale*, p. 102. See also Ginsborg, *A History of Contemporary Italy*, p. 162. In the late 1960s, the Italian economist Augusto Graziani argued that post-war economic dualism was a direct consequence of trade liberalization. For discussion of his thesis, see Sassoon, *Contemporary Italy*, pp. 29–30; Allen and Stevenson, *An Introduction to the Italian Economy*, pp. 67–8.

76 Ginsborg, *A History of Contemporary Italy*, p. 220; Zamagni, *The Economic History of Italy*, p. 373; Bevilacqua, *Breve storia dell'Italia meridionale*, p. 112; Sassoon, *Contemporary Italy*, p. 279.

77 Sassoon, *Contemporary Italy*, p. 83; Bevilacqua, *Breve storia dell'Italia meridionale*, p. 123.

78 Ginsborg, *A History of Contemporary Italy*, p. 233; Sassoon, *Contemporary Italy*, p. 50; John L. Harper, 'Italy and the World since 1945', in McCarthy (ed.), *Italy since 1945*, pp. 103–4; Zamagni, *The Economic History of Italy*, pp. 346–9.

79 Sassoon, *Contemporary Italy*, p. 33; Saul Engelbourg and Gustav Schachter, 'Two "Souths"': The United States and Italy since the 1860s', *Journal of European Economic History* 15(3) (1986), p. 581; Zamagni, 'Evolution of the Economy', p. 65; Zamagni, *The Economic History of Italy*, pp. 371–2; Bevilacqua, *Breve storia dell'Italia meridionale*, pp. 104–5; Greco, 'Institutional and Industrial Changes in the Italian South', p. 188.

80 Signorini, 'Italy's Economy' pp. 85–6. See also Barca, 'New Trends', p. 101.

81 Percy Allum, 'Italian Society Transformed', in McCarthy (ed.), *Italy since 1945*, pp. 37–8; Bevilacqua, *Breve storia dell'Italia meridionale*, pp. 121–2.

82 Luciano Cafagna, *Nord e sud. Non fare a pezzi l'unità d'Italia* (Venice: Marsilio editori, 1994); Edward C. Banfield, *The Moral Basis of a Backward Society* (Glencoe, IL: The Free Press, 1958); Leonardi, 'Regional Development in Italy', (quote from p. 170); Robert D. Putnam, *Making Democracy Work: Civic Traditions in Modern Italy* (Princeton: Princeton University Press, 1993). Diego Gambetta, *The Sicilian Mafia: The Business of Private Protection* (Cambridge, MA: Harvard University Press, 1993).

83 Rossi and Toniolo, 'Italy' pp. 443–5; Zamagni, 'Evolution of the Economy', pp. 50, 52; Clark, *Modern Italy*, pp. 377–9; Genda, Pazienza and Signorelli, 'Labour Market Performance and Job Creation', p. 152; Rey, 'Italy', pp. 518–19; Signorini, 'Italy's Economy', p. 80.

84 Cassese, 'Hypotheses on the Italian Administrative System', pp. 323, 326 (see also n. 69); Sapelli, *L'Italia di fine secolo*, p. 15; Sassoon, *Contemporary Italy*, p. 84; Zamagni, 'Evolution of the Economy', p. 66.

85 Zamagni, *The Economic History of Italy*, p. 354. See also Sebastiano Brusco and Sergio Paba, 'Per una storia dei distretti industriali italiani dal secondo dopoguerra agli anni novanta', in Barca (ed.), *Storia del capitalismo italiano*, p. 267.

86 This author has seen other estimates for the early 1990s that range from 'at least 120' to 238. Foot, *Modern Italy*, p. 142; Brusco and Paba, 'Per una storia dei distretti industriali italiani', pp. 280, 287. The problem is one of definition; the number of industrial districts varies according to the eligibility criteria employed (see Brusco and Paba, 'Per una storia dei distretti italiani', pp. 272–80).

87 Brusco and Paba, 'Per una storia del distretti industriali', pp. 274, 280; Zamagni, 'Evolution of the Economy', p. 58.

88 Suzanne Berger and Richard M. Locke, '*Il caso italiano* and globalization', *Daedalus* 130(3) (2001), p. 90; Zamagni, 'Evolution of the Economy', p. 57; Foot, *Modern Italy*, p. 144.

89 Foot, *Modern Italy*, p. 143. In 1951, Piedmont, Lombardy and Liguria had occupied the first three positions with levels of per capita income way above the national average and far higher than those of any other region of the country. Per capita income figures from Zamagni, 'Evolution of the Economy', p. 61.

90 Berger and Locke, '*Il caso italiano*', pp. 88–9; Bianchini, 'The Third Italy', pp. 338–9; Zamagni, 'Evolution of the Italian Economy', pp. 57–8.

91 Foot, *Modern Italy*, p. 143.

92 Andrea Goldstein, 'Recent Works on Italian Capitalism: A Review Essay', *Journal of Modern Italian Studies*, 3(2) (1998), p. 180.

93 For pessimistic assessments of the future of the Third Italy, see Sassoon, *Contemporary Italy*, p. 80; Bianchini, 'The Third Italy', pp. 339–41. Assessments that are more upbeat can be found in Berger and Locke, '*Il caso italiano*', pp. 94–102; Signorini, 'Italy's Economy', p. 74; Brusco and Paba, 'Per una storia del distretti industriali italiani', pp. 326–39.

94 Crafts and Toniolo, 'Postwar Growth', p. 25.

95 Stephen George and Ian Bache, *Politics in the European Union* (Oxford: Oxford University Press, 2001), p. 201.

96 Della Sala, 'Hollowing Out and Hardening the State', pp. 27, 29. See also Ginsborg, *Italy and its Discontents*, pp. 243–4. Despite the austerity drive of the 1990s, Italian governments never managed to bring the public debt under control: at the end of 2008 it stood at 104% of GDP.

97 Costis Hadjimichalis points out that under the 1974 Multi-Fibre Agreement (MFA) signed by Italy, Germany, France and the US and extended across the EU in the mid-1980s, Italian garment and textiles producers were protected from unlimited competition from low labour-cost countries in the Third World. Devaluation, a favoured tactic of Italian governments from the 1960s, designed to keep the lira low, gave exporters a significant competitive advantage in world markets. Small firms were exempt from 1970s labour legislation and the beneficiaries of a range of subsidies and tax exemptions. Costis Hadjimichalis, 'The End of Third Italy as We Knew It?', *Antipode* 38(1) (2006), pp. 86–7. See also Federico and Giannetti, 'Italy: Stalling and Surpassing', p. 142.

98 Zamagni, 'Evolution of the Economy', p. 63.

99 Aldcroft, *The European Economy*, p. 161.

100 Eric Hobsbawm, *Age of Extremes: The Short Twentieth Century 1914–1991* (London: Michael Joseph, 1994), p. 408.

101 ISTAT, 'Italy in Figures, 2007'. Accessed online at <http://www.istat.it/dati/catalogo/20070517_00/Italy2007Ing.pdf>.

102 Zamagni, 'Evolution of the Economy', pp. 60–1; Signorini and Visco, *L'economia italiana*, p. 98.

103 Barca, 'New Trends', p. 101.

104 *The Economist*, 'A Survey of Italy', 8 November 1997, p. 9.

105 Marta Petrusewicz, 'The Mezzogiorno: A Bias for Hope?', *Modern Italy* 6(1) (2001), p. 66. See also Barca, 'New Trends', pp. 98–101.

106 Andrea Goldstein, 'What Future for Italian Industry?', *Journal of Modern Italian Studies* 8(4) (2003), pp. 605–6.

107 Marcello de Cecco and Giovanni Ferri, 'Italy's Financial System: Banks and Industrial Investment', in Boltho et al., *Comparing Economic Systems*, p. 79.

108 Hadjimichalis, 'The End of Third Italy', pp. 91–100; John Peet, 'Addio, dolce vita', the *Economist*, 26 November 2005, p. 3; Simon Parker, 'Introduction: A Tale of Two Italies – Continuities and Change in the Italian Republic, 1994–2006', *Modern Italy* 12(1) (2007), pp. 2–3. In 2008, Italian per capita GDP fell below the EU average for the first time.

Chapter 9 Post-war society and culture

1 Barzini, *The Italians*, p. 214; Paola Filippucci and Perry Willson, 'Introduction', *Modern Italy* (Special Issue: Gender and the Private Sphere in Italy since 1945) 9(1) (2004), p. 6. On the one hand, the average Italian family by the 1990s was smaller than ever: 4.3 members in 1936, 3.6 in 1961, 3.01 in 1981, 2.8 in 1990. The birth rate in Italy was one of the lowest in the world (1.19 children per woman in 1998). The number of marriages (measured per thousand inhabitants) had fallen steadily over recent decades while the number of divorces – illegal until the 1970s – had doubled between the mid-1980s and mid-1990s. On the other hand, the divorce rate in Italy remained one of the lowest in Europe, there were relatively few single-parent Italian families, and the proportion of children born outside of wedlock was low. In addition, the percentage of children who continued to live in the parental home well into adulthood was extremely high in European terms. When adult children did leave home (when they got married) they continued to live in close geographical proximity to their parents. (A survey conducted in the early 1990s suggested one-third of married men saw their mothers every day!) The considerable and frequent contact between generations was (and remains) very much a feature of Italian family life. See Paul Ginsborg, 'La famiglia oltre il privato per superare l'isolamento', in Ginsborg (ed.), *Stato dell'Italia* (1994a), pp. 284–7; Ginsborg, *Italy and its Discontents*, p. 79; Antonio Mutti, 'Particularism and the Modernization Process in Southern Italy', *International Sociology* 15(4) (2000), p. 583.

2 Francesco Benigno, 'The Southern Family: A Comment on Paolo Macry', *Journal of Modern Italian Studies* 2(2) (1997), p. 215.

3 Allum, 'Italian Society Transformed', pp. 36–7.

4 Voluntary associations are considered vital to effective and stable democracy because they have the capacity to instil in participants habits of co-operation, solidarity, moderation and public spiritedness; even 'Taking part in a choral society or a bird-watching club can teach self-discipline and an appreciation for the joys of successful collaboration' (Putnam, *Making Democracy Work*, p. 90). Of course, though, as Putnam points out (n. 30, p. 221), 'Not all associations are committed to democratic goals nor organized in an egalitarian fashion', e.g. terrorist cells, racist organizations. Self-evidently, such groups do not constitute part of civil society. In this chapter, political parties and trade unions are *not* considered part of civil society. As Bagnasco notes, political parties can be excluded because of their connections to the state, unions because of their ties to the economy (market). Arnaldo Bagnasco, 'Associazionismo, quali prospettive?', in Ginsborg (ed.), *Stato dell'Italia*, p. 324.

5 Gabriel A. Almond and Sidney Verba, *The Civic Culture: Political Attitudes and Democracy in Five Nations* (Princeton: Princeton University Press, 1963), p. 402.

6 Pietro Citati, 'Una paese che non sa guardarsi allo specchio', *la Repubblica*, 23 March 2000.

7 See, for example, 'Berlusconi – Mussolini of the Media?', *The Late Show*, BBC 2, 26 September 1994. The term *apocalittici* – 'apocalyptics' – to describe those intellectuals who regarded mass culture as the beginning of the end for civilization was coined by Umberto Eco in the mid-1960s (*Apocalittici e integrati*, 1964).

8 See, for example, Simon Parker, 'Political Identities', in David Forgacs and Robert Lumley (eds), *Italian Cultural Studies: An Introduction* (Oxford: Oxford University Press, 1996), pp. 118–19.

9 Gabriella Gribaudi, 'Images of the South', in Forgacs and Lumley (eds), *Italian Cultural Studies*, p. 85.

10 See for example, Enzo Mingione, 'Italy: The Resurgence of Regionalism', *International Affairs* 62(2) (1993) pp. 317–18.

11 Dunnage, *Twentieth Century Italy*, pp. 158–9, 164; Carol Helstosky, *Garlic and Oil: Food and Politics in Italy* (Oxford and New York: Berg, 2004), p. 138. Cinema audiences rocketed in the first half of the 1950s to a peak of 819m (1955); crowds at top-flight football matches rose by 30%, 1953–63. Forgacs, *Italian Culture in the Industrial Era*, p. 127; Stefano Pivato, 'Sport', in McCarthy, *Italy since 1945*, p. 178.

12 Forgacs, *Italian Culture in the Industrial Era*, pp. 125, 128–9; David Forgacs, 'Cultural Consumption, 1940s to 1990s', in Forgacs and Lumley (eds), *Italian Cultural Studies*, p. 281; Robert Lumley, 'Peculiarities of the Italian Newspaper', in Forgacs and Lumley (eds), *Italian Cultural Studies*, p. 206.

13 Between 1951 and 1961, the number of people living in Italy's 13 largest cities – Turin, Milan, Verona, Venice, Genoa, Bologna, Florence, Rome, Naples, Bari, Palermo, Catania and Messina – grew by 21.7%. In 1951, 41.3% of Italians lived in communes with populations of more than 20,000; this had risen to 52.4% by 1971. V. Vidotto, 'La nuova società', in Sabbatucci and Vidotto (eds), *Storia d'Italia VI*, p. 28

14 Ginsborg, *A History of Contemporary Italy*, p. 324.

15 Robert C. Meade, *Red Brigades: The Story of Italian Terrorism* (Basingstoke: Macmillan, 1990), pp. 18–19.

16 Lumley estimates that 75 protesters were killed by police, 1948–54, with a further 5,000 wounded. Robert Lumley, *States of Emergency: Cultures of Revolt in Italy from 1968 to 1978* (London and New York: Verso, 1990a), p. 14.

17 V. Vidotto, 'La nuova società', p. 67.

18 Ginsborg, *A History of Contemporary Italy*, p. 323.

19 The popular Catholic press even thought it right that a husband could 'moderately chastise his wife with words or even discretely hit her', if he had cause. For its part, the PCI, although it acknowledged the right of women to equality in the public sphere (at work or within the party) and talked of 'women's emancipation', did not offer a critique of social relations and power within the home. This meant 'the status of woman as wife and mother in the family remained unquestioned, just as the implications of this situation for a sexual division of labour outside of the home were also overlooked'. As *Noi Donne*, the journal of the communist UDI (Union of Italian Women) put it: 'Our women...they're not looking for intrigue or adventure or the impossible, they're used to having calm, beautiful dreams like marrying a fine young man they love and having a little home, children and all the peace in the world'. The class struggle was, in reality, very much a male preserve. See Stefania Bernini, 'Natural Mothers: Teaching Morals and Parent-craft in Italy, 1945–60', *Modern Italy* 9(1) (2004), pp. 21–33 (quote p. 24); Lesley Caldwell, 'Italian Feminism: Some Considerations', in Zygmunt Baranski and Shirley Vinall (eds), *Women and Italy: Essays on Gender, Culture and History* (Basingstoke: Macmillan, 1991), pp. 95–116 (quotes pp. 99, 100); Nina Rothberg, 'The Catholic and Communist Women's Press in Post-war Italy: An Analysis of *Cronache* and *Noi Donne*', *Modern Italy* 11(3) (2006), pp. 285–304.

20 Forgacs, 'Cultural Consumption', p. 279.

21 Ginsborg, *A History of Contemporary Italy*, p. 244.

22 John Foot, 'The Family and the 'Economic Miracle': Social Transformation, Work, Leisure and Development at Bovisa and Comasina (Milan), 1950–70', *Contemporary European History* 4(3) (1995), p. 329.

23 The observation was made by Carla Lonzi, founder of Rivolta femminile. Quoted in Anna Di Leillo, 'Il femminismo', in Pasquino (ed.), *La politica italiana*, p. 238. The (mostly male) leaders of the student movement showed no particular interest in gender politics; women activists were usually assigned traditional female duties (duplicating leaflets, cooking meals, etc.).

24 Luisa Passerini, 'Gender Relations', in Forgacs and Lumley (eds), *Italian Cultural Studies*, p. 150.

25 Robert Lumley, 'Challenging Tradition: Social Movements, Cultural Change and the Ecology Question', in Zygmunt Baranski and Robert Lumley (eds), *Culture and Conflict in Postwar Italy* (Basingstoke: Macmillan, 1990b) p. 120.

26 Di Leillo, 'Il femminismo', p. 239.

27 Donatella della Porta, *Social Movements, Political Violence, and the State: A Comparative Analysis of Italy and Germany* (Cambridge and New York: Cambridge University Press, 1995a), p. 31; Ginsborg, *A History of Contemporary Italy*, p. 401; Lumley, *States of Emergency*, p. 329.

28 Donatella Della Porta, 'Il terrorismo', in Pasquino (ed.), *La politica italiana* (1995b), p. 536.

29 Allum, 'Italian Society Transformed', p. 28.

30 Moss estimates that the BR and other red terrorist groups killed between them 24 people in 1979, 29 in 1980, 12 in 1981 and 14 in 1982. David Moss, *The Politics of Left-wing Violence in Italy, 1969–85* (Basingstoke: Macmillan, 1989), p. 37. Neo-Fascists committed the single worst atrocity of the so-called 'years of lead' (*anni di piombi*) in August 1980 when a bomb exploded at Bologna railway station, killing 85 people and wounding hundreds more.

31 P. Sylos Labini (1986 and 1995). Figures quoted in Vidotto, 'La nuova società', p. 37. The growth of the urban middle classes has been accompanied by the continued urbanization of Italian society. In contrast to the 1950s and 1960s, however, growth was not concentrated in the major cities – in fact, the populations of Turin, Milan, Naples and Rome all shrank, 1971–91 – but rather in the smaller towns within metropolitan areas (see Vidotto, pp. 30–1).

32 Ginsborg, *A History of Contemporary Italy*, pp. 408–9, 424.

33 Forgacs, *Italian Culture in the Industrial Era*, p. 185.

34 Paolo Villa, 'Sport and Society', in Moliterno (ed.), *Encyclopedia of Contemporary Italian Culture*, p. 558; Pivato, 'Sport', pp. 179, 181.

35 Ginsborg, *Italy and its Discontents*, pp. 85–6.

36 None more so than *Dylan Dog*. The eponymous adventures of an 'investigator of nightmares', *Dylan Dog* quickly established itself after its launch in the mid-1980s as the favourite reading material of teenage Italian boys and – apparently – professional footballers. See Joe McGinniss, *The Miracle of Castel di Sangro* (London: Warner Books, 1999), p. 134.

37 Clark, *Modern Italy*, p. 405.

38 Nowhere is this contrast more evident than in the case of the monk Padre Pio, the so-called 'living crucifix', who from 1918 until his death in 1968 is alleged to have displayed the signs of the stigmata, that is, the wounds of Jesus Christ on his hands, feet and side. In the 1960s, sceptical Vatican officials ordered an investigation into the Capuchin monastery of San Giovanni Rotondo, where Padre Pio had served throughout his life. Under John Paul II, however, Padre Pio was beatified (declared blessed) in 1999 and fast-tracked to sainthood in 2002. A new church dedicated to Padre Pio opened at San Giovanni Rotondo in 2004. Millions of pilgrims visit the monastery every year. During his reign, John Paul II beatified and canonized more people than any previous pope.

39 For more on the post-war fortunes of the Church in Italy see Jeff Pratt, 'Catholic Culture', in Forgacs and Lumley (eds), *Italian Cultural Studies*, pp. 129–43; Roberto Marchisio and Maurizio Pisati, 'Belonging Without Believing: Catholics in Contemporary Italy', *Journal of Modern Italian Studies* 4(2) (1999), pp. 236–55; Franco Garelli, 'The Public Relevance of the "Church" and Catholicism in Italy', *Journal of Modern Italian Studies* 12(1) (2007), pp. 8–36; Patrick McCarthy, 'The Church in Post-war Italy', in McCarthy (ed.), *Italy since 1945*, pp. 133–52; Alberto Melloni, 'The Politics of the "Church" in the Italy of Pope Wojtyla', *Journal of Modern Italian Studies* 12(1) (2007), pp. 60–85. On popular devotions and Padre Pio, see Peter Jan Margry, 'Merchandising and Sanctity: The Invasive Cult of Padre Pio', *Journal of Modern Italian Studies* 7(1) (2002), pp. 88–115.

40 Russell King and Jacqueline Andall, 'The Geography and Economic Sociology of Recent Immigration to Italy', *Modern Italy* 4(2) (1999), pp. 137–40.

41 Putnam, *Making Democracy Work*, pp. 15, 83–120.

42 Putnam, *Making Democracy Work*, pp. 112, 121–45, 147, 167–74.

43 Putnam, *Making Democracy Work*, p. 121.

44 Putnam, *Making Democracy Work*, pp. 150–61.

45 Putnam, *Making Democracy Work*, p. 183.

46 Jude Bloomfield, 'The "Civic" in Europe', *Contemporary European History* 4(2) (1995), pp. 230–1.

47 Leonardi, 'Regional Development in Italy', p. 175.

48 Simona Piattoni, "'Virtuous Clientelism': The Southern Question Resolved?', in Schneider (ed.), *Italy's 'Southern Question'*, p. 241, n. 5 and 11; Sidney Tarrow, 'Making Social Science Work Across Space and Time: A Critical Reflection on Robert Putnam's *Making Democracy Work*', *The American Political Science Review* 90(2) (1996), p. 389, n. 4.

49 Morris, 'Challenging *meridionalismo*', p. 9.

50 Banfield, *The Moral Basis of a Backward Society*, p. 11.

51 Banfield, *The Moral Basis of a Backward Society*, pp. 85, 115, 119, 144–5, 151–2, 163.

52 Banfield, *The Moral Basis of a Backward Society*, pp. 165, 169–70, 175.

53 Gabriella Gribaudi, 'Familismo e famiglia in Napoli e nel Mezzogiorno', *Meridiana* 17 (1993), pp. 14–18; Paola Filippucci, 'Anthropological Perspectives on Culture in Italy', in Forgacs and Lumley (eds), *Italian Cultural Studies*, pp. 54–5.

54 Gribaudi, 'Familismo e famiglia', p. 40; Gabriella Gribaudi, 'Il paradigma del "familismo amorale"', in Paolo Macry and Angelo Massafia (eds), *Fra storia e storiografia: scritti in onore di Pasquale Villani* (Bologna: il Mulino, 1994), pp. 338–42, 347; Gribaudi, 'Images of the South', pp. 83–4.

55 Putnam, *Making Democracy Work*, pp. 183–5.

56 Bevilacqua, *Breve storia dell'Italia meridionale*, pp. xvi, 128.

57 Bevilacqua, *Breve storia dell'Italia meridionale*, pp. 123–34 (quote p. 125). For similar interpretations in English see Sassoon, *Contemporary Italy*, pp. 50–1 and Ch. 15; Allum, 'Italian Society Transformed', pp. 36–9.

58 For details see Patriarca, 'Italian Neopatriotism', pp. 26–30 (quotes are by Indro Montanelli).

59 Giulio Sapelli provides a good example of the latter argument:

> When industrial society arrived in Italy, it seemed to demand forms of modernization and values which were defined by horizontal rather than vertical links, and associated with the kind of virtuous modernization that people thought would be brought about by large companies and the market. However, in reality, industrial society lasted for too short a time to impose such changes in Italy (only twenty years as opposed to hundreds of years of the first industrial nations). In truth it was industrial society itself that became tangled up by a thousand threads with a past that it only re-staged.

Giulio Sapelli, 'The Italian Crises and Capitalism', *Modern Italy* 1(1) (1995), p. 91.

60 Ginsborg, 'Italian Political Culture', p. 4.

61 Charles S. Maier, 'Comments', *Journal of Modern Italian Studies* 9(4) (2004), p. 458.

62 Ginsborg in Paul Ginsborg, Perry Anderson, Simon Parker and John Foot, 'Italy in the Present Tense: A Roundtable Discussion', *Modern Italy* 5(2) (2000), p. 178.

63 Paul Ginsborg, 'Familismo', in Ginsborg (ed.), *Stato dell'Italia* (1994b), pp. 79, 81; Paul Ginsborg, 'Family, Culture and Politics in Contemporary Italy', in Baranski and Lumley (eds), *Culture and Conflict in Postwar Italy*, p. 22.

64 Ginsborg, 'Italian Political Culture', p. 7; Ginsborg, 'Familismo', pp. 81–2; Ginsborg, *A History of Contemporary Italy*, pp. 173–5; Ginsborg, *Italy and its Discontents*, p. 130.

65 See, for example, the many works of the Italian anthropologist Carlo Tullio-Altan. In the 1970s, Tullio-Altan carried out a major survey of young people's attitudes in Italy. The majority of those surveyed displayed an attachment to 'traditional' – backward – social and cultural values: familism, an indifference to others, a susceptibility to authoritarian political and social arrangements, political apathy, ethnocentrism. The same familistic attitudes, he argued, existed in Italian society as far back as the fourteenth and fifteenth centuries. The persistence of such values was due to Italy's historical 'feudal weakness'.

66 Ginsborg, 'La famiglia italiana', p. 288.

67 Ginsborg, 'Familismo', p. 80; Ginsborg, 'La famiglia italiana', pp. 288–9; Ginsborg in 'Italy in the Present Tense', p. 178; Ginsborg, *A History of Contemporary Italy*, p. 416; Ginsborg, 'Family, Culture and Politics', pp. 35, 46.

68 Ginsborg, *Italy and its Discontents*, xi.

69 Ginsborg, 'Italian Political Culture, pp. 11–13; Ginsborg, *A History of Contemporary Italy*, p. 343; Ginsborg, *Italy and its Discontents*, p. 121. After 1945 associational activity in Italy had been bound up with the dominant 'white' (Catholic) and 'red' (communist) subcultures. By the 1980s, however, the hold of Catholicism and communism over Italian society and culture had weakened significantly.

70 Ginsborg, *Italy and its Discontents*, p. 96; Ginsborg, *Silvio Berlusconi*, p. 171.

71 Ginsborg, *Italy and its Discontents*, p. 43.

72 Ginsborg, *Italy and its Discontents*, p. 43.

73 Ginsborg, *Italy and its Discontents*, p. 134.

74 Ginsborg, 'Italian Political Culture', p. 3.

75 Ginsborg, *Silvio Berlusconi*, p. 51.

76 Ginsborg, *Italy and its Discontents*, p. 322.

77 Perry Anderson in 'Italy in the Present Tense', p. 180.

78 The comments are those of Anna Cento Bull in her review of the original Italian language version of *Italy and its Discontents* (*L'Italia del tempo presente*, 1998), *Journal of Modern Italian Studies* 5(1) (2000b), p. 144. For a similar take on Italy's professional public-sector workers see John Foot, 'Heirs of Tangentopoli', *New Left Review*, 16 (July/August), 2000, p. 155.

79 Anna Cento Bull, *Social Identities and Political Cultures in Italy: Catholic, Communist and Leghist Communities between Civicness and Localism* (New York and Oxford: Berghahn Books, 2000a), pp. 204–6.

80 Davide Però, 'Next to the Dog Pound: Institutional Discourses and Practices about Rom Refugees in Left-wing Bologna', *Modern Italy* 4(2) (1999), pp. 207–24; Bruno Riccio, 'Senegalese Street-sellers, Racism and the Discourse on "Irregular Trade" in Rimini', *Modern Italy* 4(2) (1999), pp. 225–39.

81 Denis Mack Smith, for example, has written that, 'In all classes [in the south] the absence of a community sense resulted from a habit of insubordination learned in centuries of despotism'. Diego Gambetta, in his work on the Sicilian Mafia, argues that 'as a deliberate policy of divide and conquer implemented by the Spanish Hapsburgs [in the seventeenth century], *la fede pubblica* – the public trust, the basis for well-ordered society – was undermined. All that remained was *la fede privata*, that private realm populated only by kin and close friends in which people take refuge from high levels of social unpredictability, aggression and injustice'. For Gambetta, the Mafia, which he defines as 'a specific economic enterprise...which produces, promotes, and sells private protection', has to be 'understood as a response to the lack of trust specifically affecting southern Italy'. Francis Fukuyama's *Trust*, which contains a chapter on Italy, simply repeats Putnam's thesis. 'The amoral familism of the south', Fukuyama writes, 'had its origins in the Norman kingdoms in Sicily and Naples, particularly under Frederick II'. Mack Smith, *Italy*, p. 35; Diego Gambetta, *The Sicilian Mafia*, pp. 1, 77; Francis Fukuyama, *Trust: The Social Virtues and the Creation of Prosperity* (London: Penguin, 1995), p. 107.

82 Jane Schneider and Peter Schneider, *Reversible Destiny: Mafia, Anti-Mafia and the Struggle for Palermo* (Berkeley and Los Angeles: University of California Press, 2003), p. 112. Putnam remains unrepentant despite the criticisms levelled at him. In *Bowling Alone: The Collapse and Revival of American Community* (New York: Simon and Schuster, 2000), pp. 345–6, he writes: 'The historical roots of the civic community [in north and central Italy] are astonishingly deep...[they] can be traced back nearly a millennium to the eleventh century, when communal republics were established in places like Florence, Bologna, Genoa, exactly the communities that today enjoy civic engagement and successful government'.

83 'There is no contradiction in having a friend and using him or her as a resource...purely expressive bonds [of friendship] are the luxury of the young'. Jane Schneider and Peter Schneider, *Culture and Political Economy in Western Sicily* (New York and London: Academic Press, 1976), p. 104.

84 Schneider and Schneider, *Culture and Political Economy in Western Sicily*, p. 229.

85 Jane Schneider and Peter Schneider, 'Sicily: Reflections on Forty Years of Change', *Journal of Modern Italian Studies* 11(1) (2006), p. 73.

86 Schneider and Schneider, 'Sicily: Reflections', p. 76.

87 Schneider and Schneider, 'Sicily: Reflections', p. 80.

88 Ginsborg, *Italy and its Discontents*, p. 125.

89 Ginsborg, *Italy and its Discontents*, p. 98.

90 Mutti, 'Particularism and the Modernization Process in Southern Italy', p. 583. Mutti is not amongst them.

91 *Economist*, May 1990, quoted in Ginsborg, *Italy and its Discontents*, p. 68.

92 Ginsborg, 'Family, Culture and Politics', pp. 24–41.

93 Arnaldo Bagnasco (1996), quoted in Cento Bull, *Social Identities and Political Cultures in Italy*, p. 94. Not all historians concur with Bagnasco. For example, Dunnage argues the 'long family' has 'had a negative effect on the ability of young people to become independent from their families and more responsible within society'. Dunnage, *Twentieth Century Italy*, p. 206.

94 Ginsborg, *A History of Contemporary Italy*, p. 415.

95 Bull, *Social Identities and Political Cultures in Italy*, pp. 49–50, 57, 76, 92, 129.

96 Marzio Barbagli and David Kertzer, 'An Introduction to the History of Italian Family Life', *Journal of Family History* 15(4) (1990), pp. 373–5.

97 Mutti, 'Particularism and the Modernization Process in Southern Italy', p. 583.

98 Gribaudi, 'Familismo e famiglia', p. 39.

99 Jane Schneider and Peter Schneider, *Festival of the Poor: Fertility Decline and the Ideology of Class in Sicily, 1860–1980* (Tucson: University of Arizona Press, 1996).

100 Mutti, 'Particularism and the Modernization Process in Southern Italy', p. 583.

101 Defined by Amalia Signorelli (1988) as 'a system of interpersonal relations within which private ties of a kinship, ritual kinship or friendship dimension are employed in public structures so as to use public resources for private advantage'. Quoted by Ginsborg in 'Italian Political Culture', p. 6.

102 Mutti, 'Particularism and the Modernization Process in Southern Italy', p. 584.

103 Putnam, *Making Democracy Work*, p. 107.

104 Ginsborg, *Italy and its Discontents*, p. 103; Ginsborg, 'Italian Political Culture', p. 7.

105 Ginsborg, *A History of Contemporary Italy*, p. 175.

106 Ginsborg, *Italy and its Discontents*, p. 132.

107 For example, until the 1990s it was virtually impossible to find a senior Church figure in Italy willing to criticize – or even acknowledge – the Mafia. Ernesto Ruffini, the Cardinal Archbishop of Palermo from 1946 to 1967, always denied its existence, willing to ignore its activities as long as the godless communists were kept at bay. When John Paul II visited Sicily in 1982 he never once mentioned the Mafia despite the fact that Mafia murders – of both rival Mafiosi and anti-Mafia activists and public officials – were virtually a daily occurrence at the time. Only in 1993, after the murders of Falcone and Borsellino, did the Pope finally condemn 'the culture of death' perpetrated by this criminal organization.

108 Quote by Garelli, 'The Public Relevance of the Church and Catholicism in Italy', p. 21.

109 Levi, *Christ Stopped at Eboli*, p. 45; Ginsborg, *A History of Contemporary Italy*, pp. 29, 33.

110 Cento Bull, *Social Identities and Political Cultures in Italy*, p. 70.

111 Putnam, *Making Democracy Work*, pp. 108–9.

112 Garelli, 'The Public Relevance of the Church and Catholicism in Italy', p. 30.

113 Tobias Jones writes of Catholic volunteers: 'Their work is the flipside of the hierarchy's intolerance'. Jones, *The Dark Heart of Italy*, p. 169.

114 James March and Johan Olsen (1989) quoted in Putnam, *Making Democracy Work*, p. 16.

115 Foot, *Modern Italy*, p. 77.

116 Foot, *Modern Italy*, pp. 90–2.

117 Jones, *The Dark Heart of Italy*, p. 15.

118 Ginsborg, *Italy and its Discontents*, p. 217

119 Judith Chubb, *Patronage, Power, and Poverty in Southern Italy: A Tale of Two Cities* (Cambridge: Cambridge University Press, 1982), p. 247.

120 Pino Arlacchi, 'Mafia: The Sicilian Cosa Nostra', *Southern European Society and Politics* 1(1) (1996), p. 90.

121 John Dickie, *Cosa Nostra: A History of the Sicilian Mafia* (London: Hodder and Stoughton, 2004), p. 400.

122 Allum (1973) quoted in Dunnage, *Twentieth Century Italy*, p. 154.

123 Signorelli's arguments are summarized in Ginsborg, *Italy and its Discontents*, pp. 123–4.

124 'Even finding officials of the Puglia regional government in the capital city of Bari proved a challenge for us,' recalled Putnam in *Making Democracy Work*. 'Like visiting researchers, ordinary Pugliesi must first locate the nondescript regional headquarters beyond the railroad yards. In the dingy anteroom loll several indolent functionaries, though they are likely to be present only an hour or two each day and to be unresponsive even then. The persistent visitor might discover that in the offices beyond stand only ghostly rows of empty desks.' Putnam, *Making Democracy Work*, p. 5.

125 Leonardi, 'Regional Development in Italy', p. 172. For the range of protection services offered by organized crime see Gambetta, *The Sicilian Mafia*.

126 Ironically, official tax collection in Sicily was most efficient when controlled by the Mafia itself. From the 1960s until 1984, tax collection on the island was the responsibility of a private firm run by cousins Nino and Ignazio Salvo, members of the Salemi Mafia family. The Salvos took a 10% commission on all taxes collected, a ridiculously high figure, but one they were able to levy because of the backhanders they paid to politicians in return for the renewal of their contract. Because the more they collected the more money they made, and because of 'their unusual powers of persuasion', the Salvos proved to be very effective at their job. By the time of their arrest and trial (part of the maxi-trials of the mid-1980s), the Salvos were among the richest men in Sicily. Tax evasion increased significantly once tax collection returned to public control in 1984. Nino Salvo died of natural causes during the maxi-trial; Ignazio, after serving a light sentence, was killed by the Mafia in 1992. See Gambetta, *The Sicilian Mafia*, pp. 160–3; Dickie, *Cosa Nostra*, pp. 365–6, 422.

127 Paul Ginsborg, *The Politics of Everyday Life: Making Choices, Changing Lives* (Melbourne: Melbourne University Press, 2005), p. 116; Ginsborg, 'Family, Culture and Politics', p. 35; Ginsborg, *Silvio Berlusconi*, p. 109; Ginsborg, *Italy and its Discontents*, p. 110; Ginsborg in 'Italy in the Present Tense', p. 178; Ginsborg, *A History of Contemporary Italy*, p. 416.

128 Foot, 'The Family and the "Economic Miracle"', p. 331.

129 Putnam, *Bowling Alone*, pp. 224–5, 231.

130 Soria Blattman, 'A Media Conflict of Interest: Anomaly in Italy' (2003). <http://www.rsf.org/IMG/pdf/doc-2080.pdf>.

131 Berlusconi, quoted in Alexander Stille, 'Berlusconi Creates a Truman Show', *Financial Times*, 17 February 2006.

132 *La Sua Emittenza* ('His Emittence'), a long-standing nickname for Berlusconi, is a word play on *La Sua Eminenza* ('His Eminence').

133 Stille, 'Berlusconi Creates a Truman Show'. For details, see ITANES, *Perché ha vinto il centro-destra. Oltre la mera conta dei voti: chi, come, dove, perché* (Bologna: il Mulino, 2001).

134 James L. Newell and Martin J. Bull, 'Italian Politics after the 2001 Election: Plus ça change, plus c'est la même chose?', *Parliamentary Affairs* 55(4) (2002), pp. 632, 634.

135 Forgacs, 'Cultural Consumption', p. 285. To link Berlusconi's political success simply to his control of the media is also to ignore the fact that he is a very able politician. As Gianfranco Pasquino notes, Berlusconi has 'succeeded in dominating, from a political and electoral point of view, the Italian "small theatre of politics" ... not only because he is a media tycoon, but especially because he has proved to be more capable at constructing political and electoral coalitions and, above all, because he is excellent at campaigning. Indeed, he revels in it'. Gianfranco Pasquino, 'The 2008 Italian National Elections: Berlusconi's Third Victory', *South European Society and Politics* 13(3) (2008), p. 346.

136 David Forgacs, 'Scenarios for the Digital Age: Convergence, Personalization, Exclusion', *Modern Italy* 6(2) (2001), p. 132; John Agnew, 'Remaking Italy? Place Configurations and Italian Electoral Politics under the "Second Republic"', *Modern Italy* 12(1) (2007), p. 20.

137 Agnew, 'Remaking Italy?', p. 20.

138 Richard Barraclough, 'The Northern League and the 1996 General Election: Protest Vote or Political Entrepreneurship?', *The Italianist* 16(1996), p. 341.

139 Doumanis, *Italy*, p. 169.

140 Gianfranco Pasquino, 'The Italian Elections of 13 May 2001', *Journal of Modern Italian Studies* 6(3) (2001), p. 382.

141 Anna Cento Bull, 'Collective Identities: From the Politics of Inclusion to the Politics of Ethnicity and Difference', *The Global Review of Ethnopolitics* 2(3–4) (2003), p. 41.

142 Anna Cento Bull and Mark Gilbert, *The Lega Nord and the Northern Question in Italian Politics* (New York and Basingstoke: Palgrave, 2001), p. 93.

143 Benito Giordano, 'The Continuing Transformation of Italian Politics and the Contradictory Fortunes of the Lega Nord', *Journal of Modern Italian Studies* 8(2) (2003), p. 225. Giordano quotes from Cento Bull and Gilbert, *The Lega Nord*, p. 101.

144 The split between the Lega Nord and small business in the north-east has been reinforced in recent years by the Lega's anti-EU stance (the Lega in the early 1990s had been decidedly pro-European) and its increasingly strident opposition to extra-EU immigration. Neither position makes much sense to the decidedly pro-European small business owners of Third Italy, many of whom are also reliant on cheap, skilled, immigrant labour to help keep production costs down and to make good shortages in the local labour market. (See Hadjimichalis, 'The End of Third Italy?', pp. 96–100, for more on immigrant workers in industrial districts). As the 2008 general election showed, however, the *Lega* must not be written off as a political force. After a disappointing electoral showing in 2006 (4.6% of the national vote), the party enjoyed a Lazarus-like revival two years on, securing 1.3m more votes than in 2006 and increasing its share of the overall vote to 8.3%. This translated into 60 deputies (37 in 2006), and 26 senators (13 in 2006). According to Bull and Newell, the Lega 'appears to have benefited from anti-political sentiments...voters seemingly disappointed with their earlier choices and searching for an alternative radicalism'. Martin J. Bull and James L. Newell, 'The General Election in Italy, April 2008', *Electoral Studies* 28(2) (2009), p. 340. Mannheimer's analysis of the results indicate the Lega not only 'stole' many of its votes from other centre-right parties, Forza Italia especially, but also picked up a significant number of votes (8% of its total) from parties on the Left. Renato Mannheimer, 'L'8% dei voti lumbard è «rubato» alla sinistra', *Corriere della Sera*, 20 April 2008. For further analysis of the election, see Pasquino, 'The 2008 Italian National Elections'.

145 Judith Chubb, 'Comments', *Journal of Modern Italian Studies* 9(4) (2004), p. 468.

146 Chubb, 'Comments', p. 469.

147 Passerini, 'Gender Relations', pp. 152–3.

148 Passerini, 'Gender Relations', p. 157.

149 For a detailed assessment of the difficulties faced by women, see Francesca Bettio and Paola Villa, 'To What Extent Does it Pay to Be Better Educated? Education and the Work Market for Women in Italy', *South European Society and Politics* 4(2), pp. 150–70.

150 See Anna Rossi Doria, 'Una rivoluzione non ancora compiuta', and Marina Piazza, 'Il rischio di una nuova marginalità?', both in Ginsborg (ed.), *Stato dell'Italia*, pp. 262–6, 266–72.

151 Adrian Michaels, 'Naked Ambition', *Financial Times*, 13 July 2007.

152 Jones, *The Dark Heart of Italy*, p. 118.

153 Nicole Martinelli and Barbie Nadeau, 'The Stigma of Disability in Italy', *Newsweek*, 3 March 2003.

154 ISTAT press release, 4 July 2000. <http://samoa.istat.it/English/Press-rele/Outside-ca/poverty99.pdf>.

155 Doumanis, *Italy*, p. 164.

Bibliography

GENERAL HISTORIES

Absalom, R., 1995, *Italy since 1800: A Nation in the Balance?*, London and New York: Longman, 1995.

Clark, M., *Modern Italy*, 2nd edn, London: Longman, 1995.

Cohen, J. and Federico, G., *The Growth of the Italian Economy 1820–1960*, Cambridge: Cambridge University Press, 2001.

Davis, J. A., 'Modern Italy – Changing Historical Perspectives since 1945', in M. Bentley (ed.), *Companion to Historiography*, London and New York: Routledge, 1997.

Doumanis, N., *Italy*, London: Arnold, 2001.

Federico, G. (ed.), *The Economic Development of Italy since 1870*, Aldershot: Edward Elgar, 1994.

Foot, J., *Modern Italy*, Basingstoke and New York: Palgrave Macmillan, 2003.

Mack Smith, D., *Modern Italy: A Political History*, Ann Arbor: University of Michigan Press, 1997.

Zamagni, V., *The Economic History of Italy, 1860–1990*, Oxford: Clarendon Press, 1993.

PRE-UNIFICATION

Beales, D., *The Risorgimento and the Unification of Italy*, 2nd edn, London: Longman, 1981.

Riall, L., *Risorgimento: The History of Italy from Napoleon to Nation State*, Basingstoke: Palgrave Macmillan, 2009.

LIBERAL ITALY

Adamson, W. L., 'Modernism and Fascism: The Politics of Culture in Italy, 1903–1922', *American Historical Review* 95(2) (1990), pp. 359–90.

Adamson, W. L., 'The Language of Opposition in Early Twentieth-century Italy: Rhetorical Continuities between Prewar Florentine Avant-gardism and Mussolini's Fascism', *Journal of Modern History* 64(1) (1992), pp. 2–51.

Adamson, W. L., *Avant-Garde Florence: From Modernism to Fascism*, Cambridge, MA, and London: Harvard University Press, 1993.

Adamson, W. L., 'Contexts and Debates. Fascinating Futurism: The Historiographical Politics of an Historical Avant-garde', *Modern Italy* 13(1) (2008), pp. 69–85.

A'Hearn, B., 'Institutions, Externalities and Economic Growth in Southern Italy: Evidence from the Cotton Textiles Industry, 1861–1914', *Economic History Review* 51(4) (1998), pp. 734–62.

A'Hearn, B., 'Could Southern Italians Cooperate? *Banche popolari* in the *Mezzogiorno*', *Journal of Economic History* 60(1) (2000), pp. 67–93.

Banti, A. M. *Terra e denaro: una borghesia padana dell'Ottocento*, Venice: Marsilio editori, 1989.

Banti, A. M., 'Note sulle nobiltà nell'Italia dell'Ottocento', *Meridiana* 19 (1994), pp. 13–27.

Banti, A. M., 'Italian Professionals: Markets, Incomes, Estates and Identities', in M. Malatesta (ed.), *Society and the Professions in Italy, 1860–1914*, Cambridge: Cambridge University Press, 1995.

Banti, A. M., *Storia della borghesia italiana; l'età liberale (1861–1922)*, Rome: Donzelli editore, 1996.

Battente, S., 'Nation and State Building: Recent Historiographical Interpretations (1989–1997), I: Unification to Fascism', *Journal of Modern Italian Studies* 5(3) (2000), pp. 310–21.

Berghaus, G., *Futurism and Politics: Between Anarchist Rebellion and Fascist Reaction, 1909–1944*, Providence and Oxford: Berghahn Books, 1996.

Berghaus, G. (ed.), *International Futurism in Arts and Literature*, Berlin and New York: Walter de Gruyter, 2000.

Bevilacqua, P., *Breve storia dell'Italia meridionale dall'Ottocento a oggi*, Rome: Donzelli editore, 1993.

Biddiss, M., 'Intellectual and Cultural Revolution, 1890–1914', in P. Hayes (ed.), *Themes in Modern European History 1890–1945*, London and New York: Routledge, 1992.

Blackbourn, D. and Eley, G., *The Peculiarities of German History*, Oxford: Oxford University Press, 1984.

Bonelli, F. 'Il capitalismo italiano. Linee generali di interpretazione', in G. Federico (ed.), *The Economic Development of Italy since 1870*, Aldershot: Edward Elgar, 1978.

Bordogna, L., Cella, G. P. and Provasi, G., 'Labour Conflicts in Italy Before the Rise of Fascism, 1881–1923: A Quantitative Analysis', in L. H. Haimson and C. Tilly (eds), *Strikes, Wars, and Revolutions in an International Perspective: Strike Waves in the Late Nineteenth and Early Twentieth Centuries*, Cambridge: Cambridge University Press, 2002.

Bosworth, R. J. B., *Italy and the Approach of the First World War*, Basingstoke: Macmillan, 1983.

Bosworth, R. J. B., 'Historiography', in G. Moliterno (ed.), *Encyclopaedia of Contemporary Italian Culture*, London: Routledge, 2000.

Bowler, A., 'Politics as Art: Italian Futurism and Fascism', *Theory and Society* 20(6) (1991), pp. 763–94.

Buttafuoco, A., *Le Mariuccine: Storia di un'istituzione laica, l'Asilo Mariuccia*, 2nd edn, Milan: Franco Angelli, 1988.

Buttafuoco, A., 'Motherhood as a Political Strategy: The Role of the Italian Women's Movement in the Creation of the *Cassa Nazionale di Maternità*', in G. Bock and P. Thane (eds), *Gender Politics: Women and the Rise of the European Welfare States, 1880s–1950s*, London: Routledge, 1991.

Cafagna, L., 'Italy 1830–1914', in C. M. Cipolla (ed.), *The Fontana Economic History of Europe: The Emergence of Industrial Societies. Part One*, 6 vols, London: Collins-Fontana, vol. 4, 1973.

Cafagna, L., 'La questione delle origini del dualismo economico italiano', in G. Federico (ed.), *The Economic Development of Italy since 1870*, Aldershot: Edward Elgar, 1989.

Cameron, R., 'Introduction', in R. Cameron (ed.), *Banking and Economic Development: Some Lessons of History*, Oxford: Oxford University Press, 1972.

Cammarano, F., 'Nazionalizzazione della politica e politicizzazione della nazione. I dilemmi della classe dirigente nell'Italia liberale', in M. Meriggi and P. Schiera (eds), *Dalla città alla nazione: borghesie ottocentesche in Italia e in Germania*, Bologna: il Mulino, 1993.

Cardoza, A. L., *Aristocrats in Bourgeois Italy: The Piedmontese Nobility, 1861–1930*, Cambridge: Cambridge University Press, 1997a.

Cardoza, A. L., 'Review of *Gli uomini del Re* by G. Montroni, 1996', *Journal of Modern Italian Studies* 2(1) (1997b), pp. 95–7.

Castronovo, V., 'The Italian Take-off: A Critical Re-examination of the Problem', *Journal of Italian History*, 1(3) (1978), pp. 492–510.

Cento Bull, A., 'Lombard Silk-spinners in the Nineteenth Century: An Industrial Workforce in a Rural Setting', in Z. G. Baranski and S. W. Vinall (eds), *Women and Italy: Essays on Gender, Culture and History*, Basingstoke: Macmillan, 1991.

Chabod, F., *Italian Foreign Policy: The Statecraft of the Founders*, Princeton: Princeton University Press, 1996.

Ciocca, P. and Toniolo, G., 'Industry and Finance in Italy, 1918–1940', *Journal of European Economic History* (special issue) 13(2) (1984), pp. 113–36.

Cohen, J. S., 'Italy 1861–1914', in R. Cameron (ed.), *Banking and Economic Development: Some Lessons of History*, Oxford: Oxford University Press, 1972.

Cohen, J. S. and Galassi, F. L., 'Sharecropping and Productivity: "Feudal Residues" in Italian Agriculture, 1911', *Economic History Review* 43(4) (1990), pp. 646–56.

Coppa, F. J., 'The Italian Tariff and the Conflict between Agriculture and Industry: The Commercial Policy of Liberal Italy, 1860–1922', *Journal of Economic History* 30(4) (1970), pp. 742–69.

Coppa, F. J., *Planning, Protectionism and Politics in Liberal Italy: Economics and Politics in the Giolittian Age*, Washington: Catholic University of America Press, 1971.

Coppa, F. J., 'Giovanni Giolitti: Precursor of Mussolini?', *Italian Quarterly*, 27(104) (1986), pp. 45–53.

Corner, P., 'State and Society, 1901–1922', in A. Lyttleton (ed.), *Liberal and Fascist Italy*, Oxford: Oxford University Press, 2002.

Croce, B., *A History of Italy, 1871–1915*, Oxford: Clarendon Press, 1929.

Davis, J. A. (ed.), *Gramsci and Italy's Passive Revolution*, London: Croom Helm, 1979.

Davis, J. A., 'Socialism and the Italian Working Classes in Italy Before 1914', in D. Geary (ed.), *Labour and Socialist Movements in Europe before 1914*, Oxford, New York and Munich: Berg, 1989.

Davis, J. A., 'Remapping Italy's Path to the Twentieth Century', *Journal of Modern History*, 66(2) (1994), pp. 291–320.

Davis, J. A., 'Review of *La modernità squilibrata del Mezzogiorno d'Italia*, by F. Barbagallo, *Breve storia dell'Italia meridionale dall'Ottocento a oggi*, by P. Bevilacqua, and *Nord e sud. Non fare a pezzi l'unità d'Italia*, by L. Cafagna', *Journal of Modern Italian Studies*, 1(1) (1995), pp. 152–7.

Davis, J. A., 'Casting Off the "Southern Problem": Or the Peculiarities of the South Reconsidered', in J. Schneider (ed.), *Italy's 'Southern Question': Orientalism in One Country*, Oxford and New York: Berg, 1998.

Davis, J. A., 'Economy, Society, and the State', in J. A. Davis (ed.), *Italy in the Nineteenth Century*, Oxford: Oxford University Press, 2000.

De Cecco, M., 'The Economy from Liberalism to Fascism', in A. Lyttleton (ed.), *Liberal and Fascist Italy*, Oxford: Oxford University Press, 2002.

De Giorgio, M., 'The Catholic Model', in G. Fraisse and M. Perot (eds), *A History of Women in the West*, 5 vols, Cambridge, MA, and London: Harvard University Press, vol. 4, 1993a.

De Giorgio, M., *Le italiane dall'unità a oggi: modelli cuturali e comportamenti sociali*, 2nd edn, Rome-Bari: Laterza, 1993b.

De Giorgio, M., 'Women's History in Italy (Nineteenth and Twentieth Centuries)', *Journal of Modern Italian Studies* 1(3) (1996), pp. 413–31.

De Grand, A., *The Hunchback's Tailor: Giovanni Giolitti and Liberal Italy from the Challenge of Mass Politics to the Rise of Fascism, 1882–1922*, Westport: Praeger, 2001a.

De Grand, A., 'Giovanni Giolitti: A Pessimist as Modernizer', *Journal of Modern Italian Studies* 6(1) (2001b), pp. 57–67.

De Grazia, V. 'How Mussolini Ruled Women', in Françoise Thébaud (ed.), *A History of Women in the West*, 5 vols, Cambridge, MA, and London: Harvard University Press, 1994.

De Rosa, L., 'Unity or Plurality? Italian Issuing Banks, 1861–1893', *Journal of European Economic History* 23(3) (1994), pp. 453–74.

De Ruggiero, G., *The History of European Liberalism*, R. G. Collingwood (trans.), London: Oxford University Press, 1927.

Dickie, J., *Darkest Italy. The Nation and Stereotypes of the Mezzogiorno, 1860–1900*, New York: St Martin's Press, 1999.

Duggan, C., 'Francesco Crispi, "Political Education" and the Problem of Italian National Consciousness, 1860–1896', *Journal of Modern Italian Studies* 2(2) (1997), pp. 141–60.

Duggan, C., 'Review of *Sicily and the Unification of Italy: Liberal Policy and Local Power, 1859–1866*, by L. Riall', *English Historical Review* 114(459) (1999), pp. 1346–7.

Duggan, C., 'Politics in the Era of Depretis and Crispi, 1870–96', in J. A. Davis (ed.), *Italy in the Nineteenth Century*, Oxford: Oxford University Press, 2000.

Duggan, C., *Francesco Crispi, 1818–1901: From Nation to Nationalism*, Oxford: Oxford University Press, 2002.

Eckaus, R., 'The North–South Differential in Italian Economic Development', *Journal of Economic History* 21(3) (1961), pp. 285–317.

Esposto, A. G., 'Italian Industrialization and the Gerschenkronian "Great Spurt": A Regional Analysis', *Journal of Economic History* 52(2) (1992), pp. 353–62.

Esposto, A. G., 'Estimating Regional Per Capita Income: Italy, 1861–1914', *Journal of European Economic History* 26(3) (1997), pp. 585–604.

Falasca-Zamponi, S., 'The Artist to Power? Futurism, Fascism and the Avant-garde', *Theory, Culture and Society* 13(2) (1996), pp. 39–58.

Federico, G., 'Mercantilizzazione e sviluppo economico italiano (1860–1940)', in G. Federico (ed.), *The Economic Development of Italy from 1870*, Aldershot: Edward Elgar, 1986.

Federico, G., 'Heights, Calories and Welfare: A New Perspective on Italian Industrialization, 1854–1913', *Economics and Human Biology* 1(3) (2003a), pp. 289–308. http://www.iue.it/HEC/People/Faculty/Profiles/federico-publications.shtml.

Federico, G., 'Le nuove stime della produzione agricola italiana, 1860–1910: primi risultati ed implicazioni', *Rivista di storia economica* 3(19) (2003b), pp. 359–81. http://www.iue.it/HEC/People/Faculty/Profiles/federico-publications.shtml.

Federico, G., 'Protection and Italian Economic Development: Much Ado about Nothing?', in J-P. Dormois and P. Lains (eds), *Classical Trade Protectionism, 1865–1914*, London: Routledge, 2006, pp. 193–218. http://www.iue.it/HEC/People/Faculty/Profiles/federico-publications.shtml.

Federico, G. and Giannetti, R., 'Italy: Stalling and Surpassing', in J. Foreman-Peck and G. Federico (eds), *European Industrial Policy: The Twentieth-Century Experience*, Oxford: Oxford University Press, 1999.

Federico, G. and Toniolo, G., 'Italy', in R. Sylla and G. Toniolo (eds), *Patterns of European Industrialization: The Nineteenth Century*, London: Routledge, 1991.

Fenoaltea, S., 'Italy', in P. K. O'Brien (ed.), *Railways and the Economic Development of Western Europe, 1830–1914*, London: Macmillan, 1983.

Fenoaltea, S., 'Notes on the Rate of Industrial Growth in Italy, 1861–1913', *Journal of Economic History* 63(3) (2003), pp. 695–735.

Fenoaltea, S., 'The Growth of the Italian Economy, 1861–1913: Preliminary Second-generation Estimates', *European Review of Economic History* 9(3) (2005), pp. 273–312.

Forgacs, D. (ed.), *A Gramsci Reader: Selected Writings 1916–1935*, London: Lawrence & Wishart, 1988.

Gabrielli, P., 'Protagonists and Politics in the Italian Women's Movement: A Reflection on the Work of Annarita Buttafuoco', *Journal of Modern Italian Studies* 7(1) (2002), pp. 74–87.

Galassi, F. L. and Cohen, J. S., 'The Economics of Tenancy in Early Twentieth Century Southern Italy', *Economic History Review* 47(3) (1994), pp. 585–600.

Galasso, G., 'Rosario Romeo (1924–1987)', *Journal of Modern Italian Studies* 4(2) (1999), pp. 256–72.

Gay, P., *Schnitzler's Century*, London: Allen Lane, 2001.

Gentile, E., 'The Conquest of Modernity: From Modernist Nationalism to Fascism', *Modernism/Modernity* 1(3) (1994), pp. 55–78.

Gentile, E., 'Political Futurism and the Myth of the Italian Revolution', in G. Berghaus (ed.), *International Futurism in Arts and Literature*, Berlin and New York: Walter de Gruyter, 2000.

Gerschenkron, A., *Economic Backwardness in Historical Perspective: A Book of Essays*, Cambridge, MA: Harvard University Press, 1962.

Gerschenkron, A., *Continuity in History and Other Essays*, Cambridge, MA: Harvard University Press, 1968.

Gerschenkron, A., *Europe in the Russian Mirror: Four Lectures in Economic History*, Cambridge: Cambridge University Press, 1970.

Gibson, M., *Prostitution and the State in Italy, 1860–1915*, New Brunswick and London: Rutgers University Press, 1999.

Gibson, M., 'Introduction to Special Issue: Annarita Buttafuoco (1951–99) and Women's History in Italy', *Journal of Modern Italian Studies* 7(1) (2002), pp. 1–16.

Gibson, M., 'Labelling Women Deviant: Heterosexual Women, Prostitutes and Lesbians in Early Criminological Discourse', in P. Willson (ed.), *Gender, Family and Sexuality: The Private Sphere in Italy, 1860–1945*, Basingstoke: Palgrave Macmillan, 2004.

Ginsborg, P., 'Gramsci and the Era of Bourgeois Revolution in Italy', in J. A. Davis (ed.), *Gramsci and Italy's Passive Revolution*, London: Croom Helm, 1979.

Hallamore Caesar, A., 'About Town: The City and the Female Reader, 1860–1900', *Modern Italy* 7(2) (2002), pp. 129–41.

Hobsbawm, E., *The Age of Empire 1875–1914*, London: Weidenfeld & Nicolson, 1987.

Hoare, Q. and Nowell Smith, G. (eds), *Selections from the Prison Notebooks of Antonio Gramsci*, London: Lawrence & Wishart, 1971.

Kocka, J., 'The Middle Classes in Europe', in H. Kaelble (ed.), *The European Way: European Societies during the Nineteenth and Twentieth Centuries*, New York and Oxford: Berghahn, 2004.

Levy, C., 'The Centre and the Suburbs: Social Protest and Modernization in Milan and Turin, 1898–1917', *Modern Italy* 7(2) (2002), pp. 171–88.

Lupo, S., 'Tra società locale e commercio a lunga distanza: la vicenda degli agrumi Siciliana', *Meridiana*, 1 (1987), pp. 81–112.

Lupo, S., *Il giardino degli aranci: il mondo degli agrumi nella storia del Mezzogiorno*, Venice: Marsilio editore, 1990.

Lyttleton, A., 'Landlords, Peasants and the Limits of Liberalism', in J. A. Davis (ed.), *Gramsci and Italy's Passive Revolution*, London: Croom Helm, 1979.

Lyttleton, A., 'The Middle Classes in Liberal Italy', in J. A. Davis and P. Ginsborg (eds), *Society and Politics in the Age of the Risorgimento. Essays in Honour of Denis Mack Smith*, Cambridge: Cambridge University Press, 1991.

Mack Smith, D., *Italy: A Modern History*, Ann Arbor: University of Michigan Press, 1959.

Mack Smith, D., 'Benedetto Croce: History and Politics', *Journal of Contemporary History* 8(1) (1973), pp. 41–61.

Malatesta, M., 'Gli ordini professionali e la nazionalizzazione in Italia', in M. Meriggi and P. Schiera (eds), *Dalla città alla nazione: borghesie ottocentesche in Italia e in Germania*, Bologna: il Mulino, 1993.

Malatesta, M., 'The Italian Professions from a Comparative Perspective', in M. Malatesta (ed.), *Society and the Professions in Italy, 1860–1914*, Cambridge: Cambridge University Press, 1995.

Malatesta, M., 'The Landed Aristocracy during the Nineteenth and Early Twentieth Centuries', in H. Kaelble (ed.), *The European Way: European Societies during the Nineteenth and Twentieth Centuries*, New York and Oxford: Berghahn, 2004.

Maturi, W., *Interpretazioni del risorgimento: lezioni di storia della storiografia*, Turin: Einaudi, 1962.

Meriggi, M., 'Introduzione', in M. Meriggi and P. Schiera (eds), *Dalla città alla nazione: borghesie ottocentesche in Italia e in Germania*, Bologna: il Mulino, 1993a.

Meriggi, M., 'The Italian "borghesia"', in J. Kocka and A. Mitchell (eds), *Bourgeois Society in Nineteenth-century Europe*, Oxford: Berg, 1993b.

Minesso, M., 'The Engineering Profession, 1802–1923', in M. Malatesta (ed.), *Society and the Professions in Italy, 1860–1914*, Cambridge: Cambridge University Press, 1995.

Mitchell, B. R., *International Historical Statistics: Europe 1750–1993*, 4th edn, London: Macmillan, 1998.

Montroni, G., *Gli uomini del Re: la nobiltà napoletana nell'Ottocento*, Rome: Meridiana Libri, 1996.

Morris, J., *The Political Economy of Shopkeeping in Milan, 1886–1922*, Cambridge: Cambridge University Press, 1993.

Morris, J., 'Challenging *meridionalismo*: Constructing a New History for Southern Italy', in R. Lumley and J. Morris (eds), *The New History of the Italian South: The Mezzogiorno Revisited*, Exeter: University of Exeter Press, 1997.

Mosse, G. L., 'The Political Culture of Italian Futurism: A General Perspective', *Journal of Contemporary History* 25(2–3) (1990), pp. 253–68.

O'Brien, P. K., 'Do We Have a Typology for the Study of European Industrialization in the XIXth Century?', *Journal of European Economic History* 15(2) (1986), pp. 291–334.

O'Brien, P. K. and Toniolo, G., 'The Poverty of Italy and the Backwardness of its Agriculture before 1914', in B. M. S. Campbell and M. Overton (eds), *Land, Labour and Livestock: Historical Studies in European Agricultural Productivity*, Manchester: Manchester University Press, 1991.

Ortaggi Cammarosano, S., 'Labouring Women in Northern and Central Italy in the Nineteenth Century', in J. A. Davis and P. Ginsborg (eds), *Society and Politics in the Age of the Risorgimento. Essays in Honour of Denis Mack Smith*, Cambridge: Cambridge University Press, 1991.

Palazzi, M., 'Economic Autonomy and Male Authority: Female Merchants in Modern Italy', *Journal of Modern Italian Studies* 7(1) (2002), pp. 17–36.

Patriarca, S., 'Gender Trouble: Women and the Making of Italy's "Active Population", 1861–1936', *Journal of Modern Italian Studies* 3(2) (1998), pp. 144–63.

Petrusewicz, M., *Latifundium. Moral Economy and Material Life in a European Periphery*, Ann Arbor: University of Michigan Press, 1996.

Petrusewicz, M., 'The Demise of *latifondismo*', in R. Lumley and J. Morris (eds), *The New History of the Italian South: The Mezzogiorno Revisited*, Exeter: University of Exeter Press, 1997.

Pezzino, P., 'Local Power in Southern Italy', in R. Lumley and J. Morris (eds), *The New History of the Italian South: The Mezzogiorno Revisited*, Exeter: University of Exeter Press, 1997.

Randeraad, N., *Authority in Search of Liberty: The Prefects in Liberal Italy*, Amsterdam: Thesis Publishers, 1993.

Reeder, L., 1998, 'Women in the Classroom: Mass Migration, Literacy and the Nationalization of Sicilian Women at the Turn of the Century', *Journal of Social History* 32(1) (1998), pp. 101–24.

Riall, L., 'Progress and Compromise in Liberal Italy', *Historical Journal* 38(1) (1995), pp. 205–13.

Riall, L., 'Review of *Storia d'Italia I*, by G. Sabbatucci and V. Vidotto (eds)', *Journal of Modern Italian Studies* 1(3) (1996), pp. 457–9.

Romanelli, R., *Il comando impossibile: stato e società nell'Italia liberale*, Bologna: il Mulino, 1988.

Romanelli, R., 'Political Debate, Social History, and the Italian *borghesia*: Changing Perspectives in Historical Research', *Journal of Modern History* 63(3) (1991), pp. 717–39.

Romanelli, R. (ed.), *Storia dello stato italiano*, Rome: Donzelli editore, 1995.

Romeo, R., *Risorgimento e capitalismo*, 2nd edn, Bari: Laterza, 1963.

Romeo, R., *L'Italia unita e la prima guerra mondiale*, Rome-Bari: Laterza, 1978.

Salomone, A. W., *Italy in the Giolittian Era: Italian Democracy in the Making, 1900–1914*, 2nd edn, Philadelphia: University of Pennsylvania Press, 1960.

Schram, A., *Railways and the Formation of the Italian State in the Nineteenth Century*, Cambridge: Cambridge University Press, 1997.

Seymour, M., 'Keystone of the Patriarchal Family? Indissoluble Marriage, Masculinity and Divorce in Liberal Italy', *Journal of Modern Italian Studies* 10(3) (2005), pp. 302–9.

Sione, P., 'From Home to Factory: Women in the Nineteenth-century Italian Silk Industry', in D. M. Hafter (ed.), *European Women and Preindustrial Craft*, Bloomington and Indianapolis: Indiana University Press, 1995.

Snowden, F. M., *Violence and the Great Estates in the South of Italy: Apulia, 1900–1922*, Cambridge: Cambridge University Press, 1986.

Snowden, F. M., 'Fields of Death: Malaria in Italy, 1861–1962', *Modern Italy* 4(1) (1999), pp.25–57.

Socrate, F., 'Borghesie e stili di vita', in G. Sabbatucci and V. Vidotto (eds), *Storia d'Italia*, 6 vols, Rome-Bari: Laterza, vol. 3, 1995.

Soldani, S. (ed.), *L'educazione delle donne: scuole e modelli femminili nell'Italia dell'Ottocento*, Milan: Franco Angelli, 1989.

Soldani, S., 'Lo stato e il lavoro delle donne nell'Italia liberale', *Passato e Presente* 9(24) (1990), pp. 23–71.

Sternhell, Z., *The Birth of Fascist Ideology: From Cultural Rebellion to Political Revolution*, Princeton: Princeton University Press, 1994.

Tobia, B., 'Associazionismo e patriottismo: il caso del pelleginaggio nazionale a Roma del 1884', in M. Meriggi and P. Schiera (eds), *Dalla città alla nazione: borghesie ottocentesche in Italia e in Germania*, Bologna: il Mulino, 1993.

Toniolo, G., *An Economic History of Liberal Italy, 1850–1918*, London: Routledge, 1990.

Tosh, J. (ed.), *Historians on History*, Harlow: Pearson Education, 2000.

Trebilcock, C., *The Industrialization of the Continental Powers, 1780–1914*, London: Longman, 1981.

Ville, S. P., *Transport and the Development of the European Economy, 1750–1918*, London: Macmillan, 1990.

Webster, R. A., *Industrial Imperialism in Italy 1908–1915*, Berkeley: University of California Press, 1975.

Willson, P., 'Introduction: Gender and the Private Sphere in Liberal and Fascist Italy', in P. Willson (ed.), 2004, *Gender, Family and Sexuality: The Private Sphere in Italy, 1860–1945*, Basingstoke: Palgrave Macmillan, 2004.

Willson, P., 'From Margin to Centre: Recent Trends in Modern Italian Women's and Gender History', *Modern Italy* 11(3) (2006), pp. 327–37.

Zappi, E. G., *If Eight Hours Seem Too Few: Mobilization of Women Workers in the Italian Rice Fields*, Albany: State University of New York Press, 1991.

FASCIST ITALY

Abse, T., 'The Rise of Fascism in an Industrial City: The Case of Livorno, 1918–1922', in D. Forgacs (ed.), *Rethinking Italian Fascism: Capitalism, Populism and Culture*, London: Lawrence & Wishart, 1986.

Abse, T., 'Italian Workers and Italian Fascism', in R. Bessel (ed.), *Fascist Italy and Nazi Germany: Comparisons and Contrasts*, Cambridge: Cambridge University Press, 1996.

Adamson, W. L., 'Fascism and Culture: Avant-gardes and Secular Religion in the Italian Case', *Journal of Contemporary History* 24(3) (1989), pp. 411–35.

Adamson, W. L., 'Avante-garde Modernism and Italian Fascism: Cultural Politics in the Era of Mussolini', *Journal of Modern Italian Studies* 6(2) (2001), pp. 230–48.

Aquarone, A., *L'organizzazione dello stato totalitario*, Turin: Einaudi, 1965.

Azzi, S. C., 'The Historiography of Fascist Foreign Policy', *Historical Journal* 36(1) (1993), pp. 187–203.

Barzini, L., *The Italians*, London: Penguin, 1968.

Bellamy, R. and Schecter, D., *Gramsci and the Italian State*, Manchester: Manchester University Press, 1993.

Ben-Ghiat, R., 'Italian Fascism and the Aesthetics of the Third Way', *Journal of Contemporary History* 31(2) (1996), pp. 293–316.

Ben-Ghiat, R., 'Liberation: Italian Cinema and the Fascist Past', in R. J. B. Bosworth and P. Dogliani (eds), *Italian Fascism: History, Memory and Representation*, Basingstoke: Macmillan, 1999.

Berezin, M., *Making the Fascist Self: The Political Culture of Interwar Italy*, Ithaca: Cornell University Press, 1997.

Berghaus, G., 'Introduction', in G. Berghaus (ed.), *Fascism and Theatre: Comparative Studies on the Aesthetics and Politics of Performance in Europe, 1925–1945*, Oxford: Berghahn, 1996.

Berghaus, G., 'The Ritual Core of Fascist Theatre: An Anthropological Perspective', in G. Berghaus (ed.), *Fascism and Theatre: Comparative Studies on the Aesthetics and Politics of Performance in Europe, 1925–1945*, Oxford: Berghahn, 1996.

Bernadini, G., 'Anti-Semitism', in P. Cannistraro (ed.), 1982, *Historical Dictionary of Fascist Italy*, Westport, CT: Greenwood Press, 1982.

Bidussa, D., *Il mito del bravo italiano*, Milan: il Saggiatore, 1994.

Blatt, J., 'The Battle of Turin, 1933–1935: Carlo Rosselli, Giustizia e Libertà, OVRA and the Origins of Mussolini's Anti-Semitic Campaign', *Journal of Modern Italian Studies* 1(1) (1995), pp. 22–57.

Blinkhorn, M., 'The Author's Response', *Reviews in History*, 2001. http://www.history.ac.uk/reviews/paper/blinkhornMartin.html.

Bosworth, R. J. B., *The Italian Dictatorship: Problems and Perspectives in the Interpretation of Mussolini and Fascism*, London: Arnold, 1998.

Bosworth, R. J. B., 'Venice between Fascism and International Tourism, 1911–45', *Modern Italy* 4(1) (1999), pp. 5–23.

Bosworth, R. J. B., '*Per necessità famigliare*: Hypocrisy and Corruption in Fascist Italy', *European History Quarterly* 30(3) (2000), pp. 357–87.

Bosworth, R. J. B., *Mussolini's Italy: Life Under the Dictatorship, 1915–1945*, London: Allen Lane, 2005.

Braun, E., 'Expressionism as Fascist Aesthetic', *Journal of Contemporary History* 31(2) (1996), pp. 273–92.

Braun, E., 'The Visual Arts: Modernism and Fascism', in A. Lyttleton (ed.), *Liberal and Fascist Italy*, Oxford: Oxford University Press, 2002.

Burgwyn, H. J., 'Recent Books on Italian Foreign Policy in the 1930's: A Critical Essay', *Journal of Italian History* 1(3) (1978), pp. 535–53.

Burgwyn, H. J., *Italian Foreign Policy in the Interwar Period, 1918–1940*, Westport: Praeger, 1997.

Burgwyn, H. J., 'General Roatta's War Against the Partisans in Yugoslavia: 1942', *Journal of Modern Italian Studies* 9(3) (2004), pp. 314–29.

Caldwell, L., 'Reproducers of the Nation: Women and the Family in Fascist Policy', in D. Forgacs (ed.), *Rethinking Italian Fascism: Capitalism, Populism and Culture*, London: Lawrence & Wishart, 1986.

Cannistraro, P. V., 'Mussolini's Cultural Revolution: Fascist or Nationalist?', *Journal of Contemporary History* 7(3–4) (1972), pp. 115–39.

Cannistraro, P. V., 'Jacobinism, Marxism, and Fascism: The Historiographical Trajectory of Renzo De Felice', *Italian Quarterly* 36(141–2) (1999), pp. 25–32.

Caracciolo, N. (ed.), *Gli ebrei e l'Italia durante la guerra 1940–45*, Rome: Bonacci editore, 1986.

Cassels, A., *Fascist Italy*, London: Routledge and Kegan Paul, 1969.

Cassels, A., *Mussolini's Early Diplomacy*, Princeton: Princeton University Press, 1970.

Cavallo, P., 'Theatre Politics of the Mussolini Regime and their Influence on Fascist Drama', in G. Berghaus (ed.), *Fascism and Theatre: Comparative Studies on the Aesthetics and Politics of Performance in Europe, 1925–1945*, Oxford: Berghahn, 1996.

Ciocca, P., 'L'economia italiana nel contesto internazionale', in P. Ciocca and G. Toniolo (eds), *L'economia italiana nel periodo fascista*, Bologna: il Mulino, 1976.

Ciocca, P. and Toniolo, G., 'Introduzione', in P. Ciocca and G. Toniolo (eds), *L'economia italiana nel periodo fascista*, Bologna: il Mulino, 1976.

Clark, M., *Antonio Gramsci and the Revolution that Failed*, London and New Haven: Yale University Press, 1977.

Cohen, J. S., 'Un esame statistico delle opere di bonifica intraprese durante il regime fascista', in G. Toniolo (ed.), *Lo sviluppo economico italiano*, Rome-Bari: Laterza, 1973.

Cohen, J. S., 'Was Italian Fascism a Developmental Dictatorship? Some Evidence to the Contrary', *Economic History Review* 41(1) (1988), pp. 95–113.

Collotti, E., 'La politica razzista del regime fascista', 1998. http://www.novecento.org/interCollotti.html.

Collotti, E. and Klinkhammer, L., *Il fascismo e l'Italia in guerra: una conversazione fra storia e storiografia*, Rome: Edizione Ediesse, 1996.

Corner, P., *Fascism in Ferrara, 1915–1925*, Oxford: Oxford University Press, 1974.

Corner, P., 'Fascist Agrarian Policy and the Italian Economy in the Inter-war Years', in J. A. Davis (ed.), *Gramsci and Italy's Passive Revolution*, London: Croom Helm, 1979.

Corner, P., 'Italy', in S. Salter and J. Stevenson (eds), *The Working Class and Politics in Europe and America, 1929–1945*, London: Longman, 1990.

Corner, P., 'Women in Fascist Italy. Changing Family Roles in the Transition from an Agricultural to an Industrial Society', *European History Quarterly* 23(1) (1993), pp. 51–68.

Corner, P., 'State and Society, 1901–1922', in A. Lyttleton (ed.), *Liberal and Fascist Italy*, Oxford: Oxford University Press, 2002a.

Corner, P., 'The Road to Fascism: An Italian *sonderweg*?', *Contemporary European History* 11(2) (2002b), pp. 273–95.

Curami, A., 'Tecnologia e modelli di armamento', in V. Zamagni (ed.), *Come perdere la guerra e vincere la pace: l'economia italiana tra Guerra e dopoguerra, 1938–1947*, Bologna: il Mulino, 1997.

Davis, J. A. and Mack Smith, D., *Mussolini and Italian Fascism*, Coventry: Warwick History Videos, 1991.

De Bernières, L., *Captain Corelli's Mandolin*, London: Minerva, 1996.

De Felice, R., *Mussolini il Duce (I): Gli anni del consenso 1929–1936*, Turin: Einaudi, 1974.

De Felice, R., *Intervista sul fascismo*, Rome-Bari: Laterza, 1975.

De Felice, R., *Fascism: An Informal Introduction to its Theory and Practice*, New Jersey: Transaction Books, 1976.

De Felice, R., *Interpretations of Fascism*, Cambridge, MA: Harvard University Press, 1977.

De Felice, R., *Storia degli ebrei italiani sotto il fascismo*, 4th edn, Turin: Einaudi, 1993.

De Felice, R., *Rosso e Nero*, 2nd edn, Milan: Baldini and Castoldi, 1995.

De Felice, R. (ed.), *Il Fascismo. Le interpretazioni dei contemporanei e degli storici*, 2nd edn, Bari: Laterza, 1998.

De Felice, R., *Breve storia del fascismo*, Milan: Mondadori, 2001.

De Grand, A., 'Cracks in the Façade: The Failure of Fascist Totalitarianism in Italy 1935–9', *European History Quarterly* 21(4) (1991), pp. 515–35.

De Grazia, V., *The Culture of Consent: Mass Organization of Leisure in Fascist Italy*, Cambridge: Cambridge University Press, 1981.

De Grazia, V., 'Mass Culture and Sovereignty: The American Challenge to European Cinema', *Journal of Modern History* 61(1) (1989), pp. 53–87.

De Grazia, V., *How Fascism Ruled Women. Italy, 1922–1945*, Berkeley: University of California Press, 1992.

De Grazia, V., 'Nationalizing Women: The Competition Between Fascist and Commercial Cultural Models in Mussolini's Italy', in V. de Grazia (ed.), *The Sex of Things: Gender and Consumption in Historical Perspective*, Berkeley: University of California Press, 1996.

Del Boca, A., *Italiani, brava gente? Un mito duro a morire*, Vicenza: Neri Pozza, 2005.

Doumanis, N., *Myth and Memory in the Mediterranean: Remembering Fascism's Empire*, London: Macmillan, 1997.

Doumanis, N., 'Dodecanese Nostalgia for Mussolini's Rule', *History Today* 48(2) (1998), pp. 17–21.

Dunnage, J., 'Policing and Politics in the Southern Italian Community, 1943–48', in J. Dunnage (ed.), *After the War: Violence, Justice, Continuity and Renewal in Italian Society*, Market Harborough: Troubador, 1999.

Dunnage, J., 'Facing the Past and Building for the Future', in J. Dunnage (ed.), *After the War: Violence, Justice, Continuity and Renewal in Italian Society*, Market Harborough: Troubador, 1999.

Eatwell, R., 'What is Fascism?', *History Review* 26 (1996), pp. 29–35.

Falasca-Zamponi, S., *Fascist Spectacle: The Aesthetics of Power in Mussolini's Italy*, Berkeley: University of California Press, 1997.

Federico, G. and Giannetti, R., 'Italy: Stalling and Surpassing', in J. Foreman-Peck and G. Federico (eds), *European Industrial Policy: The Twentieth Century Experience*, Oxford: Oxford University Press, 1999.

Focardi, F. and Klinkhammer, L., 'The Question of Fascist Italy's War Crimes: The Construction of a Self-acquitting Myth (1943–1948)', *Journal of Modern Italian Studies* 9(3) (2004), pp. 330–48.

Fogu, C., '"To Make History": Garibaldianism and the Formation of a Fascist Historic Imaginary', in A. R. Ascoli and K. von Henneberg (eds), 2001, *Making and Remaking Italy: The Cultivation of National Identity Around the Risorgimento*, Oxford and New York: Berg, 2001.

Forgacs, D., *Italian Culture in the Industrial Era 1880–1980. Cultural Politics, Politics, and the Public*, Manchester: Manchester University Press, 1990.

Forgacs, D., '*Nostra patria*: Revisions of the Risorgimento in the Cinema, 1925–52', in A. R. Ascoli and K. von Henneberg (eds), 2001, *Making and Remaking Italy: The Cultivation of National Identity Around the Risorgimento*, Oxford and New York: Berg, 2001.

Forsyth, D. J., 'Review of *Storia economica d'Italia. Dalla Grande Guerra al miracolo economico (1918–1963)*, by R. Petri', *Journal of Modern Italian Studies* 8(1) (2003), pp. 113–15.

Fraddosio, M., 'The Fallen Hero: The Myth of Mussolini and Fascist Women in the Italian Social Republic (1943–5)', *Journal of Contemporary History* 31(1) (1996), pp. 99–124.

Gentile, E., 'The Problem of the Party in Italian Fascism', *Journal of Contemporary History* 19(2) (1984), pp. 251–74.

Gentile, E., 'Fascism in Italian Historiography: in Search of an Individual Historical Identity', *Journal of Contemporary History* 21(2) (1986a), pp. 179–208.

Gentile, E., 'From the Cultural Revolt of the Giolittian Era to the Ideology of Fascism', in F. J. Coppa (ed.), *Studies in Modern Italian History: From the Risorgimento to the Republic*, New York: Peter Lang, 1986b.

Gentile, E., 'Fascism as Political Religion', *Journal of Contemporary History* 25(2–3) (1990), pp. 229–51.

Gentile, E., *The Sacralization of Politics in Fascist Italy*, Cambridge, MA: Harvard University Press, 1996a.

Gentile, E., 'The Theatre of Politics in Fascist Italy', in G. Berghaus (ed.), *Fascism and Theatre: Comparative Studies on the Aesthetics and Politics of Performance in Europe, 1925–1945*, Oxford: Berghahn, 1996b.

Gentile, E., 'Renzo De Felice: A Tribute', *Journal of Contemporary History* 32(2) (1997), pp. 139–51.

Gentile, E., 'Paths to an Interpretation: Renzo De Felice and the Definition of Fascism', *Italian Quarterly* 36(141–2) (1999), pp. 53–70.

Gentile, E., 'Fascism in Power: The Totalitarian Experiment', in A. Lyttleton (ed.), *Liberal and Fascist Italy*, Oxford: Oxford University Press, 2002.

Gentile, E., *Renzo De Felice. Lo storico e il personaggio*, Rome-Bari: Laterza, 2003.

Ghirardo, D. Y., 'Città Fascista: Surveillance and Spectacle', *Journal of Contemporary History* 31(2) (1996), pp. 347–72.

Gillette, A., 'The Origins of the "Manifesto of Racial Scientists"', *Journal of Modern Italian Studies* 6(3) (2001), pp. 305–23.

Gregor, A. J., *Interpretations of Fascism*, New Jersey: General Learning Press, 1974a.

Gregor, A. J., 'Fascism and Modernization: Some Addenda', *World Politics* 26 (1974b), pp. 370–84.

Gregor, A. J., *Italian Fascism and Developmental Dictatorship*, Princeton: Princeton University Press, 1979.

Gregor, A. J., *Phoenix*, New Brunswick: Transaction Publishers, 1999.

Griffin, R., 'Staging the Nation's Rebirth: The Politics and Aesthetics of Performance in the Context of Fascist Studies', in G. Berghaus (ed.), *Fascism and Theatre: Comparative Studies on the Aesthetics and Politics of Performance in Europe, 1925–1945*, Oxford: Berghahn, 1996.

Griffin, R. (ed.), *International Fascism: A Reader*, London: Arnold, 1998a.

Griffin, R., 'The Sacred Synthesis: The Ideological Cohesion of Fascist Cultural Policy', *Modern Italy* 3(1) (1998b), pp. 5–23.

Griffin, R., 'Notes Towards the Definition of a Fascist Culture: The Prospects for Synergy between Marxist and Liberal Heuristics', *Culture, Theory and Critique* 42(1) (1999), pp. 95–114. http://ah.brookes.ac.uk/resources/griffin/fasaesthetics.pdf.

Griffin, R., 'How Fascist was Mussolini?', *New Perspective* 6(1) (2000), pp. 31–5. http://ah.brookes.ac.uk/resources/griffin/mussolinifascist.pdf.

Griffin, R., 'The Primacy of Italian Culture: The Current Growth (or Manufacture) of Consensus Within Fascist Studies', *Journal of Contemporary History* 37(1) (2002), pp. 21–43.

Griffin, R., 'The Palingenetic Core of Generic Fascist Ideology', in A. Campi (ed.), *Che cos'è il fascismo? Interpretazioni e prospettive di ricerche*, Rome: Ideazione Editrice, 2003, pp. 97–122. http://ah.brookes.ac.uk/resources/griffin/coreoffascism.pdf.

Grifone, P., *Capitalismo di stato e imperialismo fascista*, Milan: Mazzotta, 1975.

Guerra, E., 'Memory and Representations of Fascism: Female Autobiographical Narratives', in R. J. B. Bosworth and P. Dogliani (eds), 1999, *Italian Fascism: History, Memory and Representation*, Basingstoke: Macmillan, 1999.

Gunzberg, L. M., *Strangers at Home: Jews in the Italian Literary Imagination*, Berkeley: University of California Press, 1992.

Hughes, H. S., *Prisoners of Hope: The Silver Age of the Italian Jews 1924–74*, Cambridge, MA: Harvard University Press, 1983.

Ipsen, C., *Dictating Demography: The Problem of Population in Fascist Italy*, Cambridge: Cambridge University Press, 1996.

Kedward, R., 'Afterword: What Kind of Revisionism?', in D. Forgacs (ed.), *Rethinking Italian Fascism: Capitalism, Populism and Culture*, London: Lawrence & Wishart, 1986.

Kirkpatrick, I., *Mussolini: Study of a Demagogue*, London: Odhams, 1964.

Knox, M., 'Conquest, Foreign and Domestic, in Fascist Italy and Nazi Germany', *Journal of Modern History* 56(1) (1984), pp. 2–57.

Knox, M., 'The Fascist Regime, its Foreign Policy and its Wars: An Anti-anti-Fascist Orthodoxy?', *Contemporary European History* 4(3) (1995), pp. 347–65.

Knox, M., 'In the Duce's Defence', *Times Literary Supplement*, 26 February 1999.

Knox, M., 'Fascism: Ideology, Foreign Policy and War', in A. Lyttleton (ed.), *Liberal and Fascist Italy*, Oxford: Oxford University Press, 2002.

Ledeen, M., 'Renzo de Felice and the Question of Italian Fascism', *Society* 38(4) (2001), pp. 75–7.

Levi, C., *Christ Stopped at Eboli*, London: Penguin, 1982.

Lyttleton, A., *The Seizure of Power: Fascism in Italy 1919–1929*, 2nd edn, London: Weidenfeld & Nicolson, 1987.

Mack Smith, D., 'Mussolini, Artist in Propaganda', *History Today* 9(4) (1959), pp. 223–32.

Mack Smith, D., 'A Monument for the *Duce*', *Times Literary Supplement*, 31 October 1975.

Mack Smith, D., *Mussolini's Roman Empire*, London: Longman, 1976.

Mack Smith, D., 'Mussolini: Reservations About Renzo De Felice's Biography', *Modern Italy* 5(2) (2000), pp. 193–210.

Mallett, R., *Mussolini and the Origins of the Second World War, 1933–1940*, Basingstoke: Palgrave Macmillan, 2003.

Mason, T., 'The Turin Strikes of March 1943', in J. Caplan (ed.), *Nazism, Fascism and the Working Class*, Cambridge: Cambridge University Press, 1995.

Michaelis, M., *Mussolini and the Jews. German–Italian Relations and the Jewish Question in Italy, 1922–45*, Oxford: Clarendon Press, 1978.

Minniti, F., 'L'industria degli armamenti dal 1940 al 1943: i mercati, le produzioni', in V. Zamagni (ed.), *Come perdere la guerra e vincere la pace: l'economia italiana tra Guerra e dopoguerra, 1938–1947*, Bologna: il Mulino, 1997.

Morgan, P., '"The Years of Consent?" Popular Attitudes and Forms of Resistance to Fascism in Italy, 1925–1940', in T. Kirk and A. McElligott (eds), *Opposing Fascism. Community, Authority and Resistance in Europe*, Cambridge: Cambridge University Press, 1999.

Morgan, P., *Italian Fascism 1915–1945*, 2nd edn, Basingstoke: Palgrave, 2004.

Morgan, P., *The Fall of Mussolini. Italy, the Italians, and the Second World War*, Oxford: Oxford University Press, 2007.

Mosse, G. L., *International Fascism: New Thoughts and Approaches*, London: Sage, 1979.

Mosse, G. L., 'Fascism and the French Revolution', *Journal of Contemporary History* 24(1) (1989), pp. 5–26.

Mosse, G. L., 'Fascist Aesthetics and Society: Some Considerations', *Journal of Contemporary History* 31(2) (1996), pp. 245–52.

Paradisi, M. 'Il commercio estero e la struttura industriale', in P. Ciocca and G. Toniolo (eds), *L'economia italiana nel periodo fascista*, Bologna: il Mulino, 1976.

Passerini, L., 'Oral Memory of Fascism', in D. Forgacs (ed.), *Rethinking Italian Fascism: Capitalism, Populism and Culture*, London: Lawrence & Wishart, 1986.

Passerini, L., *Fascism in Popular Memory: The Cultural Experience of the Turin Working Class*, Cambridge: Cambridge University Press, 1987.

Pavone, C., 'Introduction', *Journal of Modern Italian Studies* 9(3) (2004), pp. 271–9.

Payne, S., *A History of Fascism*, Madison: University of Wisconsin Press, 1995.

Pertile, L., 'Fascism and Literature', in D. Forgacs (ed.), *Rethinking Italian Fascism: Capitalism, Populism and Culture*, London: Lawrence & Wishart, 1986.

Petri, R., *Storia economica d'Italia. Dalla Grande Guerra al miracolo economico (1918–1963)*, Bologna: il Mulino, 2002.

Petri, R., 'A Technocratic Strategy of Industrial Development in Italy, 1935–60', 2005. http://www.ub.es/histeco/Activitats/Petri.pdf.

Pollard, J., *The Fascist Experience in Italy*, London: Routledge, 1998.

Quartararo, R., *Roma tra Londra e Berlino: La politica estera fascista dal 1930 al 1940*, Rome: Bonacci, 1980.

Quartararo, R., *L'Anschluss come problema internazionale. Le responsabilità anglo-francesi*, Rome: Jouvence, 2005.

Ranieri, R., 'Review of *Storia economica d'Italia. Dalla Grande Guerra al miracolo economico (1918–1963)*, by R. Petri', *Business History* 45(2) (2003), pp. 115–16.

Renton, D., *Fascism: Theory and Practice*, London: Pluto Press, 1999.

Renzi, W. A., 'Italy's Neutrality and Intervention into the Great War: A Re-examination', *American Historical Review* 73(5) (1968), pp. 1414–32.

Roberts, D. D., 'How Not to Think About Fascism and Ideology, Intellectual Antecedents and Historical Meaning', *Journal of Contemporary History* 35(2) (2000), pp. 185–211.

Roberts, D. D., De Grand, A., Antliff, M. and Linehan, T., 'Comments on Roger Griffin, "The Primacy of Culture: The Current Growth (or Manufacture) of Consensus Within Fascist Studies"', *Journal of Contemporary History* 37(2) (2002), pp. 259–74.

Robertson, E., *Mussolini as Empire Builder: Europe and Africa, 1932–36*, London: Macmillan, 1977.

Rodogno, D., 'Italian Brava Gente? Fascist Italy's Policy Towards the Jews in the Balkans, April 1941–July 1943', *European History Quarterly* 35(2) (2005), pp. 213–40.

Rosselli, C., in N. Urbinati (ed.), *Liberal Socialism*, Princeton: Princeton University Press, 1994.

Rossi, N. and Toniolo, G., 'Catching up or Falling Behind? Italy's Economic Growth, 1895–1947', *Economic History Review* 45(3) (1992), pp. 537–63.

Sadkovich, J. J., 'Understanding Defeat: Reappraising Italy's Role in World War Two', *Journal of Contemporary History* 24(1) (1989), pp. 27–61.

Salvemini, G., *Under the Axe of Fascism*, London: Victor Gollancz, 1936.

Santarelli, L., 'Muted Violence: Italian War Crimes in Occupied Greece', *Journal of Modern Italian Studies* 9(3) (2004), pp. 280–99.

Sarfatti, M., 'Fascist Italy and German Jews in South-eastern France in July 1943', *Journal of Modern Italian Studies* 3(3) (1998), pp. 318–28.

Sarti, R., 'Mussolini and the Italian Industrial Leadership in the Battle of the Lira 1925–1927', *Past and Present* 47(2) (1970), pp. 97–112.

Sarti, R., *Fascism and the Industrial Leadership in Italy, 1919–40*, Berkeley: University of California Press, 1971.

Sarti, R., 'Review of *Italian Fascism and Developmental Dictatorship* and *Young Mussolini and the Intellectual Origins of Fascism*, by A. J. Gregor', *American Historical Review* 86(1) (1981), pp. 169–70.

Sarti, R., 'Fascism, Revolution, and Consensus', *Italian Quarterly* 24(93) (1983), pp. 81–7.

Schnapp, J. T., *Staging Fascism: 18BL and the Theater of the Masses for Masses*, Stanford: Stanford University Press, 1996.

Sluga, G. A., 'The Risiera di San Sabba: Fascism, Anti-Fascism and Italian Nationalism', *Journal of Modern Italian Studies* 1(3) (1996), pp. 401–12.

Sluga, G. A., 'Italian National Memory, National Identity and Fascism', in R. J. B. Bosworth and P. Dogliani (eds), *Italian Fascism: History, Memory and Representation*, Basingstoke: Macmillan, 1999.

Sluga, G. A., 'Italian National Identity and Fascism: Aliens, Allogenes and Assimilation on Italy's North-eastern Border', in G. Bedani and B. Haddock (eds), *The Politics of Italian National Identity*, Cardiff: University of Wales Press, 2000, pp. 163–90.

Sonnessa, A., 'Working Class Defence Organization, Anti-Fascist Resistance and the *Arditi del Popolo* in Turin, 1919–22', *European History Quarterly* 33(2) (2003), pp. 183–218.

Sonnessa, A., 'The 1922 Turin Massacre (*Strage di Torino*): Working Class Resistance and Conflicts Within Fascism', *Modern Italy* 10(2) (2005), pp. 187–205.

Spriano, P., *The Occupation of the Factories: Italy, 1920*, G. A. Williams (trans.), London: Pluto Press, 1975.

Steinberg, J., 'Fascism in the South: The Case of Calabria', in D. Forgacs (ed.), *Rethinking Italian Fascism: Capitalism, Populism and Culture*, London: Lawrence & Wishart, 1986.

Steinberg, J., *All or Northing: The Axis and the Holocaust, 1941–1943*, London and New York: Routledge, 1990.

Sternhell, Z., *Neither Right nor Left: Fascist Ideology in France*, Princeton: Princeton University Press, 1986.

Sternhell, Z., *The Birth of Fascist Ideology: From Cultural Rebellion to Political Revolution*, Princeton: Princeton University Press, 1994.

Stille, A., *Benevolence and Betrayal: Five Italian Jewish Families under Fascism*, London: Jonathan Cape, 1992.

Stone, M., 'Staging Fascism: The Exhibition of the Fascist Revolution', *Journal of Contemporary History* 28(2) (1993), pp. 215–43.

Stone, M., *The Patron State: Culture and Politics in Fascist Italy*, Princeton: Princeton University Press, 1998.

Stone, M., 'Challenging Cultural Categories: The Transformation of the Venice Biennale Under Fascism', *Journal of Modern Italian Studies* 4(2) (1999), pp. 184–208.

Tattara, G. and Toniolo, G., ' L'industria manifatturiera: cicli, politiche e mutamenti di struttura (1921–37)', in P. Ciocca and G. Toniolo (eds), *L'economia italiana nel periodo fascista*, Bologna: il Mulino, 1976.

Thompson, D., 'The Organisation, Fascistisation and Management of Theatre in Italy, 1925–1943', in G. Berghaus (ed.), 1996, *Fascism and Theatre: Comparative Studies on the Aesthetics and Politics of Performance in Europe, 1925–1945*, Oxford: Berghahn, 1996.

Toniolo, G. (ed.), *Lo sviluppo economico italiano*, Rome-Bari: Laterza, 1973.

Toniolo, G., *L'economia dell'Italia fascista*, Rome-Bari: Laterza, 1980.

Tranfaglia, N., *Storia d'Italia. La prima guerra mondiale e il fascismo*, vol. 22, Turin: UTET, 1995.

Tunesi, S., 'Italian Environmental Policies in the Post-war Period', in P. McCarthy (ed.), *Italy since 1945*, Oxford: Oxford University Press, 2000.

Verdone, M., 'Mussolini's "Theatre of the Masses"', in G. Berghaus (ed.), *Fascism and Theatre: Comparative Studies on the Aesthetics and Politics of Performance in Europe, 1925–1945*, Oxford: Berghahn, 1996.

Ventresca, R., 'Debating the Meaning of Fascism in Contemporary Italy', *Modern Italy* 11(2) (2006), pp. 189–209.

Ward, D., *Antifascisms: Cultural Politics in Italy, 1943–46*, Cranbury, New Jersey: Associated University Presses, 1996.

Whittam, J., *Fascist Italy*, Manchester: Manchester University Press, 1995.

Whittam, J., 'Fascism and Anti-Fascism in Italy: History, Memory and Culture', *Journal of Contemporary History* 36(1) (2001), pp. 163–71.

Willson, P., *The Clockwork Factory: Women and Work in Fascist Italy*, Oxford: Clarendon Press, 1993.

Willson, P., 'Flowers for the Doctor. Pro-natalism and Abortion in Fascist Milan', *Modern Italy* 1(2) (1996a), pp. 44–62.

Willson, P., 'Women in Fascist Italy', in R. Bessel (ed.), *Fascist Italy and Nazi Germany: Comparisons and Contrasts*, Cambridge: Cambridge University Press, 1996b.

Willson, P., 'Cooking the Patriotic Omelette: Women and the Italian Fascist Ruralization Campaign', *European History Quarterly* 27(4) (1997), pp. 531–47.

Willson, P., *Peasant Women and Politics in Fascist Italy: The Massaie Rurali*, London and New York: Routledge, 2002.

Zamagni, V., 'La dinamica dei salari nel settore industriale', in P. Ciocca and G. Toniolo (eds), *L'economia italiana nel periodo fascista*, Bologna: il Mulino, 1976.

Zamagni, V., 'Introduzione', in V. Zamagni (ed.), *Come perdere la guerra e vincere la pace: l'economia italiana tra Guerra e dopoguerra, 1938–1947*, Bologna: il Mulino, 1997.

Zimmerman, J. D., 'Introduction', in J. D. Zimmerman (ed.), *Jews in Italy under Fascist and Nazi Rule, 1922–1945*, Cambridge: Cambridge University Press, 2005.

Zuccotti, S., *The Italians and the Holocaust*, London: Peter Halban, 1987.

ITALY SINCE 1943

Absalom, R., 'Allied Escapers and the *contadini* in Occupied Italy (1943–5), *Journal of Modern Italian Studies* 10(4) (2005), pp. 413–25.

Agnew, J., 'Remaking Italy? Place Configurations and Italian Electoral Politics under the "Second Republic"', *Modern Italy* 12(1) (2007), pp. 17–38.

Aldcroft, D. H., *The European Economy 1914–2000*, 4th edn, London and New York: Routledge, 2001.

Allen, K. J. and Stevenson, A. A., *An Introduction to the Italian Economy*, London: Martin Robertson, 1974.

Allum, P., 'Italian Society Transformed', in P. McCarthy (ed.), *Italy since 1945*, Oxford: Oxford University Press, 2000.

Almond, G. A. and Verba, S., *The Civic Culture: Political Attitudes and Democracy in Five Nations*, Princeton: Princeton University Press, 1963.

Arlacchi, P., 'Mafia: the Sicilian Cosa Nostra', *Southern European Society and Politics* 1(1) (1996), pp. 74–94.

Bagnasco, A., 'Associazionismo, quali prospettive?', in P. Ginsborg (ed.), *Stato dell'Italia*, Milan: il Saggiatore/Mondadori, 1994.

Banfield, E. C., *The Moral Basis of a Backward Society*, Glencoe, IL: The Free Press, 1958.

Barbagli, M. and Kertzer, D., 'An Introduction to the History of Italian Family Life', *Journal of Family History* 15(4) (1990), pp. 369–83.

Barca, F., *Il capitalismo italiano: storia di un compromesso senza riforme*, Rome: Donzelli editore, 1999.

Barca, F., 'New Trends and the Policy Shift in the Italian Mezzogiorno', *Daedalus* 130(2) (2001), pp. 93–113.

Barca, F. and Trento, S., 'La parabola delle partecipazioni statali: una missione tradita', in F. Barca (ed.), *Storia del capitalismo italiano dal dopoguerra a oggi*, Rome: Donzelli editore, 1997.

Barca, F., Iwai, K., Pagano, U. and Trento, S., 'Divergences in Corporate Governance Models: The Role of Institutional Shocks', in A. Boltho, A. Vercelli and H. Yoshikawa (eds), *Comparing Economic Systems: Italy and Japan*, Basingstoke: Palgrave, 1997.

Barraclough, R., 'The Northern League and the 1996 General Election: Protest Vote or Political Entrepreneurship?', *The Italianist* 16 (1996), pp. 326–50.

Ben-Ghiat, R., Cafagna, L., Galli della Loggia, E., Ipsen, C. and Kertzer, D. I., 'History as it Really Wasn't: The Myths of Italian Historiography', *Journal of Modern Italian Studies* 6(3) (2001), pp. 402–19.

Benigno, F., 'The Southern Family: A Comment on Paolo Macry', *Journal of Modern Italian Studies* 2(2), pp. 215–17.

Berger, S. and Locke, R. M., '*Il caso italiano* and Globalization', *Daedalus* 130(3), pp. 85–104.

Bernini, S., 'Natural Mothers: Teaching Morals and Parent-craft in Italy, 1945–60', *Modern Italy* 9(1) (2004), pp. 21–33.

Bettio, F. and Villa, P., 'To What Extent Does it Pay to Be Better Educated? Education and the Work Market for Women in Italy', *South European Society and Politics* 4(2) (1999), pp. 150–70.

Bevilacqua, P., *Breve storia dell'Italia meridionale dall'Ottocento a oggi*, Rome: Donzelli editore, 1993.

Bevilacqua, P., 'New and Old in the Southern Question', *Modern Italy* 1(2) (1996), pp. 81–92.

Bianchini, F., 'The Third Italy: Model or Myth?', *Ekistics* 56(350–1) (1991), pp. 336–45.

Blattman, S., 'A Media Conflict of Interest: Anomaly in Italy', 2003. http://www.rsf.org/IMG/pdf/doc-2080.pdf.

Bloomfield, J., 'The "Civic" in Europe', *Contemporary European History* 4(2) (1995), pp. 223–40.

Boltho, A., 'Convergence, Competitiveness and the Exchange Rate', in N. Crafts and G. Toniolo (eds), *Economic Growth in Europe since 1945*, Cambridge: Cambridge University Press, 1996.

Bonelli, F., 'Stato ed economia nell'industrializzazione Italiana dale origini al "Welfare State"', in G. Federico (ed.), *The Economic Development of Italy since 1870*, Aldershot: Edward Elgar, 1984.

Bravo, A., 'Armed and Unarmed: Struggles Without Weapons in Europe and in Italy', *Journal of Modern Italian Studies* 10(4) (2005), pp. 468–84.

Brusco, S. and Paba, S., 'Per una storia dei distretti industriali italiani dal secondo dopoguerra agli anni novanta', in F. Barca (ed.), *Storia del capitalismo italiano dal dopoguerra a oggi*, Rome: Donzelli editore, 1997.

Bull, M. J., 'The Great Failure? The Democratic Party of the Left in Italy's Transition', in S. Gundle and S. Parker (eds), *The New Italian Republic: From the Fall of the Berlin Wall to Berlusconi*, London: Routledge, 1996.

Bull, M. J. and Newell, J. L., 'The General Election in Italy, April 2008', *Electoral Studies* 28(2) (2009), pp. 337–42.

Burnett, S. H. and Mantovani, L., *The Italian Guillotine: Operation Clean Hands and the Overthrow of Italy's First Republic*, Lanham: Rowman and Littlefield, 1998.

Cafagna, L., *Nord e sud. Non fare a pezzi l'unità d'Italia*, Venice: Marsilio editore, 1994.

Caferra, V. M., 'La corruzione', in G. Pasquino (ed.), *La politica italiana: dizionario critico 1945–95*, Rome-Bari: Laterza, 1995.

Caldwell, L., 'Italian Feminism: Some Considerations', in Z. G. Baranski and S. W. Vinall (eds), *Women and Italy: Essays on Gender, Culture and History*, Basingstoke: Macmillan, 1991.

Carnazza, P., Innocenti, A. and Vercelli, A., 'Small Firms and Manufacturing Employment', in A. Boltho, A. Vercelli and H. Yoshikawa (eds), *Comparing Economic Systems: Italy and Japan*, Basingstoke: Palgrave, 2001.

Carter, N., 'Italy: The Demise of the Post-war Partyocracy', in J. K. White and P. J. Davies (eds), *Political Parties and the Collapse of the Old Orders*, Albany: State University of New York Press, 1998.

Cassese, S., 'Hypotheses on the Italian Administrative System', *West European Politics* 16(3) (1993), pp. 316–28.

Cento Bull, A., *Social Identities and Political Cultures in Italy: Catholic, Communist and Leghist Communities between Civicness and Localism*, New York and Oxford: Berghahn Books, 2000a.

Cento Bull, A., 'Review of *L'Italia del tempo presente*, by Paul Ginsborg', *Journal of Modern Italian Studies* 5(1) (2000b), pp. 143–7.

Cento Bull, A., 'Collective Identities: From the Politics of Inclusion to the Politics of Ethnicity and Difference', *The Global Review of Ethnopolitics*, 2(3–4) (2003), pp. 41–54.

Cento Bull, A. and Gilbert, M., *The Lega Nord and the Northern Question in Italian Politics*, New York and Basingstoke: Palgrave, 2001.

Chubb, J., *Patronage, Power, and Poverty in Southern Italy: A Tale of Two Cities*, Cambridge: Cambridge University Press, 1982.

Chubb, J., 'Comments', *Journal of Modern Italian Studies* 9(4) (2004), pp. 464–72.

Citati, P., 'Una paese che non sa guardarsi allo specchio', *la Repubblica*, 23 March 2000.

Cooke, P. (ed.), *The Resistance: An Anthology*, Manchester: Manchester University Press, 1999.

Crafts, N. and Toniolo, G., 'Postwar Growth: An Overview', in N. Crafts and G. Toniolo (eds), *Economic Growth in Europe since 1945*, Cambridge: Cambridge University Press, 1996.

D'Adda, C. and Salituro, B., 'Le politiche economiche', in G. Pasquino (ed.), 1995, *La politica italiana: dizionario critico 1945–95*, Rome-Bari: Laterza, 1995.

De Cecco, M., 'Economic Policy in the Reconstruction Period 1945–51', in S. J. Woolf (ed.), *The Rebirth of Italy 1943–50*, Harlow: Longman, 1972.

De Cecco, M. and Ferri, G., 'Italy's Financial System: Banks and Industrial Investment', in A. Boltho, A. Vercelli and H. Yoshikawa (eds), *Comparing Economic Systems: Italy and Japan*, Basingstoke: Palgrave, 2001.

De Felice, R., *Rosso e Nero*, 2nd edn, Milan: Baldini and Castoldi, 1995.

De Grand, A., 'Review of *Italian Fascism: History, Memory and Representation*, by R. J. B. Bosworth and P. Dogliani (eds)', *Journal of Modern Italian Studies* 4(3) (1999), pp. 456–8.

Della Porta, D., *Social Movements, Political Violence, and the State: A Comparative Analysis of Italy and Germany*, Cambridge and New York: Cambridge University Press, 1995a.

Della Porta, D., 'Il terrorismo', in G. Pasquino (ed.), *La politica italiana: dizionario critico 1945–95*, Rome-Bari: Laterza, 1995b.

Della Sala, V., 'Hollowing Out and Hardening the State: European Integration and the Italian Economy', *West European Politics* 20(1) (1997), pp. 14–33.

Delzell, C. F., 'Renzo De Felice: An Overview', *Italian Quarterly* 36(141–2) (1999), pp. 13–24.

Dickie, J., *Cosa Nostra: A History of the Sicilian Mafia*, London: Hodder and Stoughton, 2004.

Di Leillo, A., 'Il femminismo', in G. Pasquino (ed.), *La politica italiana: dizionario critico 1945–95*, Rome-Bari: Laterza, 1995.

Di Matteo, M. and Yoshikawa, H., 'Economic Growth: The Role of Demand', in A. Boltho, A. Vercelli and H. Yoshikawa (eds), *Comparing Economic Systems: Italy and Japan*, Basingstoke: Palgrave, 2001.

The *Economist, A Survey of Italy*, 8 November 1997.

Edge, D. and Lintner, V., *Contemporary European Economics, Politics and Society*, Harlow: Prentice Hall, 1996.

Eichengreen, B., 'Economy', in M. Fulbrook (ed.), *Europe since 1945*, Oxford: Oxford University Press, 2001.

Ellwood, D. W., *Rebuilding Europe: Western Europe, America and Postwar Reconstruction*, London and New York: Longman, 1992.

Engelbourg, S. and Schachter, G., 'Two "Souths": The United States and Italy since the 1860s', *Journal of European Economic History* 15(3) (1986), pp. 563–90.

Ferraresi, F., *Threats to Democracy: the Radical Right in Italy after the War*, Princeton: Princeton University Press, 1996.

Filippucci, P., 'Anthropological Perspectives on Culture in Italy', in D. Forgacs and R. Lumley (eds), *Italian Cultural Studies: An Introduction*, Oxford: Oxford University Press, 1996.

Filippucci, P. and Willson, P., 'Introduction', *Modern Italy* (Special Issue: Gender and the Private Sphere in Italy since 1945) 9(1) (2004), pp. 5–9.

Foot, J., 'The Family and the "Economic Miracle": Social Transformation, Work, Leisure and Development at Bovisa and Comasina (Milan), 1950–70', *Contemporary European History* 4(3) (1995), pp. 315–38.

Foot, J., 'Heirs of Tangentopoli', *New Left Review* 16(July–August) (2002), pp. 153–60.

Forgacs, D., 'Cultural Consumption, 1940s to 1990s', D. Forgacs and R. Lumley (eds), *Italian Cultural Studies: An Introduction*, Oxford: Oxford University Press, 1996.

Forgacs, D., 'Scenarios for the Digital Age: Convergence, Personalization, Exclusion', *Modern Italy* 6(2) (2001), pp. 129–39.

Fukuyama, F., *Trust: The Social Virtues and the Creation of Prosperity*, London: Penguin, 1995.

Galli della Loggia, E., *La morte della patria. La crisi dell'idea di nazione tra Resistenza, antifascismo e Repubblica*, Rome-Bari: Laterza, 1996.

Gambetta, D., *The Sicilian Mafia: The Business of Private Protection*, Cambridge, MA: Harvard University Press, 1993.

Garelli, F., 'The Public Relevance of the Church and Catholicism in Italy, *Journal of Modern Italian Studies* 12(1) (2007), pp. 8–36.

Genda, Y., Grazia Pazienza, M. and Signorelli, M., 'Labour Market Performance and Job Creation', in A. Boltho, A. Vercelli and H. Yoshikawa (eds), *Comparing Economic Systems: Italy and Japan*, Basingstoke: Palgrave, 2001.

George, S. and Bache, I., *Politics in the European Union*, Oxford: Oxford University Press, 2001.

Gilbert, M., *The Italian Revolution: The End of Politics, Italian Style?*, Boulder: Westview Press, 1995.

Gilbert, M., 'Italy's Third Fall', *Journal of Modern Italian Studies* 2(2) (1997), pp. 221–31.

Ginsborg, P., *A History of Contemporary Italy: Society and Politics 1943–1988*, London: Penguin, 1989.

Ginsborg, P., 'Family, Culture and Politics in Contemporary Italy', in Z. G. Baranski and R. Lumley (eds), *Culture and Conflict in Postwar Italy*, Basingstoke: Macmillan, 1990.

Ginsborg, P., 'La famiglia oltre il privato per superare l'isolamento', in P. Ginsborg (ed.), *Stato dell'Italia*, Milan: il Saggiatore/Mondadori, 1994a.

Ginsborg, P., 'Familismo', in P. Ginsborg (ed.), *Stato dell'Italia*, Milan: il Saggiatore/Mondadori, 1994b.

Ginsborg, P., 'Explaining Italy's Crisis', in S. Gundle and S. Parker (eds), *The New Italian Republic: From the Fall of the Berlin Wall to Berlusconi*, London: Routledge, 1996.

Ginsborg, P. *Italy and its Discontents: Family, Civil Society, State, 1980–2001*, New York and London: Penguin, 2003.

Ginsborg, P., *Silvio Berlusconi: Television, Power and Patrimony*, New York: Verso, 2004.

Ginsborg, P., *The Politics of Everyday Life: Making Choices, Changing Lives*, Melbourne: Melbourne University Press, 2005.

Ginsborg, P., Anderson, P., Parker, S. and Foot, J., 'Italy in the Present Tense: A Roundtable Discussion', *Modern Italy* 5(2) (2000), pp. 175–91.

Giordano, B., 'The Continuing Transformation of Italian Politics and the Contradictory Fortunes of the Lega Nord', *Journal of Modern Italian Studies* 8(2) (2003), pp. 216–30.

Gobbi, R., *Il mito della Resistenza*, Milan: Rizzoli, 1992.

Goldstein, A., 'Recent Works on Italian Capitalism: A Review Essay', *Journal of Modern Italian Studies* 3(2) (1998), pp. 85–104.

Goldstein, A., 'What Future for Italian Industry?', *Journal of Modern Italian Studies* 8(4) (2003), pp. 175–84.

Greco, L. (2003). 'Institutional and Industrial Changes in the Italian South: The Case of Brindisi', *Modern Italy* 8(2) (2003), pp. 187–201.

Gribaudi, G., 'Familismo e famiglia in Napoli e nel Mezzogiorno', *Meridiana* 17 (1993), pp. 13–42.

Gribaudi, G., 'Il paradigma del "familismo amorale"', in P. Macry and A. Massafia (eds), *Fra storia e storiografia: scritti in onore di Pasquale Villani*, Bologna: il Mulino, 1994.

Gribaudi, G., 'Images of the South', in D. Forgacs and R. Lumley (eds), *Italian Cultural Studies: An Introduction*, Oxford: Oxford University Press, 1996.

Hadjimichalis, C., 'The End of Third Italy as We Knew it?', *Antipode* 38(1) (2006), pp. 82–106.

Harper, J. L., 'Italy and the World since 1945', in P. McCarthy (ed.), *Italy since 1945*, Oxford: Oxford University Press, 2000.

Helstosky, C., *Garlic and Oil: Food and Politics in Italy*, Oxford and New York: Berg, 2004.

Hildebrand, G., *Growth and Structure in the Economy of Modern Italy*, Cambridge, MA: Harvard University Press, 1965.

Hobsbawm, E. J., *Age of Extremes: The Short Twentieth Century 1914–1991*, London: Michael Joseph, 1994.

Hooper, J., 'Mussolini Wasn't that Bad, Says Berlusconi', *Guardian*, 12 September 2003.

Istituto nazionale di statistica (ISTAT), press release, 4 July 2000. http://samoa.istat.it/English/Press-rele/Outside-ca/poverty99.pdf.

ISTAT, 'Italy in Figures, 2007', 2007. http://www.istat.it/dati/catalogo/20070517_00/Italy2007Ing.pdf.

ITANES, *Perché ha vinto il centro-destra. Oltre la mera conta dei voti: chi, come, dove, perché*, Bologna: il Mulino, 2001.

Jones, T., *The Dark Heart of Italy: Travels Through Time and Space Across Italy*, London: Faber and Faber, 2003.

Katz, R. and Ignazi, P., 'Introduction', in R. Katz and P. Ignazi (eds), *Italian Politics: The Year of the Tycoon*, Boulder: Westview Press, 1996.

King, R., *Italy*, London: Harper and Row, 1987.

King, R. and Andall, J., 'The Geography and Economic Sociology of Recent Immigration to Italy', *Modern Italy* 4(2) (1999), pp. 135–58.

Late Show, 'Berlusconi – Mussolini of the Media?', BBC 2, 26 September 1994.

Leonardi, R., 'Regional Development in Italy: Social Capital and the Mezzogiorno', *Oxford Review of Economic Policy* 11(2) (1995), pp. 165–78.

Leonardi, R. and Wertman, D., *Italian Christian Democracy*, London: Macmillan, 1989.

Lumley, R., *States of Emergency: Cultures of Revolt in Italy from 1968 to 1978*, London and New York: Verso, 1990a.

Lumley, R., 'Challenging Tradition: Social Movements, Cultural Change and the Ecology Question', in Z. G. Baranski and R. Lumley (eds), *Culture and Conflict in Postwar Italy*, Basingstoke: Macmillan, 1990b.

Lumley, R., 'Peculiarities of the Italian Newspaper', in D. Forgacs and R. Lumley (eds), *Italian Cultural Studies: An Introduction*, Oxford: Oxford University Press, 1996.

Maier, C. S., 'Comments', *Journal of Modern Italian Studies* 9(4) (2004), pp. 455–8.

Mammone, A., 'A Daily Revision of the Past: Fascism, Anti-Fascism, and Memory in Contemporary Italy', *Modern Italy* 11(2) (2006), pp. 211–26.

Mannheimer, R., 'L'8% dei voti lumbard è «rubato» alla sinistra', *Corriere della Sera*, 20 April 2008.

Marchisio, R. and Pisati, M., 'Belonging Without Believing: Catholics in Contemporary Italy', *Journal of Modern Italian Studies* 4(2) (1999), pp. 236–55.

Margry, P. J., 'Merchandising and Sanctity: The Invasive Cult of Padre Pio', *Journal of Modern Italian Studies* 7(1) (2002), pp. 88–115.

Martinelli, N. and Nadeau, B., 'The Stigma of Disability in Italy', *Newsweek*, 3 March 2003.

Massari, O., 'La Resistenza', in G. Pasquino (ed.), *La politica italiana: dizionario critico 1945–95*, Rome-Bari: Laterza, 1995.

McCann, D., 'The "Anglo-American" Model, Privatisation and the Transformation of Private Capitalism in Italy', *Modern Italy* 5(1) (2000), pp. 47–61.

McCarthy, P., 'The Church in Post-war Italy', in P. McCarthy (ed.), *Italy since 1945*, Oxford: Oxford University Press, 2000.

McGinniss, J., *The Miracle of Castel di Sangro*, London: Warner Books, 1999.

Meade, R. C., *Red Brigades: The Story of Italian Terrorism*, Basingstoke: Macmillan, 1990.

Melloni, A., 'The Politics of the "Church" in the Italy of Pope Wojtyla', *Journal of Modern Italian Studies* 12(1) (2007), pp. 60–85.

Michaels, A., 'Naked Ambition', *Financial Times*, 13 July 2007.

Miller, J. E., 'Who Chopped Down that Cherry Tree? The Italian Resistance in History and Politics, 1945–1998', *Journal of Modern Italian Studies* 4(1) (1999), pp. 37–54.

Milward, A. S., *The Reconstruction of Western Europe, 1945–51*, London: Routledge, 1984.

Milward, A. S., *The European Rescue of the Nation State*, 2nd edn, London: Routledge, 2000.

Mingione, E., 'Italy: The Resurgence of Regionalism', *International Affairs* 62(2) pp. 305–18.

Monticelli, S., 'National Identity and the Representation of Italy at War: The Case of *Combat Film*', *Modern Italy* 5(2) (2000), pp. 133–46.

Morlino, L., 'Crisis of Parties and Change of Party System in Italy', *Party Politics* 2(1) (1996), pp. 5–30.

Moss, D., *The Politics of Left-wing Violence in Italy, 1969–85*, Basingstoke: Macmillan, 1989.

Mutti, A., 'Particularism and the Modernization Process in Southern Italy', *International Sociology* 15(4) (2000), pp. 579–90.

Nelken, D., 'A Legal Revolution? The Judges and *Tangentopoli*', in S. Gundle and S. Parker (eds), *The New Italian Republic: From the Fall of the Berlin Wall to Berlusconi*, London: Routledge, 1996.

Neppi Modona, G., 'Tangentopoli e Mani pulite: dopo le indagni, i processi', in P. Ginsborg (ed.), *Stato dell'Italia*, Milan: il Saggiatore/Mondadori, 1994.

Neri Serneri, S., 'A Past to be Thrown Away? Politics and History in the Italian Resistance', *Contemporary European History* 4(3) (1995), pp. 367–81.

Newell, J. L. and Bull, M. J., 'Italian Politics After the 2001 Election: plus ça change, plus c'est la même chose?', *Parliamentary Affairs* 55(4) (2002), pp. 626–42.

Paci, P., 'Italy', in D. A. Dyker (ed.), *The National Economies of Europe*, London and New York: Longman, 1992.

Painter, B. W., 'Renzo De Felice and the Historiography of Italian Fascism', *American Historical Review* 95(2) (1990), pp. 391–405.

Parker, S., 'Political Identities', in D. Forgacs and R. Lumley (eds), *Italian Cultural Studies: An Introduction*, Oxford: Oxford University Press, 1996.

Parker, S., 'Introduction: A Tale of two Italies – Continuities and Change in the Italian Republic, 1994–2006', *Modern Italy* 12(1) (2007), pp. 1–15.

Pasquino, G., 'Political Development', in P. McCarthy (ed.), *Italy since 1945*, Oxford: Oxford University Press, 2000.

Pasquino, G., 'The Italian Elections of 13 May 2001', *Journal of Modern Italian Studies* 6(3) (2001), pp. 371–87.

Pasquino, G., 'The 2008 Italian National Elections: Berlusconi's Third Victory', *South European Society and Politics* 13(3) (2008), pp. 345–62.

Passerini, L., 'Gender Relations', in D. Forgacs and R. Lumley (eds), *Italian Cultural Studies: An Introduction*, Oxford: Oxford University Press, 1996.

Patriarca, S., 'Italian Neopatriotism: Debating National Identity in the 1990s', *Modern Italy* 6(1) (2001), pp. 21–34.

Pavone, C., 'Le tre guerre: patriottica, civile e di classe', in M. Legnani and F. Vendramini (eds), *Guerra, Guerra di Liberazione, Guerra Civile*, Milan: Franco Angeli, 1990.

Pavone, C., *Conoscere la Resistenza*, Milan: Unicopoli, 1994.

Pavone, C., 'The General Problem of the Continuity of the State and the Legacy of Fascism', in J. Dunnage (ed.), *After the War: Violence, Justice, Continuity and Renewal in Italian Society*, Market Harborough: Troubador, 1999.

Peet, J., 'Addio, dolce vita', in The *Economist: A Survey of Italy*, 26 November, 2005, pp. 1–2.

Però, D., 'Next to the Dog Pound: Institutional Discourses and Practices about Rom Refugees in Left-wing Bologna', *Modern Italy* 4(2) (1999), pp. 207–24.

Petrusewicz, M., 'The Mezzogiorno: A Bias for Hope?', *Modern Italy* 6(1) (2001), pp. 63–7.

Piattoni, S., '"Virtuous Clientelism": The Southern Question Resolved?', in J. Schneider (ed.), *Italy's 'Southern Question': Orientalism in One Country*, Oxford and New York: Berg, 1998.

Piazza, M., 'Il rischio di una nuova marginalità?', in P. Ginsborg (ed.), *Stato dell'Italia*, Milan: il Saggiatore/Mondadori, 1994.

Pivato, S., 'Sport', in P. McCarthy (ed.), *Italy since 1945*, Oxford: Oxford University Press, 2000.

Posner, M. V. and Woolf, S. J., *Italian Public Enterprise*, London: Gerald Duckworth, 1967.

Pratt, J., 'Catholic Culture', in D. Forgacs and R. Lumley (eds), 1996, *Italian Cultural Studies: An Introduction*, Oxford: Oxford University Press, 1996.

Putnam, R. D., *Making Democracy Work: Civic Traditions in Modern Italy*, Princeton: Princeton University Press, 1993.

Putnam, D., *Bowling Alone: The Collapse and Revival of American Community*, New York: Simon and Schuster, 2000.

Quazza, G., 'The Politics of the Italian Resistance', in S. J. Woolf (ed.), *The Rebirth of Italy 1943–50*, Harlow: Longman, 1972.

Quazza, G., 'La guerra partigiana: proposte di ricerca', in F. F. Tosi, G. Grasini and M. Legnani (eds), *L'Italia nella seconda mondiale e nella Resistenza*, Milan: Franco Angeli, 1988.

Rey, G. M., 'Italy', in A. Boltho (ed.), *The European Economy: Growth and Crisis*, Oxford: Oxford University Press, 1982.

Riccio, B., 'Senegalese Street-Sellers, Racism and the Discourse on "Irregular Trade" in Rimini', *Modern Italy* 4(2) (1999), pp. 225–39.

Ricossa, S., 'Italy 1920–1970', in C. M. Cipolla (ed.), *The Fontana Economic History of Europe: Contemporary Economies, Part One*, 6 vols, Glasgow: Collins/Fontana, vol. 1, 1976.

Romero, F., 'Migration as an Issue in European Interdependence and Integration: The Case of Italy', in A. Milward, F. M. B. Lynch, R. Ranieri, F. Romero and V. Sorenson (eds), *The Frontier of National Sovereignty: History and Theory 1945–1992*, London: Routledge, 1993.

Rossi, N. and Toniolo, G., 'Italy', in N. Crafts and G. Toniolo (eds), *Economic Growth in Europe since 1945*, Cambridge: Cambridge University Press, 1996.

Rossi Doria, A., 'Una rivoluzione non ancora compiuta', in P. Ginsborg (ed.), *Stato dell'Italia*, Milan: Il Saggiatore/Mondadori, 1994.

Rothenberg, N., 'The Catholic and Communist Women's Press in Post-war Italy: An Analysis of *Cronache* and *Noi Donne*', *Modern Italy* 11(3) (2006), pp. 285–304.

Rusconi, G. E., *Resistenza e postfascismo*, Bologna: il Mulino, 1995.

Salvati, M., 'Dal miracolo economico alla moneta unica europea', in G. Sabbatucci and V. Vidotto (eds), *Storia d'Italia: L'Italia contemporanea dal 1963 a oggi*, 6 vols, Rome-Bari: Laterza, vol. 6, 1999.

Sapelli, G., 'The Italian Crises and Capitalism', *Modern Italy* 1(1) (1995), pp. 82–96.

Sapelli, G., *L'Italia di fine secolo. Economia e classi dirigente: un capitalismo senza mercato*, Venice: Marsilio editore, 1998.

Sarti, R., 'De Felice's Mussolini and the Historiography of Fascism', *Italian Quarterly* 36(141–2) (1999), pp. 45–52.

Sassoon, D., 'The 1987 Elections and the PCI', in R. Leonardi and P. Corbetta (eds), *Italian Politics: A Review*, London: Pinter, 1989.

Sassoon, D., '*Tangentopoli* or the Democratization of Corruption: Considerations on the End of Italy's First Republic', *Journal of Modern Italian Studies* 1(1) (1995), pp. 124–43.

Sassoon, D., *Contemporary Italy: Politics, Economy and Society since 1945*, 2nd edn, London: Longman, 1997.

Schneider, J. and Schneider, P., *Culture and Political Economy in Western Sicily*, New York and London: Academic Press, 1976.

Schneider, J. and Schneider, P., *Festival of the Poor: Fertility Decline and the Ideology of Class in Sicily, 1860–1980*, Tucson: University of Arizona Press, 1996.

Schneider, J. and Schneider, P., *Reversible Destiny: Mafia, Anti-Mafia and the Struggle for Palermo*, Berkeley and Los Angeles: University of California Press, 2003.

Schneider, J. and Schneider, P., 'Sicily: Reflections on Forty Years of Change', *Journal of Modern Italian Studies* 11(1) (2006), pp. 61–83.

Scoppola, P., *25 aprile. Liberazione*, Turin: Einaudi, 1995.

Seisselberg, J., 'Conditions of Success and Political Problems of a "Media-mediated Personality-party": The Case of *Forza Italia*', *West European Politics* 19(4) (1996), pp. 715–43.

Signorini, L. F., 'Italy's Economy: An Introduction', *Daedalus* 130(2) (2001), pp. 67–92.

Signorini, L. F. and Visco, I., *L'economia italiana*, Bologna: il Mulino, 1997.

Stille, A., 'A Disturbing Echo: Anti-Semitism, Fifty Years after Mussolini's Infamous Racial Laws Took Effect, is an Issue Again', *The Atlantic* 263(2) (1989), pp. 20–6.

Stille, A., 'Berlusconi Creates a Truman Show', *Financial Times*, 17 February 2006.

Tarrow, S., 'Making Social Science Work Across Space and Time: A Critical Reflection on Robert Putnam's *Making Democracy Work*', *The American Political Science Review* 90(2) (1996), pp. 389–97.

Vidotto, V., 'La nuova società', in G. Sabbatucci and V. Vidotto (eds), *Storia d'Italia: L'Italia contemporanea dal 1963 al oggi*, 2 vol, Rome-Bari: Laterza, vol. 2, 1999.

Villa, P., 'Sport and Society', in G. Moliterno (ed.), *Encyclopedia of Contemporary Italian Culture*, London: Routledge, 2000.

Zamagni, V., 'Betting on the Future: The Reconstruction of Italian Industry, 1946–1952', in J. Becker and F. Knipping (eds), *Power in Europe? Great Britain, France, Italy and Germany in a Postwar World, 1945–50*, Berlin and New York: Walter de Gruyter, 1986.

Zamagni, V., 'The Italian 'Economic Miracle' Revisited: New Markets and American Technology', in E. di Nolfo (ed.), *Power in Europe II. Britain, France, Germany and Italy and the Origins of the EEC, 1952–57*, 6 vol., Berlin and New York: Walter de Gruyter, vol. 6, 1992.

Zamagni, V., 'Evolution of the Economy', in P. McCarthy (ed.), *Italy since 1945*, Oxford: Oxford University Press, 2000.

Index